Patterns for College Writing

A Rhetorical Reader
and Guide

ELEVENTH EDITION

Patterns for College Writing

A Rhetorical Reader and Guide

LAURIE G. KIRSZNER
UNIVERSITY OF THE SCIENCES IN PHILADELPHIA

STEPHEN R. MANDELL
DREXEL UNIVERSITY

BEDFORD / ST. MARTIN'S

Boston ◆ New York

For Bedford/St. Martin's

Senior Developmental Editor: John Sullivan
Production Editor: Ryan Sullivan
Production Supervisor: Jennifer Peterson
Marketing Manager: Molly Parke
Art Director: Lucy Krikorian
Text Design: Linda Robertson
Photo Research: Helane Prottas
Cover Design: Sara Gates
Cover Art: Henri Matisse (1869–1954) © Copyright. *Interior in Yellow and Blue,* 1946. Oil on canvas. CNAC/MNAM/Dist. Réunion des Musées Nationaux/ Art Resource, NY
Composition: Pine Tree Composition, Inc.
Printing and Binding: RR Donnelley & Sons

President: Joan E. Feinberg
Editorial Director: Denise B. Wydra
Editor in Chief: Karen S. Henry
Director of Marketing: Karen R. Soeltz
Director of Editing, Design, and Production: Marcia Cohen
Assistant Director of Editing, Design, and Production: Elise S. Kaiser
Managing Editor: Shuli Traub

Library of Congress Control Number: 2009927038

Manufactured in the United States of America.

1 2 3 4 5 6   14 13 12 11 10 09

For information, write: Bedford/St. Martin's, 75 Arlington Street, Boston, MA 02116   (617-399-4000)

ISBN-10: 0-312-60152-2   ISBN-13: 978-0-312-60152-2 (paperback)
ISBN-10: 0-312-53759-X   ISBN-13: 978-0-312-53759-3 (hardcover)

Acknowledgments

For Peter Phelps (1936–1990), with thanks

Preface

Since it was first published, *Patterns for College Writing* has been adopted at more than a thousand colleges and universities. We have been delighted by the overwhelmingly positive response to the first ten editions of *Patterns*, and we continue to be gratified by the many instructors who find *Patterns* to be the most accessible and the most pedagogically sound rhetoric-reader they have ever used. In preparing this eleventh edition, we have worked hard to fine-tune the features that have made *Patterns* the most popular composition reader available today and to develop new features to enhance the book's usefulness for both instructors and students.

WHAT INSTRUCTORS AND STUDENTS LIKE ABOUT *PATTERNS FOR COLLEGE WRITING*

An Emphasis on Critical Reading

The opening chapter, "Reading to Write: How to Use This Book," prepares students to become analytical readers and writers by showing them how to apply critical reading strategies to a typical selection and by providing sample responses to the various kinds of writing prompts in the book. Not only does this chapter introduce students to the book's features, but it also prepares them to tackle reading and writing assignments in their other courses.

Extensive Coverage of the Writing Process

Part One, "The Writing Process" (Chapters 2 through 5), is a "mini-rhetoric," offering advice on drafting, writing, revising, and editing as it introduces students to activities such as freewriting, brainstorming, clustering, and journal writing. These chapters also include some twenty writing exercises to give students opportunities for immediate practice.

Detailed Coverage of the Patterns of Development

In Part Two, "Readings for Writers," Chapters 6 through 14 explain and illustrate the patterns of development that students typically use in their college writing assignments: narration, description, exemplification, process, cause and effect, comparison and contrast, classification and division, definition, and argumentation. Each chapter begins with a comprehensive introduction that presents a definition and a paragraph-length example of the pattern to be discussed and then explains the particular writing strategies and applications associated with it. Next, each chapter analyzes one or two annotated student essays to show how the pattern can be used in particular college writing situations. Chapter 15, "Combining the Patterns," illustrates how the various patterns of development discussed in Chapters 6 through 14 can work together in an essay.

A Diverse and Popular Selection of Readings

Varied in subject, style, and cultural perspective, the seventy-four professional selections engage students while providing them with outstanding models for writing. We have tried to achieve a balance between classic authors (George Orwell, Jessica Mitford, E. B. White, Martin Luther King Jr.) and newer voices (Sherman Alexie, Amy Tan, Gary Shteyngart, Meghan Daum) so that instructors have a broad range to choose from.

More Student Essays Than Any Comparable Text

To provide students with realistic models for improving their own writing, we include sixteen sample student essays (one new to this edition). These essays are also available as transparency masters so that instructors can use them more effectively in the classroom. They can be downloaded from the *Patterns for College Writing* book companion Web site, **bedfordstmartins.com/patterns**.

Helpful Coverage of Grammar Issues

Grammar in Context boxes in chapter introductions offer specific advice on how to identify and correct the grammar, mechanics, and punctuation problems that students are likely to encounter when they work on particular patterns of development. Practice exercises for mastering these grammar skills are available on *Re:Writing*, a comprehensive online exercise collection accessible at *Patterns'* companion Web site.

Apparatus Designed to Help Students Learn

Each professional essay in the text is followed by four types of questions. These questions are designed to help students assess their understanding of the essay's content and of the writer's purpose and audience; to recognize the stylistic and structural techniques used to shape the essay; and to become sensitive to the nuances of language. Each essay is also accompanied by a Journal Entry prompt, Writing Workshop topics (suggestions for the full-length writing assignments), and Thematic Connections that identify related readings in the text. Also following each essay is a Combining the Patterns feature that focuses on different patterns of development used in the essay and possible alternatives to these patterns. Each chapter ends with a list of Writing Assignments and a Collaborative Activity. Many of these assignments and activities have been updated to reflect the most current topics as well as the most up-to-date trends and sites available on the Web.

Extensive Cultural and Historical Background for All Readings

In addition to a biographical headnote, each reading is prefaced by a headnote containing essential background information to help students make connections between the reading and the historical, social, and economic forces that shaped it.

An Introduction to Visual Texts

Every rhetorical chapter includes a visual text — such as a photograph, a piece of fine art, or panels from a graphic novel — that provides an accessible introduction to each rhetorical pattern. Apparatus that helps students discuss the pattern in its visual form follows each image.

Thorough Coverage of Writing Research Papers

The appendix, "Using Research in Your Writing," which includes a student research paper that follows MLA style and format, takes students through the process of writing a research paper — from choosing a topic and finding reliable sources to avoiding plagiarism and documenting both print and online material. This appendix includes examples of MLA documentation style that follow the guidelines set forth in the *MLA Handbook for Writers of Research Papers*.

WHAT'S NEW IN THIS EDITION

Engaging New Readings

The nine images and twenty-seven compelling new professional essays treat topics of current interest. In "The Hidden Life of Garbage," Heather Rogers describes the "solution" to our wasteful, consumption-driven lives as she explores a waste disposal facility. In "Fatwa City," Cullen Murphy provides examples of dangerous new prohibitions in the United States. And in "Earth without People," Alan Weisman considers the possible effects (both positive and negative) on the environment if humans were to disappear suddenly. In all cases, readings have been carefully selected for their interesting subject matter as well as for their effectiveness as teachable models for student writing.

Argumentation Chapter Updated

The argumentation chapter has been thoroughly revised and updated to include two new debates ("What Is a Hate Crime?" and "How Big a Threat Is Global Warming?") and two new casebooks ("How Open Should Our Borders Be?" and "Is There a Case for Torture?").

More Help for Working with and Synthesizing Sources

The Research Appendix has been updated to include a new MLA sample student research paper on the dangers of using Wikipedia as an authoritative source. The Appendix also now includes a section on "synthesizing sources," and assignments that call for synthesis are now marked for quick identification. There's also more on evaluating print and online sources. Finally, new checklists help students review key concepts.

EXTENSIVE SUPPORT FOR STUDENTS AND INSTRUCTORS

Support for Student Writers

Four CD-ROMs offer students extra practice with writing and editing skills, analyzing visual texts, making arguments, and documenting sources.

- *Exercise Central to Go* contains hundreds of practice items to help students build their writing and editing skills. Drawn from the popular *Exercise Central* Web site, the practices have been extensively class-tested and provide instant feedback. No Internet connection is necessary.
- *ix: visual exercises* offers a new way for students to focus on visual rhetoric, with nine exercises that give them a vocabulary to use as they read and write about different kinds of texts.
- *i•claim: visualizing argument* offers a new way for students to see argument, with six tutorials, an illustrated glossary, and more than seventy multimedia arguments.
- *i•cite: visualizing sources* allows students to practice working with all types of sources, from Web sites to audio and video clips.

Support for Instructors

The extensive ancillary package available to instructors who adopt *Patterns* includes the following items:

- An *Instructor's Edition*, incorporating *Resources for Instructors*, gives instructors guidance in teaching from the text and provides sample answers to the questions that follow each reading. (*Resources for Instructors* is also available as a separate booklet.)
- *Transparency Masters* feature ten peer editing worksheets, ten Grammar in Context boxes, and sixteen sample student essays (available on the *Patterns for College Writing* companion Web site).

Patterns for College Writing Companion Web Site

For students who need more practice in mastering specific grammatical skills, the companion Web site at **bedfordstmartins.com/patterns** includes *Exercise Central* — a unique online collection of more than 8,000 exercise items conveniently arranged by topic that enable students to practice essential grammar skills and get immediate feedback on their progress. In addition, the companion site offers access to a free online collection of Web resources for the writing class at *Re:Writing*, including plagiarism tutorials, model documents, research guides, bibliography tools, and much more.

For instructors, the companion Web site offers a downloadable version of *Resources for Instructors to Accompany* PATTERNS FOR COLLEGE WRITING; downloadable files of the transparency masters and peer editing worksheets; access to Reading Quizzes and grade books for each reading in the book; access to TopLinks, a database that guides students to the best links available on the most commonly chosen writing topics; and access to further debate topics, Internet assignments, and author research.

ACKNOWLEDGMENTS

As always, friends, colleagues, students, and family all helped this project along. Of particular value were the responses to questionnaires sent to users of the tenth edition, and we thank each of the instructors who responded so frankly and helpfully: Heidi E. Ajrami, Victoria College; Janet Asay, Treasure Valley Community College; April D. Baker, Greenville Technical College; Liz Barnes, Daytona Beach College; Stephanie Battle, Wilbur Wright College; Kathleen Bethell, Ivy Tech Community College; Vincent Bruckert, Wright College; Nancy Mohrlock Bunker, Macon State College; Cathy Carolus, Ivy Tech Community College; Carol DeBoer-Langworthy, Brown University; DJ Dolack, Baruch College; Stephen T. Holland, Muscatine Community College; Vickie Hunt, Okaloosa-Walton College; Regina Johnson, Virgil I. Grissom High School; Dawn Jordan, John Jay College/CUNY; Jessica Kester, Daytona Beach College; Richard I. Kraskin, Daytona Beach College; Jennifer Kurtz, Virginia Western Community College; Evelyn Audi Lisi, York Country Day School; Jo Ann C. Long, Greenville Technical College; Priscilla Osovski Manwaring, Ivy Tech Community

College–Bloomington; Heather McDonald, Daytona Beach Community College; Linda S. McGann, South Plains College; Michelle Paulsen, The Victoria College; Susan F. Perry, Greenville Technical College; Hazel Peterson, Tarrant County College–South; Mary Anna Peterson, Avon High School; Deidre Dowling Price, Okaloosa-Walton College; Craig Rigg, West Prairie High School; Pamela S. Scott, Pikeville College; Rosie Soy, Hudson County Community College; Renee St. Louis, Southwestern College; Elizabeth Starr, Ivy Tech Community College; Elizabeth H. Stringer, East Mississippi Community College; Beverly Stroud, Greenville Technical College; Cheli J. Turner, Greenville Technical College; and Patrice A. Williams, Okaloosa-Walton College.

We are also grateful to those instructors who responded to an in-depth review letter: Scott E. Ash, Nassau Community College; Katherine Baker, College of Southern Nevada; Justin Barber, Stark State College; LaToya Bogard, Mississippi State University; Ruth Ann Gambino, Palo Alto College; Paullett Golden, Montgomery College; Lolann A. King, Trinity Valley Community College; Debra S. Knutson, Shawnee State University; Ann Linden, Shawnee State University; Cynthia Magno, Warren County Community College; Michael Moran, University of Georgia; Diana Nystedt, Palo Alto College; Sherry Rosenthal, College of Southern Nevada; and Beth Williams, Stark State College. We also thank our anonymous reviewers.

Special thanks go to Mark Gallaher, a true professional and a valued friend, for his help with some of the apparatus and for revising the headnotes and the *Resources for Instructors*.

Through eleven editions of *Patterns for College Writing*, we have enjoyed a wonderful working relationship with Bedford/St. Martin's. We have always found the editorial and production staff to be efficient, cooperative, and generous with their time and advice. As always, we appreciate the encouragement and advice of our longtime friend and former editor, Nancy Perry. In addition, we thank Joan Feinberg, president of Bedford/St. Martin's, for her support for this project and for her trust in us. During our work on this edition, we have benefited from our productive relationship with John Sullivan, our editor, who helped us make this edition of *Patterns* the best it could be. We are also grateful to Ryan Sullivan, project editor; Shuli Traub, managing editor; and Jennifer Peterson, production supervisor, for their work overseeing the production of this edition; to Donna Dennison, art director, for the attractive new cover and design; and to editorial assistant Alicia Young for her invaluable help with tasks large and small.

We are fortunate to have enjoyed our many years of collaboration; we know how rare a successful partnership like ours is. We also know how lucky we are to have our families — Mark, Adam, and Rebecca Kirszner and Demi, David, and Sarah Mandell — to help keep us in touch with the things that really matter.

Laurie G. Kirszner
Stephen R. Mandell

Contents

PART TWO: READINGS FOR WRITERS   *81*

6 Narration   *83*

"Gravy is the simplest, tastiest, most memory-laden dish I know how to make: a little flour, salt and pepper, crispy bits of whatever meat anchored the meal, a couple of cups of water or milk, and slow stirring to break up the lumps."

"Like me, perhaps, the people around me had in mind images from television and newspaper pictures: the collapsing buildings, the running office workers, the black plume of smoke against a bright blue sky. Like me, they were probably trying to superimpose those terrible images onto the industrious emptiness right in front of them."

"My earliest memories of Sam Cohen are of his chin, which I remember as fiercely hard and pointy."

"There's a reason landfills are tucked away, on the edge of town, in otherwise untraveled terrain, camouflaged by hydroseeded, neatly tiered slopes. If people saw what happened to their waste, lived with the stench, witnessed the scale of destruction, they might start asking difficult questions."

"My first view in the mirror blotted out the hurting. I'd seen some pretty conks, but when it's the first time, on your own head, the transformation, after the lifetime of kinks, is staggering."

"You will face a coordination problem if you are a general deploying troops, tanks, helicopters, food, tents, and medical supplies, or if you are the CEO of a large company juggling the demands of design, personnel, inventory, and production.
   And these days, you will face a coordination problem if you want to get a cup of coffee."

"If you do not think you will be able to change your appearance enough to slip past your date, you may have to find another way to depart. Back doors are the simplest; they are often located near the restrooms or are marked as fire exits. Do not open an emergency exit door if it is alarmed unless absolutely necessary; an alarm will only draw attention."

"People can be executed in places like Shea Stadium before immense paying audiences. . . . As with all sports events, a certain ritual would seem inevitable and would quickly become an expected part of the occasion."

10 Cause and Effect *321*

11 Comparison and Contrast *383*

"When Ulysses S. Grant and Robert E. Lee met in the parlor of a modest house at Appomattox Court House, Virginia, on April 9, 1865, to work out the terms for the surrender of Lee's Army of Northern Virginia, a great chapter in American life came to a close, and a great new chapter began."

"This is a tale of two sisters from Calcutta, Mira and Bharati, who have lived in the United States for some thirty-five years, but who find themselves on different sides in the current debate over the status of immigrants."

12 Classification and Division *447*

"What I wish for all students is some release from the clammy grip of the future. I wish them a chance to savor each segment of their education as an experience in itself and not as a grim preparation for the next step. I wish them the right to experiment, to trip and fall, to learn that defeat is as instructive as victory and is not the end of the world."

"With a show of energy and creativity that would be admirable if applied to the (missing) assignments in question, my students persist, week after week, semester after semester, year after year, in offering excuses about why their work is not ready. Those reasons fall into several broad categories: the family, the best friend, the evils of dorm life, the evils of technology, and the totally bizarre."

"I spend a great deal of my time thinking about the power of language — the way it can evoke an emotion, a visual image, a complex idea, or a simple truth. Language is the tool of my trade. And I use them all — all the Englishes I grew up with."

"We lie. We all do. We exaggerate, we minimize, we avoid confrontation, we spare people's feelings, we conveniently forget, we keep secrets, we justify lying to the big-guy institutions."

"Surfers have been single-minded in their concern for name anonymity, with little or no concern for profile anonymity. Privacy protection may keep our names and numbers from prying eyes, but we may never again be able to lose ourselves in cyberspace."

14 Argumentation 547

"We hold these truths to be self-evident, that all men are created equal, that they are endowed by their Creator with certain unalienable rights, that among these are life, liberty, and the pursuit of happiness."

"The history of mankind is a history of repeated injuries and usurpations on the part of man toward woman, having in direct object the establishment of an absolute tyranny over her. To prove this, let facts be submitted to a candid world."

"For years now I have heard the word 'Wait!' It rings in the ear of every Negro with piercing familiarity. This 'Wait' has almost always meant 'Never.' We must come to see, with one of our distinguished jurists, that 'justice too long delayed is justice denied.'"

"Far from being merely a prank, the hanging of nooses harks back to a shameful period in American history. . . . If we're ever going to bridge the

"We need to build a border infrastructure that is modern and effective. We can do that. . . . But we also need to find an orderly way to allow those people who are already here, who are embedded in our communities and our workforce, to be able to continue to remain."

"The problem is the second group of Hispanics. They aren't immigrants. . . . They have come here solely for jobs, which isn't the same thing at all."

"At present rates, mass immigration reinforces ethnic subcultures, reduces the incentives of newcomers to learn English, and extends the life of ethnic ghettos. . . . If we want to assimilate new immigrants — and we have no choice if we are [to] remain one nation — we must slow down the pace of immigration."

CASEBOOK: IS THERE A CASE FOR TORTURE?

"By threatening to kill for profit or idealism, [the terrorist] renounces civilized standards, and [he] can have no complaint if civilization tries to thwart him by whatever means necessary."

"If we ever did have a ticking time bomb case . . . law enforcement officials would in fact resort to physical force, even torture, as a last resort. . . . Is it better to have such torture done under the table, off the books, and below the radar screen — or in full view, with accountability and as part of our legal system?"

"Yet the 'ticking time bomb' scenario is not only extremely improbable, it's also one in which torture is most likely to be useless. If the terrorist knows the bomb will go off in two hours, all he has to do is stall by giving false information until it does go off."

"In such an urgent and rare instance, an interrogator might well try extreme measures to extract information. . . . Should he do so, and thereby save an American city or prevent another 9/11, authorities and the public would surely take this into account when judging his actions. . . . But I don't believe this scenario requires us to write into law an exception to our treaty and moral obligations that would permit cruel, inhumane, and degrading treatment."

15 Combining the Patterns *705*

"I have learned much as a scavenger. I mean to put some of what I have learned down here, beginning with the practical art of Dumpster diving and proceeding to the abstract."

"You can leave the Island, master the English language, and travel as far as you can, but if you are a Latina, especially one like me who so obviously belongs to Rita Moreno's gene pool, the Island travels with you."

"I used to think tattoos were for either lowlifes or those who wanted to pretend they were, but my mind now stands changed by the thoughtful, articulate people I talked to and the spectacular designs that had been inked into their bodies. In a word, tattoos are now officially OK by me."

"I have been assured by a very knowing American of my acquaintance in London, that a young healthy child well nursed is at a year old a most delicious, nourishing, and wholesome food, whether stewed, roasted, baked, or boiled; and I make no doubt that it will equally serve in fricassee or a ragout."

APPENDIX: USING RESEARCH IN YOUR WRITING *757*

Thematic Guide
to the Contents

Family Relationships

Language

Reading and Writing

Education

Business and Work

Sports

Race and Culture

Gender

Nature and the Environment

Media and Society

History and Politics

Ethics

Citizenship

Patterns for College Writing

A Rhetorical Reader
and Guide

1

Reading to Write: How to Use This Book

On a purely practical level, you will read the selections in this text to answer study questions and prepare for class discussions. More significantly, however, you will also read to evaluate the ideas of others, to form judgments, and to develop original viewpoints.

By introducing you to new ideas and new ways of thinking about familiar concepts, reading prepares you to respond critically to the ideas of others and to develop ideas of your own. When you read critically, you can form opinions, exchange insights with others in conversation, ask and answer questions, and develop ideas that can be further explored in writing. For all of these reasons, reading is a vital part of your education.

READING CRITICALLY

Reading is a two-way street. Readers are presented with a writer's ideas, but they also bring their own ideas to what they read. After all, readers have different national, ethnic, cultural, and geographic backgrounds and different kinds of knowledge and experiences, so they may react differently to a particular essay or story. For example, readers from an economically and ethnically homogeneous suburban neighborhood may have difficulty understanding a story about class conflict, but these readers may also be more objective than readers who are struggling with such conflict in their own lives.

These differences in readers' responses do not mean that every interpretation is acceptable, that an essay or story or poem may mean whatever a reader wants it to mean. Readers must make sure they are not distorting a writer's words, overlooking (or ignoring) significant details, or seeing things in an essay or story that do not exist. It is not important for all readers to agree on a particular interpretation of a work. It *is* important, however, for each reader to develop an interpretation that the work itself supports.

The study questions that accompany the essays in this text encourage you to think critically about writers' ideas. Although some of the questions (particularly those listed under **Comprehension**) call for fairly straight-forward, factual responses, other questions (particularly the **Journal Entry** assignments) invite more complex responses that reflect your individual reaction to the selections.

READING ACTIVELY

When you read an essay in this text, or any work that you expect to discuss in class (and perhaps to write about), you should read it carefully — and you should read it more than once.

Before You Read

Before you read, look over the essay to get an overview of its content. If the selection has a **headnote** — a paragraph or two about the author and the work — begin by reading it. (Note that each headnote in this text includes a **background** section that discusses the reading selection's cultural context.) Next, skim the work to get a general sense of the writer's ideas. As you read, note the title and any internal headings, as well as the use of boldface type, italics, and other design elements. Also pay special attention to the introductory and concluding paragraphs, where a writer is likely to make (or reiterate) key points.

As You Read

As you read, try to answer the questions in the following checklist.

✓ CHECKLIST: **Reading Actively**

- What is the writer's general subject?
- What is the writer's main point?
- Does the writer seem to have a particular purpose in mind?
- What kind of audience is the writer addressing?
- What are the writer's assumptions about audience? About subject?
- Are the writer's ideas consistent with your own?
- Does the writer reveal any biases?
- Do you have any knowledge that challenges the writer's ideas?
- Is any information missing?
- Are any sequential or logical links missing?
- Can you identify themes or ideas that also appear in other works you have read?
- Can you identify parallels with your own experience?

HIGHLIGHTING AND ANNOTATING

As you read and reread, be sure to record your reactions in writing. These notations will help you understand the writer's ideas and your own thoughts about these ideas. Every reader develops a different system of recording such responses, but many readers use a combination of *highlighting* and *annotating*.

When you **highlight**, you mark the text. You might, for example, underline important ideas, box key terms, number a series of related points, circle an unfamiliar word (or place a question mark beside it), draw a vertical line in the margin beside a particularly interesting passage, draw arrows to connect related points, or star discussions of the work's central issues or themes.

When you **annotate**, you carry on a conversation with the text in marginal notes. You might, among other things, ask questions, suggest possible parallels with other reading selections or with your own experiences, argue with the writer's points, comment on the writer's style, or define unfamiliar terms and concepts.

The following paragraph, excerpted from Maya Angelou's "Finishing School" (page 107), illustrates a student's highlighting and annotating of a text.

Date written?

Why does she mention this?

Serious or sarcastic?

Also true of boys? In North as well as South? True today?

What are these values?

Recently a white woman from Texas, who would quickly describe herself as a liberal, asked me about my hometown. When I told her that in Stamps my grandmother had owned the only Negro general merchandise store since the turn of the century, she exclaimed, "Why, you were a debutante." Ridiculous and even ludicrous. But Negro girls in small Southern towns, whether poverty-stricken or just munching along on a few of life's necessities, were given as extensive and irrelevant * preparations for adulthood as rich white girls shown in magazines. Admittedly the training was not the same. While white girls learned to waltz and sit gracefully with a tea cup balanced on their knees, we were lagging behind, learning the mid-Victorian values with very little money to indulge them.

Remember that this process of highlighting and annotating is not an end in itself but a step toward understanding what you have read. Annotations suggest questions; in your search for answers, you may ask your instructor for clarification, or you may raise particularly puzzling or provocative points during class discussion or in a study group. After your questions have been answered, you will be able to discuss and write about what you have read with greater confidence, accuracy, and authority.

The process you use when you react to a **visual text** — a photograph; an advertisement; a diagram, graph, or chart; or a work of fine art, for example — is much the same as the one you use when you respond to a written text. Here too, your goal is to understand the text, and highlighting and annotating a visual text can help you interpret it.

With visual texts, however, instead of identifying elements like particular words and ideas, you identify visual elements. These might include the use of color; the arrangement of shapes; the contrast between large and small or light and dark; and, of course, the particular images the visual includes.

The following photograph, one of four included in "Four Tattoos" (page 214), illustrates a student's highlighting and annotating of a visual text. (See page 215 for study questions about these images.)

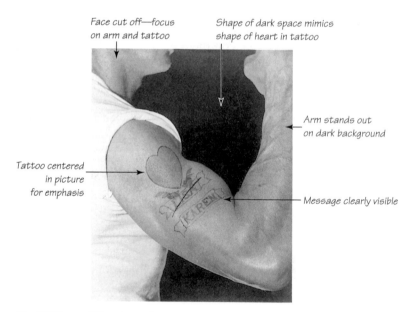

Face cut off—focus on arm and tattoo

Shape of dark space mimics shape of heart in tattoo

Arm stands out on dark background

Tattoo centered in picture for emphasis

Message clearly visible

Alex Williams, "Lisa, Karen"

READING THE ESSAYS IN THIS BOOK

The selection that follows, "'What's in a Name?'" by Henry Louis Gates Jr., is typical of the essays in this text. It is preceded by a **headnote** that gives readers information about the author's life and career. This headnote includes a **background** section that provides a social, historical, and cultural context for the essay. As you read the headnote and the essay, highlight and annotate them carefully.

HENRY LOUIS GATES JR.

"What's in a Name?"

Henry Louis Gates Jr. was born in 1950 in Keyser, West Virginia, and grew up in the small town of Piedmont. Currently W. E. B. Du Bois Professor of Humanities and director of the W. E. B. Du Bois Institute for African-American Research at Harvard, he has edited many collections of works by African-American writers and published several volumes of literary criticism. However, he is probably best known as a social critic whose books and articles for a general audience explore a wide variety of issues and themes, often focusing on race and culture. In the following essay, which originally appeared in the journal *Dissent,* Gates recalls a childhood experience that occurred during the mid-1950s.

Background on the civil rights movement

In the mid-1950s, the first stirrings of the civil rights movement were under way, and in 1954 and 1955 the U.S. Supreme Court handed down decisions declaring racial segregation unconstitutional in public schools. Still, much of the country — particularly the South — remained largely segregated until Congress passed the Civil Rights Act of 1964, which prohibited discrimination based on race, color, religion, or national origin in businesses (such as restaurants and theaters) covered by interstate commerce laws, as well as in employment. This was followed by the Voting Rights Act of 1965, which guaranteed equal access to the polls, and the Civil Rights Act of 1968, which prohibited discrimination in housing and real estate. At the time of the experience Gates recalls here — before these laws were enacted — prejudice and discrimination against African Americans were the norm in many communities, including those outside the South.

The question of color takes up much space in these pages, but the question of color, especially in this country, operates to hide the graver questions of the self.

— JAMES BALDWIN, 1961

... blood, darky, Tar Baby, Kaffir, shine ... moor, blackamoor, Jim Crow, spook ... quadroon, meriney, red bone, high yellow ... Mammy, porch monkey, home, homeboy, George ... spearchucker, schwarze, Leroy, Smokey ... mouli, buck. Ethiopian, brother, sistah.

— TREY ELLIS, 1989

I had forgotten the incident completely, until I read Trey Ellis's essay "Remember My Name" in a recent issue of the *Village Voice* (June 13, 1989). But there, in the middle of an extended italicized list of the bynames of "the race" ("the race" or "our people" being the terms my parents used in polite or reverential discourse, "jigaboo" or "nigger" more commonly used in anger, jest, or pure disgust), it was: "George." Now the events of

1

that very brief exchange return to mind so vividly that I wonder why I had forgotten it.

My father and I were walking home at dusk from his second job. He "moonlighted" as a janitor in the evenings for the telephone company. Every day but Saturday, he would come home at 3:30 from his regular job at the paper mill, wash up, eat supper, then at 4:30 head downtown to his second job. He used to make jokes frequently about a union official who moonlighted. I never got the joke, but he and his friends thought it was hilarious. All I knew was that my family always ate well, that my brother and I had new clothes to wear, and that all of the white people in Piedmont, West Virginia, treated my parents with an odd mixture of resentment and respect that even we understood at the time had something directly to do with a small but certain measure of financial security.

He had left a little early that evening because I was with him and I had to be in bed early. I could not have been more than five or six, and we had stopped off at the Cut-Rate Drug Store (where no black person in town but my father could sit down to eat, and eat off real plates with real silverware) so that I could buy some caramel ice cream, two scoops in a wafer cone, please, which I was busy licking when Mr. Wilson walked by.

Mr. Wilson was a very quiet man, whose stony, brooding, silent manner seemed designed to scare off any overtures of friendship, even from white people. He was Irish, as was one-third of our village (another third being Italian), the more affluent among whom sent their children to "Catholic School" across the bridge in Maryland. He had white straight hair, like my Uncle Joe, whom he uncannily resembled, and he carried a black worn metal lunch pail, the kind that Riley* carried on the television show. My father always spoke to him, and for reasons that we never did understand, he always spoke to my father.

"Hello, Mr. Wilson," I heard my father say.

"Hello, George."

I stopped licking my ice cream cone, and asked my Dad in a loud voice why Mr. Wilson had called him "George."

"Doesn't he know your name, Daddy? Why don't you tell him your name? Your name isn't George."

For a moment I tried to think of who Mr. Wilson was mixing Pop up with. But we didn't have any Georges among the colored people in Piedmont; nor were there colored Georges living in the neighboring towns and working at the mill.

"Tell him your name, Daddy."

"He knows my name, boy," my father said after a long pause. "He calls all colored people George."

A long silence ensued. It was "one of those things," as my Mom would put it. Even then, that early, I knew when I was in the presence of "one of

---

* EDS. NOTE — The lead character in the 1950s television program *The Life of Riley*, about a white working-class family and their neighbors.

those things," one of those things that provided a glimpse, through a rent curtain, at another world that we could not affect but that affected us. There would be a painful moment of silence, and you would wait for it to give way to a discussion of a black superstar such as Sugar Ray or Jackie Robinson.

"Nobody hits better in a clutch than Jackie Robinson."   13

"That's right. Nobody."   14

I never again looked Mr. Wilson in the eye.   15

• • •

RESPONDING TO AN ESSAY

Once you have read an essay carefully and recorded your initial reactions to it, you should be able to respond to specific questions about it.

The study questions that follow each essay in this text will guide you through the rest of the reading process and help you to **think critically** about what you are reading. Five types of questions follow each essay:

- *Comprehension* questions help you to measure your understanding of what the writer is saying.
- *Purpose and Audience* questions ask you to consider why, and for whom, each selection was written and to examine the implications of the writer's choices in view of a particular purpose or intended audience.
- *Style and Structure* questions encourage you to examine the decisions the writer has made about elements such as arrangement of ideas, paragraphing, sentence structure, word choice, and imagery.
- *Vocabulary Projects* ask you to define certain words, to consider the connotations of others, and to examine the writer's reasons for selecting particular words or patterns of language.
- *Journal Entry* assignments ask you to write a short, informal response to what you read and to speculate freely about related ideas — perhaps exploring ethical issues raised by the selection or offering your opinions about the writer's statements. Briefer, less polished, and less structured than full-length essays, journal entries may suggest ideas for more formal kinds of writing.

Following these sets of questions are three additional features:

- *Writing Workshop* assignments ask you to write essays structured according to the pattern of development explained and illustrated in the chapter.
- *Combining the Patterns* questions focus on the various patterns of development — other than the essay's dominant pattern — that the writer uses. These questions ask why a writer uses particular patterns

(narration, description, exemplification, process, cause and effect, comparison and contrast, classification and division, definition), what each pattern contributes to the essay, and what other choices the writer might have had.

- *Thematic Connections* identify other readings in this book that deal with similar themes. Reading these related works will enhance your understanding and appreciation of the original work and perhaps give you material to write about.

Following are some examples of study questions and possible responses, as well as a **Writing Workshop** assignment and **Thematic Connections**, for "'What's in a Name?'" (pages 5–7). The numbers in parentheses after quotations refer to the paragraphs in which the quotations appear.

Comprehension

1. *In paragraph 1, Gates wonders why he forgot about the exchange between his father and Mr. Wilson. Why do you think he forgot about it?*

   Gates may have forgotten about the incident simply because it was something that happened a long time ago or because such incidents were commonplace when he was a child. Alternatively, he may *not* have forgotten the exchange between his father and Mr. Wilson but pushed it out of his mind because he found it so painful. (After all, he says he never again looked Mr. Wilson in the eye.)

2. *How is the social status of Gates's family different from that of other African-American families in Piedmont, West Virginia? How does Gates account for this difference?*

   Gates's family is different from other African-American families in town in that they are treated with "an odd mixture of resentment and respect" (2) by whites. Although other blacks are not permitted to eat at the drugstore, Mr. Gates is. Gates attributes this social status to his family's "small but certain measure of financial security" (2). Even so, when Mr. Wilson insults Mr. Gates, the privileged status of the Gates family is revealed as false.

3. *What does Gates mean when he says, "It was 'one of those things,' as my Mom would put it" (12)?*

   Gates's comment indicates that the family learned to see such mistreatment as routine. In context, the word *things* in paragraph 12 refers to the kind of incident that gives Gates and his family a glimpse of the way the white world operates.

4. *Why does Gates's family turn to a discussion of a "black superstar" after a "painful moment of silence" (12) such as the one he describes?*

   Although Gates does not explain the family's behavior, we can infer that they speak of African-American heroes like prizefighter Sugar Ray Robinson and baseball player Jackie Robinson to make themselves feel better. Such discussions are a way of balancing the negative images of African Americans created by incidents such as the one Gates describes and of bolstering the low self-esteem the family felt as a result. These heroes seem to have won the respect denied to the Gates family; to mention them is to participate vicariously in their glory.

5. *Why do you think Gates "never again looked Mr. Wilson in the eye" (15)?*

Gates may have felt that Mr. Wilson was somehow the enemy, not to be trusted, because he had insulted Gates's father. Or, he may have been ashamed to look him in the eye because he believed his father should have insisted on being addressed properly.

Purpose and Audience

1. *Why do you think Gates introduces his narrative with the two quotations he selects? How do you suppose he expects his audience to react to them? How do you react?*

Gates begins with two quotations, both by African-American writers, written nearly thirty years apart. Baldwin's words seem to suggest that, in the United States, "the question of color" is a barrier to understanding "the graver questions of the self." That is, the labels *black* and *white* may mask more fundamental characteristics or issues. Ellis's list of names (many pejorative) for African Americans illustrates the fact that epithets can dehumanize people — they can, in effect, rob a person of his or her "self." This issue of the discrepancy between a name and what lies behind it is central to Gates's essay. In one sense, then, Gates begins with these two quotations because they are relevant to the issues he will discuss. More specifically, he is using the two quotations — particularly Ellis's shocking string of unpleasant names — to arouse interest in his topic and provide an intellectual and emotional context for his story. He may also be intending to make his white readers uncomfortable and his black readers angry. How you react depends on your attitudes about race (and perhaps about language).

2. *What is the point of Gates's narrative? That is, why does he recount the incident?*

Certainly Gates wishes to make readers aware of the awkward, and potentially dangerous, position of his father (and, by extension, of other African Americans) in a small southern town in the 1950s. He also shows us how names help to shape people's perceptions and actions: as long as Mr. Wilson can call all black men "George," he can continue to see them as insignificant and treat them as inferiors. The title of the piece suggests that the way names shape perceptions is the writer's main point.

3. *The title of this selection, which Gates places in quotation marks, is an allusion to act 2, scene 2, of Shakespeare's Romeo and Juliet, in which Juliet says, "What's in a name? That which we call a rose / By any other name would smell as sweet." Why do you think Gates chose this title? Does he expect his audience to recognize the quotation?*

Because his work was originally published in a journal read by a well-educated audience, Gates would have expected readers to recognize the **allusion** (and also to know a good deal about 1950s race relations). Although Gates could not have been certain that all members of this audience would recognize the reference to *Romeo and Juliet*, he could have been reasonably sure that if they did, it would enhance their understanding of the selection. In Shakespeare's play, the two lovers are kept apart essentially because of their names: she is a Capulet and he is a Montague, and the two families are involved in a bitter feud. In the speech from which Gates takes the title quotation, Juliet questions the logic of such a situation. In her view, what a person is called should not determine how he or she is regarded — and this, of course, is Gates's point as well. Even if readers do not recognize the allusion, the title still foreshadows the selection's focus on names.

Style and Structure

1. *Does paragraph 1 add something vital to the narrative, or would Gates's story make sense without the introduction? Could another kind of introduction work as well?*

    Gates's first paragraph supplies the context in which the incident is to be read — that is, it makes clear that Mr. Wilson's calling Mr. Gates "George" was not an isolated incident but part of a pattern of behavior that allowed those in positions of power to mistreat those they considered inferior. For this reason, it is an effective introduction. Although the narrative would make sense without paragraph 1, the story's full impact would probably not be as great. Still, Gates could have begun differently. For example, he could have started with the incident itself (paragraph 2) and interjected his comments about the significance of names later in the piece. He also could have begun with the exchange of dialogue in paragraphs 5 through 11 and then introduced the current paragraph 1 to supply the incident's context.

2. *What does the use of dialogue contribute to the narrative? Would the selection have a different impact without dialogue? Explain.*

    Gates was five or six years old when the incident occurred, and the dialogue helps to establish the child's innocence as well as his father's quiet acceptance of the situation. In short, the dialogue is a valuable addition to the piece because it creates two characters, one innocent and one resigned to injustice, both of whom contrast with the voice of the adult narrator: wise, worldly, but also angry and perhaps ashamed, the voice of a man who has benefited from the sacrifices of men like Gates's father.

3. *Why do you think Gates supplies the specific details he chooses in paragraphs 2 and 3? In paragraph 4? Is all this information necessary?*

    The details Gates provides in paragraphs 2 and 3 help to establish the status of his family in Piedmont; because readers have this information, the fact that the family was ultimately disregarded and discounted by some whites emerges as deeply ironic. The information in paragraph 4 also contributes to this **irony**. Here we learn that Mr. Wilson was not liked by many whites, that he looked like Gates's Uncle Joe, and that he carried a lunch box — in other words, that he had no special status in the town apart from that conferred by race.

Vocabulary Projects

1. *Define each of the following words as it is used in this selection:*
    bynames (1) — nicknames
    measure (2) — extent or degree

uncannily (4) — strangely

ensued (12) — followed

rent (12) — torn

2. *Consider the connotations of the words colored and black, both used by Gates to refer to African Americans. What different associations does each word have? Why does Gates use both — for example, colored in paragraph 9 and black in paragraph 12? What is your response to the father's use of the term boy in paragraph 11?*

In the 1950s, when the incident Gates describes took place, the term *colored* was still widely used, along with *Negro,* to designate Americans of African descent. In the 1960s, the terms *Afro-American* and *black* replaced the earlier names, with *black* emerging as the preferred term and remaining dominant through the 1980s. Today, although *black* is preferred by some, *African American* is used more and more often. Because the term *colored* is the oldest designation, it may seem old-fashioned and even racist today; *black,* which connoted a certain degree of militancy in the 1960s, is probably now considered a neutral term by most people. Gates uses both words because he is speaking from two time periods. In paragraph 9, re-creating the thoughts and words of a child in a 1950s southern town, he uses the term *colored*; in paragraph 12, the adult Gates, commenting in 1989 on the incident, uses *black.* The substitution of *African American* for the older terms might give the narrative a more contemporary flavor, but it might also seem awkward or forced — and, in paragraph 9, inappropriately formal. As far as the term *boy* is concerned, different readers are apt to have different responses. Although the father's use of the term can be seen as affectionate, it can also be seen as derisive in this context since it echoes the bigot's use of *boy* for all black males, regardless of age or accomplishments.

Journal Entry

Do you think Gates's parents should have used experiences like the one in "'What's in a Name?'" to educate him about the family's social status in the community? Why do you think they chose instead to dismiss such incidents as "one of those things" (12)?

Your responses to these questions will reflect your own opinions, based on your background and experiences as well as on your interpretation of the reading selection.

Writing Workshop

Write about a time when you, like Gates's father, could have spoken out in protest but chose not to. Would you make the same decision today?

By the time you approach the Writing Workshop assignments, you will have read an essay, highlighted and annotated it, responded to study questions about it, discussed it in class, and perhaps considered its relationship to other essays in the text. Often, your next step will be to write an essay in response to one of the Writing Workshop questions. (Chapters 2–4 follow

Laura Bobnak, a first-year composition student, through the process of writing an essay in response to this Writing Workshop assignment.)

Combining the Patterns

Although **narration** *is the pattern of development that dominates "'What's in a Name?'" and gives it its structure, Gates also uses* **exemplification***, presenting an extended example to support his thesis. What is this example? What does it illustrate? Would several brief examples have been more convincing?*

The extended example is the story of the encounter between Gates's father and Mr. Wilson, which compellingly illustrates the kind of behavior African Americans were often forced to adopt in the 1950s. Because Gates's introduction focuses on "the incident" (1), one extended example is enough (although he alludes to other incidents in paragraph 12).

Thematic Connections

- "Finishing School" (page 107)
- "The 'Black Table' Is Still There" (page 345)

As you read and think about the selections in this text, you should begin to see thematic links among them. Such parallels can add to your interest and understanding, as well as give you ideas for class discussion and writing.

For example, Maya Angelou's "Finishing School," another autobiographical essay by an African-American writer, has many similarities with Gates's. Both essays describe the uneasy position of a pre–Civil-Rights-era black child expected to conform to the white world's unfair code of behavior, and both deal squarely with the importance of being called by one's name. In fact, paragraph 26 of "Finishing School" offers some helpful insights into the problem Gates examines.

Another related work is Lawrence Otis Graham's "The 'Black Table' Is Still There." The writer, an African-American man, returns in 1991 to his junior high school, where he sees the lunch tables as segregated as they were when he was a student there. Unlike Gates's essay, which discusses a specific incident that took place in the South in the 1950s, Graham's examines an ongoing situation that may apply to schools all over the United States. Thus, it provides a more current — and, perhaps, wider — context for discussing issues of race and class.

In the process of thinking about Gates's narrative, discussing it in class, or preparing to write an essay on a related topic (such as the one listed under Writing Workshop), you might find it useful to read Angelou's and Graham's essays.

Responding to Other Texts

The first selection in Chapters 6 through 14 of this book is a visual text. It is followed by **Reading Images** questions, a **Journal Entry**, and a short list of **Thematic Connections** that will help you understand the image and shape your response to it.

The final selection in each chapter, a story or poem, is followed by **Reading Literature** questions, a **Journal Entry**, and **Thematic Connections**.

NOTE: At the end of each chapter, **Writing Assignments** offer additional practice in writing essays structured according to a particular pattern of development, and a **Collaborative Activity** suggests an idea for a group project.

PART ONE

The Writing Process

Every reading selection in this book is the result of a struggle between a writer and his or her material. If a writer's struggle is successful, the finished work is welded together without a visible seam, and readers have no sense of the frustration the writer experienced while rearranging ideas or hunting for the right word. Writing is no easy business, even for a professional writer. Still, although there is no simple formula for good writing, some approaches are easier and more productive than others.

At this point you may be asking yourself, "So what? What has this got to do with me? I'm not a professional writer." True enough, but during the next few years you will be doing a good deal of writing. Throughout your college career, you will write midterms, final exams, lab reports, essays, and research papers. In your professional life, you may write progress reports, proposals, business correspondence, and memos. As diverse as these tasks are, they have something in common: they can be made easier if you are familiar with the stages of the **writing process** — a process experienced writers follow when they write.

THE WRITING PROCESS

- **Invention** (also called **prewriting**)   During invention, you decide what to write about and gather information to support or explain what you want to say.
- **Arrangement**   During arrangement, you decide how you are going to organize your ideas.
- **Drafting and revising**   During drafting and revising, you write several drafts as you reconsider your ideas and refine your style and structure.
- **Editing and proofreading**   During editing, you focus on grammar and punctuation as well as on sentence style and word choice. During proofreading, you correct spelling, mechanical errors, and typos and check your essay's format.

Although the writing process is usually presented as a series of neatly defined steps, that model does not reflect the way people actually write. Ideas do not always flow easily, and the central point you set out to develop does not always wind up in the essay you ultimately write. In addition, writing often progresses in fits and starts, with ideas occurring sporadically or not at all. Surprisingly, much good writing occurs when a writer gets stuck or confused but continues to work until ideas begin to take shape.

Because the writing process is so erratic, its stages overlap. Most writers engage in invention, arrangement, drafting and revision, and editing simultaneously — finding ideas, considering possible methods of organization, looking for the right words, and correcting grammar and punctuation all at the same time. In fact, writing is such an idiosyncratic process that no two writers approach the writing process in exactly the same way. Some people outline; others do not. Some take elaborate notes during the invention stage; others keep track of everything in their heads.

The writing process discussed throughout this book reflects the many choices writers make at various stages of composition. But regardless of writers' different approaches, one thing is certain: the more you write, the better acquainted you will become with your personal writing process and the better you will learn how to modify it to suit various writing tasks. The four chapters that follow, which treat individual stages of the writing process, will help you define your needs as a writer and understand your options as you approach writing assignments in college and beyond.

2
Invention

Invention, or **prewriting**, is an important part of the writing process. At this stage, you discover what interests you about your subject and consider what ideas to develop in your essay.

When you are given a writing assignment, you may be tempted to start writing a first draft immediately. Before writing, however, you should be sure you understand your assignment and its limits, and you should think about what you want to say. Time spent on these issues now will pay off later when you draft your essay.

UNDERSTANDING YOUR ASSIGNMENT

Almost everything you write in college begins as an *assignment*. Some assignments will be direct and easy to understand:

Write about an experience that changed your life.

Discuss the procedure you used to synthesize ammonia.

Others will be difficult and complex:

Using Jonathan Kozol's essay "The Human Cost of an Illiterate Society" as source material, write an essay using as your thesis the following statement by James Madison: "A people who mean to be their own governors must arm themselves with the power knowledge gives."

Before beginning to write, you need to understand what your assignment is asking you to do. If the assignment is written as a question, read it carefully several times, and underline its key words. If the assignment is read aloud by your instructor, be sure to copy it accurately. (A mistaken word — *analyze* for *compare*, for example — can make quite a difference.) If you are confused about anything, ask your instructor for clarification. Remember that no matter how well written an essay is, it will fall short if it does not address the assignment.

SETTING LIMITS

Once you understand the assignment, you should consider its *length, purpose, audience,* and *occasion* and your own *knowledge* of the subject. Each of these factors helps you determine what you will say about your subject.

Length

Often, your instructor will specify the **length** of a paper, and this word or page limit has a direct bearing on your paper's focus. For example, you would need a narrower topic for a two-page essay than for a ten-page one. Similarly, you could not discuss a question as thoroughly during an hour-long exam as you might in a paper written over several days.

If your instructor sets no page limit, consider how the nature of the assignment suggests a paper's length. A *summary* of a chapter or an article, for instance, should be much shorter than the original, whereas an *analysis* of a poem will most likely be longer than the poem itself. If you are uncertain about the appropriate length for your paper, consult your instructor.

Purpose

Your **purpose** also limits what you say and how you say it. For example, if you were writing a job application letter, you would not emphasize the same elements of college life as you would in an email to a friend. In the first case, you would want to persuade the reader to hire you, so you might include your grade-point average, a list of the relevant courses you took, and perhaps the work you did for a service-learning course. In the second case, you would want to inform and perhaps entertain, so you might share anecdotes about dorm life or describe one of your favorite instructors. In each case, your purpose would help you determine what information to include to evoke a particular response in a specific audience.

In general, you can classify your purposes for writing according to your relationship to the audience.

- In **expressive writing**, you convey personal feelings or impressions to readers. Expressive writing is used in diaries, personal emails and journals, and often in narrative and descriptive essays as well.
- In **informative writing**, you inform readers about something. Informative writing is used in essay exams, lab reports, and expository essays as well as in some research papers and personal Web pages.
- In **persuasive writing**, you try to convince readers to act or think in a certain way. Persuasive writing is used in editorials, argumentative essays, research papers, and many types of electronic documents such as blogs and Web sites.

In addition to these general purposes, you might have a more specific purpose — to analyze, entertain, hypothesize, assess, summarize, question, report, recommend, suggest, evaluate, describe, recount, request, instruct, and so on. For example, suppose you wrote a report on homelessness in your community. Your general purpose might be to *inform* readers of the situation, but you might also want to *assess* the problem and *instruct* readers how to help those in need.

Audience

To be effective, your essay should be written with a particular **audience** in mind. An audience can be an *individual* (your instructor, for example), or it can be a *group* (like your classmates or coworkers). Your essay can address a *specialized* audience (such as a group of medical doctors or economists) or a *general* or *universal* audience whose members have little in common (such as the readers of a newspaper or newsmagazine).

In college, your audience is usually your instructor, and your purpose in most cases is to demonstrate your mastery of the subject matter, your reasoning ability, and your competence as a writer. Other audiences may include classmates, professional colleagues, or members of your community. Considering the age and gender of your audience, its political and religious values, its social and educational level, and its interest in your subject may help you define it.

Often, you will find that your audience is just too diverse to be categorized. In such cases, many writers imagine a general (or universal) audience and make points that they think will appeal to a variety of readers. At other times, writers identify a common denominator, a role that characterizes the entire audience. For instance, when a report on the dangers of smoking asserts, "Now is the time for health-conscious individuals to demand that cigarettes be removed from the market," it automatically casts its audience in the role of health-conscious individuals.

After you define your audience, you have to determine how much or how little its members know about your subject. This consideration helps you decide how much information your readers will need in order to understand the discussion. Are they highly informed? If so, you can present your points without much explanation. Are they relatively uninformed? If this is the case, you will have to include definitions of key terms, background information, and summaries of basic research.

Keep in mind that experts in one field will need background information in other fields. If, for example, you were writing an analysis of Joseph Conrad's *Heart of Darkness,* you could assume that the literature instructor who assigned the novel would not need a plot summary. However, if you wrote an essay for your history instructor that used *Heart of Darkness* to illustrate the evils of European colonialism in nineteenth-century Africa, you would probably include a short plot summary. (Even though your history instructor would know a lot about colonialism in Africa, she might not be familiar with Conrad's novel.)

Occasion

In general, **occasion** refers to the situation (or situations) that leads someone to write about a topic. Obviously, in an academic writing situation, the occasion is almost always a specific assignment. The occasion suggests a specific audience — for example, a history instructor — as well as a specific purpose — for example, to discuss the causes of World War I. In fact, even the format of a paper — whether you use (or do not use) headings or whether you present your response to an assignment as an essay, as a technical report, or even as a PowerPoint presentation — is determined by the occasion for your writing. For this reason, a paper suitable for a psychology or sociology class might not be suitable for a composition class.

Like college writing assignments, each writing task you do outside of school requires an approach that suits the occasion. An email to coworkers, for instance, may be less formal than a report to a manager. In addition, the occasion suggests how much (or how little) information the piece of writing includes. Finally, your occasion suggests your purpose. For example, an email to members of an online discussion group might be strictly informational, whereas an email to a state senator about preserving a local landmark would be persuasive as well as informative.

Knowledge

What you know (and do not know) about a subject determines what you can say about it. Before writing about any subject, ask yourself what you know about the subject and what do you need to find out?

Different writing situations require different kinds of knowledge. A personal essay will draw on your own experiences and observations; a term paper will require you to gain new knowledge through research. In many cases, your page limit and the amount of time you are given to do the assignment will help you decide how much information you need to gather before you can begin.

✓ **CHECKLIST: Setting Limits**

LENGTH

- Has your instructor specified a length?
- Does the nature of your assignment suggest a length?

PURPOSE

- Is your general purpose to express personal feelings? To inform? To persuade?

- In addition to your general purpose, do you have any more specific purposes?
- Does your assignment provide any guidelines about purpose?

AUDIENCE

- Is your audience a group or an individual?
- Are you going to address a specialized or a general audience?
- Should you take into consideration the audience's age, gender, education, biases, or political or social values?
- Should you cast your audience in a particular role?
- How much can you assume your audience knows about your subject?

OCCASION

- Are you writing in class or at home?
- Are you addressing a situation outside the academic setting?
- What special approaches does your occasion for writing require?

KNOWLEDGE

- What do you know about your subject?
- What do you need to find out?

Exercise 1

Decide whether or not each of the following topics is appropriate for the stated limits, and then write a few sentences to explain why each topic is or is not acceptable.

1. *A two-to-three-page paper*   A history of animal testing in medical research labs
2. *A two-hour final exam*   The effectiveness of bilingual education programs
3. *A one-hour in-class essay*   An interpretation of one of Andy Warhol's paintings of Campbell's soup cans
4. *An email to your college newspaper*   A discussion of your school's policy on plagiarism

Exercise 2

Make a list of the different audiences to whom you speak or write in your daily life. (Consider all the different people you see regularly, such as family members, your roommate, instructors, your boss, your friends, and so on.) Then, record your answers to the following questions:

1. Do you speak or write to each person in the same way and about the same things? If not, how do your approaches to these people differ?

2. List some subjects that would interest some of these people but not others. How do you account for these differences?

3. Choose one of the following subjects, and describe how you would speak or write to each audience about it.

   - A local political issue
   - Your favorite Web site
   - Random drug testing for all professional athletes
   - Identity theft

MOVING FROM SUBJECT TO TOPIC

Although many essays begin as specific assignments, some begin as broad areas of interest or concern. These **general subjects** always need to be narrowed to **specific topics** that can be discussed within the limits of the assignment. For example, a subject like stem-cell research could be interesting, but it is too complicated to write about for any college assignment except in a general way. You need to limit such a subject to a topic that can be covered within the time and space available.

GENERAL SUBJECT	SPECIFIC TOPIC
Stem-cell research	Using stem-cell research to cure multiple sclerosis
Herman Melville's *Billy Budd*	Billy Budd as a Christ figure
Constitutional law	One result of the *Miranda* ruling
The Internet	The uses of chat rooms in composition classes

Two strategies can help you narrow a general subject to a specific topic: *questions for probing* and *freewriting*.

Questions for Probing

One way to move from a general subject to a specific topic is to examine your subject by asking a series of questions about it. These **questions for probing** are useful because they reflect how your mind operates — for instance, finding similarities and differences, or dividing a whole into its parts. By asking the questions on the following checklist, you can explore your subject systematically. Not all questions will work for every subject, but any single question may elicit many different answers, and each answer is a possible topic for your essay.

✓ **CHECKLIST: Questions for Probing**

What happened?
When did it happen?
Where did it happen?
Who did it?
What does it look like?
What are its characteristics?
What impressions does it make?
What are some typical cases or examples of it?
How did it happen?
What makes it work?
How is it made?
Why did it happen?
What caused it?
What does it cause?
What are its effects?
How is it like other things?
How is it different from other things?
What are its parts or types?
How can its parts or types be separated or grouped?
Do its parts or types fit into a logical order?
Into what categories can its parts or types be arranged?
On what basis can it be categorized?
How can it be defined?
How does it resemble other members of its class?
How does it differ from other members of its class?

When applied to a subject, some of these questions can yield many workable topics, including some you might never have considered had you not asked the questions. For example, by applying this approach to the general subject "the Brooklyn Bridge," you can generate more ideas and topics than you need:

What happened? A short history of the Brooklyn Bridge

What does it look like? A description of the Brooklyn Bridge

How is it made? The construction of the Brooklyn Bridge

What are its effects? The impact of the Brooklyn Bridge on American writers

How does it differ from other members of its class? Innovations in the design of the Brooklyn Bridge

At this point in the writing process, you want to come up with possible topics, and the more ideas you have, the wider your choice. Begin by writing down all the topics you think of. (You can repeat the process of probing several times to limit topics further.) Once you have a list of topics, eliminate those that do not interest you or are too complex or too simple to fit your assignment. When you have discarded these less promising topics, you should still have several left. You can then select the topic that best suits your paper's length, purpose, audience, and occasion, as well as your interests and your knowledge of the subject.

🖳   **COMPUTER STRATEGY: Questions for Probing**

You can store the questions for probing listed on page 23 in a file that you can open whenever you have a new subject. Make sure you keep a record of your answers. If the topic you have chosen is too difficult or too narrow, you can return to the questions-for-probing file and probe your subject again.

Exercise 3

Indicate whether each of the following is a general subject or a specific topic that is narrow enough for a short essay.

1. An argument against fast-food ads aimed at young children
2. Home schooling
3. Cell phones and driving
4. Changes in U.S. immigration laws
5. Requiring college students to study a foreign language
6. The advantages of affirmative action
7. A comparison of small-town and big-city living
8. Student loans
9. The advantages of service-learning courses
10. The role of religion in people's lives

Exercise 4

In preparation for writing a 750-word essay, choose two of the following general subjects, and generate three or four specific topics from each by using as many of the questions for probing as you can.

1. Credit-card fraud
2. Job interviews
3. Identity theft
4. Gasoline prices
5. Substance abuse

6. Global warming
7. The minimum wage
8. Age discrimination
9. Parenting
10. Holidays
11. Personal triumphs
12. Rising college tuition
13. Grading
14. Television reality shows
15. The death penalty

Freewriting

Another strategy for moving from subject to topic is **freewriting**. You can use freewriting at any stage of the writing process — for example, to generate supporting information or to find a thesis. However, freewriting is a particularly useful way to narrow a general subject or assignment.

When you freewrite, you write for a fixed period, perhaps five or ten minutes, without stopping and without paying attention to spelling, grammar, or punctuation. Your goal is to get your ideas down on paper so that you can react to them and shape them. If you find you have nothing to say, write down anything until ideas begin to emerge — and in time they will. The secret is to *keep writing*. Try to focus on your subject, but don't worry if you wander off in other directions. The object of freewriting is to let your ideas flow. Often your best ideas will come from the unexpected connections you make as you write.

After completing your freewriting, read what you have written and look for ideas you can write about. Some writers underline ideas they think they might explore in their essays. Any of these ideas could become essay topics, or they could become subjects for other freewriting exercises. You might want to freewrite again, using a new idea as your focus. This process of writing more and more specific freewriting exercises — called **focused freewriting** or **looping** — can often yield a great deal of useful information and help you decide on a workable topic.

🖵 COMPUTER STRATEGY: Freewriting

If you do your freewriting on a computer, you may find that staring at your own words causes you to go blank. One possible solution is to turn down the brightness until the screen becomes dark and then to freewrite. This technique allows you to block out distracting elements and concentrate on just your ideas. Once you finish freewriting, turn up the brightness, and see what you have. If you have an interesting idea, you can move it onto a new page and use it as the subject of a new freewriting exercise.

A STUDENT WRITER: Freewriting

After reading, highlighting, and annotating Henry Louis Gates Jr.'s "'What's in a Name?'" (page 5), Laura Bobnak, a student in a composition class, decided to write an essay in response to this Writing Workshop question:

> Write about a time when you, like Gates's father, could have spoken out in protest but chose not to. Would you make the same decision today?

In an attempt to narrow this assignment to a workable topic, Laura did the following freewriting exercise:

> Write for ten minutes . . . ten minutes . . . at 9 o'clock in the morning — Just what I want to do in the morning — If you can't think of something to say, just write about anything. Right! Time to get this over with — An experience — should have talked — I can think of plenty of times I should have kept quiet! I should have brought a bottle of water to class. I wonder what the people next to me are writing about. That reminds me. Next to me. Jeff Servin in chemistry. The time I saw him cheating. I was mad but I didn't do anything. I studied so hard and all he did was cheat. I was so mad. Nobody else seemed to care. What's the difference between now and then? It's only a year and a half. . . . Honor code? Maturity? A lot of people cheated in high school. I bet I could write about this — Before and after, etc. My attitude then and now.

After some initial floundering, Laura discovered an idea that could be the basis for her essay. Although her discussion of the incident still had to be developed, Laura's freewriting helped her discover a possible topic for her essay: a time she saw someone cheating and did not speak out.

Exercise 5

Do a five-minute freewriting exercise on one of the topics you generated in Exercise 4 (pages 24–25).

Exercise 6

Read what you have just written, underline the most interesting ideas, and choose one idea as a topic you could write about in a short essay. Freewrite about this topic for another five minutes to narrow it further and to generate ideas for your essay. Underline the ideas that seem most useful.

FINDING SOMETHING TO SAY

Once you have narrowed your subject to a workable topic, you need to find something to say about it. *Brainstorming* and *journal writing* are useful tools for generating ideas, and both can be helpful at this stage of the writing process (and whenever you need to find additional material).

Brainstorming

Brainstorming is a way of discovering ideas about your topic. You can brainstorm in a group, exchanging ideas with several students in your composition class and writing down the most useful ideas. You can also brainstorm on your own, quickly writing down every fact, idea, or detail you can think of that relates to your topic. Your notes might include words, phrases, statements, questions, or even drawings or diagrams. Jot them down in the order in which you think of them. Some of the items may be inspired by your class notes; others may be ideas you got from reading or from talking with friends; and still other items may be ideas you have begun to wonder about, points you thought of while moving from subject to topic, or thoughts that occurred to you as you brainstormed.

A STUDENT WRITER: Brainstorming

To narrow her topic further and find something to say about it, Laura Bobnak made the brainstorming notes shown on page 28. After reading these notes several times, Laura decided to concentrate on the differences between her current and earlier attitudes toward cheating. She knew that she could write a lot about this idea and relate it to the assignment, and she felt confident that her topic would be interesting both to her instructor and to the other students in the class.

🖳 COMPUTER STRATEGY: Brainstorming

Brainstorming on your computer can save you time and effort. Your word-processing program makes it easy to create bulleted or numbered lists and gives you the flexibility to experiment with different ways of arranging and grouping items from your brainstorming notes. You can even use the drawing tools to make diagrams.

Journal Writing

Journal writing can be a useful source of ideas at any stage of the writing process. Many writers routinely keep a journal, jotting down experiences or exploring ideas they may want to use when they write. They write journal entries even when they have no particular writing project in mind. Often these journal entries are the kernels from which longer pieces of writing develop. Your instructor may ask you to keep a writing journal, or you may decide to do so on your own. In either case, you will find your journal entries are likely to be more narrowly focused than freewriting or brainstorming, perhaps examining a small part of a reading selection or even one particular statement. Sometimes you will write in your journal in response to specific questions, such as the Journal Entry assignments that appear throughout this book. Assignments like these can help you start thinking about a reading selection that you may later discuss in class or write about.

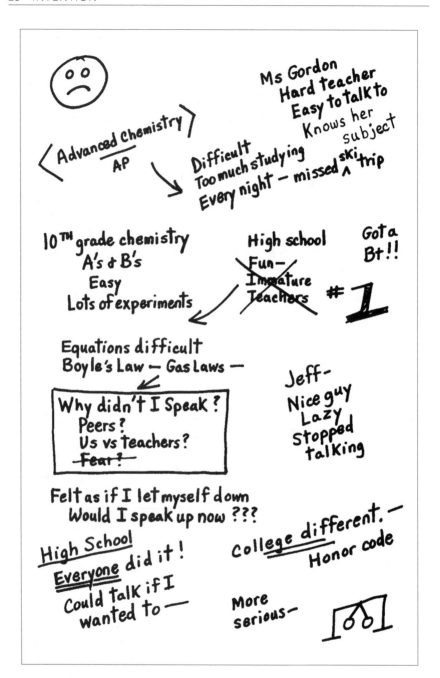

Brainstorming notes

A STUDENT WRITER: Journal Writing

In the following journal entry, Laura Bobnak explores one idea from her brainstorming notes — her thoughts about her college's honor code:

> At orientation the dean of students talked about the college's honor code. She talked about how we were a community of scholars who were here for a common purpose — to take part in an intellectual conversation. According to her, the purpose of the honor code is to make sure this conversation continues uninterrupted. This idea sounded dumb at orientation, but now it makes sense. If I saw someone cheating, I'd tell the instructor. First, though, I'd ask the student to go to the instructor. I don't see this as "telling" or "squealing." We're all here to get an education, and we should be able to assume everyone is being honest and fair. Besides, why should I go to all the trouble of studying while someone else does nothing and gets the same grade?

Even though Laura eventually included only a small part of this entry in her paper, writing in her journal helped her clarify her ideas about her topic.

🖳   **COMPUTER STRATEGY: Keeping a Journal**

Keeping your journal in a computer file has some obvious advantages. Not only can you maintain a neat record of your ideas, but you can also easily move entries from your journal into an essay without retyping them.

GROUPING IDEAS

Once you have generated material for your essay, you will want to group ideas that belong together. *Clustering* and *outlining* can help you do this.

Clustering

Clustering is a way of visually arranging ideas so that you can tell at a glance where ideas belong and whether or not you need more information. Although you can use clustering at an earlier stage of the writing process, it is especially useful now for seeing how your ideas fit together. (Clustering can also help you narrow your paper's topic even further. If you find that your cluster diagram is too detailed, you can write about just one branch of the cluster.)

Begin clustering by writing your topic in the center of a sheet of paper. After circling the topic, surround it with the words and phrases that identify the major points you intend to discuss. (You can get ideas from your brainstorming notes, from your journal, and from your freewriting.) Circle these words and phrases, and connect them to the topic in the center. Next, construct other clusters of ideas relating to each major point, and draw lines connecting them to the appropriate point. By dividing and subdividing your points, you get more specific as you move outward from the center. In the process, you identify the facts, details, examples, and opinions that illustrate and expand your main points.

A STUDENT WRITER: Clustering

Because Laura Bobnak was not very visually oriented, she chose not to use this method of grouping her ideas. If she had, however, her cluster diagram might have looked like this:

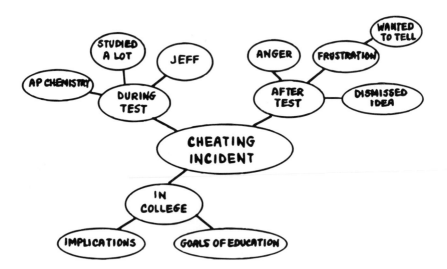

Making an Informal Outline

As an alternative or follow-up to clustering, you can organize your notes from brainstorming or other invention techniques into an **informal outline**. Informal outlines do not include all the major divisions and subdivisions of your paper or indicate the relative importance of your ideas the way formal outlines do; they simply suggest the shape of your emerging essay. Quite often an informal outline is just a list of your major points presented in a tentative order. Sometimes, however, an informal outline will include supporting details or suggest a pattern of development.

🖳   COMPUTER STRATEGY: Making an Informal Outline

If you use a computer, you can easily arrange the notes you generated in your invention activities into an informal outline. You can make an informal outline by typing words or phrases from your notes and rearranging them until the order makes sense. Later, you can use the categories from this informal outline to construct a formal outline (see page 48).

A STUDENT WRITER: Making an Informal Outline

The following informal outline shows how Laura Bobnak grouped her ideas:

During test
   Found test hard
   Saw Jeff cheating

After test
   Got angry
   Wanted to tell
   Dismissed idea

In college
   Understand implications of cheating
   Understand goals of education

Exercise 7

Continue your work on the topic you selected in Exercise 6 (page 26). Brainstorm about your topic; then, select the ideas you plan to write about in your essay, and use either clustering or an informal outline to group these ideas.

UNDERSTANDING THESIS AND SUPPORT

Once you have grouped your ideas, you need to consider your essay's thesis. A **thesis** is the main idea of your essay, its central point. The concept of *thesis and support* — stating your thesis and developing ideas that explain and expand it — is central to college writing.

The essays you write will consist of several paragraphs: an **introduction** that presents your thesis statement, several **body paragraphs** that develop and support your thesis, and a **conclusion** that reinforces your thesis and provides closure. Your thesis holds this structure together; it is the center the rest of your essay develops around.

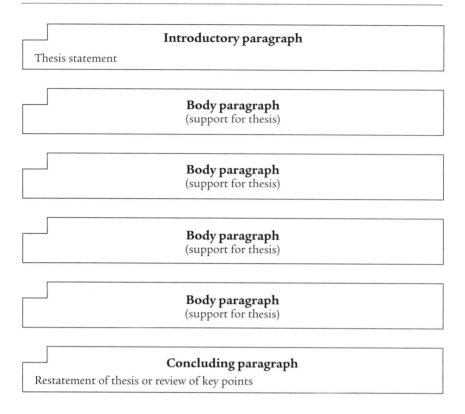

DEVELOPING A THESIS

Defining the Thesis Statement

A **thesis statement** is more than a *title*, an *announcement of your intent*, or a *statement of fact*. Although a descriptive title orients your readers, it is not detailed enough to reveal your essay's purpose or direction. An announcement of your intent can reveal more, but it is stylistically distracting. Finally, a statement of fact — such as a historical fact or a statistic — is a dead end and therefore cannot be developed into an essay. For example, a statement like "Alaska became a state in 1959" or "Tuberculosis is highly contagious" or "The population of Greece is about ten million" provides your essay with no direction. However, a judgment or opinion *can* be an effective thesis — for instance, "The continuing threat of tuberculosis, particularly in the inner cities, suggests it is necessary to frequently test high-risk populations."

Title	Hybrid Cars: Pro and Con
Announcement	I will examine the pros and cons of hybrid cars that use both gasoline and electricity.
Statement of fact	Hybrid cars are more energy efficient than cars with standard gasoline engines.

Thesis statement	Hybrid cars that use both gasoline and electricity would decrease our country's dependence on foreign oil.
Title	Orwell's "A Hanging"
Announcement	This paper will discuss George Orwell's attitude toward the death penalty in his essay "A Hanging."
Statement of fact	In his essay, Orwell describes a hanging that he witnessed in Burma.
Thesis statement	In "A Hanging," George Orwell shows that capital punishment is not only brutal but also immoral.
Title	Speaking Out
Announcement	This essay will discuss a time when I could have spoken out but did not.
Statement of fact	Once I saw someone cheating and did not speak out.
Thesis statement	As I look back at the cheating I witnessed, I wonder why I kept silent and what would have happened if I had acted.

Deciding on a Thesis

No rules determine when you formulate your thesis; the decision depends on the scope of your assignment, your knowledge of the subject, and your method of writing. When you know a lot about a subject, you may come up with a thesis before doing any invention activities (freewriting or brainstorming, for example). At other times, you may have to review your notes and then think of a single statement that communicates your position on the topic. Occasionally, your assignment may specify a thesis by telling you to take a particular position on a topic. In any case, you should decide on a thesis statement before you begin to write your first draft.

As you write, you will continue to discover new ideas, and you will probably move in directions that you did not anticipate. For this reason, the thesis statement you develop at this stage of the writing process is only **tentative**. Still, because a tentative thesis helps you to focus your ideas, it is essential at the initial stages of writing. As you draft your essay, review your thesis statement in light of the points you make, and revise it accordingly.

Stating Your Thesis

It is a good idea to include a one-sentence statement of your thesis early in your essay. An effective thesis statement has three characteristics:

1. *An effective thesis statement clearly expresses your essay's main idea.* It does more than state your topic; it indicates what you will say about your topic, and it signals how you will approach your material. The following thesis statement, from the essay "Grant and Lee: A Study in Contrasts" by Bruce Catton (page 405), clearly communicates the writer's main idea:

> They [Grant and Lee] were two strong men, these oddly different generals, and they represented the strengths of two conflicting currents that, through them, had come into final collision.

This statement says that the essay will compare and contrast Grant and Lee. Specifically, it indicates that Catton will present the two Civil War generals as symbols of two opposing historical currents. If the statement had been less fully developed — for example, had Catton written, "Grant and Lee were quite different from each other" — it would have just echoed the essay's title.

2. *An effective thesis statement communicates your essay's purpose.* Whether your purpose is to evaluate or analyze or simply to describe or inform, your thesis statement should communicate that purpose to your readers. In general terms, your thesis can be **expressive**, conveying a mood or impression; it can be **informative**, perhaps listing the major points you will discuss or presenting an objective overview of the essay; or it can be **persuasive**, taking a strong stand or outlining the position you will argue.

Each of the following thesis statements communicates a different purpose:

To express feelings	The city's homeless families live in heartbreaking surroundings.
To inform	The plight of the homeless has become so serious that it is a major priority for many city governments.
To persuade	The best way to address the problems of the homeless is to renovate abandoned city buildings to create suitable housing for homeless families.

3. *An effective thesis statement is clearly worded.* To communicate your essay's main idea, an effective thesis statement should be specifically worded. (It should also speak for itself. It is not necessary to write, "My thesis is that . . ." or "The thesis of this paper is. . . .") The thesis statement should give a clear and accurate indication of what follows and not mislead readers about the essay's direction, emphasis, scope, content, or viewpoint. Vague language, confusing abstractions, irrelevant details, and unnecessarily complex terminology have no place in a thesis statement. Keep in mind, too, that your thesis statement should not make promises that your essay is not going to keep. For example, if you are going to discuss just the *effects* of new immigration laws, your thesis statement should not emphasize the events that resulted in their passage.

Your thesis statement cannot, of course, include every point you will discuss in your essay. Still, it should be specific enough to indicate your direction and scope. The sentence "New immigration laws have failed to stem the tide of illegal immigrants" is not an effective thesis statement because it does not give your essay much focus. Which immigration laws will you be examining? Which illegal immigrants? The following sentence, however, *is* an effective thesis statement. It clearly indicates what the writer is going to discuss, and it establishes a specific direction for the essay:

> Because they do not take into account the economic causes of immigration, current immigration laws do little to decrease the number of illegal immigrants coming from Mexico into the United States.

Implying a Thesis

Like an explicitly stated thesis, an **implied thesis** conveys an essay's purpose, but it does not do so explicitly. Instead, the selection and arrangement of the essay's ideas suggest the purpose. Professional writers sometimes prefer this option because an implied thesis is subtler than a stated thesis. (An implied thesis is especially useful in narratives, descriptions, and some arguments, where an explicit thesis would seem heavy-handed or arbitrary.) In most college writing, however, you should state your thesis to avoid any risk of being misunderstood or of wandering away from your topic.

A STUDENT WRITER: Developing a Thesis

After experimenting with different ways of arranging her ideas for her essay, Laura Bobnak summed them up in a tentative thesis statement:

> As I look back at the cheating I witnessed, I wonder why I kept silent and what would have happened if I had acted.

Exercise 8

Assess the strengths and weaknesses of the following as thesis statements.

1. My instructor has an attendance policy.
2. My instructor should change her attendance policy because it is bad.
3. My instructor should change her attendance policy because it is unreasonable, inflexible, and unfair.
4. For many people, a community college makes more sense than a four-year college or university.
5. Some children show violent behavior.
6. Violence is a problem in society.
7. Conflict-resolution courses should be taught to help prevent violence in America's schools.
8. Social networking sites such as Facebook can cause problems.
9. Facebook attracts many college students.
10. College students should be careful of what material they put on their Facebook pages because prospective employers routinely check them.

Exercise 9

Rewrite the following factual statements to make them effective thesis statements. Make sure each thesis statement is a clearly and specifically worded sentence.

1. Many hospitals will not admit patients without health insurance because they are afraid that such patients will not be able to pay their bills.
2. Several Supreme Court decisions have said that art containing explicit sexual images is not necessarily pornographic.
3. Many women earn less money than men do, in part because they drop out of the workforce during their child-rearing years.
4. People who watch more than five hours of television a day tend to think the world is more violent than do people who watch less than two hours of television daily.
5. In recent years, the suicide rate among teenagers — especially middle- and upper-middle-class teenagers — has risen dramatically.

Exercise 10

Read the following sentences from "The Argument Culture" by Deborah Tannen. Then, formulate a one-sentence thesis statement that summarizes the key points Tannen makes about the naure of argument in our culture.

- "More and more, our public interactions have become like arguing with a spouse."
- "Nearly everything is framed as a battle or game in which winning or losing is the main concern."
- "The argument culture pervades every aspect of our lives today."
- "Issues from global warming to abortion are depicted as two-sided arguments, when in fact most Americans' views lie somewhere in the middle."
- "What's wrong with the argument culture is the ubiquity, the knee-jerk nature of approaching any issue, problem, or public person in an adversarial way."
- "If you fight to win, the temptation is great to deny facts that support your opponent's views and say only what supports your side."
- "We must expand the notion of 'debate' to include more dialogue."
- "Perhaps it is time to re-examine the assumption that audiences always prefer a fight."
- "Instead of insisting on hearing 'both sides,' let's insist on hearing 'all sides.'"

Exercise 11

Go through as many steps as you need to formulate an effective thesis statement for the essay you have been working on.

3

Arrangement

Each of the tasks discussed in Chapter 2 represents choices you have to make about your topic and your material. Now, before you actually begin to write, you have another choice to make — how to arrange your material into an essay.

RECOGNIZING A PATTERN

Sometimes arranging your ideas will be easy because your assignment specifies a particular pattern of development. This may be the case in a composition class, where the instructor may assign a descriptive or a narrative essay. Also, certain assignments or exam questions suggest how your material should be structured. For example, an instructor might ask you to tell about how something works, or an exam question might ask you to trace the circumstances leading up to an event. If you are perceptive, you will realize that your instructor is asking for a process essay and that the exam question is asking for either a narrative or a cause-and-effect response. The important thing is to recognize the clues such assignments give (or those you find in your topic or thesis statement) and to structure your essay accordingly.

One clue to structuring your essay may be found in the questions that proved most helpful when you probed your subject (see page 23). For example, if questions like "What happened?" and "When did it happen?" yielded the most useful information about your topic, you should consider structuring your paper as a narrative. The chart on page 38 links various questions to the patterns of development they suggest. Notice that the terms in the right-hand column — narration, description, and so on — identify patterns of development that can help order your ideas. Chapters 6 through 13 explain and illustrate each of these patterns.

✓ **CHECKLIST:** Recognizing a Pattern

What happened?
When did it happen?   } Narration
Where did it happen?
Who did it?

What does it look like?
What are its characteristics?   } Description
What impression does it make?

What are some typical cases
  or examples of it?   } Exemplification

How did it happen?
What makes it work?   } Process
How is it made?

Why did it happen?
What caused it?
What does it cause?   } Cause and effect
What are its effects?

How is it like other things?
How is it different from other } Comparison and contrast
  things?

What are its parts or types?
How can its parts or types be
  separated or grouped?
Do its parts or types fit into a
  logical order?   } Classification and division
Into what categories can its
  parts or types be arranged?
On what basis can it be
  categorized?

What is it?
How does it resemble other
  members of its class?   } Definition
How does it differ from other
  members of its class?

UNDERSTANDING THE PARTS OF THE ESSAY

No matter what pattern of development you use, your essay should have a beginning, a middle, and an end — that is, an *introduction,* a *body,* and a *conclusion.*

The Introduction

The **introduction** of your essay, usually one paragraph and rarely more than two, introduces your subject, creates interest, and often states your thesis.

You can introduce an essay and engage your readers' interest in a number of ways. Here are several options for beginning an essay (in each paragraph, the thesis statement is underlined):

1. You can begin with *background information*. This approach works well when you know the audience is already interested in your topic and you can come directly to the point. This strategy is especially useful for exams, where there is no need (or time) for subtlety.

> With inflation low, many companies have understandably lowered prices, and the oil industry should be no exception. Consequently, homeowners have begun wondering whether the high price of home heating oil is justified given the economic climate. It makes sense, therefore, for us to start examining the pricing policies of the major American oil companies. (economics essay)

2. You can introduce an essay with your own original *definition* of a relevant term or concept. This technique is especially useful for research papers or exams, where the meaning of a specific term is crucial.

> Democracy is a form of government in which power is given to and exercised by the people. This may be true in theory, but some recent elections have raised concerns about the future of democracy. Extensive voting-machine irregularities and "ghost voting" have jeopardized people's faith in the democratic process. (political science exam)

3. You can begin your essay with an *anecdote* or *story* that leads readers to your thesis.

> Three years ago, I went with my grandparents to my first auction. They live in a small town outside of Lancaster, Pennsylvania, where it is common for relatives to auction off the contents of a home when someone moves or dies. As I walked through the crowd, I smelled the funnel cakes in the food trucks, heard the hypnotic chanting of the auctioneer, and sensed the excitement of the crowd. Two hours later, I walked off with an old trunk that I had bought for thirty dollars and a passion for auctions that I still have today. (composition essay)

4. You can begin with a *question*.

> What was it like to live through the Holocaust? Elie Wiesel, in *One Generation After,* answers this question by presenting a series of accounts about ordinary people who found themselves imprisoned in Nazi death camps. As he does so, he challenges some of the assumptions we have about those who survived the Holocaust. (sociology book report)

5. You can begin with a *quotation*. If it arouses interest, it can encourage your audience to read further.

> "The rich are different," F. Scott Fitzgerald said more than seventy years ago. Apparently, they still are. <u>As an examination of the tax code shows, the wealthy receive many more benefits than the middle class or the poor do.</u>   (accounting paper)

6. You can begin with a *surprising statement*. An unexpected statement catches readers' attention and makes them want to read more.

> Believe it or not, most people who live in the suburbs are not white and rich. My family, for example, fits into neither of these categories. Ten years ago, my family and I came to the United States from Pakistan. My parents were poor then, and by some standards, they are still poor even though they both work two jobs. Still, they eventually saved enough to buy a small house in the suburbs of Chicago. <u>Throughout the country, there are many suburban families like mine who are working hard to make ends meet so that their children can get a good education and go to college.</u>   (composition essay)

7. You can begin with a *contradiction*. You can open your essay with an idea that most people believe is true and then get readers' attention by showing that it is inaccurate or ill advised.

> Many people think that after the Declaration of Independence was signed in 1776, the colonists defeated the British army in battle after battle. This commonly held belief is incorrect. The truth is that the colonial army lost most of its battles. <u>The British were defeated not because the colonial army was stronger, but because George Washington refused to be lured into a costly winner-take-all battle and because the British government lost interest in pursuing an expensive war three thousand miles from home.</u>   (history take-home exam)

8. You can begin with a *fact* or *statistic*.

> According to a recent government study, recipients of Medicare will spend billions of dollars on drugs over the next ten years. This is a very large amount of money, and it illustrates why lawmakers must do more to help older Americans with the cost of medications. <u>Although the current legislation is an important first step, more must be done to help the elderly afford the drugs they need.</u>   (public policy essay)

No matter which strategy you select, your introduction should be consistent in tone with the rest of your essay. If it is not, it can misrepresent your intentions and even damage your credibility. (For this reason, it is a good idea not to write your introduction until after you have finished the rest of your rough draft.) A technical report, for instance, should have an introduction that reflects the formality and objectivity the occasion requires. The introduction to an autobiographical essay, however, should have a more informal, subjective tone.

WHAT NOT TO DO IN AN INTRODUCTION

- **Don't apologize.** Never use phrases such as "in my opinion" or "I may not be an expert, but. . . ." By doing so, you suggest that you don't really know your subject.
- **Don't begin with a dictionary definition.** Avoid beginning an essay with phrases like "According to Webster's Dictionary. . . ." This type of introduction is overused and trite. If you want to use a definition, develop your own.
- **Don't announce what you intend to do.** Don't begin with phrases such as "In this paper I will . . ." or "The purpose of this essay is to. . . ." Use your introduction to create interest in your topic, and let readers discover your intention when they get to your thesis statement.
- **Don't wander.** Your introduction should draw readers into your essay as soon as possible. Avoid irrelevant comments or annoying digressions that will distract readers and make them want to stop reading.

Exercise 1

Look through magazine articles or the essays in this book, and find one example of each kind of introduction. Why do you think each introductory strategy was chosen? What other strategies might have worked?

The Body Paragraphs

The middle section, or **body**, of your essay develops your thesis. The body paragraphs present the support that convinces your audience your thesis is reasonable. To do so, each body paragraph should be *unified, coherent,* and *well developed.* It should also follow a particular pattern of development and should clearly support your thesis.

• *Each body paragraph should be unified.* A paragraph is **unified** when each sentence relates directly to the main idea of the paragraph. Sometimes the main idea of a paragraph is stated in a **topic sentence**. Like a thesis statement, a topic sentence acts as a guidepost, making it easy for readers to follow the paragraph's discussion. Although the placement of a topic sentence depends on a writer's purpose and subject, beginning writers often make it the first sentence of a paragraph.

Sometimes the main idea of a paragraph is not stated but **implied** by the sentences in the paragraph. Professional writers frequently use this technique because they believe that in some situations — especially narratives and descriptions — a topic sentence can seem forced or awkward. As a beginning writer, however, you will find it helpful to use topic sentences to keep your paragraphs focused.

Whether or not you include a topic sentence, remember that each sentence in a paragraph should develop the paragraph's main idea. If the sentences in a paragraph do not support the main idea, the paragraph will lack unity.

In the following excerpt from a student essay, notice how the topic sentence (underlined) unifies the paragraph by summarizing its main idea:

> <u>Another problem with fast food is that it contains additives.</u> Fast-food companies know that to keep their customers happy, they have to give them food that tastes good, and this is where the trouble starts. For example, to give fries flavor, McDonald's used to fry their potatoes in beef fat. Shockingly, their fries actually had more saturated fat than their hamburgers did. When the public found out how unhealthy their fries were, the company switched to vegetable oil. What most people don't know, however, is that McDonald's adds a chemical derived from animals to the vegetable oil to give it the taste of beef tallow.

The topic sentence, placed at the beginning of the paragraph, enables readers to grasp the writer's point immediately. The examples that follow all relate to that point, making the paragraph unified.

• *Each body paragraph should be coherent.* A paragraph is **coherent** if its sentences are smoothly and logically connected to one another. Coherence can be strengthened in three ways. First, you can repeat **key words** to carry concepts from one sentence to another and to echo important terms. Second, you can use **pronouns** to refer to key nouns in previous sentences. Finally, you can use **transitions**, words or expressions that show chronological sequence, cause and effect, and so on (see the list of transitions on page 43). These three strategies for connecting sentences — which you can also use to connect paragraphs within an essay — indicate for your readers the exact relationships among your ideas.

The following paragraph, from George Orwell's "Shooting an Elephant" (page 126), uses repeated key words, pronouns, and transitions to achieve coherence:

> I got up. The Burmans were already racing past me across the mud. It was obvious that the elephant would never rise again, but he was not dead. He was breathing very rhythmically with long rattling gasps, his great mound of a side painfully rising and falling. His mouth was wide open — I could see far down into the caverns of pale pink throat. I waited a long time for him to die, but his breathing did not weaken. Finally, I fired my two remaining shots into the spot where I thought his heart must be. The thick blood welled out of him like red velvet, but still he did not die. His body did not even jerk when the shots hit him, the tortured breathing continued without a pause. He was dying, very slowly and in great agony, but in some world remote from me where not even a bullet could damage him further. I felt that I had got to put an end to that dreadful noise. It seemed dreadful to see the great beast lying there, powerless to move and yet powerless to die, and not even to be able to finish him. I sent back for my small rifle and poured shot after shot into his heart and down his throat. They seemed to make no impression. The tortured gasps continued as steadily as the ticking of a clock.

TRANSITIONS

SEQUENCE OR ADDITION

again	first, . . . second, . . . third	next
also	furthermore	one . . . another
and	in addition	still
besides	last	too
finally	moreover	

TIME

afterward	finally	simultaneously
as soon as	immediately	since
at first	in the meantime	soon
at the same time	later	subsequently
before	meanwhile	then
earlier	next	until
eventually	now	

COMPARISON

also	likewise
in comparison	similarly
in the same way	

CONTRAST

although	in contrast	on the one hand . . .
but	instead	on the other hand . . .
conversely	nevertheless	still
despite	nonetheless	whereas
even though	on the contrary	yet
however		

EXAMPLES

for example	specifically
for instance	that is
in fact	thus
namely	

CONCLUSIONS OR SUMMARIES

as a result	in summary
in conclusion	therefore
in short	thus

CAUSES OR EFFECTS

as a result	so
because	then
consequently	therefore
since	

Orwell keeps his narrative coherent by using transitional expressions (*already, finally, when the shots hit him*) to signal the passing of time. He uses pronouns (*he, his*) in nearly every sentence to refer back to the elephant, the topic of his paragraph. Finally, he repeats key words like *shots* and *die* (and its variants *dead* and *dying*) to link the whole paragraph's sentences together.

• *Each body paragraph should be well developed.* A paragraph is **well developed** if it contains the **support** — examples, reasons, and so on — readers need to understand its main idea. If a paragraph is not adequately developed, readers will feel they have been given only a partial picture of the subject.

If you decide you need more information in a paragraph, you can look back at your brainstorming notes. If this doesn't help, you can freewrite or brainstorm again, talk with friends and instructors, read more about your topic, or (with your instructor's permission) do some research. Your assignment and your topic will determine the kind and amount of information you need.

TYPES OF SUPPORT

- **Examples**   Specific illustrations of a general idea or concept
- **Reasons**   Underlying causes or explanations
- **Facts**   Pieces of information that can be verified or proved
- **Statistics**   Numerical data (for example, results of studies by reputable authorities or organizations)
- **Details**   Parts or portions of a whole (for example, steps in a process)
- **Expert opinions**   Statements by recognized authorities in a particular field
- **Personal experiences**   Events that you lived through
- **Visuals**   Diagrams, charts, graphs, or photographs

✓ CHECKLIST: Effective Support

- **Support should be relevant.**   Body paragraphs should clearly relate to your essay's thesis. Irrelevant material — material that does not pertain to the thesis — should be deleted.
- **Support should be specific.**   Body paragraphs should contain support that is specific, not general or vague. Specific examples, clear reasons, and precise explanations engage readers and communicate your ideas to them.

- **Support should be adequate.** Body paragraphs should contain enough facts, reasons, and examples to support your thesis. How much support you need depends on your audience, your purpose, and the scope of your thesis.

- **Support should be representative.** Body paragraphs should present support that is typical, not atypical. For example, suppose you write a paper claiming that flu shots do not work. Your support for this claim is that your grandmother got the flu even though she was vaccinated. This example is not representative because studies show that most people who get vaccinated do not get the flu.

- **Support should be documented.** Support that comes from research (print sources and the Internet, for example) should be documented. (For more information on proper documentation, see the Appendix). **Plagiarism** — failure to document the ideas and words of others — is not only unfair but also dishonest. For this reason, be sure to use proper documentation to acknowledge your debt to your sources. (Keep in mind that words and ideas you borrow from the essays in this book must also be documented.)

The following student paragraph uses two examples to support its topic sentence:

Example 1
Just look at how males have been taught that extravagance is a positive characteristic. Scrooge, the main character of Dickens's *A Christmas Carol,* is portrayed as an evil man until he gives up his miserly ways and freely distributes gifts and money on Christmas day. This behavior, of course, is rewarded when people change their opinions about him and decide that he isn't such a bad person after all.

Example 2
Diamond Jim Brady is another interesting example. This individual was a nineteenth-century financier who was known for his extravagant taste in women and food. On any given night, he would eat enough food to feed at least ten of the numerous poor who roamed the streets of New York at that time. Yet, despite his selfishness and infantile self-gratification, Diamond Jim Brady's name has become associated with the good life.

- *Each body paragraph should follow a particular pattern of development.* In addition to making sure your body paragraphs are unified, coherent, and well developed, you need to organize each paragraph according to a specific pattern of development. (Chapters 6 through 13 each begin with a paragraph-length example of the pattern discussed in the chapter.)

- *Each body paragraph should clearly support the thesis statement.* No matter how many body paragraphs your essay has — three, four, five, or even more — each paragraph should introduce and develop an idea that supports the essay's thesis. Each paragraph's topic sentence should express

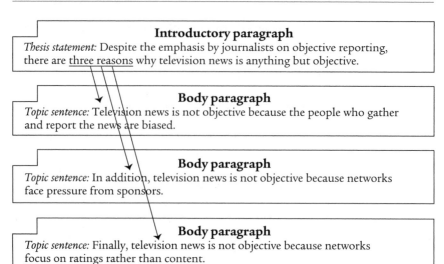

Introductory paragraph

Thesis statement: Despite the emphasis by journalists on objective reporting, there are <u>three reasons</u> why television news is anything but objective.

Body paragraph

Topic sentence: Television news is not objective because the people who gather and report the news are biased.

Body paragraph

Topic sentence: In addition, television news is not objective because networks face pressure from sponsors.

Body paragraph

Topic sentence: Finally, television news is not objective because networks focus on ratings rather than content.

Concluding paragraph

Restatement of thesis: Even though television journalists claim to strive for objectivity, the truth is that this ideal has been impossible to achieve.

one of these supporting points. The diagram above illustrates this thesis-and-support structure.

Exercise 2

Choose a body paragraph from one of the essays in this book. Using the criteria discussed on pages 41–46, decide whether the paragraph is unified, coherent, and well developed.

Exercise 3

Choose one essay in this book, and underline its thesis statement. Then, determine how its body paragraphs support that thesis statement. (Note that in a long essay, several body paragraphs may develop a single supporting point, and some paragraphs may serve as transitions from one point to another.)

The Conclusion

Since readers remember best what they read last, your **conclusion** is very important. Always end your essay in a way that reinforces your thesis and your purpose.

Like your introduction, your conclusion is rarely longer than a paragraph. Regardless of its length, however, your conclusion should be consistent with the rest of your essay. It should not introduce points you have not discussed earlier. Frequently, a conclusion will summarize your essay's main idea. Like thesis statements, effective conclusions need no announcement, so you should avoid beginning them with the artificial phrase *In conclusion.*

Here are several ways to conclude an essay:

1. You can conclude your essay by *reviewing your key points* or *restating your thesis*.

> Rotation of crops provided several benefits. It enriched soil by giving it a rest; it enabled farmers to vary their production; and it ended the cycle of "boom or bust" that had characterized the prewar South's economy when cotton was the primary crop. Of course, this innovation did not solve all the economic problems of the postwar South, but it did lay the groundwork for the healthy economy this region enjoys today.
>
> (history exam)

2. You can end a discussion of a problem with a *recommendation of a course of action*.

> Well-qualified teachers are becoming harder and harder to find. For this reason, school boards should reassess their ideas about what qualifies someone to teach. At the present time, people who have spent their lives working in a particular field are denied certification because they have not taken any education courses. This policy deprives school systems of talented teachers. In order to ensure that students have the best possible teachers, school boards should consider applicants' real-world experience when evaluating their qualifications.   (education essay)

3. You can conclude with a *prediction*. Be sure, however, that your prediction follows logically from the points you have made in the essay. Your conclusion is no place to make new points or change direction.

> Campaign advertisements should help people understand a political candidate's qualifications and where he or she stands on critical issues. They should not appeal to people's fears or greed. Above all, they should not personally attack other candidates or oversimplify complex issues. If campaign advertisements continue to do these things, the American people will disregard them and reject the candidates they promote.
>
> (political science essay)

4. You can end with a relevant *quotation*.

> In *Walden,* Henry David Thoreau says, "The mass of men lead lives of quiet desperation." This sentiment is reinforced by a drive through the Hill District of our city. Perhaps the work of the men and women who run the clinic on Jefferson Street cannot totally change this situation, but it can give us hope to know that some people, at least, are working for the betterment of us all.   (public health essay)

....

WHAT NOT TO DO IN A CONCLUSION
....

- **Don't end by repeating the exact words of your thesis and listing your main points.**   Avoid boring endings that tell readers what they already know.
- **Don't end with an empty phrase.**   Avoid ending with a cliché like "This just goes to prove that you can never be too careful."
- **Don't introduce new points or go off in new directions.**   Your conclusion should not introduce new points for discussion. It should reinforce the points you have already made in your essay.
- **Don't end with an unnecessary announcement.**   Don't end by saying that you are ending — for example, "In conclusion, let me say. . . ." The tone of your conclusion should signal that the essay is drawing to a close.

....

Exercise 4

Look through magazine articles or the essays in this book, and find one example of each kind of conclusion. Why do you think each concluding strategy was chosen? What other strategies might have worked?

CONSTRUCTING A FORMAL OUTLINE

Before you begin to write, you may decide to construct a **formal outline** to guide you. Whereas informal outlines are preliminary lists that simply remind you which points to make, formal outlines are detailed, multilevel constructions that indicate the exact order in which you will present your points. The complexity of your assignment determines which type of outline you need. For a short paper, an informal outline like the one on page 31 is usually sufficient. For a longer, more complex essay, however, you may need a formal outline.

One way to construct a formal outline is to copy down the main headings from your informal outline. Then, arrange ideas from your brainstorming notes or cluster diagram as subheadings under the appropriate headings. As you work on your outline, make sure each idea you include supports your thesis. Ideas that don't fit should be reworded or discarded. As you revise your essay, continue to refer to your outline to make sure your thesis and support are logically related. The guidelines that follow will help you prepare a formal outline.

> ✓ CHECKLIST: Constructing a Formal Outline
>
> - Write your thesis statement at the top of the page.
> - Group main headings under roman numerals (*I, II, III, IV*, and so on), and place them flush with the left-hand margin.
> - Indent each subheading under the first word of the heading above it. Use capital letters before major points and numbers before supporting details.
> - Capitalize the first letter of the first word of each heading.
> - Make your outline as simple as possible, avoiding overly complex divisions of ideas. (Try not to go beyond third-level headings — *1, 2, 3,* and so on.)
> - Construct either a **topic outline**, with headings expressed as short phrases or single words ("Advantages and disadvantages"), or a **sentence outline**, with headings expressed as complete sentences ("The advantages of advanced placement chemistry outweigh the disadvantages"). *Never use both phrases and complete sentences in the same outline.*
> - Express all headings at the same level in parallel terms. (If roman numeral *I* is a noun, *II, III,* and *IV* should also be nouns.)
> - Make sure each heading contains at least two subdivisions. You cannot have a *1* without a *2* or an *A* without a *B*.
> - Make sure your headings do not overlap.

A STUDENT WRITER: Constructing a Formal Outline

The topic outline Laura Bobnak constructed follows the guidelines discussed above. Notice that her outline focuses on the body of her paper and does not include the introduction or conclusion: these are usually developed after the body has been drafted. (Compare this formal outline with the informal outline on page 31 where Laura simply grouped her brainstorming notes under three general headings.)

Thesis statement: As I look back at the cheating I witnessed, I wonder why I kept silent and what would have happened if I had acted.

    I. The incident
       A. Test situation
       B. My observation
       C. My reactions
          1. Anger
          2. Silence

    II. Reasons for keeping silent
       A. Other students' attitudes
       B. My fears
   III. Current attitude toward cheating
       A. Effects of cheating on education
       B. Effects of cheating on students

This outline enabled Laura to arrange her points so that they supported her thesis. As she went on to draft her essay, the outline reminded her to emphasize the contrast between her present and former attitudes toward cheating.

🖳   COMPUTER STRATEGY: **Constructing a Formal Outline**

If you use a computer to construct a formal outline, you can easily arrange and rearrange your headings until your outline is logical and complete. (Your word-processing program will have an outline function that automatically indents and numbers items.) If you saved your prewriting notes in computer files, you can refer to them while working on your outline and perhaps add or modify headings to reflect what you find.

Exercise 5

Read the thesis statement you developed in Chapter 2, Exercise 11 (on page 36), as well as all the notes you made for the essay you are planning. Then, make a topic outline that lists the points you will discuss in your essay. When you are finished, check to make sure your outline conforms to the guidelines in the checklist on page 49.

4
Drafting and Revising

After you decide on a thesis and an arrangement for your ideas, you can begin to draft and revise your essay. Keep in mind that even as you carry out these activities, you may have to generate more material or revise your thesis statement.

WRITING YOUR FIRST DRAFT

The purpose of your **first draft** is to get your ideas down on paper so that you can react to them. Experienced writers know that the first draft is nothing more than a work in progress; it exists to be revised. With this in mind, you should expect to cross out and extensively rearrange material. In addition, don't be surprised if you think of new ideas as you write. If a new idea comes to you, go with it. Some of the best writing comes from unexpected turns or accidents. The following guidelines will help you prepare your first draft.

✓ CHECKLIST: Drafting

- **Begin with the body paragraphs.** Because your essay will probably be revised extensively, don't take the time at this stage to write an introduction or conclusion. Let your thesis statement guide you as you draft the body paragraphs of your essay. Later, when you have finished, you can write an appropriate introduction and conclusion.
- **Get your ideas down quickly.** Don't worry about grammar or word choice, and try not to interrupt the flow of your writing with concerns about style.
- **Take regular breaks as you write.** Don't write until you are so exhausted you can't think straight. Many writers divide their writing into stages, perhaps completing one or two body paragraphs and

(continued on next page)

(continued from previous page)
    then taking a short break. This strategy is more efficient than trying to write a complete first draft without stopping.

- **Write with revision in mind.** Leave enough space between lines so that you will have room to make changes by hand on hard copy.
- **Leave yourself time to revise.** Remember, your first draft is a *rough draft*. All writing benefits from revision, so allow enough time to write two or more drafts.

A STUDENT WRITER: Writing a First Draft

Here is the first draft of Laura Bobnak's essay on the topic "Write about a time when you, like Henry Louis Gates's father, could have spoken out but chose not to. Would you make the same decision today?"

When I was in high school, I had an experience like the one Henry Louis Gates talks about in his essay. It was then that I saw a close friend cheat in chemistry class. As I look back at the cheating I witnessed, I wonder why I kept silent and what would have happened if I had acted. 1

The incident I am going to describe took place during the final exam for my advanced placement chemistry class. I had studied hard for it, but even so, I found the test difficult. As I struggled to balance a particularly difficult equation, I noticed that my friend Jeff Servin, who was sitting across from me, was acting strangely. I noticed that he was copying material from a paper. After watching him for a while, I dismissed the incident and got back to my test. 2

After the test was over, I began to think about what I had seen. The more I thought about it the angrier I got. It seemed unfair that I had studied for weeks to memorize formulas and equations while all Jeff had done was to copy them onto a cheat sheet. For a moment I considered going to the teacher, but I quickly rejected this idea. After all, cheating was something everybody did. Besides, I was afraid if I told on Jeff, my friends would stop talking to me. 3

Now that I am in college I see the situation differently. I find it hard to believe that I could ever have been so calm about cheating. Cheating is certainly something that students should not take for granted. It undercuts the education process and is unfair to teachers and to the majority of students who spend their time studying. 4

If I could go back to high school and relive the experience, I now know that I would have gone to the teacher. Naturally Jeff would have been angry at me, but at least I would have known I had the courage to do the right thing. 5

Exercise 1

Write a draft of the essay you have been working on in Chapters 2 and 3. Be sure to look back at all your notes as well as your outline.

REVISING YOUR ESSAY

Revision is not something you do after your paper is finished. It is a continuing process during which you consider the logic and clarity of your ideas, as well as how effectively they are presented.

Revision is not simply a matter of proofreading or editing, of crossing out one word and substituting another or correcting errors in spelling and punctuation; revision involves reexamining and rethinking what you have written. When you revise, you may find yourself adding and deleting extensively, reordering whole sentences or paragraphs as you reconsider what you want to communicate to your audience.

Revision can take a lot of time, so don't be discouraged if you have to go through three or four drafts before you think your essay is ready to hand in. The following advice can help you when you revise your essay:

- *Give yourself a cooling-off period.*   Put your first draft aside for several hours or even a day or two if you can. This cooling-off period lets you distance yourself from your essay so that you can read it more objectively when you return to it. When you read it again, you will see things you missed the first time.

- *Revise on hard copy.*   Because a printed-out draft shows you your entire paper and enables you to see your handwritten edits, you should always revise on hard copy instead of directly on the computer screen.

- *Read your draft aloud.*   Before you revise, read your draft aloud to help you spot choppy sentences, missing words, or phrases that do not sound right.

- *Take advantage of opportunities to get feedback.*   Your instructor may organize peer critique sessions, distribute a revision checklist, refer students to a writing center, or schedule one-on-one conferences. Make use of as many of these opportunities for feedback as you can; each offers you a different way of gaining information about what you have written.

- *Try not to get overwhelmed.*   It is easy to become overwhelmed by all the feedback you get about your draft. To avoid this, approach revision systematically. Don't automatically make all the changes people suggest; consider the validity of each change. Also ask yourself whether comments suggest larger issues. For example, does a comment about a series of choppy sentences suggest a need for you to add transitions, or does it mean you need to rethink your ideas?

- *Don't let your ego get in the way.*   Everyone likes praise, and receiving negative criticism is never pleasant. Experienced writers know, however, that they must get feedback if they are going to improve their work. Learn to see criticism — whether from an instructor or from your peers — as a necessary part of the revision process.

- *Revise in stages.* Deal with the large elements (essay and paragraph structure) before moving on to the smaller elements (sentence structure and word choice).

How you revise — what specific strategies you decide to use — depends on your own preference, your instructor's instructions, and the time available. Like the rest of the writing process, revision varies from student to student and from assignment to assignment. Four of the most useful revision strategies are *revising with a checklist, revising with an outline, revising with a peer critique,* and *revising with your instructor's comments.*

Revising with a Checklist

If you have time, you can use the following revision checklist, adapting it to your own writing process.

✓ **CHECKLIST: Revision**

- **Thesis statement** Is your thesis statement clear and specific? Does it indicate the direction your essay is taking? Is it consistent with the body of your essay? If you departed from your essay's original direction while you were writing, you may need to revise your thesis statement so that it accurately sums up the ideas and information now contained in the body. Or, you may need to delete from the body any material that is unrelated to the thesis statement — or revise it so that it *is* relevant.

- **Body** Are the body paragraphs unified? Coherent? Well developed? If not, you might have to add more facts or examples or smoother transitions. Does each body paragraph follow a particular pattern of development? Do the points you make in these paragraphs support your thesis?

- **Introduction and conclusion** Are your introduction and your conclusion appropriate for your material, your audience, and your purpose? Are they interesting? Do they reinforce your thesis?

- **Sentences** Are your sentences effective? Interesting? Varied in length and structure? Should any sentences be deleted, combined, or moved?

- **Words** Do your words accurately express your ideas? Should you make any changes?

Revising with an Outline

If you do not have time to consult a detailed checklist, you can check your essay's structure by making a **review outline**. Either an informal outline or a formal one can show you whether you have omitted any important points. An outline can also show you whether your essay follows a particular pattern of development. Finally, an outline can clarify the relationship between your thesis statement and your body paragraphs. (See pages 48–49 for guidelines for constructing an outline.)

Revising with a Peer Critique

Another revision strategy is seeking a **peer critique** — asking a friend to read your essay and comment on it. Sometimes a peer critique can be formal. An instructor may require students to exchange papers and evaluate their classmates' work according to certain standards, perhaps by completing a **peer editing worksheet**. (See pages 57–58 for an example.) Often, however, a peer critique is informal. Even if a friend is unfamiliar with your topic, he or she can still tell you honestly whether you are getting your point across — and maybe even advise you about how to communicate more effectively. (Remember, though, that your critic should be only your reader, not your ghostwriter.)

The use of peer critiques mirrors how people in the real world actually write. Businesspeople circulate reports to get feedback from coworkers; scientists and academics routinely collaborate when they write. (And, as you may have realized, even this book is the result of a collaboration.)

Your classmates can be helpful as you write the early drafts of your essay, providing suggestions that can guide you through the revision process. In addition, they can respond to questions you may have about your essay — for example, whether your introduction works or whether one of your supporting points needs more explanation. When friends ask *you* to critique their work, the following guidelines should help you.

COMPUTER STRATEGY: Revising

When you revise, make sure you do not delete text you may need later. Move this information to the end of the draft or to a separate file. That way, if you change your mind about a deletion or if you find you need information you took out of a draft, you can recover it easily.

✓ **CHECKLIST:** Guidelines for Peer Critiques

- **Be positive.** Remember that your purpose is to help other students improve their essays.
- **Be tactful.** Be sure to emphasize the good points about the essay. Mention one or two things the writer has done particularly well before you offer your suggestions.
- **Be specific.** Offer concrete suggestions about what the writer could do better. Vague words like *good* or *bad* provide little help.
- **Be involved.** If you are doing a critique orally, make sure you interact with the writer. Ask questions, listen to responses, and explain your comments.
- **Look at the big picture.** Don't focus exclusively on issues such as spelling and punctuation. At this stage, the clarity of the thesis statement, the effectiveness of the support, and the organization of the writer's ideas are much more important.
- **Be thorough.** When possible, write down and explain your comments, either on a form your instructor provides or in the margins of the draft you are reviewing.

Revising with Your Instructor's Comments

Your instructor's **written comments** on a draft of your essay can also help you revise by suggesting changes in content, arrangement, or style. For example, these comments may question your logic, suggest a clearer thesis statement, ask for more explicit transitions, recommend that a paragraph be relocated, or even propose a new direction for your essay. They may also recommend stylistic changes or ask you to provide more support in one or more of your body paragraphs. You may decide to incorporate these suggestions into the next draft of your essay, or you may decide not to. Whatever the case, you should take your instructor's comments seriously and make reading and responding to them a part of your revision process.

Here is a paragraph from the first draft of Laura Bobnak's essay along with her instructor's comments.

Your tenative thesis statement is good — as far as it goes. It really doesn't address the second half of the assignment — namely, would you make the same decision today?

When I was in high school, I had an experience like the one Henry Louis Gates talks about in his essay. It was then that I saw a close friend cheat in chemistry class. As I look back at the cheating I witnessed, I wonder why I kept silent and what would have happened if I had acted.

COMPUTER STRATEGY: Revising

It is usually not a good idea to begin revising directly on the computer screen. Since most screens show only a portion of a page, the connections between ideas are hard to see and to keep track of. Even with the split-screen option that some word-processing programs offer, you cannot view several pages of a draft at once or easily compare one draft to another. For these reasons, you should revise on a hard copy of your essay. Once you have made your handwritten corrections, you can type them into your paper.

Your instructor's **oral comments** at a one-on-one conference can also help you revise. If your instructor encourages (or requires) you to schedule a conference, come to the conference prepared. Read all your drafts carefully and bring a copy of your most recent draft as well as a list of any questions you may have. During the conference, you can ask your instructor to clarify marginal comments or to help you revise a particular section of your essay that is giving you trouble. Make sure you take notes during the conference so that you will have a record of what you and your instructor discussed. Remember that the more prepared for the conference you are, the more you will get out of it. (Some instructors use email to answer questions and to give students feedback.)

A STUDENT WRITER: Revising a First Draft

When she revised the first draft of her essay (page 52), Laura Bobnak followed the revision process discussed above. After writing her rough draft, she put it aside for a few hours and then reread it. Later, her instructor divided the class into pairs and had them read each other's essays and fill out **peer editing worksheets**. After reading and discussing the following worksheet (filled out by one of her classmates), Laura was able to focus on a number of areas that needed revision.

📄   **PEER EDITING WORKSHEET**

1. What is the essay's thesis? Is it clearly worded? Does it provide a focus for the essay?

   "As I look back at the cheating I witnessed, I wonder why I kept silent and what would have happened if I had acted." The thesis is clear and gives a good idea of what the essay is about.

2. Do the body paragraphs clearly support the essay's thesis? Should any of the topic sentences be revised? Which, if any, could be more clearly worded?

   (continued on next page)

(continued from previous page)

> The topic sentences seem fine — each one seems to tell what the paragraph is about.

3. How do the body paragraphs develop the essay's main idea? Where could the writer have used more detail?

> Each of the body paragraphs tells a part of the narrative. You could add more detail about how the exam room was set up — I really can't picture the scene.

4. Can you follow the writer's ideas? Does the essay need transitions?

> I have no problem following your ideas. Maybe you could have added some more transitions, but I think the essay moves OK.

5. Which points are especially clear? What questions do you have that are not answered in the essay?

> I think you clearly explained what you didn't like about Jeff's cheating. I'm not sure what AP chemistry is like, though. Do people cheat because it's so hard?

6. If this were your essay, what would you change before you handed it in?

> I'd add more detail and explain more about AP chemistry. Also, what were the other students doing while the cheating was going on?

7. Overall, do you think the paper is effective? Explain.

> Good paper; cheating is a big issue, and I think your essay really gets this across.

A peer editing worksheet for each pattern of development appears at the end of the introductions for Chapters 6 through 15.

POINTS FOR SPECIAL ATTENTION: FIRST DRAFT

The Introduction

When she wrote her first draft, Laura knew she would eventually have to present more detail in her introduction. At this stage, though, she was more concerned with her thesis statement — which, as her instructor's comments pointed out, didn't address the second half of the assignment: to explain whether or not she would act differently today.

Keeping their comments in mind, Laura rewrote her introduction. First, she created a context for her discussion by specifically linking her story to Gates's essay. Next, she decided to postpone mentioning her subject — cheating — until later in the paper, hoping this strategy would stimulate the curiosity of her readers and make them want to read further.

Finally, she revised her thesis statement to reflect the specific wording of the assignment.

The Body Paragraphs

The students in her peer editing group said Laura needed to expand her body paragraphs. Although she had expected most of her readers to be familiar with courses like advanced placement chemistry, she discovered this was not the case. In addition, some students in her group thought she should expand the paragraph in which she described her reaction to the cheating. They wondered what the other students had thought about the incident. Did they know? Did they care? Laura's classmates were curious, and they thought other readers would be, too.

Before revising the body paragraphs, Laura did some brainstorming for additional ideas. She decided to describe the difficulty of advanced placement chemistry and the pressure the students in the class had felt. She also decided to summarize discussions she had had with several of her classmates after the test. In addition, she wanted to explain in more detail her present views on cheating; she felt that the paragraph presenting these ideas did not contrast enough with the paragraphs dealing with her high school experiences.

To make sure her sentences led smoothly into one another, Laura added transitions and rewrote entire sentences when necessary, signaling the progression of her thoughts by adding words and phrases such as *therefore, for this reason, for example,* and *as a result.* In addition, she tried to repeat key words so that important concepts would be reinforced.

The Conclusion

Laura's biggest concern as she revised was to make sure her readers would see the connection between her essay and the assignment. To make this connection clear, she decided to mention in her conclusion a specific effect the incident had on her: its impact on her friendship with Jeff. She also decided to link her reactions to those of Henry Louis Gates Jr. Like him, she had been upset by the actions of someone she knew. By employing this strategy, she was able to bring her essay full circle and develop an idea she had alluded to in her introduction. Thus, rewriting her conclusion helped Laura to reinforce her thesis statement and provide closure to her essay.

A STUDENT WRITER: Revising a Second Draft

The following draft incorporates Laura's revisions, as well as some preliminary editing of grammar and punctuation.

Speaking Out

In his essay "'What's in a Name?'" Henry Louis Gates Jr. recalls an incident   1
from his past in which his father did not speak up. Perhaps he kept silent because
he was afraid or because he knew that nothing he said or did would change the
situation in Piedmont, West Virginia. Although I have never encountered the kind
of prejudice Gates describes, I did have an experience in high school where, like
Gates's father, I could have spoken up but did not. As I now look back at the
cheating I witnessed, I know I would not make the same decision today.

The incident I am going to describe took place during the final examination   2
in my advanced placement chemistry class. The course was very demanding and
required hours of studying every night. Every day after school, I would meet with
other students to outline chapters and answer homework questions. Sometimes
we would even work on weekends. We would often ask ourselves whether we had
gotten in over our heads. As the semester dragged on, it became clear to me, as
well as to the other students in the class, that passing the course was not
something we could take for granted. Test after test came back with grades that
were well below the "As" and "Bs" I was used to getting in the regular chemistry
course I took in tenth grade. By the time we were ready to take the final exam,
most of us were worried that we would fail the course — despite the teacher's
assurances that she would mark on a curve.

The final examination for advanced placement chemistry was given on   3
a Friday morning from nine to twelve o'clock. As I struggled to balance a
particularly complex equation, I noticed that the person sitting across from me
was acting strangely. I thought I was imagining things, but as I stared I saw Jeff
Servin, my friend and study partner, fumbling with his test booklet. I realized
that he was copying material from a paper he had taped inside the cuff of his
shirt. After watching him for a while, I dismissed the incident and finished
my test.

Surprisingly, when I mentioned the incident to others in the class, they all   4
knew what Jeff had done. The more I thought about Jeff's actions, the angrier I
got. It seemed unfair that I had studied for weeks to memorize formulas and
equations while all Jeff had done was to copy them onto a cheat sheet. For a
moment I considered going to the teacher, but I quickly rejected this idea.
Cheating was nothing new to me or to others in my school. Many of my classmates
cheated at one time or another. Most of us saw school as a war between us and
the teachers, and cheating was just another weapon in our arsenal. The worst
crime I could commit would be to turn Jeff in. As far as I was concerned, I had no
choice. I fell in line with the values of my high school classmates and dismissed
the incident as "no big deal."

I find it hard to believe that I could ever have been so complacent about
cheating. The issues that were simple in high school now seem complex. I now ask
questions that never would have occurred to me in high school. Interestingly, Jeff
and I are no longer very close. Whenever I see him, I have the same reaction
Henry Louis Gates Jr. had when he met Mr. Wilson after he had insulted his father.

5

POINTS FOR SPECIAL ATTENTION: SECOND DRAFT

Laura could see that her second draft was stronger than her first, but
she decided to arrange a conference with her instructor to help her improve
her draft further.

The Introduction

Although Laura was satisfied with her introduction, her instructor
identified a problem during a conference. Laura had assumed that everyone reading her essay would be familiar with Gates's essay. However, her
instructor pointed out that this might not be the case. So he suggested
that she add a brief explanation of the problems Gates's father had faced
in order to accommodate readers who didn't know about or remember
Gates's comments.

The Body Paragraphs

After rereading her first body paragraph, Laura thought she could
sharpen its focus. Her instructor agreed, suggesting she delete the first sentence of the paragraph, which seemed too conversational. She also decided
she could delete the sentences that explained how difficult advanced placement chemistry was — even though she had added this material at the suggestion of a classmate. After all, cheating, not advanced placement
chemistry, was the subject of her paper. She realized that if she included
this kind of detail, she ran the risk of distracting readers from the real subject of her discussion.

Her instructor also pointed out that in the second body paragraph,
the first and second sentences did not seem to be connected, so Laura
decided to connect these ideas by adding a short discussion of her own
reaction to the test. Her instructor also suggested that Laura add more
transitional words and phrases to this paragraph to clarify the sequence of
events she was describing. Phrases such as *at first* and *about a minute passed*
would help readers follow her discussion.

Laura thought the third body paragraph was her best, but, even so, she
thought she needed to add more material. She and her instructor decided
she should expand her discussion of the students' reactions to cheating.

More information — perhaps some dialogue — would help Laura make the point that cheating was condoned by the students in her class.

The Conclusion

Laura's conclusion began by mentioning her present attitude toward cheating and then suddenly shifted to the effect cheating had on her relationship with Jeff. Her instructor suggested that she revise by taking her discussion about her current view of cheating out of her conclusion and putting it in a separate paragraph. By doing this, she could focus her conclusion on the effect cheating had on both Jeff and her. This strategy enabled Laura to present her views about cheating in more detail and also helped her end her essay forcefully.

Her instructor also suggested that Laura consider adding a quotation from Gates's essay to her conclusion. He thought that Gates's words would clearly connect his experience to Laura's. He reminded her not to forget to document the quotation and to use correct MLA documentation format (as explained and illustrated in the Appendix to this text).

The Title

Laura's original title was only a working title, and now she wanted one that would create interest and draw readers into her essay. She knew, however, that a humorous, cute, or catchy title would undermine the seriousness of her essay. After she rejected a number of possibilities, she decided on "The Price of Silence." This title was thought provoking and also descriptive, and it prepared readers for what was to follow in the essay.

CHOOSING A TITLE

Because it is the first thing in your essay that readers see, your title should create interest. Usually, single-word titles and cute ones do little to draw readers into your essay. To be effective, a title should reflect your purpose and your tone. The titles of some of the essays in this book illustrate the various kinds of titles you can use:

Statement of essay's focus: "Grant and Lee: A Study in Contrasts"
Question: "Who Killed Benny Paret?"
Unusual angle: "Thirty-Eight Who Saw Murder Didn't Call the Police"
Controversy: "A Peaceful Woman Explains Why She Carries a Gun"
Provocative wording: "Earth without People"
Quotation: "The 'Black Table' Is Still There"
Humor: "The Dog Ate My Disk and Other Tales of Woe"

A STUDENT WRITER: Preparing a Final Draft

Based on the decisions she made during and after her conference, Laura revised and edited her draft and handed in this final version of her essay.

The Price of Silence

Introduction (provides background)

Thesis statement

Narrative begins

Key incident occurs

In his essay "'What's in a Name?'" Henry Louis Gates Jr. recalls an incident from his past in which his father encountered prejudice and did not speak up. Perhaps he kept silent because he was afraid or because he knew that nothing he said or did would change the racial situation in Piedmont, West Virginia. Although I have never encountered the kind of prejudice Gates describes, I did have an experience in high school where, like Gates's father, I could have spoken out but did not. As I look back at the cheating incident that I witnessed, I realize that I have outgrown the immaturity and lack of confidence that made me keep silent. 1

In my senior year in high school I, along with fifteen other students, took advanced placement chemistry. The course was very demanding and required hours of studying every night. As the semester dragged on, it became clear to me, as well as to the other students in the class, that passing the course was not something we could take for granted. Test after test came back with grades that were well below the As and Bs I was used to getting in the regular chemistry course I had taken in tenth grade. By the time we were ready to take the final exam, most of us were worried that we would fail the course — despite the teacher's assurances that she would mark on a curve. 2

The final examination for advanced placement chemistry was given on a Friday morning between nine o'clock and noon. I had studied all that week, but, even so, I found the test difficult. I knew the material, but I had a hard time answering the long questions that were asked. As I struggled to balance a particularly complex equation, I noticed that the person sitting across from me was acting strangely. At first I thought I was imagining things, but as I stared I saw Jeff Servin, my friend and study partner, fumbling with his test booklet. About a minute passed before I realized that he was copying material 3 from a paper he had taped to the inside of his shirt cuff. After a short time, I stopped watching him and finished my test.

Narrative continues: reactions to the incident

It was not until after the test that I began thinking 4 about what I had seen. Surprisingly, when I mentioned the incident to others in the class, they all knew what Jeff had done. Some even thought that Jeff's actions were justified. "After all," one student said, "the test was hard." But the more I thought about Jeff's actions, the angrier I got. It seemed unfair that I had studied for weeks to memorize formulas and equations while all Jeff had done was copy them onto a cheat sheet. For a moment I considered going to the teacher, but I quickly rejected this idea. Cheating was nothing new to me or to others in my school. Many of my classmates cheated at one time or another. Most of us saw school as a war between us and the teachers, and cheating was just another weapon in our arsenal. The worst crime I could commit would be to turn Jeff

Narrative ends

in. As far as I was concerned, I had no choice. I fell in line with the values of my high school classmates and dismissed the incident as "no big deal."

Analysis of key incident

Now that I am in college, however, I see the situation 5 differently. I find it hard to believe that I could ever have been so complacent about cheating. The issues that were simple in high school now seem complex — especially in light of the honor code that I follow in college. I now ask questions that never would have occurred to me in high school. What, for example, are the implications of cheating? What would happen to the educational system if cheating became the norm? What are my obligations to all those who are involved in education? Aren't teachers and students interested in achieving a common goal? The answers to these questions give me a sense of the far-reaching effects of my failure to act. If confronted with the same situation today, I know I would speak out regardless of the consequences.

Jeff Servin is now a first-year student at the state 6 university and, like me, was given credit for chemistry. I feel certain that by not turning him in, I failed not only myself but also Jeff. I gave in to peer pressure instead of doing what I knew to be right. The worst that would have happened to Jeff had I spoken up is that he would have had to repeat chemistry in summer school. By doing so, he would have proven to himself that he could, like the rest of us in the class, pass on his own. In the long run, this knowledge would have served him better than the knowledge that he could cheat whenever he faced a difficult situation.

Conclusion
(aftermath
of incident)

Interestingly, Jeff and I are no longer very close. Whenever I see him, I have the same reaction Henry Louis Gates Jr. had when he met Mr. Wilson after he had insulted his father: " 'I never again looked [him] in the eye' " (7).

7

Works Cited

Gates, Henry Louis, Jr. " 'What's in a Name?' " *Patterns for College*
Writing: A Rhetorical Reader and Guide. 11th ed. Ed.
Laurie G. Kirszner and Stephen R. Mandell. New York:
Bedford, 2010. 5-7. Print.

With each draft of her essay, Laura sharpened the focus of her discussion. In the process, she clarified her thoughts about her subject and reached some new and interesting conclusions. Although much of Laura's paper is a narrative, it also includes a contrast between her current ideas about cheating and the ideas she had in high school. Perhaps Laura could have explained the reasons behind her current ideas about cheating more fully. Even so, her paper gives a straightforward account of the incident and analyzes its significance without drifting off into clichés or simplistic moralizing. Especially effective is Laura's conclusion, in which she discusses the long-term effects of her experience and quotes Gates. By placing this discussion at the end of her essay, she makes sure her readers will not lose sight of the implications of her experience. Finally, Laura documents the quotation she uses in her conclusion and includes a works-cited page at the end of her essay.

Exercise 2

Use the checklist on page 54 to help you revise your draft. If you prefer, outline your draft and use that outline to help you revise.

Exercise 3

Have another student read your second draft. Then, using the student's peer critique as your guide, revise your draft.

Exercise 4

Using the essay on pages 63–65 as your guide, label the final draft of your own essay. In addition to identifying your introduction, conclusion, and thesis statement, you should also label the main points of your essay.

5
Editing and Proofreading

When you finish revising your essay, it is tempting to print it out, hand it in, and breathe a sigh of relief. This is one temptation you should resist. You still have to *edit* and *proofread* your paper to correct any problems that may remain after you revise.

When you **edit**, you search for grammatical errors, check punctuation, and look over your sentence style and word choice one last time. When you **proofread**, you look for surface errors, such as spelling errors, typos, incorrect spacing, or problems with your essay's format. The idea is to look carefully for any error, no matter how small, that might weaken your essay's message or undermine your credibility. Remember, this is your last chance to make sure your essay says exactly what you want it to say.

EDITING FOR GRAMMAR

As you edit, keep in mind that certain grammatical errors occur more frequently than others — and even more frequently in particular kinds of writing. By concentrating on these errors, as well as on those errors you yourself are most likely to make, you will learn to edit your essays quickly and efficiently.

Learning the few rules that follow will help you identify the most common errors. Later on, when you practice writing essays in various patterns of development, you can use the **Grammar in Context** section in each chapter to help you correct any errors you find.

Be Sure Subjects and Verbs Agree

Subjects and verbs must agree in number. A singular subject takes a singular verb.

Stephanie Ericsson discusses ten kinds of liars.

A plural subject takes a plural verb.

Chronic liars are different from occasional liars.

Liars and plagiarists have a lot in common.

For information on editing for subject-verb agreement with indefinite pronoun subjects, see the Grammar in Context section of Chapter 15 (page 707).

Be Sure Verb Tenses Are Accurate and Consistent

Unintentional shifts in verb tense can be confusing to readers. Verb tenses in the same passage should be the same unless you are referring to two different time periods.

Single time period:	*past tense* Lee surrendered to Grant on April 9, 1865, *past tense* and then he addressed his men.
Two different time periods:	In "Two Ways to Belong in America," Bharati *present tense* Mukherjee compares herself and her sister, *past tense* both of whom emigrated from India.

For more information on editing for consistent verb tenses, as well as to eliminate unwarranted shifts in voice, person, and mood, see the Grammar in Context section of Chapter 9 (page 268).

Be Sure Pronoun References Are Clear

A pronoun is a word that takes the place of a noun in a sentence. Every pronoun should clearly refer to a specific **antecedent**, the word (a noun or pronoun) it replaces. Pronouns and antecedents must agree in number.
Singular pronouns refer to singular antecedents.

When she was attacked, Kitty Genovese was on her way home.

Plural pronouns refer to plural antecedents.

The people who watched the attack gave different reasons for their failure to help.

For information on editing for pronoun-antecedent agreement with indefinite pronouns, see the Grammar in Context section of Chapter 15 (page 707).

Be Sure Sentences Are Complete

A **sentence** is a group of words that includes a subject and a verb and expresses a complete thought. A **fragment** is an incomplete sentence, one that is missing a subject, a verb, or both a subject and a verb — or that has a subject and a verb but does not express a complete thought.

Sentence:	Although it was written in 1963, Martin Luther King's "Letter from Birmingham Jail" remains powerful today.
Fragment (no subject):	Remains powerful today.
Fragment (no verb):	Martin Luther King's "Letter from Birmingham Jail."
Fragment (no subject or verb):	Written in 1963.
Fragment (includes subject and verb but does not express a complete thought):	Although it was written in 1963.

To correct a sentence fragment, you need to supply the missing part of the sentence (a subject, a verb, or both — or an entire independent clause). Often, you will find that the missing words appear in an adjacent sentence in your essay.

Be Careful Not to Run Sentences Together without Proper Punctuation

There are two kinds of **run-on sentences**: *comma splices* and *fused sentences*.

A **comma splice** is an error that occurs when two independent clauses are connected by just a comma.

Comma splice:	Women who live alone need to learn to protect themselves; sometimes this means carrying a gun.

A **fused sentence** is an error that occurs when two independent clauses are connected without any punctuation.

Fused sentence:	Residents of isolated rural areas may carry guns for protection, but sometimes these guns may be used against them.

For more information on editing run-on sentences, including additional ways to correct them, see the Grammar in Context section of Chapter 6 (page 88).

Be Careful to Avoid Misplaced and Dangling Modifiers

Modifiers are words and phrases that describe other words in a sentence. To avoid confusion, place modifiers as close as possible to the words they modify.

Limited by their illiteracy, millions of Americans are ashamed to seek help.

Hoping to draw attention to their plight, Jonathan Kozol wrote *Illiterate America.*

A **misplaced modifier** appears to modify the wrong word because it is placed incorrectly in the sentence.

Misplaced modifier:	Judith Ortiz Cofer wonders why Latin women are so often stereotyped as either "hot tamales" or low-level workers in her essay "The Myth of the Latin Woman: I Just Met a Girl Named Maria" (730). (*Does Cofer's essay stereotype Latin women?*)
Correct:	In her essay "The Myth of the Latin Woman: I Just Met a Girl Named Maria," Judith Ortiz Cofer wonders why Latin women are so often stereotyped as either "hot tamales" or low-level workers (730).

A dangling modifier "dangles" because it cannot logically describe any word in the sentence.

Dangling modifier:	Going back to his old junior high school, the "black table" was still there. (*Who went back to his old school?*)
Correct:	Going back to his old junior high school, Graham discovered that the "black table" was still there.

For more information on editing to correct misplaced and dangling modifiers, see the Grammar in Context section of Chapter 7 (page 152).

Be Sure Sentence Elements Are Parallel

Parallelism is the use of matching grammatical elements (words, phrases, clauses) to express similar ideas. Used effectively — for example, with paired items or items in a series — parallelism makes the links between related ideas clear and emphasizes connections.

Paired items:	As Deborah Tannen points out, men speak more than women in public but less than women at home (436).
Items in a series:	Amy Tan says, "I spend a great deal of my time thinking about the power of language — the way it can evoke an emotion, a visual image, a complex idea, or a simple truth (477).

Faulty parallelism — using items that are not parallel in a context in which parallelism is expected — makes ideas difficult to follow and will likely confuse your readers.

Faulty parallelism:	As Deborah Tannen points out, men speak more than women in public, but at home less talking is done by them (436).
Faulty parallelism:	Amy Tan says, "I spend a great deal of my time thinking about the power of language — the way it can evoke an emotion, visual images, or complex ideas can be suggested, or communicate a simple truth" (477).

For more information on using parallelism to strengthen your writing, see the Grammar in Context section of Chapter 11 (page 390).

✓ CHECKLIST: Editing for Grammar

- **Subject-verb agreement**   Do all your verbs agree with their subjects? Remember that singular subjects take singular verbs, and plural subjects take plural verbs.
- **Verb tenses**   Are all your verb tenses accurate and consistent? Have you avoided unnecessary shifts in tense?
- **Pronoun reference**   Do pronouns clearly refer to their antecedents?
- **Sentence fragments**   Does each group of words punctuated as a sentence have both a subject and a verb and express a complete thought? If not, can you correct the fragment by adding the missing words or by attaching it to an adjacent sentence?
- **Run-on sentences**   Have you been careful not to connect two independent clauses without the necessary punctuation? Have you avoided comma splices and fused sentences?
- **Modification**   Does every modifier point clearly to the word it modifies? Have you avoided misplaced and dangling modifiers?
- **Parallelism**   Have you used matching words, phrases, or clauses to express equivalent ideas? Have you avoided faulty parallelism?

For practice in editing for grammar, visit Exercise Central online at bedfordstmartins.com/patterns.

EDITING FOR PUNCTUATION

Like grammatical errors, certain punctuation errors are more common than others, particularly in certain contexts. By understanding a few punctuation rules, you can learn to identify and correct these errors in your writing.

Learn When to Use Commas — and When Not to Use Them

Commas separate certain elements of a sentence. They are used most often in the following situations:

- To separate an introductory phrase or clause from the rest of the sentence

  In "Only Daughter," Sandra Cisneros writes about her father.

  According to Cisneros, he is very critical of her.

  Although her father has six sons, she is the only daughter.

NOTE: Do not use a comma if a dependent clause follows an independent clause: She is the only daughter although her father has six sons. *(no comma)*

- To separate two independent clauses that are joined by a coordinating conjunction

  Cisneros tries to please her father, but he is not impressed.

- To separate elements in a series

  Cisneros has written stories, essays, poems, and a novel.

For more information on using commas in a series, see the Grammar in Context section of Chapter 8 (page 205).

- To separate a **nonrestrictive clause** (a clause that does not supply information that is essential to the sentence's meaning) from the rest of the sentence

  Cisneros, who is the only daughter, feels her father would prefer her to be a son.

NOTE: Do not use commas to set off a **restrictive clause** (a clause that supplies information that is vital to the sentence's meaning).

  The child who is overlooked is often the daughter. (*no commas*)

Learn When to Use Semicolons

Semicolons, like commas, separate certain elements of a sentence. However, semicolons separate only grammatically equivalent elements — for example, two closely related independent clauses.

  In Burma, George Orwell learned something about the nature of imperialism; it was not an easy lesson.

  Shirley Jackson's "The Lottery" is fiction; however, many early readers thought it was a true story.

In most cases, commas separate items in a series. However, when one or more of the items in a series already include commas, separate the items with semicolons. This will make the sentence easier to follow.

Orwell set his works in <u>Paris, France</u>; <u>London, England</u>; and <u>Moulmein, Burma</u>.

Learn When to Use Quotation Marks

Quotation marks are used to set off quoted speech or writing.

At the end of his essay, E. B. White feels "the chill of death" (188).

Special rules govern the use of other punctuation marks with quotation marks:

- Commas and periods always go inside quotation marks.
- Colons and semicolons always go *outside* quotation marks.
- Question marks and exclamation points can go *either* inside or outside quotation marks, depending on whether or not they are part of the quoted material.

Quotation marks are also used to set off the titles of essays ("Once More to the Lake"), stories ("The Lottery"), and poems ("Five Ways to Kill a Man").

For information on integrating and formatting quotations in research papers, see the Appendix, page 757.

Learn When to Use Dashes and Colons

Dashes are occasionally used to set off and emphasize information within a sentence.

Jessica Mitford wrote a scathing critique of the funeral industry — and touched off an uproar. Her book *The American Way of Death* was widely read around the world.

However, because this usage is somewhat informal, dashes should be used in moderation in your college writing.

Colons are used to introduce lists, examples, and clarifications. A colon should always be preceded by a complete sentence.

As John De Graaf, David Wann, and Thomas H. Naylor observe in "Swollen Expectations," many middle-class people now take for granted things they once saw as luxuries: large homes, automobiles with every possible option, endless dining and beverage choices, and sophisticated electronic gadgets.

For more information on using colons, see the Grammar in Context section of Chapter 12 (page 453).

> ✓ CHECKLIST: Editing for Punctuation
>
> - **Commas**   Have you used commas when necessary — and only when necessary?
> - **Semicolons**   Have you used semicolons only between grammatically equivalent items?
> - **Quotation marks**   Have you used quotation marks to set off quoted speech or writing and to set off titles of essays, stories, and poems? Have you used other punctuation correctly with quotation marks?
> - **Dashes and colons**   Have you used dashes in moderation? Is every colon that introduces a list, an example, or a clarification preceded by a complete sentence?

> For practice in editing for punctuation, visit Exercise Central online at **bedfordstmartins.com/patterns.**

Exercise 1

Reread the essay you wrote in Chapters 2–4, and edit it for grammar and punctuation.

💻   COMPUTER STRATEGY: Editing

Just as you do when you revise, you should edit on a hard copy of your essay. Seeing your work on the printed page makes it easy for you to spot surface-level errors in grammar and punctuation. You can also run a grammar check to help you find grammar and punctuation errors, but you should keep in mind that grammar checkers are far from perfect. They often miss errors (such as faulty modification), and they frequently highlight areas of text (such as a long sentence) that may not contain an error.

Exercise 2

Run a grammar check, and then make any additional corrections you think are necessary.

EDITING FOR SENTENCE STYLE AND WORD CHOICE

As you edit your essay for grammar and punctuation, you should also be looking one last time at how you construct sentences and choose words. To make your essay as clear, readable, and convincing as possible, your sentences should be not only correct but also concise and varied. In addition, every word should mean exactly what you want it to mean, and your language should be free of clichés.

Eliminate Awkward Phrasing

As you review your essay's sentences, check carefully for awkward phrasing, and do your best to smooth it out.

Awkward:	The reason Jefferson drafted the Declaration of Independence was because he felt the king was a tyrant.
Correct:	The reason Jefferson drafted the Declaration of Independence was that he felt the king was a tyrant.

For more information about this error, see the Grammar in Context section of Chapter 10 (page 332).

Awkward:	*Work* is where you earn money.
Correct:	*Work* is the activity you do to earn money.

For more information about this error, see the Grammar in Context section of Chapter 13 (page 511).

Be Sure Your Sentences Are Concise

A **concise** sentence is efficient; it is not overloaded with extra words and complicated constructions. To make sentences concise, you need to eliminate repetition and redundancy, delete empty words and expressions, and cut everything that is not absolutely necessary.

Wordy:	Brent Staples's essay "Just Walk On By" explores his feelings, thoughts, and ideas about various events and experiences that were painful to him as a black man living in a large metropolitan city.
Concise:	Brent Staples's essay "Just Walk On By" explores his ideas about his painful experiences as a black man living in a large city.

Be Sure Your Sentences Are Varied

To add interest to your paper, vary the length and structure of your sentences, and vary the way you open them.

- Mix long and short sentences.
  As time went on, and as he saw people's hostile reactions to him, Staples grew more and more uneasy. Then, he had an idea.

- Mix simple, compound, and complex sentences.

  Simple sentence (*one independent clause*): Staples grew more and more uneasy.

  Compound sentence (*two independent clauses*): Staples grew more and more uneasy, but he stood his ground.

  Complex sentence (*dependent clause, independent clause*): Although Staples grew more and more uneasy, he continued to walk in the neighborhood.

For more information on how to form compound and complex sentences, see the Grammar in Context section of Chapter 14 (page 565).

- Vary your sentence openings. Instead of beginning every sentence with the subject (particularly with a pronoun like *he* or *this*), begin some sentences with an introductory word, phrase, or clause that ties it to the preceding sentence.

  The 1964 murder of Kitty Genovese, discussed in Martin Gansberg's "Thirty-Eight Who Saw Murder Didn't Call the Police," remains relevant today for a number of reasons. For one thing, urban crime remains a problem, particularly for women. Moreover, many people are still reluctant to report crimes. Although more than forty years have gone by, the story of Kitty Genovese and the people who watched her die and did nothing still stirs strong emotional responses.

Choose Your Words Carefully

- Choose **specific** words that identify particular examples and details.

  Vague: Violence in sports is a bad thing.

  Specific: Violence in boxing is a serious problem that threatens not just the lives of the boxers but also the sport itself.

- Avoid **clichés**, overused expressions that rely on tired figures of speech.

  Clichés: When he was hit, the boxer stood for a moment like a deer caught in the headlights, and then he fell to the mat like a ton of bricks.

  Revised: When he was hit, the boxer stood frozen for a moment, and then he fell to the mat.

✓ CHECKLIST: **Editing for Sentence Style and Word Choice**

- **Awkward phrasing**   Have you eliminated awkward constructions?
- **Concise sentences**   Have you eliminated repetition, empty phrases, and excess words? Is every sentence as concise as it can be?
- **Varied sentences**   Have you varied the length and structure of your sentences? Have you varied your sentence openings?
- **Word choice**   Have you selected specific words? Have you eliminated clichés?

For practice in editing for sentence style and word choice, visit Exercise Central online at **bedfordstmartins.com/patterns.**

Exercise 3

Check your essay's sentence style and word choice.

PROOFREADING YOUR ESSAY

When you proofread, you check your essay for surface errors, such as commonly confused words, misspellings, faulty capitalization, and incorrect italic use; then, you check for typographical errors.

Check for Commonly Confused Words

Even if you have carefully considered your choice of words during the editing stage, you may have missed some errors. As you proofread, look carefully to see if you can spot any **commonly confused words** — *its* for *it's*, *there* for *their*, or *affect* for *effect*, for example — that a spell check will not catch.

For more information on how to distinguish between *affect* and *effect*, see the Grammar in Context section of Chapter 10 (page 332).

Check for Misspellings and Faulty Capitalization

It makes no sense to work hard on an essay and then undermine your credibility with spelling and mechanical errors. If you have any doubt about how a word is spelled or whether or not to capitalize it, check a dictionary (in print or online).

Check for Correct Use of Underlining and Italics

Italics are required for titles of books and plays and for names of magazines and journals: *Life on the Mississippi, Hamlet, The Onion,* and *Publications of the Modern Language Association,* for example. However, your instructor may prefer that you underline these titles to indicate italics. When you proofread, make sure you have followed the required style.

Check for Typos

The last step in the proofreading process is to read carefully and hunt for typos. Make sure you have spaced correctly between words and have not accidentally typed an extra letter, omitted a letter, or transposed two letters. Reading your essay *backwards* — one sentence at a time — will help you focus on individual sentences, which in turn will help you see errors more clearly.

✓ CHECKLIST: Proofreading

- **Commonly confused words**   Have you proofread for errors with words that are often confused with each other?
- **Misspelled words and faulty capitalization**   Have you proofread for errors in spelling and capitalization? Have you run a spell check?
- **Italics and underlining**   Have you underlined (or typed in italics) the titles of books and plays and the names of magazines and journals?
- **Typos**   Have you checked carefully to eliminate typing errors?

For more practice with proofreading, visit Exercise Central online at **bedfordstmartins.com/patterns.**

💻   COMPUTER STRATEGY: Spell Checkers

You should certainly run a spell check to help you locate misspelled words and incorrect strings of letters caused by typos, but keep in mind that a spell checker will not find every error. For example, it will not identify many misspelled proper nouns or foreign words, nor will it highlight words that are spelled correctly but used incorrectly — *work* for *word* or *form* for *from,* for example. For this reason, you must still proofread carefully — even if you run a spell check.

Exercise 4

Proofread your essay.

CHECKING MANUSCRIPT FORMAT

The final thing to consider is manuscript format — how your paragraphs, sentences, and words look on the page. Your instructor will give you some general guidelines about format — telling you, for example, to type your last name and the page number at the top right of each page — and, of course, you should follow these guidelines. Students writing in the humanities usually follow the format illustrated below. (For information on documentation format, see the Appendix, page 757.)

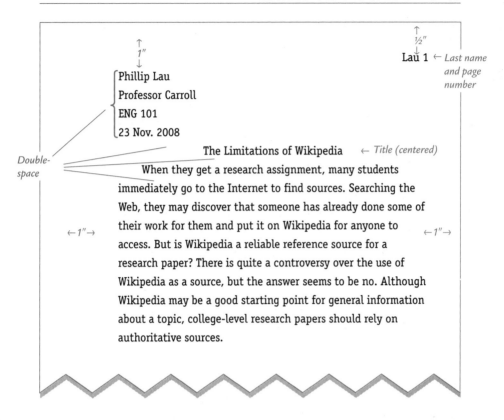

↑
1"
↓

↑
½"
↓

Lau 1 ← *Last name and page number*

Phillip Lau
Professor Carroll
ENG 101
23 Nov. 2008

The Limitations of Wikipedia   ← *Title (centered)*

Double-space

←1"→

When they get a research assignment, many students immediately go to the Internet to find sources. Searching the Web, they may discover that someone has already done some of their work for them and put it on Wikipedia for anyone to access. But is Wikipedia a reliable reference source for a research paper? There is quite a controversy over the use of Wikipedia as a source, but the answer seems to be no. Although Wikipedia may be a good starting point for general information about a topic, college-level research papers should rely on authoritative sources.

←1"→

✓ **CHECKLIST: Checking Manuscript Format**

- **Guidelines** Have you followed your instructor's manuscript guidelines?
- **Spacing** Have you double-spaced throughout?
- **Type size** Have you used ten- or twelve-point type?
- **Paragraphing** Have you indented the first line of every paragraph?
- **Visuals** If you used one or more visuals in your essay, did you insert each visual as close as possible to where it is discussed?
- **Documentation** Have you documented each source — and each visual — you used? Have you included a works-cited page?

Exercise 5

Make any necessary corrections to your essay's format, and then print out your final draft.

PART TWO

Readings for Writers

The relationship between reading and writing is a complex one. Sometimes you will write an essay based on your own experience; more often than not, however, you will respond in writing to something you have read. The essays in this book give you a chance to do both.

As you are probably aware, the fact that information appears in print or on the Internet does not mean you should take it at face value. Of course, many of the books and articles you read will be reliable, but some — especially material found on Web sites and in online discussion groups — will include contradictions, biased ideas, or even inaccurate or misleading information. For this reason, your goal should not be simply to understand what you read but to assess the credibility of the writers and, eventually, to judge the soundness of their ideas.

When you read the essays in this book, you should approach them critically. In other words, you should question (and sometimes challenge) the writer's ideas — and, in the process, try to create new interpretations that you can explore in your writing. Approaching a text in this way is not easy, for it requires you to develop your own analytical and critical skills and your own set of standards to help you judge and interpret what you read. Only after you have read and critically evaluated a text can you begin to draw your ideas together and write about them.

Every reading selection in Chapters 6 through 15 is accompanied by a series of questions intended to guide you through the reading process. In many ways, these questions are a warm-up for the intellectual workout of writing an essay. The more time you devote to them, the more you will develop your analytical skills. In a real sense, then, these questions will help you develop the critical thinking skills you will need when you write. In becoming a proficient reader, you will also gain confidence in yourself as a writer.

Each of the reading selections in Chapters 6 through 14 is organized around one dominant pattern of development. In your outside reading, however, you will often find more than one pattern used in a single piece of writing (as in Chapter 15, Combining the Patterns, page 705). When you write, then, do not feel you must follow these patterns blindly; instead, think of them as tools for making your writing more effective, and adapt them to your subject, your audience, and your writing purpose.

In addition to the reading selections, each chapter also includes a visual text — for example, a piece of fine art, an advertisement, or a photograph. By visually reinforcing the chapter's basic rhetorical concept, each visual text serves as a bridge to the chapter's essays. Following each visual is a set of questions designed to help you understand not just the image but also the pattern that is the chapter's focus.

6
Narration

WHAT IS NARRATION?

Narration tells a story by presenting events in an orderly, logical sequence. In the following paragraph from "The Stone Horse," essayist Barry Lopez recounts the history of the exploration of the California desert:

Topic sentence

Narrative traces developments through the nineteenth century

Western man did not enter the California desert until the end of the eighteenth century, 250 years after Coronado brought his soldiers into the Zuni pueblos in a bewildered search for the cities of Cibola. The earliest appraisals of the land were cursory, hurried. People traveled *through* it, en route to Santa Fe or the California coastal settlements. Only miners tarried. In 1823 what had been Spain's became Mexico's, and in 1848 what had been Mexico's became America's; but the bare, jagged mountains and dry lake beds, the vast and uniform plains of creosote bush and yucca plants, remained as obscure as the northern Sudan until the end of the nineteenth century.

Narration can be the dominant pattern in many kinds of writing (as well as in speech). Histories, biographies, and autobiographies follow a narrative form, as do personal letters, diaries, journals, and bios on personal Web pages or social networking sites, such as Facebook. Narration is the dominant pattern in many works of fiction and poetry, and it is an essential part of casual conversation. Narration also underlies folk and fairy tales and radio and television news reports. In short, anytime you tell what happened, you are using narration.

USING NARRATION

Narration can provide the structure for an entire essay, but narrative passages may also appear in essays that are not primarily narrative. In an argumentative essay supporting stricter gun-safety legislation, for example, you might devote one or two paragraphs to the story of a child accidentally killed by a handgun. In this chapter, however, we focus on narration as the dominant pattern of a piece of writing.

During your college career, many of your assignments will call for narration. In an English composition class, for instance, you may be asked to write about an experience that was important to your development as an adult; on a European history exam, you may need to relate the events that led to Napoleon's defeat at the Battle of Waterloo; and in a technical writing class, you may be asked to write a letter of complaint tracing a company's negligent actions. In each of these situations (as well as in many additional assignments), your writing has a primarily narrative structure, and the narrative supports a particular thesis.

The skills you develop in narrative writing will also help you in other kinds of writing. A *process essay,* such as an explanation of a laboratory experiment, is like a narrative because it outlines a series of steps in chronological order; a *cause-and-effect essay,* such as your answer to an exam question that asks you to analyze the events that caused the Great Depression, also resembles a narrative in that it traces a sequence of events. Although a process essay explains how to do something and a cause-and-effect essay explains why events occur, writing both these kinds of essays will be easier after you master narration. (Process essays and cause-and-effect essays are dealt with in Chapters 9 and 10, respectively.)

PLANNING A NARRATIVE ESSAY

Developing a Thesis Statement

Although the purpose of a narrative may be simply to recount events or to create a particular mood or impression, in college writing a narrative essay is more likely to present a sequence of events for the purpose of supporting a thesis. For instance, in a narrative about your problems with credit card debt, your purpose may be to show your readers that first-year college students should not have easy access to credit cards. Accordingly, you do not simply tell the story of your unwise spending. Rather, you select and arrange details to show your readers why having a credit card encouraged you to spend money you didn't have. Although it is usually best to include an explicit **thesis statement** ("My negative experiences with easy credit have convinced me that first-year college students should not have easy access to credit cards"), you may also imply your thesis through your selection and arrangement of events.

Including Enough Detail

Narratives, like other types of writing, need rich, specific details if they are to be convincing. Each detail should help to create a picture for the reader; even exact times, dates, and geographic locations can be helpful.

Look, for example, at the following paragraph from the essay "My Mother Never Worked" by Bonnie Smith-Yackel, which appears later in this chapter:

> In the winter she sewed night after night, endlessly, begging cast-off clothing from relatives, ripping apart coats, dresses, blouses, and trousers to remake them to fit her four daughters and son. Every morning and every evening she milked cows, fed pigs and calves, cared for chickens, picked eggs, cooked meals, washed dishes, scrubbed floors, and tended and loved her children. In the spring she planted a garden once more, dragging pails of water to nourish and sustain the vegetables for the family. In 1936 she lost a baby in her sixth month.

This list of details adds interest and authenticity to the narrative. The central figure in the narrative is a busy, productive woman, and readers know this because they are given an exhaustive catalog of her activities.

Varying Sentence Structure

When narratives present a long series of events, all the sentences can begin to sound alike: "She sewed dresses. She milked cows. She fed pigs. She fed calves. She cared for chickens." Such a predictable string of sentences may become monotonous for your readers. You can eliminate this monotony by varying your sentence structure — for instance, by using a variety of sentence openings or by combining simple sentences as Smith-Yackel does: "In the winter she sewed night after night, endlessly. . . . Every morning and every evening she milked cows, fed pigs and calves, cared for chickens."

Maintaining Clear Narrative Order

Many narratives present events in the exact order in which they occurred, moving from first event to last. Whether or not you follow a strict **chronological order** depends on the purpose of your narrative. If you are writing a straightforward account of a historical event or summarizing a record of poor management practices, you will probably want to move from beginning to end. In a personal-experience essay or a fictional narrative, however, you may want to engage your readers' interest by beginning with an event from the middle of your story, or even from the end, and then presenting the events that led up to it. You may also decide to begin in the present and then use one or more **flashbacks** (shifts into the past) to tell your story. To help readers follow the order of events in your narrative, it is very important to use correct verb tenses and clear transitional words and phrases.

Using Accurate Verb Tenses.   **Verb tense** is extremely important in writing that recounts events in a fixed order because tenses indicate temporal (time) relationships. When you write a narrative, you must be careful to keep verb tenses consistent and accurate so that your readers can follow the sequence of events. Naturally, you must shift tenses to reflect an actual time shift in your narrative. For instance, convention requires that you use present tense when discussing works of literature ("When Hamlet's mother *marries* his uncle . . ."), but a flashback to an earlier point in the story calls for a shift from present to past tense ("Before their marriage, Hamlet *was* . . ."). Nevertheless, you should avoid unwarranted shifts in verb tense; they will make your narrative confusing.

Using Transitions.   **Transitions** — connecting words or phrases — help link events in time, enabling narratives to flow smoothly. Without them, narratives would lack coherence, and readers would be unsure of the correct sequence of events. Transitions indicate the order of events, and they also signal shifts in time. In narrative writing, the transitions commonly used for these purposes include *first, second, next, then, later, at the same time, meanwhile, immediately, soon, before, earlier, after, afterward, now,* and *finally*. In addition to these transitional words and phrases, specific time markers — such as *three years later, in 1927, after two hours,* and *on January 3* — indicate how much time has passed between events. (A more complete list of transitions appears on page 43.)

STRUCTURING A NARRATIVE ESSAY

Like other essays, a **narrative** essay has an introduction, a body, and a conclusion. If your essay's thesis is explicitly stated, it will, in most cases, appear in the **introduction**. The **body paragraphs** of your essay will recount the events that make up your narrative, following a clear and orderly plan. Finally, the **conclusion** will give your readers the sense that your narrative is complete, perhaps by restating your thesis or by summarizing key points or events.

Suppose you are assigned a short history paper about the Battle of Waterloo. You plan to support the thesis that if Napoleon had kept more troops in reserve, he might have defeated the British troops serving under Wellington. Based on this thesis, you decide that the best way to organize your paper is to present the five major phases of the battle in chronological order. An informal outline of your essay might look like this:

Introduction:	Thesis statement — If Napoleon had kept more troops in reserve, he might have broken Wellington's line with another infantry attack and thus won the Battle of Waterloo.
Phase 1 of the battle:	Napoleon attacked the Château of Hougoumont.
Phase 2 of the battle:	The French infantry attacked the British lines.

Phase 3 of the battle:	The French cavalry staged a series of charges against the British lines that had not been attacked before; Napoleon committed his reserves.
Phase 4 of the battle:	The French captured La Haye Sainte, their first success of the day but an advantage that Napoleon, having committed troops elsewhere, could not maintain without reserves.
Phase 5 of the battle:	The French infantry was decisively defeated by the combined thrust of the British infantry and the remaining British cavalry.
Conclusion:	Restatement of thesis or review of key points or events.

By discussing the five phases of the battle in chronological order, you clearly support your thesis. As you expand your informal outline into a historical narrative, exact details, dates, times, and geographic locations are extremely important. Without them, your statements are open to question. In addition, to keep your readers aware of the order of events, you must select appropriate transitional words and phrases and pay careful attention to verb tenses.

REVISING A NARRATIVE ESSAY

When you revise a narrative essay, consider the items on the revision checklist on page 54. In addition, pay special attention to the items on the following checklist, which apply specifically to revising narrative essays.

✓ **REVISION CHECKLIST:** Narration

- Does your assignment call for narration?
- Does your essay's thesis communicate the significance of the events you discuss?
- Have you included enough specific detail?
- Have you varied your sentence structure?
- Is the order of events clear to readers?
- Have you varied sentence openings and combined simple sentences to avoid monotony?
- Do your transitions indicate the order of events and signal shifts in time?

EDITING A NARRATIVE ESSAY

When you edit your narrative essay, follow the guidelines on the editing checklists on pages 71, 74, and 76. In addition, focus on the grammar, mechanics, and punctuation issues that are particularly relevant to narrative essays. One of these issues — avoiding run-on sentences — is discussed below.

GRAMMAR IN CONTEXT: Avoiding Run-On Sentences

When writing narrative essays, particularly personal narratives and essays that include dialogue, writers can easily lose sight of sentence boundaries and create **run-on sentences**. There are two kinds of run-on sentences: *fused sentences* and *comma splices*.

A **fused sentence** occurs when two sentences are incorrectly joined without punctuation.

TWO CORRECT SENTENCES:	"The sun came out hot and bright, endlessly, day after day. The crops shriveled and died" (Smith-Yackel 115–16).
FUSED SENTENCE:	The sun came out hot and bright, endlessly, day after day the crops shriveled and died.

A **comma splice** occurs when two sentences are incorrectly joined with just a comma.

COMMA SPLICE:	The sun came out hot and bright, endlessly, day after day, the crops shriveled and died.

Five Ways to Correct These Errors:

1. Use a period to create two separate sentences.

   The sun came out hot and bright, endlessly, day after day. The crops shriveled and died.

2. Join the sentences with a comma and a **coordinating conjunction** (*and, or, nor, for, so, but, yet*).

   The sun came out hot and bright, endlessly, day after day, and the crops shriveled and died.

3. Join the sentences with a semicolon.

   The sun came out hot and bright, endlessly, day after day; the crops shriveled and died.

4. Join the sentences with a **semicolon and a transitional word or phrase** (followed by a comma), such as *however, therefore,* or *for example*. (See page 43 for a list of transitional words and phrases.)

   The sun came out hot and bright, endlessly, day after day; eventually, the crops shriveled and died.

5. Create a complex sentence by adding a subordinating conjunction (*although*, *because*, *if*, and so on) or a relative pronoun (*who*, *which*, *that*, and so on) to one of the sentences.

<u>As</u> the sun came out hot and bright, endlessly, day after day, the crops shriveled and died.

For more practice in avoiding run-ons, visit Exercise Central at **bedfordstmartins.com/patterns/runons**.

✓ **EDITING CHECKLIST: Narration**

- Have you avoided run-on sentences?
- Do your verb tenses clearly indicate time relationships between events?
- Have you avoided unnecessary tense shifts?
- If you use dialogue, have you punctuated correctly and capitalized where necessary?

A STUDENT WRITER: Narration

The following essay is typical of the informal narrative writing many students are asked to do in English composition classes. It was written by Tiffany Forte in response to the assignment "Write an essay about a goal or dream you had when you were a child."

My Field of Dreams

Introduction   When I was young, I was told that when I grew up I could be anything I wanted to be, and I always took for granted that this was true. I knew exactly what I was going to be, and I would spend hours dreaming about how wonderful my life would be when I grew up. One day, though, when I did grow *Thesis statement* up, I realized that things had not turned out the way I had always expected they would.   1

Narrative begins   When I was little, I never played with baby dolls or Barbies. I wasn't like other little girls; I was a tomboy. I was the only girl in the neighborhood where I lived, so I always played with boys. We would play army or football or (my favorite) baseball.   2

Almost every summer afternoon, all the boys in my   3
neighborhood and I would meet by the big oak tree to get a
baseball game going. Surprisingly, I was always one of the first
to be picked for a team. I was very fast, and (for my size) I
could hit the ball far. I loved baseball more than anything, and I
wouldn't miss a game for the world.

My dad played baseball too, and every Friday night I   4
would go to the field with my mother to watch him play. It was
just like the big leagues, with lots of people, a snack bar, and
lights that shone so high and bright you could see them a mile
away. I loved to go to my dad's games. When all the other kids
would wander off and play, I would sit and cheer on my dad and
his team. My attention was focused on the field, and my heart
would jump with every pitch.

Even more exciting than my dad's games were the major   5
league games. The Phillies were my favorite team, and I always
looked forward to watching them on television. My dad would
make popcorn, and we would sit and watch in anticipation of a
Phillies victory. We would go wild, yelling and screaming at all
the big plays. When the Phillies would win, I would be so
excited I couldn't sleep; when they would lose, I would go to
bed angry, just like my dad.

Key experience
introduced
(par. 6–7)

It was when my dad took me to my first major league   6
baseball game that I decided I wanted to be a major league
baseball player. The excitement began when we pulled into the
parking lot of the old Veterans Stadium. There were thousands
of cars. As we walked from the car to the stadium, my dad told
me to hold on to his hand and not to let go no matter what.
When we gave the man our tickets and entered the stadium, I
understood why. There were mobs of people everywhere. They
were walking around the stadium and standing in long lines for
hot dogs, beer, and souvenirs. It was the most wonderful thing I
had ever seen. When we got to our seats, I looked down at the
tiny baseball diamond below and felt as if I were on top of the
world.

The cheering of the crowd, the singing, and the chants   7
were almost more than I could stand. I was bursting with
enthusiasm. Then, in the bottom of the eighth inning, with the
score tied and two outs, Mike Schmidt came up to bat and hit
the game-winning home run. The crowd went crazy. Everyone in

the whole stadium was standing, and I found myself yelling and screaming along with everyone else. When Mike Schmidt came out of the dugout to receive his standing ovation, I felt a lump in my throat and butterflies in my stomach. He was everyone's hero that night, and I could only imagine the pride he must have felt. I slept the whole way home and dreamed of what it would be like to be the hero of the game.

Narrative continues

The next day, when I met with the boys at the oak tree, I   8
told them that when I grew up, I was going to be a major league baseball player. They all laughed at me and said I could never be a baseball player because I was a girl. I told them that they were all wrong and that I would show them.

Analysis of childhood experiences

In the years to follow, I played girls' softball in a   9
competitive fast-pitch league, and I was very good. I always wanted to play baseball with the boys, but there were no mixed leagues. After a few years, I realized that the boys from the oak tree were right: I was never going to be a major league baseball player. I realized that what I had been told when I was younger wasn't the whole truth. What no one had bothered to tell me was that I could be anything I wanted to be — as long as it was something that was appropriate for a girl to do.

Conclusion

In time, I would get over the loss of my dream. I found   10
new dreams, acceptable for a young woman, and I moved on to other things. Still, every time I watch a baseball game and someone hits a home run, I get those same butterflies in my stomach and think, for just a minute, about what might have been.

Points for Special Attention

Introduction.   Tiffany's introduction is straightforward, yet it arouses reader interest by setting up a contrast between what she expected and what actually happened. Her optimistic expectation — that she could be anything she wanted to be — is contradicted by her thesis statement, encouraging readers to read on to discover how things turned out and why.

Thesis Statement.   Tiffany's assignment was to write about a goal or dream she had when she was a child, but her instructor made it clear that the essay should have an explicitly stated thesis that made a point about the goal or dream. Tiffany knew she wanted to write about her passion for baseball, but she also knew that just listing a series of events would not fulfill the assignment. Her thesis statement — "One day, though, when I did grow up, I realized that things had not turned out the way I had always expected they would" — puts her memories in context, suggesting that she will use them to support a general conclusion about the gap between dreams and reality.

Structure. The body of Tiffany's essay traces the chronology of her involvement with baseball — playing with the neighborhood boys, watching her father's games, watching baseball on television, and, finally, seeing her first major league game. Each body paragraph introduces a different aspect of her experience with baseball, culminating in the vividly described Phillies game. The balance of the essay (paragraphs 8–10) summarizes the aftermath of that game, gives a brief overview of Tiffany's later years in baseball, and presents her conclusion.

Detail. Personal narratives like Tiffany's need a lot of detail because the writers want readers to see and hear and feel what they did. To present an accurate picture, Tiffany includes all the significant sights and sounds she can remember: the big oak tree, the lights on the field, the popcorn, the excited cheers, the food and souvenir stands, the crowds, and so on. She also names Mike Schmidt ("everyone's hero"), his team, and the stadium where she saw him play. Despite all these details, though, she omits some important information — for example, how old she was at each stage of her essay.

Verb Tense. Maintaining clear chronological order is very important in narrative writing, where unwarranted shifts in verb tenses can confuse readers. Knowing this, Tiffany avoids unnecessary tense shifts. In her conclusion, she shifts from past to present tense, but this shift is both necessary and clear. Elsewhere she uses *would* to identify events that recurred regularly. For example, in paragraph 5 she says, "My dad *would* make popcorn" rather than "My dad *made* popcorn," which would have suggested that he did so only once.

Transitions. Tiffany's skillful use of transitional words and expressions links her sentences and moves her readers smoothly through her essay. In addition to transitional words such as *when* and *then,* she uses specific time markers — "When I was little," "Almost every summer afternoon," "every Friday night," "As we walked," "The next day," "In the years to follow," and "After a few years" — to advance the narrative and carry her readers along.

Focus on Revision

In their responses to an earlier draft of Tiffany's essay, several students in her peer editing group recommended that she revise one particularly monotonous paragraph. (As one student pointed out, all its sentences began with the subject, making the paragraph seem choppy and its ideas disconnected.) Here is the paragraph from her draft:

> My dad played baseball too. I went to the field with my mother every Friday night to watch him play. It was just like the big leagues. There were lots of people and a snack bar. The lights shone so high and bright you could see them a mile away. I loved to go to my dad's games. All the other kids would wander off and play. I would sit and cheer on my dad and his team. My attention was focused on the field. My heart would jump with every pitch.

In the revised version of the paragraph (now paragraph 4 of her essay), Tiffany varies sentence length and opening strategies:

> My dad played baseball too, and every Friday night I would go to the field with my mother to watch him play. It was just like the big leagues, with lots of people, a snack bar, and lights that shone so high and bright you could see them a mile away. I loved to go to my dad's games. When all the other kids would wander off and play, I would sit and cheer on my dad and his team. My attention was focused on the field, and my heart would jump with every pitch.

After reading Tiffany's revised draft, another student suggested that she might still polish her essay a bit. For instance, she could add some dialogue, quoting the boys' taunts and her own reply in paragraph 8. She could also revise to eliminate **clichés** (overused expressions), substituting fresher, more original language for phrases such as "I felt a lump in my throat and butterflies in my stomach" and "felt as if I were on top of the world." In the next draft of her essay, Tiffany followed up on these suggestions. (A sample peer editing worksheet for narration appears below).

📄 **PEER EDITING WORKSHEET: Narration**

1. What point is the writer making about the essay's subject? Is this point explicitly stated in a thesis statement? If so, where? If not, can you state the essay's thesis in one sentence?
2. List some details that enrich the narrative. Where could more detail be added? What kind of detail? Be specific.
3. Does the writer vary sentence structure and avoid monotonous strings of similar sentences? Should any sentences be combined? If so, which ones? Can you suggest different openings for any sentences?
4. Should any transitions be added to clarify the order in which events occurred? If so, where?
5. Do verb tenses establish a clear chronological order? Identify any verb tenses that you believe need to be changed.

(continued on next page)

(continued from previous page)

6. Does the writer avoid run-on sentences? Point out any fused sentences or comma splices.

7. What could the writer *add* to this essay?

8. What could the writer *take out* of this essay?

9. What is the essay's greatest strength? Why?

10. What is the essay's greatest weakness? What steps should the writer take to correct this problem?

The selections that follow illustrate some of the many possibilities open to writers of narratives. The first selection, a visual text, is followed by questions designed to illustrate how narration can operate in visual form.

The Socks (Graphic Fiction)

Reading Images

1. The seven panels on page 95 (from the graphic novel *Persepolis II*) tell part of a story about changes in the life of a young girl during Iran's Islamic Revolution, which began in 1979. List the events depicted in the panels in the order in which they are shown.

2. What visual elements link each panel to the one that follows? Can you identify any verbal transitions? What additional transitional words and phrases might help to move readers from one panel to the next?

3. What do you think happened right before (and right after) the events depicted here?

Journal Entry

Write a narrative paragraph summarizing the story told in these panels. Begin with a sentence that identifies the characters and the setting. Next, write a sentence that summarizes the events that might have preceded the first panel. Then, tell the story the pictures tell. In your last sentence, bring the sequence of events to a logical close. Be sure to use present tense and to include all necessary transitions.

Thematic Connections

- "Indian Education" (page 135)
- "Just Walk On By" (page 236)
- "The Ways We Lie" (page 485)
- "The Myth of the Latin Woman: I Just Met a Girl Named Maria" (page 730)

Only Daughter

Born into a working-class family in 1954, Sandra Cisneros, the daughter of a Mexican-American mother and a Mexican father, spent much of her childhood shuttling between Chicago and Mexico City. A lonely, bookish child, Cisneros began writing privately at a young age but only began to find her voice when she was a creative-writing student at Loyola University and later at the University of Iowa Writers' Workshop. Her best-known works are the novel *The House on Mango Street* (1983) and the short-story collection *Woman Hollering Creek* (1991); she has also published several collections of poetry. Cisneros's latest novel, *Caramelo,* appeared in 2002.

Background on gender preference
In the following essay, which originally appeared in *Glamour* in 1990, Cisneros describes the difficulties of growing up as the only daughter in a Mexican-American family of six sons. Historically, sons have been valued over daughters in most cultures, as reflected in the following proverbs: "A house full of daughters is like a cellar full of sour beer" (Dutch); "Daughters pay nae [no] debts" (Scottish); "A stupid son is better than a crafty daughter" (Chinese); and "A virtuous son is the sun of his family" (Sanskrit). This was largely the case because limited employment opportunities for women meant that sons were more likely to be able to provide financial support for aging parents. Contemporary research suggests that while the preference for sons has diminished considerably in industrialized nations, a distinct preference for sons continues among many cultures in Asia and the Middle East, raising concerns among medical ethicists worldwide. And, even within the more traditional cultures of the industrialized world, old habits of mind regarding the role of women in society can die hard, as the attitudes of Cisneros's father suggest.

Once, several years ago, when I was just starting out my writing career, I was asked to write my own contributor's note for an anthology I was part of. I wrote: "I am the only daughter in a family of six sons. *That* explains everything."

Well, I've thought about that ever since, and yes, it explains a lot to me, but for the reader's sake I should have written: "I am the only daughter in a *Mexican* family of six sons." Or even: "I am the only daughter of a Mexican father and a Mexican-American mother." Or: "I am the only daughter of a working-class family of nine." All of these had everything to do with who I am today.

I was/am the only daughter and *only* a daughter. Being an only daughter in a family of six sons forced me by circumstance to spend a lot of time by myself because my brothers felt it beneath them to play with a *girl* in public. But that aloneness, that loneliness, was good for a would-be writer — it allowed me time to think and think, to imagine, to read and prepare myself.

Being only a daughter for my father meant my destiny would lead me to become someone's wife. That's what he believed. But when I was in the fifth grade and shared my plans for college with him, I was sure he understood. I remember my father saying, "*Que bueno, ni'ja*, that's good." That meant a lot to me, especially since my brothers thought the idea hilarious. What I didn't realize was that my father thought college was good for girls — good for finding a husband. After four years in college and two more in graduate school, and still no husband, my father shakes his head even now and says I wasted all that education.

In retrospect, I'm lucky my father believed daughters were meant for husbands. It meant it didn't matter if I majored in something silly like English. After all, I'd find a nice professional eventually, right? This allowed me the liberty to putter about embroidering my little poems and stories without my father interrupting with so much as a "What's that you're writing?"

But the truth is, I wanted him to interrupt. I wanted my father to understand what it was I was scribbling, to introduce me as "My only daughter, the writer." Not as "This is only my daughter. She teaches." *Es maestra* — teacher. Not even *profesora*.

In a sense, everything I have ever written has been for him, to win his approval even though I know my father can't read English words, even though my father's only reading includes the brown-ink *Esto* sports magazines from Mexico City and the bloody *¡Alarma!* magazines that feature yet another sighting of *La Virgen de Guadalupe* on a tortilla or a wife's revenge on her philandering husband by bashing his skull in with a *molcajete* (a kitchen mortar made of volcanic rock). Or the *fotonovelas,* the little picture paperbacks with tragedy and trauma erupting from the characters' mouths in bubbles.

My father represents, then, the public majority. A public who is uninterested in reading, and yet one whom I am writing about and for, and privately trying to woo.

When we were growing up in Chicago, we moved a lot because of my father. He suffered bouts of nostalgia. Then we'd have to let go of our flat, store the furniture with mother's relatives, load the station wagon with baggage and bologna sandwiches, and head south. To Mexico City.

We came back, of course. To yet another Chicago flat, another Chicago neighborhood, another Catholic school. Each time, my father would seek out the parish priest in order to get a tuition break, and complain or boast: "I have seven sons."

He meant *siete hijos,* seven children, but he translated it as "sons." "I have seven sons." To anyone who would listen. The Sears Roebuck employee who sold us the washing machine. The short-order cook where my father ate his ham-and-eggs breakfasts. "I have seven sons." As if he deserved a medal from the state.

My papa. He didn't mean anything by that mistranslation, I'm sure. 12
But somehow I could feel myself being erased. I'd tug my father's sleeve
and whisper: "Not seven sons. Six! and *one daughter*."

When my oldest brother graduated from medical school, he fulfilled 13
my father's dream that we study hard and use this — our heads, instead of
this — our hands. Even now my father's hands are thick and yellow, stubbed
by a history of hammer and nails and twine and coils and springs. "Use
this," my father said, tapping his head, "and not this," showing us those
hands. He always looked tired when he said it.

Wasn't college an investment? And hadn't I spent all those years in col- 14
lege? And if I didn't marry, what was it all for? Why would anyone go to
college and then choose to be poor? Especially someone who had always
been poor.

Last year, after ten years of writing professionally, the financial rewards 15
started to trickle in. My second National Endowment for the Arts Fellow-
ship. A guest professorship at the University of California, Berkeley. My
book, which sold to a major New York publishing house.

At Christmas, I flew home to Chicago. The house was throbbing, same 16
as always; hot *tamales* and sweet *tamales* hissing in my mother's pressure
cooker, and everybody — my mother, six brothers, wives, babies, aunts,
cousins — talking too loud and at the same time, like in a Fellini film,
because that's just how we are.

I went upstairs to my father's room. One of my stories had just been 17
translated into Spanish and published in an anthology of Chicano writing,
and I wanted to show it to him. Ever since he recovered from a stroke two
years ago, my father likes to spend his leisure hours horizontally. And that's
how I found him, watching a Pedro Infante* movie on Galavisión** and
eating rice pudding.

There was a glass filmed with milk on the bedside table. There were 18
several vials of pills and balled Kleenex. And on the floor, one black sock
and a plastic urinal that I didn't want to look at but looked at anyway.
Pedro Infante was about to burst into song, and my father was laughing.

I'm not sure if it was because my story was translated into Spanish, or 19
because it was published in Mexico, or perhaps because the story dealt with
Tepeyac, the *colonia* my father was raised in and the house he grew up in,
but at any rate, my father punched the mute button on his remote control
and read my story.

I sat on the bed next to my father and waited. He read it very slowly. As 20
if he were reading each line over and over. He laughed at all the right places
and read lines he liked out loud. He pointed and asked questions: "Is this
So-and-so?" "Yes," I said. He kept reading.

When he was finally finished, after what seemed like hours, my father 21
looked up and asked: "Where can we get more copies of this for the relatives?"

---

* EDS. NOTE — Mexican actor.
** EDS. NOTE — A Spanish-language cable channel.

Of all the wonderful things that happened to me last year, that was the   22
most wonderful.

. . .

Comprehension

1. What does Cisneros mean when she writes that being an only daughter in a family of six sons "explains everything" (1)?
2. What distinction does Cisneros make in paragraphs 2 and 3 between being "the only daughter" and being "*only* a daughter"?
3. What advantages does Cisneros see in being "the only daughter"? In being "*only* a daughter"?
4. Why does her father think she has wasted her education? What is her reaction to his opinion?
5. Why is her father's reaction to her story the "most wonderful" (22) thing that happened to Cisneros that year?

Purpose and Audience

1. Although Cisneros uses many Spanish words in her essay, in most cases she defines or explains these words. What does this decision tell you about her purpose and her audience?
2. What is Cisneros's thesis? What incidents and details support this thesis?
3. Do you think Cisneros intends to convey a sympathetic or an unsympathetic impression of her father? Explain.

Style and Structure

1. Where does Cisneros interrupt a narrative passage to comment on or analyze events? What does this strategy accomplish?
2. Are the episodes in this essay presented in chronological order? Explain.
3. What transitional expressions does Cisneros use to introduce new episodes?
4. Cisneros quotes her father several times. What do we learn about him from his words?
5. Why does Cisneros devote so much space to describing her father in paragraphs 17–21? How does this portrait compare to the one she presents in paragraphs 9–11?

Vocabulary Projects

1. Define each of the following words as it is used in this selection.

   embroidering (5)   stubbed (13)

2. What is the difference in **connotation** between *sons* and *children*? Between *teacher* and *professor*? Do you think these distinctions are as significant as Cisneros seems to think they are? Explain.

Journal Entry

In what sense do the number and gender(s) of your siblings "explain everything" about who you are today?

Writing Workshop

1. Write a narrative essay consisting of a series of related episodes that show how you gradually gained the approval and respect of one of your parents, of another relative, or of a friend.

2. In "Only Daughter," Cisneros traces the development of her identity as an adult, as a female, and as a writer. Write a narrative essay tracing the development of your own personal or professional identity. Refer in your essay to "Only Daughter," quoting relevant ideas if possible to help explain your own personal development. Be sure you document all quotations you use, and include a works-cited page. (See the Appendix for information on documentation formats.)

3. Are male and female children treated differently in your family? Have your parents had different expectations for their sons and daughters? Write a narrative essay recounting one or more incidents that illustrate these differences (or the lack of differences). If you and your siblings are all the same gender, or if you are an only child, write about another family you know well.

Combining the Patterns

Cisneros structures her essay as a narrative in which she is the main character and her brothers barely appear. To give her readers a clearer understanding of how her father's attitude toward her differs from his attitude toward her brothers, Cisneros could have added one or more paragraphs of **comparison and contrast**, focusing on the different ways she and her brothers are treated. What specific points of contrast do you think readers would find most useful? Where might such paragraphs be added?

Thematic Connections

- "My Field of Dreams" (page 89)
- "Words Left Unspoken" (page 172)
- Declaration of Sentiments and Resolutions (page 581)

Sixty-Nine Cents

Born in 1972 in what was then called Leningrad in the Soviet Union (now St. Petersburg, Russia), Gary Shteyngart immigrated to the United States with his parents when he was seven years old. After graduating from high school in New York City, Shteyngart studied political science as an undergraduate and went on to earn an M.F.A. in creative writing. His first novel, *The Russian Debutante's Handbook*, appeared in 2003, and it was followed by *Absurdistan* (2006), a satirical novel about fictional Russian (and Russian émigré) communities. In the following essay, Shteyngart writes about an incident from his adolescence.

Background on Russian Jewish immigrants to the United States

There have been four main waves of Russian Jewish immigration to the United States. At the turn of the twentieth century, many Jews fled Russia to escape increasingly violent religious persecution. A second wave of Jews joined other Russian immigrants fleeing the chaos and violence that followed in the wake of the Russian Revolution of 1917. After World War II, displaced Jews from all over Europe, including many from the Soviet Union, sought a new life in the United States. Shteyngart's family was part of the fourth wave. For years the Soviet government had refused to allow some 400,000 Jewish petitioners, who came to be called *refuseniks,* to emigrate. Beginning in 1974, however, trade pressure from the United States led to a loosening of restrictions on emigration from the Soviet Union. Over the next decade, some 250,000 Jews — ranging from political dissidents and human rights activists to artists and professionals in a variety of fields — were allowed to leave the Soviet Union. Most came from cities such as Moscow and Leningrad and settled initially in New York City. In many cases, their feelings about their new life were tinged with ambivalence. As Shteyngart noted in a recent interview, "On the one hand, I was taught that Russian culture was the best culture in the world; on the other hand, Russia was a terrible place" where his parents faced anti-Semitism.

When I was fourteen years old, I lost my Russian accent. I could, in theory, walk up to a girl and the words "Oh, hi there" would not sound like Okht Hyzer, possibly the name of a Turkish politician. There were three things I wanted to do in my new incarnation: go to Florida, where I understood that our nation's best and brightest had built themselves a sandy, vice-filled paradise; have a girl, preferably native-born, tell me that she liked me in some way; and eat all my meals at McDonald's. I did not have the pleasure of eating at McDonald's often. My parents believed that going to restaurants and buying clothes not sold by weight on Orchard Street* were things done 1

---

* EDS. NOTE — A discount shopping street on New York's Lower East Side, a destination for generations of immigrants.

only by the very wealthy or the very profligate, maybe those extravagant "welfare queens" we kept hearing about on television. Even my parents, however, as uncritically in love with America as only immigrants can be, could not resist the iconic pull of Florida, the call of the beach and the Mouse.

And so, in the midst of my Hebrew-school winter vacation, two Russian families crammed into a large used sedan and took I-95 down to the Sunshine State. The other family — three members in all — mirrored our own, except that their single offspring was a girl and they were, on the whole, more ample; by contrast, my entire family weighed three hundred pounds. There's a picture of us beneath the monorail at EPCOT Center, each of us trying out a different smile to express the déjà vu feeling of standing squarely in our new country's greatest attraction, my own megawatt grin that of a turn-of-the century Jewish peddler scampering after a potential sidewalk sale. The Disney tickets were a freebie, for which we had had to sit through a sales pitch for an Orlando time-share. "You're from Moscow?" the time-share salesman asked, appraising the polyester cut of my father's jib.

"Leningrad."

"Let me guess: mechanical engineer?"

"Yes, mechanical engineer. . . . Eh, please Disney tickets now."

The ride over the MacArthur Causeway to Miami Beach was my real naturalization ceremony. I wanted all of it — the palm trees, the yachts bobbing beside the hard-currency mansions, the concrete-and-glass condominiums preening at their own reflections in the azure pool water below, the implicit availability of relations with amoral women. I could see myself on a balcony eating a Big Mac, casually throwing fries over my shoulder into the sea-salted air. But I would have to wait. The hotel reserved by my parents' friends featured army cots instead of beds and a half-foot-long cockroach evolved enough to wave what looked like a fist at us. Scared out of Miami Beach, we decamped for Fort Lauderdale, where a Yugoslav woman sheltered us in a faded motel, beach-adjacent and featuring free UHF reception. We always seemed to be at the margins of places: the driveway of the Fontainebleau Hilton, or the glassed-in elevator leading to a rooftop restaurant where we could momentarily peek over the "Please Wait to be Seated" sign at the endless ocean below, the Old World we had left behind so far and yet deceptively near.

To my parents and their friends, the Yugoslav motel was an unquestioned paradise, a lucky coda to a set of difficult lives. My father lay magnificently beneath the sun in his red-and-black striped imitation Speedo while I stalked down the beach, past baking Midwestern girls. "Oh, hi there." The words, perfectly American, not a birthright but an acquisition, perched between my lips, but to walk up to one of those girls and say something so casual required a deep rootedness to the hot sand beneath me, a historical presence thicker than the green card embossed with my thumbprint and freckled face. Back at the motel, the *Star Trek* reruns looped endlessly on Channel 73 or 31 or some other prime number, the washed-out Technicolor planets more familiar to me than our own.

On the drive back to New York, I plugged myself firmly into my Walk-   8
man, hoping to forget our vacation. Sometime after the palm trees ran out,
somewhere in southern Georgia, we stopped at a McDonald's. I could
already taste it: the sixty-nine-cent hamburger. The ketchup, red and deca-
dent, embedded with little flecks of grated onion. The uplift of the pickle
slices; the obliterating rush of fresh Coca-Cola; the soda tingle at the back
of the throat signifying that the act was complete. I ran into the meat-
fumigated coldness of the magical place, the larger Russians following
behind me, lugging something big and red. It was a cooler, packed, before
we left the motel, by the other mother, the kindly, round-faced equivalent of
my own mother. She had prepared a full Russian lunch for us. Soft-boiled
eggs wrapped in tinfoil; *vinigret,* the Russian beet salad, overflowing a reused
container of sour cream; cold chicken served between crisp white furrows of
a *bulka.* "But it's not allowed," I pleaded. "We have to buy the food here."

I felt coldness, not the air-conditioned chill of southern Georgia but   9
the coldness of a body understanding the ramifications of its own demise,
the pointlessness of it all. I sat down at a table as far away from my parents
and their friends as possible. I watched the spectacle of the newly tanned
resident aliens eating their ethnic meal — jowls working, jowls working — the soft-boiled eggs that quivered lightly as they were brought to the
mouth; the girl, my coeval, sullen like me but with a hint of pliant equanimity; her parents, dishing out the chunks of beet with plastic spoons; my
parents, getting up to use free McDonald's napkins and straws while American motorists with their noisy towheaded children bought themselves the
happiest of meals.

My parents laughed at my haughtiness. Sitting there hungry and all   10
alone — what a strange man I was becoming! So unlike them. My pockets
were filled with several quarters and dimes, enough for a hamburger and a
small Coke. I considered the possibility of redeeming my own dignity, of
leaving behind our beet-salad heritage. My parents didn't spend money,
because they lived with the idea that disaster was close at hand, that a liver-
function test would come back marked with a doctor's urgent scrawl, that
they would be fired from their jobs because their English did not suffice. We
were all representatives of a shadow society, cowering under a cloud of bad
tidings that would never come. The silver coins stayed in my pocket, the
anger burrowed and expanded into some future ulcer. I was my parents' son.

•   •   •

Comprehension

1. Shteyngart's goals, described in paragraph 1, were to visit Florida, be
   liked by an American girl, and eat every meal at McDonald's. Why does he
   want to accomplish these three goals? How successful is he?

2. How would you characterize the fourteen-year-old Shteyngart's attitude
   toward his parents? Is he ashamed of them? Impatient with them?
   Puzzled by them? Sympathetic toward them?

3. What does Shteyngart mean when he describes the words "Oh, hi there" as "perfectly American, not a birthright but an acquisition" (7)?

4. How does Shteyngart see himself and his family as different from Americans? How does he see himself as different from his parents? Point to passages in his essay that illustrate these differences.

5. In what sense are "the washed-out Technicolor planets" (7) shown in *Star Trek* reruns more familiar to Shteyngart than his own planet?

6. Why doesn't Shteyngart use the change in his pocket to buy a hamburger and a Coke? How do you interpret the essay's last sentence?

Purpose and Audience

1. Do you see this essay's purpose as to inform, to persuade, or to express personal feelings? Can you identify elements of each purpose?

2. In paragraph 6, Shteyngart humorously describes a "half-foot-long cockroach evolved enough to wave what looked like a fist at us." In contrast, paragraph 9 describes Shteyngart feeling "the coldness of a body understanding the ramifications of its own demise, the pointlessness of it all." Do you think Shteyngart intended readers to see this essay as primarily humorous or sad?

3. Which of the following do you think is the essay's thesis statement, and why?

   • "Even my parents, however, as uncritically in love with America as only immigrants could be, could not resist the iconic pull of Florida, the call of the beach and the Mouse" (1).

   • "The ride over the MacArthur Causeway to Miami Beach was my real naturalization ceremony" (6).

   • "I was my parents' son" (10).

   Do you see any other statement in the essay that might serve as its thesis?

Style and Structure

1. Do you think "Sixty-Nine Cents" is an appropriate title for this essay? If so, why? If not, what other title can you suggest?

2. What words and phrases does Shteyngart use to move his narrative from one event to the next?

3. Paragraph 6 is full of vivid detail, both about the city of Miami Beach and about the two hotels the families stayed at. What is the effect of juxtaposing these descriptions?

4. Paragraph 8 describes the McDonald's hamburger. Why is this detailed description necessary?

5. Although his essay is very descriptive, Shteyngart includes very little description of his parents. Why? Where *does* he describe them? Do you think he should have added more detail about what they looked like? More dialogue? Explain your reasoning.

Vocabulary Projects

1. Define each of the following words as it is used in this selection.

   profligate (1)   coda (7)   equanimity (9)
   iconic (1)   ramifications (9)   towheaded (9)
   jib (2)   demise (9)   haughtiness (10)
   decamped (6)   coeval (9)   cowering (10)

2. In paragraph 2, Shteyngart uses two nouns — *déjà vu* and *megawatt* — as adjectives in the phrases "*déjà vu* feeling" and "*megawatt* smile," respectively. Where else in this essay are nouns used as adjectives? What adjectives could be substituted for the nouns in each case?

Journal Entry

What do you think the loss of his Russian accent meant to Shteyngart when he was fourteen? What do you think it signified to him when he wrote this essay?

Writing Workshop

1. Choose one of the following quotations, and use it as the thesis of an essay about an episode in your own life:

   - "_____ was my real naturalization ceremony" (6).
   - "We always seemed to be at the margins of places. . . ." (6).
   - "I was my parents' son [or daughter]" (10).

   Be sure to include documentation that identifies Shteyngart's essay as the source of the quotation you choose and to include a works-cited page. (See the Appendix for information on documentation formats.)

2. Write a narrative about a road trip you took with your family or friends.

3. Imagine that this essay appeared on Shteyngart's blog, and that his father wrote a response presenting his own narrative of the family's trip to Miami Beach. Write the father's version of the trip. Include a thesis that makes clear how his account differs from his son's, and why.

Combining the Patterns

Shteyngart's essay is highly descriptive, but (as noted in Style and Structure question 5) he includes little **description** of his parents. What kind of descriptive details could he have provided about his parents and their friends?

Thematic Connections

- "Two Ways to Belong in America" (page 411)
- "Mother Tongue" (page 477)
- "Black *and* Latino" (page 537)
- "Statement in Support of Comprehensive Immigration Reform" (page 655)

Finishing School

Maya Angelou was born Marguerita Johnson in 1928 in St. Louis and spent much of her childhood in Stamps, Arkansas, living with her grandmother. In the 1960s, she served as northern coordinator for the Southern Christian Leadership Conference, the civil rights group organized by Martin Luther King Jr. A well-known poet, Angelou composed and read "On the Pulse of Morning" for Bill Clinton's 1993 presidential inauguration. The published version of the poem was a best-seller, and her recording of it won a Grammy award. She is currently on the faculty at Wake Forest University. It is likely, however, that Angelou will be best remembered for her series of autobiographical works, beginning with the critically acclaimed *I Know Why the Caged Bird Sings* (1969), which appeared when African-American literature was just beginning to flower.

Background on "finishing schools"
In the following excerpt from *I Know Why the Caged Bird Sings,* Angelou recalls a difficult incident that occurred when she was growing up in racially segregated Stamps in the late 1930s. At this time, wealthy young white women, rather than complete a rigorous education, often attended "finishing schools," where they refined the social skills and artistic accomplishments deemed necessary for their future roles in polite society. Versions of such schools also existed (on a limited basis) for the daughters of black professionals in urban areas. However, children of the poor and the working class — both black and white — were expected to learn practical skills that would enable them to get jobs. Such employment opportunities for rural black people were limited by and large to farm work; black women were often limited to domestic service in white households, the role for which Angelou describes her training in this essay.

Recently a white woman from Texas, who would quickly describe herself as a liberal, asked me about my hometown. When I told her that in Stamps my grandmother had owned the only Negro general merchandise store since the turn of the century, she exclaimed, "Why, you were a debutante." Ridiculous and even ludicrous. But Negro girls in small Southern towns, whether poverty-stricken or just munching along on a few of life's necessities, were given as extensive and irrelevant preparations for adulthood as rich white girls shown in magazines. Admittedly the training was not the same. While white girls learned to waltz and sit gracefully with a tea cup balanced on their knees, we were lagging behind, learning the mid-Victorian values with very little money to indulge them. . . .

We were required to embroider and I had trunkfuls of colorful dishtowels, pillowcases, runners, and handkerchiefs to my credit. I mastered the art of crocheting and tatting, and there was a lifetime's supply of dainty

107

doilies that would never be used in sacheted dresser drawers. It went without saying that all girls could iron and wash, but the finer touches around
the home, like setting a table with real silver, baking roasts, and cooking
vegetables without meat, had to be learned elsewhere. Usually at the source
of those habits. During my tenth year, a white woman's kitchen became my
finishing school.

Mrs. Viola Cullinan was a plump woman who lived in a three-bedroom   3
house somewhere behind the post office. She was singularly unattractive
until she smiled, and then the lines around her eyes and mouth which
made her look perpetually dirty disappeared, and her face looked like the
mask of an impish elf. She usually rested her smile until late afternoon
when her woman friends dropped in and Miss Glory, the cook, served them
cold drinks on the closed-in porch.

The exactness of her house was inhuman. This glass went here and   4
only here. That cup had its place and it was an act of impudent rebellion to
place it anywhere else. At twelve o'clock the table was set. At 12:15 Mrs.
Cullinan sat down to dinner (whether her husband had arrived or not). At
12:16 Miss Glory brought out the food.

It took me a week to learn the difference between a salad plate, a bread   5
plate, and a dessert plate.

Mrs. Cullinan kept up the tradition of her wealthy parents. She was   6
from Virginia. Miss Glory, who was a descendant of slaves that had worked
for the Cullinans, told me her history. She had married beneath her
(according to Miss Glory). Her husband's family hadn't had their money
very long and what they had "didn't 'mount to much."

As ugly as she was, I thought privately, she was lucky to get a husband   7
above or beneath her station. But Miss Glory wouldn't let me say a thing
against her mistress. She was very patient with me, however, over the house-
work. She explained the dishware, silverware, and servants' bells. The large
round bowl in which soup was served wasn't a soup bowl, it was a tureen.
There were goblets, sherbet glasses, ice-cream glasses, wine glasses, green
glass coffee cups with matching saucers, and water glasses. I had a glass to
drink from, and it sat with Miss Glory's on a separate shelf from the others. Soup spoons, gravy boat, butter knives, salad forks, and carving platter
were additions to my vocabulary and in fact almost represented a new language. I was fascinated with the novelty, with the fluttering Mrs. Cullinan
and her Alice-in-Wonderland house.

Her husband remains, in my memory, undefined. I lumped him with   8
all the other white men that I had ever seen and tried not to see.

On our way home one evening, Miss Glory told me that Mrs. Cullinan   9
couldn't have children. She said that she was too delicate-boned. It was
hard to imagine bones at all under those layers of fat. Miss Glory went on
to say that the doctor had taken out all her lady organs. I reasoned that a
pig's organs included the lungs, heart, and liver, so if Mrs. Cullinan was
walking around without those essentials, it explained why she drank alcohol out of unmarked bottles. She was keeping herself embalmed.

When I spoke to Bailey* about it, he agreed that I was right, but he also   10
informed me that Mr. Cullinan had two daughters by a colored lady and
that I knew them very well. He added that the girls were the spitting image
of their father. I was unable to remember what he looked like, although I
had just left him a few hours before, but I thought of the Coleman girls.
They were very light-skinned and certainly didn't look very much like their
mother (no one ever mentioned Mr. Coleman).

My pity for Mrs. Cullinan preceded me the next morning like the   11
Cheshire cat's smile. Those girls, who could have been her daughters, were
beautiful. They didn't have to straighten their hair. Even when they were
caught in the rain, their braids still hung down straight like tamed snakes.
Their mouths were pouty little cupid's bows. Mrs. Cullinan didn't know
what she missed. Or maybe she did. Poor Mrs. Cullinan.

For weeks after, I arrived early, left late and tried very hard to make up   12
for her barrenness. If she had her own children, she wouldn't have had to
ask me to run a thousand errands from her back door to the back doors of
her friends. Poor old Mrs. Cullinan.

Then one evening Miss Glory told me to serve the ladies on the porch.   13
After I set the tray down and turned toward the kitchen, one of the women
asked, "What's your name, girl?" It was the speckled-faced one. Mrs.
Cullinan said, "She doesn't talk much. Her name's Margaret."

"Is she dumb?"   14

"No. As I understand it, she can talk when she wants to but she's usu-   15
ally quiet as a little mouse. Aren't you, Margaret?"

I smile at her. Poor thing. No organs and couldn't even pronounce my   16
name correctly.

"She's a sweet little thing, though."   17

"Well, that may be, but the name's too long. I'd never bother myself. I'd   18
call her Mary if I was you."

I fumed into the kitchen. That horrible woman would never have the   19
chance to call me Mary because if I was starving I'd never work for her. . . .

That evening I decided to write a poem on being white, fat, old, and   20
without children. It was going to be a tragic ballad. I would have to watch
her carefully to capture the essence of her loneliness and pain.

The very next day, she called me by the wrong name. Miss Glory and I   21
were washing up the lunch dishes when Mrs. Cullinan came to the doorway. "Mary?"

Miss Glory asked, "Who?"   22

Mrs. Cullinan, sagging a little, knew and I knew. "I want Mary to go   23
down to Mrs. Randall's and take her some soup. She's not been feeling well
for a few days."

Miss Glory's face was a wonder to see. "You mean Margaret, ma'am.   24
Her name's Margaret."

---

* EDS. NOTE — Angelou's brother.

"That's too long. She's Mary from now on. Heat that soup from last   25
night and put it in the china tureen and, Mary, I want you to carry it carefully."

Every person I knew had a hellish horror of being "called out of his   26
name." It was a dangerous practice to call a Negro anything that could be
loosely construed as insulting because of the centuries of their having been
called niggers, jigs, dinges, blackbirds, crows, boots, and spooks.

Miss Glory had a fleeting second of feeling sorry for me. Then as she   27
handed me the hot tureen she said, "Don't mind, don't pay that no mind.
Sticks and stones may break your bones, but words . . . You know, I been
working for her for twenty years."

She held the back door open for me. "Twenty years. I wasn't much older   28
than you. My name used to be Hallelujah. That's what Ma named me, but
my mistress give me 'Glory,' and it stuck. I likes it better too."

I was in the little path that ran behind the houses when Miss Glory   29
shouted, "It's shorter too."

For a few seconds it was a toss-up over whether I would laugh (imagine   30
being named Hallelujah) or cry (imagine letting some white woman rename
you for her convenience). My anger saved me from either outburst. I had to
quit the job, but the problem was going to be how to do it. Momma
wouldn't allow me to quit for just any reason.

"She's a peach. That woman is a real peach." Mrs. Randall's maid was   31
talking as she took the soup from me, and I wondered what her name used
to be and what she answered to now.

For a week I looked into Mrs. Cullinan's face as she called me Mary.   32
She ignored my coming late and leaving early. Miss Glory was a little
annoyed because I had begun to leave egg yolk on the dishes and wasn't
putting much heart in polishing the silver. I hoped that she would complain to our boss, but she didn't.

Then Bailey solved my dilemma. He had me describe the contents of   33
the cupboard and the particular plates she liked best. Her favorite piece
was a casserole shaped like a fish and the green glass coffee cups. I kept his
instructions in mind, so on the next day when Miss Glory was hanging out
clothes and I had again been told to serve the old biddies on the porch, I
dropped the empty serving tray. When I heard Mrs. Cullinan scream
"Mary!" I picked up the casserole and two of the green glass cups in readi-
ness. As she rounded the kitchen door I let them fall on the tiled floor.

I could never absolutely describe to Bailey what happened next, because   34
each time I got to the part where she fell on the floor and screwed up her
ugly face to cry, we burst out laughing. She actually wobbled around on the
floor and picked up shards of the cups and cried, "Oh, Momma. Oh, dear
Gawd. It's Momma's china from Virginia. Oh Momma, I'm sorry."

Miss Glory came running in from the yard and the women from the   35
porch crowded around. Miss Glory was almost as broken up as her mistress. "You mean to say she broke our Virginia dishes? What we gone do?"

Mrs. Cullinan cried louder. "That clumsy nigger. Clumsy little black 36
nigger."

Old speckled-face leaned down and asked, "Who did it, Viola? Was it 37
Mary? Who did it?"

Everything was happening so fast I can't remember whether her action 38
preceded her words, but I know that Mrs. Cullinan said, "Her name's
Margaret, goddamn it, her name's Margaret." And she threw a wedge of
broken plate at me. It could have been the hysteria which put her aim off,
but the flying crockery caught Miss Glory right over her ear and she started
screaming.

I left the front door wide open so all the neighbors could hear. 39

Mrs. Cullinan was right about one thing. My name wasn't Mary. 40

• • •

Comprehension

1. What is Angelou required to do in the white woman's kitchen? Why are these tasks so important to Mrs. Cullinan?

2. Why does Angelou feel sorry for Mrs. Cullinan at first? When does her attitude change? Why?

3. Why does Mrs. Cullinan's friend recommend that Angelou be called "Mary" (18)? Why does this upset Angelou so deeply?

4. When Angelou decides she wants to quit, she realizes she cannot quit "for just any reason" (30). How does her brother Bailey help her resolve her dilemma?

5. What does Angelou actually learn through her experience?

Purpose and Audience

1. Do you think Angelou wrote this essay for southerners, for blacks, for whites, or for a general audience? Identify specific details that support your answer.

2. Angelou begins her narrative by summarizing a discussion between herself and a white woman. What purpose does she have for doing this?

3. What is Angelou's thesis?

Style and Structure

1. What image does the phrase *finishing school* usually call to mind? How is the use of this phrase **ironic** in view of its meaning in this selection?

2. How does Angelou signal the passage of time in this narrative? Identify some transitional phrases that move readers from one time period to another.

3. How does the use of dialogue highlight the contrast between the black and the white characters? How does this contrast strengthen the narrative?

4. What details does Angelou use to describe Mrs. Cullinan and her home to the reader? How does this detailed description help to advance the narrative?

Vocabulary Projects

1. Define each of the following words as it is used in this selection.

tatting (2)	pouty (11)	dilemma (33)
sacheted (2)	barrenness (12)	shards (34)
impudent (4)	ballad (20)	
embalmed (9)	construed (26)	

2. According to your dictionary, what is the difference between *ridiculous* and *ludicrous* (1)? Between *soup bowl* and *tureen* (7)? Why do you think Angelou draws a distinction between the two words in each pair?

3. Try substituting an equivalent word for each of the following, paying careful attention to the context of each in the narrative.

perpetually (3)	station (7)	biddies (33)
exactness (4)	peach (31)	

Does Angelou's original choice seem more effective than your substitutions in all cases? Explain.

Journal Entry

Have you ever received any training or education that at the time you considered "extensive and irrelevant preparations for adulthood" (1)? Do you now see any value in the experience?

Writing Workshop

1. Think about a time in your life when someone in a position of authority treated you unjustly. How did you react? Write a narrative essay in which you recount the situation and your responses to it.

2. Have you, like Angelou, ever been the victim of name-calling — or participated in name-calling? Summarize your experience, including dialogue and description that will help your readers understand your motivations and reactions. Include a thesis statement that expresses your present attitude toward the situation, and try to draw parallels with Angelou's experiences.

3. Write a narrative essay that includes a brief summary of an incident from a work of fiction — specifically, an incident that serves as a character's initiation into adulthood. In your essay, focus on how the experience helps the character grow up.

Combining the Patterns

Angelou's essay is a narrative, but it is rich with descriptive detail. Identify specific passages of the essay that are structured as **descriptions** of people and places. Is the description primarily visual, or does it incorporate other senses (sound, smell, taste, and touch) as well? Do you think any person, setting, or object should be described in greater detail? Explain.

Thematic Connections

- "Midnight" (page 209)
- "The 'Black Table' Is Still There" (page 345)
- "What Work Is" (page 542)
- "Letter from Birmingham Jail" (page 588)

My Mother Never Worked

Bonnie Smith-Yackel was born into a farm family in Willmar, Minnesota, in 1937. She began writing as a young homemaker in the early 1960s and for the next fourteen years published short stories, essays, and book reviews in such publications as *Catholic Digest, Minnesota Monthly,* and *Ms.* magazine, as well as in several local newspapers. As Smith-Yackel explains it, "The catalyst for writing the [following] essay shortly after my mother's death was recounting my telephone conversation with Social Security to the lawyer who was helping me settle my mother's estate. When I told him what the SS woman had said, he responded: 'Well, that's right. Your mother didn't work, you know.' At which point I stood and said, 'She worked harder throughout her life than you or a hundred men like you!' and stomped out of his office, drove home, sat down and wrote the essay in one sitting." Although this narrative essay, first published in *Women: A Journal of Liberation* in 1975, is based on personal experience, it also makes a broader statement about how society values "women's work."

Background on Social Security benefits

Social Security is a federal insurance program that requires workers to contribute a percentage of their wages to a fund that they may draw benefits from if they become unemployed due to disability. After retirement, workers can receive a monthly income from this fund, which also provides a modest death benefit to survivors. The contribution is generally deducted directly from a worker's paycheck, and employers must contribute a matching amount. According to federal law, a woman who is a homemaker, who has never been a wage earner, is eligible for Social Security benefits only through the earnings of her deceased husband. (The same would be true for a man if the roles were reversed.) Therefore, a homemaker's survivors would not be eligible for the death benefit. Although the law has been challenged in the courts, the survivors of a homemaker who has never been a wage earner are still not entitled to a Social Security death benefit.

"Social Security Office." (The voice answering the telephone sounds very self-assured.) 1

"I'm calling about . . . my mother just died . . . I was told to call you and see about a . . . death-benefit check, I think they call it. . . ." 2

"I see. Was your mother on Social Security? How old was she?" 3

"Yes . . . she was seventy-eight. . . ." 4

"Do you know her number?" 5

"No . . . I, ah . . . don't you have a record?" 6

"Certainly. I'll look it up. Her name?" 7

"Smith. Martha Smith. Or maybe she used Martha Ruth Smith? . . .   8
Sometimes she used her maiden name . . . Martha Jerabek Smith?"

"If you'd care to hold on, I'll check our records — it'll be a few min-   9
utes."

"Yes. . . ."   10

Her love letters — to and from Daddy — were in an old box, tied with   11
ribbons and stiff, rigid-with-age leather thongs: 1918 through 1920; hers
written on stationery from the general store she had worked in full-time
and managed, single-handed, after her graduation from high school in
1913; and his, at first, on YMCA or Soldiers and Sailors Club stationery
dispensed to the fighting men of World War I. He wooed her thoroughly
and persistently by mail, and though she reciprocated all his feelings for
her, she dreaded marriage. . . .

"It's so hard for me to decide when to have my wedding day — that's all.   12
I've thought about these last two days. I have told you dozens of times that
I won't be afraid of married life, but when it comes down to setting the date
and then picturing myself a married woman with half a dozen or more kids
to look after, it just makes me sick. . . . I am weeping right now — I hope that
some day I can look back and say how foolish I was to dread it all."

They married in February, 1921, and began farming. Their first baby, a   13
daughter, was born in January, 1922, when my mother was twenty-six years
old. The second baby, a son, was born in March, 1923. They were renting
farms; my father, besides working his own fields, also was a hired man for
two other farmers. They had no capital initially, and had to gain it slowly,
working from dawn until midnight every day. My town-bred mother
learned to set hens and raise chickens, feed pigs, milk cows, plant and harvest a garden, and can every fruit and vegetable she could scrounge. She
carried water nearly a quarter of a mile from the well to fill her wash boilers
in order to do her laundry on a scrub board. She learned to shuck grain,
feed threshers, shock and husk corn, feed corn pickers. In September, 1925,
the third baby came, and in June, 1927, the fourth child — both daughters.
In 1930, my parents had enough money to buy their own farm, and that
March they moved all their livestock and belongings themselves, fifty-five
miles over rutted, muddy roads.

In the summer of 1930 my mother and her two eldest children   14
reclaimed a forty-acre field from Canadian thistles, by chopping them all
out with a hoe. In the other fields, when the oats and flax began to head
out, the green and blue of the crops were hidden by the bright yellow of
wild mustard. My mother walked the fields day after day, pulling each mustard plant. She raised a new flock of baby chicks — five hundred — and she
spaded up, planted, hoed, and harvested a half-acre garden.

During the next spring their hogs caught cholera and died. No cash   15
that fall.

And in the next year the drought hit. My mother and father trudged   16
from the well to the chickens, the well to the calf pasture, the well to the
barn, and from the well to the garden. The sun came out hot and bright,

endlessly, day after day. The crops shriveled and died. They harvested half the corn, and ground the other half, stalks and all, and fed it to the cattle as fodder. With the price at four cents a bushel for the harvested crop, they couldn't afford to haul it into town. They burned it in the furnace for fuel that winter.

In 1934, in February, when the dust was still so thick in the Minnesota air that my parents couldn't always see from the house to the barn, their fifth child — a fourth daughter — was born. My father hunted rabbits daily, and my mother stewed them, fried them, canned them, and wished out loud that she could taste hamburger once more. In the fall the shotgun brought prairie chickens, ducks, pheasant, and grouse. My mother plucked each bird, carefully reserving the breast feathers for pillows.   17

In the winter she sewed night after night, endlessly, begging cast-off clothing from relatives, ripping apart coats, dresses, blouses, and trousers to remake them to fit her four daughters and son. Every morning and every evening she milked cows, fed pigs and calves, cared for chickens, picked eggs, cooked meals, washed dishes, scrubbed floors, and tended and loved her children. In the spring she planted a garden once more, dragging pails of water to nourish and sustain the vegetables for the family. In 1936 she lost a baby in her sixth month.   18

In 1937 her fifth daughter was born. She was forty-two years old. In 1939 a second son, and in 1941 her eighth child — and third son.   19

But the war had come, and prosperity of a sort. The herd of cattle had grown to thirty head; she still milked morning and evening. Her garden was more than a half acre — the rains had come, and by now the Rural Electricity Administration and indoor plumbing. Still she sewed — dresses and jackets for the children, housedresses and aprons for herself, weekly patching of jeans, overalls, and denim shirts. She still made pillows, using feathers she had plucked, and quilts every year — intricate patterns as well as patchwork, stitched as well as tied — all necessary bedding for her family. Every scrap of cloth too small to be used in quilts was carefully saved and painstakingly sewed together in strips to make rugs. She still went out in the fields to help with the haying whenever there was a threat of rain.   20

In 1959 my mother's last child graduated from high school. A year later the cows were sold. She still raised chickens and ducks, plucked feathers, made pillows, baked her own bread, and every year made a new quilt — now for a married child or for a grandchild. And her garden, that huge, undying symbol of sustenance, was as large and cared for as in all the years before. The canning, and now freezing, continued.   21

In 1969, on a June afternoon, mother and father started out for town so that she could buy sugar to make rhubarb jam for a daughter who lived in Texas. The car crashed into a ditch. She was paralyzed from the waist down.   22

In 1970 her husband, my father, died. My mother struggled to regain some competence and dignity and order in her life. At the rehabilitation institute, where they gave her physical therapy and trained her to live use-   23 fully in a wheelchair, the therapist told me: "She did fifteen pushups today — fifteen! She's almost seventy-five years old! I've never known a woman so strong!"

From her wheelchair she canned pickles, baked bread, ironed clothes,   24
wrote dozens of letters weekly to her friends and her "half dozen or more kids," and made three patchwork housecoats and one quilt. She made balls and balls of carpet rags — enough for five rugs. And kept all her love letters.

"I think I've found your mother's records — Martha Ruth Smith; mar-   25
ried to Ben F. Smith?"

"Yes, that's right."   26

"Well, I see that she was getting a widow's pension. . . ."   27

"Yes, that's right."   28

"Well, your mother isn't entitled to our $255 death benefit."   29

"Not entitled! But why?"   30

The voice on the telephone explains patiently: 31

"Well, you see — your mother never worked."   32

•   •   •

Comprehension

1. What kind of work did Martha Smith do while her children were growing up? List some of the chores she performed.

2. Why aren't Martha Smith's survivors entitled to a death benefit when their mother dies?

3. How does the government define *work*?

Purpose and Audience

1. What point is the writer trying to make? Why do you suppose her thesis is never explicitly stated?

2. This essay appeared in *Ms.* magazine and other publications whose audiences are sympathetic to feminist goals. Could it just as easily have appeared in a magazine whose audience was not? Explain.

3. Smith-Yackel mentions relatively little about her father in this essay. How can you account for this?

4. This essay was first published in 1975. Do you think it is dated, or do you think the issues it raises are still relevant today?

Style and Structure

1. Is the essay's title effective? If so, why? If not, what alternate title can you suggest?

2. Smith-Yackel could have outlined her mother's life without framing it with the telephone conversation. Why do you think she includes this frame?

3. What strategies does Smith-Yackel use to indicate the passing of time in her narrative?

4. This narrative piles details one on top of another almost like a list. Why does the writer include so many details?

5. In paragraphs 20 and 21, what is accomplished by the repetition of the word *still*?

Vocabulary Projects

1. Define each of the following words as it is used in this selection.

scrounge (13)	rutted (13)	intricate (20)
shuck (13)	reclaimed (14)	sustenance (21)
shock (13)	flax (14)	
husk (13)	fodder (16)	

2. Try substituting equivalent words for those italicized in this sentence:

He *wooed* her *thoroughly* and *persistently* by mail, and though she *reciprocated* all his feelings for her, she *dreaded* marriage. . . (11).

How do your substitutions change the sentence's meaning?

3. Throughout her narrative, Smith-Yackel uses concrete, specific verbs. Review her choice of verbs, particularly in paragraphs 13–24, and comment on how such verbs serve the essay's purpose.

Journal Entry

Do you believe that a homemaker who has never been a wage earner should be entitled to a Social Security death benefit for her survivors? Explain your reasoning.

Writing Workshop

1. If you can, interview one of your parents or grandparents (or another person you know who reminds you of Smith-Yackel's mother) about his or her work, and write a chronological narrative based on what you learn. Include a thesis statement that your narrative can support, and quote your family member's responses when possible.

2. Write Martha Smith's obituary as it might have appeared in her hometown newspaper. (If you are not familiar with the form of an obituary, read a few in your local paper or online. You might consult Legacy.com or Obituaries.com.)

3. Write a narrative account of a typical day at the worst job you ever had. Include a thesis statement that expresses your negative feelings.

Combining the Patterns

Because of the repetitive nature of the farm chores Smith-Yackel describes in her narrative, some passages come very close to explaining a **process**, a series of repeated steps that always occur in a predictable order. Identify several such passages. If Smith-Yackel's essay were written entirely as a process explanation, what material would have to be left out? How would these omissions change the essay?

Thematic Connections

- "Midnight" (page 209)
- "I Want a Wife" (page 520)
- "What Work Is" (page 542)
- "Down and Out in Discount America" (page 638)

MARTIN GANSBERG

Thirty-Eight Who Saw Murder Didn't Call the Police

Martin Gansberg (1920–1995), a native of Brooklyn, New York, was a reporter and editor for the *New York Times* for forty-three years. The following article, written for the *Times* two weeks after the 1964 murder it recounts, earned Gansberg an award for excellence from the Newspaper Reporters Association of New York. Gansberg's thesis, though not explicitly stated, still retains its power.

Background on the Kitty Genovese murder case

The events reported here took place on March 14, 1964, as contemporary American culture was undergoing a complex transition. The relatively placid years of the 1950s were giving way to more troubling times: the Civil Rights movement was leading to social unrest in the South and in northern inner cities; the escalating war in Vietnam was creating angry political divisions; President John F. Kennedy had been assassinated just four months earlier; violent imagery was increasing in television and film; crime rates were rising; and a growing drug culture was becoming apparent. The brutal, senseless murder of Kitty Genovese — and, more important, her neighbors' failure to respond immediately to her cries for help — became a nationwide, and even worldwide, symbol for what was perceived as an evolving culture of violence and indifference.

Recently, some of the details Gansberg mentions have been challenged. For example, as the *New York Times* now acknowledges, there were only two attacks on Ms. Genovese, not three; the first attack may have been shorter than first reported; the second attack may have occurred in the apartment house foyer, where neighbors would not have been able to see Genovese; and some witnesses may, in fact, actually *have* called the police. At the time, however, the world was shocked by the incident, and even today social scientists around the world debate the causes of "the Genovese syndrome."

For more than half an hour thirty-eight respectable, law-abiding citizens in Queens watched a killer stalk and stab a woman in three separate attacks in Kew Gardens.   1

Twice their chatter and the sudden glow of their bedroom lights interrupted him and frightened him off. Each time he returned, sought her out, and stabbed her again. Not one person telephoned the police during the assault; one witness called after the woman was dead.   2

That was two weeks ago today.   3

Still shocked is Assistant Chief Inspector Frederick M. Lussen, in charge of the borough's detectives and a veteran of twenty-five years of   4 homicide investigations. He can give a matter-of-fact recitation on many murders. But the Kew Gardens slaying baffles him — not because it is a murder, but because the "good people" failed to call the police.

"As we have reconstructed the crime," he said, "the assailant had three chances to kill this woman during a thirty-five-minute period. He returned twice to complete the job. If we had been called when he first attacked, the woman might not be dead now." 5

This is what the police say happened beginning at 3:20 A.M. in the staid, middle-class, tree-lined Austin Street area: 6

Twenty-eight-year-old Catherine Genovese, who was called Kitty by almost everyone in the neighborhood, was returning home from her job as manager of a bar in Hollis. She parked her red Fiat in a lot adjacent to the Kew Gardens Long Island Rail Road Station, facing Mowbray Place. Like many residents of the neighborhood, she had parked there day after day since her arrival from Connecticut a year ago, although the railroad frowns on the practice. 7

She turned off the lights of her car, locked the door, and started to walk the one hundred feet to the entrance of her apartment at 82-70 Austin Street, which is in a Tudor building, with stores in the first floor and apartments on the second. 8

The entrance to the apartment is in the rear of the building because the front is rented to retail stores. At night the quiet neighborhood is shrouded in the slumbering darkness that marks most residential areas. 9

Miss Genovese noticed a man at the far end of the lot, near a seven-story apartment house at 82-40 Austin Street. She halted. Then, nervously, she headed up Austin Street toward Lefferts Boulevard, where there is a call box to the 102nd Police Precinct in nearby Richmond Hill. 10

She got as far as a street light in front of a bookstore before the man grabbed her. She screamed. Lights went on in the ten-story apartment house at 82-67 Austin Street, which faces the bookstore. Windows slid open and voices punctuated the early-morning stillness. 11

Miss Genovese screamed: "Oh, my God, he stabbed me! Please help me! Please help me!" 12

From one of the upper windows in the apartment house, a man called down: "Let that girl alone!" 13

The assailant looked up at him, shrugged, and walked down Austin Street toward a white sedan parked a short distance away. Miss Genovese struggled to her feet. 14

Lights went out. The killer returned to Miss Genovese, now trying to make her way around the side of the building by the parking lot to get to her apartment. The assailant stabbed her again. 15

"I'm dying!" she shrieked. "I'm dying!" 16

Windows were opened again, and lights went on in many apartments. The assailant got into his car and drove away. Miss Genovese staggered to her feet. A city bus, 0–10, the Lefferts Boulevard line to Kennedy International Airport, passed. It was 3:35 A.M. 17

The assailant returned. By then, Miss Genovese had crawled to the back of the building, where the freshly painted brown doors to the apartment house held out hope for safety. The killer tried the first door; she wasn't there. At the second door, 82-62 Austin Street, he saw her slumped on the floor at the foot of the stairs. He stabbed her a third time — fatally.   18

It was 3:50 by the time the police received their first call, from a man who was a neighbor of Miss Genovese. In two minutes they were at the scene. The neighbor, a seventy-year-old woman, and another woman were the only persons on the street. Nobody else came forward.   19

The man explained that he had called the police after much deliberation. He had phoned a friend in Nassau County for advice, and then he had crossed the roof of the building to the apartment of the elderly woman to get her to make the call.   20

"I didn't want to get involved," he sheepishly told police.   21

Six days later, the police arrested Winston Moseley, a twenty-nine-year-old business machine operator, and charged him with homicide. Moseley had no previous record. He is married, has two children, and owns a home at 133-19 Sutter Avenue, South Ozone Park, Queens. On Wednesday, a court committed him to Kings County Hospital for psychiatric observation.   22

When questioned by the police, Moseley also said that he had slain Mrs. Annie May Johnson, twenty-four, of 146-12 133d Avenue, Jamaica, on Feb. 29 and Barbara Kralik, fifteen, of 174-17 140th Avenue, Springfield Gardens, last July. In the Kralik case, the police are holding Alvin L. Mitchell, who is said to have confessed to that slaying.   23

The police stressed how simple it would have been to have gotten in touch with them. "A phone call," said one of the detectives, "would have done it." The police may be reached by dialing "0" for operator or SPring 7-3100.   24

Today witnesses from the neighborhood, which is made up of one-family homes in the $35,000 to $60,000 range with the exception of the two apartment houses near the railroad station, find it difficult to explain why they didn't call the police.   25

A housewife, knowingly if quite casually, said, "We thought it was a lovers' quarrel." A husband and wife both said, "Frankly, we were afraid." They seemed aware of the fact that events might have been different. A distraught woman, wiping her hands in her apron, said, "I didn't want my husband to get involved."   26

One couple, now willing to talk about that night, said they heard the first screams. The husband looked thoughtfully at the bookstore where the killer first grabbed Miss Genovese.   27

"We went to the window to see what was happening," he said, "but the light from our bedroom made it difficult to see the street." The wife, still apprehensive, added: "I put out the light and we were able to see better."   28

Asked why they hadn't called the police, she shrugged and replied: "I don't know."   29

A man peeked out from a slight opening in the doorway to his apart-   30
ment and rattled off an account of the killer's second attack. Why hadn't
he called the police at the time? "I was tired," he said without emotion. "I
went back to bed."

It was 4:25 A.M. when the ambulance arrived to take the body of Miss   31
Genovese. It drove off. "Then," a solemn police detective said, "the people
came out."

•   •   •

Comprehension

1. How much time elapsed between the first stabbing of Kitty Genovese and
   the time when the people finally came out?
2. What excuses do the neighbors make for not coming to Kitty Genovese's
   aid?

Purpose and Audience

1. This article appeared in 1964. What effect was it intended to have on its
   audience? Do you think it has the same impact today, or has its impact
   changed or diminished?
2. What is the article's main point? Why does Gansberg imply his thesis
   rather than state it explicitly?
3. What is Gansberg's purpose in describing the Austin Street area as "staid,
   middle-class, tree-lined" (6)?
4. Why do you suppose Gansberg provides the police department's phone
   number in his article? (Note that New York City did not have 911 emergency service in 1964.)

Style and Structure

1. Gansberg is very precise in this article, especially in his references to time,
   addresses, and ages. Why?
2. The objective newspaper style is dominant in this article, but the writer's
   anger shows through. Point to words and phrases that reveal his attitude
   toward his material.
3. Because this article was originally set in the narrow columns of a newspaper, it has many short paragraphs. Would the narrative be more effective
   if some of these brief paragraphs were combined? If so, why? If not, why
   not? Give examples to support your answer.
4. Review the dialogue. Does it strengthen Gansberg's narrative? Would the
   article be more compelling with additional dialogue? Without dialogue?
   Explain.
5. This article does not have a formal conclusion; nevertheless, the last paragraph sums up the writer's attitude. How?

Vocabulary Projects

1. Define each of the following words as it is used in this selection.

   stalk (1)   adjacent (7)   distraught (26)
   baffles (4)   punctuated (11)   apprehensive (28)
   staid (6)   sheepishly (21)

2. The word *assailant* appears frequently in this article. Why is it used so often? What impact is this repetition likely to have on readers? What other words could have been used?

Journal Entry

In a similar situation, would you have called the police? Would you have gone outside to help? What factors do you think might have influenced your decision?

Writing Workshop

1. In your own words, write a ten-sentence **summary** (see page 120) of the article. Try to reflect Gansberg's order and emphasis, as well as his ideas, and be sure to include all necessary transitions.

2. Rewrite the article as if it were a blog post by one of the thirty-eight people who watched the murder. Summarize what you saw, and explain why you decided not to call for help. (You may invent details that Gansberg does not include.) If you like, you can first visit the Web site oldkewgardens.com, which includes a detailed critique of Gansberg's article as well as photos of the area in which the crime took place.

3. If you have ever been involved in or witnessed a situation in which some-one was in trouble, write a narrative essay about the incident. If people failed to help the person in trouble, explain why you think no one acted. If people did act, tell how. Be sure to account for your own actions. In your essay's introduction, refer to Gansberg's account of Kitty Genovese's murder. If you quote Gansberg, be sure to include documentation and a works-cited page. (See the Appendix for information on documentation formats.)

Combining the Patterns

Because the purpose of this newspaper article is to give basic factual information, it has no extended descriptions of the victim, the witnesses, or the crime scene. It also does not explain *why* those who watched did not act. Where might passages of **description** or **cause and effect** be added? How might such additions change the article's impact on readers? Do you think they would strengthen the article?

Thematic Connections

- "Samuel" (page 258)
- "The Lottery" (page 311)
- "Who Killed Benny Paret?" (page 340)
- "A Peaceful Woman Explains Why She Carries a Gun" (page 357)

Shooting an Elephant

George Orwell (1903–1950) was born Eric Blair in Bengal, India, where his father was a British civil servant. Rather than attend university, Orwell joined the Imperial Police in neighboring Burma (now renamed Myanmar), where he served from 1922 to 1927. Finding himself increasingly opposed to British colonial rule, Orwell left Burma to live and write in Paris and London. A political liberal and a fierce moralist, Orwell is best known today for his novels *Animal Farm* (1945) and *1984* (1949), which portray the dangers of totalitarianism. In "Shooting an Elephant," written in 1936, he recalls an incident from his days in Burma that clarified his thinking about British colonial rule.

Background on British imperialism

The British had gradually taken over Burma through a succession of wars beginning in 1824; by 1885, the domination was complete. Like a number of other European countries, Britain had forcibly established colonial rule in countries throughout the world during the eighteenth and nineteenth centuries, primarily to exploit their natural resources. This empire building, known as *imperialism,* was justified by the belief that European culture was superior to the cultures of the indigenous peoples, particularly in Asia and Africa. Therefore, imperialist nations claimed, it was "the white man's burden" to bring civilization to these "heathen" lands. In most cases, such control could be achieved only through force. Anti-imperialist sentiment began to grow in the early twentieth century, but colonial rule continued until midcentury in much of the less-developed world. Not until the late 1940s did many European colonies begin to gain independence. The British ceded home rule to Burma in 1947.

In Moulmein, in Lower Burma, I was hated by large numbers of   1
people — the only time in my life that I have been important enough for this to happen to me. I was sub-divisional police officer of the town, and in an aimless, petty kind of way anti-European feeling was very bitter. No one had the guts to raise a riot, but if a European woman went through the bazaars alone somebody would probably spit betel juice over her dress. As a police officer I was an obvious target and was baited whenever it seemed safe to do so. When a nimble Burman tripped me up on the football field and the referee (another Burman) looked the other way, the crowd yelled with hideous laughter. This happened more than once. In the end the sneering yellow faces of young men that met me everywhere, the insults hooted after me when I was at a safe distance, got badly on my nerves. The young Buddhist priests were the worst of all. There were several thousands of them in the town and none of them seemed to have anything to do except stand on street corners and jeer at Europeans.

All this was perplexing and upsetting. For at that time I had already made up my mind that imperialism was an evil thing and the sooner I chucked up my job and got out of it the better. Theoretically — and secretly, of course — I was all for the Burmese and all against their oppressors, the British. As for the job I was doing, I hated it more bitterly than I can perhaps make clear. In a job like that you see the dirty work of Empire at close quarters. The wretched prisoners huddling in the stinking cages of the lockups, the grey, cowed faces of the long-term convicts, the scarred buttocks of the men who had been flogged with bamboos — all these oppressed me with an intolerable sense of guilt. But I could get nothing into perspective. I was young and ill-educated and I had had to think out my problems in the utter silence that is imposed on every Englishman in the East. I did not even know that the British Empire is dying, still less did I know that it is a great deal better than the younger empires that are going to supplant it.* All I knew was that I was stuck between my hatred of the empire I served and my rage against the evil-spirited little beasts who tried to make my job impossible. With one part of my mind I thought of the British Raj** as an unbreakable tyranny, as something clamped down, in *saecula saeculorum*,*** upon the will of prostrate peoples; with another part I thought that the greatest joy in the world would be to drive a bayonet into a Buddhist priest's guts. Feelings like these are the normal by-products of imperialism; ask any Anglo-Indian official, if you can catch him off duty.

One day something happened which in a roundabout way was enlightening. It was a tiny incident in itself, but it gave me a better glimpse than I had had before of the real nature of imperialism — the real motives for which despotic governments act. Early one morning the sub-inspector at a police station the other end of the town rang me up on the phone and said that an elephant was ravaging the bazaar. Would I please come and do something about it? I did not know what I could do, but I wanted to see what was happening and I got on to a pony and started out. I took my rifle, an old .44 Winchester and much too small to kill an elephant, but I thought the noise might be useful *in terrorem*.† Various Burmans stopped me on the way and told me about the elephant's doings. It was not, of course, a wild elephant, but a tame one which had gone "must."‡ It had been chained up, as tame elephants always are when their attack of "must" is due, but on the previous night it had broken its chain and escaped. Its mahout,§ the only person who could manage it when it was in that state, had set out in pursuit, but had taken the wrong direction and was now twelve hours' journey away, and in the morning the elephant had suddenly reappeared in the

---

* EDS. NOTE — Orwell was writing in 1936, when Hitler and Stalin were in power and World War II was only three years away.

** EDS. NOTE — The former British rule of the Indian subcontinent.

*** EDS. NOTE — From time immemorial.

† EDS. NOTE — For the purpose of frightening.

‡ EDS. NOTE — Was in heat, a condition likely to wear off.

§ EDS. NOTE — A keeper and driver of an elephant.

town. The Burmese population had no weapons and were quite helpless against it. It had already destroyed somebody's bamboo hut, killed a cow, and raided some fruit-stalls and devoured the stock; also it had met the municipal rubbish van and, when the driver jumped out and took to his heels, had turned the van over and inflicted violences upon it.

The Burmese sub-inspector and some Indian constables were waiting   4
for me in the quarter where the elephant had been seen. It was a very poor quarter, a labyrinth of squalid bamboo huts, thatched with palm-leaf, winding all over a steep hillside. I remember that it was a cloudy, stuffy morning at the beginning of the rains. We began questioning people as to where the elephant had gone, and, as usual, failed to get any definite information. That is invariably the case in the East; a story always sounds clear enough at a distance, but the nearer you get to the scene of events the vaguer it becomes. Some of the people said that the elephant had gone in one direction, some said that he had gone in another, some professed not even to have heard of an elephant. I had almost made up my mind that the whole story was a pack of lies, when we heard yells a little distance away. There was a loud, scandalized cry of "Go away, child! Go away this instant!" and an old woman with a switch in her hand came round the corner of a hut, violently shooing away a crowd of naked children. Some more women followed, clicking their tongues and exclaiming; evidently there was something that the children ought not to have seen. I rounded the hut and saw a man's dead body sprawling in the mud. He was an Indian, a black Dravidian coolie,* almost naked, and he could not have been dead many minutes. The people said that the elephant had come suddenly upon him round the corner of the hut, caught him with its trunk, put its foot on his back, and ground him into the earth. This was the rainy season and the ground was soft, and his face had scored a trench a foot deep and a couple of yards long. He was lying on his belly with arms crucified and head sharply twisted to one side. His face was coated with mud, the eyes wide open, the teeth bared and grinning with an expression of unendurable agony. (Never tell me, by the way, that the dead look peaceful. Most of the corpses I have seen looked devilish.) The friction of the great beast's foot had stripped the skin from his back as neatly as one skins a rabbit. As soon as I saw the dead man I sent an orderly to a friend's house nearby to borrow an elephant rifle. I had already sent back the pony, not wanting it to go mad with fright and throw me if it smelled the elephant.

The orderly came back in a few minutes with a rifle and five cartridges,   5
and meanwhile some Burmans had arrived and told us that the elephant was in the paddy** fields below, only a few hundred yards away. As I started forward practically the whole population of the quarter flocked out of the houses and followed me. They had seen the rifle and were all shouting excitedly that I was going to shoot the elephant. They had not shown much interest in the elephant when he was merely ravaging their homes, but it

---

* EDS. NOTE — An unskilled laborer.
** EDS. NOTE — Wet land for growing rice.

was different now that he was going to be shot. It was a bit of fun to them, as it would be to an English crowd; besides they wanted the meat. It made me vaguely uneasy. I had no intention of shooting the elephant — I had merely sent for the rifle to defend myself if necessary — and it is always unnerving to have a crowd following you. I marched down the hill, looking and feeling a fool, with the rifle over my shoulder and an ever-growing army of people jostling at my heels. At the bottom, when you got away from the huts, there was a metalled road and beyond that a miry waste of paddy fields a thousand yards across, not yet ploughed but soggy from the first rains and dotted with coarse grass. The elephant was standing eight yards from the road, his left side towards us. He took not the slightest notice of the crowd's approach. He was tearing up bunches of grass, beating them against his knees to clean them and stuffing them into his mouth.

I had halted on the road. As soon as I saw the elephant I knew with   6
perfect certainty that I ought not to shoot him. It is a serious matter to shoot a working elephant — it is comparable to destroying a huge and costly piece of machinery — and obviously one ought not to do it if it can possibly be avoided. And at that distance, peacefully eating, the elephant looked no more dangerous than a cow. I thought then and I think now that his attack of "must" was already passing off; in which case he would merely wander harmlessly about until the mahout came back and caught him. Moreover, I did not in the least want to shoot him. I decided that I would watch him for a little while to make sure that he did not turn savage again, and then go home.

But at that moment I glanced round at the crowd that had followed   7
me. It was an immense crowd, two thousand at the least and growing every minute. It blocked the road for a long distance on either side. I looked at the sea of yellow faces above the garish clothes — faces all happy and excited over this bit of fun, all certain that the elephant was going to be shot. They were watching me as they would watch a conjurer about to perform a trick. They did not like me, but with the magical rifle in my hands I was momentarily worth watching. And suddenly I realized that I should have to shoot the elephant after all. The people expected it of me and I had got to do it; I could feel their two thousand wills pressing me forward, irresistibly. And it was at this moment, as I stood there with the rifle in my hands, that I first grasped the hollowness, the futility of the white man's dominion in the East. Here was I, the white man with his gun, standing in front of the unarmed native crowd — seemingly the leading actor of the piece; but in reality I was only an absurd puppet pushed to and fro by the will of those yellow faces behind. I perceived in this moment that when the white man turns tyrant it is his own freedom that he destroys. He becomes a sort of hollow, posing dummy, the conventionalized figure of a sahib.* For it is the condition of his rule that he shall spend his life in trying to impress the

---

* EDS. NOTE — An official. The term was used among Hindus and Muslims in colonial India.

"natives," and so in every crisis he has got to do what the "natives" expect of him. He wears a mask, and his face grows to fit it. I had got to shoot the elephant. I had committed myself to doing it when I sent for the rifle. A sahib has got to act like a sahib; he has got to appear resolute, to know his own mind and do definite things. To come all that way, rifle in hand, with two thousand people marching at my heels, and then to trail feebly away, having done nothing — no, that was impossible. The crowd would laugh at me. And my whole life, every white man's life in the East, was one long struggle not to be laughed at.

But I did not want to shoot the elephant. I watched him beating his 8 bunch of grass against his knees, with the preoccupied grandmotherly air that elephants have. It seemed to me that it would be murder to shoot him. At that age I was not squeamish about killing animals, but I had never shot an elephant and never wanted to. (Somehow it always seems worse to kill a *large* animal.) Besides, there was the beast's owner to be considered. Alive, the elephant was worth at least a hundred pounds; dead, he would only be worth the value of his tusks, five pounds, possibly. But I had got to act quickly. I turned to some experienced-looking Burmans who had been there when we arrived, and asked them how the elephant had been behaving. They all said the same thing: he took no notice of you if you left him alone, but he might charge if you went too close to him.

It was perfectly clear to me what I ought to do. I ought to walk up to 9 within, say, twenty-five yards of the elephant and test his behavior. If he charged I could shoot, if he took no notice of me it would be safe to leave him until the mahout came back. But also I knew that I was going to do no such thing. I was a poor shot with a rifle and the ground was soft mud into which one would sink at every step. If the elephant charged and I missed him, I should have about as much chance as a toad under a steamroller. But even then I was not thinking particularly of my own skin, only of the watchful yellow faces behind. For at that moment, with the crowd watching me, I was not afraid in the ordinary sense, as I would have been if I had been alone. A white man mustn't be frightened in front of "natives"; and so, in general, he isn't frightened. The sole thought in my mind was that if anything went wrong those two thousand Burmans would see me pursued, caught, trampled on, and reduced to a grinning corpse like that Indian up the hill. And if that happened it was quite probable that some of them would laugh. That would never do. There was only one alternative. I shoved the cartridges into the magazine and lay down on the road to get a better aim.

The crowd grew very still, and a deep, low, happy sigh, as of people who 10 see the theatre curtain go up at last, breathed from innumerable throats. They were going to have their bit of fun after all. The rifle was a beautiful German thing with cross-hair sights. I did not then know that in shooting an elephant one would shoot to cut an imaginary bar running from ear-hole to ear-hole. I ought, therefore, as the elephant was sideways on, to have aimed straight at his ear-hole; actually I aimed several inches in front of this, thinking the brain would be further forward.

When I pulled the trigger I did not hear the bang or feel the kick — one   11
never does when a shot goes home — but I heard the devilish roar of glee
that went up from the crowd. In that instant, in too short a time, one would
have thought, even for the bullet to get there, a mysterious, terrible change
had come over the elephant. He neither stirred nor fell, but every line on
his body had altered. He looked suddenly stricken, shrunken, immensely
old, as though the frightful impact of the bullet had paralyzed him without knocking him down. At last, after what seemed a long time — it might
have been five seconds, I dare say — he sagged flabbily to his knees. His
mouth slobbered. An enormous senility seemed to have settled upon him.
One could have imagined him thousands of years old. I fired again into the
same spot. At the second shot he did not collapse but climbed with desperate slowness to his feet and stood weakly upright, with legs sagging and
head drooping. I fired a third time. That was the shot that did for him. You
could see the agony of it jolt his whole body and knock the last remnant of
strength from his legs. But in falling he seemed for a moment to rise, for as
his hind legs collapsed beneath him he seemed to tower upwards like a
huge rock toppling, his trunk reaching skywards like a tree. He trumpeted,
for the first and only time. And then down he came, his belly towards me,
with a crash that seemed to shake the ground even where I lay.

I got up. The Burmans were already racing past me across the mud. It   12
was obvious that the elephant would never rise again, but he was not dead.
He was breathing very rhythmically with long rattling gasps, his great
mound of a side painfully rising and falling. His mouth was wide open — I
could see far down into the caverns of pale pink throat. I waited a long
time for him to die, but his breathing did not weaken. Finally I fired my
two remaining shots into the spot where I thought his heart must be. The
thick blood welled out of him like red velvet, but still he did not die. His
body did not even jerk when the shots hit him, the tortured breathing continued without a pause. He was dying, very slowly and in great agony, but
in some world remote from me where not even a bullet could damage him
further. I felt that I had got to put an end to that dreadful noise. It seemed
dreadful to see the great beast lying there, powerless to move and yet powerless to die, and not even to be able to finish him. I sent back for my small
rifle and poured shot after shot into his heart and down his throat. They
seemed to make no impression. The tortured gasps continued as steadily
as the ticking of a clock.

In the end I could not stand it any longer and went away. I heard later   13
that it took him half an hour to die. Burmans were bringing dahs* and
baskets even before I left, and I was told they had stripped his body almost
to the bones by the afternoon.

Afterwards, of course, there were endless discussions about the shoot-   14
ing of the elephant. The owner was furious, but he was only an Indian and
could do nothing. Besides, legally I had done the right thing, for a mad
elephant has to be killed, like a mad dog, if its owner fails to control it.

---

* EDS. NOTE — Heavy knives.

Among the Europeans opinion was divided. The older men said I was right, the younger men said it was a damn shame to shoot an elephant for killing a coolie, because an elephant was worth more than any damn Coringhee coolie. And afterwards I was very glad that the coolie had been killed; it put me legally in the right and it gave me a sufficient pretext for shooting the elephant. I often wondered whether any of the others grasped that I had done it solely to avoid looking a fool.

•   •   •

Comprehension

1. Why is Orwell "hated by large numbers of people" (1) in Burma? Why does he have mixed feelings toward the Burmese people?
2. Why do the local officials want something done about the elephant? Why does the crowd want Orwell to shoot the elephant?
3. Why does Orwell finally decide to kill the elephant? What makes him hesitate at first?
4. Why does Orwell say at the end that he was glad the coolie had been killed?

Purpose and Audience

1. One of Orwell's purposes in telling his story is to show how it gave him a glimpse of "the real nature of imperialism" (3). What does he mean? How does his essay illustrate this purpose?
2. Do you think Orwell wrote this essay to inform or to persuade his audience? How did Orwell expect his audience to react to his ideas? How can you tell?
3. What is the essay's thesis?

Style and Structure

1. What does Orwell's first paragraph accomplish? Where does the introduction end and the narrative itself begin?
2. The essay includes almost no dialogue. Why do you think Orwell's voice as narrator is the only one readers hear? Is the absence of dialogue a strength or a weakness? Explain.
3. Why do you think Orwell devotes so much attention to the elephant's misery (11–12)?
4. Orwell's essay includes a number of editorial comments, which appear within parentheses or dashes. How would you characterize these comments? Why are they set off from the text?
5. Consider the following statements: "Some of the people said that the elephant had gone in one direction, some said that he had gone in another" (4); "Among the Europeans opinion was divided. The older men said I was

right, the younger men said it was a damn shame to shoot an elephant" (14). How do these comments reinforce the theme expressed in paragraph 2 ("All I knew was that I was stuck between my hatred of the empire I served and my rage against the evil-spirited little beasts")? What other comments reinforce this theme?

Vocabulary Projects

1. Define each of the following words as it is used in this selection.

baited (1)	despotic (3)	conjurer (7)
perplexing (2)	labyrinth (4)	dominion (7)
oppressors (2)	squalid (4)	magazine (9)
lockups (2)	professed (4)	cross-hair (10)
flogged (2)	ravaging (5)	remnant (11)
supplant (2)	miry (5)	trumpeted (11)
prostrate (2)	garish (7)	pretext (14)

2. Because Orwell is British, he frequently uses words or expressions that an American writer would not likely use. Substitute a contemporary American word or phrase for each of the following, making sure it is appropriate in Orwell's context.

raise a riot (1)	rubbish van (3)	a bit of fun (5)
rang me up (3)	inflicted violences (3)	I dare say (11)

What other expressions in Orwell's essay might need to be "translated" for a contemporary American audience?

Journal Entry

Do you think Orwell is a coward? Do you think he is a racist? Explain your feelings.

Writing Workshop

1. Orwell says that even though he hated British imperialism and sympathized with the Burmese people, he found himself a puppet of the system. Write a narrative essay about a time when you had to do something that went against your beliefs or convictions. Begin by summarizing Orwell's situation in Burma, and go on to show how your situation was similar to his. If you quote Orwell, be sure to include documentation and a works-cited page. (See the Appendix for information on documentation formats.)

2. Orwell's experience taught him something not only about himself but also about something beyond himself — the way British imperialism worked. Write a narrative essay that reveals how an incident in your life taught you something about some larger social or political force as well as about yourself.

3. Write an objective, factual newspaper article recounting the events Orwell describes.

Combining the Patterns

Implicit in this narrative essay is an extended **comparison and contrast** that highlights the differences between Orwell and the Burmese people. Review the essay, and list the most obvious differences Orwell perceives between himself and them. Do you think his perceptions are accurate? If all of the differences were set forth in a single paragraph, how might such a paragraph change your perception of Orwell's dilemma? Of his character?

Thematic Connections

- "Thirty-Eight Who Saw Murder Didn't Call the Police" (page 120)
- "Just Walk On By" (page 236)
- "The Power of Words in Wartime" (page 363)
- "The Untouchable" (page 512)

Indian Education (Fiction)

Sherman Alexie, the son of a Coeur d'Alene Indian father and a Spokane Indian mother, was born in 1966 and grew up on the Spokane Reservation in Wellpinit, Washington, home to some eleven hundred Spokane tribal members. Realizing as a teenager that his educational opportunities there were extremely limited, Alexie made the unusual decision to attend high school off the reservation in nearby Reardon. Later a scholarship student at Gonzaga University, he received a bachelor's degree in American studies from Washington State University at Pullman. While in college, he began publishing poetry; within a year of graduation, his first collection, *The Business of Fancydancing* (1992), appeared. This was followed by *The Lone Ranger and Tonto Fistfight in Heaven* (1993), a short-story collection, and the novels *Reservation Blues* (1995) and *Indian Killer* (1996), all of which garnered numerous awards and honors. Alexie also wrote the screenplay for the film *Smoke Signals* (1998) and wrote and directed *The Business of Fancydancing* (2002). His most recent novel, *The Absolutely True Diary of a Part-Time Indian*, won the 2007 National Book Award for Young People's Literature.

Background on the U.S. government's "Indian schools"
By the mid-1800s, most Native American tribes had been overwhelmed by the superior weapons of the U.S. military and confined to reservations. Beginning in the late 1800s and continuing into the 1950s, government policymakers established boarding schools for Native American youth to help them assimilate into the dominant culture and thus become "civilized." To this end, children were forcibly removed from their homes for long periods to separate them from native traditions. At the boarding schools, they were given a cursory academic education and spent most of their time studying Christian teachings and working to offset the cost of their schooling. Students were punished for speaking their own language or practicing their own religion. Responding to protests from the American Indian Movement in the 1970s, the government began to send fewer Native Americans to boarding schools and retreated from its goal of assimilation at boarding schools and at newly established reservation schools. Currently, government funding for Native American schools remains considerably lower than for other public schools, and students often make do with inadequate and antiquated facilities, equipment, and textbooks. In part because of such educational failures, few Native American students go on to college, and the incidence of alcohol and drug abuse among Native Americans is higher than in any other U.S. population.

First Grade

My hair was too short and my U.S. Government glasses were horn-rimmed, ugly, and all that first winter in school, the other Indian boys chased me from one corner of the playground to the other. They pushed me down, buried me in the snow until I couldn't breathe, thought I'd never breathe again.

They stole my glasses and threw them over my head, around my out- 2
stretched hands, just beyond my reach, until someone tripped me and sent me falling again, facedown in the snow.

I was always falling down; my Indian name was Junior Falls Down. 3
Sometimes it was Bloody Nose or Steal-His-Lunch. Once, it was Cries-Like-a-White-Boy, even though none of us had seen a white boy cry.

Then it was a Friday morning recess and Frenchy SiJohn threw snow- 4
balls at me while the rest of the Indian boys tortured some other *top-yogh-yaught* kid, another weakling. But Frenchy was confident enough to torment me all by himself, and most days I would have let him.

But the little warrior in me roared to life that day and knocked Frenchy 5
to the ground, held his head against the snow, and punched him so hard that my knuckles and the snow made symmetrical bruises on his face. He almost looked like he was wearing war paint.

But he wasn't the warrior. I was. And I chanted *It's a good day to die, it's a* 6
good day to die, all the way down to the principal's office.

Second Grade

Betty Towle, missionary teacher, redheaded and so ugly that no one 7
ever had a puppy crush on her, made me stay in for recess fourteen days straight.

"Tell me you're sorry," she said. 8
"Sorry for what?" I asked. 9
"Everything," she said and made me stand straight for fifteen minutes, 10
eagle-armed with books in each hand. One was a math book; the other was English. But all I learned was that gravity can be painful.

For Halloween I drew a picture of her riding a broom with a scrawny 11
cat on the back. She said that her God would never forgive me for that.

Once, she gave the class a spelling test but set me aside and gave me a 12
test designed for junior high students. When I spelled all the words right, she crumpled up the paper and made me eat it.

"You'll learn respect," she said. 13
She sent a letter home with me that told my parents to either cut my 14
braids or keep me home from class. My parents came in the next day and dragged their braids across Betty Towle's desk.

"Indians, indians, indians." She said it without capitalization. She 15
called me "indian, indian, indian."

And I said, *Yes, I am. I am Indian. Indian, I am.* 16

Third Grade

My traditional Native American art career began and ended with my 17
very first portrait: *Stick Indian Taking a Piss in My Backyard.*

As I circulated the original print around the classroom, Mrs. Schluter   18
intercepted and confiscated my art.

Censorship, I might cry now. *Freedom of expression,* I would write in edito-   19
rials to the tribal newspaper.

In third grade, though, I stood alone in the corner, faced the wall, and   20
waited for the punishment to end.

I'm still waiting.   21

Fourth Grade

"You should be a doctor when you grow up," Mr. Schluter told me,   22
even though his wife, the third grade teacher, thought I was crazy beyond
my years. My eyes always looked like I had just hit-and-run someone.

"Guilty," she said. "You always look guilty."   23

"Why should I be a doctor?" I asked Mr. Schluter.   24

"So you can come back and help the tribe. So you can heal people."   25

That was the year my father drank a gallon of vodka a day and the   26
same year that my mother started two hundred different quilts but never
finished any. They sat in separate, dark places in our HUD house and wept
savagely.

I ran home after school, heard their Indian tears, and looked in the   27
mirror. *Doctor Victor,* I called myself, invented an education, talked to my
reflection. *Doctor Victor to the emergency room.*

Fifth Grade

I picked up a basketball for the first time and made my first shot. No. I   28
missed my first shot, missed the basket completely, and the ball landed in
the dirt and sawdust, sat there just like I had sat there only minutes
before.

But it felt good, that ball in my hands, all those possibilities and angles.   29
It was mathematics, geometry. It was beautiful.

At that same moment, my cousin Steven Ford sniffed rubber cement   30
from a paper bag and leaned back on the merry-go-round. His ears rang,
his mouth was dry, and everyone seemed so far away.

But it felt good, that buzz in his head, all those colors and noises. It   31
was chemistry, biology. It was beautiful.

Oh, do you remember those sweet, almost innocent choices that the Indian   32
boys were forced to make?

Sixth Grade

Randy, the new Indian kid from the white town of Springdale, got into   33
a fight an hour after he first walked into the reservation school.

Stevie Flett called him out, called him a squawman, called him a pussy, and called him a punk. 34

Randy and Stevie, and the rest of the Indian boys, walked out into the playground. 35

"Throw the first punch," Stevie said as they squared off. 36

"No," Randy said. 37

"Throw the first punch," Stevie said again. 38

"No," Randy said again. 39

"Throw the first punch!" Stevie said for the third time, and Randy reared back and pitched a knuckle fastball that broke Stevie's nose. 40

We all stood there in silence, in awe. 41

That was Randy, my soon-to-be first and best friend, who taught me the most valuable lesson about living in the white world: *Always throw the first punch.* 42

Seventh Grade

I leaned through the basement window of the HUD house and kissed the white girl who would later be raped by her foster-parent father, who was also white. They both lived on the reservation, though, and when the headlines and stories filled the papers later, not one word was made of their color. 43

Just Indians being Indians, someone must have said somewhere and they were wrong. 44

But on the day I leaned through the basement window of the HUD house and kissed the white girl, I felt the good-byes I was saying to my entire tribe. I held my lips tight against her lips, a dry, clumsy, and ultimately stupid kiss. 45

But I was saying good-bye to my tribe, to all the Indian girls and women I might have loved, to all the Indian men who might have called me cousin, even brother. 46

I kissed that white girl and when I opened my eyes, she was gone from the reservation, and when I opened my eyes, I was gone from the reservation, living in a farm town where a beautiful white girl asked my name. 47

"Junior Polatkin," I said, and she laughed. 48

After that, no one spoke to me for another five hundred years. 49

Eighth Grade

At the farm town junior high, in the boys' bathroom, I could hear voices from the girls' bathroom, nervous whispers of anorexia and bulimia. I could hear the white girls' forced vomiting, a sound so familiar and natural to me after years of listening to my father's hangovers. 50

"Give me your lunch if you're just going to throw it up," I said to one of those girls once. 51

I sat back and watched them grow skinny from self-pity. 52

· · ·

Back on the reservation, my mother stood in line to get us commodities.   53
We carried them home, happy to have food, and opened the canned beef
that even the dogs wouldn't eat.

But we ate it day after day and grew skinny from self-pity.   54

There is more than one way to starve.   55

Ninth Grade

At the farm town high school dance, after a basketball game in an over-   56
heated gym where I had scored twenty-seven points and pulled down thirteen rebounds, I passed out during a slow song.

As my white friends revived me and prepared to take me to the emer-   57
gency room where doctors would later diagnose my diabetes, the Chicano
teacher ran up to us.

"Hey," he said. "What's that boy been drinking? I know all about these   58
Indian kids. They start drinking real young."

Sharing dark skin doesn't necessarily make two men brothers.   59

Tenth Grade

I passed the written test easily and nearly flunked the driving, but still   60
received my Washington State driver's license on the same day that Wally
Jim killed himself by driving his car into a pine tree.

No traces of alcohol in his blood, good job, wife and two kids.   61

"Why'd he do it?" asked a white Washington State trooper.   62

All the Indians shrugged their shoulders, looked down at the ground.   63

"Don't know," we all said, but when we look in the mirror, see the his-   64
tory of our tribe in our eyes, taste failure in the tap water, and shake with
old tears, we understand completely.

Believe me, everything looks like a noose if you stare at it long enough.   65

Eleventh Grade

Last night I missed two free throws which would have won the game   66
against the best team in the state. The farm town high school I play for is
nicknamed the "Indians," and I'm probably the only actual Indian ever to
play for a team with such a mascot.

This morning I pick up the sports page and read the headline: INDIANS   67
LOSE AGAIN.

Go ahead and tell me none of this is supposed to hurt me very much.   68

Twelfth Grade

I walk down the aisle, valedictorian of this farm town high school, and   69
my cap doesn't fit because I've grown my hair longer than it's ever been.

Later, I stand as the school-board chairman recites my awards, accomplishments, and scholarships.

I try to remain stoic for the photographers as I look toward the future.   70

Back home on the reservation, my former classmates graduate: a few can't   71
read, one or two are just given attendance diplomas, most look forward to
the parties. The bright students are shaken, frightened, because they don't
know what comes next.

They smile for the photographer as they look back toward tradition.   72

The tribal newspaper runs my photograph and the photograph of my   73
former classmates side by side.

Postscript: Class Reunion

Victor said, "Why should we organize a reservation high school   74
reunion? My graduating class has a reunion every weekend at the Powwow
Tavern."

•   •   •

Reading Literature

1. Instead of linking events with transitional phrases that establish chronology, Alexie uses internal headings to move readers through his story. How do these headings indicate the passage of time? Are these headings enough, or do you think Alexie should have opened each section of the story with a transitional phrase? (Try to suggest some possibilities.)

2. The narrator's experiences in each grade in school are illustrated by specific incidents. What do these incidents have in common? What do they reveal about the narrator? About his schools?

3. Explain the meaning of each of these statements in the context of the story:
   • "There is more than one way to starve" (55).
   • "Sharing dark skin doesn't necessarily make two men brothers" (59).
   • "Believe me, everything looks like a noose if you stare at it long enough" (65).

Journal Entry

What does the "Postscript: Class Reunion" section (74) tell readers about Indian education? Is this information consistent with what we have learned in the rest of the story, or does it come as a surprise? Explain.

Thematic Connections

• "College Pressures" (page 462)
• "The Dog Ate My Disk, and Other Tales of Woe" (page 471)
• The Declaration of Independence (page 575)

WRITING ASSIGNMENTS FOR NARRATION

1. Trace the path you expect to follow to establish yourself in your chosen profession, considering possible obstacles you may face and how you expect to deal with them. Include a thesis statement that conveys the importance of your goals. If you like, you may refer to some readings elsewhere in this book that focus on work — for example, "The Peter Principle" (page 216), or "What Work Is" (page 542).

2. Write a personal narrative looking back from some point in the far future on your own life as you hope others will see it. Use third person if you like, and write your own obituary; or use first person, assessing your life in a letter to your great-grandchildren.

3. Write a news article recounting in objective terms the events described in an essay that appears anywhere in this text — for example, "Who Killed Benny Paret?" (page 340) or "Grant and Lee: A Study in Contrasts" (page 405). Include a descriptive headline.

4. Write the introductory narrative for the home page of your family's (or community's) Web site. In this historical narrative, trace the roots of your family or your hometown or community. Be sure to include specific detail, dialogue, and descriptions of people and places. (You may also include visuals if you like.)

5. Write an account of one of these "firsts": your first date; your first serious argument with your parents; your first experience with physical violence or danger; your first extended stay away from home; your first encounter with someone whose culture was very different from your own; or your first experience with the serious illness or death of a close friend or relative. Make sure your essay includes a thesis statement your narrative can support.

6. Both George Orwell and Martin Gansberg deal with the consequences of failing to act. Write an essay or story recounting what would have happened if Orwell had *not* shot the elephant or if one of the eyewitnesses *had* called the police right away. Be sure to document references to Orwell or Gansberg and to include a works-cited page. (See the Appendix for information on documentation formats.)

7. Maya Angelou's "finishing school" was Mrs. Cullinan's kitchen; similarly, Gary Shteyngart's "naturalization ceremony" was the ride across the causeway to Miami Beach. Write about a place where you developed into the person you are today. What did you learn from this place, and how did this knowledge serve you later?

8. Write a narrative about a time when you were an outsider, isolated because of social, intellectual, or ethnic differences between you and others. Did you resolve the problems your isolation created? Explain. If you like, you may refer to the Angelou or Orwell essays in this chapter or to "Just Walk On By" (page 236), taking care to include parenthetical documentation and a works-cited page. (See the Appendix for information on documentation formats.)

9. Imagine a meeting between any two people who appear in this chapter's reading selections. Using dialogue and narrative, write an account of this meeting.

10. Using Alexie's story as a model, write the story of your own education.

11. List the five books you have read that most influenced you at important stages of your life. Then, write your literary autobiography, tracing your personal development through these books. (Or, write your wardrobe autobiography — discussing what you wore at different times of your life — or your music autobiography.)

COLLABORATIVE ACTIVITY FOR NARRATION

Working with a group of students of about your own age, write a history of your television-viewing habits. Start by working individually to list all your most-watched television shows in chronological order, beginning as far back as you can remember. Then, compile a single list that reflects a consensus of the group's preferences, perhaps choosing one or two representative programs for each stage of your life (preschool, elementary school, and so on). Have a different student write a paragraph on each stage, describing the chosen programs in as much detail as possible and using "we" as the subject. Finally, combine the individual paragraphs to create a narrative essay that traces the group's changing tastes in television shows. The essay's thesis statement should express what your group's television preferences reveal about your generation's development.

7
Description

WHAT IS DESCRIPTION?

You use **description** to tell readers about the physical characteristics of a person, place, or thing. Description relies on the five senses — sight, hearing, taste, touch, and smell. In the following paragraph from "Knoxville: Summer 1915," James Agee uses sight, sound, and touch to re-create a summer's evening for his audience:

Topic sentence	It is not of games children play in the evening that I want to speak now, it is of a contemporaneous atmosphere that has little to do with them; that of fathers and families, each in his space of lawn, his
Description using sight	shirt fishlike pale in the unnatural light and his face nearly anonymous, hosing their lawns. The hoses were attached to spigots that stood out of the brick foundations of the houses. The nozzles were variously set but usually so there was a long sweet
Description using touch	stream of spray, the nozzle wet in the hand, the water trickling the right forearm and the peeled-back cuff, and the water whishing out a long loose and low-curved cone, and so gentle a sound. First
Description using sound	an insane noise of violence in the nozzle, then the still irregular sound of adjustment, then the smoothing into steadiness and a pitch as accurately tuned to the size and style of stream as any violin. So many qualities of sound out of one hose: so many choral differences out of those several hoses that were in earshot. Out of any one hose, the almost dead silence of the release, and the short still arch of the separate big drops, silent as a held breath, and the only noise the flattering noise on leaves and the slapped grass at the fall of each big drop. That, and the intense hiss with the intense

> stream; that, and the same intensity not growing
> less but growing more quiet and delicate with the
> turn of the nozzle, up to that extreme tender whis-
> per when the water was just a wide bell of film.

A descriptive essay tells what something looks like or what it feels like, sounds like, smells like, or tastes like. However, description often goes beyond personal sense impressions: novelists can create imaginary land-scapes, historians can paint word pictures of historical figures, and scien-tists can describe physical phenomena they have never actually seen. When you write description, you use language to create a vivid impression for your readers.

USING DESCRIPTION

In your college writing, you use description in many different kinds of assignments. In a comparison-and-contrast essay, for example, you may describe the designs of two proposed buildings to show that one is more desirable than the other. In an argumentative essay, you may describe a fish killed in a local river to show that industrial waste dumping is a problem. Through description, you communicate your view of the world to your readers. If your readers come to understand or share your view, they are more likely to accept your observations, your judgments, and, eventually, your conclusions. Therefore, in almost every essay you write, knowing how to write effective description is important.

Understanding Objective Description

Description can be objective or subjective. In an **objective description**, you focus on the object itself rather than on your personal reactions to it. Your purpose is to present a precise, literal picture of your subject. Many writing situations require exact descriptions of apparatus or conditions, and in these cases your goal is to construct an accurate picture for your audience. A biologist describing what he sees through a microscope and a historian describing a Civil War battlefield would both write objectively. The biologist would not, for instance, say how exciting his observations were, nor would the historian say how disappointed she was at the out-come of the battle. Many newspaper reporters also try to achieve this objec-tivity, as do writers of technical reports, scientific papers, and certain types of business correspondence. Still, objectivity is an ideal that writers strive for but never fully achieve. In fact, in selecting some details and leaving out others, writers are making subjective decisions.

In the following descriptive passage, Shakespearian scholar Thomas Marc Parrott aims for objectivity by giving his readers the factual informa-tion they need to visualize Shakespeare's theater:

The main or outer stage [of Shakespeare's theatre] was a large platform, which projected out into the audience. Sections of the floor could be removed to make such things as the grave in the grave digger's scene in *Hamlet,* or they could be transformed into trapdoors through which characters could disappear, as in *The Tempest.* The players referred to the space beneath the platform as the Hell. At the rear of the platform and at the same level was the smaller, inner stage, or alcove. . . . Above the alcove at the level of the second story, there was another curtained stage, the chamber. . . . The action of the play would move from one scene to another, using one, two, or all of them. Above the chamber was the music gallery; . . . and above this were the windows, "The Huts," where characters and lookouts could appear.

Note that Parrott is not interested in responding to or evaluating the theater he describes. Instead, he chooses words that convey sizes and directions, such as *large* and *above.*

Objective descriptions are sometimes accompanied by **visuals,** such as diagrams, drawings, or photographs. A well-chosen visual can enhance a description by enabling writers to avoid tedious passages of description that might confuse readers. To be effective, a visual should clearly illustrate what is being discussed and not introduce new material.

The illustration below, which accompanies Parrott's description of Shakespeare's theater, makes the passage much easier to understand, helping readers to visualize the multiple stages where Shakespeare performed his plays.

Artist's rendering of the Globe Theatre, London.

✓ CHECKLIST: **Using Visuals Effectively**

If your instructor permits you to use visuals, ask the following questions to make sure that you have used them responsibly and effectively.

- **Does your visual add something to your paper?** For example, you could use a diagram to help explain a process, a chart or graph to clarify statistics, or a photograph to show an unusual structure.

- **Is your visual located as close as possible to where it is discussed in the paper?** This placement will establish the context for the visual and ensure that readers understand the reason why you have included it.

- **Have you documented your visual?** Like all material you borrow from a source, visuals must be documents. (For more on documentation, see the Appendix.)

💻   COMPUTER STRATEGY: **Finding Visuals**

You can find visuals on the Internet, on DVDs, or on clip-art compilations. You can also scan pictures you find in print sources or download pictures you take with a digital camera. Once the visual is downloaded onto your computer as a file, you can cut and paste it into your essay. Remember, however, that all visual material you get from a source — whether print or Internet — must be documented.

Understanding Subjective Description

In contrast to objective description, **subjective description** conveys your personal response to your subject. Here your perspective is not necessarily stated explicitly; often it is revealed indirectly, through your choice of words and phrasing. If an English composition assignment asks you to describe a place that has special meaning to you, you could give a subjective reaction to your topic by selecting and emphasizing details that show your feelings about the place. For example, you could write a subjective description of your room by focusing on particular objects — your desk, your window, and your bookshelves — and explaining the meanings these things have for you. Thus, your desk could be a "warm brown rectangle of wood whose surface reveals the scratched impressions of a thousand school assignments."

A subjective description should convey not just a literal record of sights and sounds but also their significance. For example, if you objectively described a fire, you might include its temperature, duration, and scope. In addition, you might describe, as accurately as possible, the fire's movement and intensity. If you subjectively described the fire, however, you would try to re-create for your audience a sense of how the fire made you feel — your reactions to the noise, to the dense smoke, to the destruction.

In the following passage, notice how Mark Twain subjectively describes a sunset on the Mississippi River:

> I still kept in mind a certain wonderful sunset which I witnessed when steamboating was new to me. A broad expanse of the river was turned to blood; in the middle distance the red hue brightened into gold, through which a solitary log came floating, black and conspicuous; in one place a long, slanting mark lay sparkling upon the water; in another the surface was broken by boiling, tumbling rings, that were as many-tinted as an opal.

In this passage, Twain conveys his strong emotional reaction to the sunset by using vivid, powerful images, such as the river "turned to blood," the "solitary log . . . black and conspicuous," and the "boiling, tumbling rings." He also chooses words that suggest great value, such as *gold* and *opal*.

Neither objective nor subjective description exists independently. Objective descriptions usually include some subjective elements, and subjective descriptions need some objective elements to convey a sense of reality. The skillful writer adjusts the balance between objectivity and subjectivity to suit the topic, thesis, audience, and purpose as well as occasion for writing.

Using Objective and Subjective Language

As the passages by Parrott and Twain illustrate, both objective and subjective descriptions depend on language to appeal to readers' senses. But these two types of description use language differently. Objective descriptions rely on precise, factual language that presents a writer's observations without conveying his or her attitude toward the subject. Subjective descriptions, however, often use richer and more suggestive language than objective descriptions do. They are more likely to rely on the **connotations** of words, their emotional associations, than on their **denotations**, or more direct meanings (such as those found in a dictionary). In addition, they may deliberately provoke the reader's imagination with striking phrases or vivid language, including **figures of speech** such as *simile, metaphor, personification*, and *allusion*.

- A **simile** uses *like* or *as* to compare two dissimilar things. These comparisons occur frequently in everyday speech — for example, when someone claims to be "happy as a clam," "free as a bird," or "hungry as a bear." As a rule, however, you should avoid overused expressions like these in your writing. Effective writers constantly strive to create original similes. In his essay "Once More to the Lake," for instance, E. B. White uses a striking simile to describe the annoying sound of boats on a lake when he says that in the evening "they whined around one's ears *like mosquitoes.*" Later in the same essay, he describes a thunderstorm as being *"like the revival of an old melodrama* that I had seen long ago with childish awe."

- A **metaphor** compares two dissimilar things without using *like* or *as*. Instead of saying that something is *like* something else, a metaphor says it *is* something else. Mark Twain uses a metaphor when he says, "A broad expanse of the river was turned to blood."

- **Personification** speaks of concepts or objects as if they had life or human characteristics. If you say that the wind whispered or that an engine died, you are using personification.

- An **allusion** is a reference to a person, place, event, or quotation that the writer assumes readers will recognize. In "Letter from Birmingham Jail" (page 588), for example, Martin Luther King Jr. enriches his argument by alluding to biblical passages and proverbs that he expects his audience of clergy to be familiar with.

Your purpose and audience determine whether you should use objective or subjective description. An assignment that specifically asks for reactions calls for a subjective description. Legal, medical, technical, business, and scientific writing assignments, however, usually require objective descriptions because their primary purpose is to give the audience factual information. Even in these areas, though, figures of speech are often used to describe an unfamiliar object or concept. For example, in their pioneering article on the structure of DNA, scientists James Watson and Francis Crick use a simile when they describe a molecule of DNA as looking like two spiral staircases winding around each other.

Selecting Details

Sometimes inexperienced writers pack their descriptions with general words such as *nice, great, terrific,* or *awful,* substituting their own reactions to an object for the qualities of the object itself. To produce an effective description, however, you must do more than just *say* something is wonderful — you must use details that evoke this response in your readers, as Twain does with the sunset. (Twain does use the word *wonderful* at the beginning of his description, but he then goes on to supply many specific details that make the scene he describes vivid and specific.)

All good descriptive writing, whether objective or subjective, relies on specific detail. Your aim is not simply to *tell* readers what something looks like but to *show* them. Every person, place, or thing has its special characteristics, and you should use your powers of observation to detect them. Then, you need to select the specific words that will enable your readers to imagine what you describe. Don't be satisfied with "He looked angry" when you can say, "His face flushed, and one corner of his mouth twitched as he tried to control his anger." What's the difference? In the first case, you simply identify the man's emotional state. In the second, you provide enough detail so that readers can tell not only that he was angry but also how he revealed the intensity of his anger.

Of course, you could have provided even more detail by describing the man's beard, his wrinkles, or any number of other features. Keep in mind, however, that not all details are equally useful or desirable. You should include only those that contribute to the dominant impression you wish to create. Thus, in describing a man's face to show how angry he was, you would probably not include the shape of his nose or the color of his hair. (After all, a person's hair color does not change when he or she gets angry.) In fact, the number of particulars you use is less important than their quality and appropriateness. You should select and use only those details relevant to your purpose.

Factors such as the level, background, and knowledge of your audience also influence the kinds of details you include. For example, a description of a DNA molecule written for high school students would contain more basic details than a description written for college biology majors. In addition, the more advanced description would contain details — the sequence of amino acid groups, for instance — that might be inappropriate for high school students.

PLANNING A DESCRIPTIVE ESSAY

Developing a Thesis Statement

Writers of descriptive essays often use an **implied thesis** when they describe a person, place, or thing. This technique allows them to convey an essay's point subtly, through the selection and arrangement of details. When they use description to support a particular point, however, many writers prefer to use an **explicitly stated thesis**. This strategy lets readers see immediately what point the writer is making — for example, "The sculptures that adorn Philadelphia's City Hall are a catalog of nineteenth-century artistic styles."

Whether you state or imply your thesis, the details of your descriptive essay must work together to create a single **dominant impression** — the mood or quality emphasized in the piece of writing. In many cases, your thesis may be just a statement of the dominant impression; sometimes, however, your thesis may go further and make a point about that dominant impression.

Organizing Details

When you plan a descriptive essay, you usually begin by writing down descriptive details in no particular order. You then arrange these details in a way that supports your thesis and communicates your dominant impression. As you consider how to arrange your details, keep in mind that you have a number of options. For example, you can move from a specific description of an object to a general description of other things around it. Or you can reverse this order, beginning with the general and proceeding to the specific. You can also progress from the least important feature to the most important one, from the smallest to the largest item, from the least unusual to the most unusual detail, or from left to right, right to left, top to bottom, or bottom to top. Another option is to combine approaches, using different organizing schemes in different parts of the essay. The strategy you choose depends on the dominant impression you want to convey, your thesis, and your purpose and audience.

Using Transitions

Be sure to include all the transitional words and phrases readers need to follow your description. Without them, readers will have difficulty understanding the relationship between one detail and another. Throughout your description, especially in the topic sentences of your body paragraphs, use words or phrases indicating the spatial arrangement of details. In descriptive essays, the transitions commonly used include *above, adjacent to, at the bottom, at the top, behind, below, beyond, in front of, in the middle, next to, over, under, through,* and *within.* (A more complete list of transitions appears on page 43.)

STRUCTURING A DESCRIPTIVE ESSAY

Descriptive essays begin with an **introduction** that presents the **thesis** or establishes the **dominant impression** that the rest of the essay will develop. Each **body paragraph** includes details that support the thesis or convey the dominant impression. The **conclusion** reinforces the thesis or dominant impression, perhaps echoing an idea stated in the introduction or using a particularly effective simile or metaphor.

Suppose your English composition instructor has asked you to write a short essay describing a person, place, or thing. After thinking about the assignment for a day or two, you decide to write an objective description of the National Air and Space Museum in Washington, D.C., because you have visited it recently and many details are fresh in your mind. The museum is large and has many different exhibits, so you know you cannot describe them all. Therefore, you decide to concentrate on one, the heavier-than-air flight exhibit, and you choose as your topic the display you remember most vividly — Charles Lindbergh's airplane, *The Spirit of St. Louis.* You begin by brainstorming to recall all the details you can. When you read over your notes, you realize that you could present the details of the airplane in the order in which your eye took them in, from front to rear. The dominant impression you wish to create is how small and fragile

The Spirit of St. Louis appears, and your thesis statement communicates this impression. An informal outline for your essay might look like this:

Introduction:	Thesis statement — It is startling that a plane as small as *The Spirit of St. Louis* could fly across the Atlantic.
Front of plane:	Single engine, tiny cockpit
Middle of plane:	Short wing span, extra gas tanks
Rear of plane:	Limited cargo space filled with more gas tanks
Conclusion:	Restatement of thesis or review of key points or details

REVISING A DESCRIPTIVE ESSAY

When you revise a descriptive essay, consider the items on the revision checklist on page 54. In addition, pay special attention to the items on the following checklist, which apply specifically to descriptive essays.

✓ **REVISION CHECKLIST: Description**

- Does your assignment call for description?
- Does your descriptive essay clearly communicate its thesis or dominant impression?
- Is your description primarily objective or subjective?
- If your description is primarily objective, have you used precise, factual language? Would your essay benefit from a diagram?
- If your description is primarily subjective, have you used figures of speech as well as words that convey your feelings and emotions?
- Have you included enough specific details?
- Have you arranged your details in a way that supports your thesis and communicates your dominant impression?
- Have you used the transitional words and phrases that readers need to follow your description?

EDITING A DESCRIPTIVE ESSAY

When you edit your descriptive essay, follow the guidelines in the editing checklists on pages 71, 74, and 76. In addition, focus on the grammar, mechanics, and punctuation issues particularly relevant to descriptive essays. One of these issues — avoiding misplaced and dangling modifiers — is discussed on page 152.

GRAMMAR IN CONTEXT: Avoiding Misplaced
and Dangling Modifiers

When writing descriptive essays, you use **modifying words** and **phrases** to describe people, places, and objects. Because these modifiers are important in descriptive essays, you need to place them correctly to ensure they clearly refer to the words they describe.

Avoiding Misplaced Modifiers   A **misplaced modifier** appears to modify the wrong word because it is placed incorrectly in the sentence. Sentences that contain misplaced modifiers are always illogical and frequently humorous.

> MISPLACED: E. B. White's son swam in the lake wearing an old bathing suit. (*Was the lake wearing a bathing suit?*)

> MISPLACED: From the cabin, the sounds of the woods were heard by E. B. White and his son. (*Were the sounds of the woods inside the cabin?*)

In these sentences, the phrases *wearing an old bathing suit* and *from the cabin* appear to modify words that they cannot logically modify. You can correct these errors and avoid confusion by moving each modifier as close as possible to the word it is supposed to modify.

> CORRECT: Wearing an old bathing suit, E. B. White's son swam in the lake.

> CORRECT: From the cabin, E. B. White and his son heard the sounds of the woods.

Avoiding Dangling Modifiers   A modifier "dangles" when it cannot logically modify any word that appears in the sentence. Often these **dangling modifiers** come at the beginning of sentences (as present or past participle phrases), where they illogically seem to modify the words that come immediately after them.

> DANGLING: Determined to get a better look, the viewing platform next to St. Paul's Chapel was crowded. (*Who was determined to get a better look?*)

> DANGLING: Standing on the corner, the cranes, jackhammers, and bulldozers worked feverishly at ground zero. (*Who was standing on the corner?*)

In the preceding sentences, the phrases *determined to get a better look* and *standing on the corner* seem to modify *the viewing platform* and *cranes, jackhammers, and bulldozers,* respectively. However, these sentences make no sense. How can a viewing platform get a better look? How can cranes, jackhammers, and bulldozers stand on a corner? In addition, the two sentences do not contain the words that the modifying phrases are supposed to describe. In each case, you can correct the problem by supplying the missing word and rewriting the sentence accordingly.

CORRECT: Determined to get a better look, people crowded the viewing platform next to St. Paul's Chapel.

CORRECT: Standing on the corner, people watched the cranes, jackhammers, and bulldozers work feverishly at ground zero.

> For more practice in avoiding misplaced and dangling modifiers, visit Exercise Central at **bedfordstmartins.com/patterns/modifiers**.

✓ **EDITING CHECKLIST: Description**

- Have you avoided misplaced modifiers?
- Have you avoided dangling modifiers?
- Have you used figures of speech effectively?
- Have you avoided general words such as *nice, great,* and *terrific*?

A STUDENT WRITER: Objective Description

The following essay, an **objective description** of a trailer, was written by James Greggs for a sociology class. The assignment was to write a description of the service-learning project he participated in with some classmates.

Building and Learning

Introduction   Throughout the United States, houses reflect not only   1
the lives of the people who live in them but also the diversity of
the American population. Some are large and ostentatious,
others are modest but well maintained, and still others are in
need of repair. Unfortunately, most college students know little
about homes other than those in their own neighborhood. I too
was fairly sheltered until I participated in a service-learning

Thesis statement

project for my sociology class. For this project, I, along with some classmates, added a deck to a trailer. We gained a great deal of satisfaction from this project by helping three elderly people in need.

Description of area around the trailer

The trailer we worked on was located at the end of a small dirt road about thirty minutes from campus. Patches of green and brown grass dotted the land around the trailer, and in the far right-hand corner of the property stood three tall poplar trees. Although the bushes in the front of the trailer were trimmed, the woods behind the trailer were beginning to overrun the property. (We were told that members of a local church came once a month to trim the hedges and cut back the trees.) Dominating the right front corner of the lawn was a circular concrete basin that looked like a large birdbath and that housed a white well pipe with a rusted blue cap. About thirty feet to the left of the concrete basin stood a telephone pole and a bright red metal mailbox.

General description of the trailer

Like the property where it stood, the trailer was well maintained. It was approximately thirty-five feet long and seven feet high; it rested on cinderblocks, which raised it about three feet off the ground. Under the trailer was an overturned white plastic chair. The trailer itself was covered with sheets of white vinyl siding that ran horizontally, except for the bottom panels on the right side, which ran vertically. The vinyl panels closest to the roof were slightly discolored by dirt and green moss.

Specific description of the trailer

At the left end of the trailer was a small window — about two feet wide and one foot high. Next to the window was a dark red aluminum door that was outlined in green trim. It had one window at eye level that was divided by metal strips into four small sections. The number "24" in white plastic letters was glued to the door below this window. To the right of the door was a lightbulb in a black ceramic socket. Next to the light was a large window that was actually two vertical rows of three windows — each the same size as the small window on the left. Further to the right were two smaller windows. Each of these small windows tilted upward and was framed with silver metal strips. On either side of each of these windows was a pair of green metal shutters.

Description of
steps and walkway

The deck we built replaced three wooden steps that had   5
led up to the trailer. A white metal handrail stood on the right
side of these steps. It had been newly painted and was
connected to the body of the trailer by a heart-shaped piece of
metal. In front of the steps, two worn gray wooden boards led
to the road.

Description of
new deck

The finished deck provided a much better entranceway   6
than the steps did and also gave the trailer a new look. The
deck was not very large — ten feet by eight feet — but it
extended from the doorway to the area underneath the windows
immediately to the right of the door. We built the deck out
of pressure-treated lumber so that it wouldn't rot or need
painting. We also built three steps that led from the deck to the
lawn, and we surrounded the deck with a wooden railing that
ran down the right side of the steps. After we finished, we
bought two white plastic chairs at a local thrift store and put
them on the deck.

Conclusion

Both the residents of the trailer and our class benefited   7
from the service-learning project. The residents of the trailer
were happy with the deck because it gave them a place to sit
when the weather was good. They also liked their trailer's new
look. Those of us who worked on the project learned how with
just a little bit of work we could make a difference in other
people's lives.

Points for Special Attention

Objective Description. James Greggs, a student in a sociology
course that had a service-learning component, wrote this paper describing
the project in which he participated. James knew that his instructor wanted
an objective description because she told the class not to include any subjective comments in the body of the paper. She told them that they could,
if they wished, discuss their feelings about the project in their introductions and conclusions.

Objective Language. Because his essay is an objective description,
James keeps his description straightforward. His factual, concrete language concentrates on the size, shape, and construction of the trailer as
well as on its surroundings. He uses specific measurements to convey the

dimensions of the trailer and to show the relationship of each part of the trailer to the other parts, and he uses figures of speech to help his readers visualize what he is describing — the "circular concrete basin that looked like a large birdbath" (2), for example.

Structure. James structures his description by moving from far to near. He begins by describing the land where the trailer stands. He then directs his readers' attention to specific areas — for example, the woods behind the trailer and the telephone pole and red mailbox in front of it. James gives a general description of the trailer and then, as he moves from left to right, considers its specific features. Finally, he focuses on the deck, following a general description with specific details about its construction. In his introduction, James provides the context for this description and states his thesis; in his conclusion, he reinforces the main idea of his essay and then evaluates his service-learning experience.

Selection of Detail. James's instructor defined his audience as people who would know what service learning is but who would not know about the specific project. For this reason, James does not include a definition of service learning or explain how it fits into the sociology curriculum. He does, however, provide a detailed description of the trailer and the work he and his classmates did.

Focus on Revision

The peer critics of James's paper identified three areas they thought needed work. One student said James should have included descriptions of the people who lived in the trailer. This student thought that without these descriptions, readers could not appreciate the impact the deck had on the residents. Another student suggested that James add more detail about the deck itself. She thought the deck should be the main focus of the paper, and for this reason, she thought James should spend more time describing it.

As a result of these criticisms, James decided to write a short paragraph (and insert it between paragraphs 2 and 3) describing the residents of the trailer. He also decided to add more detail about the deck itself — for example, the wishbone pattern formed by the floorboards and the decorative elements on the railing. Finally, a third student thought the description of the trailer's windows in paragraph 4 included too much unnecessary detail, so in his final draft James condensed paragraph 4.

A STUDENT WRITER: Subjective Description

The essay that follows, a subjective description of an area in Burma (renamed Myanmar after a military coup in 1989), was written by Mary Lim for her composition class. Her assignment was to write an essay about a place that had a profound effect on her. Mary's essay uses **subjective description** so that readers can share, as well as understand, her experience.

The Valley of Windmills

Introduction

In my native country of Burma, strange happenings and exotic scenery are not unusual, for Burma is a mysterious land that in some areas seems to have been ignored by time. Mountains stand jutting their rocky peaks into the clouds as they have for thousands of years. Jungles are so dense with exotic vegetation that human beings or large animals cannot even enter. But one of the most fascinating areas in Burma is

Description (identifying the scene)

the Valley of Windmills, nestled between the tall mountains near the fertile and beautiful city of Taungaleik. In this valley there is beautiful and breathtaking scenery, but there are also old, massive, and gloomy structures that can disturb a person deeply.

Description (moving toward the valley)

The road to Taungaleik twists out of the coastal flatlands into those heaps of slag, shale, and limestone that are the Tennesserim Mountains in the southern part of Burma. The air grows rarer and cooler, and stones become grayer, the highway a little more precarious at its edges, until, ahead, standing in ghostly sentinel across the lip of a pass, is a line of squat forms.

Description (immediate view)

They straddle the road and stand at intervals up hillsides on either side. Are they boulders? Are they fortifications? Are they broken wooden crosses on graves in an abandoned cemetery?

These dark figures are windmills standing in the misty atmosphere. They are immensely old and distinctly evil, some merely turrets, some with remnants of arms hanging derelict from their snouts, and most of them covered with dark green moss. Their decayed but still massive forms seem to turn and

Description (more distant view)

sneer at visitors. Down the pass on the other side is a circular green plateau that lies like an arena below, where there are still more windmills. Massed in the plain behind them, as far as the eye can see, in every field, above every hut, stand ten thousand iron windmills, silent and sailless. They seem to await only a call from a watchman to clank, whirr, flap, and groan into action. Visitors suddenly feel cold. Perhaps it is a sense of loneliness, the cool air, the desolation, or the weirdness of the arcane windmills — but something chills them.

1

2

3

Conclusion	As you stand at the lip of the valley, contrasts rush as if 4
	to overwhelm you. Beyond, glittering on the mountainside like
Description (windmills	a solitary jewel, is Taungaleik in the territory once occupied by
contrasted with city)	the Portuguese. Below, on rolling hillsides, are the dark
Thesis statement	windmills, still enveloped in morning mist. These ancient
	windmills can remind you of the impermanence of life and the
	mystery that still surrounds these hills. In a strange way, the
	scene in the valley can disturb you, but it also can give you an
	insight into the contrasts that seem to define our lives here in
	my country.

Points for Special Attention

Subjective Description.   One of the first things her classmates noticed when they read Mary's essay was her use of vivid details. The road to Taungaleik is described in specific terms: it twists "out of the coastal flatlands" into the mountains, which are "heaps of slag, shale, and limestone." The iron windmills are decayed and stand "silent and sailless" on a green plateau that "lies like an arena." Through her use of detail, Mary creates her dominant impression of the Valley of Windmills as dark, mysterious, and disquieting. The point of her essay — the thesis — is stated in the last paragraph: the Valley of Windmills embodies the contrasts that characterize life in Burma.

Subjective Language.   By describing the windmills, Mary conveys her sense of foreboding. When she first introduces them, she questions whether these "squat forms" are "boulders," "fortifications," or "broken wooden crosses," each of which has a menacing connotation. After telling readers what they are, she uses **personification**, describing the windmills as dark, evil, sneering figures with "arms hanging derelict." She sees them as ghostly sentinels awaiting "a call from a watchman" to spring into action. With this figure of speech, Mary skillfully re-creates the unearthly quality of the scene.

Structure.   Mary's purpose in this paper was to give her readers the experience of being in the Valley of Windmills. She uses an organizing scheme that takes readers along the road to Taungaleik, up into the Tennesserim Mountains, and finally to the pass where the windmills wait. From her perspective on the lip of the valley, she describes the details closest to her and then those farther away, as if following the movement of her eyes. She ends by bringing her readers back to the lip of the valley, contrasting Taungaleik "glittering on the mountainside" with the windmills "enveloped in morning mist." With her description, Mary builds up to her thesis about the nature of life in her country. She withholds the explicit statement of her main point until her last paragraph, when readers are fully prepared for it.

Focus on Revision

One of Mary's peer critics thought that her essay's thesis about life in Burma needed additional support. The student pointed out that although Mary's description is quite powerful, it does not fully convey the contrasts she alludes to in her conclusion.

Mary decided that adding another paragraph discussing something about her life (perhaps her reasons for visiting the windmills) could help supply this missing information. She could, for example, tell her readers that right after her return from the valley, she found out that a friend had been accidentally shot by border guards and that this event caused her to characterize the windmills as she did. Such information would help explain the passage's somber mood and underscore the ideas presented in the conclusion.

📄 PEER EDITING WORKSHEET: Description

1. What is the essay's dominant impression or thesis?

2. What points does the writer emphasize in the introduction? Should any other points be included? If so, which ones?

3. Would you characterize the essay as primarily an objective or subjective description? What leads you to your conclusion?

4. Point out some examples of figures of speech. Could the writer use figures of speech in other places? If so, where?

5. What specific details does the writer use to help readers visualize what is being described? Where could the writer have used more details? Would a visual have helped readers understand what is being described?

6. Are all the details necessary? Can you identify any that seem excessive or redundant? Where could the writer have provided more details to support the thesis or convey the dominant impression?

7. How are the details in the essay arranged? What other arrangement could the writer have used?

8. List some transitional words and phrases the writer uses to help readers follow the discussion. Which sentences need transitional words or phrases to link them to other sentences?

9. Do any sentences contain misplaced or dangling modifiers? If so, which ones?

10. How effective is the essay's conclusion? Does the conclusion reinforce the dominant impression?

The following selections illustrate various ways description can shape an essay. As you read them, pay particular attention to the differences between objective and subjective description. The first selection, a visual text, is followed by questions designed to illustrate how description can operate in visual form.

Dogs Playing Poker (Painting)

Reading Images

1. The painting is a whimsical picture of dogs around a poker table. Describe what you see in the picture, moving from left to right.
2. What details does the painting include? What determines how the details are arranged?
3. What dominant impression do you think the artist wants to create? How do the details in the painting communicate this dominant impression?

Journal Entry

Go to Google Images and find Paul Cezanne's *The Card Players*. Write a one-paragraph description of this painting. What dominant impression do you think Cezanne was trying to create? How is it different from the dominant impression created by *Dogs Playing Poker*?

Thematic Connections

- "Earth without People" (page 368)
- "The Dog Ate My Disk, and Other Tales of Woe" (page 471)
- "A Modest Proposal" (page 745)

DOROTHY ALLISON

Panacea

Dorothy Allison was born in Greenville, South Carolina, to a sixteen-year-old unwed mother. The first member of her family to graduate from high school, she went on to college on a National Merit Scholarship. An award-winning editor of a number of feminist journals, Allison is also the author of the best-selling novel *Bastard Out of Carolina* (1992), which was a *New York Times* Notable Book and was later made into an award-winning film.

Background on food nostalgia

In the following essay, originally published in the *New York Times Magazine* as an "Eat, Memory" feature, Allison recalls with great fondness the gravy her mother made for her and her sisters as she was growing up and her attempt to establish a similar food tradition in her own household. People of all cultures remember the foods of their childhood nostalgically. In Japan, for example, a common expression, "ofukuro no aji," translates as "taste of your mother's cooking." The English equivalent is "comfort food," a term first included in *Webster's Dictionary* in 1972. In a survey conducted by Allrecipes.com, when asked why they associated certain foods with comfort — given the choices of "Mom/Dad made it for me when I was a child," "It warms me up in the cold months of the year," "It makes me happy," "It's a family favorite that brings me home," "It's a personal favorite that defines who I am," and "Good old nostalgia for simple, safe, fun times" — fully 40 percent of respondents chose "All of the above."

Gravy is the simplest, tastiest, most memory-laden dish I know how to make: a little flour, salt and pepper, crispy bits of whatever meat anchored the meal, a couple of cups of water or milk, and slow stirring to break up lumps. That's it. It smells of home, the door locked against the night and a stillness made safe by the sound of a spoon going round in a pan. It is anticipation, the last thing prepared before the meal comes to the table, the bowl in Mama's hand closing the day out peacefully, no matter what came before.

My mother's gravy was a savory country gravy, heavy on the black pepper. Best of all was steak — cube steak. People call it country-fried steak, but Mama always called it cube steak. She began with odd, indented slabs of cheap meat carried home from the diner where she was on her feet all day. My sisters and I would pound the "steak" while she rested. The little round mouth of the Coke bottle thudded into the meat over and over until each piece was not only dimpled but flattened out half again as wide as it had been. By the time Mama stopped us, the steaks would be tenderized almost to pieces. Then she would shoo us out of the way, make up the biscuits and sift some of the flour onto a plate. Dredged in flour, the steaks went into a hot cast-iron skillet with a good covering of bacon fat. So long as we set the table and were useful, we were allowed to watch Mama cook the steaks and then set them aside on a brown paper bag. Then she took the plate of leftover flour and sprinkled it in the pan, stirring it as it browned and the pan filled with little brown flour pebbles and charred bits of meat. A lot of water and a little milk made steam rise up in a sweet cloud. Mama worked the gravy with a fork until all was smooth and silky. She might pour the gravy over the steaks or she might serve it in a bowl. It was not until I was grown that I understood that gravy poured over the meat before it came to the table meant there was not much meat.

In one tract house or another, first in South Carolina and then Florida, where we moved when I was a teenager, Mama made magic with cheap meat, flour, and determination — hiding from us how desperate things might be. She did such a good job of it that we came to believe cube steak a luxury, better than the rare T-bone our uncles might bring around as a surprise. 3

My son, Wolf, was born when I was past forty and the author of a best-selling novel. That means he has grown up a middle-class child — one who sometimes asks me for stories of my childhood but knows nothing of what it means to grow up poor and afraid. I have worked to make sure of that. His favorite foods are all dishes I never even knew existed until I was a voting adult: spinach soufflés, steamed mussels, and sautéed brussels sprouts. He has almost never eaten an egg yolk and never took an interest in gravy, not even on Thanksgiving turkey. 4

"No, thank you," he said, very politely. 5

My feelings were hurt. How could my child not like my gravy? Maybe it was the giblets I chopped and added? Next time I made a smooth, pristine gravy with no bits of anything. Wolf didn't touch it. 6

This time I sighed. I had to face the truth. My gravy was nowhere near as good as my mother's had been, and my son was not me. He had never gone to bed hungry and had no idea how important a locked door could be. I could not be unhappy about that. 7

Then there was the duck. 8

It was three years ago, and I wanted to do something special for the holidays to celebrate our aunt Mary moving up from Arizona. At the grocery, there was a big sale sign — ducks and geese at discount. A duck, a goose, a British Christmas dinner. I had read the novels. I had a brand-new roasting pan. So just because I could, I bought one of each—the goose for Christmas and the duck for New Year's. 9

Christmas was wonderful, but the goose was not a success. It came out pretty but dry. I stripped the leftovers for the dogs and worried. What was I going to do with that duck? I thought about giving up and making a ham. But my pride got in my way. I could cook. I was my mother's daughter. 10

It was clear to me that what was going to be necessary was a gravy — a good gravy. I read up on ducks and followed directions. I hung the bird over the sink in the warm kitchen and watched the fat drip off. After a while the bird looked greasy but lean. I shooed everyone out and went back 11 to basics. There was no bacon fat in my fridge, but there was bacon. I wrapped the duck in bacon, threw an obscuring layer of aluminum foil over the top and put it in the roasting pan.

You could smell the bacon in the steam coming out the top of the oven, but maybe I was the only one who noticed. It was New Year's after all, with family and friends and lots of dishes. There were greens and black-eyed peas and sweet potatoes with marshmallows. There were pies and loud music — lots of things to distract everyone away from the oven. 12

When the duck was done, I set it on a platter and disappeared the bacon slices. Then I poured off almost all the grease and took a spoon after the blackened bits in the bottom of the pan. Maybe the duck would be dry as the goose had been. But the bits in the bottom of the pan looked like great cracklings. I scraped and dredged and turned on the heat, then sprinkled flour and pepper across the oily surface. It cooked into the familiar brown pebbles. I squeezed a bite between my fingers and tasted salty, rich flavor. Uh-huh. A cup of skim milk brought up steam through which I stirred steadily. Another cup went after the first, then a cup of water. I used a fork to squash the lumps and kept stirring. Every now and then I would taste the gravy again and then go searching in my cupboard. Yes, more black pepper and a little bottled magic from K-Paul's Louisiana Kitchen.* At the last minute I reached over and spooned in some of the creamy liquid off the black-eyed peas. It made me laugh — but the gravy smelled wonderful. 13

Soon there were offers to help carry in the dishes. My son was standing by me at the stove. He was staring at the gravy I was still stirring. He leaned forward over the pan. 14

"Mmm." 15

I looked at him. His big green eyes were wide and hungry. I used a wooden spoon. Blew on the gravy to cool it, then let him lick a taste. 16

"Oh, that's wonderful!" he said. 17

After that everyone was quick to the table. The duck was perfect, everyone said so. I felt as if I had passed some ancient rite or earned some essential vindication. There was no gravy left when the meal was done. 18

Every now and then, I make duck again. But more often, I do what I know. I roast a chicken or pan-fry a steak and make pan gravy to go with it. Sometimes my boy comes to watch me cook. I watch him. He is getting so tall, now four inches taller than I and growing fast, while the world looms ever larger and more uncertain. I try not to worry. I try to make him feel he is home and safe and will always be so, no matter what comes to the door. 19

• • •

Comprehension

1. What does Allison mean when she says that gravy is "the most memory-laden dish I know how to make" (1)?

---

* EDS. NOTE — Restaurant of Chef Paul Prudhomme in New Orleans, Louisiana.

2. Why do the children have to pound the steak before it is cooked?

3. Why are Allison's feelings hurt when her son says that he doesn't care for gravy?

4. What foods does Allison's son like? How are they different from the foods that Allison ate when she was his age?

5. What does gravy mean to Allison? What do you think it meant to her mother?

Purpose and Audience

1. Does Allison seem to assume her readers come from the same background as she does? What leads you to your conclusion?

2. Is this essay just about gravy, or is it also about something else? Explain.

3. Does this essay have an explicitly stated thesis or an implied thesis? What dominant impression do you think Allison wants to convey?

Style and Structure

1. This essay is divided into three parts: the first part describes the gravy Allison's mother cooked; the second part describes Allison's son, Wolf; and the third part describes the holiday meals that Allison cooked. How does Allison signal the shift from one section of the essay to another? How effective are these shifts? What other strategies could she have used?

2. When Allison describes her son, she includes dialogue. How does this use of dialogue enrich her description? Why do you think she doesn't record her mother's comments?

3. Why does Allison spend so much time describing the gravy she made for the duck?

4. Allison ends her essay by saying of her son, "I try to make him feel he is home and safe and will always be so, no matter what comes to the door" (19). What does she mean?

5. When this essay was originally published, a detailed recipe for roast duck accompanied it. Do you think the essay would be more effective if this recipe were included, or do you think the recipe is unnecessary? Explain.

Vocabulary Projects

1. Define each of the following words as it is used in this selection.

   anticipation (1)   tract house (3)   cracklings (13)
   savory (2)   giblets (6)   rite (18)
   indented (2)   pristine (6)

2. In paragraph 2, Allison says that while most people called cube steak country-fried steak, her mother called it cube steak. This dish is also called chicken-fried steak. Go on the Web and research this type of steak. What does the information you find tell you about Allison and her mother?

3. What is the meaning of the word *panacea*? Why do you think Allison used this word as the title of her essay?

Journal Entry

What foods have special significance for you? What specific associations do these foods have?

Writing Workshop

1. Write an essay in which you describe a food that is as "memory-laden" for you as gravy is for Allison. Make sure that your essay has a clear thesis and that it includes at least one reference to Allison's essay. Be sure to document all material that you borrow from Allison's essay and to include a works-cited page. (See the Appendix for information on documentation formats.)

2. Write an email to a friend from another country in which you describe the foods you traditionally eat on a particular holiday. Assume that the person is not familiar with the food you describe. Be sure your email conveys a clear dominant impression.

3. Write an essay describing a parent or grandparent or any other older person who has had a great deal of influence on you. Make sure you include background information as well as a detailed physical description.

Combining the Patterns

In addition to describing Allison's experience with gravy, this essay also includes an extended **definition** in paragraph 1. Is this definition necessary? What purpose does it serve?

Thematic Connections

- "My Mother Never Worked" (page 114)
- "Getting Coffee Is Hard to Do" (page 287)
- "Swollen Expectations" (page 422)
- "Tortillas" (page 524)

SUZANNE BERNE

Ground Zero

Suzanne Berne has worked as a journalist and has also published book reviews and personal essays as well as three well-received novels, most recently *The Ghost at the Table* (2006). She currently teaches English at Boston College. In the following essay, which appeared on the *New York Times* op-ed page in April 2002, Berne describes a personal pilgrimage to the site of the former World Trade Center in New York City.

Background on the terrorist attacks of 9/11
The September 11, 2001, terrorist attacks that destroyed the twin towers of New York's World Trade Center and severely damaged the Pentagon stunned the nation and the world. People watched in horror as camera crews recorded the collapse of the towers while victims jumped to their deaths. The three hijacked aircraft that crashed into these targets, and a fourth that crashed into a field in rural Pennsylvania, caused the deaths of some three thousand people. An outpouring of grief, outrage, fear, and patriotism consumed the nation in the ensuing months as the possibility of war loomed large. While many, like Berne, have felt drawn to visit "ground zero" (as it has come to be called), some family members of the victims — particularly of those whose unidentified remains are still at the site — have expressed concern that it not become a tourist attraction. A memorial planned for the site will include two reflecting pools. The names of the 2,980 people who were killed in the September 11 attacks in New York City, Pennsylvnia, and Washington, D.C. as well as those killed in the 1993 World Trade Center bombings, will be inscribed around the edges of the pools. An underground museum will contain exhibits that convey the experiences of responders, victims, and witnesses.

On a cold, damp March morning, I visited Manhattan's financial district, a place I'd never been, to pay my respects at what used to be the World Trade Center. Many other people had chosen to do the same that day, despite the raw wind and spits of rain, and so the first thing I noticed when I arrived on the corner of Vesey and Church Streets was a crowd. 1

Standing on the sidewalk, pressed against aluminum police barricades, wearing scarves that flapped into their faces and woolen hats pulled over their ears, were people apparently from everywhere. Germans, Italians, Japanese. An elegant-looking Norwegian family in matching shearling coats. People from Ohio and California and Maine. Children, middle-aged couples, older people. Many of them were clutching cameras and video recorders, and they were all craning to see across the street, where there was nothing to see. 2

At least, nothing is what it first looked like, the space that is now ground zero. But once your eyes adjust to what you are looking at, "nothing" becomes something much more potent, which is absence. 3

But to the out-of-towner, ground zero looks at first simply like a construction site. All the familiar details are there: the wooden scaffolding; the cranes, the bulldozers, and forklifts; the trailers and construction workers in hard hats; even the dust. There is the pound of jackhammers, the steady beep-beep-beep of trucks backing up, the roar of heavy machinery.   4

So much busyness is reassuring, and it is possible to stand looking at the cranes and trucks and feel that mild curiosity and hopefulness so often inspired by construction sites.   5

Then gradually your eyes do adjust, exactly as if you have stepped from a dark theater into a bright afternoon, because what becomes most striking about this scene is the light itself.   6

Ground zero is a great bowl of light, an emptiness that seems weirdly spacious and grand, like a vast plaza amid the dense tangle of streets in lower Manhattan. Light reflecting off the Hudson River vaults into the site, soaking everything — especially on an overcast morning — with a watery glow. This is the moment when absence begins to assume a material form, when what is not there becomes visible.   7

Suddenly you notice the periphery, the skyscraper shrouded in black plastic, the boarded windows, the steel skeleton of the shattered Winter Garden. Suddenly there are the broken steps and cracked masonry in front of Brooks Brothers. Suddenly there are the firefighters, the waiting ambulance on the other side of the pit, the police on every corner. Suddenly there is the enormous cross made of two rusted girders.   8

And suddenly, very suddenly, there is the little cemetery attached to St. Paul's Chapel, with tulips coming up, the chapel and grounds miraculously undamaged except for a few plastic-sheathed gravestones. The iron fence is almost invisible beneath a welter of dried pine wreaths, banners, ribbons, laminated poems and prayers and photographs, swags of paper cranes, withered flowers, baseball hats, rosary beads, teddy bears. And flags, flags everywhere, little American flags fluttering in the breeze, flags on posters drawn by Brownie troops, flags on T-shirts, flags on hats, flags streaming by, tied to the handles of baby strollers.   9

It takes quite a while to see all of this; it takes even longer to come up with something to say about it.   10

An elderly man standing next to me had been staring fixedly across the street for some time. Finally he touched his son's elbow and said: "I watched those towers being built. I saw this place when they weren't there." Then he stopped, clearly struggling with, what for him, was a double negative, recalling an absence before there was an absence. His son, waiting patiently, took a few photographs. "Let's get out of here," the man said at last.   11

Again and again I heard people say, "It's unbelievable." And then they would turn to each other, dissatisfied. They wanted to say something more expressive, more meaningful. But it *is* unbelievable, to stare at so much devastation, and know it for devastation, and yet recognize that it does not look like the devastation one has imagined.   12

Like me, perhaps, the people around me had in mind images from television and newspaper pictures: the collapsing buildings, the running office   13 workers, the black plume of smoke against a bright blue sky. Like me, they were probably trying to superimpose those terrible images onto the industrious emptiness right in front of them. The difficulty of this kind of mental revision is measured, I believe, by the brisk trade in World Trade Center photograph booklets at tables set up on street corners.

Determined to understand better what I was looking at, I decided to get a ticket for the viewing platform beside St. Paul's. This proved no easy task, as no one seemed to be able to direct me to South Street Seaport, where the tickets are distributed. Various police officers whom I asked for directions waved me vaguely toward the East River, differing degrees of boredom and resignation on their faces. Or perhaps it was a kind of incredulousness. Somewhere around the American Stock Exchange, I asked a security guard for help and he frowned at me, saying, "You want tickets to the disaster?" 14

Finally I found myself in line at a cheerfully painted kiosk, watching a young juggler try to entertain the crowd. He kept dropping the four red balls he was attempting to juggle, and having to chase after them. It was noon; the next available viewing was at 4 P.M. 15

Back I walked, up Fulton Street, the smell of fish in the air, to wander again around St. Paul's. A deli on Vesey Street advertised a view of the World Trade Center from its second-floor dining area. I went in and ordered a pastrami sandwich, uncomfortably aware that many people before me had come to that same deli for pastrami sandwiches who would never come there again. But I was here to see what I could, so I carried my sandwich upstairs and sat down beside one of the big plate-glass windows. 16

And there, at last, I got my ticket to the disaster. 17

I could see not just into the pit now, but also its access ramp, which trucks had been traveling up and down since I had arrived that morning. Gathered along the ramp were firefighters in their black helmets and black coats. Slowly they lined up, and it became clear that this was an honor guard, and that someone's remains were being carried up the ramp toward the open door of an ambulance. 18

Everyone in the dining room stopped eating. Several people stood up, whether out of respect or to see better, I don't know. For a moment, everything paused. 19

Then the day flowed back into itself. Soon I was outside once more, joining the tide of people washing around the site. Later, as I huddled with a little crowd on the viewing platform, watching people scrawl their names or write "God Bless America" on the plywood walls, it occurred to me that a form of repopulation was taking effect, with so many visitors to this place, thousands of visitors, all of us coming to see the wide emptiness where so many were lost. And by the act of our visiting — whether we are motivated by curiosity or horror or reverence or grief, or by something confusing that combines them all — that space fills up again. 20

•   •   •

Comprehension

1. What does Berne mean when she says that as her eyes adjust to what she is seeing, "'nothing' becomes something much more potent, which is absence" (3)?

2. Why does it take "quite a while" (10) to see all the details at ground zero? Why does it take "even longer" (10) to think of something to say about it?

3. According to Berne, how were the television pictures of ground zero different from the actual experience of seeing it?

4. How does the area around ground zero contrast with the site itself? How does Berne react to this contrast?

5. What does Berne mean in her conclusion when she says that with so many visitors coming to see ground zero, a form of "repopulation" (20) is taking place? Do you think she is being **ironic**?

Purpose and Audience

1. Does Berne state or imply her thesis? Why do you think she makes the decision she does? State Berne's thesis in your own words.

2. What is Berne's purpose in writing her essay?

3. What assumptions does Berne make about her readers' ideas about ground zero? How can you tell?

Style and Structure

1. Why does Berne begin her essay by saying she had never before visited Manhattan's financial district?

2. What organizational scheme does Berne use? What are the advantages and disadvantages of this scheme?

3. In paragraph 3, Berne says that ground zero at first looks like "nothing"; in paragraph 4, she says that it looks like a construction site. Then, in paragraph 7, she describes ground zero as "a great bowl of light." And finally, in her conclusion, she refers to it as a pit (18). Why do you think Berne describes ground zero in so many different ways?

4. Berne leaves a space between paragraphs 17 and 18. In what way does the space (as well as paragraph 17) reinforce a shift in her essay's focus?

5. Why does Berne end her essay with a description of the crowd standing on the viewing platform? Why do you suppose she feels the need to include these observations?

6. In paragraphs 8 and 9, Berne repeats the word *suddenly*. What is the effect of this repetition? Could she have achieved this effect some other way?

Vocabulary Projects

1. Define each of the following words as it is used in this selection.

    shearling (2)   devastation (12)

potent (3)   incredulousness (14)
periphery (8)   repopulation (20)
laminated (9)

2. A **paradox** is a seemingly contradictory statement that may nonetheless be true. Find examples of paradoxes in "Ground Zero." Why do you think Berne uses these paradoxes?

3. List ten striking visual details Berne uses to describe people and objects. Can you think of other details she could have used?

4. Go to dictionary.com and look up the meaning of the term *ground zero*. What connotations does this term have? Do you think this is an appropriate title for Berne's essay?

Journal Entry

Go to the Web site wtc.vjs.org and look at film clips of Ground Zero after the twin towers collapsed. Are your reactions to these images similar to or different from Berne's?

Writing Workshop

1. Write an essay describing what you saw on the morning of September 11, 2001, when terrorists destroyed the World Trade Center. Make sure that you include an explicitly stated thesis and that you use your description to convey your reactions to the event. If you can, include a quotation from Berne's essay in your paper. Be sure to document the quotation and to include a works-cited page. (See the Appendix for information on documentation formats.)

2. Write a description of a place from several different vantage points, as Berne does. Make sure each of your perspectives provides different information about the place you are describing.

3. Write a subjective description of a scene you remember from your childhood. In your thesis statement and in your conclusion, explain how your adult impressions of the scene differ from those of your childhood.

Combining the Patterns

In addition to containing a great deal of description, this essay also uses **comparison and contrast**. In paragraphs 1 through 10, what two ways of seeing ground zero does Berne compare? What points about each view of ground zero does she contrast?

Thematic Connections

- "Shooting an Elephant" (page 126)
- "Once More to the Lake" (page 183)
- "The Case for Torture" (page 681)

Words Left Unspoken

Although she is not deaf, Leah Hager Cohen (b. 1967) lived for much of her childhood at the Lexington School for the Deaf in Queens, New York, where her mother was a teacher and her father was an administrator. (Both her paternal grandparents were deaf.) Cohen has been a writing instructor at Emerson College in Boston and an interpreter for deaf students in mainstream classes. She is also the author of four books of nonfiction and three novels, the most recent of which is *House Lights* (2007). Cohen also writes the blog *Love as a Found Object* and is a faculty mentor with Lesley University's M.F.A. program in creative writing.

Background on deaf culture

Some one million deaf people live in the United States, and more than twenty million are hearing impaired. Hearing loss is often a result of aging, but children may be born deaf or lose their hearing at an early age, usually because of infections. While improvements in hearing aids and cochlear implants have helped to mitigate some types of hearing loss, they are of only marginal help to those who are profoundly deaf. A growing segment of the deaf population has begun to urge that deafness be viewed not as an infirmity but as a cultural marker. Much debate has surrounded the question of whether deaf children should be educated to participate in the mainstream oral culture or whether they should be taught to communicate through sign language and become part of a deaf culture.

My earliest memories of Sam Cohen are of his chin, which I remember as fiercely hard and pointy. Not pointy, my mother says, jutting; Grandpa had a strong, jutting chin. But against my very young face it felt like a chunk of honed granite swathed in stiff white bristles. Whenever we visited, he would lift us grandchildren up, most frequently by the elbows, and nuzzle our cheeks vigorously. This abrasive ritual greeting was our primary means of communication. In all my life, I never heard him speak a word I could understand. [1]

Sometimes he used his voice to get our attention. It made a shapeless, gusty sound, like a pair of bellows sending up sparks and soot in a blacksmith shop. And he made sounds when he was eating, sounds that, originating from other quarters, would have drawn chiding or expulsion from the table. He smacked his lips and sucked his teeth; his chewing was moist and percussive; he released deep, hushed moans from the back of his throat, like a dreaming dog. And he burped out loud. Sometimes it was all Reba, Andy, and I could do not to catch one another's eyes and fall into giggles. [2]

Our grandfather played games with us, the more physical the better. He loved that hand game: he would extend his, palms up, and we would [3] hover ours, palms down, above his, and lower them, lower, lower, until they were just nesting, and *slap!* he'd have sandwiched one of our hands, trapping it between his. When we reversed, I could never even graze his, so fast would he snatch them away, like a big white fish.

He played three-card monte* with us, arranging the cards neatly   4
between his long fingers, showing us once the jack of diamonds smirking, red and gold, underneath. And then, with motions as swift and implausible as a Saturday morning cartoon chase, his hands darted and faked and blurred and the cards lay still, face down and impassive. When we guessed the jack's position correctly, it was only luck. When we guessed wrong, he would laugh — a fond, gravelly sound — and pick up the cards and begin again.

He mimicked the way I ate. He compressed his mouth into dainty pro-   5
portions as he nibbled air and carefully licked his lips and chewed tiny, precise bites, his teeth clicking, his eyelashes batting as he gazed shyly from under them. He could walk exactly like Charlie Chaplin and make nickels disappear, just vanish, from both his fists and up his sleeves; we never found them, no matter how we crawled over him, searching. All of this without any words.

He and my grandmother lived in the Bronx, in the same apartment my   6
father and Uncle Max had grown up in. It was on Knox Place, near Mosholu Parkway, a three-room apartment below street level. The kitchen was a tight squeeze of a place, especially with my grandmother bending over the oven, blocking the passage as she checked baked apples or stuffed cabbage, my grandfather sitting with splayed knees at the dinette. It was easy to get each other's attention in there; a stamped foot sent vibrations clearly over the short distance, and an outstretched arm had a good chance of connecting with the other party.

The living room was ampler and dimmer, with abundant floor and   7
table lamps to accommodate signed conversation. Little windows set up high revealed the legs of passersby. And down below, burrowed in black leather chairs in front of the television, we children learned to love physical comedy. Long before the days of closed captioning, we listened to our grandfather laugh out loud at the snowy black-and-white antics of Abbott and Costello, Laurel and Hardy, the Three Stooges.

During the time that I knew him, I saw his hairline shrink back and his   8
eyes grow remote behind pairs of progressively thicker glasses. His athlete's bones shed some of their grace and nimbleness; they began curving in on themselves as he stood, arms folded across his sunken chest. Even his long, thin smile seemed to recede deeper between his nose and his prominent chin. But his hands remained lithe, vital. As he teased and argued and chatted and joked, they were the instruments of his mind, the conduits of his thoughts.

---

* EDS. NOTE — A sleight-of-hand card game often played on urban streets; the dealer gets onlookers to place bets that they can pick the jack of diamonds.

As far as anyone knows, Samuel Kolominsky was born deaf (according to Lexington* records, his parents "failed to take note until child was about one and a half years old"). His birthplace was Russia, somewhere near Kiev. Lexington records say he was born in 1908; my grandmother says it was 1907. He was a child when his family fled the czarist pogroms. Lexington records have him immigrating in 1913, at age five; my grandmother says he came to this country when he was three. Officials at Ellis Island altered the family name, writing down Cohen, but they did not detect his deafness, so Sam sailed on across the last ribbon of water to America. 9

His name-sign at home: *Daddy*. His name-sign with friends: the thumb and index finger, perched just above the temple, rub against each other like grasshopper legs. One old friend attributes this to Sam's hair, which was blond and thick and wavy. Another says it derived from his habit of twisting a lock between his fingers. 10

Lexington records have him living variously at Clara, Moore, Siegel, Tehema, and Thirty-eighth streets in Brooklyn and on Avenue C in Manhattan. I knew him on Knox Place, and much later on Thieriot Avenue, in the Bronx. Wherever he lived, he loved to walk, the neighborhoods revolving silently like pictures in a Kinetoscope,** unfurling themselves in full color around him. 11

Shortly before he died, when I was thirteen, we found ourselves walking home from a coffee shop together on a warm night. My family had spent the day visiting my grandparents at their apartment. My grandmother and the rest of the family were walking half a block ahead; I hung back and made myself take my grandfather's hand. We didn't look at each other. His hand was warm and dry. His gait was uneven then, a long slow beat on the right, catch-up on the left. I measured my steps to his. It was dark except for the hazy pink cones of light cast by streetlamps. I found his rhythm, and breathed it in. That was the longest conversation we ever had. 12

He died before I was really able to converse in sign. I have never seen his handwriting. I once saw his teeth, in a glass, on the bathroom windowsill. Now everything seems like a clue. 13

• • •

Comprehension

1. Why was Cohen's grandfather unable to speak? How did Cohen communicate with him?
2. What kind of relationship did Cohen have with her grandfather? Warm? Distant?

---

* EDS. NOTE — The Lexington School for the Deaf, where Cohen's grandfather was once a student.
** EDS. NOTE — A device for viewing a sequence of moving pictures as it rotates over a light source, creating the illusion of motion.

3. What does Cohen mean when she says, "That was the longest conversation we ever had" (12)?

4. In paragraph 13, Cohen says that now, after her grandfather's death, "everything seems like a clue." What does she mean?

5. What is the significance of the essay's title? What do you think the "words left unspoken" are? Is the speaker of these words Cohen, her grandfather, or both? Explain.

Purpose and Audience

1. Does "Words Left Unspoken" have an explicitly stated thesis? Why, or why not?

2. What dominant impression is Cohen trying to create in this essay? How successful is she?

3. How much do you think Cohen expects her readers to know about deaf culture? How can you tell?

Style and Structure

1. Why do you think Cohen begins her essay with a description of her grandfather's chin?

2. What is the organizing principle of this essay? Would another organizing principle be more effective? Explain.

3. Are you able to picture Cohen's grandfather after reading her description? Do you think she expects you to?

4. Does Cohen develop her description fully enough? At what points could she have provided more detail?

5. What figures of speech does Cohen use in this essay? Where might additional figures of speech be helpful?

Vocabulary Projects

1. Define each of the following words as it is used in this selection.

honed (1)	abundant (7)
expulsion (2)	prominent (8)
percussive (2)	lithe (8)
smirking (4)	conduits (8)
splayed (6)	gait (12)

2. Supply a synonym for each of the words listed. How is each synonym different from the original word?

Journal Entry

How does Cohen's grandfather fit the traditional stereotype of a grandfather? How does he not fit this stereotype?

Writing Workshop

1. Write a description of a person. Concentrate on one specific feature or quality you associate with this person (as Cohen does in her essay).

2. Choose three or four members of your family, and write a one-paragraph description of each. Combine these descriptions into a "family album" essay that has an introduction, a thesis statement, and a conclusion.

3. Write an essay describing your earliest memories of a family member or close family friend. Before you write, decide on the dominant impression you want to convey.

Combining the Patterns

Cohen uses **narration** to develop paragraph 9. Why does she include this narrative paragraph? Does it add to or detract from the dominant impression she wants to convey? Explain.

Thematic Connections

- "Only Daughter" (page 97)
- "Panacea" (page 162)
- "Mother Tongue" (page 477)

The Hidden Life of Garbage

Journalist Heather Rogers has written articles on the environmental effects of mass production and consumption for the *New York Times Magazine*, the *Utne Reader*, *Architecture*, and a variety of other publications. Her 2002 documentary film *Gone Tomorrow: The Hidden Life of Garbage* has been screened at festivals around the world and served as the basis for a book of the same title. Named an Editor's Choice by the *New York Times* and the *Guardian*, the book, published in 2005, traces the history and politics of household garbage in the United States, drawing connections between modern industrial production, consumer culture, and our contemporary throwaway lifestyle. In the following excerpt from the book, Rogers provides a detailed description of a giant landfill in central Pennsylvania and asks readers to think about the ramifications of accumulating so much trash.

Background on waste disposal

With the establishment of permanent settlements some ten thousand years ago, humans faced the question of how to dispose of garbage. The first city dump was established in ancient Athens, and the government of Rome had begun the collection of municipal trash by 200 C.E. Over the ensuing years and even as late as the 1800s, garbage was, at worst, simply thrown out into city streets or dumped into rivers and ditches; in more enlightened communities, it might have been carted to foul-smelling open dumps or burned in incinerators, creating clouds of dense smoke. Experiments with systematically covering the garbage in dumps began as early as the 1920s, and the first true "sanitary landfill," as it was called, was created in Fresno, California, in 1937. Today, more than 60 percent of the solid waste in the United States ends up in landfills, and the amount of waste seems to keep growing. According to the Energy Information Administration, the amount of waste produced in the United States has more than doubled in the last thirty years, and it is estimated that the average American generates an astounding 4.5 pounds of trash every day.

In the dark chill of early morning, heavy steel garbage trucks chug and creep along neighborhood collection routes. A worker empties the contents of each household's waste bin into the truck's rear compaction unit. Hydraulic compressors scoop up and crush the dross, cramming it into the enclosed hull. When the rig is full, the collector heads to a garbage depot called a "transfer station" to unload. From there the rejectamenta is taken to a recycling center, an incinerator or, most often, to what's called a "sanitary landfill."

Land dumping has long been the favored disposal method in the U.S. thanks to the relative low cost of burial and North America's abundant supply of <u>unused</u> acreage. Although the great majority of our castoffs go to landfills, they are places the public is not meant to see. Today's garbage graveyards are sequestered, guarded, veiled. They are also high-tech, and, increasingly, located in rural areas that receive much of their rubbish from urban centers that no longer bury their own wastes.

There's a reason landfills are tucked away, on the edge of town, in otherwise untraveled terrain, camouflaged by hydroseeded, neatly tiered slopes. If people saw what happened to their waste, lived with the stench, witnessed the scale of destruction, they might start asking difficult questions. Waste Management Inc., the largest rubbish handling corporation in the world, operates its Geological Reclamation Operations and Waste Systems (GROWS) landfill just outside Morrisville, Pennsylvania — in the docile river valley near where Washington momentously crossed the Delaware leading his troops into Trenton in 1776. Sitting atop the landfill's 300-foot-high butte composed entirely of garbage, the logic of our society's unrestrained consuming and wasting quickly unravels.

Up here is where the dumping takes place; it is referred to as the fill's "working face." Clusters of trailer trucks, <u>yellow</u> earthmovers, compacting machines, steamrollers, and water tankers populate this bizarre, thirty-acre nightmare. Churning in slow motion through the surreal landscape, these machines are remaking the earth in the image of garbage. Scores of seagulls hover overhead then suddenly drop into the rotting piles. The ground underfoot is torn from the metal treads of the equipment. Potato chip wrappers, tattered plastic bags, and old shoes poke through the dirt as if floating to the surface. The smell is sickly and sour.

The aptly named GROWS landfill is part of Waste Management Inc.'s (WMI) 6,000-acre garbage treatment complex, which includes a second landfill, an incinerator, and a state-mandated leaf composting lot. GROWS is one of a new breed of waste burial sites referred to as "mega-fills." These high-tech, high-capacity dumps are comprised of a series of earth covered "cells" that can be ten to one hundred acres across and up to hundreds of feet deep — or tall, as is the case at GROWS. (One Virginia whopper has disposal capacity equivalent to the length of one thousand football fields and the height of the Washington Monument.) As of 2002, GROWS was the single largest recipient of New York City's garbage in Pennsylvania, a state that is the country's biggest depository for exported waste.

WMI's Delaware-side operation sits on land that has long served the interests of industry. Overlooking a <u>rambling, mostly decommissioned US Steel</u> factory, WMI now occupies the former grounds of the Warner Company. In the previous century, Warner surface mined the area for gravel and sand, much of which was shipped to its cement factory in Philadelphia. The area has since been converted into a reverse mine of sorts; instead of extraction, workers dump, pack, and fill the earth with almost forty million pounds of municipal wastes daily.

Back on top of the GROWS landfill, twenty-ton dump trucks gather at the low end of the working face, where they discharge their fetid cargo. Several feet up a <u>dirt</u> bank, a string of large trailers are being detached from

3

4

5

6

7

semi trucks. In rapid succession each container is tipped almost vertical by a giant hydraulic lift and, within seconds, twenty-four tons of putrescence cascades down into the day's menacing valley of trash. In the middle of the dumping is a "landfill compactor" — which looks like a bulldozer on steroids with mammoth metal spiked wheels — that pitches back and forth, its fifty tons crushing the detritus into the earth. A smaller vehicle called a "track loader" maneuvers on tank treads, channeling the castoffs from kitchens and offices into the compactor's path. The place runs like a well-oiled machine, with only a handful of workers orchestrating the burial.

Get a few hundred yards from the landfill's working face and it's hard to smell the rot or see the debris. The place is kept tidy with the help of thirty-five-foot tall fencing made of "litter netting" that surrounds the perimeter of the site's two landfills. As a backup measure, teams of "paper pickers" constantly patrol the area retrieving discards carried off by the wind. Small misting machines dot fence tops, roads, and hillsides, spraying a fine, invisible chemical-water mixture into the air, which binds with odor molecules and pulls them to the ground.   8

In new state-of-the-art landfills, the cells that contain the trash are built on top of what is called a "liner." The liner is a giant underground bladder intended to prevent contamination of groundwater by collecting leachate — liquid wastes and the rainwater that seeps through buried trash — and channeling it to nearby water treatment facilities. WMI's two Morrisville landfills leach on average 100,000 gallons daily. If this toxic stew contaminated the site's groundwater it would be devastating.   9

Once a cell is filled, which might take years, it is closed off or "capped." The capping process entails covering the garbage with several feet of dirt, which gets graded, then packed by steamrollers. After that, layers of clay-embedded fabric, synthetic mesh, and plastic sheeting are draped across the top of the cell and joined with the bottom liner (which is made of the same materials) to encapsulate all those outmoded appliances, dirty diapers, and discarded wrappers.   10

Today's landfill regulations, ranging from liner construction to post-capping oversight, mean that disposal areas like WMI's GROWS are potentially less dangerous than the dumps of previous generations. But the fact remains that these systems are short-term solutions to the garbage problem. While they may not seem toxic now, all those underground cells packed with plastics, solvents, paints, batteries and other hazardous materials will someday have to be treated since the liners won't last forever. Most liners are expected to last somewhere between thirty and fifty years. That time frame just happens to coincide with the post-closure liability private landfill operators are subject to: thirty years after a site is shuttered, its owner is no longer responsible for contamination, the public is.   11

There is a palpable tension at waste treatment facilities, as though at any minute the visitor will uncover some illegal activity. But what's most striking at these places isn't what they might be hiding; it's what's in plain view. The lavish resources dedicated to destroying used commodities and making that obliteration acceptable, even "green," is what's so astounding.   12

Each landfill (not to mention garbage collection systems, transfer stations, recycling centers, and incinerators) is an expensive, complex operation that uses the latest methods developed and perfected at laboratories, universities, and corporate campuses across the globe.

The more state-of-the-art, the more "environmentally responsible" the   13
operation, the more the repressed question pushes to the surface: what if we didn't have so much trash to get rid of?

•   •   •

Comprehension

1. According to Rogers, why are landfills "tucked away, on the edge of town, in otherwise untraveled terrain" (3)?
2. What is the landfill's "working face" (4)? How does it compare with other parts of the landfill?
3. Why does Rogers think that the GROWS landfill is aptly named? What **connotations** do you think Waste Management Inc. intended the name GROWS to have? What connotations does Rogers think the name has?
4. What are the dangers of the new "state-of-the-art landfills" (9)? What point does Rogers make about liners being "expected to last somewhere between thirty and fifty years" (11)?
5. According to Rogers, what is the "repressed question" (13) that is not being asked?

Purpose and Audience

1. At what point in the essay does Rogers state her thesis? Why do you think she places the thesis where she does?
2. What dominant impression does Rogers try to create in her description? Is she successful?
3. What is Rogers's attitude toward waste disposal in general — and toward disposal companies like Waste Management Inc. in particular? Do you share her feelings?

Style and Structure

1. Rogers begins her essay with a description of garbage trucks collecting trash. What specific things does she describe? How does this description establish the context for the rest of the essay?
2. What determines the order in which details are arranged in Rogers's essay?
3. Is this essay a subjective or objective description of the landfill? Explain.
4. In paragraph 13, why does Rogers put the phrase *environmentally responsible* in quotation marks? What impression is she trying to convey?
5. Rogers never offers a solution to the problems she writes about. Should she have done so? Is her failure to offer a solution a shortcoming of the essay?

Vocabulary Projects

1. Define each of the following words as it is used in this selection.

   hydraulic (1)   putrescence (7)
   rejectamenta (1)   cascades (7)
   sequestered (2)   leach (9)
   hydroseeded (3)   encapsulate (10)
   butte (3)   palpable (12)
   aptly (5)   lavish (12)
   fetid (7)   obliteration (12)

2. Some critics of waste disposal methods accuse both municipalities and waste disposal companies of "environmental racism." Research this term on the Web. Do you think the methods described by Rogers are examples of environmental racism? Explain.

3. Underline the adjectives Rogers uses when she describes garbage in paragraph 7. How do these adjectives help her make her point?

Journal Entry

What do you think you and your family could do to reduce the amount of garbage you produce? How realistic are your suggestions?

Writing Workshop

1. Write an essay in which you describe the waste that you see generated at your school, home, or job. Like Rogers, write your description in a way that will motivate people to do something about the problem. In your essay, use a quotation from Rogers's essay. Make sure you document the quotation and include a works-cited page. (See the Appendix for information on documentation formats.)

2. In 1986, the city of Philadelphia hired a company to dispose of waste from a city incinerator. Over thirteen thousand tons of waste — some of which was hazardous — was loaded onto a ship called the *Khian Sea,* which unsuccessfully tried to dispose of it. After two years, the cargo mysteriously disappeared. Go to Google Images and find several pictures of the *Khian Sea.* Then, write a description of the ship and its cargo. Make sure the thesis statement of your description clearly conveys your dominant impression. If you wish, you may insert one of the images you found into your essay. Make sure that you document the image and include a works-cited page. (See the Appendix for information on documentation formats.)

3. Describe a place that has played an important role in your life. Include a narrative passage that conveys the place's significance to you.

Combining the Patterns

In paragraphs 9 and 10, Rogers includes a **definition** as well as a **process** description. Explain how these paragraphs help Rogers develop her description.

Thematic Connections

- "Earth without People" (page 368)
- "Swollen Expectations" (page 422)
- "The Time to Act Is Now" (page 617)
- "On Dumpster Diving" (page 714)

E. B. WHITE

Once More to the Lake

Elwyn Brooks White was born in 1899 in Mount Vernon, New York. He joined the newly founded *New Yorker* in 1925 and was associated with the magazine until his death in 1985. In 1937, White moved his family to a farm in Maine and began a monthly column for *Harper's* magazine titled "One Man's Meat." A collection of some of these essays appeared under the same title in 1942. In addition to this and other essay collections, White published two popular children's books, *Stuart Little* (1945) and *Charlotte's Web* (1952). He also wrote a classic writer's handbook, *The Elements of Style* (1959), a revision of a text by one of his Cornell professors, William Strunk.

Background on continuity and change

In a sense, White's essay is a reflection on continuity and change. While much had remained the same at the Maine lake since 1904, the year White began coming with his parents, the world outside had undergone a significant transformation. Auto and air travel had become commonplace; the invention of innumerable electrical appliances and machines had revolutionized the home and the workplace; movies had gone from primitive, silent, black-and-white shorts to sophisticated productions with sound and sometimes color; and the rise of national advertising had spurred a new and greatly expanded generation of consumer products. Moreover, the country had suffered through World War I, enjoyed a great economic expansion, experienced a period of social revolution, and been devastated by a great economic depression. Within this context, White relives his childhood through his son's eyes.

One summer, along about 1904, my father rented a camp on a lake in Maine and took us all there for the month of August. We all got ringworm from some kittens and had to rub Pond's Extract on our arms and legs night and morning, and my father rolled over in a canoe with all his clothes on; but outside of that the vacation was a success and from then on none of us ever thought there was any place in the world like that lake in Maine. We returned summer after summer — always on August 1st for one month. I have since become a salt-water man, but sometimes in summer there are days when the restlessness of the tides and the fearful cold of the sea water and the incessant wind which blows across the afternoon and into the evening make me wish for the placidity of a lake in the woods. A few weeks ago this feeling got so strong I bought myself a couple of bass hooks and a spinner and returned to the lake where we used to go, for a week's fishing and to revisit old haunts. 1

I took along my son, who had never had any fresh water up his nose and who had seen lily pads only from train windows. On the journey over 2 to the lake I began to wonder what it would be like. I wondered how time would have marred this unique, this holy spot — the coves and streams, the hills that the sun set behind, the camps and the paths behind the camps. I was sure that the tarred road would have found it out and I wondered in what other ways it would be desolated. It is strange how much you can remember about places like that once you allow your mind to return into the grooves which lead back. You remember one thing, and that suddenly reminds you of another thing. I guess I remembered clearest of all the early mornings, when the lake was cool and motionless, remembered how the bedroom smelled of the lumber it was made of and the wet woods whose scent entered through the screen. The partitions in the camp were thin and did not extend clear to the top of the rooms, and as I was always the first up I would dress softly so as not to wake the others, and sneak out into the sweet outdoors and start out in the canoe, keeping close along the shore in the long shadows of the pines. I remembered being very careful never to rub my paddle against the gunwale for fear of disturbing the stillness of the cathedral.

The lake had never been what you would call a wild lake. There were 3 cottages sprinkled around the shores, and it was in farming country although the shores of the lake were quite heavily wooded. Some of the cottages were owned by nearby farmers, and you would live at the shore and eat your meals at the farmhouse. That's what our family did. But although it wasn't wild, it was a fairly large and undisturbed lake and there were places in it which, to a child at least, seemed infinitely remote and primeval.

I was right about the tar: it led to within half a mile of the shore. But 4 when I got back there, with my boy, and we settled into a camp near a farmhouse and into the kind of summertime I had known, I could tell that it was going to be pretty much the same as it had been before — I knew it, lying in bed the first morning, smelling the bedroom, and hearing the boy sneak quietly out and go off along the shore in a boat. I began to sustain the illusion that he was I, and therefore, by simple transposition, that I was my father. This sensation persisted, kept cropping up all the time we were there. It was not an entirely new feeling, but in this setting it grew much stronger. I seemed to be living a dual existence. I would be in the middle of some simple act, I would be picking up a bait box or laying down a table fork, or I would be saying something, and suddenly it would be not I but my father who was saying the words or making the gesture. It gave me a creepy sensation.

We went fishing the first morning. I felt the same damp moss covering 5 the worms in the bait can, and saw the dragonfly alight on the tip of my rod as it hovered a few inches from the surface of the water. It was the arrival of this fly that convinced me beyond any doubt that everything was as it always had been, that the years were a mirage and there had been no years. The small waves were the same, chucking the rowboat under the chin as we fished at anchor, and the boat was the same boat, the same color green and the ribs broken in the same places, and under the floor-boards the same freshwater leavings and débris — the dead helgramite,* the wisps of moss, the rusty discarded fishhook, the dried blood from yesterday's catch. We stared silently at the tips of our rods, at the dragonflies that came and went. I lowered the tip of mine into the water, tentatively, pensively dislodging the fly, which darted two feet away, poised, darted two feet back, and came to rest again a little farther up the rod. There had been no years between the ducking of this dragonfly and the other one — the one that was part of memory. I looked at the boy, who was silently watching his fly, and it was my hands that held his rod, my eyes watching. I felt dizzy and didn't know which rod I was at the end of.

We caught two bass, hauling them in briskly as though they were   6
mackerel, pulling them over the side of the boat in a businesslike manner without any landing net, and stunning them with a blow on the back of the head. When we got back for a swim before lunch, the lake was exactly where we had left it, the same number of inches from the dock, and there was only the merest suggestion of a breeze. This seemed an utterly enchanted sea, this lake you could leave to its own devices for a few hours and come back to, and find that it had not stirred, this constant and trustworthy body of water. In the shallows, the dark, water-soaked sticks and twigs, smooth and old, were undulating in clusters on the bottom against the clean ribbed sand, and the track of the mussel was plain. A school of minnows swam by, each minnow with its small individual shadow, doubling the attendance, so clear and sharp in the sunlight. Some of the other campers were in swimming, along the shore, one of them with a cake of soap, and the water felt thin and clear and unsubstantial. Over the years there had been this person with the cake of soap, this cultist, and here he was. There had been no years.

Up to the farmhouse to dinner through the teeming, dusty field, the   7
road under our sneakers was only a two-track road. The middle track was missing, the one with the marks of the hooves and the splotches of dried, flaky manure. There had always been three tracks to choose from in choosing which track to walk in; now the choice was narrowed down to two. For a moment I missed terribly the middle alternative. But the way led past the tennis court, and something about the way it lay there in the sun reassured me; the tape had loosened along the backline, the alleys were green with plantains and other weeds, and the net (installed in June and removed in September) sagged in the dry noon, and the whole place steamed with midday heat and hunger and emptiness. There was a choice of pie for dessert, and one was blueberry and one was apple, and the waitresses were the same country girls, there having been no passage of time, only the illusion of it as in a dropped curtain — the waitresses were still fifteen; their hair had been washed, that was the only difference — they had been to the movies and seen the pretty girls with the clean hair.

Summertime, oh summertime, pattern of life indelible, the fade-proof   8
lake, the woods unshatterable, the pasture with the sweetfern and the

---

* EDS. NOTE — An insect larva often used as bait.

juniper forever and ever, summer without end; this was the background, and the life along the shore was the design, the cottages with their innocent and tranquil design, their tiny docks with the flagpole and the American flag floating against the white clouds in the blue sky, the little paths over the roots of the trees leading from camp to camp and the paths leading back to the outhouses and the can of lime for sprinkling, and at the souvenir counters at the store the miniature birch-bark canoes and the post cards that showed things looking a little better than they looked. This was the American family at play, escaping the city heat, wondering whether the newcomers in the camp at the head of the cove were "common" or "nice," wondering whether it was true that the people who drove up for Sunday dinner at the farmhouse were turned away because there wasn't enough chicken.

It seemed to me, as I kept remembering all this, that those times and those summers had been infinitely precious and worth saving. There had been jollity and peace and goodness. The arriving (at the beginning of August) had been so big a business in itself, at the railway station the farm wagon drawn up, the first smell of the pine-laden air, the first glimpse of the smiling farmer, and the great importance of the trunks and your father's enormous authority in such matters, and the feel of the wagon under you for the long ten-mile haul, and at the top of the last long hill catching the first view of the lake after eleven months of not seeing this cherished body of water. The shouts and cries of the other campers when they saw you, and the trunks to be unpacked, to give up their rich burden. (Arriving was less exciting nowadays, when you sneaked up in your car and parked it under a tree near the camp and took out the bags and in five minutes it was all over, no fuss, no loud wonderful fuss about trunks.)

Peace and goodness and jollity. The only thing that was wrong now, really, was the sound of the place, an unfamiliar nervous sound of the outboard motors. This was the note that jarred, the one thing that would sometimes break the illusion and set the years moving. In those other summertimes all motors were inboard; and when they were at a little distance, the noise they made was a sedative, an ingredient of summer sleep. They were one-cylinder and two-cylinder engines, and some were make-and-break and some were jump-spark, but they all made a sleepy sound across the lake. The one-lungers throbbed and fluttered, and the twin-cylinder ones purred and purred, and that was a quiet sound too. But now the campers all had outboards. In the daytime, in the hot mornings, these motors made a petulant, irritable sound; at night, in the still evening when the afterglow lit the water, they whined about one's ears like mosquitoes. My boy loved our rented outboard, and his great desire was to achieve singlehanded mastery over it, and authority, and he soon learned the trick of choking it a little (but not too much), and the adjustment of the needle valve. Watching him I would remember the things you could do with the old one-cylinder engine with the heavy flywheel, how you could have it eating out of your hand if you got really close to it spiritually. Motor boats in those days didn't have clutches, and you would make a landing by shutting

9

10

off the motor at the proper time and coasting in with a dead rudder. But there was a way of reversing them, if you learned the trick, by cutting the switch and putting it on again exactly on the final dying revolution of the flywheel, so that it would kick back against compression and begin reversing. Approaching a dock in a strong following breeze, it was difficult to slow up sufficiently by the ordinary coasting method, and if a boy felt he had complete mastery over his motor, he was tempted to keep it running beyond its time and then reverse it a few feet from the dock. It took a cool nerve, because if you threw the switch a twentieth of a second too soon you could catch the flywheel when it still had speed enough to go up past center, and the boat would leap ahead, charging bull-fashion at the dock.

We had a good week at the camp. The bass were biting well and the sun shone endlessly, day after day. We would be tired at night and lie down in the accumulated heat of the little bedrooms after the long hot day and the breeze would stir almost imperceptibly outside and the smell of the swamp drift in through the rusty screens. Sleep would come easily and in the morning the red squirrel would be on the roof, tapping out his gay routine. I kept remembering everything, lying in bed in the mornings — the small steamboat that had a long rounded stern like the lip of a Ubangi,* how quietly she ran on the moonlight sails, when the older boys played their mandolins and the girls sang and we ate doughnuts dipped in sugar, and how sweet the music was on the water in the shining night, and what it had felt like to think about girls then. After breakfast we would go up to the store and the things were in the same place — the minnows in a bottle, the plugs and spinners disarranged and pawed over by the youngsters from the boys' camp, the fig newtons and the Beeman's gum. Outside, the road was tarred and cars stood in front of the store. Inside, all was just as it had always been, except there was more Coca-Cola and not so much Moxie** and root beer and birch beer and sarsaparilla.*** We would walk out with a bottle of pop apiece and sometimes the pop would backfire up our noses and hurt. We explored the streams, quietly, where the turtles slid off the sunny logs and dug their way into the soft bottom; and we lay on the town wharf and fed worms to the tame bass. Everywhere we went I had trouble making out which was I, the one walking at my side, the one walking in my pants.

One afternoon while we were there at that lake a thunderstorm came up. It was like the revival of an old melodrama that I had seen long ago with childish awe. The second-act climax of the drama of the electrical disturbance over a lake in America had not changed in any important respect. This was the big scene, still the big scene. The whole thing was so familiar, the first feeling of oppression and heat and a general air around camp of

11

12

---

* EDS. NOTE — A member of an African tribe known for wearing mouth ornaments that stretch the lips into a saucerlike shape.
** EDS. NOTE — A soft drink that was popular in the early twentieth century.
*** EDS. NOTE — A sweetened carbonated beverage flavored with birch oil and sassafras.

not wanting to go very far away. In midafternoon (it was all the same) a curious darkening of the sky, and a lull in everything that had made life tick; and then the way the boats suddenly swung the other way at their moorings with the coming of a breeze out of the new quarter, and the premonitory rumble. Then the kettle drum, then the snare, then the bass drum and cymbals, then crackling light against the dark, and the gods grinning and licking their chops in the hills. Afterward the calm, the rain steadily rustling in the calm lake, the return of light and hope and spirits, and the campers running out in joy and relief to go swimming in the rain, their bright cries perpetuating the deathless joke about how they were getting simply drenched, and the children screaming with delight at the new sensation of bathing in the rain, and the joke about getting drenched linking the generations in a strong indestructible chain. And the comedian who waded in carrying an umbrella.

When the others went swimming my son said he was going in too. He 13 pulled his dripping trunks from the line where they had hung all through the shower, and wrung them out. Languidly, and with no thought of going in, I watched him, his hard little body, skinny and bare, saw him wince slightly as he pulled up around his vitals the small, soggy, icy garment. As he buckled the swollen belt suddenly my groin felt the chill of death.

• • •

Comprehension

1. How are the writer and his son alike? How are they different? What does White mean when he says, "I seemed to be living a dual existence" (4)?
2. In paragraph 5, White says that "no years" seemed to have gone by between past and present; elsewhere, he senses that things are different. How do you account for these conflicting feelings?
3. Why does White feel disconcerted when he discovers that the road to the farmhouse has two tracks, not three? What do you make of his comment that "now the choice was narrowed down to two" (7)?
4. How does sound "break the illusion and set the years moving" (10)?
5. What is White referring to in the essay's last sentence?

Purpose and Audience

1. What is the thesis of this essay? Is it stated or implied?
2. Do you think White expects the ending of his essay to surprise his audience? Explain.
3. What age group do you think this essay would appeal to most? Why?

Style and Structure

1. List the specific changes that have taken place on the lake. Does White emphasize these changes or play them down? Explain.

2. What ideas and images does White repeat throughout his essay? What is the purpose of this repetition?

3. White goes to great lengths to describe how things look, feel, smell, taste, and sound. How does this help him achieve his purpose in this essay?

4. How does White's conclusion echo the first paragraph of the essay?

Vocabulary Projects

1. Define each of the following words as it is used in this selection.

placidity (1)	pensively (5)	melodrama (12)
gunwale (2)	jollity (9)	premonitory (12)
primeval (3)	petulant (10)	perpetuating (12)
transposition (4)	imperceptibly (11)	languidly (13)

2. Underline ten words in the essay that refer to one of the five senses, and make a list of synonyms you could use for these words. How close do your substitutions come to capturing White's meaning?

Journal Entry

Do you identify more with the father or with the son in this essay? Why?

Writing Workshop

1. Write a description of a scene you remember from your childhood. In your essay, discuss how your current view of the scene differs from the view you had when you were a child.

2. Assume you are a travel agent. Write a descriptive brochure designed to bring tourists to the lake. Be specific, and stress the benefits White mentions in his essay.

3. Write an essay describing yourself from the perspective of one of your parents. Make sure your description conveys both the qualities your parent likes and the qualities he or she would want to change.

Combining the Patterns

White opens his essay with a short narrative about his first trip to the lake in 1904. How does this use of **narration** provide a context for the entire essay?

Thematic Connections

- "Only Daughter" (page 97)
- "Earth without People" (page 368)
- "Swollen Expectations" (page 422)

The Storm (Fiction)

Kate Chopin (1851–1904) was born Catherine O'Flaherty. In 1870, she married Oscar Chopin and moved with him to New Orleans. After suffering business reversals, the Chopins relocated to Cloutierville, Louisiana, to be closer to Oscar's extended Creole family. Oscar Chopin died suddenly in 1882, and Kate Chopin, left with six children to raise, returned to St. Louis. There she began writing short stories, many set in the colorful Creole country of central Louisiana. Her first collection, *Bayou Folk*, was published in 1894, followed by *A Night in Arcadie* in 1897. Her literary success was cut short, however, with the publication of her first novel, *The Awakening* (1899), a story of adultery that outraged many of her critics and readers because it was told sympathetically from a woman's perspective. Her work languished until the middle of the twentieth century, when it was rediscovered, largely by feminist literary scholars.

Background on Creole culture

The following story was probably written about the same time as *The Awakening*, but Chopin never attempted to publish it. Its frank sexuality — franker than that depicted in her controversial novel — and its focus on a liaison between two lovers (Calixta and Alcée) married to others would have been too scandalous for middle-class readers of the day. Even within the more liberal Creole culture in which the story is set, Calixta's actions would have been outrageous. While Creole men were expected to have mistresses (usually black or mixed-race women), Creole wives were expected to remain true to their wedding vows. The Creoles themselves were descendants of the early Spanish and French settlers in Louisiana, and they lived lives quite separate from — and, they believed, superior to — those whose ancestors were British. Their language became a mix of French and English, as did their mode of dress and cuisine. A strong Creole influence can still be found in New Orleans and the surrounding Louisiana countryside; Mardi Gras, for example, is a Creole tradition.

I

The leaves were so still that even Bibi thought it was going to rain. 1
Bobinôt, who was accustomed to converse on terms of perfect equality with his little son, called the child's attention to certain sombre clouds that were rolling with sinister intention from the west, accompanied by a sullen, threatening roar. They were at Friedheimer's store and decided to remain there till the storm had passed. They sat within the door on two empty kegs. Bibi was four years old and looked very wise.

"Mama'll be 'fraid, yes," he suggested with blinking eyes. 2

"She'll shut the house. Maybe she got Sylvie helpin' her this evenin'," 3
Bobinôt responded reassuringly.

"No; she ent got Sylvie. Sylvie was helpin' her yistiday," piped Bibi.   4

Bobinôt arose and going across to the counter purchased a can of   5
shrimps, of which Calixta was very fond. Then he returned to his perch on
the keg and sat stolidly holding the can of shrimps while the storm burst.
It shook the wooden store and seemed to be ripping great furrows in the
distant field. Bibi laid his little hand on his father's knee and was not
afraid.

II

Calixta, at home, felt no uneasiness for their safety. She sat at a side   6
window sewing furiously on a sewing machine. She was greatly occupied
and did not notice the approaching storm. But she felt very warm and
often stopped to mop her face on which the perspiration gathered in beads.
She unfastened her white sacque at the throat. It began to grow dark, and
suddenly realizing the situation she got up hurriedly and went about closing windows and doors.

Out on the small front gallery she had hung Bobinôt's Sunday clothes   7
to air and she hastened out to gather them before the rain fell. As she
stepped outside, Alcée Laballière rode in at the gate. She had not seen him
very often since her marriage, and never alone. She stood there with
Bobinôt's coat in her hands, and the big rain drops began to fall. Alcée rode
his horse under the shelter of a side projection where the chickens had
huddled and there were plows and a harrow piled up in the corner.

"May I come and wait on your gallery till the storm is over, Calixta?" he   8
asked.

"Come 'long in, M'sieur Alcée."   9

His voice and her own startled her as if from a trance, and she seized   10
Bobinôt's vest. Alcée, mounting to the porch, grabbed the trousers and
snatched Bibi's braided jacket that was about to be carried away by a sudden gust of wind. He expressed an intention to remain outside, but it was
soon apparent that he might as well have been out in the open: the water
beat in upon the boards in driving sheets, and he went inside, closing the
door after him. It was even necessary to put something beneath the door to
keep the water out.

"My! what a rain! It's good two years sence it rain' like that," exclaimed   11
Calixta as she rolled up a piece of bagging and Alcée helped her to thrust it
beneath the crack.

She was a little fuller of figure than five years before when she married;   12
but she had lost nothing of her vivacity. Her blue eyes still retained their
melting quality; and her yellow hair, dishevelled by the wind and rain,
kinked more stubbornly than ever about her ears and temples.

The rain beat upon the low, shingled roof with a force and clatter that   13
threatened to break an entrance and deluge them there. They were in the
dining room — the sitting room — the general utility room. Adjoining was
her bed room, with Bibi's couch along side her own. The door stood open,

and the room with its white, monumental bed, its closed shutters, looked dim and mysterious.

Alcée flung himself into a rocker and Calixta nervously began to gather up from the floor the lengths of a cotton sheet which she had been sewing. 14

"If this keeps up, *Dieu sait** if the levees goin' to stan' it!" she exclaimed. 15

"What have you got to do with the levees?" 16

"I got enough to do! An' there's Bobinôt with Bibi out in that storm — if he only didn't left Friedheimer's!" 17

"Let us hope, Calixta, that Bobinôt's got sense enough to come in out of a cyclone." 18

She went and stood at the window with a greatly disturbed look on her face. She wiped the frame that was clouded with moisture. It was stiflingly hot. Alcée got up and joined her at the window, looking over her shoulder. The rain was coming down in sheets obscuring the view of far-off cabins and enveloping the distant wood in a gray mist. The playing of the lightning was incessant. A bolt struck a tall chinaberry tree at the edge of the field. It filled all visible space with a blinding glare and the crash seemed to invade the very boards they stood upon. 19

Calixta put her hands to her eyes, and with a cry, staggered backward. Alcée's arm encircled her, and for an instant he drew her close and spasmodically to him. 20

"*Bonté!*"** she cried, releasing herself from his encircling arm and retreating from the window, "the house'll go next! If I only knew w'ere Bibi was!" She would not compose herself; she would not be seated. Alcée clasped her shoulders and looked into her face. The contact of her warm, palpitating body when he had unthinkingly drawn her into his arms, had aroused all the old-time infatuation and desire for her flesh. 21

"Calixta," he said, "don't be frightened. Nothing can happen. The house is too low to be struck, with so many tall trees standing about. There! aren't you going to be quiet? say, aren't you?" He pushed her hair back from her face that was warm and steaming. Her lips were as red and moist as pomegranate seed. Her white neck and a glimpse of her full, firm bosom disturbed him powerfully. As she glanced up at him the fear in her liquid blue eyes had given place to a drowsy gleam that unconsciously betrayed a sensuous desire. He looked down into her eyes and there was nothing for him to do but to gather her lips in a kiss. It reminded him of Assumption.*** 22

"Do you remember — in Assumption, Calixta?" he asked in a low voice broken by passion. Oh! she remembered; for in Assumption he had kissed her and kissed and kissed her; until his senses would well nigh fail, and to 23

---

* Eds. note — God knows.
** Eds. note — Goodness!
*** Eds. note — A parish near New Orleans.

save her he would resort to a desperate flight. If she was not an immaculate dove in those days, she was still inviolate; a passionate creature whose very defenselessness had made her defense, against which his honor forbade him to prevail. Now — well, now — her lips seemed in a manner free to be tasted, as well as her round, white throat and her whiter breasts.

They did not heed the crashing torrents, and the roar of the elements   24 made her laugh as she lay in his arms. She was a revelation in that dim, mysterious chamber; as white as the couch she lay upon. Her firm, elastic flesh that was knowing for the first time its birthright, was like a creamy lily that the sun invites to contribute its breath and perfume to the undying life of the world.

The generous abundance of her passion, without guile or trickery, was   25 like a white flame which penetrated and found response in depths of his own sensuous nature that had never yet been reached.

When he touched her breasts they gave themselves up in quivering   26 ecstasy, inviting his lips. Her mouth was a fountain of delight. And when he possessed her, they seemed to swoon together at the very borderland of life's mystery.

He stayed cushioned upon her, breathless, dazed, enervated, with his   27 heart beating like a hammer upon her. With one hand she clasped his head, her lips lightly touching his forehead. The other hand stroked with a soothing rhythm his muscular shoulders.

The growl of the thunder was distant and passing away. The rain beat   28 softly upon the shingles, inviting them to drowsiness and sleep. But they dared not yield.

The rain was over; and the sun was turning the glistening green world   29 into a palace of gems. Calixta, on the gallery, watched Alcée ride away. He turned and smiled at her with a beaming face; and she lifted her pretty chin in the air and laughed aloud.

III

Bobinôt and Bibi, trudging home, stopped without at the cistern to   30 make themselves presentable.

"My! Bibi, w'at will yo' mama say! You ought to be asham'. You oughtn'   31 put on those good pants. Look at 'em! An' that mud on yo' collar! How you got that mud on yo' collar, Bibi? I never saw such a boy!" Bibi was the picture of pathetic resignation. Bobinôt was the embodiment of serious solicitude as he strove to remove from his own person and his son's the signs of their tramp over heavy roads and through wet fields. He scraped the mud off Bibi's bare legs and feet with a stick and carefully removed all traces from his heavy brogans. Then, prepared for the worst — the meeting with an over-scrupulous housewife, they entered cautiously at the back door.

Calixta was preparing supper. She had set the table and was dripping   32 coffee at the hearth. She sprang up as they came in.

"Oh, Bobinôt! You back! My! but I was uneasy. W'ere you been during   33
the rain? An' Bibi? he ain't wet? he ain't hurt?" She had clasped Bibi and
was kissing him effusively. Bobinôt's explanations and apologies which he
had been composing all along the way, died on his lips as Calixta felt him
to see if he were dry, and seemed to express nothing but satisfaction at
their safe return.

"I brought you some shrimps, Calixta," offered Bobinôt, hauling the   34
can from his ample side pocket and laying it on the table.

"Shrimps! Oh, Bobinôt! you too good fo' anything!" and she gave him   35
a smacking kiss on the cheek that resounded. *"J'vous réponds,** we'll have a
feas' tonight! umph-umph!"

Bobinôt and Bibi began to relax and enjoy themselves, and when the   36
three sated themselves at table they laughed much and so loud that anyone
might have heard them as far away as Laballière's.

IV

Alcée Laballière wrote to his wife, Clarisse, that night. It was a loving   37
letter, full of tender solicitude. He told her not to hurry back, but if she and
the babies liked it at Biloxi, to stay a month longer. He was getting on
nicely; and though he missed them, he was willing to bear the separation a
while longer — realizing that their health and pleasure were the first things
to be considered.

V

As for Clarisse, she was charmed upon receiving her husband's letter.   38
She and the babies were doing well. The society was agreeable; many of her
old friends and acquaintances were at the bay. And the first free breath
since her marriage seemed to restore the pleasant liberty of her maiden
days. Devoted as she was to her husband, their intimate conjugal life was
something which she was more than willing to forego for a while.

So the storm passed and everyone was happy.   39

. . .

Reading Literature

1. How does the storm help set in motion the action of the story? List the
   events caused by the storm.
2. Is the last line of the story to be taken literally, or is it meant to be **ironic**
   (that is, does it actually suggest the opposite meaning)? Explain.
3. What do the story's specific descriptive details tell us about Calixta?

---

* EDS. NOTE — I tell you.

Journal Entry

On one level, the story's title refers to the storm that takes place through much of the story. To what else could the story's title refer?

Thematic Connections

- "Why Marriage Is Good for You" (page 227)
- "Sex, Lies, and Conversation" (page 436)
- "The Ways We Lie" (page 485)

WRITING ASSIGNMENTS FOR DESCRIPTION

1. Choose a character from a book or movie who you think is interesting. Write a descriptive essay conveying what makes this character so special.

2. Several of the essays in this chapter deal with the way journeys change how the writers see themselves. For example, in "Once More to the Lake," a visit to a campground forces E. B. White to confront his own mortality, and in "The Hidden Life of Garbage," a visit to a landfill outside Morrisville, Pennsylvania, enables Heather Rogers to grasp the enormity of the task of disposing of garbage in the United States. Write an essay describing a place that you traveled to. Make sure that, in addition to describing the place, you explain how it has taught you something about yourself.

3. Locate some photographs of your relatives. Describe three of these pictures, including details that provide insight into the lives of the people you discuss. Use your descriptive passages to support a thesis about your family.

4. Visit an art museum (or go to a museum site on the Web), and select a painting that interests you. Study it carefully, and then write an essay-length description of it. Before you write, decide how you will organize your details and whether you will write a subjective or an objective description. If possible, include a photograph of the painting in your essay. Be sure to document the photograph and to include a works-cited page. (See the Appendix for information on documentation formats.)

5. Select an object you are familiar with, and write an objective description of it. Include a diagram.

6. Assume you are writing an email to someone in another country who knows little about life in the United States. Describe to this person something you consider typically American — for example, a baseball stadium or a food court in a shopping mall.

7. Visit your college library, and write a brochure in which you describe the reference area. Be specific, and select an organizing scheme before you begin your description. Your purpose is to acquaint students with some of the reference materials they will use. If possible, include a diagram that will help orient students to this section of the library.

8. Describe your neighborhood to a visitor who knows nothing about it. Include as much specific detail as you can.

9. After reading "Ground Zero," write a description of a sight or scene that fascinated, surprised, or shocked you. Your description should explain why you were so deeply affected by what you saw.

10. Write an essay describing an especially frightening horror film. What specific sights and sounds make this film so horrifying? Include a thesis statement assessing the film's success as a horror film. (Be careful not to simply summarize the plot of the film.)

COLLABORATIVE ACTIVITY FOR DESCRIPTION

Working in groups of three or four students, select a famous person — one you can reasonably expect your classmates to recognize. Then, work as a group to write a description of that individual, including as much physical detail as possible. (Avoid any details that will be an instant giveaway.) Give your description a general title — *politician, television star,* or *person in the news,* for example. Finally, have one person read the description aloud to the class, and see whether your classmates can guess the person's identity.

8
Exemplification

WHAT IS EXEMPLIFICATION?

Exemplification uses one or more particular cases, or **examples**, to illustrate or explain a general point or an abstract concept. In the following paragraph from *Sexism and Language,* Alleen Pace Nilsen uses a number of well-chosen examples to illustrate her statement that the armed forces use words that have positive masculine connotations to encourage recruitment:

Topic sentence

> The armed forces, particularly the Marines, use the positive masculine connotation as part of their recruitment psychology. They promote the idea that to join the Marines (or the Army, Navy, or Air Force) guarantees that you will become a man. But this brings up a problem, because much of the work that is necessary to keep a large organization running is what is traditionally thought of as *woman's work.* Now, how can the Marines ask someone who has signed up for a *man-sized job* to do *woman's work?* Since they can't, they euphemize and give the jobs titles that are more prestigious or, at least, don't make people think of females. Waitresses are called *orderlies,* secretaries are called *clerktypists,* nurses are called *medics,* assistants are called *adjutants,* and cleaning up an area is called *policing* the area. The same kind of word glorification is used in civilian life to bolster a man's ego when he is doing such tasks as cooking and sewing. For example, a *chef* has higher prestige than a *cook* and a *tailor* has higher prestige than a *seamstress.*

Series of related examples

USING EXEMPLIFICATION

You have probably noticed, when watching television talk shows or listening to classroom discussions, that the most effective exchanges occur when participants support their points with specific examples. Sweeping generalizations and vague statements are not nearly as effective as specific observations, anecdotes, details, and opinions. It is one thing to say, "The mayor is corrupt and should not be reelected" and another to illustrate your point by saying, "The mayor should not be reelected because he has fired two city workers who refused to contribute to his campaign fund, has put his family and friends on the city payroll, and has used public employees to make improvements to his home." The same principle applies to writing: many of the most effective essays use examples extensively. Exemplification is used in every kind of writing situation to explain and clarify, to add interest, and to persuade.

Using Examples to Explain and Clarify

On a midterm exam in a film course, you might write, "Even though horror movies seem modern, they really aren't." You may think your statement is perfectly clear, but if this is all you say about horror movies, you should not be surprised if your exam comes back with a question mark in the margin next to this sentence. After all, you have only made a general statement about your subject. It is not specific, nor does it anticipate readers' questions about how horror movies are not modern. To be certain your audience knows exactly what you mean, state your point precisely: "Despite the fact that horror movies seem modern, two of the most memorable ones are adaptations of nineteenth-century Gothic novels." Then, use examples to ensure clarity and avoid ambiguity. For example, you could illustrate your point by discussing two films — *Frankenstein*, directed by James Whale, and *Dracula*, directed by Todd Browning — and linking them to the nineteenth-century novels they are based on. With the benefit of these specific examples, readers would know what you mean — that the literary roots of such movies are in the past, not that their cinematic techniques or production methods are dated. Moreover, readers would know which particular horror movies you are discussing.

Using Examples to Add Interest

Writers use well-chosen examples to add interest as well as to clarify their points. Laurence J. Peter and Raymond Hull do this in their essay "The Peter Principle," which appears later in this chapter. Their claim that employees in a system rise to a level of authority where they are incompetent is not particularly engaging. This statement becomes interesting, however, when supported by specific examples — the affable foreman who becomes the indecisive supervisor, the exacting mechanic who becomes the disorganized foreman, and the effective battlefield general who becomes the ineffective and self-destructive field marshal.

When you use exemplification, look for examples that are interesting as well as pertinent. Test the effectiveness of your examples by putting yourself in your readers' place. If you don't find your essay lively and absorbing, chances are your readers won't either. If this is the case, try to add more thought-provoking and spirited examples. After all, your goal is to communicate ideas to your readers, and imaginative examples can make the difference between an engrossing essay and one that is a chore to read.

Using Examples to Persuade

Although you may use examples to explain or to add interest, examples are also an effective way of persuading people that what you are saying is reasonable and worth considering. A few well-chosen examples can provide effective support for otherwise unconvincing general statements. For instance, a broad statement that school districts across the country cannot cope with the numerous students with limited English skills is one that needs support. If you make such a statement on an exam, you need to back it up with appropriate examples — such as that in one state, North Carolina, the number of students with limited English skills increased from 8,900 in 1993 to 52,500 in 2008. Similarly, a statement in a biology paper that DDT should continue to be banned is unconvincing without persuasive examples such as these to support it:

- Although DDT has been banned since December 31, 1972, scientists are finding traces in the eggs of various fish and waterfowl.
- Certain lakes and streams cannot be used for sport and recreation because DDT levels are dangerously high, presumably because of farmland runoff.
- Because of its stability as a compound, DDT does not degrade quickly; therefore, existing residues will threaten the environment well into the twenty-first century.

PLANNING AN EXEMPLIFICATION ESSAY

Developing a Thesis Statement

The **thesis statement** of an exemplification essay makes a point that the rest of the essay will support with examples. This statement usually identifies your topic as well as the main point you want to make about it.

The examples you gather during the invention stage of the writing process can help you develop your thesis. By doing so, they can help you test your ideas as well as the ideas of others. For instance, suppose you plan to write a paper for a composition class about students' writing skills. Your tentative thesis is that writing well is an inborn talent and that teachers can do little to help people write better. But is this really true? Has it been true in your own life? To test your point, you brainstorm about the various teachers you have had who tried to help you improve your writing.

As you assemble your list, you remember Mrs. Colson, a teacher you had in high school. She was strict, required lots of writing, and seemed to accept nothing less than perfection. At the time, neither you nor your class-mates liked her. But looking back, you recall her one-on-one conferences, her organized lessons, and her helpful comments on your essays. You real-ize that after completing her class, you felt much more comfortable writ-ing. When examining some papers you saved, you are surprised to see how much your writing actually improved during that year. These examples lead you to reevaluate your ideas and to revise your thesis:

> Even though some people seem to have a natural flair for writing, a good teacher can make a difference.

Providing Enough Examples

Unfortunately, no general rule exists to tell you when you have enough examples to support your ideas. The number you use depends on your the-sis statement. If, for instance, your thesis is that an educational institution, like a business, needs careful financial management, a single detailed examination of one college or university could provide all the information you need to make your point.

If, however, your thesis is that conflict between sons and fathers is a major theme in Franz Kafka's writing, more than one example would be necessary. A single example would show only that the theme is present in *one* of Kafka's works. In this case, the more examples you include, the more effectively you support your point.

For some thesis statements, however, even several examples would not be enough. Examples alone, for instance, could not demonstrate convinc-ingly that children from small families have more successful careers than children from large families. This thesis would have to be supported with a **statistical study** — that is, by collecting and interpreting numerical data representing a great many examples.

Choosing a Fair Range of Examples

Selecting a sufficient **range of examples** is just as important as choos-ing an appropriate number. If you want to persuade readers that Colin Powell was an able general, you should choose examples from several stages of his military career. Likewise, if you want to convince readers that out-door advertising ruins the scenic views from major highways, you should discuss an area larger than your immediate neighborhood. Your objective in each case is to choose a cross section of examples to represent the full range of your topic.

Similarly, if you want to argue for a ban on smoking in all public buildings, you should not limit your examples to restaurants. To be convincing, you should include examples involving many public places, such as office buildings, hotel lobbies, and sports stadiums. For the same reason, one person's experience is not enough to support a general conclusion involving many people unless you can establish that the experience is typical.

If you decide you cannot cite a fair range of examples that support your thesis, reexamine it. Rather than switching to a new topic, try to narrow your thesis. After all, the only way your paper will be convincing is if your readers believe that your thesis is supported by your examples and that your examples fairly represent the scope of your topic.

Of course, to be convincing you must not only *choose* examples effectively but also *use* them effectively. You should keep your thesis statement in mind as you write, taking care not to get so involved with one example that you digress from your main point. No matter how carefully developed, no matter how specific, lively, and appropriate, your examples accomplish nothing if they do not support your essay's main idea.

Using Transitions

Be sure to use transitional words and phrases to introduce your examples. Without them, readers will have difficulty seeing the connection between an example and the general statement it is illustrating. In some cases, transitions will help you connect examples to your thesis statement ("*Another* successful program for the homeless provides telephone answering services for job seekers"). In other cases, transitions will link examples to topic sentences ("*For instance,* I have written articles for my college newspaper"). In exemplification essays, the most frequently used transitions include *for example, for instance, in fact, namely, specifically, that is,* and *thus.* (A more complete list of transitions appears on page 43.)

STRUCTURING AN EXEMPLIFICATION ESSAY

Exemplification essays usually begin with an **introduction** that includes the **thesis statement**, which is supported by examples in the body of the essay. Each **body paragraph** may develop a separate example, present a point illustrated by several brief examples, or explore one aspect of a single extended example that is developed throughout the essay. The **conclusion** reinforces the essay's main idea, perhaps restating the thesis. At times, however, variations of this basic pattern are advisable and even necessary. For instance, beginning your paper with a striking example might stimulate your reader's interest and curiosity; ending with one might vividly reinforce your thesis.

Exemplification presents one special organizational problem. If you do not select your examples carefully and arrange them effectively, your paper can become a thesis statement followed by a list or by ten or fifteen brief, choppy paragraphs. One way to avoid this problem is to develop your best examples fully in separate paragraphs and to discard the others. Another effective strategy is to group related examples together in one paragraph.

Within each paragraph, you can arrange examples **chronologically**, beginning with those that occurred first and moving to those that occurred later. You can also arrange examples **in order of increasing complexity**, beginning with the simplest and moving to the most difficult or complex. Finally, you can arrange examples **in order of importance**, beginning with those that are less significant and moving to those that are most significant or persuasive.

The following informal outline for an essay evaluating the nursing care at a hospital illustrates one way to arrange examples. Notice how the writer presents his examples in order of increasing importance under three general headings — *patient rooms, emergency room,* and *clinics.*

Introduction:	Thesis statement — Because of its focus on the patient, the nursing care at Montgomery Hospital can serve as a model for other medical facilities.

In Patient Rooms

Example 1:	Being responsive
Example 2:	Establishing rapport
Example 3:	Delivering bedside care

In Emergency Room

Example 4:	Staffing treatment rooms
Example 5:	Circulating among patients in the waiting room
Example 6:	Maintaining good working relationships with physicians

In Clinics

Example 7:	Preparing patients
Example 8:	Assisting during treatment
Example 9:	Instructing patients after treatment
Conclusion:	Restatement of thesis or review of key points or examples

REVISING AN EXEMPLIFICATION ESSAY

When you revise an exemplification essay, consider the items on the revision checklist on page 54. In addition, pay special attention to the items on the following checklist, which apply specifically to exemplification essays.

✓ **REVISION CHECKLIST:** Exemplification

- Does your assignment call for exemplification?
- Does your essay have a clear thesis statement that identifies the point you will illustrate?
- Do your examples explain and clarify your thesis statement?
- Have you provided enough examples?
- Have you used a range of examples?
- Are your examples persuasive?
- Do your examples add interest?
- Have you used transitional words and phrases that reinforce the connection between your examples and your thesis statement?

EDITING AN EXEMPLIFICATION ESSAY

When you edit your exemplification essay, follow the guidelines on the editing checklists on pages 71, 74, and 76. In addition, focus on the grammar, mechanics, and punctuation issues that are most relevant to exemplification essays. One of these issues — using commas in a series — is discussed here.

GRAMMAR IN CONTEXT: Using Commas in a Series

When you write an exemplification essay, you often use a **series of examples** to support a statement or to illustrate a point. When you use a series of three or more examples in a sentence, you must remember to separate them with commas.

- Always use commas to separate three or more items — words, phrases, or clauses — in a series.

In "Just Walk On By," Brent Staples says, "I was surprised, embarrassed, and dismayed all at once" (237).

In "Just Walk On By," Staples observes that the woman thought she was being stalked by a mugger, by a rapist, or by something worse (237).

In "The Peter Principle," Laurence Peter says, "For example, my principal's main concerns were that all window shades be at the same level, that classrooms should be quiet, and that no one step on or near the rose beds" (Peter and Hull 216).

(continued on next page)

(continued from previous page)

According to Jonathan Kozol in "The Human Cost of an Illiterate Society," <u>illiterates cannot help with homework</u>, <u>they cannot write notes to teachers</u>, and <u>they cannot read school notices</u> (250).

NOTE: Although newspaper and magazine writers routinely leave out the comma before the last item in a series of three or more items, you should always include this comma in your college writing.

• Do not use a comma after the final element in a series of three or more items.

Incorrect: Staples was <u>shocked</u>, <u>horrified</u>, and <u>disillusioned</u>, to be taken for a mugger.

Correct: Staples was <u>shocked</u>, <u>horrified</u>, and <u>disillusioned</u> to be taken for a mugger.

• Do not use commas if all the elements in a series of three or more items are separated by coordinating conjunctions (*and, or, but,* and so on).

Peter and Hull believe that the Peter Principle controls everyone <u>in business</u> and <u>in government</u> and <u>in education</u>. *(no commas)*

For more practice in using commas in a series, visit Exercise Central at **bedfordstmartins.com/patterns/commas.**

✓ **EDITING CHECKLIST: Exemplification**

• Have you used commas to separate three or more items in a series?
• Have you made sure not to use a comma after the last element in a series?
• Have you made sure not to use a comma in a series with items separated by coordinating conjunctions?
• Are all the elements in a series stated in **parallel** terms (see page 390)?

A STUDENT WRITER: Exemplification

Exemplification is frequently used in nonacademic writing situations, such as business reports, memos, and proposals. One of the most important situations for using exemplification* is in a letter you write to apply for a job. Kristy Bredin's letter of application to a prospective employer follows.

---

* EDS. NOTE — In business letters, paragraphs are not indented and extra space is added between paragraphs.

1028 Geissinger Street
Bethlehem, PA 18018
September 7, 2008

Kim Goldstein
Rolling Stone
1290 Avenue of the Americas
New York, NY 10104

Dear Ms. Goldstein:

Introduction

I am writing to apply for the editorial internship with *Rolling Stone* magazine that you posted on Moravian College's

Thesis statement

employment Web site. I believe that both my academic experience and my experience in publishing qualify me for the position you advertised.   1

Examples

I am currently a senior at Moravian College, where I am majoring in English (with a concentration in creative writing) and music. Throughout my college career, I have maintained a 3.4 average. After I graduate in May, I would like to find a full-time job in publishing. For this reason, I am very interested in your internship. It would not only give me additional editorial and administrative experience, but it would also give me insight into a large-scale publishing operation. An internship at *Rolling Stone* would also enable to me to read, edit, and possibly write articles about popular music — a subject I know a lot about.   2

Examples

Throughout college, I have been involved in writing and editing. I have served as both secretary and president of the Literary Society and have written, edited, and published its annual newsletter. I have also worked as a tutor in Moravian's Writing Center; as a literature editor for the *Manuscript*, Moravian's literary magazine; and as a features editor for the *Comeneian*, the student newspaper. In these jobs I have gained a good deal of practical experience in publishing as well as insight into dealing with people. In addition, I acquired professional editing   3 experience this past semester when I worked as an intern for Taylor and Francis (Routledge) Publishing in New York.

Conclusion   I believe that my education and experience make me a   4
good candidate for your position. As your ad requested, I
have enclosed my résumé, three letters of reference,
information on Moravian's internship program, and
several writing samples for your consideration. You
can contact me by phone at (484) 625-6731 or by e-mail
at stkab@moravian.edu. I will be available for an
interview anytime after September 23. I look forward to
meeting with you to discuss my qualifications.

Sincerely,

Kristy Bredin

Kristy Bredin

Points for Special Attention

Organization.   Exemplification is ideally suited for letters of application. The only way Kristy Bredin can support her claims about her qualifications for the internship at *Rolling Stone* is to give examples of her educational and professional qualifications. For this reason, the body of her letter is divided into two categories — her educational record and her editorial experience.

Each of the body paragraphs has a clear purpose and function. The second paragraph contains two examples pertaining to Kristy's educational record. The third paragraph contains examples of her editorial experience. These examples tell the prospective employer what qualifies Kristy for the internship. Within these two body paragraphs, she arranges her examples in order of increasing importance. Because her practical experience as an editor relates directly to the position she is applying for, Kristy considers this her strongest point and presents it last.

Kristy ends her letter on a strong note, expressing her willingness to be interviewed and giving the first date she will be available for an interview. Because people remember best what they read last, a strong conclusion is essential here, just as it is in other writing situations.

Persuasive Examples.   To support a thesis convincingly, examples should convey specific information, not generalizations. Saying "I am a good student who is not afraid of responsibility" means very little. It is far better to say, as Kristy does, "Throughout my college career, I have maintained a 3.4 average" and "I have served as both secretary and president of the Literary Society." A letter of application should specifically show a prospective employer how your strengths and background correspond to the employer's needs; well-chosen examples can help you accomplish this goal.

Focus on Revision

After reading her letter, the students in Kristy's peer editing group identified several areas that they thought needed work.

One student thought Kristy should have mentioned her computer experience: she had taken a desktop publishing course as an elective and worked with publishing and graphics software when she was the features editor of the student newspaper. Kristy agreed that this expertise would make her a more attractive candidate for the job and thought she could work these examples into her third paragraph.

Another student asked Kristy to explain how her experience as secretary and president of the Literary Society relates to the job she is applying for. If her purpose is to show that she can assume responsibility, she should say so; if it is to illustrate that she can supervise others, she should make this clear.

Finally, a student suggested that she expand the discussion of her internship with Taylor and Francis Publishing in New York. Examples of her duties there would be persuasive because they would give her prospective employer a clear idea of her editorial experience. (A peer editing worksheet for exemplification can be found on pages 212–13.)

A STUDENT WRITER: Exemplification

The following essay by Grace Ku was written for a composition class in response to the following assignment: "Write an essay about the worst job you (or someone you know) ever had. If you can, include a quotation from one of the essays in your textbook. Make sure you include documentation as well as a works-cited page."

Midnight

Introduction   It was eight o'clock, and I was staring at the television   1
set wondering what kind of lesson Dr. Huxtable would teach his
children next on a rerun of *The Cosby Show*. I was glued to the
set like an average eleven-year-old couch potato while leisurely
eating cold Chef Boyardee spaghetti out of the can. As I
watched the show, I fell asleep on the floor fully clothed in a

pair of jeans and a T-shirt, wondering when my parents would come home. Around midnight I woke up to a rustling noise: my parents had finally arrived from a long day at work. I could see in their tired faces the grief and hardship of working at a dry-cleaning plant.

Thesis statement

Transitional paragraph provides background

Although my parents lived in the most technologically advanced country in the world, their working conditions were like those of nineteenth-century factory workers. Because they were immigrants with little formal education and spoke broken English, they could get jobs only as laborers. Therefore, they worked at a dry-cleaning plant that was as big as a factory, a place where hundreds of small neighborhood cleaners sent their clothes to be processed. Like Bonnie Smith-Yackel's mother in the essay "My Mother Never Worked," my parents constantly "struggled to regain some competence and dignity and order" in their lives (116).

Quotation from essay in textbook

Series of brief examples: physical demands

At work, my parents had to meet certain quotas. Each day they had to clean and press several hundred garments — shirts, pants, and other clothing. By themselves, every day, they did the work of four laborers. The muscles of my mother's shoulders and arms grew hard as iron from working with the press, a difficult job even for a man. In addition to pressing, my father operated the washing machines. As a result, his work clothes always smelled of oil.

Example: long hours

Not only were my parents' jobs physically demanding, but they also required long hours. My parents went to work at five o'clock in the morning and came home between nine o'clock at night and midnight. Each day they worked over twelve hours at the dry-cleaning plant, where eight-hour workdays and labor unions did not exist. They were allowed to take only two ten- to twenty-minute breaks — one for lunch and one for dinner. They did not stop even when they were burned by a hot iron or by steam rising from a press. The scars on their arms made it obvious that they worked at a dry-cleaning plant. My parents' burned skin would blister and later peel off, exposing raw flesh. In time, these injuries would heal, but other burns would soon follow.

Example: frequent burns

Example: low pay

In addition to having to work long hours and suffering painful injuries, my parents were paid below minimum wage. Together their paychecks were equal to that of a single

2

3

4

5

unionized worker (even though they did the work of four). They used this money to feed and care for a household of five people.

Conclusion

As my parents silently entered our home around midnight, they did not have to complain about their jobs. I could see their anguish in their faces and their fatigue in the slow movements of their bodies. Even though they did not

Restatement of thesis

speak, their eyes said, "We hate our jobs, but we work so that our children will have better lives than we do."

6

Works Cited

Smith-Yackel, Bonnie. "My Mother Never Worked." *Patterns for College Writing: A Rhetorical Reader and Guide*. 11th ed. Ed. Laurie G. Kirszner and Stephen R. Mandell. New York: Bedford, 2010. 114. Print.

Points for Special Attention

Organization.   Grace Ku begins her introduction by describing herself as an eleven-year-old sitting on the floor watching television. At first, her behavior seems typical of many American children, but two things suggest problems: first, she is eating her cold dinner out of a can, and, second, even though it is late in the evening, she is still waiting for her parents to return from work. This opening prepares readers for her thesis that her parents' jobs produce only grief and hardship.

In the body of her essay, Grace presents the examples that support her thesis statement. In paragraph 2, she sets the stage for the discussion to follow, explaining that her parents' workingw conditions were similar to those of nineteenth-century factory workers. At the end of paragraph 2, Grace includes a quotation from Bonnie Smith-Yackel's essay "My Mother Never Worked" that helps her put her parents' struggles in perspective. In paragraph 3, she presents a series of examples that illustrate how physically demanding her parents' jobs were. In the remaining body paragraphs, she gives three other examples to show how unpleasant the jobs were — how long her parents worked, how often they were injured, and how little they were paid.

Grace concludes her essay by returning to the scene in her introduction, using a quotation that she wants to stay with her readers after they have finished the essay.

Enough Examples.   Certainly no single example, no matter how graphic, could adequately support the thesis of this essay. To establish the pain and difficulty of her parents' jobs, Grace uses several examples. Although additional examples would have added even more depth to the essay, the ones she uses are vivid and compelling enough to reinforce her thesis that her parents had to endure great hardship to make a living.

Range of Examples. Grace selects examples that illustrate the full range of her subject. She draws from her parents' daily experience and does not include atypical examples. She also includes enough detail so that her readers, who she assumes do not know much about working in a dry-cleaning plant, will understand her points. She does not, however, provide so much detail that her readers get bogged down and lose interest.

Effective Examples. All of Grace's examples support her thesis statement. While developing these examples, she never loses sight of her main idea; consequently, she does not get sidetracked in irrelevant discussions. She also avoids the temptation to preach to her readers about the injustice of her parents' situation. By allowing her examples to speak for themselves, Grace paints a powerful portrait of her parents and their hardships.

Focus on Revision

After reading this draft, a peer critic thought Grace could go into more detail about her parents' situation and could explain her examples in more depth — perhaps writing about the quotas her parents had to meet or the other physical dangers of their jobs.

Grace herself thought she should expand the discussion in paragraph 5 about her parents' low wages, perhaps anticipating questions some of her readers might have about working conditions. For example, was it legal for her parents' employer to require them to work overtime without compensation or to pay them less than the minimum wage? If not, how was the employer able to get away with such practices?

Grace also thought she should move the information about her parents' work-related injuries from paragraph 4 to paragraph 3, where she discusses the physical demands of their jobs.

Finally, she decided to follow the advice of another student and include comments by her parents to make their experiences more immediate to readers.

📄 **PEER EDITING WORKSHEET: Exemplification**

1. What strategy does the writer use in the essay's introduction? Would another strategy be more effective?

2. What is the essay's thesis? Does it make a point that the rest of the essay will support with examples?

3. What specific points do the body paragraphs make?

4. Does the writer use one example or several to illustrate each point? Should the writer use more examples? Fewer? Explain.

5. Does the writer use a sufficient range of examples? Are they explained in enough depth?

6. Do the examples add interest? How persuasive are they? List a few other examples that might be more persuasive.

7. What transitional words and phrases does the writer use to introduce examples? What other transitional words and phrases should be added? Where?

8. In what order are the examples presented? Would another order be more effective? Explain.

9. Has the writer used a series of three or more examples in a single sentence? If so, are these examples separated by commas?

10. What strategy does the writer use in the conclusion? What other strategy could be used?

The selections in this chapter all depend on exemplification to explain and clarify, to add interest, or to persuade. The first selection, a visual text, is followed by questions designed to illustrate how exemplification can operate in visual form.

ALEX WILLIAMS, JOEL GORDON,
CHARLES GATEWOOD, AND BOB DAEMMRICH*

Four Tattoos (Photos)

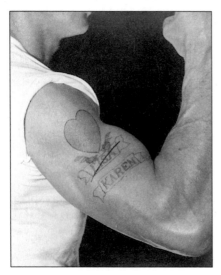

Alex Williams, "~~Lisa~~, Karen"

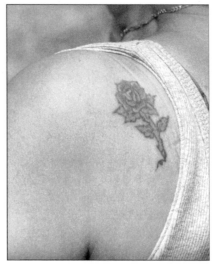

Joel Gordon, "Rose"

Bob Daemmrich, "Jiminy Cricket"

Charles Gatewood, "Body Art"

---

* Photos shown clockwise from top left.

. . .

Reading Images

1. How would you describe each of the four tattoos pictured on the previous page? List the prominent features of each, and then write two or three sentences that describe each of them.

2. After studying the four pictures (and reviewing your answer to question 1), write a one-sentence general statement that sums up your ideas about tattoos. For example, why do you think people get tattoos? Do you see them as a way for people to express themselves? As a way of demonstrating individuality? As a form of rebellion? As an impulsive act? As something else?

3. List several examples that support the general statement you made in question 2. What examples could you use to support this general statement?

Journal Entry

Would you ever get a tattoo? Write a paragraph answering this question. Use your answers to the questions above to support the main idea in your topic sentence. (If you have a tattoo, give several reasons why you decided to get it.)

Thematic Connections

- "Medium Ash Brown" (page 275)
- "My First Conk" (page 282)
- "The Embalming of Mr. Jones" (page 304)
- "The Wife-Beater" (page 528)

The Peter Principle

Laurence J. Peter (1919–1990), an academic and education specialist, and Raymond Hull (1919–1985), a humorist and playwright, collaborated on the 1969 best-seller *The Peter Principle: Why Things Always Go Wrong*. In the preface to the book, Hull explained that he had become increasingly appalled at the number of problems people experienced with businesses and organizations, from those of trifling significance (bills going to an old address despite numerous attempts to give the business a new one) to ones of catastrophic importance (bridges collapsing only a few years after construction). Dr. Peter, Hull discovered, had the explanation for such widespread ineptitude: within any hierarchy, employees tend to be promoted to a level where they are incompetent to perform the duties of the position. Within a short time of the publication of their book, the term *Peter Principle* had entered the language.

Background on corporations

During the 1950s, large corporations were widely perceived as models of efficiency. By the late 1960s, however, large bureaucracies seemed to be increasingly unresponsive, riddled with red tape, and demoralizing for workers. Peter and Hull's idea that most corporations were run by executives and managers who were simply out of their depth flew in the face of conventional 1950s wisdom and provided an explanation for 1960s corporate failings. The meteoric rise and subsequent crash of many Web-based business ventures in the late 1990s and the stunning demise in the years that followed of supposedly model corporations (such as Enron and WorldCom) suggest that Peter and Hull's analysis may still be valid.

When I was a boy I was taught that the men upstairs knew what they 1
were doing. I was told, "Peter, the more you know, the further you go." So I stayed in school until I graduated from college and then went forth into the world clutching firmly these ideas and my new teaching certificate. During the first year of teaching I was upset to find that a number of teachers, school principals, supervisors, and superintendents appeared to be unaware of their professional responsibilities and incompetent in executing their duties. For example, my principal's main concerns were that all window shades be at the same level, that classrooms should be quiet, and that no one step on or near the rose beds. The superintendent's main concerns were that no minority group, no matter how fanatical, should ever be offended and that all official forms be submitted on time. The children's education appeared farthest from the administrator's mind.

At first I thought this was a special weakness of the school system in   2
which I taught so I applied for certification in another province.* I filled
out the special forms, enclosed the required documents, and complied willingly with all the red tape. Several weeks later, back came my application
and all the documents!

No, there was nothing wrong with my credentials; the forms were cor-   3
rectly filled out; an official departmental stamp showed that they had been
received in good order. But an accompanying letter said, "The new regulations require that such forms cannot be accepted by the Department of
Education unless they have been registered at the Post Office to ensure safe
delivery. Will you please remail the forms to the Department, making sure
to register them this time?"

I began to suspect that the local school system did not have a monop-   4
oly on incompetence.

As I looked further afield, I saw that every organization contained a   5
number of persons who could not do their jobs.

A Universal Phenomenon

Occupational incompetence is everywhere. Have you noticed it? Prob-   6
ably we have all noticed it.

We see indecisive politicians posing as resolute statesmen and the   7
"authoritative source" who blames his misinformation on "situational
imponderables." Limitless are the public servants who are indolent and
insolent, military commanders whose behavioral timidity belies their
dreadnought rhetoric, and governors whose innate servility prevents their
actually governing. In our sophistication, we virtually shrug aside the
immoral cleric, corrupt judge, incoherent attorney, author who cannot
write, and English teacher who cannot spell. At universities we see procla-
mations authored by administrators whose own office communications
are hopelessly muddled, and droning lectures from inaudible or incompre-
hensible instructors.

Seeing incompetence at all levels of every hierarchy — political, legal,   8
educational, and industrial — I hypothesized that the cause was some
inherent feature of the rules governing the placement of employees. Thus
began my serious study of the ways in which employees move upward
through a hierarchy, and of what happens to them after promotion.

For my scientific data hundreds of case histories were collected. Here   9
are three typical examples.

---

* EDS. NOTE — An administrative district of a country, similar to a state; in this case,
in Canada.

Municipal Government File, Case No. 17

J. S. Minion* was a maintenance foreman in the public works department of Excelsior City. He was a favorite of the senior officials at City Hall. They all praised his unfailing affability.

"I like Minion," said the superintendent of works. "He has good judgment and is always pleasant and agreeable."

This behavior was appropriate for Minion's position: he was not supposed to make policy, so he had no need to disagree with his superiors.

The superintendent of works retired and Minion succeeded him. Minion continued to agree with everyone. He passed to his foreman every suggestion that came from above. The resulting conflicts in policy, and the continual changing of plans, soon demoralized the department. Complaints poured in from the Mayor and other officials, from taxpayers and from the maintenance-workers' union.

Minion still says "Yes" to everyone, and carries messages briskly back and forth between his superiors and his subordinates. Nominally a superintendent, he actually does the work of a messenger. The maintenance department regularly exceeds its budget, yet fails to fulfill its program of work. In short, Minion, a competent foreman, became an incompetent superintendent.

Service Industries File, Case No. 3

E. Tinker was exceptionally zealous and intelligent as an apprentice at G. Reece Auto Repair Inc., and soon rose to journeyman mechanic. In this job he showed outstanding ability in diagnosing obscure faults, and endless patience in correcting them. He was promoted to foreman of the repair shop.

But here his love of things mechanical and his perfectionism became liabilities. He will undertake any job that he thinks looks interesting, no matter how busy the shop may be. "We'll work it in somehow," he says.

He will not let a job go until he is fully satisfied with it.

He meddles constantly. He is seldom to be found at his desk. He is usually up to his elbows in a dismantled motor and while the man who should be doing the work stands watching, other workmen sit around waiting to be assigned new tasks. As a result the shop is always overcrowded with work, always in a muddle, and delivery times are often missed.

Tinker cannot understand that the average customer cares little about perfection — he wants his car back on time! He cannot understand that most of his men are less interested in motors than in their pay checks. So Tinker cannot get on with his customers or with his subordinates. He was a competent mechanic, but is now an incompetent foreman.

---

* Some names have been changed, in order to protect the guilty.

Military File, Case No. 8

Consider the case of the late renowned General A. Goodwin. His hearty,   20
informal manner, his racy style of speech, his scorn for petty regulations,
and his undoubted personal bravery made him the idol of his men. He led
them to many well-deserved victories.

When Goodwin was promoted to field marshal he had to deal, not   21
with ordinary soldiers, but with politicians and allied generalissimos.

He would not conform to the necessary protocol. He could not turn   22
his tongue to the conventional courtesies and flatteries. He quarreled with
all the dignitaries and took to lying for days at a time, drunk and sulking,
in his trailer. The conduct of the war slipped out of his hands into those of
his subordinates. He had been promoted to a position that he was incompetent to fill.

An Important Clue

In time I saw that all such cases had a common feature. The employee   23
had been promoted from a position of competence to a position of incompetence. I saw that, sooner or later, this could happen to every employee in
every hierarchy.

Hypothetical Case File, Case No. 1

Suppose you own a pill-rolling factory, Perfect Pill Incorporated. Your   24
foreman pill roller dies of a perforated ulcer. You need a replacement. You
naturally look among your rank-and-file pill rollers.

Miss Oval, Mrs. Cylinder, Mr. Ellipse, and Mr. Cube all show various   25
degrees of incompetence. They will naturally be ineligible for promotion.
You will choose — other things being equal — your most competent pill
roller, Mr. Sphere, and promote him to foreman.

Now suppose Mr. Sphere proves competent as foreman. Later, when   26
your general foreman, Legree, moves up to Works Manager, Sphere will be
eligible to take his place.

If, on the other hand, Sphere is an incompetent foreman, he will get no   27
more promotion. He has reached what I call his "level of incompetence."
He will stay there till the end of his career.

Some employees, like Ellipse and Cube, reach a level of incompetence   28
in the lowest grade and are never promoted. Some, like Sphere (assuming
he is not a satisfactory foreman), reach it after one promotion.

E. Tinker, the automobile repair-shop foreman, reached his level of   29
incompetence on the third stage of the hierarchy. General Goodwin reached
his level of incompetence at the very top of the hierarchy.

So my analysis of hundreds of cases of occupational incompetence led   30
me on to formulate *The Peter Principle:*

In a Hierarchy Every Employee Tends to Rise to His Level of Incompetence.

A New Science!

Having formulated the Principle, I discovered that I had inadvertently   31
founded a new science, hierarchiology, the study of hierarchies.

The term "hierarchy" was originally used to describe the system of   32
church government by priests graded into ranks. The contemporary meaning includes any organization whose members or employees are arranged
in order of rank, grade, or class.

Hierarchiology, although a relatively recent discipline, appears to have   33
great applicability to the fields of public and private administration.

This Means You!

My Principle is the key to an understanding of all hierarchical systems,   34
and therefore to an understanding of the whole structure of civilization. A
few eccentrics try to avoid getting involved with hierarchies, but everyone
in business, industry, trade-unionism, politics, government, the armed
forces, religion, and education is so involved. All of them are controlled by
the Peter Principle.

Many of them, to be sure, may win a promotion or two, moving from   35
one level of competence to a higher level of competence. But competence in
that new position qualifies them for still another promotion. For each
individual, for *you,* for *me,* the final promotion is from a level of competence to a level of incompetence.*

So, given enough time — and assuming the existence of enough ranks   36
in the hierarchy — each employee rises to, and remains at, his level of
incompetence. Peter's Corollary states:

> *In time, every post tends to be occupied by an employee who is incompetent to carry
> out its duties.*

Who Turns the Wheels?

You will rarely find, of course, a system in which *every* employee has   37
reached his level of incompetence. In most instances, something is being
done to further the ostensible purposes for which the hierarchy exists.

> *Work is accomplished by those employees who have not yet reached their level of
> incompetence.*

·   ·   ·

---

* The phenomena of "percussive sublimation" (commonly referred to as "being
kicked upstairs") and of "the lateral arabesque" are not, as the casual observer might
think, exceptions to the Principle. They are only pseudo-promotions. . . .

Comprehension

1. What things disillusioned Peter during his first year of teaching? What did he discover about organizations?

2. What is the Peter Principle? According to Peter and Hull, what happens when employees reach their "level of incompetence" (30)?

3. What do Peter and Hull mean by *hierarchiology* (31)? How did hierarchiology lead Peter to the Peter Principle?

4. If the Peter Principle operates in hierarchies such as corporations, who does the work?

Purpose and Audience

1. Is this essay aimed at a general audience or an expert audience? What led you to your conclusion?

2. What is the essay's thesis? At what point in the essay does the thesis statement appear? Why do you think Peter and Hull wait so long to state it?

3. How serious are Peter and Hull? What words or phrases indicate whether their purpose is to instruct or to entertain — or both?

Style and Structure

1. Why do you think Peter and Hull begin the essay with an example? Why do they present a series of brief examples before introducing the typical case histories?

2. Why do Peter and Hull say they collected hundreds of case histories for data? How are the three case histories analyzed here typical?

3. Does the use of hypothetical examples strengthen or weaken the writers' case? Explain.

4. Do Peter and Hull use a sufficiently wide range of examples? Explain.

Vocabulary Projects

1. Define each of the following words as it is used in this selection.

imponderables (7)	incomprehensible (7)	protocol (22)
indolent (7)	hypothesized (8)	subordinates (22)
insolent (7)	hierarchy (8)	eccentrics (34)
dreadnought (7)	minion (10)	ostensible (37)
inaudible (7)	dismantled (18)	

2. Do Peter and Hull use **figures of speech** in their discussion? Why do you think they do or do not?

Journal Entry

What examples of the Peter Principle have you encountered in your life?

Writing Workshop

1. Do Peter and Hull overstate their case? Write an email to them in the form of an exemplification essay pointing out the weaknesses of their position.

2. Study a school, business, or organization that you know well. Write an exemplification essay showing how the Peter Principle applies (or does not apply).

3. Do you know someone who has progressed to the highest level of his or her incompetence? Assume that you are that person's supervisor and that you have been told to write an evaluation of his or her job performance. Write your evaluation in the form of an exemplification essay. Supporting your thesis with several examples, show how the Peter Principle does (or does not) apply. If you can, use ideas (or a quotation) from "The Peter Principle" to support your points. Make sure that you document words and ideas from "The Peter Principle" and that you include a works-cited page. (See the Appendix for information on documentation formats.)

Combining the Patterns

Peter and Hull use a series of narrative examples. What are the advantages and disadvantages of using **narration** here? Would other kinds of examples — such as statistics — have been more effective? Explain.

Thematic Connections

- "Shooting an Elephant" (page 126)
- "Getting Coffee Is Hard to Do" (page 287)
- "Fame-iness" (page 532)
- "What Work Is" (page 542)
- "The Case for Wal-Mart" (page 631)

DAVID J. BIRNBAUM

The Catbird Seat

David J. Birnbaum was born in 1963 in Brooklyn, New York. A manager with AT&T, he also contributes essays to a number of publications. As he explains in the following essay, he lost the use of his legs in an auto accident and now uses a wheelchair to move about. The essay originally appeared in 1998 in the *New York Times Magazine*'s "Lives" column, where people from a variety of backgrounds write about their experiences.

Background on the 1990 Americans with Disabilities Act

Approximately 19 percent of Americans, representing about 49 million people, have some form of disability, and almost half of these are considered severely disabled. An estimated 15 percent (about 38 million people) have disabilities that limit their physical activity.

The 1990 Americans with Disabilities Act, which Birnbaum refers to in paragraph 11, requires that reasonable accommodation be made in areas of educational opportunity, employment, government services, and access to businesses open to the general public, and it further prohibits discrimination against people with disabilities. Noncompliance with the act can result in fines, and perceived noncompliance has resulted in a number of lawsuits, which have raised questions about who can legitimately be considered disabled and what, in fact, constitutes "reasonable" accommodation. As Birnbaum suggests, due to various ambiguities in the wording of the act and to some of the loopholes contained in it, many establishments are still not in full compliance; this remains a sore point for advocates for the disabled.

1   I wasn't in a hurry to get back to my hospital room, but I had a lot on my mind. I was adjusting to my new fate, quadriplegia. Besides, I had been waiting at least three minutes for the elevator, which in teenage time is three years. When I heard the ding, I dashed into the car, unintentionally cutting off the handful of other riders.

2   "What's the big hurry?" a pregnant woman asked. An elderly Asian man chimed in: "Leave the young man alone. He's in a wheelchair!"

3   That was the first time I felt my new place in society. A few months later, my friend Roy and I were in the back of a ticketholders' line that was clogging 34th Street waiting to see *The Empire Strikes Back* at the Murray Hill cinema. Suddenly an usher appeared and asked us to follow him into the theater. Despite the drizzle, the other patrons didn't seem to mind that we were cutting ahead. I was the only one in line that had a chair to sit in. Yet I didn't have to wait. Thereafter, I began to cut ahead often. Cashing a check at Chase, I'd ignore the velvet ropes and go straight to a teller. Registering for classes at N.Y.U., I cut three lines in one day: department approval, course selection, and, finally, registrar payment. Older people

who only a few months earlier would have ignored a teenager with long hair began acting very friendly. Senior citizens still smile at me seventeen years after I crashed my car in Park Slope, breaking my neck, just days before my eighteenth birthday. Are they trying to cheer me up? Maybe they just see me as nonthreatening. They're probably thinking, "This guy is less than half my age, but I can still beat him up."

Soon after leaving the hospital, I realized I could now break rules. I would sneak cans of beer into concerts at Madison Square Garden. At the queue where teenagers are routinely patted down, the guards held up the process for me: "Please step back, we gotta wheelchair coming through!"

When I leave Staples, I tell the security guard that I need the plastic shopping basket to carry my goods to my van. He nods his head trustingly, on the assumption that I'll unload and return it. I have five of these red baskets in my hallway closet. I don't know what I'm going to do with them. I just get a kick driving them home.

Before I left Jamaica last January, I hid a box of Cuban cigars in my canvas case. As I passed through customs at Newark International Airport, a woman in a brown uniform looked at my two large bags suspiciously. Perusing the card I filled out on the plane, she asked, "Nothing to declare?"

"Nothing."

"What's the canvas bag for?"

"It's a portable handicap shower seat," I replied truthfully.

"Oh . . . I'm so sorry. Go ahead."

Cutting the lines at the Department of Motor Vehicles to renew my driver's license, getting out of speeding tickets and arriving late to work without a reprimand are my "even uppers" for my physical limitations and for the difficulties caused by establishments not complying with the Americans with Disabilities Act. I had to sit behind the last row in a theater, separated from my college friends, only once before I stopped being too proud to accept the senior citizens' discount offered by sympathetic employees. When the purser offered to bump me up into first class on that flight from Jamaica, I didn't say: "No, thank you. I've accepted my disability, I have a successful career and live independently. Please treat me like everyone else." I didn't care whether she was condescending, sympathizing, or patronizing. I was just glad to be in "2B" sipping Chardonnay while I eyed the coach passengers frantically seeking space for their carry-on luggage and duty-free rum.

After sneaking my cigars through customs, I headed upstairs to get a taxi. Three carloads of tired travelers, dragging luggage with and without wheels, were waiting for a single elevator to arrive. I waited like an Olympic sprinter anticipating the starting gun. I began inching my wheelchair forward, but accidentally wheeled over some guy's foot.

"Oww!" he turned around, saw my wheelchair and then followed nervously with, "Oh, I'm ss . . . sss . . . sorry." He stepped to the side, leaving me perfectly positioned in front of the sliding aluminum doors. The "L" on the display lighted, the ding went off, the doors opened, and I swiftly pushed my chair forward into the car.

"What's wrong with you?" A well-tanned girl asked me angrily. I looked her in the eye with cockiness, expecting my usual support from others. But it didn't come. 14

"Have some respect, for God's sake!" she continued, holding the door open for a middle-aged man with dark glasses and a white cane. 15

There in the elevator, as everyone looked at me in disgust, I learned the pecking order: blind trumps wheelchair; wheelchair trumps pregnant; pregnant trumps old; old trumps whatever is left. 16

· · ·

Comprehension

1. What "new place in society" does Birnbaum occupy after his accident (3)?
2. How does Birnbaum take advantage of his new status?
3. According to Birnbaum, how are cutting in line, avoiding speeding tickets, and getting to work late his "even uppers" (11)?
4. What incident causes Birnbaum to realize that the advantages he gets from his disability have limitations?

Purpose and Audience

1. What preconceptions about the disabled does Birnbaum assume his readers have? How can you tell?
2. Why does Birnbaum wait until paragraph 16 to state his thesis? Should he have stated it sooner? Explain.
3. Birnbaum is aiming his essay at a general audience. How would his essay be different if he were addressing health-care professionals? Other people with disabilities?
4. What is Birnbaum's purpose in writing this essay? For example, does he want to educate his readers? To persuade them? Or does he have some other purpose?

Style and Structure

1. Birnbaum begins his essay with an example. Is this an effective introductory strategy? Should he have used a more formal introduction?
2. All of Birnbaum's examples are drawn from his own experience. Does this reliance on personal experience make his essay more (or less) convincing? Explain.
3. How does Birnbaum arrange his examples? Is this arrangement effective? Explain.
4. How are the ideas in Birnbaum's first example (1–2) echoed in his conclusion?

Vocabulary Projects

1. Define each of the following words as it is used in this selection.

   quadriplegia (1)   patronizing (11)
   reprimand (11)   Chardonnay (11)
   purser (11)   trumps (16)
   condescending (11)

2. What terms does Birnbaum use to refer to his physical condition? What other terms could he have used? What different connotations do these terms have?

3. Someone in a positon of power or prominence is said to be "in the catbird seat." Why does Birnbaum use this expression as his title? Is he being serious or **ironic**?

Journal Entry

Do you think people with disabilities have advantages that others do not have? Do you think Birnbaum should have special privileges because of his disability?

Writing Workshop

1. Write an email to Birnbaum agreeing or disagreeing with his actions. Do you think he should reject the benefits conferred on him because he has a disability? Or do you think these benefits are justified given his physical limitations?

2. A **stereotype** is an oversimplified concept or image. Write an essay discussing three stereotypes of people with disabilities that many people share. How accurate are these stereotypes? What could (or should) be done to eliminate them?

3. Write an editorial for your school newspaper discussing how your school could do more to help students with physical disabilities. To support your thesis, include specific examples of changes that could be made. You might begin by visiting the Americans with Disabilities Web site at ada.gov.

Combining the Patterns

Choose four or five examples that Birnbaum uses in his essay. What other patterns of development does he use in presenting these examples? Does any single pattern predominate? If so, why?

Thematic Connections

- "Words Left Unspoken" (page 172)
- "The Human Cost of an Illiterate Society" (page 248)
- "On Dumpster Diving" (page 714)

Why Marriage Is Good for You

Maggie Gallagher (b. 1960) is a nationally syndicated columnist whose essays have appeared in *Newsday, USA Today,* the *New York Times,* and elsewhere. A former editor with the conservative weekly *National Review,* she is a founding senior editor of the Manhattan Institute's *City Journal,* where the following essay originally appeared. A one-time single mother, Gallagher has become a leading voice in promoting the value of marriage, both as president of the Institute for Marriage and Public Policy and as the author of books such as *The Case for Marriage: Why Married People Are Happier, Healthier, and Better-Off Financially* (2001) and *The Case for Staying Married* (2005), both with Linda J. Waite. She makes frequent media appearances and is a popular lecturer on a variety of social issues.

Background on marriage trends

Attitudes toward marriage and divorce have shifted dramatically in the United States over the last half century. Sixty years ago, marriage was the norm, and most children grew up with both biological parents in the household; today that figure has dropped to only about 60 percent. Of women who married in the 1950s, only 14 percent would eventually divorce; today, close to half of all marriages end in divorce, and the number of single mothers has risen from around two million to more than ten million. At the same time, marriage rates have declined, and the number of unmarried heterosexual couples living together — an arrangement almost unheard of in the 1950s — has climbed to five million; in fact, a majority of marriages today begin with cohabitation. The number of people who have never been married is up 6 percent from the 1950s, and people who marry do so later (the average age for marriage is now twenty-six, five years older than it was in 1950). Even as marriage rates have declined among heterosexual couples, same-sex couples have petitioned to be allowed to marry; while only two states, Massachusetts and California, sanction same-sex marriage, eight other states and the District of Columbia grant legal domestic partnerships or civil unions to same-sex couples. It is within this context that a "new marriage" movement, of which Gallagher is a part, has arisen, promoting a return to more traditional views of marriage.

When Americans debate the value of marriage, most attention focuses on the potential harm to children of divorce or illegitimacy, and for good reason. Mountains of research tell us that children reared outside of intact marriages are much more likely than other kids to slip into poverty, become victims of child abuse, fail at school and drop out, use illegal drugs, launch into premature sexual activity, become unwed teen mothers, divorce, commit suicide and experience other signs of mental illness, become physically ill, and commit crimes and go to jail. On average, children reared outside

1

of marriage are less successful in their careers, even after controlling not only for income but also for parental conflict.

Yes, marriage protects children. And yes, marriage therefore protects   2
taxpayers and society from a broad and deep set of costs, personal and communal. But there is another case for marriage, equally significant, that you probably haven't heard. Marriage is a powerful creator and sustainer of human and social capital for adults as well as children, about as important as education when it comes to promoting the health, wealth, and well-being of adults and communities. For most Americans, this is news. When it comes to adults, the case for lifelong marriage has been framed in exclusively moral, spiritual, and emotional terms: one side argues for personal liberation from marriage, the other urges parents to sacrifice for God's and/or the kids' sake.

These are important considerations to be sure. Parents surely should   3
be willing to make appropriate sacrifices for their kids' sake. But framing the marriage debate solely in those terms obscures as much as it reveals. It misses the profound benefits that lasting marriage confers on adults. And it overestimates considerably the likelihood that divorce will, in fact, lead to greater happiness for the individual.

Recently, I had the opportunity to review the scientific evidence on the   4
consequences of marriage for adults with University of Chicago scholar Linda J. Waite for our new book, *The Case for Marriage*. What I found surprised me. Quietly, with little fanfare, a broad and deep body of scientific literature has been accumulating that affirms what Genesis teaches: it is not good for man to be alone — no, nor woman neither. In virtually every way that social scientists can measure, married people do much better than the unmarried or divorced: they live longer, healthier, happier, sexier, and more affluent lives.

How big a difference does marriage make? If David Letterman were to   5
compile a Top Ten list for marriage, it might look something like this:

Top Ten Reasons Why Marriage Is Good For You

10. It's Safer.

Marriage lowers the risk that both men and women will become vic-   6
tims of violence, including domestic violence. A 1994 Justice Department report, based on the National Crime Victimization Survey, found that single and divorced women were four to five times more likely to be victims of violence in any given year than wives; bachelors were four times more likely to be violent-crime victims than husbands. Two-thirds of acts of violence against women committed by intimate partners were not committed by husbands but by boyfriends (whether live-in or not) or former husbands or boyfriends. As one scholar sums up the relevant research: "Regardless of methodology, the studies yielded similar results: cohabitors engage in more violence than spouses." Linda Waite conducted an analysis of the National Survey of Families and Households for our new book. She found that, even

after controlling for education, race, age, and gender, people who live together are still three times more likely to say their arguments got physical (such as kicking, hitting, or shoving) in the past year than married couples.

9. It Can Save Your Life.

Married people live longer and healthier lives. The power of marriage   7
is particularly evident in late middle age. When Linda Waite and a colleague, for example, analyzed mortality differentials in a very large, nationally representative sample, they found an astonishingly large "marriage gap" in longevity: nine out of ten married guys who are alive at forty-eight will make it to age sixty-five, compared with just six in ten comparable single guys (controlling for race, education, and income). For women, the protective benefits of marriage are also powerful, though not quite as large. Nine out of ten wives alive at age forty-eight will live to be senior citizens, compared with just eight out of ten divorced and single women.

In fact, according to statisticians Bernard Cohen and I-Sing Lee, who   8
compiled a catalog of relative mortality risks, "being unmarried is one of the greatest risks that people voluntarily subject themselves to." Having heart disease, for example, reduces a man's life expectancy by just under six years, while being unmarried chops almost ten years off a man's life. This is not just a selection effect: even controlling for initial health status, sick people who are married live longer than their unmarried counterparts. Having a spouse, for example, lowers a cancer patient's risk of dying from the disease as much as being in an age category ten years younger. A recent study of outcomes for surgical patients found that just being married lowered a patient's risk of dying in the hospital. For perhaps more obvious reasons, the risk a hospital patient will be discharged to a nursing home was two and a half times greater if the patient was unmarried. Scientists who have studied immune functioning in the laboratory find that happily married couples have better-functioning immune systems. Divorced people, even years after the divorce, show much lower levels of immune function.

8. It Can Save Your Kid's Life.

Children lead healthier, longer lives if parents get and stay married.   9
Adults who fret about second-hand smoke and drunk driving would do well to focus at least some of their attention on this point. In one long-term study that followed a sample of highly advantaged children (middle-class whites with IQs of at least 135) up through their seventies, a parent's divorce knocked four years off the adult child's life expectancy. Forty-year-olds from divorced homes were three times more likely to die from all causes than forty-year-olds whose parents stayed married.

7. You Will Earn More Money.

Men today tend to think of marriage as a consumption item — a financial burden. But a broad and deep body of scientific literature suggests that   10 for men especially, marriage is a productive institution — as important as education in boosting a man's earnings. In fact, getting a wife may increase an American male's salary by about as much as a college education. Married men make, by some estimates, as much as 40 percent more money than comparable single guys, even after controlling for education and job history. The longer a man stays married, the higher the marriage premium he receives. Wives' earnings also benefit from marriage, but they decline when motherhood enters the picture. Childless white wives get a marriage wage premium of 4 percent, and black wives earn 10 percent more than comparable single women.

6. Did I Mention You'll Get Much Richer?

Married people not only make more money, they manage money better   11
and build more wealth together than either would alone. At identical income levels, for example, married people are less likely to report "economic hardship" or trouble paying basic bills. The longer you stay married, the more assets you build; by contrast, length of cohabitation has no relationship to wealth accumulation. On the verge of retirement, the average married couple has accumulated assets worth about $410,000, compared with $167,000 for the never-married and $154,000 for the divorced. Couples who stayed married in one study saw their assets increase twice as fast as those who had remained divorced over a five-year period.

5. You'll Tame His Cheatin' Heart (Hers, Too).

Marriage increases sexual fidelity. Cohabiting men are four times more   12
likely to cheat than husbands, and cohabiting women are eight times more likely to cheat than wives. Marriage is also the only realistic promise of permanence in a romantic relationship. Just one of ten cohabiting couples are still cohabiting after five years. By contrast, 80 percent of couples marrying for the first time are still married five years later, and close to 60 percent (if current divorce rates continue) will marry for life. One British study found that biological parents who marry are three times more likely still to be together two years later than biological two-parent families who cohabit, even after controlling for maternal age, education, economic hardship, previous relationship failure, depression, and relationship quality. Marriage may be riskier than it once was, but when it comes to making love last, there is still no better bet.

4. You Won't Go Bonkers.

Marriage is good for your mental health. Married men and women are   13
less depressed, less anxious, and less psychologically distressed than single, divorced, or widowed Americans. By contrast, getting divorced lowers both men's and women's mental health, increasing depression and hostility, and lowering one's self-esteem and sense of personal mastery and purpose in life.

And this is not just a statistical illusion: careful researchers who have   14
tracked individuals as they move toward marriage find that it is not just

that happy, healthy people marry; instead, getting married gives individuals a powerful mental health boost. Nadine Marks and James Lambert looked at changes in the psychological health of a large sample of Americans in the late eighties and early nineties. They measured psychological well-being at the outset and then watched what happened to individuals over the next years as they married, remained single, or divorced. When people married, their mental health improved — consistently and substantially. When people divorced, they suffered substantial deterioration in mental and emotional well-being, including increases in depression and declines in reported happiness. Those who divorced over this period also reported a lower sense of personal mastery, less positive relations with others, less sense of purpose in life, and lower levels of self-acceptance than their married peers did.

Married men are only half as likely as bachelors and one-third as likely   15
as divorced guys to take their own lives. Wives are also much less likely to commit suicide than single, divorced, or widowed women. Married people are much less likely to have problems with alcohol abuse or illegal drugs. In a recent national survey, one out of four single men ages nineteen to twenty-six say their drinking causes them problems at work or problems with aggression, compared with just one out of seven married guys this age.

3. It Will Make You Happy.

For most people, the joys of the single life and of divorce are overrated.   16
Overall, 40 percent of married people, compared with about a quarter of singles or cohabitors, say they are "very happy" with life in general. Married people are also only about half as likely as singles or cohabitors to say they are unhappy with their lives.

How happy are the divorced? If people divorce in order to be happy, as   17
we are often told, the majority should demand their money back. Just 18 percent of divorced adults say they are "very happy," and divorced adults are twice as likely as married folk to say they are "not too happy" with life in general. Only a minority of divorcing adults go on to make marriages that are happier than the one they left. "Divorce or be miserable," certain cultural voices tell us, but, truth be told, "Divorce *and* be miserable" is at least as likely an outcome.

This is not just an American phenomenon. One recent study by Steven   18
Stack and J. Ross Eshleman of seventeen developed nations found that "married persons have a significantly higher level of happiness than persons who are not married," even after controlling for gender, age, education, children, church attendance, financial satisfaction, and self-reported health. Further, "the strength of the association between being married and being happy is remarkably consistent across nations." Marriage boosted financial satisfaction and health. But being married conferred a happiness advantage over and above its power to improve the pocketbook and the health chart. Cohabitation, by contrast, did not increase financial satisfaction or perceived health, and the boost to happiness from having a

live-in lover was only about a quarter of that of being married. Another large study, of 100,000 Norwegians, found that, with both men and women, "the married have the highest level of subjective well-being, followed by the widowed." Even long-divorced people who cohabited were not any happier than singles.

2. Your Kids Will Love You More.

Divorce weakens the bonds between parents and children over the long run. Adult children of divorce describe relationships with both their mother and their father less positively, on average, and they are about 40 percent less likely than adults from intact marriages to say they see either parent at least several times a week. 19

1. You'll Have Better Sex, More Often.

Despite the lurid *Sex in the City* marketing that promises singles erotic joys untold, both husbands and wives are more likely to report that they have an extremely satisfying sex life than are singles or cohabitors. (Divorced women were the least likely to have a sex life they found extremely satisfying emotionally.) For one thing, married people are more likely to *have* a sex life. Single men are twenty times more likely, and single women ten times more likely, not to have had sex even once in the past year than the married. (Almost a quarter of single guys and 30 percent of single women lead sexless lives.) 20

Married people are also the most likely to report a highly satisfying sex life. Wives, for example, are almost twice as likely as divorced and never-married women to have a sex life that a) exists and b) is extremely satisfying emotionally. Contrary to popular lore, for men, having a wife beats shacking up by a wide margin: 50 percent of husbands say sex with their partner is extremely satisfying physically, compared with 39 percent of cohabiting men. 21

How can a piece of paper work such miracles? For surprisingly, the piece of paper, and not just the personal relationship, matters a great deal. People who live together, for the most part, don't reap the same kinds of benefits that men and women who marry do. Something about marriage as a social institution — a shared aspiration and a public, legal vow — gives wedlock the power to change individuals' lives. 22

By increasing confidence that this partnership will last, marriage allows men and women to specialize — to take on those parts of life's tasks, from developing an interesting social life to getting money out of insurance companies, that one person does better or enjoys more than the other. Though this specialization is often along traditional gender lines, it doesn't have to be. Even childless married couples benefit from splitting up the work. Married households have twice the talent, twice the time, and twice the labor pool of singles. Over time, as spouses specialize, each actually produces more in both market and non-market goods than singles who have to shoulder all of life's tasks on their own. 23

But because marriage is a partnership in the whole of life, backed up   24
by family, community, and religious values, marriage can do what economic partnerships don't: give a greater sense of meaning and purpose to
life (a reason to exercise or cut back on booze, work harder, and to keep
plugging even in the middle of those times when the marriage may not feel
gratifying at all). Married people are both responsible for and responsible
to another human being, and both halves of that dynamic lead the married
to live more responsible, fruitful, and satisfying lives. Marriage is a transformative act, changing the way two people look at each other, at the
future, and at their roles in society. And it changes the way significant others — from family to congregation to insurance companies and the
IRS — look at and treat that same couple. Sexual fidelity, an economic
union, a parenting alliance, the promise of care that transcends day-to-day
emotions: all these are what give a few words mumbled before a clergyman
or judge the power to change lives.

What proportion of unhappily married couples who stick it out stay   25
miserable? The latest data show that within five years, just 12 percent of
very unhappily married couples who stick it out are still unhappy; 70 percent of the unhappiest couples now describe their marriage as "very" or
"quite" happy.

Just as good marriages go bad, bad marriages go good. And they have a   26
better chance of doing so in a society that recognizes the value of marriage
than one that sings the statistically dubious joys of divorce.

• • •

Comprehension

1. What does Gallagher mean when she says, "Marriage is a powerful creator
   and sustainer of human and social capital for adults as well as children" (2)?
2. What objection does Gallagher have to framing the marriage debate "in
   exclusively moral, spiritual, and emotional" terms (2)?
3. Why does Gallagher think that unmarried people are not as happy as
   married people? Does she state her reasons directly, or does she imply
   them?
4. According to Gallagher, how does marriage give so many benefits to so
   many people?
5. In paragraph 24, Gallagher calls marriage a "transformative act." What
   does she mean?

Purpose and Audience

1. At what point does Gallagher state her thesis? Why does she state it where
   she does?
2. Why does Gallagher think that she has to defend marriage? What preconceptions about marriage does she assume her readers have?

3. At whom do you think this essay is aimed? Young adults? Married people? Divorced people? Others? On what do you base your conclusions?

Style and Structure

1. Gallagher begins her essay by addressing some misconceptions people have about marriage. Is this an effective introductory strategy? What other strategy could she have used?

2. In what order does Gallagher present her Top Ten list for marriage? Would another order have made more sense?

3. Throughout her essay, Gallagher uses examples in the form of statistics to support her points. Locate several of these statistics. How effectively do they support Gallagher's points? Should she have documented her statistics more fully? Why or why not?

4. Do you think Gallagher makes a fair case for marriage, or do you think she overstates her case? Should Gallagher have discussed the possible disadvantages of marriage? Would including this material have made her essay more convincing? Explain.

5. When Gallagher discusses marriage, she specifically talks about traditional heterosexual marriage. Does she allow for other family structures — for example, gay marriage or civil unions? Should she have acknowledged these arrangements? Would this shift in focus have strengthened or weakened her essay?

Vocabulary Projects

1. Define each of the following words as it is used in this selection.

illegitimacy (1)	affirms (4)	fret (9)
premature (1)	domestic (6)	reap (22)
communal (2)	cohabitators (6)	aspiration (22)
sustainer (2)	mortality (7)	dubious (26)

2. At a number of points in her essay, Gallagher uses colloquial words and phrases — for example, "kids" (2), "guy" (7), and "go bonkers" (13). Why do you think she does this? Underline five of these words and phrases, and determine what would be gained or lost by using more formal language.

Journal Entry

Write a one-paragraph conclusion to Gallagher's essay. Then, write a few sentences analyzing what your conclusion adds to the essay.

Writing Workshop

1. Do you think Gallagher is treating her subject objectively, or do you think she has an underlying agenda? Write an essay in which you explain your

response to this question, including specific references to Gallagher's points. Make sure that you document all material you borrow from Gallagher and that you include a works-cited page. (See the Appendix for information on documentation formats.)

2. Review Gallagher's Top Ten list, and choose the three reasons you think are the most important. Then, write an essay in which you agree or disagree with these reasons. Use examples from the essay to support your points. Make sure that you document all material you borrow from Gallagher and that you include a works-cited page. (See the Appendix for information on documentation formats.)

3. Make your own Top Five list of reasons why marriage is good or bad for people. Then, write an essay in which you explain your position. Support your points with examples from your own experience.

Combining the Patterns

Gallagher uses **cause and effect** in paragraphs 1 and 2 to introduce her essay. What are the advantages of this strategy? Could she have used other patterns — for example, **comparison and contrast** to show how her ideas about marriage contrast with popular opinion? Would these paragraphs have added to the essay's impact? Explain.

Thematic Connections

- "My Mother Never Worked" (page 114)
- "I Want a Wife" (page 520)
- "The Wife-Beater" (page 528)
- Declaration of Sentiments and Resolutions (page 581)

BRENT STAPLES

Just Walk On By: A Black Man Ponders His Power to Alter Public Space

Born in Chester, Pennsylvania, in 1951, Brent Staples joined the staff of the *New York Times* in 1985, writing on culture and politics, and he became a member of its editorial board in 1990. His columns appear regularly on the paper's op-ed pages. Staples has also written a memoir, *Parallel Time: Growing Up in Black and White* (1994), about his escape from the poverty and violence of his childhood.

Background on racial profiling

"Just Walk On By" can be read in the light of current controversies surrounding racial profiling of criminal suspects, which occurs, according to the American Civil Liberties Union, "when the police target someone for investigation on the basis of that person's race, national origin, or ethnicity. Examples of profiling are the use of race to determine which drivers to stop for minor traffic violations ('driving while black') and the use of race to determine which motorists or pedestrians to search for contraband." Although law enforcement officials have often denied that they profile criminals solely on the basis of race, studies have shown a high prevalence of police profiling directed primarily at African and Hispanic Americans. A number of states have enacted laws barring racial profiling, and some people have won court settlements when they objected to being interrogated by police solely because of their race. Since the terrorist attacks of September 11, 2001, people of Arab descent have been targets of heightened interest at airports and elsewhere, which has added to the continuing controversy surrounding the association of criminal behavior with particular ethnic groups.

My first victim was a woman — white, well dressed, probably in her early twenties. I came upon her late one evening on a deserted street in Hyde Park, a relatively affluent neighborhood in an otherwise mean, impoverished section of Chicago. As I swung onto the avenue behind her, there seemed to be a discreet, uninflammatory distance between us. Not so. She cast back a worried glance. To her, the youngish black man — a broad six feet two inches with a beard and billowing hair, both hands shoved into the pockets of a bulky military jacket — seemed menacingly close. After a few more quick glimpses, she picked up her pace and was soon running in earnest. Within seconds she disappeared into a cross street.

That was more than a decade ago. I was twenty-two years old, a graduate student newly arrived at the University of Chicago. It was in the echo of that terrified woman's footfalls that I first began to know the unwieldy inheritance I'd come into — the ability to alter public space in ugly ways. It was clear that she thought herself the quarry of a mugger, rapist, or worse. Suffering a bout of insomnia, however, I was stalking sleep, not defenseless wayfarers. As a softy who is scarcely able to take a knife to a raw chicken — let alone hold it to a person's throat — I was surprised, embarrassed, and dismayed all at once. Her flight made me feel like an accomplice in tyranny. It also made it clear that I was indistinguishable from the muggers who occasionally seeped into the area from the surrounding ghetto. That first encounter, and those that followed, signified that a vast, unnerving gulf lay between nighttime pedestrians — particularly women — and me. And I soon gathered that being perceived as dangerous is a hazard in itself. I only needed to turn a corner into a dicey situation, or crowd some frightened, armed person in a foyer somewhere, or make an errant move after being pulled over by a policeman. Where fear and weapons meet — and they often do in urban America — there is always the possibility of death.

In that first year, my first away from my hometown, I was to become   3
thoroughly familiar with the language of fear. At dark, shadowy intersections in Chicago, I could cross in front of a car stopped at a traffic light and elicit the *thunk, thunk, thunk, thunk* of the driver — black, white, male, or female — hammering down the door locks. On less traveled streets after dark, I grew accustomed to but never comfortable with people who crossed to the other side of the street rather than pass me. Then there were the standard unpleasantries with police, doormen, bouncers, cab drivers, and others whose business it is to screen out troublesome individuals *before* there is any nastiness.

I moved to New York nearly two years ago and I have remained an avid   4
night walker. In central Manhattan, the near-constant crowd cover minimizes tense one-on-one street encounters. Elsewhere — visiting friends in SoHo, where sidewalks are narrow and tightly spaced buildings shut out the sky — things can get very taut indeed.

Black men have a firm place in New York mugging literature. Norman   5
Podhoretz in his famed (or infamous) 1963 essay, "My Negro Problem — and Ours," recalls growing up in terror of black males; they "were tougher than we were, more ruthless," he writes — and as an adult on the Upper West Side of Manhattan, he continues, he cannot constrain his nervousness when he meets black men on certain streets. Similarly, a decade later, the essayist and novelist Edward Hoagland extols a New York where once "Negro bitterness bore down mainly on other Negroes." Where some see mere panhandlers, Hoagland sees "a mugger who is clearly screwing up his nerve to do more than just *ask* for money." But Hoagland has "the New Yorker's quick-hunch posture for broken-field maneuvering," and the bad guy swerves away.

I often witness that "hunch posture," from women after dark on the   6
warrenlike streets of Brooklyn where I live. They seem to set their faces on neutral and, with their purse straps strung across their chests bandolier style, they forge ahead as though bracing themselves against being tackled.

I understand, of course, that the danger they perceive is not a hallucination. Women are particularly vulnerable to street violence, and young black males are drastically overrepresented among the perpetrators of that violence. Yet these truths are no solace against the kind of alienation that comes of being ever the suspect, against being set apart, a fearsome entity with whom pedestrians avoid making eye contact.

It is not altogether clear to me how I reached the ripe old age of twenty-two without being conscious of the lethality nighttime pedestrians attributed to me. Perhaps it was because in Chester, Pennsylvania, the small, angry industrial town where I came of age in the 1960s, I was scarcely noticeable against a backdrop of gang warfare, street knifings, and murders. I grew up one of the good boys, had perhaps a half-dozen fist fights. In retrospect, my shyness of combat has clear sources.   7

Many things go into the making of a young thug. One of those things is the consummation of the male romance with the power to intimidate. An infant discovers that random flailings send the baby bottle flying out of the crib and crashing to the floor. Delighted, the joyful babe repeats those motions again and again, seeking to duplicate the feat. Just so, I recall the points at which some of my boyhood friends were finally seduced by the perception of themselves as tough guys. When a mark cowered and surrendered his money without resistance, myth and reality merged — and paid off. It is, after all, only manly to embrace the power to frighten and intimidate. We, as men, are not supposed to give an inch of our lane on the highway; we are to seize the fighter's edge in work and in play and even in love; we are to be valiant in the face of hostile forces.   8

Unfortunately, poor and powerless young men seem to take all this nonsense literally. As a boy, I saw countless tough guys locked away; I have since buried several, too. They were babies, really — a teenage cousin, a brother of twenty-two, a childhood friend in his mid-twenties — all gone down in episodes of bravado played out in the streets. I came to doubt the virtues of intimidation early on. I chose, perhaps even unconsciously, to remain a shadow — timid, but a survivor.   9

The fearsomeness mistakenly attributed to me in public places often has a perilous flavor. The most frightening of these confusions occurred in the late 1970s and early 1980s when I worked as a journalist in Chicago. One day, rushing into the office of a magazine I was writing for with a deadline story in hand, I was mistaken for a burglar. The office manager called security and, with an ad hoc posse, pursued me through the labyrinthine halls, nearly to my editor's door. I had no way of proving who I was. I could only move briskly toward the company of someone who knew me.   10

Another time I was on assignment for a local paper and killing time before an interview. I entered a jewelry store on the city's affluent Near North Side. The proprietor excused herself and returned with an enormous red Doberman pinscher straining at the end of a leash. She stood, the dog extended toward me, silent to my questions, her eyes bulging nearly   11 out of her head. I took a cursory look around, nodded, and bade her good night. Relatively speaking, however, I never fared as badly as another black male journalist. He went to nearby Waukegan, Illinois, a couple of summers ago to work on a story about a murderer who was born there. Mistaking the reporter for the killer, police hauled him from his car at gunpoint and but for his press credentials would probably have tried to book him. Such episodes are not uncommon. Black men trade tales like this all the time.

In "My Negro Problem — and Ours," Podhoretz writes that the hatred   12
he feels for blacks makes itself known to him through a variety of avenues — one being his discomfort with that "special brand of paranoid touchiness" to which he says blacks are prone. No doubt he is speaking here of black men. In time, I learned to smother the rage I felt at so often being taken for a criminal. Not to do so would surely have led to madness — via that special "paranoid touchiness" that so annoyed Podhoretz at the time he wrote the essay.

I began to take precautions to make myself less threatening. I move   13
about with care, particularly late in the evening. I give a wide berth to nervous people on subway platforms during the wee hours, particularly when I have exchanged business clothes for jeans. If I happen to be entering a building behind some people who appear skittish, I may walk by, letting them clear the lobby before I return, so as not to seem to be following them. I have been calm and extremely congenial on those rare occasions when I've been pulled over by the police.

And on late-evening constitutionals along streets less traveled by, I   14
employ what has proved to be an excellent tension-reducing measure: I whistle melodies from Beethoven and Vivaldi and the more popular classical composers. Even steely New Yorkers hunching toward nighttime destinations seem to relax, and occasionally they even join in the tune. Virtually everybody seems to sense that a mugger wouldn't be warbling bright, sunny selections from Vivaldi's *Four Seasons*. It is my equivalent of the cowbell that hikers wear when they know they are in bear country.

• • •

Comprehension

1. Why does Staples characterize the woman he encounters in paragraph 1 as a "victim"?
2. What does Staples mean when he says he has the power to "alter public space" (2)?
3. Why does Staples walk the streets at night?
4. What things, in Staples's opinion, contribute to "the making of a young thug" (8)? According to Staples, why are young, poor, and powerless men especially likely to become thugs?
5. How does Staples attempt to make himself less threatening?

Purpose and Audience

1. What is Staples's thesis? Does he state it or imply it?

2. Does Staples use logic, emotion, or a combination of the two to appeal to his readers? How appropriate is his strategy?

3. What preconceptions does Staples assume his audience has? How does he challenge these preconceptions?

4. What is Staples trying to accomplish with his first sentence? Do you think he succeeds? Why or why not?

Style and Structure

1. Why does Staples mention Norman Podhoretz? Could he make the same points without referring to Podhoretz's essay?

2. Staples begins his essay with an anecdote. How effective is this strategy? Do you think another opening strategy would be more effective? Explain.

3. Does Staples present enough examples to support his thesis? Are they representative? Would other types of examples be more convincing? Explain.

4. In what order does Staples present his examples? Would another order be more effective? Explain.

Vocabulary Projects

1. Define each of the following words as it is used in this selection.

discreet (1)	quarry (2)	constrain (5)
uninflammatory (1)	insomnia (2)	bravado (9)
billowing (1)	wayfarers (2)	constitutionals (14)

2. In his essay, Staples uses the word *thug*. List as many synonyms as you can for this word. Do all these words convey the same idea, or do they differ in their connotations? Explain. (If you like, consult an online thesaurus at thesaurus.reference.com.)

Journal Entry

Have you ever been in a situation such as the ones Staples describes, where you perceived someone (or someone perceived you) as threatening? How did you react? After reading Staples's essay, do you think you would react the same way now?

Writing Workshop

1. Use your journal entry to help you write an essay using a single long example to support this statement: "When walking alone at night, you can (or cannot) be too careful."

2. Relying on examples from your own experience and from Staples's essay, write an essay discussing what part you think race plays in people's reactions to Staples. Do you think his perceptions are accurate? Make sure that you document Staples's words and ideas and that you include a works-cited page. (See the Appendix for information on documentation formats.)

3. How accurate is Staples's observation concerning the "male romance with the power to intimidate" (8)? What does he mean by this statement? What examples from your own experience support (or do not support) the idea that this "romance" is an element of male upbringing in our society?

Combining the Patterns

In paragraph 8, Staples uses **cause and effect** to demonstrate what goes "into the making of a young thug." Would several **examples** have better explained how a youth becomes a thug?

Thematic Connections

- "Finishing School" (page 107)
- "The 'Black Table' Is Still There" (page 345)
- "The Ways We Lie" (page 485)
- "The Wife-Beater" (page 528)

Fatwa City

Writer and editor Cullen Murphy (b. 1952) is currently an editor-at-large for *Vanity Fair*. His books include a collection of essays that originally appeared in the *Atlantic*, an examination of trash-disposal practices in the United States, an exploration of women and the Bible, and, most recently, *Are We Rome?:The Fall of an Empire and the Fate of America* (2007). As John Cullen Murphy, he also wrote the *Prince Valiant* newspaper comic strip for some twenty years.

Background on *fatwa*

A *fatwa* is a religious ruling issued by an accepted scholarly authority on a point of Islamic law. Traditionally, to be valid a fatwa must coincide with proofs derived from the Koran, be the work of a knowledgeable person or group with sincere intentions, not benefit the one issuing the fatwa or depend on political whim, and correspond with the needs of the contemporary world. Fatwa from different sources may conflict with one another — and, in fact, according to religious teaching, they are considered binding only on their author (although some religious authorities misleadingly present fatwa as obligatory for all Muslims). In recent times, fatwa have sometimes become overtly politicized, and some even call for the death of individuals seen to have defamed Islam. Islamic extremists use the term to justify acts that would not be allowed under Islamic law; for example, it is said that Osama bin Laden received a fatwa to launch his attack on the United States. In the West, the word has come to be applied to any sweeping decree, as in "The mayor's office issued a fatwa to purge the streets of homeless people."

"Underwear is called underwear for a reason — because it is normally worn under your clothes." This explanation was offered to fellow legislators earlier this year by a member of Virginia's House of Delegates. It came amid a searing floor debate over a measure introduced by Algie T. Howell, a Democrat from Norfolk, that would levy a $50 fine for the wearing of pants that droop, hip-hop style, allowing underwear to show. Supporters of the bill hoped that it would begin to stem the "coarsening of society." Opponents, including the American Civil Liberties Union, argued that the fine amounted to racial profiling, because the fashion statement at issue is associated with African-American males. The House of Delegates passed the bill by a wide margin, but then, in the face of nationwide ridicule, a committee of Virginia's senate convened a special meeting and killed it. 1

During most of my lifetime America has been a land where governments took little regulatory interest in the nanobehavior of everyday life. To be sure, there were plenty of so-called blue laws* back in Colonial times, 2 some of which remain on the books. (Even now local lore holds that it is technically illegal to kiss in front of a church in the city of Boston.) There was also the failed experiment of Prohibition. And to this day that tag on mattresses cannot be torn off without risk of *peine forte et dure.*** But in recent decades we have not had to live according to *fatwas* like those of Iraq's Grand Ayatollah Ali Sistani, who has decreed, for instance, in Fatwa 2648: "It is unworthy to drink too much water, to drink water after eating fatty food, and to drink water while standing during the night." (Or this, Fatwa 2479: "A man cannot marry a girl who has been suckled fully by his mother or paternal grandmother.") We have not been forced to adhere to fastidious strictures like those of Singapore, where the offense of spitting on the sidewalk carries a $600 fine. The ongoing "Let us trim our hair in accordance with Socialist lifestyle" campaign in North Korea has posed no imminent threat of infiltration here. If anything, the tendency in late-twentieth-century America was in exactly the opposite direction — toward moral laissez-faire.

That said, and despite the failure of the "droopy drawers" bill, the tide now appears to be turning, and turning fast. My files are far from exhaustive, but they overflow with examples. In Texas a Republican lawmaker has proposed a bill that would require teenagers under eighteen to have a grade-point average of 2.0 or above in order to be issued a driver's license. Arguing that "parents with young children should not have to explain to them what a four-hour erection is," a Virginia congressman, Jim Moran, introduced an amendment (to H.R. 310) that would outlaw TV ads for erectile-dysfunction drugs between 6:00 A.M. and 10:00 P.M. The state of Arkansas has now mandated that all schoolchildren be evaluated for their body-mass index, and that they receive an annual BMI "report card." In Alabama proponents of a law forbidding the sale of sex toys are breathing easier (and opponents less heavily) after the collapse in February of a legal challenge mounted by the ACLU, which argued that the ban violated the right to privacy; the U.S. Supreme Court declined to consider the matter. In Sutter, California, students this year were issued radio identification tags in order to automate the monitoring of attendance (and, parents wondered, who knew what else?). In Hawaii legislators are considering a prohibition on smoking at public beaches and parks — the first extension by any state of smoking bans to the outdoors. Meanwhile, the same Virginia legislator who was troubled by exposed underwear has introduced legislation that would penalize drivers for playing music too loudly in their cars or for slouching too far back in their seats.

Language, of course, has long been a target of those who would legislate morality, and the Federal Communications Commission under Michael Powell was an increasingly stern watchdog. Earlier this year PBS

3

4

---

* EDS. NOTE — Laws prohibiting businesses from opening on Sunday.
** EDS. NOTE — French legal term for "hard and forceful punishment."

distributed to its affiliates only the expurgated version of *A Company of Soldiers*, a *Frontline* documentary about American forces in Iraq, because of concerns that obscenities shouted by military personnel during an ambush might bring censure from the FCC; it released the unbleeped version only to those local stations willing to sign waivers absolving PBS of liability for any fines. In Congress, Representative Douglas Ose, a Republican from California, is pushing legislation (H.R. 3687) that would explicitly forbid certain words from being broadcast in America under any circumstances. Thirty years ago the comedian George Carlin built a routine around the seven forbidden words, the words that "curve your spine and grow hair on your hands." Congressman Ose's list is nearly the same as Carlin's, except that Ose would for some reason permit the use of "tits" but proscribe the use of "asshole." The fine-tuning of linguistic etiquette is not confined to the United States. Our British cousins, through the auspices of the *British Medical Journal*, have proposed the eradication of a dozen terms, including "911" (the easy shorthand conceals the enormity of thousands of deaths) and "kiddie porn" (it sounds too chirpy for something so terrible). The journal's editor, Richard Smith, observes, "The proposal to ban a word focuses attention on the many wrong assumptions, prejudices, and even evil thoughts that might be contained within a word."

Legislating morality takes many forms; it doesn't require actual legislation. One indication of a creeping moralism is the application of a religious gloss to activities or phenomena where previously there had been none. On the outskirts of Tampa, Florida, a developer named Bill Martin plans to open a refuge called Club Natura, a nudist camp with an overtly Christian theme, which aims to offer an experience of the virtuous life in the Garden of Eden (and which will not tolerate any tasting of the forbidden fruit, unlike other nudist camps Martin could name). *Cosmopolitan* magazine, once a lodestar of earthly pleasuring, has hired a spirituality editor, its first, for the British edition. The editor, Hannah Borno, writes, "I've come to the painful realization that men and shoes are not enough to make me happy." Cleaning up nuclear contamination is too important to be left to the scientists: Madonna, whose interest in kabbalah is well known, was recently observed (by an undercover BBC reporter, according to the *New York Post*) trying to rid Chernobyl* of excessive radiation by means of "a weird religious service, which started with prayer readings and chanting that culminated in everyone turning to the east, pushing the air with their hands, and crying out 'Cher-er-er-er-nobyl' at the top of their voices." Even devil worship, once widely regarded as outside the religious fold almost by definition, has received the balm of sanctification: the Royal Navy now recognizes devil worship as a religion, opening the way for a seaman named Chris Cranmer, a technician on the HMS *Cumberland*, to perform Satanist rituals aboard ship and, in the event he falls in battle, to have a Church of

5

---

* EDS. NOTE — Ukrainian city; site of 1986 nuclear power plant accident.

Satan funeral (which brings up an intriguing theological point: if killed during a conflict with the Axis of Evil, should he be denied a Satanic service?).

"We shouldn't legislate morality," the liberals say, to which a social conservative like John Ashcroft* would (and does) reply, "I think *all* we should legislate is morality. We shouldn't legislate *im*morality." No one wants to get caught between the antagonists in this debate. Like most Americans, I take a libertotalitarian stance, believing that government should not legislate my morality but in certain areas could do a lot more legislating of other people's. That's not a very helpful guide to good public policy, but maybe this is: if instead of referring to legislation as H.R. 310 or H.R. 3687 we referred to Fatwa 310 or Fatwa 3687, we might instinctively know better where to draw a line.

6

• • •

Comprehension

1. What is the "droopy drawers" bill? Why did Algie T. Howell introduce it?
2. What does Murphy mean when he says, "Despite the failure of the 'droopy drawers' bill, the tide now appears to be turning, and turning fast" (3)?
3. What areas of life are being focused on, according to Murphy, by people who want to legislate morality?
4. What is the "creeping moralism" that Murphy refers to in paragraph 5? What is his opinion of this phenomenon? How do you know?
5. According to Murphy, what contrasting positions do liberals and conservatives take on the issue of legislating morality? What does he mean when he says, "No one wants to get caught between the antagonists in this debate" (6)?

Purpose and Audience

1. Does Murphy have a serious message to convey, or do you think he is just trying to entertain his readers?
2. What preconceptions does Murphy seem to have about his audience? For example, does he think they are interested in his topic? Does he think they know a lot about it? How can you tell?
3. Where in the essay does Murphy state his thesis? Why does he state it where he does?

* Eds. note — Attorney General who served during the first term of George W. Bush.

Style and Structure

1. Murphy begins his essay by discussing a bill that tried to fine anyone wearing droopy pants. Why does Murphy begin his essay with this example? Do you think this is a good choice?

2. What three different types of examples does Murphy discuss? How does he introduce each type of example?

3. Does Murphy present a sufficient number of examples? Are there any places where he should have included more examples?

4. Does Murphy give a fair range of examples, or does he seem to be "stacking the deck" in any way? Explain.

5. In his conclusion, Murphy quotes former Attorney General John Ashcroft. How do you interpret Ashcroft's statement? In what way does this quotation help Murphy make his point?

Vocabulary Projects

1. Define each of the following words as it is used in this selection.

levy (1)	stern (4)	eradication (4)
coarsening (1)	expurgated (4)	gloss (5)
fastidious (2)	linguistic (4)	lodestar (5)
laissez-faire (2)	etiquette (4)	kabbalah (5)
mandated (3)	auspices (4)	

2. Go to an online encyclopedia such as reference.com and look up the term *blue laws* (2). What point is Murphy making by using this term in his essay?

3. In paragraph 2, Murphy coins the term *nanobehavior,* and in paragraph 6, he coins the term *libertotalitarian.* What do you think these coinages mean? Why doesn't Murphy use more traditional language to convey these concepts?

Journal Entry

What types of personal behavior do you think the government should try to control? What types of behavior (if any) do you believe should be off limits?

Writing Workshop

1. Do you think government can ever successfully regulate "the nanobehavior of everyday life" (2)? Why or why not? Give some examples from your own experience to support your thesis.

2. Is Murphy's use of the term *fatwa* appropriate here, or is it insensitive or unfair? Go to an online encyclopedia such as reference.com and look up *fatwa.* Then, write an essay in which you criticize or support Murphy's use of this term in his essay. Make sure that you document any ideas you bor-

row from a source and that you include a works-cited page. (See the Appendix for information on documentation formats.)

3. Would you have voted for or against Algie T. Howell's "droopy drawers" bill? Write an email to Howell in which you defend your vote. Make sure that you document any ideas you take from Murphy's essay and that you include a works-cited page. (See the Appendix for information on documentation formats.)

Combining the Patterns

In paragraph 2, Murphy uses **comparison and contrast**. What two things is Murphy comparing? In what way does this comparison help him set up the rest of his essay?

Thematic Connections

- "The Socks" (page 95)
- "The Catbird Seat" (page 223)
- "The Lottery" (page 311)

JONATHAN KOZOL

The Human Cost of an Illiterate Society

Jonathan Kozol was born in Boston in 1936. After studying in England, he began teaching in public schools in Boston's inner city. His experiences there provided the source material for his first book, *Death at an Early Age* (1967), a startling indictment of the system's failure to provide an adequate education to poor, mostly minority children. Kozol also wrote *Illiterate America* (1985), an examination of the human and financial costs of illiteracy in the United States, from which the following essay was taken. In the years since, Kozol has continued to use firsthand experience to write about the poorest in our society. His books have focused on homelessness, on the inequities between schools in poor neighborhoods and those in affluent ones, and on what he calls "apartheid schooling" in America.

Background on illiteracy in the United States

In *Illiterate America*, Kozol estimates that more than 35 million Americans read below the level needed to function in society. A comprehensive survey published in 1993 seemed to support Kozol's estimates, reporting that more than 40 million adults — as much as 23 percent of the population — scored at the lowest of five levels on a series of standardized reading tests. Some critics have claimed that these results are misleading because the lowest level included some people who could not read at all and others who were functional readers who could perform some reading tasks. Still, literacy in the United States remains a matter of concern. In a recent report by the Educational Testing Service, analysis of the results of the 1993 U.S. study and a later international literacy study found that the United States ranked only twelfth in terms of literacy among twenty comparably wealthy nations and ranked first or second in terms of inequality in the distribution of literacy skills.

PRECAUTIONS. READ BEFORE USING.
Poison: Contains sodium hydroxide (caustic soda-lye).
Corrosive: Causes severe eye and skin damage, may cause blindness.
Harmful or fatal if swallowed.
If swallowed, give large quantities of milk or water.
Do not induce vomiting.
Important: Keep water out of can at all times to prevent contents
from violently erupting. . . .

–WARNING ON A CAN OF DRANO

Questions of literacy, in Socrates' belief, must at length be judged as matters of morality. Socrates could not have had in mind the moral compromise peculiar to a nation like our own. Some of our Founding Fathers did, however, have this question in their minds. One of the wisest of those

Founding Fathers (one who may not have been most compassionate but surely was more prescient than some of his peers) recognized the special dangers that illiteracy would pose to basic equity in the political construction that he helped to shape.

"A people who mean to be their own governors," James Madison wrote, "must arm themselves with the power knowledge gives. A popular government without popular information or the means of acquiring it, is but a prologue to a farce or a tragedy, or perhaps both."

Tragedy looms larger than farce in the United States today. Illiterate citizens seldom vote. Those who do are forced to cast a vote of questionable worth. They cannot make informed decisions based on serious print information. Sometimes they can be alerted to their interests by aggressive voter education. More frequently, they vote for a face, a smile, or a style, not for a mind or character or body of beliefs.

The number of illiterate adults exceeds by 16 million the entire vote cast for the winner in the 1980 presidential contest. If even one third of all illiterates could vote, and read enough and do sufficient math to vote in their self-interest, Ronald Reagan would not likely have been chosen president. There is, of course, no way to know for sure. We do know this: democracy is a mendacious term when used by those who are prepared to countenance the forced exclusion of one third of our electorate. So long as 60 million people are denied significant participation, the government is neither of, nor for, nor by, the people. It is a government, at best, of those two-thirds whose wealth, skin color, or parental privilege allows them opportunity to profit from the provocation and instruction of the written word.

The undermining of democracy in the United States is one "expense" that sensitive Americans can easily deplore because it represents a contradiction that endangers citizens of all political positions. The human price is not so obvious at first.

Since I first immersed myself within this work I have often had the following dream: I find that I am in a railroad station or a large department store within a city that is utterly unknown to me and where I cannot understand the printed words. None of the signs or symbols is familiar. Everything looks strange: like mirror writing of some kind. Gradually I understand that I am in the Soviet Union. All the letters on the walls around me are Cyrillic. I look for my pocket dictionary but I find that it has been mislaid. Where have I left it? Then I recall that I forgot to bring it with me when I packed my bags in Boston. I struggle to remember the name of my hotel. I try to ask somebody for directions. One person stops and looks at me in a peculiar way. I lose the nerve to ask. At last I reach into my wallet for an ID card. The card is missing. Have I lost it? Then I remember that my card was confiscated for some reason, many years before. Around this point, I wake up in a panic.

This panic is not so different from the misery that millions of adult illiterates experience each day within the course of their routine existence in the U.S.A.

Illiterates cannot read the menu in a restaurant.   8

They cannot read the cost of items on the menu in the *window* of the   9
restaurant before they enter.

Illiterates cannot read the letters that their children bring home from   10
their teachers. They cannot study school department circulars that tell
them of the courses that their children must be taking if they hope to
pass the SAT exams. They cannot help with homework. They cannot write
a letter to the teacher. They are afraid to visit in the classroom. They do not
want to humiliate their child or themselves.

Illiterates cannot read instructions on a bottle of prescription medi-   11
cine. They cannot find out when a medicine is past the year of safe consumption; nor can they read of allergenic risks, warnings to diabetics, or
the potential sedative effect of certain kinds of nonprescription pills. They
cannot observe preventive health care admonitions. They cannot read
about "the seven warning signs of cancer" or the indications of blood-sugar
fluctuations or the risks of eating certain foods that aggravate the likelihood of cardiac arrest.

Illiterates live, in more than literal ways, an uninsured existence. They   12
cannot understand the written details on a health insurance form. They
cannot read the waivers that they sign preceding surgical procedures. Several women I have known in Boston have entered a slum hospital with the
intention of obtaining a tubal ligation and have emerged a few days later
after having been subjected to a hysterectomy. Unaware of their rights,
incognizant of jargon, intimidated by the unfamiliar air of fear and atmosphere of ether that so many of us find oppressive in the confines even of
the most attractive and expensive medical facilities, they have signed their
names to documents they could not read and which nobody, in the hectic
situation that prevails so often in those overcrowded hospitals that serve
the urban poor, had even bothered to explain.

Childbirth might seem to be the last inalienable right of any female   13
citizen within a civilized society. Illiterate mothers, as we shall see, already
have been cheated of the power to protect their progeny against the likelihood of demolition in deficient public schools and, as a result, against the
verbal servitude within which they themselves exist. Surgical denial of the
right to bear that child in the first place represents an ultimate denial, an
unspeakable metaphor, a final darkness that denies even the twilight
gleamings of our own humanity. What greater violation of our biological,
our biblical, our spiritual humanity could possibly exist than that which
takes place nightly, perhaps hourly these days, within such overburdened
and benighted institutions as the Boston City Hospital? Illiteracy has many
costs; few are so irreversible as this.

Even the roof above one's head, the gas or other fuel for heating that   14
protects the residents of northern city slums against the threat of illness in
the winter months become uncertain guarantees. Illiterates cannot read
the lease that they must sign to live in an apartment which, too often, they
cannot afford. They cannot manage check accounts and therefore seldom

pay for anything by mail. Hours and entire days of difficult travel (and the cost of bus or other public transit) must be added to the real cost of whatever they consume. Loss of interest on the check accounts they do not have, and could not manage if they did, must be regarded as another of the excess costs paid by the citizen who is excluded from the common instruments of commerce in a numerate society.

"I couldn't understand the bills," a woman in Washington, D.C., reports, "and then I couldn't write the checks to pay them. We signed things we didn't know what they were."   15

Illiterates cannot read the notices that they receive from welfare offices or from the IRS. They must depend on word-of-mouth instruction from the welfare worker — or from other persons whom they have good reason to mistrust. They do not know what rights they have, what deadlines and requirements they face, what options they might choose to exercise. They are half-citizens. Their rights exist in print but not in fact.   16

Illiterates cannot look up numbers in a telephone directory. Even if they can find the names of friends, few possess the sorting skills to make use of the yellow pages; categories are bewildering and trade names are beyond decoding capabilities for millions of nonreaders. Even the emergency numbers listed on the first page of the phone book — "Ambulance," "Police," and "Fire" — are too frequently beyond the recognition of nonreaders.   17

Many illiterates cannot read the admonition on a pack of cigarettes. Neither the Surgeon General's warning nor its reproduction on the package can alert them to the risks. Although most people learn by word of mouth that smoking is related to a number of grave physical disorders, they do not get the chance to read the detailed stories which can document this danger with the vividness that turns concern into determination to resist. They can see the handsome cowboy or the slim Virginia lady lighting up a filter cigarette; they cannot heed the words that tell them that this product is (not "may be") dangerous to their health. Sixty million men and women are condemned to be the unalerted, high-risk candidates for cancer.   18

Illiterates do not buy "no-name" products in the supermarkets. They must depend on photographs or the familiar logos that are printed on the packages of brand-name groceries. The poorest people, therefore, are denied the benefits of the least costly products.   19

Illiterates depend almost entirely upon label recognition. Many labels, however, are not easy to distinguish. Dozens of different kinds of Campbell's soup appear identical to the nonreader. The purchaser who cannot read and does not dare to ask for help, out of the fear of being stigmatized (a fear which is unfortunately realistic), frequently comes home with something which she never wanted and her family never tasted.   20

Illiterates cannot read instructions on a pack of frozen food. Packages sometimes provide an illustration to explain the cooking preparations; but illustrations are of little help to someone who must "boil water, drop the   21 food — *within* its plastic wrapper — in the boiling water, wait for it to simmer, instantly remove."

Even when labels are seemingly clear, they may be easily mistaken. A 22 woman in Detroit brought home a gallon of Crisco for her children's dinner. She thought that she had bought the chicken that was pictured on the label. She had enough Crisco now to last a year — but no more money to go back and buy the food for dinner.

Recipes provided on the packages of certain staples sometimes tempt a 23 semiliterate person to prepare a meal her children have not tasted. The longing to vary the uniform and often starchy content of low-budget meals provided to the family that relies on food stamps commonly leads to ruinous results. Scarce funds have been wasted and the food must be thrown out. The same applies to distribution of food-surplus produce in emergency conditions. Government inducements to poor people to "explore the ways" by which to make a tasty meal from tasteless noodles, surplus cheese, and powdered milk are useless to nonreaders. Intended as benevolent advice, such recommendations mock reality and foster deeper feelings of resentment and of inability to cope. (Those, on the other hand, who cautiously refrain from "innovative" recipes in preparation of their children's meals must suffer the opprobrium of "laziness," "lack of imagination. . . .")

Illiterates cannot travel freely. When they attempt to do so, they 24 encounter risks that few of us can dream of. They cannot read traffic signs and, while they often learn to recognize and to decipher symbols, they cannot manage street names which they haven't seen before. The same is true for bus and subway stops. While ingenuity can sometimes help a man or woman to discern directions from familiar landmarks, buildings, cemeteries, churches, and the like, most illiterates are virtually immobilized. They seldom wander past the streets and neighborhoods they know. Geographical paralysis becomes a bitter metaphor for their entire existence. They are immobilized in almost every sense we can imagine. They can't move up. They can't move out. They cannot see beyond. Illiterates may take an oral test for drivers' permits in most sections of America. It is a questionable concession. Where will they go? How will they get there? How will they get home? Could it be that some of us might like it better if they stayed where they belong?

Travel is only one of many instances of circumscribed existence. Choice, 25 in almost all of its facets, is diminished in the life of an illiterate adult. Even the printed TV schedule, which provides most people with the luxury of preselection, does not belong within the arsenal of options in illiterate existence. One consequence is that the viewer watches only what appears at moments when he happens to have time to turn the switch. Another consequence, a lot more common, is that the TV set remains in operation night and day. Whatever the program offered at the hour when he walks into the room will be the nutriment that he accepts and swallows. Thus, to passivity, is added frequency — indeed, almost uninterrupted continuity.

Freedom to select is no more possible here than in the choice of home or surgery or food.

"You don't choose," said one illiterate woman. "You take your wishes from somebody else." Whether in perusal of a menu, selection of highways, purchase of groceries, or determination of affordable enjoyment, illiterate Americans must trust somebody else: a friend, a relative, a stranger on the street, a grocery clerk, a TV copywriter.

"All of our mail we get, it's hard for her to read. Settin' down and writing a letter, she can't do it. Like if we get a bill . . . we take it over to my sister-in-law. . . . My sister-in-law reads it."

Billing agencies harass poor people for the payment of the bills for purchases that might have taken place six months before. Utility companies offer an agreement for a staggered payment schedule on a bill past due. "You have to trust them," one man said. Precisely for this reason, you end up by trusting no one and suspecting everyone of possible deceit. A submerged sense of distrust becomes the corollary to a constant need to trust. "They are cheating me. . . . I have been tricked. . . . I do not know. . . ."

Not knowing: This is a familiar theme. Not knowing the right word for the right thing at the right time is one form of subjugation. Not knowing the world that lies concealed behind those words is a more terrifying feeling. The longitude and latitude of one's existence are beyond all easy apprehension. Even the hard, cold stars within the firmament above one's head begin to mock the possibilities for self-location. Where am I? Where did I come from? Where will I go?

"I've lost a lot of jobs," one man explains. "Today, even if you're a janitor, there's still reading and writing. . . . They leave a note saying 'Go to room so-and-so. . . .' You can't do it. You can't read it. You don't know."

"The hardest thing about it is that I've been places where I didn't know where I was. You don't know where you are. . . . You're lost."

"Like I said: I have two kids. What do I do if one of my kids starts choking? I go running to the phone. . . . I can't look up the hospital phone number. That's if we're at home. Out on the street, I can't read the sign. I get to a pay phone. 'Okay, tell us where you are. We'll send an ambulance.' I look at the street sign. Right there, I can't tell you what it says. I'd have to spell it out, letter for letter. By that time, one of my kids would be dead. . . . These are the kinds of fears you go with, every single day. . . ."

"Reading directions, I suffer with. I work with chemicals. . . . That's scary to begin with. . . ."

"You sit down. They throw the menu in front of you. Where do you go from there? Nine times out of ten you say, 'Go ahead. Pick out something for the both of us.' I've eaten some weird things, let me tell you!"

Menus. Chemicals. A child choking while his mother searches for a word she does not know to find assistance that will come too late. Another mother speaks about the inability to help her kids to read: "I can't read to them. Of course that's leaving them out of something they should have. Oh, it matters. You *believe* it matters! I ordered all these books. The kids belong to a book club. Donny wanted me to read a book to him. I told Donny: 'I can't read.' He said: 'Mommy, you sit down. I'll read it to you.' I tried it one day, reading from the pictures. Donny looked at me. He said, 'Mommy, that's not right.' He's only five. He knew I couldn't read. . . ."

A landlord tells a woman that her lease allows him to evict her if her baby cries and causes inconvenience to her neighbors. The consequence of challenging his words conveys a danger which appears, unlikely as it seems, even more alarming than the danger of eviction. Once she admits that she can't read, in the desire to maneuver for the time in which to call a friend, she will have defined herself in terms of an explicit impotence that she cannot endure. Capitulation in this case is preferable to self-humiliation. Resisting the definition of oneself in terms of what one cannot do, what others take for granted, represents a need so great that other imperatives (even one so urgent as the need to keep one's home in winter's cold) evaporate and fall away in face of fear. Even the loss of home and shelter, in this case, is not so terrifying as the loss of self. 36

"I come out of school. I was sixteen. They had their meetings. The directors meet. They said that I was wasting their school paper. I was wasting pencils. . . ." 37

Another illiterate, looking back, believes she was not worthy of her teacher's time. She believes that it was wrong of her to take up space within her school. She believes that it was right to leave in order that somebody more deserving could receive her place. 38

Children choke. Their mother chokes another way: on more than chicken bones. 39

People eat what others order, know what others tell them, struggle not to see themselves as they believe the world perceives them. A man in California speaks about his own loss of identity, of self-location, definition: 40

"I stood at the bottom of the ramp. My car had broke down on the freeway. There was a phone. I asked for the police. They was nice. They said to tell them where I was. I looked up at the signs. There was one that I had seen before. I read it to them: ONE WAY STREET. They thought it was a joke. I told them I couldn't read. There was other signs above the ramp. They told me to try. I looked around for somebody to help. All the cars was going by real fast. I couldn't make them understand that I was lost. The cop was nice. He told me: 'Try once more.' I did my best. I couldn't read. I only knew the sign above my head. The cop was trying to be nice. He knew that I was trapped. 'I can't send out a car to you if you can't tell me where you are.' I felt afraid. I nearly cried. I'm forty-eight years old. I only said: 'I'm on a one-way street. . . .'" 41

The legal problems and the courtroom complications that confront illiterate adults have been discussed above. The anguish that may underlie such matters was brought home to me this year while I was working on this book. I have spoken [in an earlier part of the book] of a sudden phone 42 call from one of my former students, now in prison for a criminal offense. Stephen is not a boy today. He is twenty-eight years old. He called to ask me to assist him in his trial, which comes up next fall. He will be on trial for murder. He has just knifed and killed a man who first enticed him to his home, then cheated him, and then insulted him — as "an illiterate subhuman."

Stephen now faces twenty years to life. Stephen's mother was illiterate.   43
His grandparents were illiterate as well. What parental curse did not destroy was killed off finally by the schools. Silent violence is repaid with interest. It will cost us $25,000 yearly to maintain this broken soul in prison. But what is the price that has been paid by Stephen's victim? What is the price that will be paid by Stephen?

Perhaps we might slow down a moment here and look at the realities   44
described above. This is the nation that we live in. This is a society that most of us did not create but which our president and other leaders have been willing to sustain by virtue of malign neglect. Do we possess the character and courage to address a problem which so many nations, poorer than our own, have found it natural to correct?

The answers to these questions represent a reasonable test of our belief   45
in the democracy to which we have been asked in public school to swear allegiance.

• • •

Comprehension

1. In what sense is illiteracy a danger to a democratic society?
2. According to Kozol, why do our reactions to the problem of illiteracy in America test our belief in democracy?
3. What does Kozol mean when he says that an illiterate person leads a "circumscribed existence" (25)? How does being illiterate limit a person's choices?
4. What legal problems and courtroom complications confront illiterate adults?
5. According to Kozol, what are people doing to solve the problem of illiteracy in the United States?

Purpose and Audience

1. What is Kozol's thesis? Where does he state it?
2. Kozol aims his essay at a general audience. How does he address the needs of this audience? How would his discussion differ if it were intended for an audience of reading specialists? Of politicians?
3. Is Kozol's purpose to inform, to persuade, to express emotions, or some combination of these three? Does he have additional, more specific purposes as well? Explain.

Style and Structure

1. Why does Kozol introduce his essay with references to Socrates and James Madison? How does this strategy help him support his thesis?

2. In paragraph 6, Kozol recounts a dream he often has. Why does he include this anecdote? How does it help him make the transition from his introduction to the body of his essay?

3. Kozol uses many short examples to make his point. Do you think fewer examples developed in more depth would be more effective? Why or why not?

4. How effective is Kozol's use of statistics? Do the statistics support or undercut his examples of the personal cost of illiteracy?

Vocabulary Projects

1. Define each of the following words as it is used in this selection.

prescient (1)	sedative (11)	opprobrium (23)
farce (2)	admonitions (11)	concession (24)
mendacious (4)	incognizant (12)	firmament (29)
countenance (4)	jargon (12)	capitulation (36)
Cyrillic (6)	numerate (14)	

2. Reread paragraphs 24 and 25, and determine which words or phrases convey Kozol's feelings toward his subject. Rewrite these two paragraphs, eliminating as much subjective language as you can. Do you think your changes make the paragraphs more (or less) appealing to a general audience? To a group of sociologists? To a group of reading teachers?

Journal Entry

Keep a detailed record of your activities for a day. Then, discuss the difficulty you would have carrying out each activity in your daily routine if you were illiterate.

Writing Workshop

1. Using your journal entry as a starting point, write an essay describing the tasks you would have difficulty accomplishing if you could not read. Include an explicit thesis statement, and use examples to illustrate your points.

2. Six hundred years ago, most people could not read, but they could still function in society. Similarly, many people today are not computer literate. Do you believe such people can still function well as citizens, as employees, and as parents?

3. Using Kozol's essay as source material, write an essay using as your thesis James Madison's statement, "A people who mean to be their own governors must arm themselves with the power knowledge gives" (2). Be sure to

document any information you borrow from Kozol and to include a works-cited page. (See the Appendix for information on documentation formats.)

Combining the Patterns

Why does Kozol choose to end his essay with a **narrative** about Stephen, one of his former students, who is in jail awaiting trial for murder? How does this anecdote help Kozol set up his concluding remarks in paragraphs 44 and 45?

Thematic Connections

- "Words Left Unspoken" (page 172)
- "The Catbird Seat" (page 223)
- "Mother Tongue" (page 477)
- "The Untouchable" (page 512)

Samuel (Fiction)

Initially interested in poetry, Grace Paley (1922–2007) began writing short fiction in the 1950s while raising a family and participating in a number of political causes. Her stories have been published in the collections *Little Disturbances of Man* (1959), *Enormous Changes at the Last Minute* (1974), and *Later the Same Day* (1985). Her *Collected Stories* appeared in 1994 and was nominated for a National Book Award. "Samuel," originally published in *The Atlantic Monthly,* was reprinted in Paley's 1974 collection of stories.

Background on the generation gap

During the 1960s, the term *generation gap* was coined to describe the differences in attitudes toward drug use, the Vietnam War, fashion, music, lifestyle, and politics between parents and their teenage children. While generational differences have always existed, the gap between the "baby-boomers" and their parents seemed to be magnified significantly — perhaps because of the vast size of the baby-boom generation. "Samuel" is set during the 1960s and reflects the social and political upheaval within American society at that time. Much of the younger generation was rebelling against government policies and cultural conformity, while many older people felt fearful of or antagonistic toward the young people and minorities who were challenging the status quo. "Samuel" touches on these issues and raises difficult questions about responsibility and loss.

Some boys are very tough. They're afraid of nothing. They are the ones who climb a wall and take a bow at the top. Not only are they brave on the roof, but they make a lot of noise in the darkest part of the cellar where even the super hates to go. They also jiggle and hop on the platform between the locked doors of the subway cars. [1]

Four boys are jiggling on the swaying platform. Their names are Alfred, Calvin, Samuel, and Tom. The men and women in the cars on either side watch them. They don't like them to jiggle or jump but don't want to interfere. Of course some of the men in the cars were once brave boys like these. One of them had ridden the tail of a speeding truck from New York to Rockaway Beach without getting off, without his sore fingers losing hold. Nothing happened to him then or later. He had made a compact with other boys who preferred to watch: starting at Eighth Avenue and Fifteenth Street, he would get to some specified place, maybe Twenty-third and the river, by hopping the tops of the moving trucks. This was hard to do when one truck turned a corner in the wrong direction and the nearest truck was a couple of feet too high. He made three or four starts before succeeding. He had gotten this idea from a film at school called *The Romance of Logging.* He had finished high school, married a good friend, was in a responsible job, and going to night school. [2]

These two men and others looked at the four boys jumping and jig- 3
gling on the platform and thought, It must be fun to ride that way, especially now the weather is nice and we're out of the tunnel and way high over
the Bronx. Then they thought, These kids do seem to be acting sort of stupid. They *are* little. Then they thought of some of the brave things they had
done when they were boys and jiggling didn't seem so risky.

The ladies in the car became very angry when they looked at the four 4
boys. Most of them brought their brows together and hoped the boys could
see their extreme disapproval. One of the ladies wanted to get up and say,
be careful you dumb kids, get off that platform or I'll call a cop. But three
of the boys were Negroes and the fourth was something else she couldn't
tell for sure. She was afraid they'd be fresh and laugh at her and embarrass
her. She wasn't afraid they'd hit her, but she was afraid of embarrassment.
Another lady thought, Their mothers never know where they are. It wasn't
true in this particular case. Their mothers all knew that they had gone to
see the missile exhibit on Fourteenth Street.

Out on the platform, whenever the train accelerated, the boys would 5
raise their hands and point them up to the sky to act like rockets going off,
then they rat-tat-tatted the shatterproof glass pane like machine guns,
although no machine guns had been exhibited.

For some reason known only to the motorman, the train began a sud- 6
den slowdown. The lady who was afraid of embarrassment saw the boys
jerk forward and backward and grab the swinging guard chains. She had
her own boy at home. She stood up with determination and went to the
door. She slid it open and said, "You boys will be hurt. You'll be killed. I'm
going to call the conductor if you don't just go into the next car and sit
down and be quiet."

Two of the boys said, "Yes'm," and acted as though they were about to 7
go. Two of them blinked their eyes a couple of times and pressed their lips
together. The train resumed its speed. The door slid shut, parting the lady
and the boys. She leaned against the side door because she had to get off at
the next stop.

The boys opened their eyes wide at each other and laughed. The lady 8
blushed. The boys looked at her and laughed harder. They began to pound
each other's back. Samuel laughed the hardest and pounded Alfred's back
until Alfred coughed and the tears came. Alfred held tight to the chain
hook. Samuel pounded him even harder when he saw the tears. He said,
"Why you bawling? You a baby, huh?" and laughed. One of the men whose
boyhood had been more watchful than brave became angry. He stood up
straight and looked at the boys for a couple of seconds. Then he walked in
a citizenly way to the end of the car, where he pulled the emergency cord.
Almost at once, with a terrible hiss, the pressure of air abandoned the
brakes and the wheels were caught and held.

People standing in the most secure places fell forward, then backward. 9
Samuel had let go of his hold on the chain so he could pound Tom as well
as Alfred. All the passengers in the cars whipped back and forth, but he

pitched only forward and fell head first to be crushed and killed between the cars.

The train had stopped hard, halfway into the station, and the conduc- 10
tor called at once for the trainmen who knew about this kind of death and
how to take the body from the wheels and brakes. There was silence except
for passengers from the other cars who asked, What happened! What happened! The ladies waited around wondering if he might be an only child.
The men recalled other afternoons with very bad endings. The little boys
stayed close to each other, leaning and touching shoulders and arms and
legs.

When the policeman knocked at the door and told her about it, 11
Samuel's mother began to scream. She screamed all day and moaned all
night, though the doctors tried to quiet her with pills.

Oh, oh, she hopelessly cried. She did not know how she could ever find 12
another boy like that one. However, she was a young woman and she
became pregnant. Then for a few months she was hopeful. The child born
to her was a boy. They brought him to be seen and nursed. She smiled. But
immediately she saw that this baby wasn't Samuel. She and her husband
together have had other children, but never again will a boy exactly like
Samuel be known.

* * *

Reading Literature

1. The story begins with the observation, "Some boys are very tough." Is
   Samuel really tough? What do you think Paley wants her readers to realize about Samuel?

2. What point do you think the story makes about bravery? Which of the
   characters do you consider brave? Why?

3. What effect does the incident have on the other characters? What do their
   reactions reveal about them?

Journal Entry

Do you consider Samuel a hero? Is it true, as the narrator asserts, that
"never again will a boy exactly like Samuel be known" (12)?

Thematic Connections

- "The Socks" (page 95)
- "Thirty-Eight Who Saw Murder Didn't Call the Police" (page 120)
- "Who Killed Benny Paret?" (page 340)
- "Suicide Note" (page 377)

WRITING ASSIGNMENTS FOR EXEMPLIFICATION

1. Interview several businesspeople in your community. Begin by explaining the Peter Principle to them if they are unfamiliar with it. Then, ask them to give their opinions of this concept, and take notes on their responses. Finally, write an essay about your findings that includes quotations from your notes. Document your sources, and include a works-cited page. (See the Appendix for information on documentation formats.)

2. Write a humorous essay about a ritual, ceremony, or celebration you experienced and the types of people who participated in it. Make a point about the event, and use the participants as examples to support your point.

3. Write an essay establishing that you are an optimistic (or pessimistic) person. Use examples to support your case.

4. If you could change three or four things at your school, what would they be? Use examples from your own experience to support your recommendations, and tie your recommendations together in your thesis statement.

5. Write an essay discussing two or three of the greatest challenges facing the United States today. If you like, you may refer to essays in this chapter, such as "Just Walk On By" (page 236) or "The Human Cost of an Illiterate Society" (page 248), or to essays elsewhere in this book, such as "Two Ways to Belong in America" (page 411) or "On Dumpster Diving" (page 714). Make sure that you document any material you get from your sources, and that you include a works-cited page. (See the Appendix for information on documentation formats.)

6. Using your family and friends as examples, write an essay suggesting some of the positive or negative characteristics of Americans.

7. Write an essay presenting your formula for achieving success in college. You may, if you wish, talk about things such as scheduling time, maintaining a high energy level, and learning how to relax. Use examples from your own experience to make your point. You may wish to refer to "College Pressures" (page 462).

8. Write an exemplification essay discussing how cooperation has helped you achieve some important goal. Support your thesis with a single well-developed example.

9. Choose an event that you believe illustrates a less-than-admirable moment in your life. Then, write an essay explaining your feelings.

10. The popularity of the TV show *American Idol* has revealed once again Americans' long-standing infatuation with music icons. Choose several pop groups or stars, old and new — such as Elvis Presley, the Beatles, Michael Jackson, Madonna, Fergie, Alicia Keys, 50 Cent, Amy Winehouse, and The Dixie Chicks, to name only a few — and use them to illustrate the characteristics that you think make pop stars so appealing.

COLLABORATIVE ACTIVITY FOR EXEMPLIFICATION

The following passage appeared in a handbook given to parents of entering students at a midwestern university:

The freshman experience is like no other — at once challenging, exhilarating, and fun. Students face academic challenges as they are exposed to many new ideas. They also face personal challenges as they meet many new people from diverse backgrounds. It is a time to mature and grow. It is an opportunity to explore new subjects and familiar ones. There may be no more challenging and exciting time of personal growth than the first year of university study.

Working in groups of four, brainstorm to identify examples that support or refute the idea that there "may be no more challenging and exciting time of personal growth" than the first year of college. Then, choose one person from each group to tell the class the position the group took and explain the examples you collected. Finally, work together to write an essay that presents your group's position. Have one student write the first draft, two others revise this draft, and the last student edit and proofread the revised draft.

9
Process

WHAT IS PROCESS?

A **process** essay explains how to do something or how something occurs. It presents a sequence of steps and shows how those steps lead to a particular result. In the following paragraph from *Language in Thought and Action,* the semanticist S. I. Hayakawa uses process to explain how a dictionary editor decides on a word's definition:

<table>
<tr>
<td>

Process presents series of steps in chronological order

</td>
<td>

To define a word, then, the dictionary-editor places before him the stack of cards illustrating that word; each of the cards represents an actual use of the word by a writer of some literary or historical importance. He reads the cards carefully, discards some, rereads the rest, and divides up the stack according to what he thinks are the several senses of the word. Finally, he writes his definitions, following the hard-and-fast rule that each definition *must* be based on what the quotations in front of him reveal about the meaning of the word. The editor cannot be influenced by what *he* thinks a

</td>
</tr>
<tr>
<td>

Topic sentence

</td>
<td>

given word *ought* to mean. He must work according to the cards or not at all.

</td>
</tr>
</table>

Process, like narration, presents events in chronological order. Unlike a narrative, however, a process essay explains a particular series of events that produces the same outcome whenever it is duplicated. Because these events form a sequence with a fixed order, clarity is extremely important. Whether your readers will actually perform the process or are simply trying to understand how it occurs, your essay must make clear the exact order of the individual steps, as well as their relationships to one another and to the process as a whole. This means you need to provide clear, logical transitions between the steps in a process, and you also need to present the steps in *strict* chronological order — that is, in the exact order in which they occur or are to be performed.

Depending on its purpose, a process essay can be either a set of *instructions* or a *process explanation.*

Understanding Instructions

The purpose of **instructions** is to enable readers to perform a process. A recipe, a handout about using your library's online databases, and the operating manual for your DVD player are all written in the form of instructions. So are directions for locating an office building in Washington, D.C., or for driving from Houston to Pensacola. Instructions use the present tense and, like commands, they use the imperative mood, speaking directly to readers: "*Disconnect* the system, and *check* the electrical source."

Understanding Process Explanations

The purpose of a **process explanation** is not to enable readers to perform a process but rather to help them understand how it is carried out. Such essays may examine anything from how silkworms spin their cocoons to how Michelangelo and Leonardo da Vinci painted their masterpieces on plaster walls and ceilings.

A process explanation may use the first person (*I, we*) or the third (*he, she, it, they*), the past tense or the present. Because its readers need to understand the process, not perform it, a process explanation does not use the second person (*you*) or the imperative mood (commands). The style of a process explanation varies, depending on whether a writer is explaining a process that takes place regularly or one that occurred in the past and also depending on whether the writer or someone else carries out the steps. The following chart suggests the stylistic options available to writers of process explanations.

	First person	*Third person*
Present tense	"After I place the chemicals in the tray, I turn out the lights in the darkroom." *(habitual process performed by the writer)*	"After photographers place the chemicals in the tray, they turn out the lights in the darkroom." *(habitual process performed by someone other than the writer)*
Past tense	"After I placed the chemicals in the tray, I turned out the lights in the darkroom." *(process performed in the past by the writer)*	"After the photographer placed the chemicals in the tray, she turned out the lights in the darkroom." *(process performed in the past by someone other than the writer)*

USING PROCESS

College writing frequently calls for instructions or process explanations. In a biology paper on genetic testing, you might devote a paragraph to an explanation of the process of amniocentesis; in an editorial about the negative side of fraternity life, you might include a brief account of the process of pledging. You can also organize an entire paper around a process pattern: in a literature essay, you might trace a fictional character's progress toward some new insight; on a finance midterm, you might explain the procedure for approving a commercial loan.

PLANNING A PROCESS ESSAY

As you plan a process essay, remember that your primary goal is to depict the process accurately. This means you need to distinguish between what usually or always happens and what occasionally or rarely happens, between necessary steps and optional ones. You should also mentally test all the steps in sequence to be sure the process really works as you say it does, checking carefully for omitted steps or incorrect information. If you are writing about a process you witnessed, try to test the accuracy of your explanation by observing the process again.

Accommodating Your Audience

As you write, remember to keep your readers' needs in mind. When necessary, explain the reasons for performing the steps, describe unfamiliar materials or equipment, define terms, and warn readers about possible problems that may occur during the process. (Sometimes you may want to include illustrations.) Besides complete information, your readers need a clear and consistent discussion without ambiguities or digressions. For this reason, you should avoid unnecessary shifts in tense, person, voice, and mood. You should also be careful not to omit articles (*a, an,* and *the*) so that your discussion moves smoothly, like an essay — not abruptly, like a cookbook.

Developing a Thesis Statement

Both instructions and process explanations can be written either to persuade or simply to present information. If its purpose is persuasive, a process essay may take a strong stand in a **thesis statement**, such as "Applying for food stamps is a needlessly complex process that discourages many qualified recipients" or "The process of slaughtering baby seals is inhumane and sadistic." Many process essays, however, communicate nothing more debatable than the procedure for blood typing. Even in such a case, though, a process should have a clear thesis statement that identifies the process and perhaps tells why it is performed: "Typing their own blood can familiarize students with some fundamental laboratory procedures."

Using Transitions

Throughout your essay, be sure to use transitional words and phrases to ensure that each step, each stage, and each paragraph leads logically to the next. Transitions such as *first, second, meanwhile, after this, next, then, at the same time, when you have finished,* and *finally* help to establish sequential and chronological relationships so that readers can follow the process. (A more complete list of transitions appears on page 43.)

STRUCTURING A PROCESS ESSAY

Like other essays, a process essay generally consists of three sections. The **introduction** identifies the process and indicates why and under what circumstances it is performed. This section may include information about materials or preliminary preparations, or it may present an overview of the process, perhaps even listing its major stages. The paper's thesis is also usually stated in the introduction.

Each paragraph in the **body** of the essay typically treats one major stage of the process. Each stage may group several steps, depending on the nature and complexity of the process. These steps are presented in chronological order, interrupted only for essential definitions, explanations, or cautions. Every step must be included and must appear in its proper place.

A short process essay may not need a formal **conclusion**. If an essay does have a conclusion, however, it will often briefly review the procedure's major stages. Such an ending is especially useful if the paper has outlined a technical procedure that may seem complicated to general readers. The conclusion may also reinforce the thesis by summarizing the results of the process or explaining its significance.

Suppose you are taking a midterm examination in a course in childhood and adolescent behavior. One essay question calls for a process explanation: "Trace the stages that children go through in acquiring language." After thinking about the question, you formulate the following thesis statement: "Although individual cases may differ, most children acquire language in a predictable series of stages." You then plan your essay and develop an informal outline, which might look like this:

Introduction:	Thesis statement — Although individual cases may differ, most children acquire language in a predictable series of stages.
First stage (two to twelve months):	Prelinguistic behavior, including "babbling" and appropriate responses to nonverbal cues.
Second stage (end of first year):	Single words as commands or requests; infant catalogs his or her environment.

Third stage (beginning of second year):	Expressive jargon (flow of sounds that imitates adult speech); real words along with jargon.
Fourth and final stage (middle of second year to beginning of third year):	Two-word phrases; longer strings; missing parts of speech.
Conclusion:	Restatement of thesis or review of major stages of process.

This essay, when completed, will show not only what the stages of the process are but also how they relate to one another. In addition, it will support the thesis that children learn language through a well-defined process.

REVISING A PROCESS ESSAY

When you revise a set of instructions or a process explanation, consider the items on the revision checklist on page 54. In addition, pay special attention to the items on the following checklist, which apply specifically to revising process essays.

✓ **REVISION CHECKLIST: Process**

- Does your assignment call for a set of instructions or a process explanation?
- Is your essay's style appropriate for the kind of process essay (instructions or process explanation) you are writing?
- Does your essay have a clearly stated thesis that identifies the process and perhaps tells why it is (or was) performed?
- Have you included all necessary reminders and cautions?
- Have you included all necessary steps?
- Are the steps presented in strict chronological order?
- Do transitions clearly indicate where one step ends and the next begins?

EDITING A PROCESS ESSAY

When you edit your process essay, follow the guidelines on the editing checklists on pages 71, 74, and 76. In addition, focus on the grammar, mechanics, and punctuation issues that are particularly relevant to process essays. One of these issues — avoiding unnecessary shifts in tense, person, voice, and mood — is discussed on pages 268-69.

GRAMMAR IN CONTEXT: Avoiding Unnecessary Shifts

To explain a process to readers, you need to use consistent verb **tense** (past or present), **person** (second or third), **voice** (active or passive), and **mood** (statements or commands). Unnecessary shifts in tense, person, voice, or mood can confuse readers and make it difficult for them to follow your process.

Avoiding Shifts in Tense   Use present tense for a process that is performed regularly.

"The body is first laid out in the undertaker's morgue — or rather, Mr. Jones is reposing in the preparation room — to be readied to bid the world farewell" (Mitford 305).

Use past tense for a process that was performed in the past.

"He peeled the potatoes and thin-sliced them into a quart-sized Mason fruit jar" (Malcolm X 283).

Shift from present to past tense only when you need to indicate a change in time: Usually, I study several days before a test, but this time I studied the night before.

Avoiding Shifts in Person   In process explanations, use first or third person.

FIRST PERSON (*I*):	"I reached for the box of Medium Ash Brown hair dye just as my friend Veronica grabbed the box labeled Sparkling Sherry" (Hunt 275).
FIRST PERSON (*WE*):	"We decided to use my bathroom to dye our hair" (Hunt 275).
THIRD PERSON (*HE*):	"The embalmer, having allowed an appropriate interval to elapse, returns to the attack, but now he brings into play the skill and equipment of sculptor and cosmetician" (Mitford 307).

In instructions, use second person.

SECOND PERSON (*YOU*):	"If you sometimes forget to pay bills, or if you have large student loans, you may have a problem" (McGlade 270).

When you give instructions, be careful not to shift from third to second person.

INCORRECT:	If a person sometimes forgets to pay bills, or if someone has large student loans, you may have a problem.
CORRECT:	If you sometimes forget to pay bills, or if you have large student loans, you may have a problem. (second person)

Avoiding Shifts in Voice Use active voice when you want to emphasize the person performing the action.

"In the last four years, I have moved eight times, living in three dorm rooms, two summer sublets, and three apartments in three different cities." (McGlade 270).

Use passive voice to emphasize the action itself, not the person performing it.

"The patching and filling completed, Mr. Jones is now shaved, washed, and dressed" (Mitford 308).

Do not shift between the active and the passive voice, especially within a sentence, unless your intent is to change your emphasis.

INCORRECT:	The first draft of my essay was completed, and then I started the second draft.
CORRECT:	I completed the first draft of my essay, and then I started the second draft. (active voice)

Avoiding Shifts in Mood Use the indicative mood (statements) for process explanations.

"He draped the towel around my shoulders, over my rubber apron, and began again vaselining my hair" (Malcolm X 283).

Use the imperative mood (commands) only in instructions.

"Call a friend or relative for help" (Piven et al. 291).

Be careful not to shift from the imperative mood to the indicative mood.

INCORRECT:	First, check your credit report for errors, and you should report any errors you find.
CORRECT:	First, check your credit report for errors, and report any errors you find. (imperative)
CORRECT:	First, you should check your credit report for errors, and you should report any errors you find. (indicative)

For more practice in avoiding unnecessary shifts, visit Exercise Central at **bedfordstmartins.com/patterns/shifts.**

✓ **EDITING CHECKLIST: Process**

- Have you used commas correctly in a series of three or more steps, including a comma before the *and*?
- Have you used parallel structure for items in a series?
- Have you avoided unnecessary shifts in tense?
- Have you avoided unnecessary shifts in person?
- Have you avoided unnecessary shifts in voice?
- Have you avoided unnecessary shifts in mood?

A STUDENT WRITER: Instructions

The following student essay, "The Search," by Eric McGlade, gives readers **instructions** on how to find an apartment. It was written for a composition class in response to the assignment, "Write an essay giving practical instructions for doing something most people you know will need to do at one time or another."

The Search

Introduction

In the last four years, I have moved eight times, living in three dorm rooms, two summer sublets, and three apartments in three different cities. I would not recommend this experience to anyone. Finding an apartment is time consuming, stressful, and expensive, so the best advice is to stay where you are. However, if you must move, here are a few tips to help you survive the search.

Thesis statement

First major stage of process: before the search

Before you begin your search, take some time to plan. First, figure out what you can afford. (Here's a hint — you can afford less than you think.) Most experts say you should spend no more than one-third of your net income on rent. Find a budgeting worksheet online, and see for yourself how car insurance, electricity, and cable can add up. Remember, your new landlord may charge a security deposit and the first month's rent, and there may be pet, parking, cleaning, or moving-in fees.

First step: review your finances

Second step: check your credit history

Next, consider your credit history. If you sometimes forget to pay bills, or if you have large student loans, you may

1

2

3

have a problem. Landlords usually run a credit check on potential renters. If you are particularly concerned about your credit rating, order a credit report from one of the three main credit bureaus: TransUnion, Equifax, or Experian. If you find that your credit isn't perfect, don't panic. First, check your credit report for errors, and report any errors you find to the credit bureau. Second, adopt good financial habits immediately. Start paying bills on time, and try to consolidate any debts at a lower interest rate. If a landlord does question your credit, be prepared to explain any extenuating circumstances of the past and to point out your current good behavior.

Third step: consider where to live

After you know what you can afford, you need to figure out where you want to (and can afford to) live. Keep in mind important factors such as how close the apartment is to your school or workplace and how convenient the neighborhood is. Is public transportation located nearby? Is on-street parking available? Can you easily get to a supermarket, coffee shop, convenience store, and Laundromat? If possible, visit each potential neighborhood both during the day and at night. A business district may be bustling during the day but deserted (and even dangerous) at night. If you visit both early and late, you will get a more accurate impression of how safe the neighborhood feels. 4

Fourth step: consider a roommate

During this stage, consider whether or not you are willing to live with a roommate. You will sacrifice privacy, but you will be able to afford a better apartment. If you do decide to live with a roommate, the easiest way to proceed is to find a friend who also needs an apartment. If this isn't possible, try to find an apartment that comes with a roommate — one with one roommate moving out but the other roommate remaining in the apartment. The third option is to find another apartment seeker and go apartment hunting together. Some Web sites, such as www.roommates.com, cater to this type of search, but, unfortunately, most require a fee. However, your school housing office might have a list of students looking for roommates. 5

Transitional paragraph

Now, you are ready to start looking. You can find the perfect apartment through a real estate agent, by checking your local newspaper or school's housing listings, by asking your friends and family, or by visiting Web sites such as www.craigslist.org. 6

Second major stage
of process: during
the search

Each of these methods has pros and cons. A real estate   7
agent might help you find your dream apartment quickly, but
you will usually have to pay for this speedy service. As for
newspaper listings, stick to your local paper; unless you are
looking for a second vacation home in Maui, national

First step: do
research

newspapers are not your best bet. An even better idea is to
check your school's housing listings, where you are likely to
find fellow students in search of apartments in your price range.

Second step: spread
the word

Meanwhile, spread the word. Tell everyone you know that   8
you are apartment hunting. After all, your stepsister's uncle's
mother-in-law may live in a building with a newly vacant
apartment. This method isn't the most efficient, but the results
can be amazing. As a bonus, you will receive practical advice
about your neighborhood, such as what to watch out for and
what problems other renters have had.

Third step: try
Craigslist

Finally, if you are hunting in a major city, I have but one   9
word: Craigslist. Craigslist.org has free apartment listings
arranged by city and neighborhood. You can hunt for an
apartment by price, by number of bedrooms, or by length of
lease. If you are on a tight moving schedule and need a place
immediately, this Web site is especially helpful because of the
sheer volume of its listings. Craigslist also has the added benefit
of providing a general price range for your ideal neighborhood.

Fourth step: visit
apartments

Once you have identified some possibilities, it's time to   10
visit the apartments. Get a good look at each one. Is it
furnished or unfurnished? Look closely at the kitchen. Are all
the appliances in good working order? How big is your
bedroom? Will your bed fit? How much closet space will you
have? Are there phone, cable, and Internet hookups? Is it a
sunny apartment (south facing), or is it dark (north facing)? In
the bathroom, turn on the faucets in the sink and shower;
check for rust and poor water pressure. As you walk through the
apartment, check the cell-phone reception (leaning out the
window of your bathroom to talk on the phone is not fun). Most
important, do not forget to take notes. After seeing fourteen
apartments, you may confuse Apartment A, with the six pets
and funny smell, with Apartment G, with the balcony and
renovated kitchen.

Third major stage
of process: after
the search

And now, at last, the search is over: you have found your   11
apartment. Congratulations! Unfortunately, your work is not

First step: check your lease   yet over. Now, it is time to read your lease. It will be long and boring, but it is a very important document. Among other things, your lease should specify the length of the lease, a rent due date, fees for late rent payments, the amount of the security deposit, and the conditions required for the return of the security deposit. If you have decided to live with a roommate, you might ask the landlord to divide the rent on your lease. This way, if your roommate moves to Brazil, you will not have to pay his share of the rent. Be sure to read your lease thoroughly and bring up any concerns with your landlord.

Second step: get insurance and activate utilities   Before you move in, you have a few more things to do: 12 get renter's insurance to protect you from theft or damage to your possessions; arrange to get your utilities hooked up; submit a change-of-address form at the post office; and inform your bank or credit-card company about your future move. Finally, start packing!

Conclusion   If you plan ahead and shop smart, you can find your   13 perfect apartment. Remember to figure out what you can afford, check out the neighborhoods, consider a roommate, use multiple search methods, and take careful notes when you visit potential apartments. Yes, happy endings do occur. I am now in the third month of a two-year lease, and I have no plans to move anytime soon.

Points for Special Attention

Introduction.   The first paragraph of Eric McGlade's essay begins by giving readers some background on his own experience as an apartment hunter. This strategy gives him some credibility, establishing him as an "expert" who can explain the process. Eric then narrows his focus to the difficulties of apartment hunting and ends his introduction with a thesis statement telling readers that the process can be made easier.

Structure.   Eric divides his essay into the three major stages of apartment hunting: what to do before, during, and after the search. After his introduction, Eric includes four paragraphs that explain what to do before the search gets under way. In paragraphs 6 through 10, he explains how to go about the actual hunt for an apartment. Then, in paragraphs 11 and 12, he tells readers what they should do after they locate an apartment (but before they move in). In his conclusion, he restates his thesis, summarizes the steps in the process, and returns to his own experience to reassure readers that a positive outcome is possible.

Purpose and Style. Because Eric's assignment asked him to give practical advice for a process readers could expect to perform, he decided to write the essay as a set of instructions. Therefore, he uses the second person ("If *you* find that *your* credit isn't perfect, don't panic") and the present tense, with many of his verbs in the form of commands ("First, *figure* out what you can afford").

Transitions. To make his essay clear and easy to follow, Eric includes transitions that indicate the order in which each step is to be performed ("First," "Next," "Now," "Meanwhile," "Finally," and so on), as well as expressions such as "During this stage." He also includes transitional sentences to move his essay from one stage of the process to the next:

- "Before you begin your search, take some time to plan" (2).
- "Now, you are ready to start looking" (6).
- "Once you have identified some possibilities, it's time to visit the apartments" (10).
- "And now, at last, the search is over: you have found your apartment" (11).

Finally, paragraph 6 serves as a transitional paragraph, moving readers from the preliminary steps to the start of the actual search for an apartment.

Focus on Revision

When he met with his peer editing group, Eric found that they had all gone through the apartment-hunting process and therefore had some practical suggestions to make. In the draft they reviewed, Eric included a good deal of information about his own experiences, but his readers felt those narratives, although amusing, were distracting and got in the way of the process. Eric agreed, and he deleted these anecdotes. His readers thought that mentioning his experiences briefly in his introduction would be sufficient, but Eric decided to also return briefly to his own story in his conclusion, adding the two "happy ending" sentences that now conclude his essay. In addition, he followed his readers' suggestion to add a review of the steps of the process to his conclusion to help readers remember what they had read. These additions gave him a fully developed conclusion.

In terms of his essay's content, his reviewers were most concerned with paragraph 10, which they felt seemed to rush through a very important part of the process: visiting the apartments. They also observed that the information in this paragraph was not arranged in any logical order and that Eric had failed to mention other considerations (for example, whether the apartment needed repairs or painting, whether it was noisy, whether it included air conditioning). One reader suggested that Eric expand his discussion and divide the information into two separate paragraphs, one on the apartment's mechanical systems (plumbing, electricity, and so on) and another on its physical appearance (size of rooms, light, and so on). In the final draft of his essay, Eric did just that. (A sample peer editing worksheet for process appears on pages 278–79.)

A STUDENT WRITER: Process Explanation

The essay that follows, "Medium Ash Brown," by Melany Hunt, is a **process explanation**. It was written for a composition class in response to the assignment, "Write an essay explaining a process that changed your appearance in some way."

Medium Ash Brown

Introduction	The beautiful chestnut-haired woman pictured on the box seemed to beckon to me. I reached for the box of Medium Ash Brown hair dye just as my friend Veronica grabbed the box labeled Sparkling Sherry. I can't remember our reasons for wanting to change our hair color, but they seemed to make sense at the time. Maybe we were just bored. I do remember that the idea of transforming our appearance came up unexpectedly. Impulsively, we decided to change our hair	1
Thesis statement	color — and, we hoped, ourselves — that very evening. The process that followed taught me that some impulses should definitely be resisted.	
Materials assembled	We decided to use my bathroom to dye our hair. Inside each box of hair color, we found two little bottles and a small tube wrapped in a page of instructions. Attached to the instruction page itself were two very large, one-size-fits-all plastic gloves, which looked and felt like plastic sandwich bags. The directions recommended having some old towels around to soak up any spills or drips that might occur. Under the sink we found some old, frayed towels that I figured my mom had	2
First stage of process: preparing the dye	forgotten about, and we spread them around the bathtub. After we put our gloves on, we began the actual dyeing process. First we poured the first bottle into the second, which was half-full of some odd-smelling liquid. The smell was not much better after we combined the two bottles. The directions advised us to cut off a small section of hair to use as a sample. For some reason, we decided to skip this step.	
Second stage of process: applying the dye	At this point, Veronica and I took turns leaning over the tub to wet our hair for the dye. The directions said to leave the dye on the hair for fifteen to twenty minutes, so we found a	3

little timer and set it for fifteen minutes. Next, we applied the dye to our hair. Again, we took turns, squeezing the bottle in order to cover all our hair. We then wrapped the old towels around our sour-smelling hair and went outside to get some fresh air.

Third stage of process: rinsing

After the fifteen minutes were up, we rinsed our hair. According to the directions, we were to add a little water and scrub as if we were shampooing our hair. The dye lathered up, and we rinsed our hair until the water ran clear. So far, so good. 4

Last stage of process: applying conditioner

The last part of the process involved applying the small tube of conditioner to our hair (because dyed hair becomes brittle and easily damaged). We used the conditioner as directed, and then we dried our hair so that we could see the actual color. Even before I looked in the mirror, I heard Veronica's gasp. 5

Outcome of process

"Nice try," I said, assuming she was just trying to make me nervous, "but you're not funny." 6

"Mel," she said, "look in the mirror." Slowly, I turned around. My stomach turned into a lead ball when I saw my reflection. My hair was the putrid greenish-brown color of a winter lawn, dying in patches yet still a nice green in the shade. 7

The next day in school, I wore my hair tied back under a baseball cap. I told only my close friends what I had done. After they were finished laughing, they offered their deepest, most heartfelt condolences. They also offered many suggestions — none very helpful — on what to do to get my old hair color back. 8

Conclusion

It is now three months later, and I still have no idea what prompted me to dye my hair. My only consolation is that I resisted my first impulse — to dye my hair a wild color, like blue or fuchsia. Still, as I wait for my hair to grow out, and as I assemble a larger and larger collection of baseball caps, it is small consolation indeed. 9

Points for Special Attention

Structure. In her opening paragraph, Melany's thesis statement makes it very clear that the experience she describes is not one she would recommend to others. The temptation she describes in her introduction's first few sentences lures readers into her essay, just as the picture on the box lured her. Her second paragraph lists the contents of the box of hair dye and explains how she and her friend assembled the other necessary materials. Then, she explains the first stage in the process: preparing the dye. Paragraphs 3–5 describe the other stages in the process in chronological order, and paragraphs 6–8 record Melany's and Veronica's reactions to their experiment. In paragraph 9, Melany sums up the impact of her experience and once again expresses her annoyance with herself for her impulsive act.

Purpose and Style.   Melany's purpose is not to enable others to duplicate the process she explains; on the contrary, she wants to discourage readers from doing what she did. Consequently, she presents her process not as a set of instructions but as a process explanation, using first person and past tense to explain her and her friend's actions. She also largely eliminates cautions and reminders that her readers, who are not likely to undertake the process, will not need to know.

Detail.   Melany's essay includes vivid descriptive detail that gives readers a clear sense of the process and its outcome. Throughout, her emphasis is on the negative aspects of the process — the "odd-smelling liquid" and the "putrid greenish-brown color" of her hair, for instance — and this emphasis is consistent with her essay's purpose.

Transitions.   To move readers smoothly through the process, Melany includes clear transitions ("First," "At this point," "Next," "then") and clearly identifies the beginning of the process ("After we put our gloves on, we began the actual dyeing process") and the end ("The last part of the process").

Focus on Revision

Students who read Melany's essay thought it was clearly written and structured and that its ironic, self-mocking tone was well suited to her audience and purpose. They felt, however, that some minor revisions would make her essay even more effective. Specifically, they thought that paragraph 2 began too abruptly: paragraph 1 recorded the purchase of the hair dye, and paragraph 2 opened with the sentence "We decided to use my bathroom to dye our hair," leaving readers wondering how much time had passed between purchase and application. Because the thesis rests on the idea of the foolishness of an impulsive gesture, it is important for readers to understand that the girls presumably went immediately from the store to Melany's house.

After thinking about this criticism, Melany decided to write a clearer opening for paragraph 2: "As soon as we paid for the dye, we returned to my house, where, eager to begin our transformation, we locked ourselves in my bathroom. Inside each box . . . ." She also decided to divide paragraph 2 into two paragraphs, one describing the materials and another beginning with "After we put our gloves on," which introduces the first step in the process.

Another possible revision Melany considered was developing Veronica's character further. Although both girls purchase and apply hair color, readers never learn what happens to Veronica. Melany knew she could easily add a brief paragraph after paragraph 7, describing Veronica's "Sparkling Sherry" hair in humorous terms, and she planned to do so in her paper's final draft.

Finally, one student suggested that Melany refer in her essay to Malcolm X's "My First Conk" (page 282). After all, Malcolm X had also tried to change his appearance and had also been sorry afterward. (In fact, the class's assignment — "Write an essay explaining a process that changed your appearance in some way" — was inspired by their reading of "My First Conk.") Melany considered this suggestion but ultimately decided not to take her classmate's advice. She realized that Malcolm X's initial response to his transformation (unlike hers) was positive; only later did he realize that his desire to transform his looks to conform to a white ideal was "ridiculous" (page 284), a "step toward self-degradation" (page 284). Moreover, Melany thought Malcolm X's serious analysis would not be a good fit for her lighthearted essay. So, even though the topic of Malcolm X's essay was similar to hers, Melany decided that referring to his experience would trivialize his ideas and be out of place in her essay.

📄 **PEER EDITING WORKSHEET: Process**

1. What process does this essay describe?
2. Does the writer include all the information the audience needs? Is any vital step or piece of information missing? Is any step or piece of information irrelevant? Is any necessary definition, explanation, or caution missing or incomplete?
3. Is the essay a set of instructions or a process explanation? How can you tell? Why do you think the writer chose this strategy rather than the alternative? Do you think this was the right choice?
4. Does the writer consistently follow the stylistic conventions for the strategy — instructions or process explanation — he or she has chosen?
5. Are the steps presented in clear, logical order? Are they grouped logically into paragraphs? Should any steps be combined or relocated? If so, which ones?
6. Does the writer use enough transitions to move readers through the process? Should any transitions be added? If so, where?
7. Does the writer need to revise to correct confusing shifts in tense, person, voice, and mood? If so, where?

8. Is the essay interesting? What descriptive details would add interest to the essay? Would a visual be helpful?

9. How would you characterize the writer's opening strategy? Is it appropriate for the essay's purpose and audience? What alternative strategy might be more effective?

10. How would you characterize the writer's closing strategy? Would a different conclusion be more effective? Explain.

The reading selections that follow illustrate how varied the uses of process writing can be. The first selection, a visual text, is followed by questions designed to illustrate how process can operate in visual form.

How to Change a Flat Tire (Illustration)

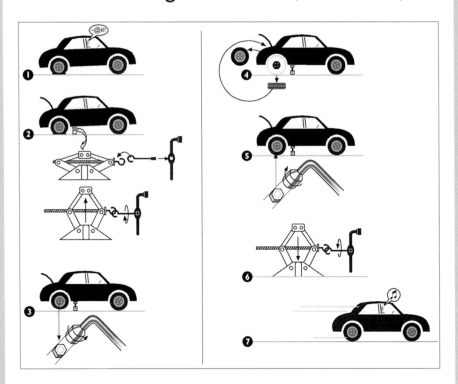

Reading Images

1. Look closely at the series of illustrations above. Do the illustrations give you enough information to enable you to perform the process? What specific details, if any, are missing?

2. Consulting the illustrations, list the steps involved in the process of changing a tire. Are the steps labeled number 1 and number 7 actually part of the process? Explain.

3. What cautions or reminders might be helpful to someone who wanted to follow these instructions?

Journal Entry

Write a one-paragraph set of instructions (straightforward or humorous) for changing a tire. Using commands and present tense, explain each step in order. Then, add an introductory sentence to identify the process and a concluding sentence to sum it up.

Thematic Connections

- "The Human Cost of an Illiterate Society" (page 248)
- "How to Escape from a Bad Date" (page 291)

My First Conk

Malcolm X was born Malcolm Little in Omaha, Nebraska, in 1925. As a young man, he had a number of run-ins with the law, and he wound up in prison on burglary charges before he was twenty-one. There he pursued his education and was influenced by the writings of Elijah Muhammed, the founder of the Black Muslims (now known as the Nation of Islam), a black separatist organization. On his release from prison, Malcolm X became a highly visible member of this group and a disciple of its leader. He left the movement in 1963, later converting to orthodox Islam and founding a rival African-American political organization. He was assassinated in 1965.

Background on conks and other African-American hair styles
The Autobiography of Malcolm X (written with Alex Haley) was published in 1964. The following excerpt from that book describes the painful and painstaking process many African-American men once endured to achieve a style of straight hair called a "conk." (The term probably comes from Congolene, the brand name of one commercial hair straightener.) First popularized in the 1920s by black entertainers such as Cab Calloway, the style continued to be fashionable until the 1960s, when more natural styles, including the Afro, became a symbol of black pride, and conked hair came to be seen as a self-loathing attempt to imitate whites. Ironically, perhaps, some contemporary African Americans still distinguish between "good" (that is, naturally straight) and "bad" (that is, naturally curly) hair. Today, cosmetically straightened hair (a process that is no longer so arduous) is considered one fashion option among many, including shaved heads, closely cropped hair, braids, cornrows, and dreadlocks.

1   Shorty soon decided that my hair was finally long enough to be conked. He had promised to school me in how to beat the barber shops' three- and four-dollar price by making up congolene, and then conking ourselves.

2   I took the little list of ingredients he had printed out for me, and went to a grocery store, where I got a can of Red Devil lye, two eggs, and two medium-sized white potatoes. Then at a drugstore near the poolroom, I asked for a large jar of vaseline, a large bar of soap, a large-toothed comb and a fine-toothed comb, one of those rubber hoses with a metal spray-head, a rubber apron, and a pair of gloves.

3   "Going to lay on that first conk?" the drugstore man asked me. I proudly told him, grinning, "Right!"

4   Shorty paid six dollars a week for a room in his cousin's shabby apartment. His cousin wasn't at home. "It's like the pad's mine, he spends so much time with his woman," Shorty said. "Now, you watch me — "

He peeled the potatoes and thin-sliced them into a quart-sized Mason   5
fruit jar, then started stirring them with a wooden spoon as he gradually
poured in a little over half the can of lye. "Never use a metal spoon; the lye
will turn it black," he told me.

A jelly-like, starchy-looking glop resulted from the lye and potatoes,   6
and Shorty broke in the two eggs, stirring real fast — his own conk and
dark face bent down close. The congolene turned pale-yellowish. "Feel the
jar," Shorty said. I cupped my hand against the outside, and snatched it
away. "Damn right, it's hot, that's the lye," he said. "So you know it's going
to burn when I comb it in — it burns bad. But the longer you can stand it,
the straighter the hair."

He made me sit down, and he tied the string of the new rubber apron   7
tightly around my neck, and combed up my bush of hair. Then, from the
big vaseline jar, he took a handful and massaged it hard all through my hair
and into the scalp. He also thickly vaselined my neck, ears, and forehead.
"When I get to washing out your head, be sure to tell me anywhere you feel
any little stinging," Shorty warned me, washing his hands, then pulling on
the rubber gloves, and tying on his own rubber apron. "You always got to
remember that any congolene left in burns a sore into your head."

The congolene just felt warm when Shorty started combing it in. But   8
then my head caught fire.

I gritted my teeth and tried to pull the sides of the kitchen table   9
together. The comb felt as if it was raking my skin off.

My eyes watered, my nose was running. I couldn't stand it any longer; I   10
bolted to the washbasin. I was cursing Shorty with every name I could
think of when he got the spray going and started soap lathering my head.

He lathered and spray-rinsed, lathered and spray-rinsed, maybe ten or   11
twelve times, each time gradually closing the hot-water faucet, until the
rinse was cold, and that helped some.

"You feel any stinging spots?"   12

"No," I managed to say. My knees were trembling.   13

"Sit back down, then. I think we got it all out okay."   14

The flame came back as Shorty, with a thick towel, started drying my   15
head, rubbing hard. *"Easy, man, easy!"* I kept shouting.

"The first time's always worst. You get used to it better before long.   16
You took it real good, homeboy. You got a good conk."

When Shorty let me stand up and see in the mirror, my hair hung down   17
in limp, damp strings. My scalp still flamed, but not as badly; I could bear
it. He draped the towel around my shoulders, over my rubber apron, and
began again vaselining my hair.

I could feel him combing, straight back, first the big comb, then the   18
fine-tooth one.

Then, he was using a razor, very delicately, on the back of my neck.   19
Then, finally, shaping the sideburns.

My first view in the mirror blotted out the hurting. I'd seen some pretty   20
conks, but when it's the first time, on your *own* head, the transformation,
after the lifetime of kinks, is staggering.

The mirror reflected Shorty behind me. We both were grinning and   21
sweating. And on top of my head was this thick, smooth sheen of shining
red hair — real red — as straight as any white man's.

How ridiculous I was! Stupid enough to stand there simply lost in   22
admiration of my hair now looking "white," reflected in the mirror in
Shorty's room. I vowed that I'd never again be without a conk, and I never
was for many years.

This was my first really big step toward self-degradation: when I   23
endured all of that pain, literally burning my flesh to have it look like a
white man's hair. I had joined that multitude of Negro men and women in
America who are brainwashed into believing that the black people are "inferior" — and white people "superior" — that they will even violate and muti-
late their God-created bodies to try to look "pretty" by white standards.

Look around today, in every small town and big city, from two-bit cat-   24
fish and soda-pop joints into the "integrated" lobby of the Waldorf-Astoria,
and you'll see conks on black men. And you'll see black women wearing
these green and pink and purple and red and platinum-blonde wigs. They're
all more ridiculous than a slapstick comedy. It makes you wonder if the
Negro has completely lost his sense of identity, lost touch with himself.

You'll see the conk worn by many, many so-called "upper class" Negroes,   25
and, as much as I hate to say it about them, on all too many Negro entertainers. One of the reasons that I've especially admired some of them, like Lionel
Hampton and Sidney Poitier, among others, is that they have kept their natural hair and fought to the top. I admire any Negro man who has never had
himself conked, or who has had the sense to get rid of it — as I finally did.

I don't know which kind of self-defacing conk is the greater shame — the   26
one you'll see on the heads of the black so-called "middle class" and "upper
class," who ought to know better, or the one you'll see on the heads of the
poorest, most downtrodden, ignorant black men. I mean the legal-
minimum-wage ghetto-dwelling kind of Negro, as I was when I got my first
one. It's generally among these poor fools that you'll see a black kerchief
over the man's head, like Aunt Jemima; he's trying to make his conk last
longer, between trips to the barbershop. Only for special occasions is this
kerchief-protected conk exposed — to show off how "sharp" and "hip" its
owner is. The ironic thing is that I have never heard any woman, white or
black, express any admiration for a conk. Of course, any white woman with
a black man isn't thinking about his hair. But I don't see how on earth a
black woman with any race pride could walk down the street with any black
man wearing a conk — the emblem of his shame that he is black.

To my own shame, when I say all of this, I'm talking first of all about   27
myself — because you can't show me any Negro who ever conked more
faithfully than I did. I'm speaking from personal experience when I say of
any black man who conks today, or any white-wigged black woman, that if
they gave the brains in their heads just half as much attention as they do
their hair, they would be a thousand times better off.

·   ·   ·

Comprehension

1. What exactly is a conk? Why does Malcolm X want to get his hair conked? What does the conk symbolize to him at the time he gets it? What does it symbolize at the time he writes about it?

2. List the materials Shorty asks Malcolm X to buy. Is the purpose of each explained? If so, where?

3. Outline the major stages in the procedure Malcolm X describes. Are they presented in chronological order? Which, if any, of the major stages are out of place?

Purpose and Audience

1. Why was this selection written as a process explanation instead of as a set of instructions?

2. This selection has an explicitly stated thesis that makes its purpose clear. What is this thesis?

3. *The Autobiography of Malcolm X* was published in 1964, when many African Americans regularly straightened their hair. Is the thesis of this excerpt from the book still relevant today?

4. Why do you think Malcolm X includes so many references to the pain and discomfort he endured as part of the process?

5. What is the relationship between Malcolm X's personal experience and his universal statement about conking?

Style and Structure

1. Identify some of the transitional words Malcolm X uses to move from step to step.

2. Only about half of this selection is devoted to the process explanation. Where does the process begin? Where does it end?

3. In paragraphs 22–26, Malcolm X encloses several words in quotation marks, occasionally prefacing them with the phrase *so-called.* What is the effect of these quotation marks?

Vocabulary Projects

1. Define each of the following words as it is used in this selection.

vowed (22)	mutilate (23)	downtrodden (26)
self-degradation (23)	slapstick (24)	emblem (26)
multitude (23)	self-defacing (26)	

2. Because this is an informal piece of writing, Malcolm X uses many **colloquialisms** and **slang** terms. Substitute a more formal word for each of the following.

beat (1)	glop (6)	"sharp" (26)
pad (4)	real (6)	"hip" (26)

Evaluate the possible impact of your substitutions. Do they improve the essay or weaken it?

Journal Entry

Did you ever engage in behavior that you later came to view as unacceptable as your beliefs changed or as your social consciousness developed? What made you change your attitude toward this behavior?

Writing Workshop

1. Write a process explanation of an unpleasant experience you or someone you know has often gone through to conform to others' standards of physical beauty (for instance, dieting or undertaking strenuous exercise). Include a thesis statement that conveys your disapproval of the process.

2. Rewrite Malcolm X's process explanation as he might have written it when he still considered conking a desirable process, worth all the trouble. Include all his steps, but change his thesis and choose words that make conking sound painless and worthwhile. If you quote Malcolm X's words, be sure to include parenthetical documentation and a works-cited page. (See the Appendix for information on documentation formats.)

3. Rewrite this essay as a set of instructions that Shorty might have written for a friend about to help someone conk his hair. Begin by telling the friend what materials to purchase.

Combining the Patterns

Although "My First Conk" is very detailed, it does not include an extended **definition** of a conk. Do you think a definition paragraph should be added? If so, where could it be inserted? What patterns could be used to develop such a definition?

Thematic Connections

- "Finishing School" (page 107)
- "Four Tattoos" (page 214)
- "Just Walk On By" (page 236)
- "Medium Ash Brown" (page 275)
- "Inked Well" (page 738)

STANLEY FISH

Getting Coffee Is Hard to Do

Literary critic and legal scholar Stanley Fish (b. 1938) has had a long and distinguished academic career. He is currently Davidson-Kahn Distinguished Professor of Humanities and a professor of law at Florida International University in Miami. An authority on the seventeenth-century poet John Milton, Fish is also widely recognized for his revolutionary approach to literary criticism, as summarized in his groundbreaking book *Is There a Text in This Class?: The Authority of Interpretive Communities* (1980). A regular contributor to popular journals and op-ed pages in newspapers nationwide, Fish has also been a guest columnist for the *New York Times*, where the following essay originally appeared.

Background on U.S. coffee drinking trends
Coffee consumption in the United States goes back to the earliest English settlers. In fact, the British tax imposed on tea that led to the rebellious Boston Tea Party resulted in coffee's becoming the most popular American drink. However, the popularity of gourmet coffees can be traced back to 1966, when Dutch immigrant Alfred Peet, a coffee importer who was unhappy with the general quality of coffee in the United States, opened a shop in Berkeley, California, where he sold his own special roast. Trained in coffee roasting by Peet, the founders of Starbucks opened their first outlet in Seattle in 1971, selling quality coffee beans and coffeemaking equipment. Returning from a buying trip to Italy in 1985, then-marketing director Howard Schultz suggested that Starbucks become a true coffee house in the Italian tradition, a gathering spot where people could enjoy freshly roasted and brewed coffee. Despite being met with skepticism, Schultz would eventually take over the business and turn it into a worldwide phenomenon.

1   A coordination problem (a term of art in economics and management) occurs when you have a task to perform, the task has multiple and shifting components, the time for completion is limited, and your performance is affected by the order and sequence of the actions you take. The trick is to manage it so that the components don't bump into each other in ways that produce confusion, frustration, and inefficiency.

2   You will face a coordination problem if you are a general deploying troops, tanks, helicopters, food, tents, and medical supplies, or if you are the CEO of a large company juggling the demands of design, personnel, inventory, and production.

3   And these days, you will face a coordination problem if you want to get a cup of coffee.

4   It used to be that when you wanted a cup of coffee you went into a nondescript place fitted out largely in linoleum, Formica, and neon, sat

down at a counter, and, in response to a brisk "What'll you have, dear?" said, "Coffee and a cheese Danish." Twenty seconds later, tops, they arrived, just as you were settling into the sports page.

Now it's all wood or concrete floors, lots of earth tones, soft, high-style 5
lighting, open barrels of coffee beans, folk-rock and indie music, photographs of urban landscapes, and copies of *The Onion*. As you walk in, everything is saying, "This is very sophisticated, and you'd better be up to it."

It turns out to be hard. First you have to get in line, and you may have 6
one or two people in front of you who are ordering a drink with more parts than an internal combustion engine, something about "double shot," "skinny," "breve," "grande," "au lait" and a lot of other words that never pass my lips. If you are patient and stay in line (no bathroom breaks), you get to put in your order, but then you have to find a place to stand while you wait for it. There is no such place. So you shift your body, first here and then there, trying not to get in the way of those you can't help get in the way of.

Finally, the coffee arrives. 7

But then your real problems begin when you turn, holding your prize, 8
and make your way to where the accessories — things you put in, on, and around your coffee — are to be found. There is a staggering array of them, and the order of their placement seems random in relation to the order of your needs. There is no "right" place to start, so you lunge after one thing and then after another with awkward reaches.

Unfortunately, two or three other people are doing the same thing, and 9
each is doing it in a different sequence. So there is an endless round of "excuse me," "no, excuse me," as if you were in an old Steve Martin routine.

But no amount of politeness and care is enough. After all, there are so 10
many items to reach for — lids, cup jackets, straws, napkins, stirrers, milk, half and half, water, sugar, Splenda, the wastepaper basket, spoons. You and your companions may strive for a ballet of courtesy, but what you end up performing is more like bumper cars. It's just a question of what will happen first — getting what you want or spilling the coffee you are trying to balance in one hand on the guy reaching over you.

I won't even talk about the problem of finding a seat. 11

And two things add to your pain and trouble. First, it costs a lot, $3 and 12
up. And worst of all, what you're paying for is the privilege of doing the work that should be done by those who take your money. The coffee shop experience is just one instance of the growing practice of shifting the burden of labor to the consumer — gas stations, grocery and drug stores, bagel shops (why should I put on my own cream cheese?), airline check-ins, parking lots. It's insert this, swipe that, choose credit or debit, enter your PIN, push the red button, error, start again. At least when you go on a "vacation" that involves working on a ranch, the work is something you've chosen. But none of us has chosen to take over the jobs of those we pay to serve us.

Well, it's Sunday morning, and you're probably reading this with a cup 13
of coffee. I hope it was easy to get.

·   ·   ·

Comprehension

1. How does Fish describe the traditional process of getting a cup of coffee (4)? What does he see as the main difference between getting a cup of coffee in a diner or coffee shop and getting coffee in today's coffee bars?
2. According to Fish, how do the two kinds of coffee shops differ in terms of their physical setting?
3. List some of the obstacles Fish says customers face in a modern-day coffee bar.
4. Whom, or what, does Fish blame for the situation he describes?

Purpose and Audience

1. What purpose do the first two paragraphs of this essay serve? Are they necessary, or could the essay begin with paragraph 3?
2. What is the point of this essay? Is Fish simply trying to explain how difficult it has become to get a cup of coffee (as his title suggests), or does he have a more specific — and perhaps more serious — purpose in mind? (Read paragraph 12 carefully before you answer this question.)
3. In one sentence, state this essay's thesis. Does this thesis statement appear in the essay? If so, where?
4. Do you think Fish is exaggerating the difficulty of getting a cup of coffee? If so, what might be his purpose for doing so?
5. Who is the "you" Fish addresses in this essay?

Style and Structure

1. This essay includes several one-sentence paragraphs. Locate each one, and explain why you think it is so short. Should any of these one-sentence paragraphs be developed further? If so, how? Should any be combined with an adjacent paragraph?
2. List the steps in the process Fish describes. Then, group the steps into stages in the process.
3. Where does Fish include cautions and reminders? Give some examples. Given his audience's likely familiarity with the process he describes, are these tips necessary? If not, why do you think he includes them?
4. This essay is a process explanation. Do you think it would have been more effective if Fish had written it in the form of instructions? Explain.
5. Would you characterize Fish's tone as amused? Annoyed? Puzzled? What is his attitude toward the process he describes?

Vocabulary Projects

1. Define each of the following words as it is used in this selection.

deploying (2)   nondescript (4)   staggering (8)

2. As Fish illustrates, the world of the coffee bar has its own vocabulary. List and define five words that are part of this specialized vocabulary. (You can define words Fish includes here, or you can make your own list.)

Journal Entry

Do you agree with Fish that the process he describes is a problem? Why or why not?

Writing Workshop

1. Write an essay describing another process that is "hard to do" — specifically, something that is more complicated today than it used to be. For possible topics, see paragraph 12 of Fish's essay. If you like, you may quote the fourth sentence of this essay in your essay — but if you do, be sure to include parenthetical documentation and a works-cited page. (See the Appendix for information on documentation formats.)

2. Write a set of instructions for ordering, eating, and cleaning up after a meal in a fast-food restaurant. Assume your audience has never eaten in a fast-food restaurant before. Use "Getting Fast Food Is Easy to Do" as your essay's title.

Combining the Patterns

Fish includes several other patterns of development in his process essay. Locate examples of **definition, comparison and contrast, description, exemplification,** and **narration**. How do these passages support the process explanation?

Thematic Connections

- "Panacea" (page 162)
- "Swollen Expectations" (page 422)
- "Tortillas" (page 524)
- "Down and Out in Discount America" (page 638)

JOSHUA PIVEN, DAVID BORGENICHT,
AND JENNIFER WORICK

How to Escape from a Bad Date

Joshua Piven and David Borgenicht are the authors of the runaway best-seller *The Worst-Case Scenario Survival Handbook* (1999), having consulted numerous experts to enable them to provide advice for such dilemmas as "How to Break into a Parked Car" and "How to Escape from a Mountain Lion." The book's success sparked a series that now includes *The Worst-Case Scenario Survival Handbook: Travel* (2001), *The Worst-Case Scenario Survival Handbook: Holidays* (2002), *The Worst-Case Scenario Survival Handbook: College* (2004), and *The Worst-Case Scenario Survival Handbook: Weddings* (2004) as well as the reality-television show *Worst-Case Scenario*. In 2001, they collaborated on *The Worst-Case Scenario Survival Handbook: Dating and Sex* with Jennifer Worick, who is also the author of *Backcountry Betty: Roughing It in Style* (2007).

Background on self-help and "how-to" books
The United States has a long history of "how-to," advice, and self-improvement books dating back to Benjamin Franklin's *Poor Richard's Almanack* (1732–1757), but, beginning in the 1930s, the genre proliferated when publications such as Dale Carnegie's *How to Win Friends and Influence People* topped the best-seller lists. The "Self-Help" and "How-To" sections are now among the largest in many bookstores, and the success of the "for Dummies" series suggests the wide range of topics covered by such advice books. The books in the *Worst-Case Scenario* series, however, are generally shelved in bookstores' "Humor" sections because they offer tongue-in-cheek advice not really intended to be followed.

Fake an Emergency

1. Excuse Yourself from the Table.

Tell your date that you are going to the restroom to "wash up." Take   1
your cell phone with you. If you do not have one, locate a restaurant phone that's out of your date's line of vision. Bring a restaurant matchbook or a business card that includes the restaurant's phone number.

2. Call a Friend or Relative for Help.

Tell them to call you (either on your cell phone or on the restaurant's   2
phone) and pretend there has been an emergency. Believable emergencies are:

- Personal Crisis: "My friend just broke up with her husband — she's having a breakdown. I have to go."

- Business Crisis: "My boss just called — she's in Seattle for a major presentation, and has lost all her files. I have to email them to her immediately."
- Health Crisis: "My sister just called — our grandmother is alone and ill."

3. Leave Quickly before Your Date Can Protest.

Apologize, but refuse any attempt your date makes to accompany you. If you leave swiftly and without hesitation, your date won't have time to understand what's happening or to object.

3

Slip Away Unnoticed

1. Identify Your Escape Route.

Observe your surroundings. Take note of the exits, especially the back doors. Look for the best way out and an alternative.

4

2. Plan to Alter Your Appearance.

Think about your most distinctive features and figure out how to hide or disguise them. The person you are trying to leave is going to see a figure moving past and away at a distance and will be focusing on the first impression. If you are not familiar to him and are uninteresting, you will not get a second look.

5

3. Excuse Yourself from the Table.

Move to the restroom or any private area with a mirror to begin your transformation. Your date will probably wait only two or three minutes before expecting you to return, so act quickly, before he begins looking for you.

6

4. Add or Remove Clothing.

Layering garments will change your body shape and even suggest a different gender. A long coat will obscure your body type. Hats are especially useful because they conceal your hair and facial features. Eyeglasses, whether added or removed, work wonders. A shopping bag is a handy prop and can be used to hold your belongings.

7

5. Change Your Walk and Posture.

If you usually walk quickly, move slowly. If you stand up straight, hunch over. To alter your gait, slip a pebble in one shoe or bind one of your knees with a piece of string or cloth.

8

6. Use or Remove Cosmetics.

Lipstick can change the shape of your mouth, heighten the color in your cheeks and nose, and even give you tired eyes if dabbed and blended

9

Add—or remove—eyeglasses. Roll or unroll your sleeves; tuck in or untuck your blouse. Modify your hairstyle.

From *The Worst-Case Scenario Survival Handbook: Dating and Sex.* © 2001 by Quirk Productions, Inc. Used with permission of Chronicle Books LLC, San Francisco. Visit ChronicleBooks.com.

on your eyelids. An eyebrow pencil can be used to add age lines, change the shape of your eyes and brows, or create facial hair.

7. Change Your Hairstyle or Color.

A rubberband, hairspray, water, or any gooey substance can be useful for changing a hairstyle, darkening your hair, or altering a hairline. Borrow flour from the kitchen to lighten or gray your hair color.   10

8. Adopt a Cover Role.

A waiter in the restaurant may have an apron and be carrying a tray. If you can manage to procure these items, add or subtract a pair of eyeglasses,   11 and alter your hairline or hairstyle, you can become invisible as you are moving out of the restaurant, into the kitchen, and out the rear door. Or you can take on the role of a maintenance worker; carry a convenient potted plant out the front door and no one will think twice.

9. Make Your Move.

Do not look at your date.   12

Slip Out the Window

If you do not think you will be able to change your appearance enough   13
to slip past your date, you may have to find another way to depart. Back doors are the simplest; they are often located near the restrooms or are marked as fire exits. Do not open an emergency exit door if it is alarmed unless absolutely necessary; an alarm will only draw attention. If there are no accessible alternate doors, you will need to find a window.

1. Locate a Usable Window.

Avoid windows with chicken wire or large plate glass. Bathroom win-   14
dows often work best. If you are not on the ground floor, be sure there is a fire escape.

2. Attempt to Open the Window.

Do not immediately break the window, no matter how dire your need   15
to get out.

3. Prepare to Break the Window if You Cannot Open It.

Make sure no one is around. If you can, lock the bathroom door.   16

4. Find an Implement to Break the Window.

Try to avoid using your elbow, fist, or foot. Suitable implements are: 17

- Wastebasket
- Toilet plunger
- Handbag or briefcase
- Paper towel dispenser

5. Strike the Center of the Glass with the Implement.

If the hand holding the implement will come within a foot of the win-   18
dow as you break it, wrap it with a jacket or sweater before attempting to break the glass. If no implement is available, use your heavily wrapped hand; be sure you wrap your arm as well, beyond the elbow.

6. Punch Out Any Remaining Shards of Glass.

Cover your fist with a jacket or sweater before removing the glass.   19

Strike the center of the glass with the implement.

7. Make Your Escape.

Do not worry about any minor nicks and cuts. Run.   20

Get Your Date to Leave

1. Say Something Offensive.

If you know your date is of a particular religion or ethnicity, make   21
inappropriate comments.

2. Behave Inappropriately.

Do things that you think he will find unattractive or distasteful: chew   22
with your mouth open, eat with your fingers, argue with the waiter, close
your eyes and pretend to sleep, light matches and drop them on your plate,
ignore everything he says, and/or call someone else on your cell phone.

3. Send Your Date on a "Fool's Errand."

• Tell him you want to go to a specific nightclub, but explain that it   23
gets very crowded and that if you are not in line by a certain time (say,

fifteen minutes from then), you won't get in. Tell your date that you have arranged to have your friend stop by the restaurant with guest passes, but that if your date does not go ahead to the nightclub to get in line, you'll never make it inside. If your date wants your cell phone number, give the number willingly but make sure you change one digit. Promise you will see your date within half an hour. Never show.

• Fake an allergy attack, and insist that he leave in search of the appropriate over-the-counter allergy medicine. Explain that you must have been allergic to something in the drink/appetizer/food/taxicab, and that if you do not obtain your medicine you will break out in hives. When your date dutifully leaves, slip away.

Be Aware

Blind dates are the riskiest form of dating — it is best to check out a   24
potential suitor extensively before the date.

• Have a friend agree to check out your potential suitor and call you before you enter the bar/restaurant. Send your friend in with a cell phone. Situate yourself at a bar nearby, and await her call. Have her contact you when she has identified the mark.

• If you discover unsavory facts about someone you're supposed to meet, call immediately to cancel the date. Blame work and say that you have to stay late at the office, or say that you're experiencing car trouble. A more permanent solution is to say that an old flame has reentered your life; this will prevent your blind date from calling you again and asking for a rain check.

•   •   •

Comprehension

1. According to the authors, what four basic strategies can be used by someone who wants to escape from a bad date?
2. Which of the four strategies seems most plausible? Why?
3. What kind of date do the authors seem to be imagining? Where does the date take place? How can you tell? Can the "escape" strategies the authors describe be modified for other kinds of dates as well?

Purpose and Audience

1. Do the authors expect readers to take their advice seriously? How do you know?
2. What purpose do visuals usually serve in instructions? What purpose do the visuals serve in this selection?
3. What thesis is implied in this set of instructions? Write a sentence that could serve as the thesis statement. Should such a sentence be added? If so, where?

4. Is the intended audience of this selection men, women, or both? How can you tell?

5. The writers never define what they mean by a "bad date." Why not?

Style and Structure

1. This selection is neither structured nor formatted like most of the other essays in this text. What does it include that other essays do not? What elements are missing that other essays include?

2. What stylistic features tell you this is a set of instructions rather than a process explanation?

3. Instructions are directed at people who will actually perform the process described. Is that the case here? Explain.

4. Where do the authors include the cautions and reminders that characterize instructions? Are these warnings and reminders actually necessary here?

5. Look carefully at the steps listed under each of the essay's five strategy headings ("Fake an Emergency," and so on). How do the authors move readers from one step to the next? Would transitional words and expressions be helpful additions? If so, suggest some transitions to add.

Vocabulary Projects

1. Define each of the following words as it is used in this selection.

obscure (7)   dire (15)
gait (8)   implement (17)
procure (11)   unsavory (24)

2. Despite its informal style and tone, "How to Escape from a Bad Date" uses some terms — for example, "escape route" (4) and "prop" (7) — designed to make it sound like an authentic set of instructions. Identify other examples of such language. Do these expressions make the selection seem more serious? More credible?

Journal Entry

Think about a date you wanted to "escape" from but couldn't. Which of the strategies presented here might have been useful to you? Why?

Writing Workshop

1. Although this is a humorous essay, the writers nevertheless do give some useful advice. Write a more serious version of these instructions, including only steps that you see as realistic and sensible. In your introduction, give some reasons someone might need to escape from a date; in your

conclusion, make recommendations for avoiding this problem in the future.

2. Rewrite one of the selection's four strategy sections, replacing the authors' specific advice with your own advice — for example, your own steps for faking an emergency or getting your date to leave. Add an introduction and a conclusion to make your instructions into a complete essay.

3. Write an essay in the form of a set of instructions for how to escape from a bad party. Use the four strategy headings of "How to Escape from a Bad Date" as topic sentences of your essay's body paragraphs, acknowledging your borrowing with parenthetical documentation — for example, "The first strategy to try is to 'fake an emergency'" (Piven et al. 291). Then, use your body paragraphs to explain how you will accomplish each strategy. (Do not use numbered steps.) Include a works-cited page. (See the Appendix for information on documentation formats.)

Combining the Patterns

"How to Escape from a Bad Date" presents the steps in a process but considers neither the causes nor the effects of the "escape." What might cause someone to need to escape from a date? What might the effects of such an escape be? Should the authors have included sections of **cause and effect** to answer these questions?

Thematic Connections

- "Sex, Lies, and Conversation" (page 436)
- "The Dog Ate My Disk, and Other Tales of Woe" (page 471)
- "The Ways We Lie" (page 485)

Get It Right: Privatize Executions

One of the leading playwrights of the twentieth century, Arthur Miller (1915–2005) had his first play produced on Broadway in 1944. Though it was not a success, his next Broadway production, *All My Sons* (1947), received positive reviews and the New York Drama Critics' Circle Award. However, it was his 1949 play *Death of a Salesman* that established Miller as a major voice in the American theater: opening to ecstatic reviews, it went on to win the Pulitzer Prize. Another important play, *The Crucible* (1953), was set during the Salem witch trials of the late seventeenth century but was written as an allegory for the persecution of suspected Communists in the 1950s. (Miller himself was called before the House Un-American Activities Committee and convicted of contempt of Congress because he refused to cooperate by naming one-time Communist sympathizers.) While his plays from the 1960s on did not achieve the success of his earlier works, Miller's artistic legacy is assured; his moral vision, as evidenced in the following 1992 essay, continues to move readers and playgoers around the world.

Background on public executions

Public executions of convicted felons can be traced back at least as far as the ancient civilizations of Greece and Rome and were common in European countries until well into the nineteenth century (public executions were conducted in England, for example, until 1868). Over time, they have been carried out by crucifixion, stoning, burning at the stake, and beheading, among other methods. However, by the 1600s in England and in the American colonies, public executions were most often accomplished by hanging, usually in a public square. These hangings, which were meant to teach spectators a moral lesson, ironically took on a festive, carnival-like air and were considered a form of free entertainment. By the early 1800s, authorities in a number of states began to require that hangings be performed in the privacy of prisons — in part because the crowds witnessing them had become so rowdy and in part because it was felt that public executions could stir sentiments against capital punishment. Still, public executions persisted in some areas of the United States until the twentieth century; the last was performed in 1936 in Owensboro, Kentucky. Today, public executions continue in countries operating under Muslim law and under repressive regimes, such as that of North Korea. In this essay, Miller makes the somewhat radical suggestion that public execution be "privatized" — that is, run not by government but by private companies.

The time has come to consider the privatization of executions.   1

There can no longer be any doubt that government — society itself — is   2
incapable of doing anything right, and this certainly applies to the executions of convicted criminals.

At present, the thing is a total loss, to the convicted person, to his family, and to society. It need not be so.

People can be executed in places like Shea Stadium before immense paying audiences. The income from the spectacle could be distributed to the prison that fed and housed him or to a trust fund for prisoner rehabilitation and his own family and/or girlfriend, as he himself chose.

The condemned would of course get a percentage of the gate, to be negotiated by his agent or a promoter, if he so desired.

The take would, without question, be sizable, considering the immense number of Americans in favor of capital punishment. A \$200 to \$300 ringside seat would not be excessive, with bleachers going for, say, \$25.

As with all sports events, a certain ritual would seem inevitable and would quickly become an expected part of the occasion. The electric chair would be set on a platform, like a boxing ring without the rope, around second base.

Once the audience was seated, a soprano would come forward and sing "The Star-Spangled Banner." When she stepped down, the governor, holding a microphone, would appear and describe the condemned man's crimes in detail, plus his many failed appeals.

Then the governor would step aside and a phalanx of police officers or possibly National Guard or Army troops would mount the platform and surround the condemned. This climactic entrance might be accompanied by a trumpet fanfare or other musical number by the police or Army band, unless it was thought to offend good taste.

Next, a minister or priest would appear and offer a benediction, asking God's blessing on the execution.

The condemned, should he desire, could make a short statement and even a plea of innocence. This would only add to the pathos of the occasion and would of course not be legally binding. He would then be strapped into the chair.

Finally, the executioner, hooded to protect himself from retaliation, would proceed to the platform. He would walk to a console where, on a solemn signal from the governor, he would pull the switch.

The condemned man would instantly surge upward against his bindings, with smoke emitting from his flesh. This by itself would provide a most powerful lesson for anyone contemplating murder. For those not contemplating murder, it would be a reminder of how lucky they are to have been straight and honest in America.

For the state, this would mean additional income; for the audience, an intense and educational experience — people might, for example, wish to bring their children.

And for the condemned, it would have its achievement aspect, because he would know that he had not lived his life for nothing.

Some might object that such proceedings are so fundamentally attractive that it is not too much to imagine certain individuals contemplating murder in order to star in the program. But no solution to any profound social problem is perfect.

Finally, and perhaps most important, it is entirely possible that after   17
witnessing a few dozen privatized executions, the public might grow tired
of the spectacle — just as it seizes on all kinds of entertainment only to lose
interest once their repetitiousness becomes too tiresomely apparent.

Then perhaps we might be willing to consider the fact that in execut-   18
ing prisoners we merely add to the number of untimely dead without
diminishing the number of murders committed.

At that point, the point of boredom, we might begin asking why it is   19
that Americans commit murder more often than any other people. At the
moment, we are not bored enough with executions to ask this question;
instead, we are apparently going to demand more and more of them, most
probably because we never get to witness any in person.

My proposal would lead us more quickly to boredom and away from   20
our current gratifying excitement — and ultimately perhaps to a wiser use
of alternating current.

• • •

Comprehension

1. What process does Miller describe? List the individual steps in this
   process.
2. Which of Miller's recommendations are most outrageous? Is any part of
   his scheme actually plausible?
3. In paragraph 6, Miller notes that many Americans support capital punishment. Do you think Miller is one of these people? Why, or why not?
4. Why, according to Miller, do executions need to be privatized rather than
   performed by the government?
5. What specific benefits does Miller say will result from his scheme?
6. In paragraph 20, Miller suggests that his proposal might ultimately lead
   to "a wiser use of alternating current." What does he mean?

Purpose and Audience

1. This essay begins with an abrupt statement of a very controversial thesis.
   Why does Miller choose this approach? How successful is it?
2. What kind of reaction do you think Miller would like to get from his
   audience? For instance, does he want them to be amused? Shocked?
   Guilty? Angry? Explain.
3. What is Miller's real purpose in writing this essay? What do you think he
   hopes to accomplish?

Style and Structure

1. Because this essay was first published in a newspaper and set in columns,
   it has relatively short paragraphs. Which paragraphs, if any, could be

combined? Which would you leave as they are? Are there any advantages
to using one- or two-sentence paragraphs in this essay?

2. Where does the actual process begin? Where does it end?

3. What words and phrases does Miller use to link the steps in the process?
Do you think he needs any additional transitions? If so, where?

4. Much of this essay's tone is ironic, and Miller clearly intends that many of
his statements not be taken literally. How do you suppose he expects
readers to react to each of the following?

   - "unless it was thought to offend good taste" (9)
   - "he would know that he had not lived his life for nothing" (15)
   - "no solution to any profound social problem is perfect" (16)

5. Miller seems to suggest that executions are not unlike sporting events.
How, according to Miller, are they alike? Is this a valid **analogy**?

Vocabulary Projects

1. Define each of the following words as it is used in this selection.

   privatization (1)   fanfare (9)
   phalanx (9)   pathos (11)
   climactic (9)   emitting (13)

2. Miller repeats variations of the word *execution* many times. What alternatives does he have? What different connotations does each of these possible alternatives suggest?

Journal Entry

Many people who support capital punishment see it as a deterrent to crime.
Do you think Miller's scheme, if enacted, would be a deterrent?

Writing Workshop

1. Using past tense, rewrite the process section of Miller's essay from the
point of view of someone who has just witnessed a public execution. Give
the condemned person an identity, a history, and a family, and explain
the crime for which he or she is being punished. In your thesis, take a
stand on whether or not this person deserves to be executed.

2. Write an email to the editor of a newspaper expressing your strong disapproval of the idea of public executions. Quoting Miller where necessary,
and acknowledging the source of these qotations, use the steps in the
process he describes to support your position. To convince readers this
practice is inhumane, add descriptive details — for example, information
about the observers' reactions and the sensationalist TV news coverage.

Combining the Patterns

Although the body of this essay is structured as a process, the essay as a whole makes a powerful **argument**. Does Miller have a debatable thesis? Do you think he needs more evidence to support his thesis, or is the process itself enough? Does he consider the possible objections of his audience? Does he refute these objections?

Thematic Connections

- "Shooting an Elephant" (page 126)
- "The Lottery" (page 311)
- "Who Killed Benny Paret?" (page 340)
- "Five Ways to Kill a Man" (page 501)
- "A Modest Proposal" (page 745)

The Embalming of Mr. Jones

Jessica Mitford (1917–1996) was born in Batsford Mansion, England, to a wealthy, aristocratic family. Rebelling against her sheltered upbringing, she became involved in left-wing politics and eventually immigrated to the United States. Mitford wrote two volumes of autobiography — *Daughters and Rebels* (1960), about her eccentric family, and *A Fine Old Conflict* (1976). In the 1950s, she began a career in investigative journalism, which produced the books *The American Way of Death* (1963), about abuses in the funeral business; *Kind and Usual Punishment* (1973), about the U.S. prison system; and *The American Way of Birth* (1992), about the crisis in American obstetrical care.

Background on the funeral industry

"The Embalming of Mr. Jones" is excerpted from *The American Way of Death,* a scathing critique of the funeral industry in the United States. The book prompted angry responses from morticians but also led to increased governmental regulation, culminating in a 1984 Federal Trade Commission ruling requiring funeral homes to disclose in writing the prices for all goods and services, as well as certain consumer rights; barring funeral homes from forcing consumers to purchase more than they really want; and forbidding funeral directors from misleading consumers regarding state laws governing the disposal of bodies. Still, industry critics charge that many abuses continue. While funeral services can be purchased for less than a thousand dollars, the standard rate is between two and four thousand dollars — and it can go much higher. The difference in cost is based largely on the price of a casket, and grieving family members are often strongly pressured into buying the most expensive caskets, which may be marked up as much as 500 percent. Advocates for reform suggest that consumers choose cremation over burial (of the approximately 2.5 million people who died in the United States in 2006, only some 800,000 were cremated) and that they hold memorial services in churches or other settings, where costs are much lower than in funeral homes.

Embalming is indeed a most extraordinary procedure, and one must wonder at the docility of Americans who each year pay hundreds of millions of dollars for its perpetuation, blissfully ignorant of what it is all about, what is done, how it is done. Not one in ten thousand has any idea of what actually takes place. Books on the subject are extremely hard to come by. They are not to be found in most libraries or bookshops.

In an era when huge television audiences watch surgical operations in the comfort of their living rooms, when, thanks to the animated cartoon, the geography of the digestive system has become familiar territory even to the nursery school set, in a land where the satisfaction of curiosity about almost all matters is a national pastime, the secrecy surrounding embalming can, surely, hardly be attributed to the inherent gruesomeness of the subject. Custom in this regard has within this century suffered a complete reversal. In the early days of American embalming, when it was performed in the home of the deceased, it was almost mandatory for some relative to stay by the embalmer's side and witness the procedure. Today, family members who might wish to be in attendance would certainly be dissuaded by the funeral director. All others, except apprentices, are excluded by law from the preparation room.

A close look at what does actually take place may explain in large measure the undertaker's intractable reticence concerning a procedure that has become his major *raison d'être.** Is it possible he fears that public information about embalming might lead patrons to wonder if they really want this service? If the funeral men are loath to discuss the subject outside the trade, the reader may, understandably, be equally loath to go on reading at this point. For those who have the stomach for it, let us part the formaldehyde curtain. . . . 3

The body is first laid out in the undertaker's morgue — or rather, Mr. Jones is reposing in the preparation room — to be readied to bid the world farewell. 4

The preparation room in any of the better funeral establishments has the tiled and sterile look of a surgery, and indeed the embalmer-restorative artist who does his chores there is beginning to adopt the term "dermasurgeon" (appropriately corrupted by some mortician-writers as "demisurgeon") to describe his calling. His equipment, consisting of scalpels, scissors, augers, forceps, clamps, needles, pumps, tubes, bowls, and basin, is crudely imitative of the surgeon's as is his technique, acquired in a nine- or twelve-month post-high-school course in an embalming school. He is supplied by an advanced chemical industry with a bewildering array of fluids, sprays, pastes, oils, powders, creams, to fix or soften tissue, shrink or distend it as needed, dry it here, restore the moisture there. There are cosmetics, waxes, and paints to fill and cover features, even plaster of Paris to replace entire limbs. There are ingenious aids to prop and stabilize the cadaver: a Vari-Pose Head Rest, the Edwards Arm and Hand Positioner, the Repose Block (to support the shoulders during the embalming), and the Throop Foot Positioner, which resembles an old-fashioned stocks. 5

Mr. John H. Eckels, president of the Eckels College of Mortuary Science, thus describes the first part of the embalming procedure: "In the hands of a skilled practitioner, this work may be done in a comparatively short time and without mutilating the body other than by slight incision — so slight that it scarcely would cause serious inconvenience if made upon a living person. It is necessary to remove all the blood, and doing this not only helps in the disinfecting, but removes the principal cause of disfigurements due to discoloration." 6

---

* Eds. note — Reason for being (French).

Another textbook discusses the all-important time element: "The ear- 7
lier this is done, the better, for every hour that elapses between death and
embalming will add to the problems and complications encountered. . . ."
Just how soon should one get going on the embalming? The author tells
us, "On the basis of such scanty information made available to this profession through its rudimentary and haphazard system of technical research,
we must conclude that the best results are to be obtained if the subject is
embalmed before life is completely extinct — that is, before cellular death
has occurred. In the average case, this would mean within an hour after
somatic death." For those who feel that there is something a little rudimentary, not to say haphazard, about this advice, a comforting thought is
offered by another writer. Speaking of fears entertained in early days of
premature burial, he points out, "One of the effects of embalming by
chemical injection, however, has been to dispel fears of live burial." How
true; once the blood is removed, chances of live burial are indeed remote.

To return to Mr. Jones, the blood is drained out through the veins and 8
replaced by embalming fluid pumped in through the arteries. As noted in
The Principles and Practices of Embalming, "every operator has a favorite injection and drainage point — a fact which becomes a handicap only if he fails
or refuses to forsake his favorites when conditions demand it." Typical
favorites are the carotid artery, femoral artery, jugular vein, subclavian vein.
There are various choices of embalming fluid. If Flextone is used, it will
produce a "mild, flexible rigidity. The skin retains a velvety softness, the
tissues are rubbery and pliable. Ideal for women and children." It may be
blended with B. and G. Products Company's Lyf-Lyk tint, which is guaranteed to reproduce "nature's own skin texture . . . the velvety appearance of
living tissue." Suntone comes in three separate tints: Suntan; Special Cosmetic Tint, a pink shade "especially indicated for young female subjects";
and Regular Cosmetic Tint, moderately pink.

About three to six gallons of a dyed and perfumed solution of formal- 9
dehyde, glycerin, borax, phenol, alcohol, and water is soon circulating
through Mr. Jones, whose mouth has been sewn together with a "needle
directed upward between the upper lip and gum and brought out through
the left nostril," with the corners raised slightly "for a more pleasant expression." If he should be buck-toothed, his teeth are cleaned with Bon Ami
and coated with colorless nail polish. His eyes, meanwhile, are closed with
flesh-tinted eye caps and eye cement.

The next step is to have at Mr. Jones with a thing called a trocar. This is 10
a long, hollow needle attached to a tube. It is jabbed into the abdomen,
poked around the entrails and chest cavity, the contents of which are
pumped out and replaced with "cavity fluid." This done, and the hole in
the abdomen sewed up, Mr. Jones's face is heavily creamed (to protect the
skin from burns which may be caused by leakage of the chemicals), and he
is covered with a sheet and left unmolested for a while. But not for
long — there is more, much more, in store for him. He has been embalmed,
but not yet restored, and the best time to start restorative work is eight to
ten hours after embalming, when the tissues have become firm and dry.

The object of all this attention to the corpse, it must be remembered, is   11
to make it presentable for viewing in an attitude of healthy repose. "Our
customs require the presentation of our dead in the semblance of normal-
ity . . . unmarred by the ravages of illness, disease, or mutilation," says Mr. J.
Sheridan Mayer in his *Restorative Art.* This is rather a large order since few
people die in the full bloom of health, unravaged by illness and unmarked
by some disfigurement. The funeral industry is equal to the challenge: "In
some cases the gruesome appearance of a mutilated or disease-ridden subject may be quite discouraging. The task of restoration may seem impossible and shake the confidence of the embalmer. This is the time for
intestinal fortitude and determination. Once the formative work is begun
and affected tissues are cleaned or removed, all doubts of success vanish. It
is surprising and gratifying to discover the results which may be obtained."

The embalmer, having allowed an appropriate interval to elapse,   12
returns to the attack, but now he brings into play the skill and equipment
of sculptor and cosmetician. Is a hand missing? Casting one in plaster of
Paris is a simple matter. "For replacement purposes, only a cast of the back
of the hand is necessary; this is within the ability of the average operator
and is quite adequate." If a lip or two, a nose or an ear should be missing,
the embalmer has at hand a variety of restorative waxes with which to
model replacements. Pores and skin texture are simulated by stippling with
a little brush, and over this cosmetics are laid on. Head off? Decapitation
cases are rather routinely handled. Ragged edges are trimmed, and head
joined to torso with a series of splints, wires, and sutures. It is a good idea
to have a little something at the neck — a scarf or high collar — when time
for viewing comes. Swollen mouth? Cut out tissue as needed from inside
the lips. If too much is removed, the surface contour can easily be restored
by padding with cotton. Swollen necks and cheeks are reduced by removing tissue through vertical incisions made down each side of the
neck. "When the deceased is casketed, the pillow will hide the suture incisions. . . . as an extra precaution against leakage, the suture may be painted
with liquid sealer."

The opposite condition is more likely to present itself — that of emaci-   13
ation. His hypodermic syringe now loaded with massage cream, the
embalmer seeks out and fills the hollowed and sunken areas by injection.
In this procedure the backs of the hands and fingers and the underchin
area should not be neglected.

Positioning the lips is a problem that recurrently challenges the inge-   14
nuity of the embalmer. Closed too tightly, they tend to give a stern, even
disapproving expression. Ideally, embalmers feel, the lips should give the
impression of being ever so slightly parted, the upper lip protruding
slightly for a more youthful appearance. This takes some engineering, however, as the lips tend to drift apart. Lip drift can sometimes be remedied by
pushing one or two straight pins through the inner margin of the lower lip
and then inserting them between the two front upper teeth. If Mr. Jones
happens to have no teeth, the pins can just as easily be anchored in
his Armstrong Face Former and Denture Replacer. Another method to

maintain lip closure is to dislocate the lower jaw, which is then held in its new position by a wire run through holes which have been drilled through the upper jaws at the midline. As the French are fond of saying, *il faut souf-frir pour être belle.**

If Mr. Jones has died of jaundice, the embalming fluid will very likely   15
turn him green. Does this deter the embalmer? Not if he has intestinal for-titude. Masking pastes and cosmetics are heavily laid on, burial garments and casket interiors are color-correlated with particular care, and Jones is displayed beneath rose-colored lights. Friends will say, "How *well* he looks." Death by carbon monoxide, on the other hand, can be rather a good thing from an embalmer's viewpoint: "One advantage is the fact that this type of discoloration is an exaggerated form of a natural pink coloration." This is nice because the healthy glow is already present and needs but little atten-tion.

The patching and filling completed, Mr. Jones is now shaved, washed,   16
and dressed. Cream-based cosmetic, available in pink, flesh, suntan, bru-nette, and blonde, is applied to his hands and face, his hair is shampooed and combed (and, in the case of Mrs. Jones, set), his hands manicured. For the horny-handed son of toil special care must be taken; cream should be applied to remove ingrained grime, and the nails cleaned. "If he were not in the habit of having them manicured in life, trimming and shaping is advised for better appearance — never questioned by kin."

Jones is now ready for casketing (this is the present participle of the   17
verb "to casket"). In this operation his right shoulder should be depressed slightly "to turn the body a bit to the right and soften the appearance of lying flat on the back." Positioning the hands is a matter of importance, and special rubber positioning blocks may be used. The hands should be cupped slightly for a more lifelike, relaxed appearance. Proper placement of the body requires a delicate sense of balance. It should lie as high as pos-sible in the casket, yet not so high that the lid, when lowered, will hit the nose. On the other hand, we are cautioned, placing the body too low "cre-ates the impression that the body is in a box."

Jones is next wheeled into the appointed slumber room where a few   18
last touches may be added — his favorite pipe placed in his hand or, if he was a great reader, a book propped into position. (In the case of little Mas-ter Jones a Teddy bear may be clutched.) Here he will hold open house for a few days, visiting hours 10 A.M. to 9 P.M.

·   ·   ·

Comprehension

1. How, according to Mitford, has the public's knowledge of embalming changed? How does she explain this change?

---

* EDS. NOTE — It is necessary to suffer in order to be beautiful.

2. To what other professionals does Mitford compare the embalmer? Are these analogies flattering or critical? Explain.

3. What are the major stages in the process of embalming and restoration?

Purpose and Audience

1. Mitford's purpose in this essay is to convince her audience of something. What is her thesis?

2. Do you think Mitford expects her audience to agree with her thesis? How can you tell?

3. In one of her books, Mitford refers to herself as a *muckraker,* one who informs the public of misconduct. Does she achieve this status here? Cite specific examples.

4. Mitford's tone in this essay is subjective, even judgmental. What effect does her tone have on you? Does it encourage you to trust her? Should she have presented her facts in a more objective way? Explain.

Style and Structure

1. Identify the stylistic features that distinguish this process explanation from a set of instructions.

2. In this selection, as in many process essays, a list of necessary materials comes before the procedure. What additional details does Mitford include in her list in paragraph 5? How do these additions affect you?

3. Locate Mitford's remarks about the language of embalming. How do her comments about euphemisms, newly coined words, and other aspects of language help to support her thesis?

4. Throughout the essay, Mitford quotes various experts. How does she use their remarks to support her thesis?

5. Give examples of phrases that serve as transitions that link the various stages of Mitford's process.

6. Mitford uses a good deal of sarcasm and biased language in this essay. Identify some examples. Do you think this kind of language strengthens or weakens her essay? Why?

Vocabulary Projects

1. Define each of the following words as it is used in this selection.

perpetuation (1)	rudimentary (7)	stippling (12)
inherent (2)	haphazard (7)	emaciation (13)
mandatory (2)	entertained (7)	recurrently (14)
dissuaded (2)	pliable (8)	jaundice (15)
intractable (3)	repose (11)	toil (16)
reticence (3)	unravaged (11)	
loath (3)	fortitude (11)	

2. Substitute another word for each of the following.

territory (2)   ingenious (5)   presentable (11)
gruesomeness (2)   jabbed (10)

How does each of your substitutions change Mitford's meaning?

3. Reread paragraphs 5–9 carefully. Then, list all the words in this section of the essay that suggest surgical technique and all the words that suggest cosmetic artistry. What do your lists tell you about Mitford's intent in these paragraphs?

Journal Entry

What are your thoughts about how your religion or culture deals with death and dying? What practices, if any, make you uncomfortable? Why?

Writing Workshop

1. Rewrite this process explanation as a set of instructions for undertakers, condensing it so that your essay is about five hundred words long. Unlike Mitford, keep your essay objective.

2. In the role of a funeral director, write a blog post taking issue with Mitford's essay. As you explain the process of embalming, paraphrase or quote two or three of Mitford's statements and argue against them, making sure to identify the source of these quotations. Your objective is to defend the practice of embalming as necessary and practical.

3. Write an explanation of a process you personally find disgusting — or delightful. Make your attitude clear in your thesis statement and in your choice of words.

Combining the Patterns

Although Mitford structures this essay as a process, many passages rely heavily on subjective **description**. Where is her focus on descriptive details most obvious? What is her purpose in describing particular individuals and objects as she does? How do these descriptive passages help to support her essay's thesis?

Thematic Connections

- "My First Conk" (page 282)
- "The Ways We Lie" (page 485)
- "A Modest Proposal" (page 745)

SHIRLEY JACKSON

The Lottery (Fiction)

Shirley Jackson (1919–1965) is best known for her subtly macabre stories of horror and suspense, most notably her best-selling novel *The Haunting of Hill House* (1959), which Stephen King has called "one of the greatest horror stories of all time." She also published wryly humorous reflections on her experiences as a wife and mother of four children. Many of her finest stories and novels were not anthologized until after her death.

Background on the initial reaction to "The Lottery"

"The Lottery" first appeared in *The New Yorker* in 1948, three years after the end of World War II. Jackson was living somewhat uneasily in the New England college town of Bennington, Vermont, a village very similar to the setting of "The Lottery." She felt herself an outsider there, a sophisticated intellectual in an isolated, closely knit community suspicious of strangers. Here, Jackson (whose husband was Jewish) experienced frequent encounters with anti-Semitism. At the time, the full atrocity of Germany's wartime program to exterminate Jews, now called the Holocaust, had led many social critics to contemplate humanity's terrible capacity for evil. Most Americans, however, wished to put the horrors of the war behind them, and many readers reacted with outrage to Jackson's tale of an annual small-town ritual, calling it "nasty," "nauseating," and even "perverted." Others, however, immediately recognized its genius, its power, and its many layers of meaning. This classic tale is now one of the most widely anthologized of twentieth-century short stories.

The morning of June 27th was clear and sunny, with the fresh warmth 1
of a full-summer day; the flowers were blossoming profusely and the grass was richly green. The people of the village began to gather in the square, between the post office and the bank, around ten o'clock; in some towns there were so many people that the lottery took two days and had to be started on June 26th, but in this village, where there were only about three hundred people, the whole lottery took less than two hours, so it could begin at ten o'clock in the morning and still be through in time to allow the villagers to get home for noon dinner.

The children assembled first, of course. School was recently over for 2
the summer, and the feeling of liberty sat uneasily on most of them; they tended to gather together quietly for a while before they broke into boisterous play, and their talk was still of the classroom and the teacher, of books and reprimands. Bobby Martin had already stuffed his pockets full of stones, and the other boys soon followed his example, selecting the smoothest and roundest stones; Bobby and Harry Jones and Dickie Delacroix — the villagers pronounced his name "Dellacroy" — eventually made a great pile

of stones in one corner of the square and guarded it against the raids of the other boys. The girls stood aside, talking among themselves, looking over their shoulders at the boys, and the very small children rolled in the dust or clung to the hands of their older brothers or sisters.

Soon the men began to gather, surveying their own children, speaking of planting and rain, tractors and taxes. They stood together, away from the pile of stones in the corner, and their jokes were quiet and they smiled rather than laughed. The women, wearing faded house dresses and sweaters, came shortly after their menfolk. They greeted one another and exchanged bits of gossip as they went to join their husbands. Soon the women, standing by their husbands, began to call to their children, and the children came reluctantly, having to be called four or five times. Bobby Martin ducked under his mother's grasping hand and ran, laughing, back to the pile of stones. His father spoke up sharply, and Bobby came quickly and took his place between his father and his oldest brother.

The lottery was conducted — as were the square dances, the teenage club, the Halloween program — by Mr. Summers, who had time and energy to devote to civic activities. He was a round-faced, jovial man and he ran the coal business, and people were sorry for him, because he had no children and his wife was a scold. When he arrived in the square, carrying the black wooden box, there was a murmur of conversation among the villagers, and he waved and called "Little late today, folks." The postmaster, Mr. Graves, followed him, carrying a three-legged stool, and the stool was put in the center of the square and Mr. Summers set the black box down on it. The villagers kept their distance, leaving a space between themselves and the stool, and when Mr. Summers said, "Some of you fellows want to give me a hand?" there was a hesitation before two men, Mr. Martin and his oldest son, Baxter, came forward to hold the box steady on the stool while Mr. Summers stirred up the papers inside it.

The original paraphernalia for the lottery had been lost long ago, and the black box now resting on the stool had been put into use even before Old Man Warner, the oldest man in town, was born. Mr. Summers spoke frequently to the villagers about making a new box, but no one liked to upset even as much tradition as was represented by the black box. There was a story that the present box had been made with some pieces of the box that had preceded it, the one that had been constructed when the first people settled down to make a village here. Every year, after the lottery, Mr. Summers began talking about a new box, but every year the subject was allowed to fade off without anything's being done. The black box grew shabbier each year; by now it was no longer completely black but splintered badly along one side to show the original wood color, and in some places faded and stained.

Mr. Martin and his oldest son, Baxter, held the black box securely on the stool until Mr. Summers had stirred the papers thoroughly with his hand. Because so much of the ritual had been forgotten or discarded, Mr. Summers had been successful in having slips of paper substituted for the chips of wood that had been used for generations. Chips of wood, Mr. Summers had argued, had been all very well when the village was tiny, but now that the population was more than three hundred and likely to keep on growing, it was necessary to use something that would fit more easily into the black box. The night before the lottery, Mr. Summers and Mr. Graves made up the slips of paper and put them in the box, and it was then taken to the safe of Mr. Summers' coal company and locked up until Mr. Summers was ready to take it to the square the next morning. The rest of the year, the box was put away, sometimes one place, sometimes another; it had spent one year in Mr. Graves' barn and another year underfoot in the post office, and sometimes it was set on a shelf in the Martin grocery and left there.

There was a great deal of fussing to be done before Mr. Summers   7
declared the lottery open. There were the lists to make up — of heads of families, heads of households in each family, members of each household in each family. There was the proper swearing-in of Mr. Summers by the postmaster, as the official of the lottery; at one time, some people remembered, there had been a recital of some sort, performed by the official of the lottery, a perfunctory, tuneless chant that had been rattled off duly each year; some people believed that the official of the lottery used to stand just so when he said or sang it, others believed that he was supposed to walk among the people, but years and years ago this part of the ritual had been allowed to lapse. There had been, also, a ritual salute, which the official of the lottery had had to use in addressing each person who came up to draw from the box, but this also had changed with time, until now it was felt necessary only for the official to speak to each person approaching. Mr. Summers was very good at all this; in his clean white shirt and blue jeans, with one hand resting carelessly on the black box, he seemed very proper and important as he talked interminably to Mr. Graves and the Martins.

Just as Mr. Summers finally left off talking and turned to the assembled   8
villagers, Mrs. Hutchinson came hurriedly along the path to the square, her sweater thrown over her shoulders, and slid into place in the back of the crowd. "Clean forgot what day it was," she said to Mrs. Delacroix, who stood next to her, and they both laughed softly. "Thought my old man was out back stacking wood," Mrs. Hutchinson went on, "and then I looked out the window and the kids were gone, and then I remembered it was the twenty-seventh and came a-running." She dried her hands on her apron, and Mrs. Delacroix said, "You're in time, though. They're still talking away up there."

Mrs. Hutchinson craned her neck to see through the crowd and found   9
her husband and children standing near the front. She tapped Mrs. Delacroix on the arm as a farewell and began to make her way through the crowd. The people separated good-humoredly to let her through; two or three people said, in voices just loud enough to be heard across the crowd, "Here comes your Missus, Hutchinson," and "Bill, she made it after all." Mrs. Hutchinson reached her husband, and Mr. Summers, who had been waiting, said cheerfully, "Thought we were going to have to get on without

you, Tessie." Mrs. Hutchinson said, grinning, "Wouldn't have me leave m'dishes in the sink, now, would you, Joe?" and soft laughter ran through the crowd as the people stirred back into position after Mrs. Hutchinson's arrival.

"Well, now," Mr. Summers said soberly, "guess we better get started, get this over with, so's we can go back to work. Anybody ain't here?" 10

"Dunbar," several people said. "Dunbar, Dunbar." 11

Mr. Summers consulted his list. "Clyde Dunbar," he said. "That's right. He's broke his leg, hasn't he? Who's drawing for him?" 12

"Me, I guess," a woman said, and Mr. Summers turned to look at her. "Wife draws for her husband," Mr. Summers said. "Don't you have a grown boy to do it for you, Janey?" Although Mr. Summers and everyone else in the village knew the answer perfectly well, it was the business of the official of the lottery to ask such questions formally. Mr. Summers waited with an expression of polite interest while Mrs. Dunbar answered. 13

"Horace's not but sixteen yet," Mrs. Dunbar said regretfully. "Guess I gotta fill in for the old man this year." 14

"Right," Mr. Summers said. He made a note on the list he was holding. Then he asked, "Watson boy drawing this year?" 15

A tall boy in the crowd raised his hand. "Here," he said. "I'm drawing for m'mother and me." He blinked his eyes nervously and ducked his head as several voices in the crowd said things like "Good fellow, Jack," and "Glad to see your mother's got a man to do it." 16

"Well," Mr. Summers said, "guess that's everyone. Old Man Warner make it?" 17

"Here," a voice said, and Mr. Summers nodded. 18

A sudden hush fell on the crowd as Mr. Summers cleared his throat and looked at the list. "All ready?" he called. "Now, I'll read the names — heads of families first — and the men come up and take a paper out of the box. Keep the paper folded in your hand without looking at it until everyone has had a turn. Everything clear?" 19

The people had done it so many times that they only half listened to the directions; most of them were quiet, wetting their lips, not looking around. Then Mr. Summers raised one hand high and said, "Adams." A man disengaged himself from the crowd and came forward. "Hi, Steve," Mr. Summers said, and Mr. Adams said, "Hi, Joe." They grinned at one another humorlessly and nervously. Then Mr. Adams reached into the black box and took out a folded paper. He held it firmly by one corner as he turned and went hastily back to his place in the crowd, where he stood a little apart from his family, not looking down at his hand. 20

"Allen," Mr. Summers said. "Anderson. . . . Betham." 21

"Seems like there's no time at all between lotteries any more," Mrs. Delacroix said to Mrs. Graves in the back row. "Seems like we got through the last one only last week." 22

"Time sure goes fast," Mrs. Graves said. 23

"Clark. . . . Delacroix."   24

"There goes my old man," Mrs. Delacroix said. She held her breath   25
while her husband went forward.

"Dunbar," Mr. Summers said, and Mrs. Dunbar went steadily to the   26
box while one of the women said, "Go on, Janey," and another said, "There
she goes."

"We're next," Mrs. Graves said. She watched while Mr. Graves came   27
around from the side of the box, greeted Mr. Summers gravely, and selected
a slip of paper from the box. By now, all through the crowd there were men
holding the small folded papers in their large hands, turning them over
and over nervously. Mrs. Dunbar and her two sons stood together, Mrs.
Dunbar holding the slip of paper.

"Harburt. . . . Hutchinson."   28

"Get up there, Bill," Mrs. Hutchinson said, and the people near her   29
laughed.

"Jones."   30

"They do say," Mr. Adams said to Old Man Warner, who stood next to   31
him, "that over in the north village they're talking of giving up the lottery."

Old Man Warner snorted. "Pack of crazy fools," he said. "Listening to   32
the young folks, nothing's good enough for *them.* Next thing you know,
they'll be wanting to go back to living in caves, nobody work any more, live
that way for a while. Used to be a saying about 'Lottery in June, corn be
heavy soon.' First thing you know, we'd all be eating stewed chickweed and
acorns. There's *always* been a lottery," he added petulantly. "Bad enough to
see young Joe Summers up there joking with everybody."

"Some places have already quit lotteries," Mrs. Adams said.   33

"Nothing but trouble in *that*," Old Man Warner said stoutly. "Pack of   34
young fools."

"Martin." And Bobby Martin watched his father go forward.   35
"Overdyke. . . . Percy."

"I wish they'd hurry," Mrs. Dunbar said to her older son. "I wish they'd   36
hurry."

"They're almost through," her son said.   37

"You get ready to run tell Dad," Mrs. Dunbar said.   38

Mr. Summers called his own name and then stepped forward precisely   39
and selected a slip from the box. Then he called, "Warner."

"Seventy-seventh year I been in the lottery," Old Man Warner said as he   40
went through the crowd. "Seventy-seventh time."

"Watson." The tall boy came awkwardly through the crowd. Someone   41
said, "Don't be nervous, Jack," and Mr. Summers said, "Take your time,
son."

"Zanini."   42

After that, there was a long pause, a breathless pause, until Mr.   43
Summers, holding his slip of paper in the air, said, "All right fellows." For a
minute, no one moved, and then all the slips of paper were opened.

Suddenly, all the women began to speak at once, saying, "Who is it," "Who's got it?," "Is it the Dunbars?," "Is it the Watsons?" Then the voices began to say, "It's Hutchinson. It's Bill," "Bill Hutchinson's got it."

"Go tell your father," Mrs. Dunbar said to her older son.   44

People began to look around to see the Hutchinsons. Bill Hutchinson   45
was standing quiet, staring down at the paper in his hand. Suddenly, Tessie
Hutchinson shouted to Mr. Summers, "You didn't give him time enough
to take any paper he wanted. I saw you. It wasn't fair!"

"Be a good sport, Tessie," Mrs. Delacroix called, and Mrs. Graves said,   46
"All of us took the same chance."

"Shut up, Tessie," Bill Hutchinson said.   47

"Well, everyone," Mr. Summers said, "That was done pretty fast, and   48
now we've got to be hurrying a little more to get it done in time." He consulted his next list. "Bill," he said, "you draw for the Hutchinson family.
You got any other households in the Hutchinsons?"

"There's Don and Eva," Mrs. Hutchinson yelled. "Make *them* take their   49
chance!"

"Daughters draw with their husbands' families, Tessie," Mr. Summers   50
said gently. "You know that as well as anyone else."

"It wasn't *fair*," Tessie said.   51

"I guess not, Joe," Bill Hutchinson said regretfully. "My daughter draws   52
with her husband's family, that's only fair. And I've got no other family
except the kids."

"Then, as far as drawing for families is concerned, it's you," Mr.   53
Summers said in explanation, "and as far as drawing for households is concerned, that's you, too. Right?"

"Right," Bill Hutchinson said.   54

"How many kids, Bill?" Mr. Summers asked formally.   55

"Three," Bill Hutchinson said. "There's Bill, Jr., and Nancy, and little   56
Dave. And Tessie and me."

"All right, then," Mr. Summers said. "Harry, you got their tickets   57
back?"

Mr. Graves nodded and held up the slips of paper. "Put them in the   58
box, then," Mr. Summers directed. "Take Bill's and put it in."

"I think we ought to start over," Mrs. Hutchinson said, as quietly as she   59
could. "I tell you it wasn't *fair*. You didn't give him time enough to choose.
*Every*body saw that."

Mr. Graves had selected the five slips and put them in the box, and he   60
dropped all the papers but those onto the ground, where the breeze caught
them and lifted them off.

"Listen, everybody," Mrs. Hutchinson was saying to the people around   61
her.

"Ready, Bill?" Mr. Summers asked, and Bill Hutchinson, with one   62
quick glance around at his wife and children, nodded.

"Remember," Mr. Summers said, "take the slips and keep them folded   63
until each person has taken one. Harry, you help little Dave." Mr. Graves

took the hand of the little boy, who came willingly with him up to the box. "Take a paper out of the box, Davy," Mr. Summers said. Davy put his hand into the box and laughed. "Take just *one* paper," Mr. Summers said. "Harry, you hold it for him." Mr. Graves took the child's hand and removed the folded paper from the tight fist and held it while little Dave stood next to him and looked up at him wonderingly.

"Nancy next," Mr. Summers said. Nancy was twelve, and her school 64
friends breathed heavily as she went forward, switching her skirt, and took a slip daintily from the box. "Bill, Jr.," Mr. Summers said, and Billy, his face red and his feet over-large, nearly knocked the box over as he got a paper out. "Tessie," Mr. Summers said. She hesitated for a minute, looking around defiantly, and then set her lips and went up to the box. She snatched a paper out and held it behind her.

"Bill," Mr. Summers said, and Bill Hutchinson reached into the box 65
and felt around, bringing his hand out at last with the slip of paper in it.

The crowd was quiet. A girl whispered, "I hope it's not Nancy," and the 66
sound of the whisper reached the edges of the crowd.

"It's not the way it used to be," Old Man Warner said clearly. "People 67
ain't the way they used to be."

"All right," Mr. Summers said. "Open the papers. Harry, you open little 68
Dave's."

Mr. Graves opened the slip of paper and there was a general sigh 69
through the crowd as he held it up and everyone could see that it was blank. Nancy and Bill, Jr., opened theirs at the same time, and both beamed and laughed, turning around to the crowd and holding their slips of paper above their heads.

"Tessie," Mr. Summers said. There was a pause, and then Mr. Summers 70
looked at Bill Hutchinson, and Bill unfolded his paper and showed it. It was blank.

"It's Tessie," Mr. Summers said, and his voice was hushed. "Show us 71
her paper, Bill."

Bill Hutchinson went over to his wife and forced the slip of paper out 72
of her hand. It had a black spot on it, the black spot Mr. Summers had made the night before with the heavy pencil in the coal-company office. Bill Hutchinson held it up, and there was a stir in the crowd.

"All right, folks," Mr. Summers said. "Let's finish quickly." 73

Although the villagers had forgotten the ritual and lost the original 74
black box, they still remembered to use stones. The pile of stones the boys had made earlier was ready; there were stones on the ground with the blowing scraps of paper that had come out of the box. Mrs. Delacroix selected a stone so large she had to pick it up with both hands and turned to Mrs. Dunbar. "Come on," she said. "Hurry up."

Mrs. Dunbar had small stones in both hands, and she said, gasping for 75
breath, "I can't run at all. You'll have to go ahead and I'll catch up with you."

The children had stones already, and someone gave little Davy 76
Hutchinson a few pebbles.

Tessie Hutchinson was in the center of a cleared space by now, and she held her hands out desperately as the villagers moved in on her. "It isn't fair," she said. A stone hit her on the side of the head. 77

Old Man Warner was saying, "Come on, come on, everyone." Steve Adams was in the front of the crowd of villagers, with Mrs. Graves beside him. 78

"It isn't fair, it isn't right," Mrs. Hutchinson screamed, and then they were upon her. 79

• • •

Reading Literature

1. List the stages in the process of the lottery. Then, identify passages explaining the reasons behind each step. How logical are these explanations?

2. What is the significance of the fact that the process has continued essentially unchanged for so many years? What does this fact suggest about the people in the town?

3. Do you see this story as an explanation of a brutal process carried out in one town, or do you see it as a universal statement about dangerous tendencies in modern society — or in human nature? Explain your reasoning.

Journal Entry

What do you think it would take to stop a process like the lottery? What would have to be done — and who would have to do it?

Thematic Connections

- "Thirty-Eight Who Saw Murder Didn't Call the Police" (page 120)
- "Shooting an Elephant" (page 126)
- "Samuel" (page 258)
- "Get It Right: Privatize Executions" (page 299)

WRITING ASSIGNMENTS FOR PROCESS

1. Jessica Mitford describes the process of doing a job. Write an essay summarizing the steps you took in applying for, performing, or quitting a job.

2. Write a set of instructions explaining in objective terms how the lottery Shirley Jackson describes should be conducted. Imagine you are setting these steps down in writing for generations of your fellow townspeople to follow.

3. Write a consumer-oriented article for your school newspaper explaining how to apply for financial aid, a work-study job, or an internship.

4. List the steps in the process you follow when you study for an important exam. Then, interview two friends about how they study, and take notes about their usual routine. Finally, combine the most helpful strategies into a set of instructions aimed at students entering your school.

5. Think of a series of steps in a bureaucratic process, a process you had to go through to accomplish something — getting a driver's license or becoming a U.S. citizen, for instance. Write an essay explaining that process, and include a thesis statement that evaluates the process's efficiency.

6. Imagine you have encountered a visitor from another country (or another planet) who is not familiar with a social ritual you take for granted. Try to outline the steps involved in the ritual you are familiar with — for instance, choosing sides for a game or pledging a fraternity or sorority.

7. Write a process essay explaining how you went about putting together a collection, a scrapbook, a writing portfolio, or an album of some kind. Be sure your essay makes clear why you collected or compiled your materials.

8. Explain how a certain ritual or ceremony is conducted in your religion. Make sure someone of another faith could understand the process, and include a thesis statement that explains why the ritual is important.

9. Think of a process you believe should be modified or discontinued. Formulate a thesis that presents your negative feelings, and then explain the process so that you make your objections clear to your readers.

10. Write an essay explaining a process you experienced but would not recommend to others — for example, getting a tattoo or a body piercing.

11. Give readers instructions for participating in a potentially dangerous but worthwhile physical process — for example, rock climbing or white-water rafting. Be sure to include all necessary cautions.

COLLABORATIVE ACTIVITY FOR PROCESS

Working with three other students, create an illustrated instructional pamphlet to help new students survive four of your college's first "ordeals" — for example, registering for classes, purchasing textbooks, eating in the cafeteria, and moving into a dorm. Before beginning, decide as a group which processes to write about, whether you want your pamphlet to be practical and serious or humorous and irreverent, and what kinds of illustrations it should include. Then, decide who will write about which process — each student should do one — and who will provide the illustrations. When all of you are ready, assemble your individual efforts into a single unified piece of writing.

10
Cause and Effect

WHAT IS CAUSE AND EFFECT?

Process describes *how* something happens; **cause and effect** analyzes *why* something happens. Cause-and-effect essays examine causes, describe effects, or do both. In the following paragraph, journalist Tom Wicker considers the effects of a technological advance on a village in India:

Cause

Effects

Topic sentence

When a solar-powered water pump was provided for a well in India, the village headman took it over and sold the water, until stopped. The new liquid abundance attracted hordes of unwanted nomads. Village boys who had drawn water in buckets had nothing to do, and some became criminals. The gap between rich and poor widened, since the poor had no land to benefit from irrigation. Finally, village women broke the pump, so they could gather again around the well that had been the center of their social lives. Moral: technological advances have social, cultural, and economic consequences, often unanticipated.

Cause and effect, like narration, links situations and events together in time, with causes preceding effects. But causality involves more than sequence: cause-and-effect analysis explains why something happened — or is happening — and predicts what probably will happen.

Sometimes many different causes can be responsible for one effect. For example, as the following diagram illustrates, many elements may contribute to an individual's decision to leave his or her country of origin for the United States:

Causes   *Effect*

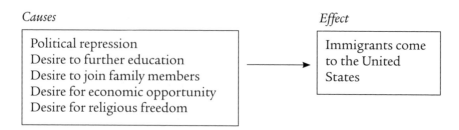

Similarly, a single cause can produce many different effects. Immigration, for instance, has had a variety of effects on the United States:

Cause   *Effects*

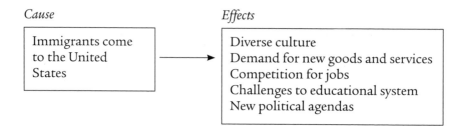

USING CAUSE AND EFFECT

Of course, causal relationships are rarely as neat as the boxes above suggest; in fact, such relationships are often subtle and complex. As you examine situations that seem suited to cause-and-effect analysis, you will discover that most complex situations involve numerous causes and many different effects.

Consider the two examples that follow.

The Case of the Losing Team Suppose a professional basketball team, recently stocked with the best players money can buy, has had a mediocre season. Because the individual players are talented and were successful under other coaches, fans blame the current coach for the team's losing streak and want him fired. But is the coach alone responsible? Maybe the inability of the players to function well as a team contributed to their poor performance. Perhaps some of the players are suffering from injuries, personal problems, or drug dependency. Or maybe the lack of support among fans has affected the team's morale. Clearly, other elements besides the new coach could have caused the losing streak. (And, of course, the team's losing streak might have any number of consequences, from declining attendance at games to the city's refusal to build a new arena.)

The Case of the Declining SAT Scores   For more than twenty years, from the 1960s to the 1980s, the college-board scores of high school seniors steadily declined and educators began to look for causes.* The decline began soon after television became popular, and therefore many people concluded that the two events were connected. This idea is plausible because children did seem to be reading less to watch television more, and reading comprehension is one of the chief skills the tests evaluate.

But many other elements might have contributed to the decline of test scores. During the same period, for example, many schools reduced the number of required courses and deemphasized traditional subjects and skills, such as reading. Adults were reading less than they used to, and perhaps they were not encouraging their children to read. Furthermore, during the 1960s and 1970s, many colleges changed their policies and admitted students who previously would not have qualified. These new admission standards encouraged students who would not have taken college boards in earlier years to take the tests. Therefore, the scores may have been lower because they measured the top third of high school seniors rather than the top fifth. In any case, the reason for the lower scores during that twenty-year period remains unclear. Perhaps television was the main cause after all, but nobody knows for sure. In such a case, it is easy — too easy — to claim a cause-and-effect relationship without the evidence to support it.

Just as the drop in scores may have had many causes, television watching may have had many effects. For instance, it may have made those same students better observers and listeners even if they did less well on standardized written tests. It may have encouraged them to have a national or even international outlook instead of a narrower local perspective. In other words, even if watching television did limit young people in some ways, it might also have expanded their horizons in other ways.

Remember, when you write about situations such as those described above, you need to give a balanced analysis. This means that you should try to consider all possible causes and effects, not just the most obvious ones or the first ones you think of.

Understanding Main and Contributory Causes

Even when you have identified several causes of a particular effect, one — the *main cause* — is always more important than the others, the *contributory causes*. Understanding the distinction between the **main** (most important) **cause** and the **contributory** (less important) **causes** is vital for planning a cause-and-effect paper because once you identify the main

---

* Today, with 2006 SAT scores showing their biggest decline since 1975 and the average SAT verbal scores falling five points, educators continue to search for causes, including changes in the test itself and the fact that fewer students are taking the test more than once.

cause, you can emphasize it in your paper and downplay the other causes. How, then, can you tell which cause is most important? Sometimes the main cause is obvious, but often it is not, as the following example shows.

The Case of the Hartford Roof Collapse During one winter a number of years ago, an unusually large amount of snow accumulated on the roof of the Civic Center Auditorium in Hartford, Connecticut, and the roof fell in. Newspapers reported that the weight of the snow had caused the collapse, and they were partly right. Other buildings, however, had not been flattened by the snow, so the main cause seemed to lie elsewhere. Insurance investigators eventually decided that the roof design, not the weight of the snow (which was a contributory cause), was the main cause of the collapse.

These cause-and-effect relationships are shown in this diagram:

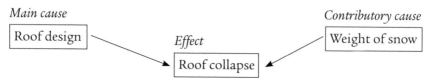

Because the main cause is not always the most obvious one, you should be sure to consider the significance of each cause very carefully as you plan your essay — and to continue to evaluate the importance of each cause as you write and revise.

Understanding Immediate and Remote Causes

Another important distinction is the difference between an immediate cause and a remote cause. An **immediate cause** closely precedes an effect and is therefore relatively easy to recognize. A **remote cause** is less obvious, perhaps because it involves something in the past or far away. Assuming that the most obvious cause is always the most important can be dangerous as well as shortsighted.

Reconsidering the Hartford Roof Collapse Most people agreed that the snow was the immediate, or most obvious, cause of the roof collapse. But further study by insurance investigators suggested remote causes that were not so apparent. The design of the roof was the most important remote cause of the collapse, but other remote causes were also examined. Perhaps the materials used in the roof's construction were partly to blame. Maybe maintenance crews had not done their jobs properly, or necessary repairs had not been made. If you were the insurance investigator analyzing the causes of this event, you would want to assess all possible contributing factors rather than just the most obvious. If you did not consider the remote as well as the immediate causes, you would reach an oversimplified and perhaps incorrect conclusion.

This diagram shows the cause-and-effect relationships just summarized:

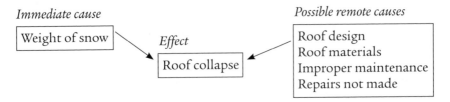

Remember, remote causes can be extremely important. In the roof-collapse situation, as we have seen, a remote cause — the roof design — was actually the main cause of the accident.

Understanding Causal Chains

Sometimes an effect can also be a cause. This is true in a **causal chain**, where A causes B, B causes C, C causes D, and so on, as shown here:

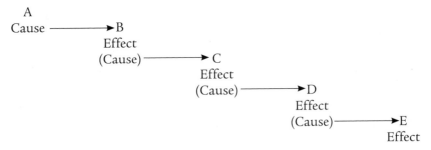

In causal chains, the result of one action is the cause of another. Leaving out any link in the chain, or putting any link in improper order, destroys the logic and continuity of the chain.

A simple example of a causal chain is the recent suggestion by a group of retired generals that global warming might be a threat to U.S. national security. According to these generals, global warming causes worldwide climate changes, such as droughts, which in turn create a refugee crisis as people leave their homelands in search of clean water. The resulting refugee camps, the generals claim, become a breeding ground for terrorists, and it is these terrorists who threaten our nation's security.

Here is another example of a causal chain.

The Case of the Disappearing Bicycle   In the past thirty years, the bicycle as a form of transportation for children has become increasingly rare, with fewer than one percent of children now riding bicycles to school. In addition, fewer children ride bicycles for recreation. Causes cited for this decline include the absence of sidewalks in many newer suburban communities, parents' rising fears about crime and traffic accidents, the rise in the number of students who schedule back-to-back after-school activities (perhaps due in part to the increased number of households with both parents working), the growing popularity of computer games, and the increased availability of after-school jobs for teenagers (who often need cars, not bikes, to get to work). The decreasing number of children who ride bikes has contributed to a corresponding steady decline, since the 1970s, in the sale of bicycles.

As a result of the decline in bicycle sales, bicycle thefts have decreased sharply, and bicycle deaths involving children under sixteen have also dropped dramatically (although this is due in part to increased use of helmets). However, the number of American children who are obese has doubled since the mid-1980s — in part because children get less and less exercise. So, factors such as fewer sidewalks and more working teenagers have led to a decline in bicycle sales, which in turn has had a far-reaching impact on children's health.

If your analysis of a situation reveals a causal chain, this discovery can be useful as you plan your essay. The very operation of a causal chain suggests an organizational pattern for a paper, and following the chain helps you to discuss items in their logical order. Be careful, however, to keep your emphasis on the causal connections and not to lapse into narration.

Avoiding *Post Hoc* Reasoning

When developing a cause-and-effect paper, you should not assume that just because event A *precedes* event B, event A has *caused* event B. This illogical assumption, called **post hoc reasoning**, equates a chronological sequence with causality. When you fall into this trap — assuming, for instance, that you failed an exam because a black cat crossed your path the day before — you are mistaking coincidence for causality.

Consider a classic example of *post hoc* reasoning.

The Case of the Magical Maggots Until the late nineteenth century, many scientists accepted the notion of spontaneous generation — that is, they believed living things could arise directly from nonliving matter. To support their beliefs, they pointed to specific situations. For instance, they observed that maggots, the larvae of the housefly, seemed to arise directly from the decaying flesh of dead animals.

These scientists were confusing sequence with causality, assuming that because the presence of decaying meat preceded the appearance of maggots, the two were connected in a causal relationship. In fact, because the dead animals were exposed to the air, flies were free to lay eggs in the animals' bodies, and these eggs hatched into maggots. Therefore, the living maggots were not a direct result of the presence of nonliving matter. Although these scientists were applying the best technology and scientific theory of their time, hindsight reveals that their conclusions were not valid.

Here is a more recent example of *post hoc* reasoning.

The Case of the Female Centenarians Several years ago, medical researchers published findings reporting that female centenarians — women who reached the age of one hundred — were four times as likely to have given birth when they were past forty as were women in a control group who died at the age of seventy-three. Researchers saw no causal connection between childbirth after forty and long life, suggesting only that the centenarians might have been predisposed to live longer because they reached menopause later than the other women. Local television newscasts and tabloid newspapers, however, misinterpreted the study's implications, presenting the relationship between late childbearing and long life as a causal one. In a vivid example of *post hoc* reasoning, one promotional spot for a local television newscast proclaimed, "Having kids late in life can help you live longer."

In your writing, as well as in your observations, it is neither logical nor fair to assume that a causal relationship exists unless clear, strong evidence supports the connection. When you revise a cause-and-effect paper, make sure you have not confused words such as *because, therefore,* and *consequently* (words that indicate a causal relationship) with words such as *then, next, subsequently, later,* and *afterward* (words that indicate a chronological relationship). When you use a word like *because,* you are signaling to readers that you are telling *why* something happened; when you use a word like *later,* you are only showing *when* it happened.

The ability to identify and analyze cause-and-effect relationships; to distinguish causes from effects and recognize causal chains; and to distinguish immediate from remote, main from contributory, and logical from illogical causes are all skills that will improve your writing. Understanding the nature of various cause-and-effect relationships will help you decide when and how to use this pattern in a paper.

PLANNING A CAUSE-AND-EFFECT ESSAY

After you have sorted out the cause-and-effect relationships you will write about, you are ready to plan your paper. You have three basic options — to discuss causes, to discuss effects, or to discuss both causes and effects. Often your assignment will suggest which of these options to use. Here are a few likely topics for cause-and-effect treatment:

Focus on finding causes	Discuss the factors that contributed to the declining population of state mental hospitals in the 1960s. (social work paper)
	Identify some possible causes of collective obsessional behavior. (psychology exam)

Focus on describing or predicting effects	Evaluate the probable effects of moving elementary school children from a highly structured classroom to a relatively open classroom. (education paper) Discuss the impact of World War I on two of Ernest Hemingway's characters. (literature exam)
Focus on both causes and effects	The 1840s were volatile years in Europe. Choose one social, political, or economic event that occurred during those years, analyze its causes, and briefly note how the event influenced later developments in European history. (history exam)

Developing a Thesis Statement

Of course, a cause-and-effect essay usually does more than just enumerate causes or effects; more often, it presents and supports a particular thesis. For example, an economics paper treating the major effects of the Vietnam War on the U.S. economy could be just a straightforward presentation of factual information — an attempt to inform readers of the war's economic impact. It is more likely, however, that the paper would indicate the significance of the war's effects, not just list these effects. In fact, cause-and-effect analysis often requires you to judge various factors so that you can assess their relative significance.

When you formulate a **thesis statement**, be sure it identifies the relationships among the specific causes or effects you will discuss. This thesis statement should tell your readers three things: the issues you plan to consider, the position you will take, and whether your emphasis is on causes, effects, or both. Your thesis statement may also indicate explicitly or implicitly the cause or effect you consider most important and the order in which you will present your points.

Arranging Causes and Effects

When deciding on the sequence in which you will present causes or effects, you have several options. One option, of course, is chronological order: you can present causes or effects in the order in which they occurred. Another option is to introduce the main cause first and then the contributory causes — or you can do just the opposite. If you want to stress positive consequences, begin by briefly discussing the negative ones; if you plan to emphasize negative results, summarize the less important positive effects first. Still another possibility is to begin by dismissing any events that were *not* causes and then explain what the real causes were. (This method is especially effective if you think your readers are likely to jump to *post hoc* conclusions.) Finally, you can begin with the most obvious causes or effects and move on to more subtle factors — and then to your analysis and conclusion.

Using Transitions

Cause-and-effect essays rely on clear transitions — *the first cause, the second cause; one result, another result* — to distinguish causes from effects and to help move readers through the discussion. In essays that analyze complex causal relationships, transitions are even more important because they can help readers distinguish main from contributory causes (*the most important cause, another cause*) and immediate from remote causes (*the most obvious cause, a less apparent cause*). Transitions are also essential in a causal chain, where they can help readers sort out the sequence (*then, next*) as well as the causal relationships (*because, as a result, for this reason*). A more complete list of transitions appears on page 43.

STRUCTURING A CAUSE-AND-EFFECT ESSAY

Finding Causes

Suppose you are planning the social work paper mentioned earlier: "Discuss the factors that contributed to the declining population of state mental hospitals in the 1960s." Your assignment specifies an effect — the declining population of state mental hospitals — and asks you to discuss possible causes, which might include the following:

- An increasing acceptance of mental illness in our society
- Prohibitive costs of in-patient care
- Increasing numbers of mental health professionals, which made it possible to treat patients outside of hospitals

Many health professionals, however, believe that the most important cause was the development and use of psychotropic drugs, such as chlorpromazine (Thorazine), which can alter behavior. To emphasize this cause in your paper, you could formulate the following thesis statement:

Less important causes	Although society's increasing acceptance of the mentally ill, the high cost of in-patient care, and the rise in the number of mental health professionals were all influential in reducing the population of state mental hospitals, the most important cause of this decline was the development and use of psychotropic drugs.
Effect	
Most important cause	

This thesis statement fully prepares your readers for your essay. It identifies the points you will consider, and it reveals your position — your assessment of the relative significance of the causes you identify. It states the less important causes first and indicates their secondary importance with *although*. In the body of your essay, the less important causes would come first so that the essay could gradually build up to the most convincing material. An informal outline for your paper might look like this:

Introduction:	Thesis statement — Although society's increasing acceptance of the mentally ill, the high cost of in-patient care, and the rise in the number of mental health professionals were all influential in reducing the population of state mental hospitals, the most important cause of this decline was the development and use of psychotropic drugs.
First cause:	Increasing acceptance of the mentally ill
Second cause:	High cost of in-patient care
Third cause:	Rise in the number of mental health professionals
Fourth (and most important) cause:	Development and use of psychotropic drugs
Conclusion:	Restatement of thesis or summary of key points

Describing or Predicting Effects

Suppose you were planning the education paper mentioned earlier: "Evaluate the probable effects of moving elementary school children from a highly structured classroom to a relatively open classroom." Here you would focus on effects rather than on causes. After brainstorming and deciding which specific points to discuss, you might formulate this thesis statement:

Cause	Moving children from a highly structured classroom to a relatively open one is desirable because it
Effects	is likely to encourage more independent play, more flexibility in forming friendship groups, and, ultimately, more creativity.

This thesis statement clearly tells readers the stand you will take and the main points you will consider in your essay. The thesis also clearly indicates that these points are *effects* of the open classroom. After introducing the cause, your essay would treat these three effects in the order they are presented in the thesis statement, building up to the most important point. An informal outline of your paper might look like this:

Introduction:	Thesis statement — Moving children from a highly structured classroom to a relatively open one is desirable because it is likely to encourage more independent play, more flexibility in forming friendship groups, and, ultimately, more creativity.

First effect:	More independent play
Second effect:	More flexible friendship groups
Third (and most important) effect:	More creativity
Conclusion:	Restatement of thesis or summary of key points

REVISING A CAUSE-AND-EFFECT ESSAY

When you revise a cause-and-effect essay, consider the items on the revision checklist on page 54. In addition, pay special attention to the items on the following checklist, which apply specifically to cause-and-effect essays.

✓ **REVISION CHECKLIST: Cause and Effect**

- Does your assignment call for a discussion of causes, of effects, or of both causes and effects?
- Does your essay have a clearly stated thesis that indicates whether you will focus on causes, effects, or both?
- Have you considered all possible causes and all possible effects?
- Have you distinguished between the main (most important) cause and the contributory (less important) causes?
- Have you distinguished between immediate and remote causes?
- Have you identified a causal chain in your reasoning?
- Have you avoided *post hoc* reasoning?
- Have you used transitional words and phrases to show how the causes and effects you discuss are related?

EDITING A CAUSE-AND-EFFECT ESSAY

When you edit your cause-and-effect essay, follow the guidelines on the editing checklists on pages 71, 74, and 76. In addition, focus on the grammar, mechanics, and punctuation issues that are particularly relevant to cause-and-effect essays. Two of these issues — avoiding faulty "the reason is because" constructions and using *affect* and *effect* correctly — are discussed here.

GRAMMAR IN CONTEXT: Avoiding "The reason is because";
Using *Affect* and *Effect* Correctly

Avoiding "the reason is because" When you discuss causes and
effects, you may find yourself writing the phrase "the reason is." If you
follow this phrase with *because* ("the reason is *because*"), you will create
an error.

The word *because* means "for the reason that." Therefore, it is redundant to say "the reason is because" (which literally means "the reason is
for the reason that"). You can correct this error by substituting *that* for
because ("the reason is *that*").

INCORRECT: Robin Tolmach Lakoff believes that one <u>reason</u> soldiers
are able to kill in wartime <u>is because</u> they use language to
dehumanize their enemies (363).

CORRECT: Robin Tolmach Lakoff believes that one <u>reason</u> soldiers
are able to kill in wartime <u>is that</u> they use language to
dehumanize their enemies (363).

Using *Affect* and *Effect* Correctly When you write a cause-and-
effect essay, you will most likely use the words *affect* and *effect* quite often.
For this reason, it is important that you know the difference between
affect and *effect.*

- *Affect,* usually a verb, means "to influence."

  Linda M. Hasselstrom believes that carrying a gun has <u>affected</u> her life
  in a positive way (357).

- *Effect,* usually a noun, means "a result."

  Linda M. Hasselstrom believes that carrying a gun has had a positive
  <u>effect</u> on her life (357).

NOTE: *Effect* can also be a verb meaning "to bring about" ("She worked
hard to <u>effect</u> change in the community").

For more practice in avoiding faulty constructions and commonly confused words,
visit Exercise Central at bedfordstmartins.com/patterns/faultyconstructions
or bedfordstmartins.com/patterns/confusedwords.

✓EDITING CHECKLIST: Cause and Effect

- Have you used verb tenses correctly to distinguish among events
  that happened earlier, at the same time, and later?
- Have you placed a comma **after** every dependent clause introduced by *because* ("Because the rally was so crowded, we left

early") but *not* used a comma **before** a dependent clause introduced by *because* ("We left early because the rally was so
crowded")?

- Have you used "the reason is that" (not "the reason is because")?
- Have you used *affect* and *effect* correctly?

A STUDENT WRITER: Cause and Effect

The following midterm exam, written for a history class, analyzes both
the causes and the effects of the Irish potato famine that occurred during
the 1840s. Notice how the writer, Evelyn Pellicane, concentrates on causes
but also discusses briefly the effects of this tragedy, just as the exam question directs.

Question: The 1840s were volatile years in Europe. Choose one social, political, or economic event that occurred during those years, analyze its causes,
and briefly note how the event influenced later developments in European
history.

The Irish Famine, 1845-1849

Thesis statement   The Irish famine, which brought hardship and tragedy to   1
Ireland during the 1840s, was caused and prolonged by four
basic factors: the failure of the potato crop, the landlord-tenant
system, errors in government policy, and the long-standing
prejudice of the British toward Ireland.

First cause   The immediate cause of the famine was the failure of   2
the potato crop. In 1845, potato disease struck the crop, and
potatoes rotted in the ground. The 1846 crop also failed, and
before long people were eating weeds. The 1847 crop was
healthy, but there were not enough potatoes to go around,
and in 1848 the blight struck again, leading to more and
more evictions of tenants by landlords.

Second cause   The tenants' position on the land had never been very   3
secure. Most had no leases and could be turned out by their
landlords at any time. If a tenant owed rent, he was
evicted — or, worse, put in prison, leaving his family to starve.
The threat of prison caused many tenants to leave their land;
those who could leave Ireland did so, sometimes with money
provided by their landlords. Some landlords did try to take care
of their tenants, but most did not. Many were absentee
landlords who spent their rent money abroad.

Third cause   Government policy errors, although not an immediate   4
cause of the famine, played an important role in creating an

unstable economy and perpetuating starvation. In 1846, the government decided not to continue selling corn, as it had during the first year of the famine, claiming that low-cost purchases of corn by Ireland had paralyzed British trade by interfering with free enterprise. Therefore, 1846 saw a starving population, angry demonstrations, and panic; even those with money were unable to buy food. Still, the government insisted that if it sent food to Ireland, prices would rise in the rest of the United Kingdom and that this would be unfair to hardworking English and Scots. As a result, no food was sent. Throughout the years of the famine, the British government aggravated an already grave situation: they did nothing to improve agricultural operations, to help people adjust to another crop, to distribute seeds, or to reorder the landlord-tenant system that made the tenants' position so insecure.

Fourth cause

    At the root of this poor government policy was the long-standing British prejudice against the Irish. Hostility between the two countries went back some six hundred years, and the British were simply not about to inconvenience themselves to save the Irish. When the Irish so desperately needed grain to replace the damaged potatoes, it was clear that grain had to be imported from England. This meant, however, that the Corn Laws, which had been enacted to keep the price of British corn high by taxing imported grain, had to be repealed. The British were unwilling to repeal the Corn Laws. Even when they did supply cornmeal, they made no attempt to explain to the Irish how to cook this unfamiliar food. Moreover, the British government was determined to make Ireland pay for its own poor, so it forced the collection of taxes. Since many landlords could not collect the tax money, they were forced to evict their tenants. The British government's callous and indifferent treatment of the Irish has been called genocide.

5

Effects

    As a result of this devastating famine, the population of Ireland was reduced from about nine million to about six and one-half million. During the famine years, men roamed the streets looking for work, begging when they found none. Epidemics of "famine fever" and dysentery reduced the population drastically. The most important historical result of the famine, however, was the massive immigration to the United States, Canada, and Great Britain of poor, unskilled people who

6

had to struggle to fit into a skilled economy and who brought with them a deep-seated hatred of the British. (This same hatred remained strong in Ireland itself — so strong that during World War II, Ireland, then independent, remained neutral rather than coming to England's aid.) Irish immigrants faced slums, fever epidemics, joblessness, and hostility — even anti-Catholic and anti-Irish riots — in Boston, New York, London, Glasgow, and Quebec. In Ireland itself, poverty and discontent continued, and by 1848 those emigrating from Ireland included a more highly skilled class of farmers, the ones Ireland needed to recover and to survive.

Conclusion (includes restatement of thesis)   The Irish famine, one of the great tragedies of the nineteenth century, was a natural disaster compounded by the insensitivity of the British government and the archaic agricultural system of Ireland. Although the deaths that resulted depleted Ireland's resources even more, the men and women who immigrated to other countries permanently enriched those nations.

7

Points for Special Attention

Structure.   This is a relatively long essay; if it were not so clearly organized, it would be difficult to follow. Because the essay was to focus primarily on causes, Evelyn first introduces the effect — the famine itself — and then considers its causes. After she examines the causes, she moves on to the results of the famine, treating the most important result last. In this essay, then, the famine is first treated as an effect and then, toward the end, as a cause. In fact, it is the central link in a causal chain.

Evelyn devotes one paragraph to her introduction and one to each cause; she sums up the famine's results in a separate paragraph and devotes the final paragraph to her conclusion. (Depending on a particular paper's length and complexity, more — or less — than one paragraph may be devoted to each cause or effect.) An informal outline for her paper might look like this:

Introduction (including thesis statement)
First cause: Failure of the potato crop
Second cause: The landlord-tenant system
Third cause: Errors in government policy
Fourth cause: British prejudice
Results of the famine
Conclusion

Because Evelyn saw all the causes as important and interrelated, she did not present them in order of increasing importance. Instead, she begins with the immediate cause of the famine — the failure of the potato crop — and then digs more deeply until she arrives at the most remote cause, British prejudice. The immediate cause is also the main (most important) cause; the other situations had existed before the famine began.

Transitions. Because Evelyn considers a series of relationships as well as an intricate causal chain, the cause-and-effect relationships in this essay are both subtle and complex. Throughout the essay, many words suggest cause-and-effect connections: *brought, caused, leading to, therefore, as a result, so, since,* and the like. These words help readers sort out the causal connections.

Answering an Exam Question. Before planning and writing her answer, Evelyn read the exam question carefully. She saw that it asked for both causes and effects but that its wording directed her to spend more time on causes ("analyze") than on effects ("briefly note"), so she organized her discussion to conform to these directions. In addition, she indicated *explicitly* which were the causes ("government policy . . . played an important role") and which were the effects ("The most important historical result").

Evelyn's purpose was to convey factual information and, in doing so, to demonstrate her understanding of the course material. Rather than waste her limited time choosing a clever opening strategy or making elaborate attempts to engage her audience, she began her essay with a direct statement of her thesis.

Evelyn was obviously influenced by outside sources; the ideas in the essay are not completely her own. Because this was an exam, however, and because the instructor expected that students would base their essays on class notes and assigned readings, Evelyn did not have to document her sources.

Focus on Revision

Because this essay was written as an exam answer, Evelyn had no time — and no need — to revise it further. If she had been preparing this assignment outside of class, however, she might have done more. For example, she could have added a more arresting opening, such as a brief eyewitness account of the famine's effects. Her conclusion — appropriately brief and straightforward for an exam answer — could also have been developed further, perhaps with the addition of information about the nation's eventual recovery. Finally, adding statistics, quotations by historians, or a brief summary of Irish history before the famine could have further enriched the essay.

📄   **PEER EDITING WORKSHEET: Cause and Effect**

1. Paraphrase the essay's thesis. Is it explicitly stated? Should it be?

2. Does the essay focus on causes, effects, or both? Does the thesis statement clearly identify this focus? If not, how should the thesis statement be revised?

3. Does the writer consider *all* relevant causes or effects? Are any key causes or effects omitted? Are any irrelevant causes or effects included?

4. Make an informal outline of the essay. What determines the order of the causes or effects? Is this the most effective order? If not, what revisions do you suggest?

5. List the transitional words and phrases used to indicate causal connections. Are any additional transitions needed? If so, where?

6. Does the writer use *post hoc* reasoning? Point out any examples of illogical reasoning.

7. Are more examples or details needed to help readers understand causal connections? If so, where?

8. Do you agree with the writer's conclusions? Why or why not?

9. Has the writer used any "the reason is because" constructions? If so, suggest revisions.

10. Are *affect* and *effect* used correctly? Point out any errors.

All the selections that follow focus on cause-and-effect relationships. Some readings focus on causes, others on effects. The first selection, a visual text, is followed by questions designed to illustrate how cause and effect can operate in visual form.

Major League Baseball Brawl (Photo)

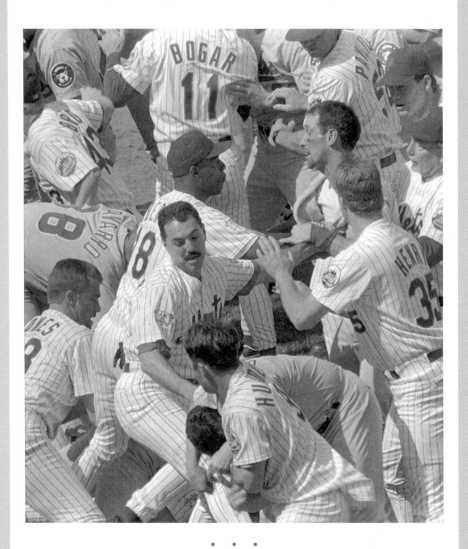

• • •

Reading Images

1. Study the photo above. What might have caused the situation on the field? Consider remote as well as immediate causes.

2. What outcomes might you expect from this fight? Consider the effects on the players on the field, on the players waiting in the dugout, and on the fans in the stands.

3. Consider the fight on the field as part of a causal chain. Diagram that chain of events, using arrows to point from one event to the next.

Journal Entry

Write a paragraph suggesting ways to prevent situations such as the one shown in the picture. For example, might high fines deter players from losing their tempers?

Thematic Connections

- "My Field of Dreams" (page 89)
- "Who Killed Benny Paret?" (page 340)

NORMAN COUSINS

Who Killed Benny Paret?

Norman Cousins (1915–1990) began his career in journalism writing for the *New York Evening Post* and *Current History* magazine. In 1940, Cousins joined the *Saturday Review,* where he served as editor from 1942 to 1978. A noted social critic, Cousins lectured widely on world affairs. An adjunct professor in the department of psychiatry at the UCLA School of Medicine from 1978 until his death, he is particularly remembered for his many books urging a positive outlook to combat illness, including *Anatomy of an Illness* (1979).

Background on the hazards of boxing

Cousins's classic 1962 essay "Who Killed Benny Paret?" focuses on a brutal boxing match at Madison Square Garden between Emile Griffith and Benny (Kid) Paret — a fight that led to Paret's death after nine days in a coma. The event, witnessed by millions of shocked television viewers, is the subject of a 2004 documentary, *Ring of Fire.* The fight went twelve rounds and ended with Griffith driving Paret onto the ropes and relentlessly beating him. Some newspapers reported that Griffith was angry because Paret had questioned his manhood, calling him, in Spanish (Paret was Cuban), a *maricón* (a derogatory name for a gay man). In the aftermath of the fight, many demanded that boxing be banned altogether. As a result, a number of rules for professional boxing were changed, but boxing remains an inherently dangerous sport. More than five hundred ring deaths have occurred in the past century; as recently as 2005, a professional boxer died following a knockout in the ring. In addition, many boxers suffer from chronic latent brain damage, known medically as *dementia pugilistica.* In answering the question posed by his essay's title, Cousins takes a strong stand against violence in boxing.

1   Sometime about 1935 or 1936 I had an interview with Mike Jacobs, the prize-fight promoter. I was a fledgling reporter at that time; my beat was education but during the vacation season I found myself on varied assignments, all the way from ship news to sports reporting. In this way I found myself sitting opposite the most powerful figure in the boxing world.

2   There was nothing spectacular in Mr. Jacobs' manner or appearance; but when he spoke about prize fights, he was no longer a bland little man but a colossus who sounded the way Napoleon must have sounded when he reviewed a battle. You knew you were listening to Number One. His saying something made it true.

3   We discussed what to him was the only important element in successful promoting — how to please the crowd. So far as he was concerned, there was no mystery to it. You put killers in the ring and the people filled your arena. You hire boxing artists — men who are adroit at feinting, parrying,

weaving, jabbing, and dancing, but who don't pack dynamite in their fists — and you wind up counting your empty seats. So you searched for the killers and sluggers and maulers — fellows who could hit with the force of a baseball bat.

I asked Mr. Jacobs if he was speaking literally when he said people came out to see the killer.   4

"They don't come out to see a tea party," he said evenly. "They come out to see the knockout. They come out to see a man hurt. If they think anything else, they're kidding themselves."   5

Recently, a young man by the name of Benny Paret was killed in the ring. The killing was seen by millions; it was on television. In the twelfth round, he was hit hard in the head several times, went down, was counted out, and never came out of the coma.   6

The Paret fight produced a flurry of investigations. Governor Rockefeller was shocked by what happened and appointed a committee to assess the responsibility. The New York State Boxing Commission decided to find out what was wrong. The District Attorney's office expressed its concern. One question that was solemnly studied in all three probes concerned the action of the referee. Did he act in time to stop the fight? Another question had to do with the role of the examining doctors who certified the physical fitness of the fighters before the bout. Still another question involved Mr. Paret's manager; did he rush his boy into the fight without adequate time to recuperate from the previous one?   7

In short, the investigators looked into every possible cause except the real one. Benny Paret was killed because the human fist delivers enough impact, when directed against the head, to produce a massive hemorrhage in the brain. The human brain is the most delicate and complex mechanism in all creation. It has a lacework of millions of highly fragile nerve connections. Nature attempts to protect this exquisitely intricate machinery by encasing it in a hard shell. Fortunately, the shell is thick enough to withstand a great deal of pounding. Nature, however, can protect a man against everything except man himself. Not every blow to the head will kill a man — but there is always the risk of concussion and damage to the brain. A prize fighter may be able to survive even repeated brain concussions and go on fighting, but the damage to his brain may be permanent.   8

In any event, it is futile to investigate the referee's role and seek to determine whether he should have intervened to stop the fight earlier. That is not where the primary responsibility lies. The primary responsibility lies with the people who pay to see a man hurt. The referee who stops a fight too soon from the crowd's viewpoint can expect to be booed. The crowd wants the knockout; it wants to see a man stretched out on the canvas. This is the supreme moment in boxing. It is nonsense to talk about prize fighting as a test of boxing skills. No crowd was ever brought to its feet screaming and cheering at the sight of two men beautifully dodging and weaving out of each other's jabs. The time the crowd comes alive is when a man is hit hard over the heart or the head, when his mouthpiece   9 flies out, when the blood squirts out of his nose or eyes, when he wobbles under the attack and his pursuer continues to smash at him with pole-axe impact.

Don't blame it on the referee. Don't even blame it on the fight manag-   10
ers. Put the blame where it belongs — on the prevailing mores that regard prize fighting as a perfectly proper enterprise and vehicle of entertainment. No one doubts that many people enjoy prizefighting and will miss it if it should be thrown out. And that is precisely the point.

• • •

Comprehension

1. Why, according to Mike Jacobs, do people come to see a prizefight? Does Cousins agree with him?
2. What was the immediate cause of Paret's death? What remote causes did the investigators consider? What, according to Cousins, was the main cause? That is, where does the "primary responsibility" (9) lie?
3. Why does Cousins believe "it is futile to investigate the referee's role" (9)?
4. Cousins ends his essay with "And that is precisely the point." What is the "point" he refers to?

Purpose and Audience

1. This persuasive essay has a strong thesis. What is it?
2. This essay appeared on May 5, 1962, a month after Paret died. What do you suppose its impact was on its audience? Do you think the impact on readers is the same today?
3. At whom is this essay aimed — boxing enthusiasts, sportswriters, or a general audience? On what do you base your conclusion?
4. Does Cousins expect his audience to agree with his thesis? How does he try to win sympathy for his position?

Style and Structure

1. Do you think Cousins includes enough detail to convince readers? Where, if anywhere, might more detail be helpful?
2. Sort out the complex cause-and-effect relationships discussed in paragraph 9.
3. What strategy does Cousins use in his conclusion? Is it effective? Explain your reasoning.

Vocabulary Projects

1. Define each of the following words as it is used in this selection.

   promoter (1)   feinting (3)   lacework (8)
   fledgling (1)   parrying (3)   encasing (8)
   colossus (2)   maulers (3)   intervened (9)

2. The specialized vocabulary of boxing is prominent in this essay, but the facts Cousins presents would apply equally well to any sport in which violence is a potential problem.

   a. Imagine you are writing a similar essay about football, hockey, rugby, or another sport. Think about your audience, and substitute an appropriate equivalent word or phrase for each of the following:

      promoter (1)   feinting, parrying, weaving,   knockout (5)
      prize fights (2)   jabbing, and dancing (3)   referee (7)
      in the ring (3)   killers and sluggers   fighters/fight (7)
      boxing artists (3)   and maulers (3)

   b. Rewrite this sentence so that it suits the sport you have chosen: "The crowd wants the knockout; it wants to see a man stretched out on the canvas. . . . It is nonsense to talk about prize fighting as a test of boxing skills. No crowd was ever brought to its feet screaming and cheering at the sight of two men beautifully dodging and weaving out of each other's jabs" (9).

Journal Entry

Do Cousins's graphic descriptions convince you that boxing should be outlawed? Explain.

Writing Workshop

1. Write a cause-and-effect essay examining how the demands of the public affect professional athletes. For example, you might examine steroid use in baseball, violence in hockey or football, or how an individual player cultivates a glamorous image for fans.

2. Write a cause-and-effect essay about a time when, in response to peer pressure, you encouraged someone to do something you felt was dishonest or unwise. Be sure to identify what caused your actions.

3. Why do you think a young person might turn to a career in boxing? Write a cause-and-effect essay examining the possible motives.

Combining the Patterns

This essay begins with five paragraphs of **narration** that summarize a meeting between Cousins and Mike Jacobs. What function does this narrative introduction serve in the essay? Once Paret's death is mentioned and the persuasive portion of the essay begins, Cousins never resumes the narrative. Do you think he should have returned to this narrative? If so, where might he have continued the story?

Thematic Connections

- "Thirty-Eight Who Saw Murder Didn't Call the Police" (page 120)
- "Shooting an Elephant" (page 126)
- "Get It Right: Privatize Executions" (page 299)
- "The Lottery" (page 311)

LAWRENCE OTIS GRAHAM

The "Black Table" Is Still There

Lawrence Otis Graham was born in 1962 into one of the few African-American families then living in an upper-middle-class community in Westchester County, near New York City. A graduate of Princeton University and Harvard Law School, Graham works as a corporate attorney in Manhattan and teaches at Fordham University. He is the author of some dozen books, most recently *Our Kind of People: Inside America's Black Upper Class* (1999) and *Proversity: Getting Past Face Value* (1997). The following essay, originally published in the *New York Times* in 1991, is included in Graham's 1995 essay collection, *Member of the Club: Reflections on Life in a Racially Polarized World.*

Background on school segregation
In "The 'Black Table' Is Still There," Graham returns to his largely white junior high school and discovers to his dismay how little has changed since the 1970s. Since the 1950s, the United States government has strongly supported integration of public schools. For example, the Supreme Court in 1955 found segregation of public schools unconstitutional; the Civil Rights Act of 1964 required public school systems to implement integration programs; and in 1971, the Supreme Court upheld court-ordered busing as a means of achieving integration. The results of these policies were dramatic. From the mid-1960s to 1972, the number of African-American students attending desegregated schools jumped from 12 percent to 44 percent. By the 1990s, however, this had begun to change as the Supreme Court began to lift desegregation orders in response to local school boards' promises to desegregate voluntarily through magnet schools and the like. A study published in 2003 showed that two-thirds of African-American students attend schools that are predominantly minority and more than 15 percent attend schools that are 99 to 100 percent minority, a significant rise since 1989. Ironically, as Graham observes, when students are given the choice, self-segregation seems to be the norm.

During a recent visit to my old junior high school in Westchester County, I came upon something that I never expected to see again, something that was a source of fear and dread for three hours each school morning of my early adolescence: the all-black lunch table in the cafeteria of my predominantly white suburban junior high school. 1

As I look back on twenty-seven years of often being the first and only black person integrating such activities and institutions as the college newspaper, the high school tennis team, summer music camps, our all-white suburban neighborhood, my eating club at Princeton, or my private social club at Harvard Law School, the one scenario that puzzled me the most then and now is the all-black lunch table. 2

Why was it there? Why did the black kids separate themselves? What did the table say about the integration that was supposedly going on in homerooms and gym classes? What did it say about the black kids? The white kids? What did it say about me when I refused to sit there, day after day, for three years? 3

Each afternoon, at 12:03 P.M., after the fourth period ended, I found myself among six hundred 12-, 13-, and 14-year-olds who marched into the brightly-lit cafeteria and dashed for a seat at one of the twenty-seven blue formica lunch tables. 4

No matter who I walked in with — usually a white friend — no matter what mood I was in, there was one thing that was certain: I would not sit at the black table. 5

I would never consider sitting at the black table. 6

What was wrong with me? What was I afraid of? 7

I would like to think that my decision was a heroic one, made in order to express my solidarity with the theories of integration that my community was espousing. But I was just twelve at the time, and there was nothing heroic in my actions. 8

I avoided the black table for a very simple reason: I was afraid that by sitting at the black table I'd lose all my white friends. I thought that by sitting there I'd be making a racist, anti-white statement. 9

Is that what the all-black table means? Is it a rejection of white people? I no longer think so. 10

At the time, I was angry that there was a black lunch table. I believed that the black kids were the reason why other kids didn't mix more. I was ready to believe that their self-segregation was the cause of white bigotry. 11

Ironically, I even believed this after my best friend (who was white) told me I probably shouldn't come to his bar mitzvah because I'd be the only black and people would feel uncomfortable. I even believed this after my Saturday afternoon visit, at age ten, to a private country club pool prompted incensed white parents to pull their kids from the pool in terror. 12

In the face of this blatantly racist (anti-black) behavior I still somehow managed to blame only the black kids for being the barrier to integration in my school and my little world. What was I thinking? 13

I realize now how wrong I was. During that same time, there were at least two tables of athletes, an Italian table, a Jewish girls' table, a Jewish boys' table (where I usually sat), a table of kids who were into heavy metal music and smoking pot, a table of middle-class Irish kids. Weren't these tables just as segregationist as the black table? At the time, no one thought so. At the time, no one even acknowledged the segregated nature of these other tables. 14

Maybe it's the color difference that makes all-black tables or all-black groups attract the scrutiny and wrath of so many people. It scares and angers people; it exasperates. It did those things to me, and I'm black. 15

As an integrating black person, I know that my decision *not* to join the black lunch table attracted its own kinds of scrutiny and wrath from my 16 classmates. At the same time that I heard angry words like "Oreo" and "white boy" being hurled at me from the black table, I was also dodging impatient questions from white classmates: "Why do all those black kids sit together?" or "Why don't you ever sit with the other blacks?"

The black lunch table, like those other segregated tables, is a comment   17
on the superficial inroads that integration has made in society. Perhaps I should be happy that even this is a long way from where we started. Yet, I can't get over the fact that the twenty-seventh table in my junior high school cafeteria is still known as the "black table" — fourteen years after my adolescence.

• • •

Comprehension

1. What exactly is the "black table"?
2. In paragraph 1, Graham says that on a recent visit to his old junior high school he "came upon something that [he] never expected to see again." Why do you think the sight of the all-black lunch table was such a surprise to him?
3. In Graham's junior high school, what factors determined where students sat?
4. Why didn't Graham sit at the "black table" when he was in junior high?
5. When he was a junior high school student, whom did Graham blame for the existence of the exclusively black lunch table? Whom or what does he now see as the cause of the table's existence?

Purpose and Audience

1. What is Graham's thesis?
2. Rather than introducing outside supporting information — such as statistics, interviews with educators, or sociological studies — Graham relies on his own opinions and on anecdotal evidence to support his thesis. Do you think this is enough? Explain your reasoning.
3. Why does Graham give background information about himself in this essay — for example, in paragraphs 2 and 12? How does this information affect your reaction to him as a person? Your reaction to his essay? Do you think he needs to supply additional information about himself or about his junior high school? If so, what kind of information would be helpful?
4. Do you think Graham's primary purpose here is to criticize a system he despises, to change his audience's views about segregated lunch tables, or to justify his own behavior? Explain your conclusion.
5. In paragraph 5, Graham tells readers that he usually entered the cafeteria with a white friend; in paragraph 12, he reveals that his best friend was white. Why do you suppose he wants his audience to know these facts?

Style and Structure

1. Throughout his essay, Graham asks **rhetorical questions**. Identify as many of these questions as you can. Are they necessary? Provocative? Distracting? Explain.

2. In paragraph 16, Graham quotes his long-ago classmates. What do these quotations reveal? Should he have included more of them?

3. Is Graham's focus on finding causes, describing effects, or both? Explain.

4. This essay uses first-person pronouns and contractions. Do you think Graham would have more credibility if he used a less personal and more formal style?

Vocabulary Projects

1. Define each of the following words as it is used in this selection.

   scenario (2)   incensed (12)   scrutiny (15)
   espousing (8)   blatantly (13)   inroads (17)

2. Does the phrase *black table* have a negative connotation for you? Do you think Graham intends it to? What other names could he give to the table that might present it in a more neutral, even positive, light? What names could he give to the other tables he lists in paragraph 14?

Journal Entry

Graham sees the continued presence of the "black table" as a serious problem. Do you agree?

Writing Workshop

1. In paragraph 14, Graham mentions other lunch tables that were limited to certain groups and asks, "Weren't these tables just as segregationist as the black table?" Answer his question in a cause-and-effect essay explaining why you believe "black tables" still exist. In your introduction, quote Graham's question, and be sure to include parenthetical documentation and a works-cited page. (See the Appendix for information on documentation formats.)

2. In addition to self-segregated lunch tables, many colleges also have single-race social clubs, dormitories, fraternities, and even graduation ceremonies. Do you see such self-segregation as something that divides our society (that is, as a cause) or as something that reflects divisions that already exist (that is, as an effect)? Write an essay discussing this issue, supporting your thesis with examples from your own experience.

3. Do the people at your school or workplace tend to segregate themselves according to race, gender, or some other principle? Do you see a problem in such behavior? Write an email to your school's dean of students or to

your employer explaining what you believe causes this pattern and what effects, positive or negative, you have observed.

Combining the Patterns

In paragraph 14, Graham uses **classification and division**. What is he categorizing? What categories does he identify? What other categories might he include? Why is this pattern of development particularly appropriate for this essay?

Thematic Connections

- "Indian Education" (page 135)
- "Just Walk On By" (page 236)
- "College Pressures" (page 462)
- "The Myth of the Latin Woman: I Just Met a Girl Named Maria" (page 730)

LILLIAN B. RUBIN

Guns and Grief

Sociologist and psychologist Lillian B. Rubin (b. 1926) grew up in a poor immigrant family in the Bronx, New York. Now retired from the sociology department at Queens College, City University of New York, she continues her affiliation with the Institute for the Study of Social Change at Berkeley. Rubin is the author of twelve books, including *The Transcendent Child: Tales of Triumph over the Past* (1996), *The Man with the Beautiful Voice, and More Stories from the Other Side of the Couch* (2003), and *60 on Up: The Truth about Aging in America* (2007). The following essay appeared in the liberal periodical *Dissent*.

Background on school safety
On April 20, 1999, two armed teenagers walked into Columbine High School in Littleton, Colorado, and killed twelve students and a teacher, injuring twenty-three others before killing themselves. Since then, many schools across the country have instituted emergency response programs in coordination with public safety agencies. They have also expanded mental health programs and made greater attempts to identify students at risk for violence. Government funding has put more security officers in public schools, and more than half of the states have passed laws requiring zero-tolerance for school violence. In addition, a number of schools have provided the means for students to report anonymously — either through a "concerned student" note to an administrator or through commercial telephone help lines and Web sites — any behavior they believe may lead to violence. Finally, a variety of high schools and colleges have been experimenting with the use of email and text-message warning systems when violence threatens. Still, as the following essay argues, tragic campus violence — particularly gun-related violence — is still a reality.

Dawn broke on April 16, 2007, as it does always, but this day would soon reveal itself to be unlike any other. For this was the day that a twenty-three-year-old student walked onto the campus at Virginia Tech carrying two semi-automatic pistols — a Glock 9 mm and a Walther P22 — and fired close to two hundred rounds, killing thirty-two people and injuring scores more in the deadliest shooting rampage in our nation's history. Minutes later, long before anyone knew any of the facts, reporters filled the airwaves, the Web buzzed with headlines, and the show was on — a spectacle nearly as obscene as the massacre itself.

As reporters dug for the story behind the killing spree and found that the shooter, Cho Seung-Hui, had been ordered by a judge to undergo outpatient treatment after he was diagnosed in December 2005 as "mentally ill and in need of hospitalization," the din increased, and the psychology of the killer moved to center stage. Nearly every news show featured its very own mental health "expert" — psychologists and psychiatrists, none of whom had ever met Cho Seung-Hui and knew almost nothing about him, yet had no problem offering up instant, and often contradictory, psychological analyses to explain why he did it. Having spent over three decades of my professional life in clinical practice and knowing its uncertainties, I wondered how these guys (and they were almost always "guys") dared to speak with such assurance, as if psychology were a mathematics-like science where it's perfectly clear that if you add two and two, you will always get four. It's as if they had a recipe: pour a little anger into the pot, mix well with violent fantasies, add a big dollop of alienation, and you'll have yourself a mass murderer. Sounds like a lot of teenagers and young adults we all know, doesn't it?

I listened to my local public radio station most of that day, then turned   3
to various television news programs during the evening, waiting in vain for one of these experts to acknowledge that, whatever Cho's psychological state, he couldn't have killed and injured so many people if he hadn't had two semi-automatic weapons in his hands. Instead, I heard an orgy of blame.

Because the theory to which most mental health professionals have   4
dedicated their lives tells them that the seeds of the son's problems must lie in the family, the parents were at the top of the list. This must be a seriously dysfunctional family, they announced. Didn't these people talk to their son? How could they not have known that this young man was so troubled? Never mind that the parents had tried unsuccessfully to get help for their son, and that this was widely reported. Never mind, either, the obvious fact that whatever our individual differences may be, our psychology is born and takes root in a social environment whose reach is well beyond the bounds of family, an environment in which it is all too easy to get the guns to carry out the violent fantasies. Theory trumped fact.

If not the family, who else to blame? The school officials, obviously.   5
Why didn't they intervene when they saw earlier signs that he was a troubled young man? Why, when two people were shot dead two hours before the massacre, didn't they lock down the campus? Good questions, but they still avoid the central one: how is it possible to protect against this kind of mass violence in a society where such a vast number of guns circulate so freely?

The professors, too, got their share of blame. Why didn't they take   6
more seriously the rage and violence he expressed in written assignments? But real life doesn't mimic television, and unlike the show in which FBI profilers always catch their prey because they can accurately assess "the criminal mind," it's virtually impossible for even the professionally trained to predict when a young person's violent and/or suicidal fantasies are anything more than an outlet for blowing off steam.

Meanwhile, in the midst of all the talk, the grief counselors were gath-   7
ering, ready to "help" the students, teachers, and their families through the

trauma and teach them to express their grief and rage "constructively." Plug grief counseling into Google and you come up with 1.2 million hits and what seems like an endless list of professionals and organizations offering what one Web site calls "the uncharted waters of the grieving process." Uncharted waters? It has been nearly forty years since the five stages of grief — denial, anger, bargaining, depression, and acceptance — as laid out by Elisabeth Kubler-Ross entered public consciousness to become the basis for a burgeoning grief industry, in which mental health professionals of all stripes counsel people on how to do it right, as if they hadn't been grieving without a map since the beginning of time.

I'm not arguing for or against the idea of stages of grief, although my   8
experience as a psychotherapist warns me against taking as gospel any notion that lays out a series of universal steps necessary to complete or resolve any psychological process. Kubler-Ross's five stages make some intellectual sense. Whether they make emotional sense for all or even most people is quite another question — one few mental health professionals ask.

So what's wrong with all the psychologizing if it helps us understand   9
such tragic events better, gets us through the grieving process a little easier? What's wrong is that it focuses entirely on the individual, with little or no attempt to put that behavior into its social context. What's wrong is that it assumes that if we understand the psychology, we can change the behavior and save ourselves from future atrocities like Virginia Tech or Columbine or the shootings in various post offices and corporate headquarters in recent years. But that isn't true. Despite the National Rifle Association's insistence that "Guns don't kill people, people kill people," people couldn't kill on a mass scale without guns.

Yes, I know, guns aren't the only culprits in violent assaults. And I   10
know, too, that we need to do better in identifying people like Cho Seung-Hui before they wreak their havoc. But we already know that we won't always be able to do this, that there will probably be a next person and a next who is troubled enough to exact his revenge (and it is, so far, almost always a "he") on some community for real or imagined slights. The question now is, will he have access to guns, our uniquely American weapon of mass destruction, that will allow him to kill scores of people in a few minutes?

Look at the statistics. In a single year, close to 20,000 Americans suffer   11
nonfatal gun injuries, while 34,000 more, including over 3,000 children and teenagers, are killed by gunfire. That's one child killed every three hours, nine children every day, and more than sixty children every week. In the same year not a single Japanese child died of gunshot wounds, Great Britain had 19 deaths, Germany 57, France 109, and Canada 153.

In the aftermath of the Virginia Tech murders, we've had a litany of   12
suggestions for prevention, almost all of them focused on individual behav-

ior, with the exception of the favored bogeyman: television and film violence. I'm not suggesting that we should be complacent about the violence that's so plentiful in our media or that the incivility and vulgarity so prominent in our culture today isn't worthy of comment and discussion. But appeals to strengthening family values, more religious training and involvement in church, and early identification of potentially violent individuals are truly, as Bob Dylan would have it, "blowin' in the wind."

Although any or all of the suggested interventions may have some   13
value, they will not by themselves eliminate the mass shootings in schools or the thirty-odd thousand deaths by gunfire outside the schoolyard. Only eliminating guns will do the job. And I don't mean just closing the loopholes in laws we already know don't work or promulgating new ones that will just as easily be subverted. I'm speaking of federal and state laws that will take the existing stockpile of two hundred million guns out of the hands of ordinary citizens and ban the further sale and possession of handguns except for people who have some legitimate, professional reason to carry them.

Ah, yes, I forgot for a moment: there's that pesky Second Amendment   14
to the Bill of Rights that declares, "A well regulated militia, being necessary to the security of a free state, the right of the people to keep and bear arms, shall not be infringed." These twenty-seven words continue to be the historical justification for millions of guns in private hands. I'm not a constitutional lawyer and not qualified to join the esoteric debate about what the framers meant when they wrote these words. But then, whether opponents of gun control or proponents, they don't know either; it's all speculation based on the political/social philosophy that's dominant at any given time.

What I do know is that the Bill of Rights was ratified in 1791, when   15
this country was still in need of its "well regulated militia" to ensure the security of its new and untried government. What does that have to do with handguns owned and used today by ordinary citizens who are not part of any organized militias? Or with a powerful government whose "security as a free state" is not in question, at least not from its own people?

It's time to put an end to the arguments about the meaning of the Sec-   16
ond Amendment and come to terms with the social and political realities of the twenty-first century. Guns kill; it's what they're meant to do. And no spin by those stalwarts who insist on our right to carry guns can change the fact that their unregulated use has unleashed a murderous plague that kills and injures far too many victims every year. Yes, people will continue to kill each other even if we ban guns. But all the evidence, not to mention plain common sense, tells us that they can't do it so efficiently and in such large numbers without the aid of a gun.

• • •

Comprehension

1. What does Rubin mean when she says that the media's reaction to the shooting was "a spectacle nearly as obscene as the massacre itself" (1)? Do you agree, or do you think she is overstating her case?

2. According to experts interviewed on news shows, what caused the massacre? Why does Rubin disagree with them?

3. What does Rubin mean in paragraph 4 when she says, "Theory trumped fact"?

4. When asking who, or what, caused the deadly shootings, Rubin considers the young man's mental health, his family, school officials, professors, and television and film violence. In what sense might each of these have been responsible?

5. According to Rubin, what is the main cause of the shootings? What are the contributory causes?

6. Rubin begins paragraph 9 with a question. Paraphrase her answers.

7. In paragraph 12, Rubin dismisses what she considers some minor causes of shootings like the one at Virginia Tech. Is her dismissal convincing, or does she need more evidence?

8. Where in this essay does Rubin make specific recommendations about how to prevent gun violence? What does she recommend?

9. How does Rubin deal with the "pesky Second Amendment" (14)? Is her argument persuasive? Why or why not?

Purpose and Audience

1. In paragraph 2, Rubin presents her professional credentials. Where else does she do so? Why? Do you think these credentials qualify her as an expert on the topic she discusses? Explain.

2. What is Rubin's attitude toward the mental health professionals interviewed by the media? Toward the grief counselors? How can you tell? Why do you suppose she includes their opinions in her essay?

3. Why does Rubin present statistics in paragraph 11? Are these statistics convincing? How do they support her thesis?

4. Rubin's main purpose in this essay is to argue that guns are inherently dangerous. Where does she begin this argument? Should she have introduced this idea earlier? Explain.

Style and Structure

1. Throughout this essay, Rubin — a sociologist and psychologist — uses a very informal style. Give some examples. Why do you think she uses this kind of language instead of a more formal or more professional style? Does such language strengthen or weaken her credibility?

2. When Rubin asks rhetorical questions ("So what's wrong . . . ," 9), uses *we* and *us,* and addresses the reader directly ("Yes, I know, guns aren't the

only culprits in violent assaults," 10), what is she trying to accomplish? Is she successful?

3. In paragraph 10, Rubin refers to guns as "our uniquely American weapon of mass destruction." Do you see this language as fair, or do you think Rubin is being manipulative?

4. This essay focuses on a search for causes of the shootings. Does it also consider effects? If so, where?

Vocabulary Projects

1. Define each of the following words as it is used in this selection.

rampage (1)	culprit (10)	complacent (12)
trumped (4)	wreak (10)	promulgating (13)
uncharted (7)	exact (10)	subverted (13)
burgeoning (7)	aftermath (12)	esoteric (14)
stripes (7)	litany (12)	stalwarts (16)

2. Look up the word *grief* in a variety of different print and online dictionaries. Which meaning do you think Rubin had in mind when she chose her essay's title? Do you think juxtaposing *guns* and *grief* is an effective strategy?

Journal Entry

What do you see as the main cause of massacres like the one at Virginia Tech?

Writing Workshop

1. Assume that you are a school counselor who treated the Virginia Tech shooter, and write a report explaining his possible motives for the massacre. Consider all the causes — immediate and remote, main and contributory — that might have led to his decision to commit this terrible crime.

2. The Virginia Tech shooter had been a student in several creative writing courses. Assume you are one of his creative writing instructors. Write an article for the school newspaper (or a speech to be delivered at a university-wide assembly) in which you briefly summarize the causes of the tragedy but focus on the specific *effects* of the crime on various segments of the university community.

3. Referring to William Zinsser's "College Pressures" (page 462) as well as to "Guns and Grief," write an essay in which you trace a **causal chain** that begins when an alienated and mentally disturbed young man like the Virginia Tech shooter arrives at college. Begin by summarizing the young man's psychiatric problems, and then speculate about social, academic, and family pressures that might have compounded these problems. Make sure that you document your references to the two essays and that you

include a works-cited page. (See the Appendix for information on documentation formats.)

Combining the Patterns

To support her cause-and-effect essay, Rubin uses many examples, and she also includes passages of **narration**. Identify these narrative passages. How do they strengthen her essay?

Thematic Connections

- "Shooting an Elephant" (page 126)
- "A Peaceful Woman Explains Why She Carries a Gun" (page 357)
- "College Pressures" (page 462)

LINDA M. HASSELSTROM

A Peaceful Woman Explains
Why She Carries a Gun

Linda M. Hasselstrom (b. 1943) grew up in rural South Dakota in a cattle ranching family. After receiving a master's degree in journalism from the University of Missouri, she returned to South Dakota to run her own ranch and now divides her time between South Dakota and Cheyenne, Wyoming. A highly respected poet, essayist, and writing teacher, she often focuses on everyday life in the American West in her work. Her publications include the poetry collections *Caught by One Wing* (1984), *Roadkill* (1987), and *Dakota Bones* (1991); the essay collection *Land Circle* (1991); and several books about ranching, including *Feels Like Far: A Rancher's Life on the Great Plains* (1999) and *Between Grass and Sky: Where I Live and Work* (2002). In this essay from *Land Circle,* Hasselstrom explains her reluctant decision to become licensed to carry a concealed handgun.

Background on incidences of sexual assault

Hasselstrom's gun ownership can certainly be considered in the context of the ongoing debate over how (and even whether) stricter gun safety measures should be enacted in the United States. Equally important, however, is the fact that her reason for carrying a gun is to protect herself from sexual assault. According to the 2006 National Crime Victimization survey, almost 250,000 women reported being sexually assaulted in this country in 2006. It is estimated that only one in six instances of sexual assault is actually reported to the police, so the number of such attacks is, in reality, much higher.

I am a peace-loving woman. But several events in the past ten years 1 have convinced me I'm safer when I carry a pistol. This was a personal decision, but because handgun possession is a controversial subject, perhaps my reasoning will interest others.

I live in western South Dakota on a ranch twenty-five miles from the 2 nearest town: for several years I spent winters alone here. As a freelance writer, I travel alone a lot — more than 100,000 miles by car in the last four years. With women freer than ever before to travel alone, the odds of our encountering trouble seem to have risen. Distances are great, roads are deserted, and the terrain is often too exposed to offer hiding places.

A woman who travels alone is advised, usually by men, to protect her- 3 self by avoiding bars and other "dangerous situations," by approaching her car like an Indian scout, by locking doors and windows. But these precautions aren't always enough. I spent years following them and still found myself in dangerous situations. I began to resent the idea that just because I am female, I have to be extra careful.

A few years ago, with another woman, I camped for several weeks in the West. We discussed self-defense, but neither of us had taken a course in it. She was against firearms, and local police told us Mace was illegal. So we armed ourselves with spray cans of deodorant tucked into our sleeping bags. We never used our improvised Mace because we were lucky enough to camp beside people who came to our aid when men harassed us. But on one occasion we visited a national park where our assigned space was less than fifteen feet from other campers. When we returned from a walk, we found our closest neighbors were two young men. As we gathered our cooking gear, they drank beer and loudly discussed what they would do to us after dark. Nearby campers, even families, ignored them: rangers strolled past, unconcerned. When we asked the rangers point-blank if they would protect us, one of them patted my shoulder and said, "Don't worry, girls. They're just kidding." At dusk we drove out of the park and hid our camp in the woods a few miles away. The illegal spot was lovely, but our enjoyment of that park was ruined. I returned from the trip determined to reconsider the options available for protecting myself.

At that time, I lived alone on the ranch and taught night classes in town. Along a city street I often traveled, a woman had a flat tire, called for help on her CB radio, and got a rapist who left her beaten. She was afraid to call for help again and stayed in her car until morning. For that reason, as well as because CBs work best along line-of-sight, which wouldn't help much in the rolling hills where I live, I ruled out a CB.

As I drove home one night, a car followed me. It passed me on a narrow bridge while a passenger flashed a blinding spotlight in my face. I braked sharply. The car stopped, angled across the bridge, and four men jumped out. I realized the locked doors were useless if they broke the windows of my pickup. I started forward, hoping to knock their car aside so I could pass. Just then another car appeared, and the men hastily got back in their car. They continued to follow me, passing and repassing. I dared not go home because no one else was there. I passed no lighted houses. Finally they pulled over to the roadside, and I decided to use their tactic: fear. Speeding, the pickup horn blaring, I swerved as close to them as I dared as I roared past. It worked: they turned off the highway. But I was frightened and angry. Even in my vehicle I was too vulnerable.

Other incidents occurred over the years. One day I glanced out at a field below my house and saw a man with a shotgun walking toward a pond full of ducks. I drove down and explained that the land was posted. I politely asked him to leave. He stared at me, and the muzzle of the shotgun began to rise. In a moment of utter clarity I realized that I was alone on the ranch, and that he could shoot me and simply drive away. The moment passed: the man left.

One night, I returned home from teaching a class to find deep tire ruts in the wet ground of my yard, garbage in the driveway, and a large gas tank empty. A light shone in the house: I couldn't remember leaving it on. I was too embarrassed to drive to a neighboring ranch and wake someone up. An hour of cautious exploration convinced me the house was safe, but once inside, with the doors locked, I was still afraid. I kept thinking of how vulnerable I felt, prowling around my own house in the dark.

My first positive step was to take a kung fu class, which teaches evasive or protective action when someone enters your space without permission. I learned to move confidently, scanning for possible attackers. I learned how to assess danger and techniques for avoiding it without combat.   9

I also learned that one must practice several hours every day to be good at kung fu. By that time I had married George: when I practiced with him, I learned how *close* you must be to your attacker to use martial arts, and decided a 120-pound woman dare not let a six-foot, 220-pound attacker get that close unless she is very, very good at self-defense. I have since read articles by several women who were extremely well trained in the martial arts, but were raped and beaten anyway.   10

I thought back over the times in my life when I had been attacked or threatened and tried to be realistic about my own behavior, searching for anything that had allowed me to become a victim. Overall, I was convinced that I had not been at fault. I don't believe myself to be either paranoid or a risk-taker, but I wanted more protection.   11

With some reluctance I decided to try carrying a pistol. George had always carried one, despite his size and his training in martial arts. I practiced shooting until I was sure I could hit an attacker who moved close enough to endanger me. Then I bought a license from the county sheriff, making it legal for me to carry the gun concealed.   12

But I was not yet ready to defend myself. George taught me that the most important preparation was mental: convincing myself I could actually *shoot a person*. Few of us wish to hurt or kill another human being. But there is no point in having a gun — in fact, gun possession might increase your danger — unless you know you can use it. I got in the habit of rehearsing, as I drove or walked, the precise conditions that would be required before I would shoot someone.   13

People who have not grown up with the idea that they are capable of protecting themselves — in other words, most women — might have to work hard to convince themselves of their ability, and of the necessity. Handgun ownership need not turn us into gunslingers, but it can be part of believing in, and relying on, *ourselves* for protection.   14

To be useful, a pistol has to be available. In my car, it's within instant reach. When I enter a deserted rest stop at night, it's in my purse, with my hand on the grip. When I walk from a dark parking lot into a motel, it's in my hand, under a coat. At home, it's on the headboard. In short, I take it with me almost everywhere I go alone.   15

Just carrying a pistol is not protection; avoidance is still the best approach to trouble. Subconsciously watching for signs of danger, I believe I've become more alert. Handgun use, not unlike driving, becomes instinctive. Each time I've drawn my gun — I have never fired it at another human being — I've simply found it in my hand.   16

I was driving the half-mile to the highway mailbox one day when I saw   17
a vehicle parked about midway down the road. Several men were standing
in the ditch, relieving themselves. I have no objection to emergency urina-
tion, but I noticed they'd dumped several dozen beer cans in the road.
Besides being ugly, cans can slash a cow's feet or stomach.

The men noticed me before they finished and made quite a perfor-   18
mance out of zipping their trousers while walking toward me. All four of
them gathered around my small foreign car, and one of them demanded
what the hell I wanted.

"This is private land. I'd appreciate it if you'd pick up the beer cans."   19

"What beer cans?" said the belligerent one, putting both hands on the   20
car door and leaning in my window. His face was inches from mine, and the
beer fumes were strong. The others laughed. One tried the passenger door,
locked; another put his foot on the hood and rocked the car. They circled,
lightly thumping the roof, discussing my good fortune in meeting them
and the benefits they were likely to bestow upon me. I felt very small and
very trapped and they knew it.

"The ones you just threw out," I said politely.   21

"I don't see no beer cans. Why don't you get out here and show them to   22
me, honey?" said the belligerent one, reaching for the handle inside my
door.

"Right over there," I said, still being polite. " — there, and over there." I   23
pointed with the pistol, which I'd slipped under my thigh. Within one minute the cans and the men were back in the car and headed down the road.

I believe this incident illustrates several important principles. The men   24
were trespassing and knew it: their judgment may have been impaired by
alcohol. Their response to the polite request of a woman alone was to use
their size, numbers, and sex to inspire fear. The pistol was a response in the
same language. Politeness didn't work: I couldn't match them in size or
number. Out of the car, I'd have been more vulnerable. The pistol just
changed the balance of power. It worked again recently when I was driving
in a desolate part of Wyoming. A man played cat-and-mouse with me for
thirty miles, ultimately trying to run me off the road. When his car passed
mine with only two inches to spare, I showed him my pistol, and he disappeared.

When I got my pistol, I told my husband, revising the old Colt slogan,   25
"God made men *and women,* but Sam Colt made them equal." Recently I
have seen a gunmaker's ad with a similar sentiment. Perhaps this is an idea
whose time has come, though the pacifist inside me will be saddened if the
only way women can achieve equality is by carrying weapons.

We must treat a firearm's power with caution. "Power tends to corrupt,   26
and absolute power corrupts absolutely," as a man (Lord Acton) once said.
A pistol is not the only way to avoid being raped or murdered in today's
world, but, intelligently wielded, it can shift the balance of power and provide a measure of safety.

•　　•　　•

Comprehension

1. According to Hasselstrom, why does she carry a gun? In one sentence, summarize her rationale.

2. List the specific events that led Hasselstrom to her decision to carry a gun.

3. Other than carrying a gun, what means of protecting herself did Hasselstrom try? Why did she find them unsatisfactory? Can you think of other strategies she could have adopted instead of carrying a gun?

4. Where in the essay does Hasselstrom express her reluctance to carry a gun?

5. In paragraph 13, Hasselstrom says, "gun possession might increase your danger unless you know you can use it." Where else does she touch on the possible pitfalls of carrying a gun?

6. What does Hasselstrom mean when she says, "The pistol just changed the balance of power" (24)?

Purpose and Audience

1. How does paragraph 1 establish Hasselstrom's purpose for writing this essay? What other purpose might she have?

2. What purpose does paragraph 5 serve? Is it necessary?

3. Do you think this essay is aimed at a particular gender? If so, do you think it is directed at men or at women? Why?

4. Do you think Hasselstrom expects her readers to agree with her position? Where does she indicate that she expects them to challenge her? How does she address this challenge?

Style and Structure

1. This essay is written in the first person, and it relies heavily on personal experience. Do you see this as a strength or a weakness? Explain.

2. What is the main cause in this cause-and-effect essay — that is, what is the most important reason Hasselstrom gives for carrying a gun? Can you identify any contributory causes?

3. Could you argue that simply being a woman is justification enough for carrying a gun? Do you think this is Hasselstrom's position? Explain.

4. Think of Hasselstrom's essay as the first step in a possible causal chain. What situations might result from her decision to carry a gun?

5. In paragraph 25, Hasselstrom says, "the pacifist inside me will be saddened if the only way women can achieve equality is by carrying weapons." In her title and elsewhere in the essay, Hasselstrom characterizes herself as a "peaceful woman." Do you think she is successful in using language like this to portray herself as a peace-loving woman who only reluctantly carries a gun?

Vocabulary Projects

1. Define each of the following words as it is used in this selection.

   posted (7)   belligerent (20)   wielded (26)
   muzzle (7)   bestow (20)

2. Some of the words and phrases Hasselstrom uses in this essay suggest that she sees her pistol as an equalizer, something that helps to compensate for her vulnerability. Identify the words and phrases she uses to characterize her gun in this way.

Journal Entry

Do you agree that carrying a gun is Hasselstrom's only choice, or do you think she could take other steps to ensure her safety? Explain.

Writing Workshop

1. Hasselstrom lives in a rural area, and the scenarios she describes apply to rural life. Rewrite this essay as "A Peaceful Urban (or Suburban) Woman Explains Why She Carries a Gun."

2. What reasons might a "peace-loving" man have for carrying a gun? Write a cause-and-effect essay outlining such a man's motives, using any of Hasselstrom's reasons that might apply to him as well. If you quote Hasselstrom in your essay, be sure to include parenthetical documentation and a works-cited page. (See the Appendix for information on documentation formats.)

3. Write a cause-and-effect essay presenting reasons to support a position that opposes Hasselstrom's: "A Peaceful Woman (or Man) Explains Why She (or He) Will Not Carry a Gun."

Combining the Patterns

Several times in her essay, Hasselstrom uses **narration** to support her position. Identify these narrative passages. Are they absolutely essential to the essay? Could they be briefer? Could some be deleted? Explain.

Thematic Connections

- "Shooting an Elephant" (page 126)
- "Just Walk On By" (page 236)
- "Guns and Grief" (page 350)
- "The Wife-Beater" (page 528)

ROBIN TOLMACH LAKOFF

The Power of Words in Wartime

Linguist Robin Tolmach Lakoff has taught at the University of California at Berkeley since 1971. Her first book, *Language and Woman's Place* (1975), was a groundbreaking study of the effect of language on gender roles. Other important works include *Talking Power: The Politics of Language in Our Lives* (1990) and *The Language War* (2000), an analysis of language, politics, and the media. The following essay appeared on the op-ed page of the *New York Times* in May 2004.

Background on what wartime enemies have called Americans
During World War II, the German Nazis denigrated Americans as "mongrels" (because the U.S. population was made up of so many nationalities), creating an image of Americans as ill-bred animals. To the Japanese, Americans were "monsters" and "devils" as well as "mongrels," and American soldiers were referred to in Japanese films of the time simply as "they" or "them." During the subsequent Korean War, Korean communist propaganda called Americans "apes" and "beasts," while during the Vietnam War, Vietnamese communists referred to Americans generally as "imperialists" and to American soldiers as "killers" and "American aggressors." More recently, extremists in the Muslim world have referred to America as "the Great Satan," echoing the words of Iran's Ayatollah Khomeini, and have referred to Americans in general as "infidels."

An American soldier refers to an Iraqi prisoner as "it." A general speaks not of "Iraqi fighters" but of "the enemy." A weapons manufacturer doesn't talk about people but about "targets."   1

Bullets and bombs are not the only tools of war. Words, too, play their part.   2

Human beings are social animals, genetically hardwired to feel compassion toward others. Under normal conditions, most people find it very difficult to kill.   3

But in war, military recruits must be persuaded that killing other people is not only acceptable but even honorable.   4

The language of war is intended to bring about that change, and not only for soldiers in the field. In wartime, language must be created to enable combatants and noncombatants alike to see the other side as killable, to overcome the innate queasiness over the taking of human life. Soldiers, and those who remain at home, learn to call their enemies by names that make them seem not quite human — inferior, contemptible, and not like "us."   5

The specific words change from culture to culture and war to war. The names need not be obviously demeaning. Just the fact that *we* can name   6

363

them gives us a sense of superiority and control. If, in addition, we give them nicknames, we can see them as smaller, weaker, and childlike — not worth taking seriously as fully human.

The Greeks and Romans referred to everyone else as "barbarians" — etymologically those who only babble, only go "barbar." During the American Revolution, the British called the colonists "Yankees," a term with a history that is still in dispute. While the British intended it disparagingly, the Americans, in perhaps the first historical instance of reclamation, made the word their own and gave it a positive spin, turning the derisive song "Yankee Doodle" into our first, if unofficial, national anthem. 7

In World War I, the British gave the Germans the nickname "Jerries," from the first syllable of German. In World War II, Americans referred to the Japanese as "Japs." 8

The names may refer to real or imagined cultural and physical differences that emphasize the ridiculous or the repugnant. So in various wars, the British called the French "Frogs." Germans have been called "Krauts," a reference to weird and smelly food. The Vietnamese were called "Slopes" and "Slants." The Koreans were referred to simply as "Gooks." 9

The war in Iraq has added new examples. Some American soldiers refer to the Iraqis as "Hadjis," used in a derogatory way, apparently unaware that the word, which comes from the Arabic term for a pilgrimage to Mecca, is used as a term of respect for older Muslim men. 10

The Austrian ethologist Konrad Lorenz suggested that the more clearly we see other members of our own species as individuals, the harder we find it to kill them. 11

So some terms of war are collective nouns, encouraging us to see the enemy as an undifferentiated mass, rather than as individuals capable of suffering. Crusaders called their enemy "the Saracen," and in World War I, the British called Germans "the Hun." 12

American soldiers are trained to call those they are fighting against "the enemy." It is easier to kill an enemy than an Iraqi. 13

The word "enemy" itself provides the facelessness of a collective noun. Its nonspecificity also has a fear-inducing connotation; enemy means simply "those we are fighting," without reference to their identity. 14

The terrors and uncertainties of war make learning this kind of language especially compelling for soldiers on the front. But civilians back home also need to believe that what their country is doing is just and necessary, and that the killing they are supporting is in some way different from the killing in civilian life that is rightly punished by the criminal justice system. The use of the language developed for military purposes by civilians reassures them that war is not murder. 15

The linguistic habits that soldiers must absorb in order to fight make atrocities like those at Abu Ghraib virtually inevitable. The same language that creates a psychological chasm between "us" and "them," and enables American troops to kill in battle, makes enemy soldiers fit subjects for tor- 16 ture and humiliation. The reasoning is: they are not really human, so they will not feel the pain.

Once language draws that line, all kinds of mistreatment become 17 imaginable, and then justifiable. To make the abuses at Abu Ghraib unthinkable, we would have to abolish war itself.

•   •   •

Comprehension

1. According to Lakoff, exactly what power do words have in wartime?

2. Do you think Lakoff attributes too much power to language in the circumstances she describes, or do you think she is right?

3. Do you see this essay as primarily about language or about war? Explain your conclusion.

4. What other factors, besides language, might cause soldiers (and civilians) to see their enemies as "inferior, contemptible, and not like 'us'" (5)? Does Lakoff consider these other factors? If not, do you think she should have?

5. Lakoff focuses here on one effect of language on people's behavior. What other effects do you think such language might have on the people who use it?

6. In paragraph 16, Lakoff says, "The linguistic habits that soldiers must absorb in order to fight make atrocities like those at Abu Ghraib virtually inevitable." Do you agree, or do you think she is exaggerating?

7. When Lakoff discusses U.S. enemies — for example, the Germans and the Japanese in World War II and the Iraqi insurgents today — she does not mention that among these groups, too, language is used to dehumanize their enemies. Do you think this information is implicit, or does her failure to illustrate that, in times of war, Americans are also *victims* of the power of words weaken her essay?

Purpose and Audience

1. Paraphrase Lakoff's thesis. Do you think most readers would be likely to accept this thesis? Does Lakoff convince you?

2. In paragraph 11, Lakoff paraphrases Konrad Lorenz. What purpose does this paragraph serve?

3. Is Lakoff's primary purpose to analyze language, or is this essay really about something else? (Before you answer this question, reread the essay's last sentence.)

Style and Structure

1. Lakoff opens her essay with a series of examples. Is this an effective opening strategy? What other options did she have?

2. In this cause-and-effect essay, is language a cause, an effect, or both? Explain.

3. What words does Lakoff use to signal to readers that she is focusing on cause-and-effect relationships?

4. Lakoff considers language the main, or most important, cause of our ability to dehumanize our enemies. Do you agree, or do you see it as just a contributory cause? In what sense can it also be seen as a remote cause? Explain.

5. In paragraphs 7–9, Lakoff lists historical examples to support her thesis. Do such examples constitute sufficient support? What other kinds of support might she have used?

6. Do you see Lakoff's central argument as logical, or do you think she is guilty of *post hoc* reasoning?

Vocabulary Projects

1. Define each of the following words as it is used in this selection.

   innate (5)   derogatory (10)
   etymologically (7)   ethologist (11)
   disparagingly (7)   undifferentiated (12)
   reclamation (7)   chasm (16)

2. In this essay on a very serious topic, Lakoff uses colloquialisms such as "hardwired" (3) and "spin" (7). Can you identify other examples? Do you think such language is appropriate?

Journal Entry

Lakoff asserts that language can make it easier for us to dismiss or discount our enemies. Do you think the kinds of pejorative names Lakoff discusses can also have such power in situations outside of wartime?

Writing Workshop

1. Write a cause-and-effect essay explaining how derogatory terms applied to particular groups of people — for example, people from developing nations, migrant workers, undocumented immigrants, or individuals with disabilities — make it possible for others to ignore, dislike, or even mistreat them.

2. Young children often direct hurtful language at their peers without recognizing or understanding its impact. What effects does such language have on children? Write an essay discussing the power of words on the playground. Edit Lakoff's words in pararaph 2 to construct your thesis statement. Be sure to acknowledge Lakoff as your source and to include a works-cited page. (See the Appendix for infomation on documentation formats.)

3. What might cause parents to use abusive language to belittle a child? How might repeated instances of such verbal abuse affect a child? Write a cause-and-effect essay that traces the causal chain that this type of abuse initiates.

Combining the Patterns

Although Lakoff focuses primarily on causes and effects, this essay also relies heavily on **exemplification**. Are some of her examples more convincing than others? Should other kinds of examples be added?

Thematic Connections

- " 'What's in a Name?' " (page 5)
- "Shooting an Elephant" (page 126)
- "The Embalming of Mr. Jones" (page 304)
- "The Ways We Lie" (page 485)
- "The Untouchable" (page 512)

ALAN WEISMAN

Earth without People

Alan Weisman (b. 1947) is an associate professor of journalism and Latin American studies at the University of Arizona and a senior editor and producer for Homeland Productions, an independent, nonprofit journalism collective specializing in issues-oriented radio documentaries. He is the author of five books, including *Gaviotas: A Village to Reinvent the World* (1998), which won the Social Inventions award from the Global Ideas Bank. His writing on Latin America has been featured in *Harper's, Atlantic Monthly, Mother Jones,* and the *New York Times Magazine,* and his radio documentaries have aired on National Public Radio. The following essay, originally published in *Discover* magazine, grew out of his work on his most recent book, *The World without Us* (2007).

Background on wilderness

"Earth without People" imagines the return to wilderness that would occur on the planet over time if human beings simply disappeared. In fact, the opposite is taking place as humans increasingly encroach on wilderness areas. About 46 percent of the world's land mass is considered wilderness, and only a small fraction of these lands fall under governmental protection to limit damage to their ecosystems. (In the lower forty-eight United States, the figure is just 2 percent.) Humans alter wilderness for the worse in ways large and small. Individuals pollute the environment by racing dirt bikes, snowmobiles, all-terrain vehicles, and jet skis. Developers create populous subdivisions in what were once undeveloped areas. Multinational corporations clear-cut forests, drill for oil, engage in mining activities, and otherwise exploit resources in wilderness areas. All of these actions have led to dramatic declines in biodiversity, and, despite the efforts of a multitude of conservation organizations, the problems continue to grow.

Given the mounting toll of fouled oceans, overheated air, missing top-soil, and mass extinctions, we might sometimes wonder what our planet would be like if humans suddenly disappeared. Would Superfund sites revert to Gardens of Eden? Would the seas again fill with fish? Would our concrete cities crumble to dust from the force of tree roots, water, and weeds? How long would it take for our traces to vanish? And if we could answer such questions, would we be more in awe of the changes we have wrought, or of nature's resilience?

A good place to start searching for answers is in Korea, in the 155-mile-long, 2.5-mile-wide mountainous Demilitarized Zone, or DMZ, set up by the armistice ending the Korean War. Aside from rare military patrols or desperate souls fleeing North Korea, humans have barely set foot in the strip since 1953. Before that, for five thousand years, the area was populated by rice farmers who carved the land into paddies. Today those paddies have become barely discernible, transformed into pockets of marsh, and the new occupants of these lands arrive as dazzling white squadrons of red-crowned cranes that glide over the bulrushes in perfect formation, touching down so lightly that they detonate no land mines. Next to whooping cranes, they are the rarest such birds on Earth. They winter in the DMZ alongside the endangered white-naped cranes, revered in Asia as sacred portents of peace.

If peace is ever declared, suburban Seoul, which has rolled ever north-   3
ward in recent decades, is poised to invade such tantalizing real estate. On the other side, the North Koreans are building an industrial megapark. This has spurred an international coalition of scientists called the DMZ Forum to try to consecrate the area for a peace park and nature preserve. Imagine it as "a Korean Gettysburg and Yosemite rolled together," says Harvard University biologist Edward O. Wilson, who believes that tourism revenues could trump those from agriculture or development.

As serenely natural as the DMZ now is, it would be far different if   4
people throughout Korea suddenly disappeared. The habitat would not revert to a truly natural state until the dams that now divert rivers to slake the needs of Seoul's more than 20 million inhabitants failed — a century or two after the humans had gone. But in the meantime, says Wilson, many creatures would flourish. Otters, Asiatic black bears, musk deer, and the

In a city bereft of humans, concrete cracks, weeds invade, and mammals multiply. Paper money stored in a sealed safe could remain intact for eons. Photo illustration by Glen Wexler © 2005

nearly vanquished Amur leopard would spread into slopes reforested with young daimyo oak and bird cherry. The few Siberian tigers that still prowl the North Korean–Chinese borderlands would multiply and fan across Asia's temperate zones. "The wild carnivores would make short work of livestock," he says. "Few domestic animals would remain after a couple of hundred years. Dogs would go feral, but they wouldn't last long: they'd never be able to compete."

If people were no longer present anywhere on Earth, a worldwide   5
shakeout would follow. From zebra mussels to fire ants to crops to kudzu, exotics would battle with natives. In time, says Wilson, all human attempts to improve on nature, such as our painstakingly bred horses, would revert to their origins. If horses survived at all, they would devolve back to Przewalski's horse, the only true wild horse, still found in the Mongolian steppes. "The plants, crops, and animal species man has wrought by his own hand would be wiped out in a century or two," Wilson says. In a few thousand years, "the world would mostly look as it did before humanity came along — like a wilderness."

The new wilderness would consume cities, much as the jungle of   6
northern Guatemala consumed the Mayan pyramids and megalopolises of overlapping city-states. From A.D. 800 to 900, a combination of drought and internecine warfare over dwindling farmland brought two thousand years of civilization crashing down. Within ten centuries, the jungle swallowed all.

Mayan communities alternated urban living with fields sheltered by   7
forests, in contrast with today's paved cities, which are more like man-made deserts. However, it wouldn't take long for nature to undo even the likes of a New York City. Jameel Ahmad, civil engineering department chair at Cooper Union College in New York City, says repeated freezing and thawing common in months like March and November would split cement within a decade, allowing water to seep in. As it, too, froze and expanded, cracks would widen. Soon, weeds such as mustard and goosegrass would invade. With nobody to trample seedlings, New York's prolific exotic, the Chinese ailanthus tree, would take over. Within five years, says Dennis Stevenson, senior curator at the New York Botanical Garden, ailanthus roots would heave up sidewalks and split sewers.

That would exacerbate a problem that already plagues New York — rising groundwater. There's little soil to absorb it or vegetation to transpire it,   8
and buildings block the sunlight that could evaporate it. With the power off, pumps that keep subways from flooding would be stilled. As water sluiced away soil beneath pavement, streets would crater.

Eric Sanderson of the Bronx Zoo Wildlife Conservation Society heads   9
the Mannahatta Project, a virtual re-creation of pre-1609 Manhattan. He says there were thirty to forty streams in Manhattan when the Dutch first arrived. If New Yorkers disappeared, sewers would clog, some natural watercourses would reappear, and others would form. Within twenty years, the water-soaked steel columns that support the street above the East Side's

subway tunnels would corrode and buckle, turning Lexington Avenue into a river.

New York's architecture isn't as flammable as San Francisco's clap- 10
board Victorians, but within two hundred years, says Steven Clemants, vice president of the Brooklyn Botanic Garden, tons of leaf litter would over-flow gutters as pioneer weeds gave way to colonizing native oaks and maples in city parks. A dry lightning strike, igniting decades of uncut, knee-high Central Park grass, would spread flames through town.

As lightning rods rusted away, roof fires would leap among buildings 11
into paneled offices filled with paper. Meanwhile, native Virginia creeper and poison ivy would claw at walls covered with lichens, which thrive in the absence of air pollution. Wherever foundations failed and buildings tumbled, lime from crushed concrete would raise soil pH, inviting buck-thorn and birch. Black locust and autumn olive trees would fix nitrogen, allowing more goldenrods, sunflowers, and white snakeroot to move in along with apple trees, their seeds expelled by proliferating birds. Sweet carrots would quickly devolve to their wild form, unpalatable Queen Anne's lace, while broccoli, cabbage, brussels sprouts, and cauliflower would regress to the same unrecognizable broccoli ancestor.

Unless an earthquake strikes New York first, bridges spared yearly 12
applications of road salt would last a few hundred years before their stays and bolts gave way (last to fall would be Hell Gate Arch, built for railroads and easily good for another thousand years). Coyotes would invade Central Park, and deer, bears, and finally wolves would follow. Ruins would echo the love song of frogs breeding in streams stocked with alewives, herring, and mussels dropped by seagulls. Missing, however, would be all fauna that have adapted to humans. The invincible cockroach, an insect that origi-nated in the hot climes of Africa, would succumb in unheated buildings. Without garbage, rats would starve or serve as lunch for peregrine falcons and red-tailed hawks. Pigeons would genetically revert back to the rock doves from which they sprang.

It's unclear how long animals would suffer from the urban legacy of 13
concentrated heavy metals. Over many centuries, plants would take these up, recycle, redeposit, and gradually dilute them. The time bombs left in petroleum tanks, chemical plants, power plants, and dry-cleaning plants might poison the earth beneath them for eons. One intriguing example is the former Rocky Mountain Arsenal next to Denver International Airport. There a chemical weapons plant produced mustard and nerve gas, incendi-ary bombs, napalm, and after World War II, pesticides. In 1984 it was con-sidered by the arsenal commander to be the most contaminated spot in the United States. Today it is a national wildlife refuge, home to bald eagles that feast on its prodigious prairie dog population.

However, it took more than $130 million and a lot of man-hours to 14
drain and seal the arsenal's lake, in which ducks once died minutes after landing and the aluminum bottoms of boats sent to fetch their carcasses rotted within a month. In a world with no one left to bury the bad stuff,

decaying chemical containers would slowly expose their lethal contents. Places like the Indian Point nuclear power plant, thirty-five miles north of Times Square, would dump radioactivity into the Hudson long after the lights went out.

Old stone buildings in Manhattan, such as Grand Central Station or the Metropolitan Museum of Art, would outlast every modern glass box, especially with no more acid rain to pock their marble. Still, at some point thousands of years hence, the last stone walls — perhaps chunks of St. Paul's Chapel on Wall Street, built in 1766 from Manhattan's own hard schist — would fall. Three times in the past 100,000 years, glaciers have scraped New York clean, and they'll do so again. The mature hardwood forest would be mowed down. On Staten Island, Fresh Kills's four giant mounds of trash would be flattened, their vast accumulation of stubborn PVC plastic and glass ground to powder. After the ice receded, an unnatural concentration of reddish metal — remnants of wiring and plumbing — would remain buried in layers. The next toolmaker to arrive or evolve might discover it and use it, but there would be nothing to indicate who had put it there.

Before humans appeared, an oriole could fly from the Mississippi to the Atlantic and never alight on anything other than a treetop. Unbroken forest blanketed Europe from the Urals to the English Channel. The last remaining fragment of that primeval European wilderness — half a million acres of woods straddling the border between Poland and Belarus, called the Bialowieza Forest — provides another glimpse of how the world would look if we were gone. There, relic groves of huge ash and linden trees rise 138 feet above an understory of hornbeams, ferns, swamp alders, massive birches, and crockery-size fungi. Norway spruces, shaggy as Methuselah, stand even taller. Five-century-old oaks grow so immense that great spotted woodpeckers stuff whole spruce cones in their three-inch-deep bark furrows. The woods carry pygmy owl whistles, nutcracker croaks, and wolf howls. Fragrance wafts from eons of mulch.

High privilege accounts for such unbroken antiquity. During the fourteenth century, a Lithuanian duke declared it a royal hunting preserve. For centuries it stayed that way. Eventually, the forest was subsumed by Russia and in 1888 became the private domain of the czars. Occupying Germans took lumber and slaughtered game during World War I, but a pristine core was left intact, which in 1921 became a Polish national park. Timber pillaging resumed briefly under the Soviets, but when the Nazis invaded, nature fanatic Hermann Göring decreed the entire preserve off limits. Then, following World War II, a reportedly drunken Josef Stalin agreed one evening in Warsaw to let Poland retain two-fifths of the forest.

To realize that all of Europe once looked like this is startling. Most unexpected of all is the sight of native bison. Just six hundred remain in the wild, on both sides of an impassable iron curtain erected by the Soviets in 1980 along the border to thwart escapees to Poland's renegade Solidarity movement. Although wolves dig under it, and roe deer are believed to leap over it, the herd of the largest of Europe's mammals remains divided, and thus its gene pool. Belarus, which has not removed its statues of Lenin, has no specific plans to dismantle the fence. Unless it does, the bison may suffer genetic degradation, leaving them vulnerable to a disease that would wipe them out.

If the bison herd withers, they would join all the other extinct mega-   19
fauna that even our total disappearance could never bring back. In a glass case in his laboratory, paleoecologist Paul S. Martin at the University of Arizona keeps a lump of dried dung he found in a Grand Canyon cave, left by a sloth weighing two hundred pounds. That would have made it the smallest of several North American ground sloth species present when humans first appeared on this continent. The largest was as big as an ele-phant and lumbered around by the thousands in the woodlands and des-erts of today's United States. What we call pristine today, Martin says, is a poor reflection of what would be here if *Homo sapiens* had never evolved.

"America would have three times as many species of animals over 1,000   20
pounds as Africa does today," he says. An amazing megafaunal menagerie roamed the region: Giant armadillos resembling armor-plated autos; bears twice the size of grizzlies; the hoofed, herbivorous toxodon, big as a rhinoc-eros; and saber-toothed tigers. A dozen species of horses were here, as well as the camel-like litoptern, giant beavers, giant peccaries, woolly rhinos, mammoths, and mastodons. Climate change and imported disease may have killed them, but most paleontologists accept the theory Martin advo-cates: "When people got out of Africa and Asia and reached other parts of the world, all hell broke loose." He is convinced that people were respon-sible for the mass extinctions because they commenced with human arrival everywhere: first, in Australia 60,000 years ago, then mainland America 13,000 years ago, followed by the Caribbean islands 6,000 years ago, and Madagascar 2,000 years ago.

Yet one place on Earth did manage to elude the intercontinental holo-   21
caust: the oceans. Dolphins and whales escaped for the simple reason that prehistoric people could not hunt enough giant marine mammals to have a major impact on the population. "At least a dozen species in the ocean Columbus sailed were bigger than his biggest ship," says marine paleoecol-ogist Jeremy Jackson of the Smithsonian Tropical Research Institute in Panama. "Not only mammals — the sea off Cuba was so thick with 1,000-pound green turtles that his boats practically ran aground on them." This was a world where ships collided with schools of whales and where sharks were so abundant they would swim up rivers to prey on cattle. Reefs swarmed with 800-pound goliath grouper, not just today's puny aquarium species. Cod could be fished from the sea in baskets. Oysters filtered all the water in Chesapeake Bay every five days. The planet's shores teemed with millions of manatees, seals, and walrus.

Within the past century, however, humans have flattened the coral   22
reefs on the continental shelves and scraped the sea grass beds bare; a dead zone bigger than New Jersey grows at the mouth of the Mississippi; all the world's cod fisheries have collapsed. What Pleistocene humans did in 1,500 years to terrestrial life, modern man has done in mere decades to the

oceans — "almost," Jackson says. Despite mechanized overharvesting, satellite fish tracking, and prolonged butchery of sea mammals, the ocean is still bigger than we are. "It's not like the land," he says. "The great majority of sea species are badly depleted, but they still exist. If people actually went away, most could recover."

Even if global warming or ultraviolet radiation bleaches the Great Barrier Reef to death, Jackson says, "it's only seven thousand years old. New reefs have had to form before. It's not like the world is a constant place." Without people, most excess industrial carbon dioxide would dissipate within two hundred years, cooling the atmosphere. With no further chlorine and bromine leaking skyward, within decades the ozone layer would replenish, and ultraviolet damage would subside. Eventually, heavy metals and toxins would flush through the system; a few intractable PCBs might take a millennium. 23

During that same span, every dam on Earth would silt up and spill over. Rivers would again carry nutrients seaward, where most life would be, as it was long before vertebrates crawled onto the shore. Eventually, that would happen again. The world would start over. 24

. . .

Comprehension

1. This essay focuses on effects. According to Weisman, what cause is responsible for all the effects he describes?
2. Why does Weisman begin his essay by focusing on Korea's DMZ?
3. Why do you suppose Weisman chooses New York City as the setting for his disaster scenario?
4. Beginning with paragraph 16, Weisman shifts his focus from the future to the present, and then to the past. Why? What do paragraphs 16–18 contribute to the essay? How is the description of the Bialowieza Forest different from the essay's earlier descriptions?
5. In paragraph 20, Weisman quotes paleoecologist Paul S. Martin. How do Martin's comments support Weisman's thesis?
6. How is the situation of the oceans different from that of terrestrial life?
7. Does Weisman see "earth without people" as a positive or a negative outcome? Explain.
8. Weisman ends his essay with the sentence, "The world would start over" (24). Do you see this statement as optimistic, pessimistic, or neutral? Why?

Purpose and Audience

1. Do you think Weisman's purpose here is to inform? To persuade? To warn? To inspire? To frighten? What makes you think so? (Reread paragraph 1 carefully before you respond to this question.)

2. Where does Weisman cite experts? What do their comments add to his discussion?

3. This essay was published in *Discover*, a popular science magazine. How can you tell that Weisman assumes his audience is made up of readers who are interested in, and knowledgeable about, his topic?

4. What is Weisman's thesis? Does he state it? If so, where?

Style and Structure

1. Paragraphs 7 and 8 describe a **causal chain**. Diagram this causal chain. What other causal chains can you identify in this essay?

2. To describe animals and plants, Weisman frequently uses **similes**, such as "as big as an elephant" (19), and **analogies**, such as "twice the size of grizzlies" (20). Identify as many of these comparisons as you can, and explain why Weisman uses them.

3. Near the end of paragraph 21 (beginning with "This was a world . . . ,"), Weisman describes the oceans in prehistoric times. What impact does the style of this passage have on you? Why?

4. Throughout the essay, Weisman piles up series and catalogs of details. Point to a few places where he does this. What is the effect of such lists of details? Are they absolutely necessary, or could the essay make its point without them?

5. What do the visuals contribute to this essay? How would the essay be different without them? If you were choosing alternative (or additional) visuals for this essay, what kind would you choose, and where would you place them?

Vocabulary Projects

1. Define each of the following words as it is used in this selection.

wrought (1)	feral (4)	prodigious (13)
portents (2)	shakeout (5)	primeval (16)
consecrate (3)	megalopolises (6)	wafts (16)
trump (3)	exacerbate (8)	subsumed (17)
slake (4)	devolve (11)	pristine (19)

2. List a few scientific terms Weisman uses, and define each for a popular audience.

3. In paragraph 21, Weisman uses the term "intercontinental holocaust" for the destruction he describes. Why do you think Weisman uses this term? Investigate the origin and changing meanings of the word *holocaust*, and then consider whether it is an accurate term for the effects Weisman describes.

Journal Entry

Write a few paragraphs from the point of view of one of the surviving creatures in the "earth without people" world Weisman imagines.

Writing Workshop

1. Imagine you are the last person in New York City. Write a diary entry describing what you see around you and explaining how you have adapted to the changes Weisman outlines in paragraphs 7–15. If you quote Weisman's essay, be sure to include parenthetical documentation. (See the Appendix for information on documentation formats.)

2. Watch a movie that depicts "earth without people" — for example, *The World, the Flesh, and the Devil* (1959), *The Omega Man* (1971), or *I Am Legend* (2007). Write an essay in which you discuss both the causes and the effects of the scenario presented in the film you have chosen. Your thesis statement should evaluate the film's success as social criticism.

Combining the Patterns

Weisman uses **narration, description, comparison and contrast,** and **exemplification** to develop his cause-and-effect essay. Identify passages of each pattern. Where do you think Weisman might add passages of **definition**? Would such additions strengthen his essay, or might they be distracting?

Thematic Connections

- "The Valley of Windmills" (page 157)
- "Ground Zero" (page 167)
- "The Hidden Life of Garbage" (page 177)
- "Once More to the Lake" (page 183)
- "The Time to Act Is Now" (page 617)

Suicide Note (Poetry)

Janice Mirikitani, a third-generation Japanese American, was born in San Francisco in 1942 and graduated from the University of California at Los Angeles in 1962. In her poetry, Mirikitani often considers how racism in the United States affects Asian Americans, particularly the thousands of Japanese Americans held in internment camps during World War II. Her collections include *Awake in the River* (1978), *Shedding Silence* (1987), and *We, the Dangerous: New and Selected Poems* (1995). She has also edited anthologies of Japanese-American and developing-nation literature, as well as several volumes giving voice to children living in poverty. For many years, she has been president of the Glide Foundation, which sponsors outreach programs for the poor and homeless of San Francisco. Mirikitani is the current poet laureate of San Francisco.

Background on teenage suicide
The following poem, which appears in *Shedding Silence,* takes the form of a suicide note written by a young Asian-American college student to her family and reveals the extreme pressure to excel placed on her by her parents and her culture. The theme, however, has considerable relevance beyond the Asian-American community. Tragically, some five thousand teenagers and young adults commit suicide annually in the United States (there are thirty to fifty times as many attempts), and suicide is the third leading cause of death among fifteen- to twenty-four-year-olds. Among college students, suicide is the second leading cause of death; some one thousand college students take their own lives every year. Indicating the extent of the problem, in 2004 Congress passed a bill, signed into law by President Bush, authorizing funding of $82 million for programs to help prevent youth suicides.

How many notes written . . .
ink smeared like birdprints in snow.

not good enough   not pretty enough   not smart enough

dear mother and father.
I apologize   5
for disappointing you.
I've worked very hard,

not good enough

harder, perhaps to please you.
If only I were a son, shoulders broad   10
as the sunset threading through pine,

I would see the light in my mother's
eyes, or the golden pride reflected
in my father's dream
of my wide, male hands worthy of work   15
and comfort.
I would swagger through life
muscled and bold and assured,
drawing praises to me
like currents in the bed of wind, virile   20
with confidence.

    not good enough   not strong enough   not good enough

I apologize.
Tasks do not come easily.
Each failure, a glacier.
Each disapproval, a bootprint.   25
Each disappointment,
ice above my river.
So I have worked hard.

           not good enough   30

My sacrifice I will drop
bone by bone, perched
on the ledge of my womanhood,
fragile as wings.

           not strong enough   35

It is snowing steadily
surely not good weather
for flying — this sparrow
sillied and dizzied by the wind
on the edge.   40

           not smart enough

I make this ledge my altar
to offer penance.
This air will not hold me,
the snow burdens my crippled wings,   45
my tears drop like bitter cloth
softly into the gutter below.

    not good enough   not strong enough   not smart enough

Choices thin as shaved
ice. Notes shredded   50
drift like snow

on my broken body,
cover me like whispers
of sorries
sorries.   55
Perhaps when they find me
they will bury
my bird bones beneath
a sturdy pine
and scatter my feathers like   60
unspoken song
over this white and cold and silent
breast of earth.

•   •   •

Reading Literature

1. An author's note that originally introduced this poem explained the
   main cause of the student's death:

   An Asian-American college student was reported to have jumped to her death
   from her dormitory window. Her body was found two days later under a deep
   cover of snow. Her suicide note contained an apology to her parents for having
   received less than a perfect four-point grade average.

   What other causes might have contributed to her suicide?

2. Why does the speaker believe her life would be happier if she were male?
   Do you think she is correct?

3. What words, phrases, and images are repeated in this poem? What effect
   do these repetitions have on you?

Journal Entry

Whom (or what) do you blame for teenage suicides such as the one the
poem describes? How might such deaths be eliminated?

Thematic Connections

• "Only Daughter" (page 97)
• "College Pressures" (page 462)

WRITING ASSIGNMENTS FOR CAUSE AND EFFECT

1. "Thirty-Eight Who Saw Murder Didn't Call the Police" (page 120), "Who Killed Benny Paret?" (page 340), and "On Dumpster Diving" (page 714) all encourage readers, either directly or indirectly, to take action rather than remain uninvolved. Using information gleaned from these essays (or from others in the text) as support for your thesis, write an essay exploring either the possible consequences of apathy, the possible causes of apathy, or both. Be sure to provide parenthetical documentation for any words or ideas that are not your own, and include a works-cited page. (See the Appendix for more information on documentation formats.)

2. Write an updated version of one of this chapter's essays. For example, you might explore the kinds of pressure Lawrence Otis Graham ("The 'Black Table' Is Still There") might face as a middle-school student today.

3. Various technological and social developments have contributed to the decline of formal letter writing. One of these is the telephone; others are text-messaging and email. Consider some other possible causes, and write an essay explaining why letter writing has all but disappeared. You may also consider the *effects* (both positive and negative) of this development.

4. How do you account for the popularity of one of the following: email, blogs, hip-hop, video games, home schooling, reality TV, fast food, or sensationalist tabloids such as the *Star*? Write an essay considering remote as well as immediate causes for the success of the phenomenon you choose.

5. Between 1946 and 1964, the U.S. birth rate increased considerably. Some of the effects attributed to this "baby boom" include the 1960s antiwar movement, an increase in the crime rate, and the development of the women's movement. Write an essay exploring some possible effects on the nation's economy and politics of the baby-boom generation's growing older. What trends would you expect to find now that the first baby boomers have turned sixty?

6. Write an essay tracing a series of events in your life that constitutes a causal chain. Indicate clearly both the sequence of events and the causal connections among them, and be careful not to confuse coincidence with causality.

7. Almost half of American marriages now end in divorce. To what do you attribute this high divorce rate? Be as specific as possible, citing "case studies" of families you are familiar with.

8. What do you see as the major cause of any one of these problems: binge drinking among college students, voter apathy, school shootings, or academic cheating? Based on your identification of its cause, formulate some specific solutions for the problem you select.

9. Write an essay considering the likely effects of a severe, protracted shortage of one of the following commodities: clean water, rental housing, flu vaccine, books, or gasoline. You may consider a community-, city-, or statewide shortage or a nation- or worldwide crisis.

10. Write an essay exploring the causes, effects, or both of increased violence among children in the United States. If you choose to cite the media as a

main cause, you may refer to the essays on media violence in Chapter 14, "Argumentation."

COLLABORATIVE ACTIVITY FOR CAUSE AND EFFECT

Working in groups of four, discuss your thoughts about the increasing homeless population, and then list four effects the presence of homeless people is having on you, your community, and our nation. Assign each member of your group to write a paragraph explaining one of the effects the group identifies. Then, arrange the paragraphs by increasing importance, moving from the least to the most significant consequence. Finally, work together to turn your individual paragraphs into an essay: write an introduction, a conclusion, and transitions between paragraphs, and include a thesis statement in paragraph 1.

11
Comparison and Contrast

WHAT IS COMPARISON AND CONTRAST?

In the narrowest sense, *comparison* shows how two or more things are similar, and *contrast* shows how they are different. In most writing situations, however, the two related processes of **comparison and contrast** are used together. In the following paragraph from *Disturbing the Universe*, scientist Freeman Dyson compares and contrasts two different styles of human endeavor, which he calls "the gray and the green":

<table>
<tr>
<td>Topic sentence (outlines elements of comparison)

Point-by-point comparison</td>
<td>In everything we undertake, either on earth or in the sky, we have a choice of two styles, which I call the gray and the green. The distinction between the gray and green is not sharp. Only at the extremes of the spectrum can we say without qualification, this is green and that is gray. The difference between green and gray is better explained by examples than by definitions. Factories are gray, gardens are green. Physics is gray, biology is green. Plutonium is gray, horse manure is green. Bureaucracy is gray, pioneer communities are green. Self-reproducing machines are gray, trees and children are green. Human technology is gray, God's technology is green. Clones are gray, clades* are green. Army field manuals are gray, poems are green.</td>
</tr>
</table>

A special form of comparison, called **analogy**, explains one thing by comparing it to a second, more familiar thing. In the following paragraph from *The Shopping Mall High School*, Arthur G. Powell, Eleanor Farrar, and David K. Cohen use analogy to shed light on the nature of contemporary American high schools:

> If Americans want to understand their high schools at work, they should imagine them as shopping malls. Secondary education is another

---

* EDS. NOTE — A group of organisms that evolved from a common ancestor.

consumption experience in an abundant society. Shopping malls attract a broad range of customers with different tastes and purposes. Some shop at Sears, others at Woolworth's or Bloomingdale's. In high schools a broad range of students also shop. They too can select from an astonishing variety of products and services conveniently assembled in one place with ample parking. Furthermore, in malls and schools many different kinds of transactions are possible. Both institutions bring hopeful purveyors and potential purchasers together. The former hope to maximize sales but can take nothing for granted. Shoppers have a wide discretion not only about what to buy but also about whether to buy.

USING COMPARISON AND CONTRAST

Throughout our lives, we are bombarded with information from newspapers, television, radio, the Internet, and personal experience: the police strike in Memphis; city workers walk out in Philadelphia; the Senate debates government spending; taxes are raised in New Jersey. Somehow we must make sense of the jumbled facts and figures that surround us. One way we have of understanding information like this is to put it side by side with other data and then to compare and contrast. Do the police in Memphis have the same complaints as the city workers in Philadelphia? What are the differences between the two situations? Is the national debate on spending analogous to the New Jersey debate on taxes? How do they differ?

We apply comparison and contrast every day to matters that directly affect us. When we make personal decisions, we consider alternatives, asking ourselves whether one option seems better than another. Should I major in history or business? What job opportunities will each major offer me? Should I register as a Democrat or a Republican, or should I join a third party? What are the positions of each political party on government spending, health care, and taxes? To answer questions like these, we use comparison and contrast.

PLANNING A COMPARISON-AND-CONTRAST ESSAY

Because comparison and contrast is central to our understanding of the world, this way of thinking is often called for in papers and on essay exams:

Compare and contrast the attitudes toward science and technology expressed in Fritz Lang's *Metropolis* and George Lucas's *Star Wars*. (film)

What are the similarities and differences between mitosis and meiosis? (biology)

Discuss the relative merits of establishing a partnership or setting up a corporation. (business law)

Discuss the advantages and disadvantages of bilingual education. (education)

Recognizing Comparison-and-Contrast Assignments

You are not likely to sit down and say to yourself, "I think I'll write a comparison-and-contrast essay today. Now what can I write about?" Instead, your assignment will suggest comparison and contrast, or you will decide comparison and contrast suits your purpose. In the preceding examples, for instance, the instructors phrased their questions to tell students how to treat the material. When you read these questions, certain key words and phrases — *compare and contrast, similarities and differences, relative merits, advantages and disadvantages* — indicate you should use a comparison-and-contrast pattern to organize your essay. Sometimes you may not even need a key phrase. Consider the question, "Which of the two Adamses, John or Samuel, had the greater influence on the timing and course of the American Revolution?" Here the word *greater* is enough to suggest a contrast.

Even when your assignment is not worded to suggest comparison and contrast, your purpose may point to this pattern of development. For instance, when you **evaluate**, you frequently use comparison and contrast. If, as a student in a management course, you are asked to evaluate two health-care systems, you can begin by researching the standards experts use in their evaluations. You can then compare each system's performance with those standards and contrast the systems with each other, concluding perhaps that both systems meet minimum standards but that one is more cost-efficient than the other. Or, if you are evaluating two of this year's new cars for a consumer newsletter, you can establish some criteria — fuel economy, safety features, handling, comfort, style — and compare and contrast the cars on each criterion. If each of the cars is better in different categories, your readers will have to decide which features matter most to them.

Establishing a Basis for Comparison

Before you can compare and contrast two things, you must be sure a **basis for comparison** exists — that the two things have enough in common to justify the comparison. For example, although cats and dogs are very different, they share several significant elements: they are mammals, they make good pets, and they are intelligent. Without these shared elements, there would be no basis for analysis and nothing of importance to discuss.

A comparison should lead you beyond the obvious. For instance, at first the idea of a comparison-and-contrast essay based on an analogy between bees and people might seem absurd: after all, these two creatures differ in species, physical structure, and intelligence. In fact, their differences are so obvious that an essay based on them might seem pointless. But after further analysis, you might decide that bees and people have quite a few similarities. Both are social animals that live in complex social structures, and both have tasks to perform and roles to fulfill in their respective societies. Therefore, you *could* write about them, but you would focus on the common elements that seem most provocative — social structures and roles — rather than on dissimilar elements. If you tried to draw an analogy between bees and SUVs or humans and golf tees, however, you would run into trouble. Although some points of comparison could be found, they would be trivial. Why bother to point out that both bees and SUVs can travel great distances or that both people and tees are needed to play golf? Neither statement establishes a significant basis for comparison.

When two subjects are very similar, the contrast may be worth writing about. And when two subjects are not very much alike, you may find that the similarities are worth considering.

Selecting Points for Discussion

After you decide which subjects to compare and contrast, you need to select the points you want to discuss. You do this by determining your emphasis — on similarities, differences, or both — and the major focus of your paper. If your purpose in comparing two types of house plants is to explain that one is easier to grow than the other, you would select points having to do with plant care, not those having to do with plant biology.

When you compare and contrast, make sure you treat the same (or at least similar) elements for each subject you discuss. For instance, if you were going to compare and contrast two novels, you might consider the following elements in both works:

NOVEL A	NOVEL B
Minor characters	Minor characters
Major characters	Major characters
Themes	Themes

Try to avoid the common error of discussing entirely different elements for each subject. Such an approach obscures any basis for comparison that might exist. The two novels, for example, could not be meaningfully compared or contrasted if you discussed dissimilar elements:

NOVEL A	NOVEL B
Minor characters	Author's life
Major characters	Plot
Themes	Symbolism

Developing a Thesis Statement

After selecting the points you want to discuss, you are ready to develop your thesis statement. This **thesis statement** should tell readers what to expect in your essay, identifying not only the subjects to be compared and contrasted but also the point you will make about them. Your thesis statement should also indicate whether you will concentrate on similarities or differences or both. In addition, it may list the points of comparison and contrast in the order in which they will be discussed in the essay.

The structure of your thesis statement can indicate the emphasis of your essay. As the following sentences illustrate, a thesis statement should highlight the essay's central concern by presenting it in the independent, rather than the dependent, clause of the sentence. Notice that the structure of the first thesis statement emphasizes similarities, while the structure of the second highlights differences:

> Despite the fact that television and radio are distinctly different media, they use similar strategies to appeal to their audiences.

> Although Melville's *Moby-Dick* and London's *The Sea Wolf* are both about the sea, the minor characters, major characters, and themes of *Moby-Dick* establish its greater complexity.

STRUCTURING A COMPARISON-AND-CONTRAST ESSAY

Like every other type of essay in this book, a comparison-and-contrast essay has an **introduction**, several **body paragraphs**, and a **conclusion**. Within the body of your paper, you can use either of two basic comparison-and-contrast strategies — **subject by subject** or **point by point**.

As you might expect, each organizational strategy has advantages and disadvantages. In general, you should use subject-by-subject comparison when your purpose is to emphasize overall similarities or differences, and you should use point-by-point comparison when your purpose is to emphasize individual points of similarity or difference.

Using Subject-by-Subject Comparison

In a **subject-by-subject comparison**, you essentially write a separate essay about each subject, but you discuss the same points for both subjects. Use your basis for comparison to guide your selection of points, and arrange these points in some logical order, usually in order of their increasing significance. The following informal outline illustrates a subject-by-subject comparison:

Introduction:	Thesis statement — Despite the fact that television and radio are distinctly different media, they use similar strategies to appeal to their audiences.

Television audiences

Point 1:	Men
Point 2:	Women
Point 3:	Children

Radio audiences
Point 1:	Men
Point 2:	Women
Point 3:	Children
Conclusion:	Restatement of thesis or review of key points

Subject-by-subject comparisons are most appropriate for short, uncomplicated papers. In longer papers, where you might make many points about each subject, this organizational strategy demands too much of your readers, requiring them to keep track of all your points throughout your paper. In addition, because of the length of each section, your paper may seem like two completely separate essays. For longer or more complex papers, then, it is often best to use point-by-point comparison.

Using Point-by-Point Comparison

In a **point-by-point comparison**, you first make a point about one subject and then follow it with a comparable point about the other. This alternating pattern continues throughout the body of your essay until all your points have been made. The following informal outline illustrates a point-by-point comparison:

Introduction:	Thesis statement — Although Melville's *Moby-Dick* and London's *The Sea Wolf* are both about the sea, the minor characters, major characters, and themes of *Moby-Dick* establish its greater complexity.

Minor characters
Book 1:	*The Sea Wolf*
Book 2:	*Moby-Dick*

Major characters
Book 1:	*The Sea Wolf*
Book 2:	*Moby-Dick*

Themes
Book 1:	*The Sea Wolf*
Book 2:	*Moby-Dick*
Conclusion:	Restatement of thesis or review of key points

Point-by-point comparisons are useful for longer, more complicated essays in which you discuss many different points. (If you treat only one or two points of comparison, you should consider a subject-by-subject organization.) In a point-by-point essay, readers can follow comparisons or contrasts more easily and do not have to wait several paragraphs to find out, for example, the differences between minor characters in *Moby-Dick* and *The Sea Wolf* or to remember on page five what was said on page three. Nevertheless, it is easy to fall into a monotonous, back-and-forth movement between points when you write a point-by-point comparison. To avoid this problem, vary your sentence structure as you move from point to point.

Using Transitions

Transitions are especially important in comparison-and-contrast essays because you must supply readers with clear signals that identify individual similarities and differences. Without these cues, readers will have trouble following your discussion and may lose track of the significance of the points you are making. Some transitions indicating comparison and contrast are listed in the following box. (A more complete list of transitions appears on page 43.)

USEFUL TRANSITIONS FOR COMPARISON AND CONTRAST

COMPARISON

in comparison	like
in the same way	likewise
just as . . . so	similarly

CONTRAST

although	nevertheless
but	nonetheless
conversely	on the contrary
despite	on the one hand . . . on the other hand
even though	still
however	unlike
in contrast	whereas
instead	yet

Longer essays frequently include **transitional paragraphs** that connect one part of an essay to another. A transitional paragraph can be a single sentence that signals a shift in focus or a longer paragraph that provides a concise summary of what was said before. In either case, transitional paragraphs enable readers to pause and consider what has already been said before moving on to a new subject.

REVISING A COMPARISON-AND-CONTRAST ESSAY

When you revise your comparison-and-contrast essay, consider the items on the revision checklist on page 54. In addition, pay special attention to the items on the following checklist, which apply specifically to comparison-and-contrast essays.

✓ **REVISION CHECKLIST:** Comparison and Contrast

- Does your assignment call for comparison and contrast?
- What basis for comparison exists between the two subjects you are comparing?
- Does your essay have a clear thesis statement that identifies both the subjects you are comparing and the points you are making about them?
- Do you discuss the same or similar points for both subjects?
- If you have written a subject-by-subject comparison, have you included a transition paragraph that connects the two sections of the essay?
- If you have written a point-by-point comparison, have you included appropriate transitions and varied your sentence structure to indicate your shift from one point to another?
- Have you included transitional words and phrases that indicate whether you are discussing similarities or differences?

EDITING A COMPARISON-AND-CONTRAST ESSAY

When you edit your comparison-and-contrast essay, follow the guidelines on the editing checklists on pages 71, 74, and 76. In addition, focus on the grammar, mechanics, and punctuation issues that are particularly relevant to comparison-and-contrast essays. One of these issues — using parallel structure — is discussed below.

GRAMMAR IN CONTEXT: Using Parallelism

Parallelism — the use of matching nouns, verbs, phrases, or clauses to express the same or similar ideas — is often used in comparison-and-contrast essays to emphasize the similarities or differences between one point or subject and another.

• Always use parallel structure with paired items or with items in a series.

"I am an American citizen and she is not" (Mukherjee 411).

"For women, as for girls, intimacy is the fabric of relationships, and talk is the thread from which it is woven" (Tannen 437).

"Lee was tidewater Virginia, and in his background were family, culture, and tradition . . . the age of chivalry transplanted to a New World which was making its own legends and its own myths" (Catton 405).

According to Bruce Catton, Lee was <u>strong</u>, <u>aristocratic</u>, and <u>dedicated to the Confederacy</u> (406).

• Be sure to use parallel structure with paired items linked by correlative conjunctions (*not only/but also, both/and, neither/nor, either/or,* and so on).

"In everything we undertake, **either** <u>on earth</u> **or** <u>in the sky</u>, we have a choice of two styles, which I call the gray and the green" (Dyson 383).

Not only <u>does Catton admire Grant</u>, **but** <u>he</u> **also** <u>respects him</u>.

• Finally, use parallel structure to emphasize the contrast between paired items linked by *as* or *than*.

According to Deborah Tannen, women's conversation is **as** <u>frustrating for men</u> **as** <u>men's is for women</u> (Tannen 439).

As Deborah Tannen observes, most men are socialized <u>to communicate through actions</u> **rather than** <u>to communicate through conversation</u> (437).

For more practice in using parallelism, visit Exercise Central at
bedfordstmartins.com/patterns/parallelism.

✓ **EDITING CHECKLIST: Comparison and Contrast**

- Have you used parallel structure with parallel elements in a series?
- Have you used commas to separate three or more parallel elements in a series?
- Have you used parallel structure with paired items linked by correlative conjunctions?
- Have you used parallel structure with paired items linked by *as* or *than*?

A STUDENT WRITER: Subject-by-Subject Comparison

The following essay, by Mark Cotharn, is a subject-by-subject comparison. It was written for a composition class whose instructor asked students to write an essay comparing two educational experiences.

Brains versus Brawn

Introduction

When people think about discrimination, they usually 1
associate it with race or gender. But discrimination can take
other forms. For example, a person can gain an unfair advantage
at a job interview by being attractive, by knowing someone who
works at the company, or by being able to talk about something
(like sports) that has nothing to do with the job. Certainly, the
people who do not get the job would claim that they were
discriminated against, and to some extent they would be
right. As a high school athlete, I experienced both sides of
discrimination. When I was a sophomore, I benefited from
discrimination. When I was a junior, however, I was penalized
by it, treated as if there were no place for me in a classroom. As

*Thesis statement
(emphasizing
differences)*

a result, I learned that discrimination, whether it helps you or
hurts you, is wrong.

*First subject:
Mark helped by
discrimination*

At my high school, football was everything, and the 2
entire town supported the local team. In the summer,

Status of football

merchants would run special football promotions. Adults would
wear shirts with the team's logo, students would collect money
to buy equipment, and everyone would go to the games and
cheer the team on. Coming out of junior high school, I was
considered an exceptional athlete who was eventually going to
start as varsity quarterback. Because of my status, I was
enthusiastically welcomed by the high school. Before I entered
the school, the varsity coach visited my home, and the principal
called my parents and told them how well I was going to do.

Treatment by teachers

I knew that high school would be different from junior 3
high, but I wasn't prepared for the treatment I received from my
teachers. Many of them talked to me as if I were their friend,
not their student. My math teacher used to keep me after class
just to talk football; he would give me a note so I could be late
for my next class. My biology teacher told me I could skip the
afternoon labs so that I would have some time for myself before
practice. Several of my teachers told me that during football
season, I didn't have to hand in homework because it might
distract me during practice. My Spanish teacher even told me
that if I didn't do well on a test, I could take it over after the
season. Everything I did seemed to be perfect.

*Mark's reaction to
treatment*

Despite this favorable treatment, I continued to study 4
hard. I knew that if I wanted to go to a good college, I would

have to get good grades, and I resented the implication that the only way I could get good grades was by getting special treatment. I had always been a good student, and I had no intention of changing my study habits now that I was in high school. Each night after practice, I stayed up late outlining my notes and completing my class assignments. Any studying I couldn't do during the week, I would complete on the weekends. Of course my social life suffered, but I didn't care. I was proud that I never took advantage of the special treatment my teachers were offering me.

Transitional paragraph: signals shift from one subject to another

Then, one day, the unthinkable happened. The township redrew the school-district lines, and I suddenly found myself assigned to a new high school — one that was academically more demanding than the one I attended and, worse, one that had a weak football team. When my parents appealed to the school board to let me stay at my current school, they were told that if the board made an exception for me, it would have to make exceptions for others, and that would lead to chaos. My principal and my coach also tried to get the board to change its decision, but they got the same response. So, in my junior year, at the height of my career, I changed schools. 5

Second subject: Mark hurt by discrimination

Status of football

Unlike the people at my old school, no one at my new school seemed to care much about high school football. Many of the students attended the games, but their primary focus was on getting into college. If they talked about football at all, they usually discussed the regional college teams. As a result, I didn't have the status I had when I attended my former school. When I met with the coach before school started, he told me the football team was weak. He also told me that his main goal was to make sure everyone on the team had a chance to play. So, even though I would start, I would have to share the quarterback position with two seniors. Later that day, I saw the principal, who told me that although sports were an important part of school, academic achievement was more important. He made it clear that I would play football only as long as my grades did not suffer. 6

Treatment by teachers

Unlike the teachers at my old school, the teachers at my new school did not give any special treatment to athletes. When I entered my new school, I was ready for the challenge. What I was not ready for was the hostility of most of my new teachers. 7

Mark's reaction to treatment

From the first day, in just about every class, my teachers made it obvious that they had already made up their minds about what kind of student I was going to be. Some teachers told me I shouldn't expect any special consideration just because I was the team's quarterback. One even said in front of the class that I would have to study as hard as the other students if I expected to pass. I was hurt and embarrassed by these comments. I didn't expect anyone to give me anything, and I was ready to get the grades I deserved. After all, I had gotten good grades up to this point, and I had no reason to think that the situation would change. Even so, my teachers' preconceived ideas upset me.

Just as I had in my old school, I studied hard, but I didn't know how to deal with the prejudice I faced. At first, it really bothered me and even affected my performance on the football field. However, after awhile, I decided that the best way to show my teachers that I was not the stereotypical jock was to prove to them what kind of student I really was. In the long run, far from discouraging me, their treatment motivated me, and I decided to work as hard in the classroom as I did on the football field. By the end of high school, not only had the team won half of its games (a record season), but I had also proved to my teachers that I was a good student. (I still remember the surprised look on the face of my chemistry teacher when she handed my first exam back to me and told me that I had received the second highest grade in the class.)

Conclusion

Before I graduated, I talked to the teachers about how they had treated me during my junior year. Some admitted they had been harder on me than on the rest of the students, but others denied they had ever discriminated against me. Eventually, I realized that some of them would never understand what they had done. Even so, my experience did have some positive effects. I learned that you should judge people on their merits, not by your own set of assumptions. In addition, I learned that although some people are talented intellectually, others have special skills that should also be valued. And, as I found out, discriminatory treatment, whether it helps you or hurts you, is no substitute for fairness.

Restatement of thesis

8

9

Points for Special Attention

Basis for Comparison.   Mark knew he could easily compare his two experiences. Both involved high school, and both focused on the treatment he had received as an athlete. In one case, Mark was treated better than other students because he was the team's quarterback; in the other, he was stereotyped as a "dumb jock" because he was a football player. Mark also knew that his comparison would make an interesting (and perhaps unexpected) point — that discrimination is unfair even when it gives a person an advantage.

Selecting Points for Comparison.   Mark wanted to make certain that he would discuss the same (or at least similar) points for the two experiences he was going to compare. As he planned his essay, he consulted his brainstorming notes and made the following informal outline:

EXPERIENCE 1 (gained an advantage)	EXPERIENCE 2 (was put at a disadvantage)
Status of football	Status of football
Treatment by teachers	Treatment by teachers
My reaction	My reaction

Structure.   Mark's essay makes three points about each of the two experiences he compares. Because his purpose was to convey the differences between the two experiences, he decided to use a subject-by-subject strategy. In addition, Mark thought he could make his case more convincingly if he discussed the first experience fully before moving on to the next one, and he believed readers would have no trouble keeping his individual points in mind as they read. Of course, Mark could have decided to do a point-by-point comparison. He rejected this strategy, though, because he thought that shifting back and forth between subjects would distract readers from his main point.

Transitions.   Without adequate transitions, a subject-by-subject comparison can read like two separate essays. Notice that in Mark's essay, paragraph 5 is a **transitional paragraph** that connects the two sections of the essay. In it, Mark sets up the comparison by telling how he suddenly found himself assigned to another high school.

In addition to connecting the sections of an essay, transitional words and phrases can identify individual similarities or differences. Notice, for example, how the transitional word *however* emphasizes the contrast between the following sentences from paragraph 1:

WITHOUT TRANSITION

When I was a sophomore, I benefited from discrimination. When I was a junior, I was penalized by it.

WITH TRANSITION

When I was a sophomore, I benefited from discrimination. When I was a junior, *however,* I was penalized by it.

Topic Sentences.   Like transitional phrases, topic sentences help to guide readers through an essay. When reading a comparison-and-contrast essay, readers can easily forget the points being compared, especially if the paper is long or complex. Direct, clearly stated topic sentences act as guide-posts, alerting readers to the comparisons and contrasts you are making. For example, Mark's straightforward topic sentence at the beginning of paragraph 5 dramatically signals the movement from one experience to the other ("Then, one day, the unthinkable happened"). In addition, as in any effective comparison-and-contrast essay, each point discussed in con-nection with one subject is also discussed in connection with the other. Mark's topic sentences reinforce this balance:

FIRST SUBJECT

At my high school, football was everything, and the entire town supported the local team.

SECOND SUBJECT

Unlike the people at my old school, no one at my new school seemed to care much about high school football.

Focus on Revision

Mark's peer critics thought he could have spent more time talking about what he did to counter the preconceptions about athletes that teachers in *both* his schools had.

One student pointed out that the teachers at both schools seemed to think athletes were weak students. The only difference was that the teach-ers at Mark's first school were willing to make allowances for athletes, while the teachers at his second school were not. The student thought that although Mark alluded to this fact, he should have made his point more explicitly. Another student suggested that Mark use a quotation from David J. Birnbaum's essay "The Catbird Seat." The student pointed out that Birnbaum, like Mark, was given an advantage that he considered unfair.

After rereading his essay, along with his classmates' comments, Mark decided to add information about how demanding football practice was. Without this information, readers would have a hard time understanding how difficult it was for him to keep up with his studies. Mark also decided to refer to Birnbaum's essay in the next draft of his paper. (Adding this ref-erence would require him to include parenthetical documentation and a works-cited page.)

Another peer critic thought Mark should concede that some student athletes *do* fit the teachers' stereotypes (although many do not). This information would reinforce his thesis and help him demonstrate how unfair his treatment was. (A sample peer editing worksheet for comparison and contrast appears on page 402.)

A STUDENT WRITER: Point-by-Point Comparison

The following essay, by Maria Tecson, is a point-by-point comparison. It was written for a class in educational psychology whose instructor asked students to compare two Web sites about a health issue and to determine which is the more reliable information source.

A Comparison of Two Web Sites on Attention Deficit Disorder

Introduction   At first glance, the National Institute of Mental Health 1 (NIMH) Web site on Attention Deficit Hyperactivity Disorder (nimh.nih.gov) and AdultADD.com — two Web sites on Attention Deficit Disorder (ADD) — look a lot alike. Both have good designs, informative headings, and links to other Web sites. Because anyone can publish on the Internet, however, Web sites cannot be judged simply on how they look. Colorful graphics and an appealing layout can often hide shortcomings *Thesis statement* that make sites unsuitable for use as research sources. As a *(emphasizing differences)* comparison of the NIMH and AdultADD.com Web sites shows, one site is definitely a more reliable source of information than the other.

First point: comparing   The first difference between the two Web sites is the 2 *homepages* design of their homepages. The nimh.nih.gov homepage looks *NIMH homepage* clear and professional. For example, the logos, tabs, links, search boxes, and text columns are placed carefully on the page (see fig. 1). Words are spelled correctly; tabs help users to navigate; and content is arranged topically, with headers such as "What is Attention Deficit Hyperactivity Disorder?" and "Signs & Symptoms." The text, set in columns, looks like a newspaper page. Throughout the Web site, links connect to a reference page that lists sources for articles, and footnotes document information. In addition, the nimh.nih.gov site contains links to other reliable Web sites, both governmental and academic. Finally, the site accommodates sight-disabled people by giving them the option of viewing enlarged text.

Adult ADD homepage   The AdultADD.com homepage looks more open than the 3 NIMH homepage; it has less text and contains fewer design elements (see fig. 2). Even so, the arrangement of text on the

Fig. 1. NIMH homepage

page, the no-nonsense style, and the lack of misspellings indicate that it has been carefully designed. The homepage is straightforward and businesslike and looks like a PowerPoint slide. It is easy to navigate and contains simple headings, such as "Find a Physician" and "Treatment for Adults." Despite the clean, direct design, however, the layout raises a question: why isn't this site linked to any other Web sites about ADD or ADHD? Unlike nimh.nih.gov, the AdultADD.com Web site has no reference page and no footnotes. In addition, it does not accommodate sight-disabled users.

Second point: comparing sponsors

NIMH site sponsor

Another difference between the two Web sites is who posted them. One look at the URL for the NIMH Web site indicates that it is a *.gov* — a Web site created by a branch of the United States government. The logo in the upper left-hand corner of the homepage identifies the National Institute of Mental Health (NIMH) as the sponsor of the site. In addition, every article on the Web site has a listed author, so users know exactly who is responsible for the content. The "About NIMH"

4

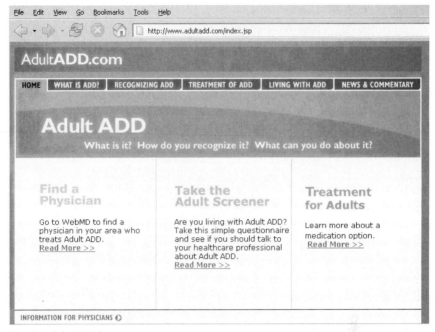

Fig. 2. Adult ADD homepage

tab on the upper-right of the homepage takes users to a description of NIMH, as well as to contact information. Here visitors to the site find out that NIMH is part of the National Institutes of Health, which is, in turn, a part of the U.S. Department of Health and Human Services. Furthermore, NIMH is the "lead Federal agency for research on mental and behavioral disorders." This description also makes clear the NIMH Web site's purpose: to give the American public the latest information about ADHD. For this reason, the Web site lists all the medications used to treat ADHD and evaluates the various treatment options available to patients.

AdultADD site sponsor   The URL for the AdultADD.com Web site ends with *.com,*   5
indicating that it is a commercial site that promotes a product. It is not immediately clear, however, who (or what) sponsors the Web site. The home page has no corporate logo and no identifying information. Across the top of the homepage are a series of links — "What is ADD?" "Recognizing ADD," and so on. Each of these links leads to a page that contains a video clip of a television commercial that promotes Strattera, a new drug manufactured by the Eli Lilly pharmaceutical company for the

treatment of ADD. If you click on the links in the middle of the page, however, you never encounter this information. For this reason, there is a possibility that much of the information these links lead to is biased. In other words, Lilly could be highlighting treatments that involve its own product and disregarding treatments that involve products made by other pharmaceutical companies.

Third point: comparing frequency of updates

NIMH updates

A final difference between the two Web sites is how   6
frequently they are updated. The NIMH Web site makes a
point of staying up-to-date, presenting the most current
information on its subject. The bottom left-hand corner of the
NIMH homepage contains the exact date the site was last
updated, and each page on the Web site has a different date,
so it is clear when every article on the site was written and
posted.

Adult ADD updates

The AdultADD.com Web site, however, is less clear about   7
updates. The date on the bottom of the homepage indicates
only that the Web site was copyrighted in 2003; it does not
indicate when the Web site itself was updated. This omission
makes it very difficult for a visitor to the site to determine how
current the information on the site actually is.

Conclusion

A comparison of the NIMH Web site and AdultADD.com   8
Web site shows some clear differences between the two. The
NIMH Web site makes it easy for users to find out who posted
the site, who wrote material on it, and when the site was last
updated. The AdultADD.com Web site, however, hides its
commercial purpose and makes it difficult for visitors to the site
to find out who posted the material and when it was last

Restatement of thesis

updated. For these reasons, the NIMH Web site is a more
trustworthy source of information than the AdultADD.com
Web site.

Points for Special Attention

Structure.   Maria's purpose in writing this essay was to compare two Web sites that deal with Attention Deficit Hyperactivity Disorder and to determine which is the better, more reliable source of information. She structured her essay as a point-by-point comparison, carefully discussing the same points for each subject. With this method of organization, she can be sure her readers will understand the specific differences between the

NIMH Web site and the AdultADD.com Web site. Had Maria used a subject-by-subject comparison, her readers would have had to keep turning back to match the points she made about one Web site with those she made about the other.

Topic Sentences.   Without clear topic sentences, Maria's readers would have had difficulty determining where each discussion of the NIMH Web site ended and each one about the AdultADD.com Web site began. Maria uses topic sentences to distinguish the two subjects of her comparison and to make the contrast between them clear.

Point 1
> The nimh.nih.gov homepage looks clear and professional.
>
> The AdultADD.com homepage looks more open than the NIMH homepage; it has less text and contains fewer design elements.

Point 2
> One look at the URL (Uniform Resource Locator) for the NIMH Web site indicates that it is a *.gov* — a Web site created by a branch of the United States government.
>
> The URL for the AdultADD.com Web site ends with *.com,* indicating that it is a commercial site that promotes a product.

Point 3
> The NIMH Web site makes a point of staying up-to-date, presenting the most current information on its subject.
>
> The AdultADD.com Web site, however, is less clear about updates.

Transitions.   In addition to clear and straightforward topic sentences, Maria included **transitional sentences** to help readers move through the essay. These sentences identify the three points of contrast in the essay and, by establishing a parallel structure, they form a pattern that reinforces the essay's thesis.

> The first difference between the two Web sites is the design of their homepages.

> Another difference between the two Web sites is who posted them.

> A final difference between the two Web sites is how frequently they are updated.

Focus on Revision

Maria's peer critics thought the greatest strength of her essay was its use of detail, which made the contrast between the two Web sites clear, but they thought that even more detail would improve her essay. For example, in paragraph 6, Maria could include a few titles of the articles the NIMH Web site lists, along with their dates of publication. In paragraph 7, she could also list some of the specific information on the AdultADD.com

Web site and explain why it is necessary to know when the information was written and posted.

Maria agreed with these suggestions. She also thought she could improve her conclusion: although it summed up the main points of her essay, it contained little that would stay with readers after they finished. A sentence or two to caution readers about the need to carefully evaluate the information they find on Web sites would be an improvement.

PEER EDITING WORKSHEET: Comparison and Contrast

1. Does the essay have a clearly stated thesis? What is it?
2. What two things are being compared? What basis for comparison exists between the two?
3. Does the essay treat the same or similar points for each of its two sub-jects? List the points discussed.

FIRST SUBJECT	SECOND SUBJECT
a.	a.
b.	b.
c.	c.
d.	d.

   Are these points discussed in the same order for both subjects? Are the points presented in parallel terms?
4. Does the essay use a point-by-point or subject-by-subject strategy? Is this the best choice? Why?
5. Are transitional words and phrases used appropriately to identify points of comparison and contrast? List some of the transitions used.
6. Are additional transitions needed? If so, where?
7. How could the introductory paragraph be improved?
8. How could the concluding paragraph be improved?

The selections that follow illustrate both subject-by-subject and point-by-point comparisons. The first selection, a pair of visual texts, is followed by questions designed to illustrate how comparison and contrast can operate in visual form.

The Kiss (Sculpture)

LOVE (Sculpture)

• • •

Reading Images

1. What significant characteristics do the two sculptures pictured above and on the preceding page share? Do they share enough characteristics to establish a basis for comparison? Explain.

2. Make a list of points you could discuss if you were comparing the two sculptures.

3. What general statement could you make about these two sculptures? Do the points you listed in question 2 provide enough support for this general statement?

Journal Entry

How does each sculpture convey the idea of love? Which one do you believe conveys this idea more effectively? Why?

Thematic Connections

- "The Storm" (page 190)
- "How to Escape from a Bad Date" (page 291)
- "Sex, Lies, and Conversation" (page 436)

BRUCE CATTON

Grant and Lee: A Study in Contrasts

Bruce Catton (1899–1978) was a respected journalist and an authority on the American Civil War. His studies were interrupted by his service during World War I, after which he worked as a journalist and then for various government agencies. Catton edited *American Heritage* magazine from 1954 until his death. Among his many books are *Mr. Lincoln's Army* (1951); *A Stillness at Appomattox* (1953), which won both a Pulitzer Prize and a National Book Award; and *Gettysburg: The Final Fury* (1974). Catton also wrote a memoir, *Waiting for the Morning Train* (1972), in which he recalls listening as a young boy to the reminiscences of Union Army veterans.

Background on Grant and Lee
"Grant and Lee: A Study in Contrasts," which first appeared in a collection of historical essays titled *The American Story,* focuses on the two generals who headed the opposing armies during the Civil War (1861–1865). Robert E. Lee led the Army of Northern Virginia, the backbone of the Confederate forces, throughout much of the war. Ulysses S. Grant was named commander in chief of the Union troops in March 1864. By the spring of 1865, although it seemed almost inevitable that the Southern forces would be defeated, Lee made an attempt to lead his troops to join another Confederate army in North Carolina. Finding himself virtually surrounded by Grant's forces near the small town of Appomattox Court House, Lee chose to surrender to Grant. The following essay considers these two great generals in terms of both their differences and their important similarities.

When Ulysses S. Grant and Robert E. Lee met in the parlor of a modest house at Appomattox Court House, Virginia, on April 9, 1865, to work out the terms for the surrender of Lee's Army of Northern Virginia, a great chapter in American life came to a close, and a great new chapter began.   1

These men were bringing the Civil War to its virtual finish. To be sure, other armies had yet to surrender, and for a few days the fugitive Confederate government would struggle desperately and vainly, trying to find some way to go on living now that its chief support was gone. But in effect it was all over when Grant and Lee signed the papers. And the little room where they wrote out the terms was the scene of one of the poignant, dramatic contrasts in American history.   2

They were two strong men, these oddly different generals, and they represented the strengths of two conflicting currents that, through them, had come into final collision.   3

Back of Robert E. Lee was the notion that the old aristocratic concept might somehow survive and be dominant in American life.   4

Lee was tidewater Virginia, and in his background were family, culture, and tradition . . . the age of chivalry transplanted to a New World which   5 was making its own legends and its own myths. He embodied a way of life that had come down through the age of knighthood and the English country squire. America was a land that was beginning all over again, dedicated to nothing much more complicated than the rather hazy belief that all men had equal rights and should have an equal chance in the world. In such a land Lee stood for the feeling that it was somehow of advantage to human society to have pronounced inequality in the social structure. There should be a leisure class, backed by ownership of land; in turn, society itself should be keyed to the land as the chief source of wealth and influence. It would bring forth (according to this ideal) a class of men with a strong sense of obligation to the community; men who lived not to gain advantage for themselves, but to meet the solemn obligations which had been laid on them by the very fact that they were privileged. From them the country would get its leadership; to them it could look for the higher values — of thought, of conduct, of personal deportment — to give it strength and virtue.

Lee embodied the noblest elements of this aristocratic ideal. Through   6
him, the landed nobility justified itself. For four years, the Southern states had fought a desperate war to uphold the ideals for which Lee stood. In the end, it almost seemed as if the Confederacy fought for Lee; as if he himself was the Confederacy . . . the best thing that the way of life for which the Confederacy stood could ever have to offer. He had passed into legend before Appomattox. Thousands of tired, underfed, poorly clothed Confederate soldiers, long since past the simple enthusiasm of the early days of the struggle, somehow considered Lee the symbol of everything for which they had been willing to die. But they could not quite put this feeling into words. If the Lost Cause, sanctified by so much heroism and so many deaths, had a living justification, its justification was General Lee.

Grant, the son of a tanner on the Western frontier, was everything Lee   7
was not. He had come up the hard way and embodied nothing in particular except the eternal toughness and sinewy fiber of the men who grew up beyond the mountains. He was one of a body of men who owed reverence and obeisance to no one, who were self-reliant to a fault, who cared hardly anything for the past but who had a sharp eye for the future.

These frontier men were the precise opposites of the tidewater aristo-   8
crats. Back of them, in the great surge that had taken people over the Alleghenies and into the opening Western country, there was a deep, implicit dissatisfaction with a past that had settled into grooves. They stood for democracy, not from any reasoned conclusion about the proper ordering of human society, but simply because they had grown up in the middle of democracy and knew how it worked. Their society might have privileges, but they would be privileges each man had won for himself. Forms and patterns meant nothing. No man was born to anything, except perhaps to a chance to show how far he could rise. Life was competition.

Yet along with this feeling had come a deep sense of belonging to a   9
national community. The Westerner who developed a farm, opened a shop,

or set up in business as a trader, could hope to prosper only as his own community prospered — and his community ran from the Atlantic to the Pacific and from Canada down to Mexico. If the land was settled, with towns and highways and accessible markets, he could better himself. He saw his fate in terms of the nation's own destiny. As its horizons expanded, so did his. He had, in other words, an acute dollars-and-cents stake in the continued growth and development of his country.

And that, perhaps, is where the contrast between Grant and Lee becomes most striking. The Virginia aristocrat, inevitably, saw himself in relation to his own region. He lived in a static society which could endure almost anything except change. Instinctively, his first loyalty would go to the locality in which that society existed. He would fight to the limit of endurance to defend it, because in defending it he was defending everything that gave his own life its deepest meaning.

The Westerner, on the other hand, would fight with an equal tenacity for the broader concept of society. He fought so because everything he lived by was tied to growth, expansion, and a constantly widening horizon. What he lived by would survive or fall with the nation itself. He could not possibly stand by unmoved in the face of an attempt to destroy the Union. He would combat it with everything he had, because he could only see it as an effort to cut the ground out from under his feet.

So Grant and Lee were in complete contrast, representing two diametrically opposed elements in American life. Grant was the modern man emerging; beyond him, ready to come on the stage, was the great age of steel and machinery, of crowded cities and a restless burgeoning vitality. Lee might have ridden down from the old age of chivalry, lance in hand, silken banner fluttering over his head. Each man was the perfect champion of his cause, drawing both his strengths and his weaknesses from the people he led.

Yet it was not all contrast, after all. Different as they were — in background, in personality, in underlying aspiration — these two great soldiers had much in common. Under everything else, they were marvelous fighters. Furthermore, their fighting qualities were really very much alike.

Each man had, to begin with, the great virtue of utter tenacity and fidelity. Grant fought his way down the Mississippi Valley in spite of acute personal discouragement and profound military handicaps. Lee hung on in the trenches at Petersburg after hope itself had died. In each man there was an indomitable quality . . . the born fighter's refusal to give up as long as he can still remain on his feet and lift his two fists.

Daring and resourcefulness they had, too; the ability to think faster and move faster than the enemy. These were the qualities which gave Lee the dazzling campaigns of Second Manassas and Chancellorsville and won Vicksburg for Grant.

Lastly, and perhaps greatest of all, there was the ability, at the end, to turn quickly from war to peace once the fighting was over. Out of the way these two men behaved at Appomattox came the possibility of a peace of reconciliation. It was a possibility not wholly realized, in the years to come, but which did, in the end, help the two sections to become one nation again . . . after a war whose bitterness might have seemed to make such a reunion wholly impossible. No part of either man's life became him more than the part he played in this brief meeting in the McLean house at Appomattox. Their behavior there put all succeeding generations of Americans in their debt. Two great Americans, Grant and Lee — very different, yet under everything very much alike. Their encounter at Appomattox was one of the great moments of American history.

• • •

Comprehension

1. What took place at Appomattox Court House on April 9, 1865? Why did the meeting at Appomattox signal the closing of "a great chapter in American life" (1)?

2. How does Robert E. Lee represent aristocracy? How does Ulysses S. Grant represent Lee's opposite?

3. According to Catton, where is it that "the contrast between Grant and Lee becomes most striking" (10)?

4. What similarities does Catton see between the two men?

5. Why, according to Catton, are "succeeding generations of Americans" (16) in debt to Grant and Lee?

Purpose and Audience

1. Catton's purpose in contrasting Grant and Lee is to make a statement about the differences between two currents in American history. Summarize these differences. Do you think the differences still exist today? Explain.

2. Is Catton's purpose in comparing Grant and Lee the same as his purpose in contrasting them? That is, do their similarities also make a statement about U.S. history? Explain.

3. State the essay's thesis in your own words.

Style and Structure

1. Does Catton use subject-by-subject or point-by-point comparison? Why do you think he chooses the strategy he does?

2. In this essay, topic sentences are extremely helpful to the reader. Explain the functions of the following sentences: "Grant . . . was everything Lee was not" (7); "So Grant and Lee were in complete contrast" (12); "Yet it was not all contrast, after all" (13); and "Lastly, and perhaps greatest of all . . ." (16).

3. Catton uses transitions skillfully in his essay. Identify the transitional words or expressions that link each paragraph to the preceding one.

4. Why do you suppose Catton provides the background for the meeting at Appomattox but presents no information about the dramatic meeting itself?

Vocabulary Projects

1. Define each of the following words as it is used in this selection.

poignant (2)   obeisance (7)   tenacity (14)
chivalry (5)   implicit (8)   fidelity (14)
deportment (5)   inevitably (10)   indomitable (14)
sanctified (6)   diametrically (12)   reconciliation (16)
embodied (7)   burgeoning (12)
sinewy (7)   aspiration (13)

2. Go to the online thesaurus at dictionary.com, and look up **synonyms** for each of the following words. Then, determine whether each synonym would be as effective as the word used in this essay.

deportment (5)   obeisance (7)   indomitable (14)
sanctified (6)   diametrically (12)

Journal Entry

Compare your attitudes about the United States with those held by Grant and by Lee. With which man do you agree?

Writing Workshop

1. Write a "study in contrasts" about two people you know well — two teachers, your parents, two relatives, two friends — or about two fictional characters you are very familiar with. Be sure to include a thesis statement.

2. Write a dialogue between two people you know that reveals their contrasting attitudes toward school, work, or any other subject.

3. Write an essay about two individuals from a period of American history other than the Civil War to make the same points Catton makes. If you do research, make sure you document your sources and include a works-cited page. (See the Appendix for information on documentation formats.)

Combining the Patterns

In several places, Catton uses **exemplification** to structure a paragraph. For instance, in paragraph 7, he uses examples to support the topic sentence "Grant, the son of a tanner on the Western frontier, was everything Lee was not." Identify three paragraphs that use examples to support the topic sentence, and bracket the examples. How do these examples in these paragraphs reinforce the similarities and differences between Grant and Lee?

Thematic Connections

- "Sixty-Nine Cents" (page 102)
- "Fatwa City" (page 242)
- The Declaration of Independence (page 575)
- "Letter from Birmingham Jail" (page 588)

BHARATI MUKHERJEE

Two Ways to Belong in America

Born in 1940 in Calcutta, India, novelist Bharati Mukherjee immigrated to the United States in 1961. Now a naturalized U.S. citizen, she teaches at the University of California at Berkeley. Mukherjee's novels include *Tiger's Daughter* (1972), *Jasmine* (1989), *Leave It to Me* (1997), *Desirable Daughters* (2002), and *The Tree Bride* (2004); her story collections are *Darkness* (1975) and the prize-winning *The Middleman and Other Stories* (1988). Her fiction often explores the tensions between the traditional role of women in Indian society and their very different role in the United States.

Background on U.S. immigration policy
The following essay, originally published in 1996, was written in response to proposals in Congress (eventually defeated) to enact legislation denying government benefits, such as Social Security, to resident aliens. Not to be confused with illegal immigrants, resident aliens — also called *legal permanent residents* — are immigrants who live in the United States legally, sometimes for their whole lives, but do not apply for citizenship. Most work and pay taxes like any citizen. According to the 2000 census, the United States population includes more than 30 million foreign-born residents, accounting for about 11 percent of the population. Of these, 9.3 million are legal permanent residents, 9.2 million are naturalized citizens, and an estimated 8.5 million are in the country illegally (some experts think this number is much higher); most of the rest are refugees seeking political asylum and students and temporary workers with visas. Although various issues related to immigration policy have been hotly debated for many years, particularly as large numbers of immigrants entered the country in the 1990s, the terrorist attacks of September 2001 have led to greater restrictions on and closer screenings of foreigners who want to enter the United States, especially those applying for student visas.

This is a tale of two sisters from Calcutta, Mira and Bharati, who have lived in the United States for some 35 years, but who find themselves on different sides in the current debate over the status of immigrants. I am an American citizen and she is not. I am moved that thousands of long-term residents are finally taking the oath of citizenship. She is not.

Mira arrived in Detroit in 1960 to study child psychology and pre-school education. I followed her a year later to study creative writing at the University of Iowa. When we left India, we were almost identical in appearance and attitude. We dressed alike, in saris; we expressed identical views on politics, social issues, love, and marriage in the same Calcutta convent-school accent. We would endure our two years in America, secure our degrees, then return to India to marry the grooms of our father's choosing.

1

2

Instead, Mira married an Indian student in 1962 who was getting his   3
business administration degree at Wayne State University. They soon
acquired the labor certifications necessary for the green card of hassle-free
residence and employment.

Mira still lives in Detroit, works in the Southfield, Mich., school sys-   4
tem, and has become nationally recognized for her contributions in the
fields of pre-school education and parent-teacher relationships. After 36
years as a legal immigrant in this country, she clings passionately to her
Indian citizenship and hopes to go home to India when she retires.

In Iowa City in 1963, I married a fellow student, an American of Cana-   5
dian parentage. Because of the accident of his North Dakota birth, I
bypassed labor-certification requirements and the race-related "quota" system that favored the applicant's country of origin over his or her merit. I
was prepared for (and even welcomed) the emotional strain that came with
marrying outside my ethnic community. In 33 years of marriage, we have
lived in every part of North America. By choosing a husband who was not
my father's selection, I was opting for fluidity, self-invention, blue jeans
and T-shirts, and renouncing 3,000 years (at least) of caste-observant, "pure
culture" marriage in the Mukherjee family. My books have often been read
as unapologetic (and in some quarters overenthusiastic) texts for cultural
and psychological "mongrelization." It's a word I celebrate.

Mira and I have stayed sisterly close by phone. In our regular Sunday   6
morning conversations, we are unguardedly affectionate. I am her only
blood relative on this continent. We expect to see each other through the
looming crises of aging and ill health without being asked. Long before
Vice President Gore's "Citizenship U.S.A." drive, we'd had our polite arguments over the ethics of retaining an overseas citizenship while expecting
the permanent protection and economic benefits that come with living
and working in America.

Like well-raised sisters, we never said what was really on our minds, but   7
we probably pitied one another. She, for the lack of structure in my life, the
erasure of Indianness, the absence of an unvarying daily core. I, for the nar-
rowness of her perspective, her uninvolvement with the mythic depths or
the superficial pop culture of this society. But, now, with the scapegoatings
of "aliens" (documented or illegal) on the increase, and the targeting of
long-term legal immigrants like Mira for new scrutiny and new self-
consciousness, she and I find ourselves unable to maintain the same polite
discretion. We were always unacknowledged adversaries, and we are now,
more than ever, sisters.

"I feel used," Mira raged on the phone the other night. "I feel manipu-   8
lated and discarded. This is such an unfair way to treat a person who was
invited to stay and work here because of her talent. My employer went to
the I.N.S. and petitioned for the labor certification. For over 30 years, I've
invested my creativity and professional skills into the improvement of *this*
country's pre-school system. I've obeyed all the rules, I've paid my taxes, I
love my work, I love my students, I love the friends I've made. How dare
America now change its rules in midstream? If America wants to make new

rules curtailing benefits of legal immigrants, they should apply only to immigrants who arrive after those rules are already in place."

To my ears, it sounded like the description of a long-enduring, comfortable yet loveless marriage, without risk or recklessness. Have we the right to demand, and to expect, that we be loved? (That, to me, is the subtext of the arguments by immigration advocates.) My sister is an expatriate, professionally generous and creative, socially courteous and gracious, and that's as far as her Americanization can go. She is here to maintain an identity, not to transform it.   9

I asked her if she would follow the example of others who have decided to become citizens because of the anti-immigration bills in Congress. And here, she surprised me. "If America wants to play the manipulative game, I'll play it, too," she snapped. "I'll become a U.S. citizen for now, then change back to India when I'm ready to go home. I feel some kind of irrational attachment to India that I don't to America. Until all this hysteria against legal immigrants, I was totally happy. Having my green card meant I could visit any place in the world I wanted to and then come back to a job that's satisfying and that I do very well."   10

In one family, from two sisters alike as peas in a pod, there could not be a wider divergence of immigrant experience. America spoke to me — I married it — I embraced the demotion from expatriate aristocrat to immigrant nobody, surrendering those thousands of years of "pure culture," the saris, the delightfully accented English. She retained them all. Which of us is the freak?   11

Mira's voice, I realize, is the voice not just of the immigrant South Asian community but of an immigrant community of the millions who have stayed rooted in one job, one city, one house, one ancestral culture, one cuisine, for the entirety of their productive years. She speaks for greater numbers than I possibly can. Only the fluency of her English and the anger, rather than fear, born of confidence from her education, differentiate her from the seamstresses, the domestics, the technicians, the shop owners, the millions of hard-working but effectively silenced documented immigrants as well as their less fortunate "illegal" brothers and sisters.   12

Nearly 20 years ago, when I was living in my husband's ancestral homeland of Canada, I was always well-employed but never allowed to feel part of the local Quebec or larger Canadian society. Then, through a Green Paper that invited a national referendum on the unwanted side effects of "nontraditional" immigration, the Government officially turned against its immigrant communities, particularly those from South Asia.   13

I felt then the same sense of betrayal that Mira feels now. I will never forget the pain of that sudden turning, and the casual racist outbursts the Green Paper elicited. That sense of betrayal had its desired effect and drove me, and thousands like me, from the country.   14

Mira and I differ, however, in the ways in which we hope to interact with the country that we have chosen to live in. She is happier to live in America as expatriate Indian than as an immigrant American. I need to feel like a part of the community I have adopted (as I tried to feel in Canada as   15 well). I need to put roots down, to vote and make the difference that I can. The price that the immigrant willingly pays, and that the exile avoids, is the trauma of self-transformation.

• • •

Comprehension

1. At first, how long did Mukherjee and her sister intend to stay in America? Why did they change their plans?

2. What does Mukherjee mean when she says she welcomed the "emotional strain" of "marrying outside [her] ethnic community" (5)?

3. In what ways is Mukherjee different from her sister? What kind of relationship do they have?

4. Why does Mukherjee's sister feel used? Why does she say that America has "'change[d] its rules in midstream'" (8)?

5. According to Mukherjee, how is her sister like all immigrants who "have stayed rooted in one job, one city, one house, one ancestral culture, one cuisine, for the entirety of their productive years" (12)?

Purpose and Audience

1. What is Mukherjee's thesis? At what point does she state it?

2. At whom is Mukherjee aiming her remarks? Immigrants like herself? Immigrants like her sister? General readers? Explain.

3. What is Mukherjee's purpose? Is she trying to inform? To move readers to action? To accomplish something else? Explain.

Style and Structure

1. What basis for comparison exists between Mukherjee and her sister? Where in the essay does Mukherjee establish this basis?

2. Is this essay a point-by-point or a subject-by-subject comparison? Why do you think Mukherjee chose the strategy she did?

3. What points does Mukherjee discuss for each subject? Should she have discussed any other points?

4. What transitional words and phrases does Mukherjee use to signal shifts from one point to another?

5. How effective is Mukherjee's conclusion? Does it summarize the essay's major points? Would another strategy be more effective? Explain.

Vocabulary Projects

1. Define each of the following words as it is used in this selection.

certifications (3)	perspective (7)	superficial (7)
mongrelization (5)	mythic (7)	scrutiny (7)

discretion (7)   divergence (11)   saris (11)
curtailing (8)   expatriate (11)   trauma (15)

2. What, according to Mukherjee, is the difference between an *immigrant* and an *exile* (15)? What are the connotations of these two words? Do you think the distinction Mukherjee makes is valid?

Journal Entry

Do you think Mukherjee respects her sister's decision? From your perspective, which sister has made the right choice?

Writing Workshop

1. Assume that her sister, Mira, has just read Mukherjee's essay and wants to respond to it. Write an email from Mira comparing her position about assimilation to that of Mukherjee. Make sure you explain Mira's position and address Mukherjee's points about assimilation.

2. Have you ever moved from one town or city to another? Write an essay comparing the two places. Your thesis statement should indicate whether you are emphasizing similarities or differences and convey your opinion of the new area. (If you have never moved, write an essay comparing two places you are familiar with — your college and your high school, for example.)

3. Assume you had to move to another country. Where would you move? Would you, like Mukherjee, assimilate into your new culture, or would you, like her sister, retain your own cultural values? Write an essay comparing life in your new country with life in the United States. (If you have already moved from another country, compare your life in the United States with your life in your country of origin.) Include at least one quotation from Mukherjee's essay in your introduction, and be sure to document the quotation and to include a works-cited page. (See the Appendix for information on documentation formats.)

Combining the Patterns

Do you think Mukherjee should have used **cause and effect** to structure a section explaining why she and her sister are so different? Explain what such a section would add to or take away from the essay.

Thematic Connections

- "Only Daughter" (page 97)
- "Sixty-Nine Cents" (page 102)
- "The Untouchable" (page 512)
- "The Myth of the Latin Woman: I Just Met a Girl Named Maria" (page 730)

ELLEN LAIRD

I'm Your Teacher, Not Your Internet-Service Provider

An educator and essayist for over thirty years, Ellen Laird believes that technology has forever changed both teaching and learning, as the following essay, originally published in the *Chronicle of Higher Education*, suggests.

Background on "distance learning"

Correspondence schools began to appear in the United States in the late nineteenth century, facilitated to a large degree by an extensive and efficient national postal service. These schools allowed students to receive study materials by mail and to complete examinations and other written work that they then submitted, again by mail, to a central departmental office for response and grading by instructors. For the most part, correspondence schools tended to focus on technical curricula, although some programs were geared toward a more traditional liberal arts curriculum. By the 1930s, correspondence schools had entered a period of decline as an increase in the number of high school graduates and the rise of junior colleges meant that students were more likely to have hands-on educational opportunities close to home. Then, beginning in the 1960s, the concept was revived through the broadcast of publicly funded televised courses, again with a mail-based system for transmitting written materials. Today, many universities have Internet-based distance-learning programs.

The honeymoon is over. My romance with distance teaching is losing its spark. Gone are the days when I looked forward to each new online encounter with students, when preparing and posting a basic assignment was a thrilling adventure, when my colleagues and friends were well-wishers, cautiously hopeful about my new entanglement. What remains is this instructor, alone, often in the dark of night, facing the reality of my online class and struggling to make it work.

After four years of Internet teaching, I must pause. When pressed to demonstrate that my online composition class is the equivalent of my classroom-based composition sections, I can do so professionally and persuasively. On the surface, course goals, objectives, standards, outlines, texts, Web materials, and so forth, are identical. But my fingers are crossed.

The two experiences are as different as a wedding reception and a rave. The nonlinear nature of online activity and the well-ingrained habits of Web use involve behavior vastly different from that which fosters success in the traditional college classroom. Last fall, my online students ranged from ages fifteen to fifty, from the home-schooled teen to the local union presi-

dent. Yet all brought to class assumptions and habits that sometimes inter-
fered with learning and often diminished the quality of the experience for
all of us. As a seasoned online instructor, I knew what to expect and how to
help students through the inevitable. But for the uninitiated, the reality of
online teaching can be confounding and upsetting. It can make a talented
teacher feel like an unmitigated failure.

If faculty members, whether well established or new, are to succeed in   4
online teaching, they must be prepared for attitudes and behaviors that
permeate Web use but undermine teaching and learning in the Web classroom. Potential online instructors are generally offered technical training
in file organization, course-management software use, and the like. But
they would be best served by an unfiltered look at what really happens
when the student logs into class, however elegantly designed the course
may be. A few declarative sentences drafted for my next online syllabus may
suffice:

The syllabus is not a restaurant menu.

In sections offered in campus classrooms, my students regard the syl-   5
labus as a fixed set of requirements, not as a menu of choices. They accept
the sequence and format in which course material is provided for them.
They do not make selections among course requirements according to
preference.

Online? Not so. Each semester, online students howl electronically   6
about having to complete the same assignments in the same sequence
required of my face-to-face students. Typical Internet users, these students
are accustomed to choices online. They enjoy the nonlinear nature of Web
surfing; they would be hard pressed to replicate the sequence of their activity without the down arrow beside the URL box on their browsers.

To their detriment, many of these students fail to consider that Web   7
learning is different from Web use, particularly in a skills-based course like
composition. They find it hard to accept, for example, that they must focus
on writing a solid thesis before tackling a research paper. Most would prefer to surf from one module of material to the next and complete what
appeals to them rather than what is required of them.

The difference between students' expectations and reality frustrates us   8
all. In traditional classrooms, students do not pick up or download only
the handouts that appeal to them; most do not try to begin the semester's
final project without instruction in the material on which it is based. Yet,
online students expect such options.

Even Cinderella had a deadline.

Students in my traditional classes certainly miss deadlines. But they   9
generally regard deadlines as real, if not observable; they recognize an

instructor's right to set due dates; and they accept the consequences of missing them to be those stated on the syllabus.

Not so with my online students. Neither fancy font nor flashing bullet can stir the majority to submit work by the published deadline. Students seem to extend the freedom to choose the time and place of their course work to every aspect of the class. Few request extensions in the usual manner. Instead, they announce them. One student, for example, emailed me days after a paper was due, indicating that he had traveled to New York for a Yankees' game and would submit the essay in a couple of weeks. 10

All course components do not function at the speed of the Internet.

As relaxed as my online students are about meeting deadlines, they begin the course expecting instantaneous service. The speed of Internet transmission seduces them into seeking and expecting speed as an element of the course. Naturally, students' emphasis on rapidity works against them. The long, hard, eventually satisfying work of thinking, doing research, reading, and writing has no relationship to bandwidth, processor speed, or cable modems. 11

At the same time, it takes me a long time to respond thoughtfully to students' work, particularly their writing. Each semester, online students require help in understanding that waiting continues to be part of teaching and learning, that the instructor is not another version of an Internet-service provider, to be judged satisfactory or not by processing speed and 24/7 availability. 12

There are no sick or personal days in cyberspace.

In my traditional classes, I refrain from informing students that I will be out of town for a weekend, that I need a root canal, or that my water heater failed before work. My face-to-face students can read my expression and bearing when they see me; thus, I can usually keep personal explanations to a professional minimum. 13

In my online class, however, students cannot see the bags under my eyes or the look of exuberance on my face. They cannot hear the calm or the shake in my voice. Thus, for the smooth functioning of the course, I willingly provide details about where I am and what I am doing, so students can know what to expect. 14

However, I am still troubled by the email message from an online student that began, "I know you are at your father's funeral right now, but I just wondered if you got my paper." Surely, he hesitated before pushing "send," but his need for reassurance prevailed. And so it goes, all semester long. There simply isn't room in an online class for the messiness of ordinary life, the students' or mine. Nor is there room for the extraordi- 15 nary — the events of September 11, for example. As long as the server functions, the course is always on, bearing down hard on both students and instructor.

Still, students will register for online classes under circumstances that would prohibit them from enrolling in a course on the campus. The welder compelled to work mandatory overtime, the pregnant woman due before midsemester, and the newly separated security guard whose wife will not surrender the laptop all arrive online with the hope and the illusion that, in cyberspace, they can accomplish what is temporarily impossible for them on campus.

I am not on your buddy list.

The egalitarian atmosphere of the Internet chat room transfers rapidly and inappropriately to the online classroom. Faceless and ageless online, I am, at first, addressed as a peer. If students knew that I dress like many of their mothers, or that my hair will soon be more gray than brown, would their exchanges with me be different? I reveal what I want them to know — the date of my marathon, my now-deceased dog's consumption of a roll of aluminum foil, my one gig as a cocktail-lounge pianist — but little of what one good look at me, in my jumper and jewelry, would tell them.

They, on the other hand, hold back nothing. Confessional writing, always a challenge in composition, can easily become the norm online. So can racist, sexist, and otherwise offensive remarks — even admissions of crimes. The lack of a face to match with a rhetorical voice provides the illusion of anonymity, and thus the potential for a no-holds-barred quality to every discussion thread. The usual restraint characterizing conversation among classroom acquaintances evaporates online within about two weeks. Private conversations fuse with academic discussion before an instructor can log in.

Are there strategies to manage these and similar difficulties? Of course there are. Thus, I continue with online teaching and welcome both its challenges and its rewards. But educators considering online teaching need to know that instruction in person and online are day and night. They must brace themselves for a marriage of opposites, and build large reserves of commitment, patience, and wherewithal if the relationship is to succeed.

•   •   •

Comprehension

1. Why does Laird say that her "honeymoon" with distance learning is over (1)?
2. According to Laird, why are Internet teaching and classroom-based teaching different? How does she explain the differences?

3. What does Laird mean when she says that potential online instructors "would be best served by an unfiltered look at what really happens when the student logs into class" (4)?

4. In what way does classroom-based teaching limit students' choices? How is Internet teaching different?

5. In paragraph 11, Laird says that "the long, hard, eventually satisfying work of thinking, doing research, reading, and writing has no relationship to bandwidth, processor speed, or cable modems." What does she mean?

Purpose and Audience

1. What is the thesis of this essay?

2. To whom do you think Laird is addressing her essay? Instructors? Students? Both?

3. What do you think Laird is trying to accomplish in her essay? Is she successful?

4. Does Laird assume that her readers are familiar with Internet-based teaching, or does she assume they are relatively unfamiliar with it? How can you tell?

Style and Structure

1. Is this essay a point-by-point or subject-by-subject comparison? Why do you think Laird chose this strategy?

2. Laird highlights "a few declarative sentences" (4) in boldface throughout her essay. What is the function of these sentences?

3. Does Laird seem to favor one type of teaching over another? Is she optimistic or pessimistic about the future of Internet teaching? Explain.

4. Does Laird indicate how students feel about Internet teaching? Should she have spent more time exploring this issue?

5. In her conclusion, Laird asks, "Are there strategies to manage these and similar difficulties?" Her answer: "Of course there are." Should she have listed some of these strategies in her conclusion? Why do you think she does not?

Vocabulary Projects

1. Define each of the following words as it is used in this selection.

   nonlinear (3)   permeate (4)
   inevitable (3)   declarative (4)
   uninitiated (3)   consequences (9)
   unmitigated (3)   wherewithal (19)

2. Laird spends four paragraphs introducing the points she intends to discuss. What words and phrases in these paragraphs indicate that she intends to write a comparison?

3. In paragraph 3, Laird says, "The two experiences are as different as a wedding reception and a rave." What are the denotations and connotations of

wedding reception and *rave*? What point is Laird trying to make with this comparison?

Journal Entry

Do you agree or disagree with Laird's assessment of Internet learning and classroom-based leaning? (If you have never taken an Internet course, discuss only her analysis of classroom-based learning.)

Writing Workshop

1. Write an essay in which you discuss whether you would like to take a distance-learning writing course. How do you think such a course would compare with a traditional classroom-based course? (If you are already taking such a course, compare it with a traditional writing course.)

2. Write an email to Laird in which you explain that like her, students also have difficulty adapting to Internet instruction. Address the specific difficulties that students encounter in such courses, and compare these difficulties with those they experience when they take a classroom-based course.

3. Read the following list of advantages of taking online courses:

   * A student who is ill will not miss classes.
   * Students who are employed and cannot come to campus can take courses.
   * Nontraditional students — the elderly and disabled, for example — can take courses.
   * Courses are taken at any time, day or night.
   * Guest speakers who cannot travel to campus can be integrated into the course.

   Then, make a list of disadvantages (for example, students never have face-to-face contact with an instructor). Finally, write an essay in which you discuss whether the advantages of online instruction outweigh the disadvantages.

Combining the Patterns

Laird begins her essay with two **narrative** paragraphs. What is the purpose of these paragraphs? What other strategy could Laird have used to introduce her essay?

Thematic Connections

* "The Human Cost of an Illiterate Society" (page 248)
* "The Dog Ate My Disk, and Other Tales of Woe" (page 471)
* "On the Internet, There's No Place to Hide" (page 495)

JOHN DE GRAAF, DAVID WANN, AND THOMAS H. NAYLOR

Swollen Expectations

Over the past several decades, John De Graaf has written and produced fifteen programs for public television, including *Circle of Plenty, Green Plans,* and *Genetic Time Bomb.* He has received more than a hundred awards for his filmmaking. David Wann is a former official with the Environmental Protection Agency who now writes extensively about sustainable lifestyles. He is the author of the books *Deep Design: Pathways to a Livable Future* (1995) and *Simple Prosperity: Finding Real Wealth in a Sustainable Lifestyle* (2007). Thomas H. Naylor is professor emeritus of economics at Duke University, where he taught for thirty years. An international strategic management consultant to governments and corporations in more than thirty nations, Naylor has authored or coauthored a number of books, including *The Search for Meaning* (1994) and *Downsizing the U.S.A.* (1997). The following chapter from the three authors' book *Affluenza: The All-Consuming Epidemic* (2001) is based on a television program by De Graaf comparing the American passion for consumption to a disease.

Background on American consumerism in the 1950s

Following the economic hardships created by the Great Depression of the 1930s and the war years of the 1940s (when goods were scarce), the 1950s saw an explosion in American consumerism. The postwar economy was booming, incomes doubled over the decade, and the government's G.I. Bill provided low-cost mortgages to veterans, allowing many more Americans to own their own homes, often in new suburban developments. Television sets, which were once very expensive, came within the price range of the average consumer. Soon a majority of American families owned one, along with other basic appliances, such as a range, a refrigerator, and a washing machine (clothes dryers and dishwashers were much rarer). Still, as the following selection points out, material expectations were considerably lower in the 1950s than they are for many today. The average home was far smaller. People generally had many fewer possessions, as demonstrated by the fewer and smaller closets built into most 1950s homes. And, while car ownership became increasingly common over the decade, most households owned only one car. The average family traveled modestly as well, generally vacationing in spots that could easily be reached by car; airline travel was, by and large, limited to the wealthy.

Take a walk down memory lane. Way down. If you're as old as we are, your memories carry you back to the 1950s, at least. The Second World War and the Great Depression were over, and America was on the move. Suburban houses going up everywhere. New cars rolling from the assembly lines and out onto new pavement. Ground breaking for the National

Defense Interstate Highway System, soon to stretch from sea to shining sea. A TV dinner (introduced in 1953) in every oven.

"It's a great life, eh Bob?" a man in a '50s commercial intones as a young couple and their tow-headed son sit on a couch watching the tube. "And tomorrow will be even better, for you and for all the people." Of course, the great life wasn't great for the millions who were poor or discriminated against. And even for middle-class America, it wasn't worry-free. On the same day in 1957 (October 4th) that *Leave It To Beaver* premiered on American television, those pesky Russians shot Sputnik* into space. Nikita Khrushchev** promised to bury us "in the peaceful field of economic competition." We know how that came out.

But 1957 was important for another less-heralded reason. It was the year the percentage of Americans describing themselves as "very happy" reached a peak never to be exceeded for the rest of the Twentieth Century.[1] The following year, a year when Americans bought 200 million "hula hoops," economist John Kenneth Galbraith published an influential book calling the United States "the affluent society."

We *felt* richer then than we do now. Most Americans today don't really think of themselves as affluent, says psychologist Paul Wachtel, "even though in terms of Gross National Product we have more than twice as much as we did then. Everybody's house has twice as much stuff in it. But the feeling of affluence, the experience of well-being, is no higher and perhaps even lower."[2]

Liberal economists argue that since about 1973 the real wages earned by middle-class Americans haven't really risen much and, for many workers, have actually declined. Young couples talk of not being able to afford what their parents had. By contrast, conservative economists contend that the rate of inflation as calculated by the federal government has been overstated and, therefore, that real wages have actually risen considerably. But one thing is incontestable: *We have a lot more stuff and much higher material expectations than previous generations did.*

Starter Castles

Take housing, for example. The average size of new homes is now more than double what it was in the 1950s, while families are smaller. LaNita Wacker, who owns Dream House Realty in Seattle, has been selling homes for more than a quarter of a century. She takes us on a drive through the neighborhoods near her office to explain what's happened.

She shows us houses built during every decade since World War II and describes how they've gotten bigger and bigger. Right after World War II, Wacker points out, 750 square feet was the norm (in Levittown, for example). "Then in the '50s," she says, "they added 200 square feet, so 950

---

* EDS. NOTE — The first artificial satellite.
** EDS. NOTE — Premier of the Soviet Union during the 1950s and 1960s.

was the norm." By the '60s, 1,100 square feet was typical, and by the '70s, 1,350. Now it's 2,300.

LaNita Wacker started selling homes in 1972, "right about the time we moved from a single bath to the demand for a double bath."[3] Two-car garages came in then too, and by the late '80s many homes were being built with three-car garages. That's 600 to 900 square feet of garage space alone, "as much square footage as an entire family used in the early '50s," Wacker says. "It would house an entire family. But we have acquired a lot of stuff to store." 8

To drive the point home, Wacker takes us by a huge home with a four-car garage. Expensive cars and a boat are parked outside. The owner comes out wondering why LaNita is so interested in his place. "I own Dream House Realty," she says. "And yours is a dream house." "It was built to the specifications of my charming wife," the man replies with a laugh. "So why four garages?" asks LaNita. "It's probably because of storage," the man replies, explaining that the garages are filled with family possessions. "You never have enough storage so you can never have enough garages," he adds cheerfully. LaNita asks if he has children. "They're gone now," he replies. "It's just me and the wife." 9

The four-car garage is an exception, no doubt. But everyone expects larger homes now. "A master bedroom in the '50s would be about 130 square feet," explains Wacker. "Now, even in moderately priced homes, you're talking about maybe 300 square feet devoted to the master bedroom." 10

In recent years more than ever, homes have become a symbol of conspicuous consumption, as beneficiaries of the recent stock market boom and unparalleled economic expansion have begun, in many communities, to buy real estate, bulldoze existing (and perfectly functional) homes, and replace them with megahouses of 10,000 square feet and more. "Starter castles," some have named them. Others call them "Monster Homes." 11

On America's Streets of Dreams, the competition is fierce. McMansions . . . Double McMansions . . . Deluxe McMansions . . . Deluxe McMansions with Cheese . . . Full Garage Deals . . . each one a little bigger and glitzier, popping up like mushrooms in a frenzy of home wars. In places like the spectacular mountain towns of the West, many such megahomes are actually *second homes,* mere vacation destinations for the newly rich. 12

Better than Tail Fins

A similar story presents itself with automobiles. In 1957, when Ford had a better idea called the Edsel,* cars were big and chromey, but they were far from the sophisticated machines we drive today. A 1960 Ford commercial shows crowds of people admiring new Fairlanes, Thunderbirds, and Falcons, surrounded by twinkling stars as if touched by Tinkerbell. It is, the ad proclaims, "the Wonderful New World of Ford." But in that won- 13

---

* EDS. NOTE — A famously unsuccessful Ford model.

derful new world, much of what we now take for granted as standard automobile features wasn't even available in luxury models.

In 1960, for example, fewer than five percent of new cars had air condi-   14
tioning. Now 90 percent do. Mike Sillivan, a veteran Toyota salesman in
Seattle, says that "today, people's expectations are much higher. They want
amenities — power steering, power brakes as standard, premium sound
systems."[4] The car of today is a different animal from that of a generation
ago. Filled with computer technology. And, after a decade's hiatus following the "energy crisis" of the mid '70s, big is back.

Until the recent price hike, gasoline costs for Americans were at an all-   15
time low in real dollar terms. Worries about fuel efficiency were forgotten
as we bought gas-guzzling four-wheel drive wagons called sport utility
vehicles (some call them Suburban Assault Vehicles). In the late '90s half of
all new cars sold were SUVs and light trucks, exempted from federal fuel
efficiency standards. Roomy, comfy, and costly, SUVs just keep getting
bigger.

Car Wars

Until recently, the 18-foot-long Chevy Suburban set the standard for   16
gigantism. Now, not to be outdone, Ford has introduced the Excursion, a
7,000-pound titan that is a foot longer than the Suburban. Ford Motors
Chairman William Ford even apologized for making so many SUVs, calling
his Excursion "the Ford Valdez"* for its propensity to consume fuel. He
condemned SUVs as wasteful and polluting, but said Ford would continue
to manufacture them anyway because they are extremely profitable.

"For a lot of people an SUV is a status symbol," says car salesman   17
Sillivan. "So they're willing to pay the thirty- to forty-odd thousand dollars
to drive one of these vehicles."

Never one to give up without a fight, General Motors has come charg-   18
ing back at Ford, acquiring ownership of the Hummer, a more luxurious
version of the military transport vehicle used during the Gulf War. GM is
"placing a big bet that the decade-long trend toward ever larger and more
aggressive-looking sport utility vehicles would continue," according to *The
New York Times*.[5] "It's like a tank with fashion," says one teenager quoted
by the *Times*. The kid says he loves the Hummer because "I like something
where I can look down into another car and give that knowing smile that
says 'I'm bigger than you.' It makes me feel powerful." More than a foot
wider than the Excursion, the Hummer retails for $93,000. GM predicts
these behemoths will be especially popular in (we are not making this
up) Manhattan, which is probably a good thing because you need to be on
the viewing platform of the Empire State Building to see over them.
But now what will Ford counter with, an even bigger SUV called The
Extinction?

---

* EDS. NOTE — Alaskan site of a dangerous 1989 oil tanker spill.

Weightless Tourism

Hummers on the streets of Manhattan. You might call them Saddam's   19
revenge. Or Ho-Hummers, if you compare them with yet another way to
drop nearly a hundred grand. Check out spacevoyages.com to find out
what may be the ultimate in swollen expectations. Just plop down $98 K,
including a $6 K deposit, and you, dear reader, can be an astronaut. Some-
time between 2003 and 2005, you'll be able to take a two-hour trip on a
rocket ship and spend about five weightless minutes in actual outer space.
Besides that, you'll get an "original and exclusive Space Adventures sub-
orbital flight certificate," a flight training suit, astronaut wings, a medal-
lion, a travel bag, photos, and a lifetime membership in the Space
Adventurers Club — all for less than a hundred thousand dollars. If that
sounds like a deal, you might want to stick a thermometer in your mouth
right away. Ten . . . nine . . . eight . . .*

Let's Do Lunch

Consider food. The '50s did give us TV dinners. Turkey, peas, and   20
mashed potatoes in a throwaway tray for sixty-nine cents, thank you Swan-
son's. As kids, we considered them delectable. Our standard diets were
pretty bland. Exotic meant soggy egg rolls, chow mein, and chop suey. Mexican was tacos and tamales (how did we cope without chimichangas and
chalupas?). Thai wasn't even part of our vocabulary. Now, city streets and
even suburban malls sport a United Nations of restaurants. We remember
waiting for certain fruits and vegetables to be in season. Now, there is no
season; everything is always available. When it's winter here, it's summer in
New Zealand, after all. Yet we often feel deprived. Strawberries lose their
flavor when you can have them all the time. More choices and more diversity certainly aren't a bad thing, but they come at a cost. The exotic quickly
becomes commonplace and boring, requiring ever newer and more expensive menus.

Take coffee. Until recently, we took it as watery brown stuff made bear-   21
able by gobs of sugar. Now, specialty coffees are everywhere. NPR radio
host Scott Simon was surprised a few years ago when he stopped at a service station in rural Washington State. In the station's mini-mart was an
espresso stand with so many types of coffee drinks to offer that Simon
longed for an Italian dictionary to identify them. No need. The kid behind
the counter with his baseball cap on backwards knew them all.

Eating out used to be a special occasion. Now we spend more money   22
on restaurant food than on the food we cook ourselves. Swelling expectations. Swelling stomachs too, but that's another symptom.

---

* EDS. NOTE — As of this writing, private space vehicles are not expected to take paying passengers until at least 2009.

Invention Is the Mother of Necessity

Consider, also, the kinds of goods that were deemed luxuries as recently   23
as 1970, but are now found in well over half of U.S. homes, and thought of
by a majority of Americans as necessities: dishwashers, clothes dryers,
central heating and air conditioning, color and cable TV.[6] And back in
1970, there were no microwave ovens, VCRs, CD players, cell phones, fax
machines, compact discs, leaf blowers, Pokemon, or personal computers.
Now, more than half of us take all of these goods for granted and would
feel deprived without them. Well, OK, so you wouldn't feel deprived without Pokemon.

There always seems to be a "better" model that we've just gotta have.   24
Writing about Compaq's new iPaq 3600 Pocket PC, *Seattle Times* technology reporter Paul Andrews warns that the iPaq, with its "sleek Porsche-like
case and striking color screen," costs $500 more than an ordinary Palm
Pilot. "But without the color display, music, and photos of the iPaq, life
seems pretty dull," he laments.[7]

And take travel. We drive twice as much per capita as we did a half cen-   25
tury ago, and fly an amazing twenty-five times as much.[8] Middle-income
Americans seldom ventured more than a few hundred miles from home
then, even during two-week summer vacations. Now, many of us (not just
the rich) expect to spend occasional long weekends in Puerto Vallarta, or
(in the case of New Yorkers) in Paris. Everywhere, humble motels have been
replaced by elegant "inns," humble resorts by Club Meds. Now, "I need a
vacation" means I need to change continents for a few days.

The Changing Joneses

"Greed has infected our society. It is the worst infection," says the real   26
Patch Adams, the doctor who was portrayed by Robin Williams in a popular Hollywood film.[9] He's right only to a degree. It may be fear rather than
greed that primarily drives our swelling expectations. Fear of not succeeding in the eyes of others. In one magazine ad from the '50s, readers are
encouraged to "keep up with the Joneses" by driving what they're driving: a
Chevy. A Chevy sedan at that, not even a Corvette. Just about the cheapest
car around, even then.

But the mythical Joneses don't drive Chevrolets any more. And they're   27
no longer your next door neighbors either, folks who make roughly what
you do. Economist Juliet Schor studied people's attitudes about consumption in a large corporation and found that most Americans now compare
themselves with coworkers or television characters when they think about
what they "need."

But corporations have become increasingly stratified economically in   28
recent years. One frequently comes into contact with much-better-paid colleagues than oneself. Their cars, clothes, and travel plans reflect their
higher incomes, yet set the standards for everyone in the firm.

Likewise, says Schor, "TV shows a very inflated standard of living rela-   29
tive to what the true standard of living of the American public is. People on
television tend to be upper middle class or even rich, and people who watch
a lot of TV have highly inflated views of what the average American has.
For example, people who are heavy TV watchers vastly exaggerate the number of Americans with swimming pools, tennis courts, maids, and planes,
and their own expectations of what they should have also become inflated,
so they tend to spend more and save less."[10]

Schor says that as the gap between rich and poor grew during the   30
1980s, people with relatively high incomes began to feel deprived in comparison to those who were suddenly making even more. "They started to
feel 'poor on $100,000 a year' as the well-known phrase puts it, because
they were comparing themselves to the Donald Trumps and the other
newly wealthy." It happened all the way down the income line, Schor says.
"Everybody felt worse compared to the role models, those at the top." Polls
now show that Americans believe they need $75,000 (for a family of four)
just to lead a "minimum" middle-class life.

I've Got Mine, Jack

In the years just after World War II, the super-rich sought to conceal   31
their profligacy, but since Ronald Reagan's first inaugural ball many have
begun to flaunt it again. As economist Robert Frank points out, there's
been a rush on $15,000 purses, $10,000 watches, even $65 million private
jets. Twenty million Americans now own big-screen TVs costing at least
$2,000 each. Some buy their children $5,000 life-size reproductions of
Darth Vader and $18,000 replicas of Range Rovers, $25,000 birthday parties and million-dollar bar mitzvahs.[11]

Thus from the hot zones of popular culture and stratified workplaces,   32
our new Joneses — consciously or otherwise — spread the affluenza virus,
swelling our expectations as never before. And stuffing us up.

•   •   •

Endnotes

1. David Meyer, *The American Paradox*, p. 136.
2. Personal interview, April 1996.
3. Personal interview, September 1996.
4. Personal interview, September 1996.
5. Keith Bradshear, "GM Has High Hopes for Road Warriors," *New York Times,* August 6, 2000.
6. See the wealth of information on changing expectations in Richard McKenzie's *The Paradox of Progress*.
7. Paul Andrews, "Compaq's new iPac may be the PC for your pocket," *Seattle Times,* November 5, 2000.

8.   *All-Consuming Passion,* p. 4.

9.   Personal interview, October 1987.

10.   Personal interview, May 1997.

11.   James Lardner, "The Urge to Splurge," *U.S. News and World Report,* May 24, 1998.

Comprehension

1. Why do De Graaf, Wann, and Naylor think that 1957 was an important year? What is odd about the fact that most Americans today do not consider themselves affluent?

2. What do liberal economists say about wages? How do their ideas differ from those of conservative economists?

3. How are houses built today different from those built in the 1950s, 1960s, 1970s, and 1980s? How are these differences significant?

4. According to the authors, why do Americans seem to be buying bigger and bigger automobiles? What do the authors see as the implications of this trend?

5. What do most Americans compare themselves to when they form their attitudes about consumption? How do these comparisons cause dissatisfaction?

Purpose and Audience

1. At what point do the authors state their thesis? Why do they state it where they do?

2. What preconceptions do the authors seem to have about their readers? How can you tell?

3. What is the authors' purpose? To instruct? To persuade? To entertain? Do they have any other purpose? Explain.

Style and Structure

1. Why do the authors begin with "a walk down memory lane" (1)? What does this look at the past contribute to the essay?

2. What two things are the authors comparing? Is this selection organized as a subject-by-subject or a point-by-point comparison? Why do you think the authors chose the strategy they did?

3. What purpose do the headings serve? Are these headings helpful, or do they just get in the way?

4. What transitions do the authors use to signal their movement from one point to another?

5. What strategy do the authors use in their conclusion? Is the strategy effective? Why or why not?

Vocabulary Projects

1. Define each of the following words as it is used in this selection.

intones (2)	consumption (11)	exotic (20)
affluent (3)	hiatus (14)	stratified (28)
inflation (5)	status (17)	conceal (31)
conspicuous (11)	behemoths (18)	flaunt (31)

2. In their conclusion, the authors coin (invent) a new word: *affluenza*. What two words did they use to form this new word? What do you think this word means? Did the authors have to coin a word, or could they have used a word already in the language? Explain.

Journal Entry

Do you think the authors characterize society accurately, or do they overstate their case? For example, do you know people who suffer from *affluenza*?

Writing Workshop

1. Write an essay comparing your home or car with the ones the authors discuss in their essay.
2. Interview your parents or grandparents, and ask them about the trends the authors discuss. Then, write an essay agreeing or disagreeing with their thesis. Support your thesis by comparing the authors' observations with those of the people you interviewed.
3. Do you expect to be more or less affluent than your parents? Write an essay comparing where your parents are now to where you expect to be when you are their age. Your essay can be either serious or humorous.

Combining the Patterns

This essay contains a number of **exemplification** paragraphs — for example, paragraphs 6 and 9. What do these paragraphs add to the essay? Would more such paragraphs be helpful?

Thematic Connections

- "Once More to the Lake" (page 183)
- "The Human Cost of an Illiterate Society" (page 248)
- "The 'Black Table' Is Still There" (page 345)
- "On Dumpster Diving" (page 714)

ALEX WRIGHT

Friending, Ancient or Otherwise

Alex Wright is a writer and information design consultant whose design work has won numerous industry awards, including a Webby nomination and Adobe System's American Graphic Design Award. His writing has appeared in such publications as Salon.com, the *Christian Science Monitor*, the *Utne Reader*, *Yankee*, and *Library Journal*, and he is also a popular speaker and lecturer. Wright's first book, *Glut: Mastering Information through the Ages*, was published in 2007. The following essay originally appeared on the op-ed page of the *New York Times*.

Background on social networking sites

Social networking sites began to appear with little fanfare in the late 1990s, but it was the debut of Friendster in early 2003 that ushered in a boom in such sites. (Friendster signed up three million members within its first six months.) Started as a way for people to meet potential dates by networking among friends of friends, Friendster was soon eclipsed by the more generally "friend"-oriented MySpace (which started out by allowing members to post lists of their favorite music). MySpace remains the most popular social networking site, with over fifty million members; others include Facebook, Xanga, Orcut, Bebo, Tribe, and Linkedin (as well as special-interest sites). In all, well over 100 million people are registered on such sites worldwide. While for the most part a relatively harmless way for friends to stay in touch, sites like MySpace have proved perilous as well. Young people, in particular, have often failed to consider the consequences of posting private information and revealing pictures in these very public forums. Even more seriously, such sites have become an easy place for sexual predators to find young victims, using false profiles to lure vulnerable teenagers into dangerous face-to-face meetings.

The growing popularity of social networking sites like Facebook, MySpace, and Second Life has thrust many of us into a new world where we make "friends" with people we barely know, scrawl messages on each other's walls, and project our identities using totem-like visual symbols. 1

We're making up the rules as we go. But is this world as new as it seems? 2

Academic researchers are starting to examine that question by taking an unusual tack: exploring the parallels between online social networks and tribal societies. In the collective patter of profile-surfing, messaging and "friending," they see the resurgence of ancient patterns of oral communication. 3

"Orality is the base of all human experience," says Lance Strate, a communications professor at Fordham University and devoted MySpace user. 4

He says he is convinced that the popularity of socal networks stems from their appeal to deep-seated, prehistoric patterns of human communication. "We evolved with speech," he says. "We didn't evolve with writing."

The growth of social networks — and the Internet as a whole — stems largely from an outpouring of expression that often feels more like "talking" than writing: blog posts, comments, homemade videos and, lately, an outpouring of epigrammatic one-liners broadcast using services like Twitter and Facebook status updates (usually proving Gertrude Stein's* maxim that "literature is not remarks").   5

"If you examine the Web through the lens of orality, you can't help but see it everywhere," says Irwin Chen, a design instructor at Parsons who is developing a new course to explore the emergence of oral culture online. "Orality is participatory, interactive, communal, and focused on the present. The Web is all of these things."   6

An early student of electronic orality was the Rev. Walter J. Ong, a professor at St. Louis University and student of Marshall McLuhan** who coined the term "secondary orality" in 1982 to describe the tendency of electronic media to echo the cadences of earlier oral cultures. The work of Father Ong, who died in 2003, seems especially prescient in light of the social-networking phenomenon. "Oral communication," as he put it, "unites people in groups."   7

In other words, oral culture means more than just talking. There are subtler—and perhaps more important—social dynamics at work.   8

Michael Wesch, who teaches cultural anthropology at Kansas State University, spent two years living with a tribe in Papua New Guinea, studying how people forge social relationships in a purely oral culture. Now he applies the same ethnographic research methods to the rites and rituals of Facebook users.   9

"In tribal cultures, your identity is completely wrapped up in the question of how people know you," he says. "When you look at Facebook, you can see the same pattern at work: people projecting their identities by demonstrating their relationships to each other. You define yourself in terms of who your friends are."   10

In tribal societies, people routinely give each other jewelry, weapons, and ritual objects to cement their social ties. On Facebook, people accomplish the same thing by trading symbolic sock monkeys, disco balls, and hula girls.   11

"It's reminiscent of how people exchange gifts in tribal cultures," says Dr. Strate, whose MySpace page lists his 1,335 "friends" along with his academic credentials and his predilection for *Battlestar Galactica*.   12

---

* EDS. NOTE — Gertrude Stein (1874–1946), American writer who became a major figure in the development of modern art and literature.

** EDS. NOTE — Marshall McLuhan (1911–1980), a Canadian communications theorist.

As intriguing as these parallels may be, they only stretch so far. There 13
are big differences between real oral cultures and the virtual kind. In tribal
societies, forging social bonds is a matter of survival; on the Internet, far
less so. There is presumably no tribal antecedent for popular Facebook rituals like "poking," virtual sheep-tossing, or drunk-dialing your friends.

Then there's the question of who really counts as a "friend." In tribal 14
societies, people develop bonds through direct, ongoing face-to-face contact. The Web eliminates that need for physical proximity, enabling people
to declare friendships on the basis of otherwise flimsy connections.

"With social networks, there's a fascination with intimacy because it 15
simulates face-to-face communication," Dr. Wesch says. "But there's also
this fundamental distance. That distance makes it safe for people to connect through weak ties where they can have the appearance of a connection
because it's safe."

And while tribal cultures typically engage in highly formalized rituals, 16
social networks seem to encourage a level of casualness and familiarity that
would be unthinkable in traditional oral cultures. "Secondary orality has a
leveling effect," Dr. Strate says. "In a primary oral culture, you would probably refer to me as 'Dr. Strate,' but on MySpace, everyone calls me 'Lance.'"

As more of us shepherd our social relationships online, will this level- 17
ing effect begin to shape the way we relate to each other in the offline world
as well? Dr. Wesch, for one, says he worries that the rise of secondary orality may have a paradoxical consequence: "It may be gobbling up what's left
of our real oral culture."

The more time we spend "talking" online, the less time we spend, well, 18
talking. And as we stretch the definition of a friend to encompass people
we may never actually meet, will the strength of our real-world friendships
grow diluted as we immerse ourselves in a lattice of hyperlinked "friends"?

Still, the sheer popularity of social networking seems to suggest that 19
for many, these environments strike a deep, perhaps even primal chord.
"They fulfill our need to be recognized as human beings, and as members
of a community," Dr. Strate says. "We all want to be told: You exist."

•   •   •

Comprehension

1. Why are academic researchers examining the similarities between "online
   social networks and tribal societies" (3)?

2. According to Lance Strate, what is the reason for the popularity of online
   social networks?

3. How are the rituals of Facebook users similar to those of tribal cultures?

4. What are the differences between "real oral cultures" and virtual cultures
   (13)?

5. According to Michael Wesch, how could online relationships damage our
   relationships in the real world?

Purpose and Audience

1. In paragraph 2, Wright states his thesis as a question. Would a declarative sentence have been more effective? Explain.
2. What is Wright's purpose in writing his essay? Does he achieve this purpose?
3. Does Wright assume that his readers are already familiar with social networking sites like Facebook and MySpace? How do you know?

Style and Structure

1. Why does Wright open his essay with a discussion of the "newness" of social networking sites?
2. What subjects is Wright comparing? Is he using a point-by-point or a subject-by-subject organization for his comparison? What are the advantages of the strategy he uses?
3. What transitions does Wright use to signal the shift from one subject to another? Could he have signaled these shifts more clearly? If so, how?
4. Does Wright make the same (or similar) points about both social networks and tribal societies? If not, what is missing?
5. Throughout his essay, Wright quotes a number of experts. How effectively do these quotations support his points?
6. What strategy does Wright use in his conclusion? Is this strategy effective? Why, or why not?

Vocabulary Projects

1. Define each of the following words as it is used in this selection.

scrawl (1)	dynamics (8)
totem (1)	ethnographic (9)
patter (3)	antecedent (13)
epigrammatic (5)	proximity (14)
maxim (5)	paradoxical (17)
cadences (7)	hyperlinked (18)
prescient (7)	

2. This essay contains a number of rather difficult words. Choose five of these words from the list above, and find synonyms for them in the online thesaurus at dictionary.com. Then, looking at the sentences that contain the original words, decide whether or not the synonyms you chose are superior to the original words.
3. In paragraph 7, Wright says that Walter J. Ong coined the term *secondary orality*. What does this coined term mean? Why do you think Ong felt he needed to coin a term to make his point?

Journal Entry

Do you believe that extensive use of social networking sites somehow impairs people's ability to interact with others in the real world?

Writing Workshop

1. Write an essay in which you tell how being involved with a social networking site has affected your life. Make sure you compare your life before you began using the social networking site with your life after you started to use it. Your essay can be either humorous or serious.
2. What rules govern communication on social networking sites? How are they different from the rules that govern face-to-face communication?
3. Expand your journal entry into an essay. Do you believe that "talking online" (18) impairs your ability to make friends in the real world? Include a quotation from Wright's essay in your discussion, and be sure to document it and include a works-cited page. (See the Appendix for information on documentation formats.)

Combining the Patterns

Wright uses two **cause-and-effect** paragraphs (17–18) at the end of his essay. Why does he include these two paragraphs? Why does he present the possible effects of social networking sites before he states his conclusion?

Thematic Connections

- "Once More to the Lake" (page 183)
- "College Pressures" (page 462)
- "On the Internet, There's No Place to Hide" (page 495)

DEBORAH TANNEN

Sex, Lies, and Conversation

Deborah Tannen was born in Brooklyn, New York, in 1945 and currently teaches at Georgetown University. Tannen has written and edited several scholarly books on the problems of communicating across cultural, class, ethnic, and sexual divides. She has also presented her research to the general public in newspapers and magazines and in her best-selling books *That's Not What I Meant!* (1986), *You Just Don't Understand: Women and Men in Conversation* (1990), and *Talking from 9 to 5* (1994). Her latest book is *You're Wearing That?: Understanding Mothers and Daughters in Conversation* (2006).

Background on men's and women's communication styles
Tannen wrote "Sex, Lies, and Conversation" because the chapter in *That's Not What I Meant!* on the difficulties men and women have communicating with one another got such a strong response. She realized the chapter might raise some controversy — that discussing their different communication styles might be used to malign men or to put women at a disadvantage — and indeed, some critics have seen her work as reinforcing stereotypes. Still, her work on the subject, along with that of other writers (most notably John Gray in his *Men Are from Mars, Women Are from Venus* series), has proved enormously popular. Much of the research about male and female differences in terms of brain function, relational styles and expectations, and evolutionary roles is still very controversial and continues to stir debate.

I was addressing a small gathering in a suburban Virginia living room — a women's group that had invited men to join them. Throughout the evening, one man had been particularly talkative, frequently offering ideas and anecdotes, while his wife sat silently beside him on the couch. Toward the end of the evening, I commented that women frequently complain that their husbands don't talk to them. This man quickly concurred. He gestured toward his wife and said, "She's the talker in our family." The room burst into laughter; the man looked puzzled and hurt. "It's true," he explained. "When I come home from work I have nothing to say. If she didn't keep the conversation going, we'd spend the whole evening in silence."

This episode crystallizes the irony that although American men tend to talk more than women in public situations, they often talk less at home. And this pattern is wreaking havoc with marriage.

The pattern was observed by political scientist Andrew Hacker in the late '70s. Sociologist Catherine Kohler Riessman reports in her new book *Divorce Talk* that most of the women she interviewed — but only a few of the men — gave lack of communication as the reason for their divorces.

Given the current divorce rate of nearly 50 percent, that amounts to millions of cases in the United States every year — a virtual epidemic of failed conversation.

In my own research, complaints from women about their husbands most often focused not on tangible inequities such as having given up the chance for a career to accompany a husband to his, or doing far more than their share of daily life-support work like cleaning, cooking, social arrangements, and errands. Instead, they focused on communication: "He doesn't listen to me," "He doesn't talk to me." I found, as Hacker observed years before, that most wives want their husbands to be, first and foremost, conversational partners, but few husbands share this expectation of their wives.

In short, the image that best represents the current crisis is the stereotypical cartoon scene of a man sitting at the breakfast table with a newspaper held up in front of his face, while a woman glares at the back of it, wanting to talk.

Linguistic Battle of the Sexes

How can women and men have such different impressions of communication in marriage? Why the widespread imbalance in their interests and expectations?

In the April issue of *American Psychologist,* Stanford University's Eleanor Maccoby reports the results of her own and others' research showing that children's development is most influenced by the social structure of peer interactions. Boys and girls tend to play with children of their own gender, and their sex-separate groups have different organizational structures and interactive norms.

I believe these systematic differences in childhood socialization make talk between women and men like cross-cultural communication, heir to all the attraction and pitfalls of that enticing but difficult enterprise. My research on men's and women's conversations uncovered patterns similar to those described for children's groups.

For women, as for girls, intimacy is the fabric of relationships, and talk is the thread from which it is woven. Little girls create and maintain friendships by exchanging secrets; similarly, women regard conversation as the cornerstone of friendship. So a woman expects her husband to be a new and improved version of a best friend. What is important is not the individual subjects that are discussed but the sense of closeness, of a life shared, that emerges when people tell their thoughts, feelings, and impressions.

Bonds between boys can be as intense as girls', but they are based less on talking, more on doing things together. Since they don't assume talk is the cement that binds a relationship, men don't know what kind of talk women want, and they don't miss it when it isn't there.

Boys' groups are larger, more inclusive, and more hierarchical, so boys must struggle to avoid the subordinate position in the group. This may play a role in women's complaints that men don't listen to them. Some men really don't like to listen, because being the listener makes them feel one-down, like a child listening to adults or an employee to a boss.

But often when women tell men, "You aren't listening," and the men protest, "I am," the men are right. The impression of not listening results from misalignments in the mechanics of conversation. The misalignment begins as soon as a man and a woman take physical positions. This became clear when I studied videotapes made by psychologist Bruce Dorval of children and adults talking to their same-sex best friends. I found that at every age, the girls and women faced each other directly, their eyes anchored on each other's faces. At every age, the boys and men sat at angles to each other and looked elsewhere in the room, periodically glancing at each other. They were obviously attuned to each other, often mirroring each other's movements. But the tendency of men to face away can give women the impression they aren't listening even when they are. A young woman in college was frustrated: Whenever she told her boyfriend she wanted to talk to him, he would lie down on the floor, close his eyes, and put his arm over his face. This signaled to her, "He's taking a nap." But he insisted he was listening extra hard. Normally, he looks around the room, so he is easily distracted. Lying down and covering his eyes helped him concentrate on what she was saying.

Analogous to the physical alignment that women and men take in conversation is their topical alignment. The girls in my study tended to talk at length about one topic, but the boys tended to jump from topic to topic. The second-grade girls exchanged stories about people they knew. The second-grade boys teased, told jokes, noticed things in the room, and talked about finding games to play. The sixth-grade girls talked about problems with a mutual friend. The sixth-grade boys talked about 55 different topics, none of which extended over more than a few turns.

Listening to Body Language

Switching topics is another habit that gives women the impression men aren't listening, especially if they switch to a topic about themselves. But the evidence of the 10th-grade boys in my study indicates otherwise. The 10th-grade boys sprawled across their chairs with bodies parallel and eyes straight ahead, rarely looking at each other. They looked as if they were riding in a car, staring out the windshield. But they were talking about their feelings. One boy was upset because a girl had told him he had a drinking problem, and the other was feeling alienated from all his friends.

Now, when a girl told a friend about a problem, the friend responded by asking probing questions and expressing agreement and understanding. But the boys dismissed each other's problems. Todd assured Richard that his drinking was "no big problem" because "sometimes you're funny when you're off your butt." And when Todd said he felt left out, Richard responded, "Why should you? You know more people than me."

Women perceive such responses as belittling and unsupportive. But   16
the boys seemed satisfied with them. Whereas women reassure each other
by implying, "You shouldn't feel bad because I've had similar experiences,"
men do so by implying, "You shouldn't feel bad because your problems
aren't so bad."

There are even simpler reasons for women's impression that men don't   17
listen. Linguist Lynette Hirschman found that women make more listener-
noise, such as "mhm," "uhuh," and "yeah," to show "I'm with you." Men,
she found, more often give silent attention. Women who expect a stream of
listener-noise interpret silent attention as no attention at all.

Women's conversational habits are as frustrating to men as men's are   18
to women. Men who expect silent attention interpret a stream of listener-
noise as overreaction or impatience. Also, when women talk to each other
in a close, comfortable setting, they often overlap, finish each other's sentences, and anticipate what the other is about to say. This practice, which I
call "participatory listenership," is often perceived by men as interruption,
intrusion, and lack of attention.

A parallel difference caused a man to complain about his wife, "She   19
just wants to talk about her own point of view. If I show her another view,
she gets mad at me." When most women talk to each other, they assume a
conversationalist's job is to express agreement and support. But many men
see their conversational duty as pointing out the other side of an argument. This is heard as disloyalty by women, and refusal to offer the requi-
site support. It is not that women don't want to see other points of view,
but that they prefer them phrased as suggestions and inquiries rather than
as direct challenges.

In his book *Fighting for Life,* Walter Ong points out that men use   20
"agonistic," or warlike, oppositional formats to do almost anything; thus
discussion becomes debate, and conversation a competitive sport. In contrast, women see conversation as a ritual means of establishing rapport. If
Jane tells a problem and June says she has a similar one, they walk away feeling closer to each other. But this attempt at establishing rapport can backfire when used with men. Men take too literally women's ritual "troubles
talk," just as women mistake men's ritual challenges for real attack.

The Sounds of Silence

These differences begin to clarify why women and men have such dif-   21
ferent expectations about communication in marriage. For women, talk
creates intimacy. Marriage is an orgy of closeness: you can tell your feelings
and thoughts, and still be loved. Their greatest fear is being pushed away.
But men live in a hierarchical world, where talk maintains independence
and status. They are on guard to protect themselves from being put down
and pushed around.

This explains the paradox of the talkative man who said of his silent   22
wife, "She's the talker." In the public setting of a guest lecture, he felt

challenged to show his intelligence and display his understanding of the lecture. But at home, where he has nothing to prove and no one to defend against, he is free to remain silent. For his wife, being home means she is free from the worry that something she says might offend someone, or spark disagreement, or appear to be showing off; at home she is free to talk.

The communication problems that endanger marriage can't be fixed by mechanical engineering. They require a new conceptual framework about the role of talk in human relationships. Many of the psychological explanations that have become second nature may not be helpful, because they tend to blame either women (for not being assertive enough) or men (for not being in touch with their feelings). A sociolinguistic approach by which male-female conversation is seen as cross-cultural communication allows us to understand the problem and forge solutions without blaming either party.   23

Once the problem is understood, improvement comes naturally, as it did to the young woman and her boyfriend who seemed to go to sleep when she wanted to talk. Previously, she had accused him of not listening, and he had refused to change his behavior, since that would be admitting fault. But then she learned about and explained to him the differences in women's and men's habitual ways of aligning themselves in conversation. The next time she told him she wanted to talk, he began, as usual, by lying down and covering his eyes. When the familiar negative reaction bubbled up, she reassured herself that he really was listening. But then he sat up and looked at her. Thrilled, she asked why. He said, "You like me to look at you when we talk, so I'll try to do it." Once he saw their differences as cross-cultural rather than right and wrong, he independently altered his behavior.   24

Women who feel abandoned and deprived when their husbands won't listen to or report daily news may be happy to discover their husbands trying to adapt once they understand the place of small talk in women's relationships. But if their husbands don't adapt, the women may still be comforted that for men, this is not a failure of intimacy. Accepting the difference, the wives may look to their friends or family for that kind of talk. And husbands who can't provide it shouldn't feel their wives have made unreasonable demands. Some couples will still decide to divorce, but at least their decisions will be based on realistic expectations.   25

In these times of resurgent ethnic conflicts, the world desperately needs cross-cultural understanding. Like charity, successful cross-cultural communication should begin at home.   26

• • •

Comprehension

1. What pattern of communication does Tannen identify at the beginning of her essay?
2. According to Tannen, what do women complain about most in their marriages?

3. What gives women the impression that men do not listen?

4. What characteristics of women's speech do men find frustrating?

5. According to Tannen, what can men and women do to remedy the communication problems that exist in most marriages?

Purpose and Audience

1. What is Tannen's thesis?

2. What is Tannen's purpose in writing this essay? Do you think she wants to inform or to persuade? On what do you base your conclusion?

3. Is Tannen writing for an expert audience or for an audience of general readers? To men, women, or both? How can you tell?

Style and Structure

1. What does Tannen gain by stating her thesis in paragraph 2 of the essay? Would there be any advantage in postponing the thesis statement until the end? Explain.

2. Is this essay a subject-by-subject or a point-by-point comparison? What does Tannen gain by organizing her essay the way she does?

3. Throughout her essay, Tannen cites scholarly studies and quotes statistics. How effectively does this information support her points? Could she have made a strong case without this material? Why, or why not?

4. Would you say Tannen's tone is hopeful, despairing, sarcastic, angry, or something else? Explain.

5. Tannen concludes her essay with a far-reaching statement. What do you think she hopes to accomplish with this conclusion? Is she successful? Explain your reasoning.

Vocabulary Projects

1. Define each of the following words as it is used in this selection.

concurred (1)	pitfalls (8)	rapport (20)
crystallizes (2)	subordinate (11)	ritual (20)
inequities (4)	misalignment (12)	orgy (21)
imbalance (6)	analogous (13)	sociolinguistic (23)
peer (7)	alienated (14)	forge (23)
organizational (7)	intrusion (18)	

2. Where does Tannen use professional **jargon** in this essay? Would the essay be more or less effective without these words? Explain.

Journal Entry

Based on your own observations of male-female communication, how accurate is Tannen's analysis? Can you relate an anecdote from your own life that illustrates (or contradicts) her thesis?

Writing Workshop

1. In another essay, Tannen contrasts the communication patterns of male and female students in classroom settings. After observing a few of your own classes, write an essay also drawing a comparison between the communication patterns of your male and female classmates.
2. Write an essay comparing the way male and female characters speak in films or on television. Use examples to support your points.
3. Write an essay comparing the vocabulary used in two different sports. Does one sport use more violent language than the other? For example, baseball uses the terms *bunt* and *sacrifice,* and football uses the terms *blitz* and *bomb.* Use as many examples as you can to support your points.

Combining the Patterns

Tannen begins her essay with an anecdote. Why does she begin with a paragraph of **narration**? How does this story set the tone for the rest of the essay?

Thematic Connections

- "Only Daughter" (page 97)
- "Why Marriage Is Good for You" (page 227)
- "I Want a Wife" (page 520)
- "The Wife-Beater" (page 528)

Sadie and Maud (Poetry)

Poet Gwendolyn Brooks (1917–2000) was born in Topeka, Kansas, and graduated from Wilson Junior College in Chicago, where she lived most of her life. She was on the faculty of Columbia College and Northeastern Illinois State College, and she was named the poet laureate of Illinois. Her first volume of poetry was *A Street in Bronzeville* (1945), named for the African-American neighborhood on the South Side of Chicago where she grew up. Among her many later collections are *Annie Allen* (1949), for which she was the first African American to win a Pulitzer Prize; *Riot* (1969), based on the violent unrest that gripped many inner-city neighborhoods following the assassination of Martin Luther King Jr.; and *Blacks* (1987). She also published books for children, a novel, and two volumes of her memoirs. The following poem is from *A Street in Bronzeville*.

Background on African Americans in the 1940s
Because deed restrictions in Chicago in the 1940s prevented blacks from buying property outside of Bronzeville, the area was home to African Americans from all income levels as well as to many thriving black-owned businesses. Still, the opportunities available to women like Sadie and Maud in the 1940s were limited. Only about 12 percent of African Americans completed four years of high school (although numbers were higher in the North than in the South), and many fewer went on to college. Six out of ten African-American women were employed in low-paying domestic service positions, while fewer than one percent held professional positions, primarily as teachers in segregated schools.

Maud went to college.
Sadie stayed at home.
Sadie scraped life
With a fine-tooth comb.

She didn't leave a tangle in.   5
Her comb found every strand.
Sadie was one of the livingest chits
In all the land.

Sadie bore two babies
Under her maiden name.   10
Maud and Ma and Papa
Nearly died of shame.

When Sadie said her last so-long
Her girls struck out from home.
(Sadie had left as heritage   15
Her fine-tooth comb.)

Maud, who went to college,
Is a thin brown mouse.
She is living all alone
In this old house.   20

. . .

Reading Literature

1. What two ideas is Brooks comparing in the poem? How does the speaker let readers know when she is shifting her focus from one subject to another?
2. How accurate do you think the speaker's portrayals are? Is the speaker stereotyping the two women?
3. What comment do you think the poem is making about education? About society? About women? About African-American women?

Journal Entry

Brooks wrote "Sadie and Maud" in 1945. What changes do you think she would have to make if she wrote her poem today?

Thematic Connections

- "Finishing School" (page 107)
- Declaration of Sentiments and Resolutions (page 581)
- "The Myth of the Latin Woman: I Just Met a Girl Named Maria" (page 730)

WRITING ASSIGNMENTS FOR COMPARISON AND CONTRAST

1. Find a description of the same news event in two different magazines or newspapers. Write a comparison-and-contrast essay discussing the similarities and differences between the two stories.

2. In the library, locate two children's books on the same subject — one written in the 1950s and one written within the past ten years. Write an essay discussing which elements are the same and which are different. Include a thesis statement about the significance of the differences between the two books. Make sure that you document all material you take from the two books and that you include a works-cited page. (See the Appendix for information on documentation formats.)

3. Write an essay about a relative or friend you have known since you were a child. Consider how your opinion of this person is different now from what it was then.

4. Write an essay comparing and contrasting the expectations that college professors and high school teachers have for their students. Cite your own experiences as examples.

5. Since you started college, how have you changed? Write an essay that answers this question.

6. Taking careful notes, watch a local television news program and then a national news broadcast. Write an essay comparing the two programs, paying particular attention to the news content and to the journalists' broadcasting styles.

7. Write an essay comparing your own early memories of school with those of a parent or an older relative.

8. How are the attitudes toward education different among students who work to finance their own education and students who do not? Your thesis statement should indicate what differences exist and why.

9. Compare and contrast the college experiences of commuters and students who live in dorms on campus. Interview people in your classes to use as examples.

10. Write an essay comparing any two groups that have divergent values — vegetarians and meat eaters or smokers and nonsmokers, for example.

11. How is being a participant — playing a sport or acting in a play, for instance — different from being a spectator? Write a comparison-and-contrast essay in which you answer this question.

COLLABORATIVE ACTIVITY FOR COMPARISON AND CONTRAST

Form groups of four students each. Assume your college has hired these groups as consultants to suggest solutions for several problems students have been complaining about. Select the four areas — food, campus safety, parking, and class scheduling, for example — you think need improvement. Then, as a group, write a short report to your college describing the present conditions in these areas, and compare them to the improvements you envision. (Be sure to organize your report as a comparison-and-contrast essay.) Finally, have one person from each group read the group's report to the class. Decide as a class which group has the best suggestion.

12

Classification and Division

WHAT IS CLASSIFICATION AND DIVISION?

Division is the process of breaking a whole into parts; **classification** is the process of sorting individual items into categories. In the following paragraph from "Pregnant with Possibility," Gregory J. E. Rawlins divides Americans into categories based on their access to computer technology:

Topic sentence identifies categories

Today's computer technology is rapidly turning us into three completely new races: the superpoor, the rich, and the superrich. The superpoor are perhaps eight thousand in every ten thousand of us. The rich — me and you — make up most of the remaining two thousand, while the superrich are perhaps the last two of every ten thousand. Roughly speaking, the decisions of two superrich people control what almost two thousand of us do, and our decisions, in turn, control what the remaining eight thousand do. These groups are really like races since the group you're born into often determines which group your children will be born into.

Through **classification and division**, we can make sense of seemingly random ideas by putting scattered bits of information into useful, coherent order. By breaking a large group into smaller categories and assigning individual items to larger categories, we can identify relationships between a whole and its parts and relationships among the parts themselves. Remember, though, that classification involves more than simply comparing two items or enumerating examples; when you classify, you sort individual examples into a variety of different categories.

In countless practical situations, classification and division bring order to chaos. For example, your iPod will *classify* your music, sorting individual songs into distinct genres — alternative rock, classical, country,

Latin, and so on. Similarly, numbers listed in your cell phone's address book are *divided* into three clearly defined categories: home, work, and mobile. Thus, order can be brought to your music and your phone numbers — just as it is brought to newspapers, department stores, supermarkets, biological hierarchies, and libraries — when a whole is divided into categories or sections and individual items are assigned to one or another of these subgroups.

Understanding Classification

Even though the interrelated processes of classification and division invariably occur together, they are two separate operations. When you **classify**, you begin with individual items and sort them into categories. Since a given item invariably has several different attributes, it can be classified in various ways. For example, the most obvious way to classify the students who attend your school might be according to their year in college. But you could also classify students according to their major, racial or ethnic background, home state, grade-point average, or any number of other principles. The **principle of classification** you choose — the quality your items have in common — would depend on how you wish to approach the members of this large and diverse group.

Understanding Division

Division is the opposite of classification. When you **divide**, you start with a whole (an entire class) and break it into its individual parts. For example, you might start with the large general class *television shows* and divide it into categories: *sitcoms, action/adventure, reality shows,* and so forth. You could then divide each of these still further. *Action/adventure programs,* for example, might include *Westerns, crime dramas, spy dramas,* and so on — and each of these categories could be further divided as well. Eventually, you would need to identify a particular principle of classification to help you assign specific programs to one category or another — that is, to classify them.

USING CLASSIFICATION AND DIVISION

Whenever you write an essay, you use classification and division to bring order to the invention stage of the writing process. For example, when you brainstorm, as Chapter 2 explains, you begin with your paper's topic and list all the ideas you can think of. Next, you *divide* your topic into logical categories and *classify* the items in your brainstorming notes into one category or another, perhaps narrowing, expanding, or eliminating some categories — or some ideas — as you go along. This sorting and grouping enables you to condense and shape your material until it eventually suggests a thesis and the main points your essay will develop.

More specifically, certain topics and questions, because of the way they are worded, immediately suggest a classification-and-division pattern. Suppose, for example, you are asked, "What kinds of policies can government implement to reduce the nation's budget deficit?" Here, the word *kinds* suggests classification and division. Other words — such as *types, varieties, aspects,* and *categories* — can also indicate that this pattern of development is called for.

PLANNING A CLASSIFICATION-AND-DIVISION ESSAY

Once you decide to use a classification-and-division pattern, you need to identify a **principle of classification**. Every group of people, things, or ideas can be categorized in many different ways. When you are at your college bookstore with limited funds, the cost of different books may be the only principle of classification you use when deciding which ones to buy. As you consider which books to carry across campus, however, weight may matter more. Finally, as you study and read, the usefulness of the books will determine which ones you concentrate on. Similarly, when you organize an essay, the principle of classification you choose is determined by your writing situation — your assignment, your purpose, your audience, and your special knowledge and interests.

Selecting and Arranging Categories

After you define your principle of classification and apply it to your topic, you should select your categories by dividing a whole class into parts and grouping a number of different items together within each part. Next, you should decide how you will treat the categories in your essay. Just as a comparison-and-contrast essay makes comparable points about its subjects, so your classification-and-division essay should treat all categories similarly. When you discuss comparable points for each category, your readers are able to understand your distinctions among categories as well as your definition of each category.

Finally, you should arrange your categories in some logical order so that readers can see how the categories are related and what their relative importance is. Whatever order you choose, it should be consistent with your purpose and with your essay's thesis.

✓ **CHECKLIST:** Establishing Categories

- **All the categories should derive from the same principle.** If you decide to divide *television shows* into *soap operas, crime shows,* and the like, it is not logical to include *children's programs,* for this category results from one principle (target audience) while the others result from another principle (genre). Similarly, if you were classifying undergraduates at your school according to their year, you would not include the category *students receiving financial aid.*

- **All the categories should be at the same level.** In the series *sitcoms, action/adventure,* and *Westerns,* the last item, *Westerns,* does not belong because it is at a lower level — that is, it is a subcategory of *action/adventure.* Likewise, *sophomores* (a subcategory of *undergraduates*) does not belong in the series *undergraduates, graduate students, continuing education students.*

- **You should treat all categories that are significant and relevant to your discussion.** Include enough categories to make your point, with no important omissions and no overlapping categories. In a review of a network's fall television lineup, the series *sitcoms, soap operas, crime shows,* and *detective shows* is incomplete because it omits important categories such as *news programs, game shows, reality shows,* and *documentaries;* moreover, *detective shows* may overlap with *crime shows.* In the same way, the series *freshmen, sophomores, juniors,* and *transfers* is illogical: the important group *seniors* has been omitted, and *transfers* may include *freshmen, sophomores,* and *juniors.*

Developing a Thesis Statement

Like other kinds of essays, a classification-and-division essay should have a thesis. Your **thesis statement** should identify your subject, introduce the categories you will discuss, and perhaps show readers the relationships of your categories to one another and to the subject as a whole. In addition, your thesis statement should tell your readers why your categories are significant or establish their relative value. For example, simply listing different kinds of investments would be pointless. Instead, your thesis statement might note their relative strengths and weaknesses and perhaps make recommendations based on your assessment. Similarly, a research paper about a writer's major works would accomplish little if it merely categorized his or her writings. Instead, your thesis statement should communicate your evaluation of these works, perhaps demonstrating that some deserve higher public regard than others.

Using Transitions

When you write a classification-and-division essay, you use transitional words and phrases both to introduce your categories (*the first category, one category*, and so on) and to move readers from one category to the next (*the second category, another category*, and so on). In addition, transitional words and expressions can show readers the relationships between categories — for example, whether one category is more important than another (*a more important category, the most important category*, and so on). A more complete list of transitions appears on page 43.

STRUCTURING A CLASSIFICATION-AND-DIVISION ESSAY

Once you have formulated your essay's thesis and established your categories, you should plan your classification-and-division essay around the same three major sections that other essays have: *introduction, body,* and *conclusion.* Your **introduction** should orient your readers by mentioning your topic, the principle for classifying your material, and the individual categories you plan to discuss; your thesis is also usually stated in the introduction. In the **body paragraphs**, you should treat the categories one by one in the same order as in your introduction. Finally, your **conclusion** should restate your thesis, summing up the points you have made and perhaps considering their implications.

Suppose you are preparing a research paper on Mark Twain's nonfiction works for an American literature course. You have read selections from *Roughing It, Life on the Mississippi,* and *The Innocents Abroad.* Besides these travel narratives, you have read parts of Twain's autobiography and some of his correspondence and essays. When you realize that the works you have studied can easily be classified as four different types of Twain's nonfiction — travel narratives, essays, letters, and autobiography — you decide to use classification and division to structure your essay. Therefore, you first divide the large class *Twain's nonfiction prose* into major categories — his travel narratives, essays, autobiography, and letters. Then, you classify the individual works, assigning each work to one of these categories, which you will discuss one at a time. Your purpose is to persuade readers to reconsider the reputations of some of these works, and you word your thesis statement accordingly. You might then prepare a formal outline like the one that follows for the body of your paper:

Thesis statement: Most readers know Mark Twain as a novelist, but his nonfiction works — his travel narratives, essays, letters, and especially his autobiography — deserve more attention.

I. Travel narratives
   A. Roughing It
   B. The Innocents Abroad
   C. Life on the Mississippi

    II. Essays
       A. "Fenimore Cooper's Literary Offenses"
       B. "How to Tell a Story"
       C. "The Awful German Language"
    III. Letters
       A. To W. D. Howells
       B. To his family
    IV. Autobiography

Because this will be a long essay, each of the outline's divisions will have several subdivisions, and each subdivision might require several paragraphs.

This outline illustrates the characteristics of an effective classification-and-division essay. To begin with, Twain's nonfiction works are classified according to a single principle of classification — literary genre. (Depending on your purpose, of course, another principle — such as theme or subject matter — could work just as well.) The outline also reveals that the paper's four categories are on the same level (each is a different literary genre) and that all relevant categories are included. Had you left out *essays,* for example, you would have been unable to classify several significant works of nonfiction.

This outline also arranges the four categories so that they will support your thesis most effectively. Because you believe Twain's travel narratives are somewhat overrated, you plan to discuss them early in your paper. Similarly, because you think the autobiography would make your best case for the merit of the nonfiction works as a whole, you decide it should be placed last. (Of course, you could arrange your categories in several other orders, such as from shorter to longer works or from least to most popular, depending on the thesis your paper will support.)

Finally, this outline reminds you to treat all categories comparably in your paper. Your case would be weakened if, for example, you inadvertently skipped style in your discussion of Twain's letters while discussing style for every other category. This omission might lead your readers to suspect that you had not done enough research on the letters or that the style of Twain's letters did not measure up to the style of his other works.

REVISING A CLASSIFICATION-AND-DIVISION ESSAY

When you revise a classsification-and-division essay, consider the items on the revision checklist on page 54. In addition, pay special attention to the items on the following checklist, which apply specifically to revising classification-and-division essays.

✓ **REVISION CHECKLIST:** Classification and Division

- Does your assignment call for classification and division?
- Have you identified a principle of classification for your material?

- Have you identified the categories you plan to discuss and decided how you will treat them?
- Have you arranged your categories in a logical order?
- Have you treated all categories similarly?
- Does your essay have a clearly stated thesis that identifies your subject and the categories you will discuss and indicates the significance of your classification?
- Have you used transitional words and phrases to show the relationships among categories?

EDITING A CLASSIFICATION-AND-DIVISION ESSAY

When you edit your classification-and-division essay, you should follow the guidelines on the editing checklists on pages 71, 74, and 76. In addition, you should focus on the grammar, mechanics, and punctuation issues that are particularly relevant to classification-and-division essays. One of these issues — using a colon to introduce your categories — is discussed below.

GRAMMAR IN CONTEXT: Using a Colon to Introduce Your Categories

When you state the thesis of a classification-and-division essay, you often give readers an overview by listing the categories you will discuss. You introduce this list of categories with a **colon**, a punctuation mark whose purpose is to direct readers to look ahead for a series, list, clarification, or explanation.

When you use a colon to introduce your categories, the colon must be preceded by a complete sentence.

CORRECT: "I see four kinds of pressure working on college students today: economic pressure, parental pressure, peer pressure, and self-induced pressure" (Zinsser 463).

INCORRECT: Four kinds of pressure working on college students today are: economic pressure, parental pressure, peer pressure, and self-induced pressure.

In any list or series of three or more categories, the categories should be separated by commas, with a comma preceding the *and* that separates the last two items. This last comma prevents confusion by ensuring that readers will be able to see at a glance exactly how many categories you are discussing.

(continued on next page)

(continued from previous page)

CORRECT: economic pressure, parental pressure, peer pressure, and self-induced pressure (four categories)

INCORRECT: economic pressure, parental pressure, peer pressure and self-induced pressure (without the final comma, it might appear you are only discussing three categories)

NOTE: Items in a list or series are always stated in **parallel** terms.

For more practice in using colons correctly, visit Exercise Central at **bedfordstmartins.com/patterns/colons**.

✓**EDITING CHECKLIST: Classification and Division**

- Do you introduce your list of categories with a colon preceded by a complete sentence?
- Are the items on your list of categories separated by commas?
- Do you include a comma before the *and* that connects the last two items in your list?
- Do you state the items on your list in parallel terms?

A STUDENT WRITER: Classification and Division

The following classification-and-division essay was written by Josie Martinez for an education course. Her assignment was to look back at her own education and to consider what she had learned so far, referring in her essay to William Zinsser's "College Pressures" (page 462). Josie's essay divides a whole — college classes — into four categories.

What I Learned (and Didn't Learn) in College

Introduction   In "College Pressures," William Zinsser notes the   1
disappearance of a time when college students "journeyed through college with a certain relaxation, sampling a wide variety of courses — music, art, philosophy, classics, anthropology, poetry, religion — that would send them out as liberally educated men and women" (464). The change in college students' focus is even more noticeable today than when Zinsser wrote his essay, and it represents a real loss for students. Taking a variety of different kinds of courses can educate students about a wide range of subjects, and it can also teach them about themselves.

Categories listed and explained

Despite the variety of experiences that different students have with different courses, most college classes can be classified into one of four categories: ideal classes, worthless classes, disappointing classes, and unexpectedly valuable classes. First are courses that students love — ideal learning environments in which they enjoy both the subject matter and the professor-student interaction. Far from these ideal courses are those that students find completely worthless in terms of subject matter, atmosphere, and teaching style. Somewhere between these two extremes are two kinds of courses that can be classified into another pair of opposites: courses that students expect to enjoy and to learn much from but are disappointing and courses that students are initially not interested in but that exceed their expectations. Knowing that these four categories exist can help students accept the fact that one disappointing class is not a disaster and can encourage them to try classes with different kinds of subjects, class sizes, and instructors.

Thesis statement

2

First category: ideal class

One of the best courses I have taken so far as a college student was my Shakespeare class. The professor who taught it had a great sense of humor and was liberal in terms of what she allowed in her classroom — for example, controversial Shakespeare adaptations and virtually any discussion, relevant or irrelevant. The students in the class — English majors and non-English majors, those who were interested in the plays as theater and those who preferred to study them as literature — shared an enthusiasm for Shakespeare, and they were eager to engage in lively discussions. This class gave us a thorough knowledge of Shakespeare's plays (tragedies, histories, comedies) as well as an understanding of his life. We also developed our analytical skills through our discussions of the plays and films, as well as through special projects — for example, a character profile presentation and an abstract art presentation relating a work of art to one of the plays. This class was an ideal learning environment not only because of the wealth of material we were exposed to but also because of the respect with which our professor treated us: we were her colleagues, and she was as willing to learn from us as we were to learn from her.

3

Second category: worthless class

In contrast to this ideal class, one of the most worthless courses I have taken in college was Movement Education. As an education major, I expected to like this class, and several other students who had taken it told me it was both easy and enjoyable. The class consisted of playing children's games and learning what made certain activities appropriate and inappropriate for children of various ages. The only requirement for this class was that we had to write note cards explaining how to play each game so that we could use them for reference in our future teaching experiences. Unfortunately, I never really enjoyed the games we played, and I have long since discarded my note cards and forgotten how to play the games — or even what they were.

4

Third category: disappointing class

Although I looked forward to taking Introduction to Astronomy, I was very disappointed in this class. I had hoped to satisfy my curiosity about the universe outside our solar system, but the instructor devoted most of the semester to a detailed study of the earth and the other bodies in our own solar system. In addition, a large part of our work included charting orbits and processing distance equations — work that I found both difficult and boring. Furthermore, we spent little class time learning how to use a telescope and locate objects in the sky. In short, I gained little information from the class, learning only how to solve equations I would never confront again and how to chart orbits that had already been charted.

5

Fourth category: unexpectedly valuable class

In direct contrast to my astronomy class, a religion class called Paul and the Early Church was much more rewarding than I had anticipated. Having attended Catholic school for thirteen years, I assumed this course would offer me little that was new to me. However, because the class took a historical approach to studying Paul's biblical texts, I found that I learned more about Christianity than I had in all my previous religion classes. We learned about the historical validity of Paul and other texts in the Bible and how they were derived from various sources and passed orally through several generations before being written down and translated into different languages. We approached the texts from a linguistic perspective, determining the significance of certain words and how various meanings can be derived from different translations of the same passage. This class was unlike any of my other religion classes in that it

6

encouraged me to study the texts objectively, leaving me with a new and valuable understanding of material I had been exposed to for most of my life.

Conclusion

Although each student's learning experience in college   7
will be different — because every student has a different learning style, is interested in different subjects, and takes courses at different schools taught by different professors — all

Summary of four categories

college students' experiences are similar in one respect. All students will encounter the same kinds of courses: those that are ideal, those that are worthless, those that they learn little from despite their interest in the subject, and those that they learn from and become engaged in despite their low

Restatement of thesis

expectations. Understanding that these categories exist is important because it gives students the freedom and courage to try new things, as college students did years ago. After all, even if one course is a disappointment, another may be more interesting — or even exciting. For this reason, they should not be discouraged by a course they do not like; the best classes are almost certainly still in their future.

Work Cited

Zinsser, William. "College Pressures." *Patterns for College Writing: A Rhetorical Reader and Guide*. 11th ed. Ed. Laurie G. Kirszner and Stephen R. Mandell. New York: Bedford, 2010. 462-70. Print.

Points for Special Attention

Citing a Source. Josie's teacher asked students to cite William Zinsser's "College Pressures," which they had just discussed, somewhere in their own essays. Josie knew that the passage she chose to quote or paraphrase would have to be directly relevant to her own paper's subject, so she knew it would have to focus on academic (rather than economic or social) pressures. When she discovered Zinsser's comments on students' tendency not to experiment with a wide variety of courses, she knew she had found material that could give her essay a more global, less personal focus. For this reason, she decided to refer to Zinsser in her essay's first paragraph. (Note that she includes parenthetical documentation and a works-cited list.)

Thesis and Support. Josie's purpose in writing this essay was to communicate to her professor and the other students in her education class what she had learned from the classes she had taken so far in college, and both the thesis she states in paragraph 2 and the restatement of this thesis in her conclusion make this clear: what she has learned is to take a wide variety of courses. Knowing that few, if any, students in her class would have taken any of the courses she took, Josie realized she had to provide a lot of detail to show what these classes taught her.

Organization. As she reviewed the various courses she had taken and took stock of their strengths and weaknesses, Josie saw a classification scheme emerging. As soon as she noticed this, she organized her material into four categories. Rather than discuss the four kinds of classes from best to worst or from worst to best, Josie decided to present them as two opposing pairs: ideal class and worthless class, surprisingly disappointing class and unexpectedly worthwhile class. In paragraph 2, Josie lists the four categories she plans to discuss in her essay and gives readers an overview of these categories to help prepare them for her thesis.

Transitions between Categories. Josie uses clear topic sentences to move readers from one category to the next and indicate the relationship of each category to another.

> "One of the best college courses I have taken so far as a college student was my Shakespeare class." (3)

> "In contrast to this ideal class, one of the most worthless courses I have taken in college was Movement Education." (4)

> "Although I looked forward to taking Introduction to Astronomy, I was very disappointed in this class." (5)

> "In direct contrast to my astronomy class, a religion class called Paul and the Early Church was much more rewarding than I had anticipated." (6)

These four sentences distinguish the four categories from one another and also help to communicate Josie's direction and emphasis.

Focus on Revision

An earlier draft of Josie's essay, which she discussed with her classmates in a peer editing session, did not include very helpful topic sentences. Instead, the sentences were vague and unfocused:

> "One class I took in college was a Shakespeare course."

> "Another class I took was Movement Education."

> "I looked forward to taking Introduction to Astronomy."

> "My experience with a religion class was very different."

Although her essay's second paragraph listed the categories and explained how they differed, Josie's classmates advised her to revise her topic sentences so that it would be clear which category she was discussing in each body paragraph. Josie took the advice of her peer editing group and revised these topic sentences. After reading her next draft, she felt confident that her categories — listed in paragraph 2 and repeated in her topic sentences and again in her conclusion — were clear and distinct.

Even after making these revisions, however, Josie felt her paper needed some additional fine-tuning. For example, in her final draft, she planned to add some material to paragraphs 4 and 5. At first, because she had dismissed Movement Education as completely worthless and Introduction to Astronomy as disappointing, Josie felt she did not have to say much about them. When she reread her paper, however, she realized she needed to explain the shortcomings of the two classes more fully so that her readers would understand why these classes had little value for her.

📄 **PEER EDITING WORKSHEET: Classification and Division**

1. Paraphrase the essay's thesis.

2. What whole is being divided into parts in this essay? Into what general categories is the whole divided?

3. Is each category clearly identified and explained? If not, what revisions can you suggest? (For example, can you suggest a different title for a particular category? A different topic sentence to introduce it?)

4. Where does the writer list the categories to be discussed? Is the list introduced by a colon (preceded by a complete sentence)? If not, suggest revisions.

5. Are the categories arranged in a logical order, one that indicates their relationships to one another and their relative importance? If not, how could they be rearranged?

6. Does the writer treat all relevant categories and no irrelevant ones? Which categories, if any, should be added, deleted, or combined?

7. Does the writer include all necessary items, and no unnecessary ones, within each category? What additional items could be added? Should any items be located elsewhere?

8. Does the writer treat all categories similarly, discussing comparable points for each? Should any additional points be discussed? If so, where?

9. Do topic sentences clearly signal the movement from one category to the next? Should any topic sentences be strengthened to mark the boundaries between categories more clearly? If so, which ones?

10. Could the writer use another pattern of development to structure this essay, or is classification and division the best choice? Explain.

Each of the following selections is developed by means of classification and division. In some cases, the pattern is used to explain ideas; in others, it is used to persuade the reader. The first selection, a visual text, is followed by questions designed to illustrate how classification and division can operate in visual form.

Key to Chalk Marks Designating Medical Conditions of Immigrants, Ellis Island (Chart)

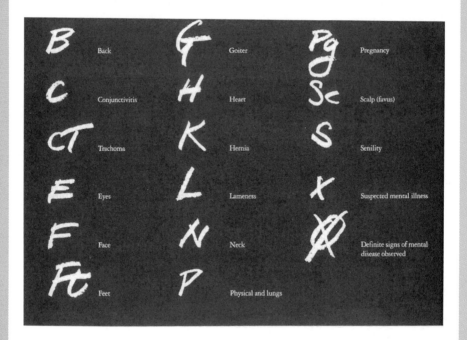

B	Back	G	Goiter	Pg	Pregnancy
C	Conjunctivitis	H	Heart	Sc	Scalp (favus)
CT	Trachoma	K	Hernia	S	Senility
E	Eyes	L	Lameness	X	Suspected mental illness
F	Face	N	Neck	Ⓧ	Definite signs of mental disease observed
Ft	Feet	P	Physical and lungs		

• • •

Reading Images

1. The photo above shows symbols, written in chalk on early-twentieth-century immigrants' clothing, representing medical conditions that could disqualify them from entry into the United States. What different principles of classification might be used to sort these symbols into categories? Which principle of classification seems to make the most sense? Why?

2. Guided by the principle of classification you selected in question 1, arrange the various symbols into three or four logical categories. Are there any that do not fit into your classification scheme?

3. The chalk mark system illustrated here is no longer in use, but visitors' health is still a consideration. What medical conditions do you think should disqualify a visitor for entry into the United States today? List some possible criteria for exclusion, and arrange these criteria into categories.

Journal Entry

Do you think the United States should exclude any potential immigrants solely for medical reasons? Why or why not?

Thematic Connections

- "Words Left Unspoken" (page 172)
- "The Catbird Seat" (page 223)
- "Statement in Support of Comprehensive Immigration Reform" (page 655)

WILLIAM ZINSSER

College Pressures

William Zinsser has worked as a newspaper and magazine writer and has taught English at Yale University. He is also author of numerous books on writing, including *On Writing Well: The Classic Guide to Writing Nonfiction* (twenty-fifth anniversary edition, 2001) and *Writing about Your Life: A Journey into the Past* (2004). His works on American culture include *Spring Training* (1989), about the culture of baseball, and *Easy to Remember: Great American Songwriters and Their Songs* (2001).

Background on college pressures today
Although the following essay focuses on the kinds of pressures facing Yale students in 1979, many of these remain relevant (and, in some cases, even more relevant) for college students today. These pressures include the need to develop time management and study skills appropriate for college work, the desire for good grades, the desire to meet familial expectations, and the need to find employment in a competitive job market after graduation. In addition, many college students today face pressures unknown to most students in the late 1970s. According to the U.S. Department of Education's National Center for Education Statistics, only about 25 percent of current undergraduates fit the "traditional" model of eighteen- to twenty-two-year-old full-time students still supported primarily by their parents. Increasingly, college undergraduates are adults, supporting themselves — and sometimes families — and funding their own education through full- or part-time employment. Moreover, the average student faces more than $20,000 of college-related debt by the time he or she graduates.

Dear Carlos: I desperately need a dean's excuse for my chem midterm which will begin in about one hour. All I can say is that I totally blew it this week. I've fallen incredibly, inconceivably behind. 1

Carlos: Help! I'm anxious to hear from you. I'll be in my room and won't leave it until I hear from you. Tomorrow is the last day for . . . 2

Carlos: I left town because I started bugging out again. I stayed up all night to finish a take home make-up exam and am typing it to hand in on the 10th. It was due on the 5th. P.S. I'm going to the dentist. Pain is pretty bad. 3

Carlos: Probably by Friday I'll be able to get back to my studies. Right now I'm going to take a long walk. This whole thing has taken a lot out of me. 4

Carlos: I'm really up the proverbial creek. The problem is I really *bombed* the history final. Since I need that course for my major . . . 5

Carlos: Here follows a tale of woe. I went home this weekend, had to help my Mom, & caught a fever so didn't have much time to study. My professor . . . 6

Carlos: Aargh! Nothing original but everything's piling up at once. To be   7
brief, my job interview . . .

Hey Carlos, good news! I've got mononucleosis.   8

Who are these wretched supplicants, scribbling notes so laden with   9
anxiety, seeking such miracles of postponement and balm? They are men
and women who belong to Bradford College, one of the twelve residential
colleges at Yale University, and the messages are just a few of the hundreds
that they left for their dean, Carlos Hortas — often slipped under his door
at 4 A.M. — last year.

But students like the ones who wrote those notes can also be found on   10
campuses from coast to coast — especially in New England and at many
other private colleges across the country that have high academic standards and highly motivated students. Nobody could doubt that the notes
are real. In their urgency and their gallows humor they are authentic voices
of a generation that is panicky to succeed.

My own connection with the message writers is that I am master of   11
Bradford College. I live in its Gothic quadrangle and know the students
well. (We have 485 of them.) I am privy to their hopes and fears — and also
to their stereo music and their piercing cries in the dead of night ("Does
anybody *ca-a-are?*"). If they went to Carlos to ask how to get through tomorrow, they come to me to ask how to get through the rest of their lives.

Mainly I try to remind them that the road ahead is a long one and that   12
it will have more unexpected turns than they think. There will be plenty of
time to change jobs, change careers, change whole attitudes and approaches.
They don't want to hear such liberating news. They want a map — right
now — that they can follow unswervingly to career security, financial security, Social Security, and, presumably, a prepaid grave.

What I wish for all students is some release from the clammy grip of   13
the future. I wish them a chance to savor each segment of their education
as an experience in itself and not as a grim preparation for the next step. I
wish them the right to experiment, to trip and fall, to learn that defeat is as
instructive as victory and is not the end of the world.

My wish, of course, is naive. One of the few rights that America does   14
not proclaim is the right to fail. Achievement is the national god, venerated
in our media — the million-dollar athlete, the wealthy executive — and glo-
rified in our praise of possessions. In the presence of such a potent state
religion, the young are growing up old.

I see four kinds of pressure working on college students today: eco-   15
nomic pressure, parental pressure, peer pressure, and self-induced pressure. It is easy to look around for villains — to blame the colleges for
charging too much money, the professors for assigning too much work,
the parents for pushing their children too far, the students for driving
themselves too hard. But there are no villains, only victims.

"In the late 1960s," one dean told me, "the typical question that I   16
got from students was 'Why is there so much suffering in the world?' or

'How can I make a contribution?' Today it's 'Do you think it would look better for getting into law school if I did a double major in history and political science, or just majored in one of them?'" Many other deans confirmed this pattern. One said: "They're trying to find an edge — the intangible something that will look better on paper if two students are about equal."

Note the emphasis on looking better. The transcript has become a sacred document, the passport to security. How one appears on paper is more important than how one appears in person. *A* is for Admirable and *B* is for Borderline, even though, in Yale's official system of grading, *A* means "excellent" and *B* means "very good." Today, looking very good is no longer good enough, especially for students who hope to go on to law school or medical school. They know that entrance into the better schools will be an entrance into the better law firms and better medical practices where they will make a lot of money. They also know that the odds are harsh. Yale Law School, for instance, matriculates 170 students from an applicant pool of 3,700; Harvard enrolls 550 from a pool of 7,000.

It's all very well for those of us who write letters of recommendation for our students to stress the qualities of humanity that will make them good lawyers or doctors. And it's nice to think that admission officers are really reading our letters and looking for the extra dimension of commitment or concern. Still, it would be hard for a student not to visualize these officers shuffling so many transcripts studded with *A*s that they regard a *B* as positively shameful.

The pressure is almost as heavy on students who just want to graduate and get a job. Long gone are the days of the "gentleman's *C*," when students journeyed through college with a certain relaxation, sampling a wide variety of courses — music, art, philosophy, classics, anthropology, poetry, religion — that would send them out as liberally educated men and women. If I were an employer I would rather employ graduates who have this range and curiosity than those who narrowly pursued safe subjects and high grades. I know countless students whose inquiring minds exhilarate me. I like to hear the play of their ideas. I don't know if they're getting *A*s or *C*s, and I don't care. I also like them as people. The country needs them, and they will find satisfying jobs. I tell them to relax. They can't.

Nor can I blame them. They live in a brutal economy. Tuition, room, and board at most private colleges now comes to at least $7,000, not counting books and fees.* This might seem to suggest that the colleges are getting rich. But they are equally battered by inflation. Tuition covers only 60 percent of what it costs to educate a student, and ordinarily the remainder comes from what colleges receive in endowments, grants, and gifts. Now the remainder keeps being swallowed by cruel costs — higher every year — of just opening the doors. Heating oil is up. Insurance is up. Postage is up.

17

18

19

20

---

* EDS. NOTE — Zinsser's essay was published in 1979; the figures quoted for tuition and other expenses would be much higher today.

Health-premium costs are up. Everything is up. Deficits are up. We are witnessing in America the creation of a brotherhood of paupers — colleges, parents, and students, joined by the common bond of debt.

Today it is not unusual for a student, even if he works part-time at college and full time during the summer, to accrue $5,000 in loans after four years — loans that he must start to repay within one year after graduation. Exhorted at commencement to go forth into the world, he is already behind as he goes forth. How could he not feel under pressure throughout college to prepare for this day of reckoning? I have used "he" incidentally, only for brevity. Women at Yale are under no less pressure to justify their expensive education to themselves, their parents, and society. In fact, they are probably under more pressure. For although they leave college superbly equipped to bring fresh leadership to traditionally male jobs, society hasn't yet caught up with this fact.

Along with economic pressure goes parental pressure. Inevitably, the two are deeply intertwined.

I see many students taking pre-medical courses with joyless tenacity. They go off to their labs as if they were going to the dentist. It saddens me because I know them in other corners of their life as cheerful people.

"Do you want to go to medical school?" I ask them.

"I guess so," they say, without conviction, or "Not really."

"Then why are you going?"

"Well, my parents want me to be a doctor. They're paying all this money and . . ."

Poor students, poor parents. They are caught in one of the oldest webs of love and duty and guilt. The parents mean well; they are trying to steer their sons and daughters toward a secure future. But the sons and daughters want to major in history or classics or philosophy — subjects with no "practical" value. Where's the payoff on the humanities? It's not easy to persuade such loving parents that the humanities do indeed pay off. The intellectual faculties developed by studying subjects like history and classics — an ability to synthesize and relate, to weigh cause and effect, to see events in perspective — are just the faculties that make creative leaders in business or almost any general field. Still, many fathers would rather put their money on courses that point toward a specific profession — courses that are pre-law, pre-medical, pre-business, or, as I sometimes heard it put, "pre-rich."

But the pressure on students is severe. They are truly torn. One part of them feels obliged to fulfill their parents' expectations; after all, their parents are older and presumably wiser. Another part tells them that the expectations that are right for their parents are not right for them.

I know a student who wants to be an artist. She is very obviously an artist and will be a good one — she has already had several modest exhibits. Meanwhile she is growing as a well-rounded person and taking humanistic subjects that will enrich the inner resources out of which her art will grow. But her father is strongly opposed. He thinks that an artist is a "dumb" thing to be. The student vacillates and tries to please everybody. She keeps up with her art somewhat furtively and takes some of the "dumb" courses her father wants her to take — at least they are dumb courses for her. She is a free spirit on a campus of tense students — no small achievement in itself — and she deserves to follow her muse.

Peer pressure and self-induced pressure are also intertwined, and they begin almost at the beginning of freshman year. 31

"I had a freshman student I'll call Linda," one dean told me, "who came in and said she was under terrible pressure because her roommate, Barbara, was much brighter and studied all the time. I couldn't tell her that Barbara had come in two hours earlier to say the same thing about Linda." 32

The story is almost funny — except that it's not. It's symptomatic of all the pressures put together. When every student thinks every other student is working harder and doing better, the only solution is to study harder still. I see students going off to the library every night after dinner and coming back when it closes at midnight. I wish they could sometimes forget about their peers and go to a movie. I hear the clacking of typewriters in the hours before dawn. I see the tension in their eyes when exams are approaching and papers are due: *Will I get everything done?* 33

Probably they won't. They will get sick. They will get "blocked." They will sleep. They will oversleep. They will bug out. *Hey Carlos, help!* 34

Part of the problem is that they do more than they are expected to do. A professor will assign five-page papers. Several students will start writing ten-page papers to impress him. Then more students will write ten-page papers, and a few will raise the ante to fifteen. Pity the poor student who is still just doing the assignment. 35

"Once you have twenty or thirty percent of the student population deliberately overexerting," one dean points out, "it's bad for everybody. When a teacher gets more and more effort from his class, the student who is doing normal work can be perceived as not doing well. The tactic works, psychologically." 36

Why can't the professor just cut back and not accept longer papers? He can, and he probably will. But by then the term will be half over and the damage done. Grade fever is highly contagious and not easily reversed. Besides, the professor's main concern is with his course. He knows his students only in relation to the course and doesn't know that they are also overexerting in their other courses. Nor is it really his business. He didn't sign up for dealing with the student as a whole person and with all the emotional baggage the student brought along from home. That's what deans, masters, chaplains, and psychiatrists are for. 37

To some extent this is nothing new: a certain number of professors have always been self-contained islands of scholarship and shyness, more comfortable with books than with people. But the new pauperism has widened the gap still further, for professors who actually like to spend time with students don't have as much time to spend. They also are overexerting. If they are young, they are busy trying to publish in order not to per- 38 ish, hanging by their fingernails onto a shrinking profession. If they are old and tenured, they are buried under the duties of administering departments — as departmental chairmen or members of committees — that have been thinned out by the budgetary axe.

Ultimately it will be the students' own business to break the circles in which they are trapped. They are too young to be prisoners of their parents' dreams and their classmates' fears. They must be jolted into believing in themselves as unique men and women who have the power to shape their own future.   39

"Violence is being done to the undergraduate experience," says Carlos Hortas. "College should be open-ended: at the end it should open many, many roads. Instead, students are choosing their goal in advance, and their choices narrow as they go along. It's almost as if they think that the country has been codified in the type of jobs that exist — that they've got to fit into certain slots. Therefore, fit into the best-paying slot.   40

"They ought to take chances. Not taking chances will lead to a life of colorless mediocrity. They'll be comfortable. But something in the spirit will be missing."   41

I have painted too drab a portrait of today's students, making them seem a solemn lot. That is only half of their story; if they were so dreary I wouldn't so thoroughly enjoy their company. The other half is that they are easy to like. They are quick to laugh and to offer friendship. They are not introverts. They are usually kind and are more considerate of one another than any student generation I have known.   42

Nor are they so obsessed with their studies that they avoid sports and extracurricular activities. On the contrary, they juggle their crowded hours to play on a variety of teams, perform with musical and dramatic groups, and write for campus publications. But this in turn is one more cause of anxiety. There are too many choices. Academically, they have 1,300 courses to select from; outside class they have to decide how much spare time they can spare and how to spend it.   43

This means that they engage in fewer extracurricular pursuits than their predecessors did. If they want to row on the crew and play in the symphony they will eliminate one; in the '60s they would have done both. They also tend to choose activities that are self-limiting. Drama, for instance, is flourishing in all twelve of Yale's residential colleges as it never has before. Students hurl themselves into these productions — as actors, directors, carpenters, and technicians — with a dedication to create the best possible play, knowing that the day will come when the run will end and they can get back to their studies.   44

They also can't afford to be the willing slave of organizations like the *Yale Daily News*. Last spring at the one-hundredth anniversary banquet of that paper — whose past chairmen include such once and future kings as Potter Stewart, Kingman Brewster, and William F. Buckley, Jr.* — much   45

---

* Eds. note — Stewart was a U.S. Supreme Court Justice, Brewster was a president of Yale, and Buckley was a conservative editor and columnist.

was made of the fact that the editorial staff used to be small and totally committed and that "newsies" routinely worked fifty hours a week. In effect they belonged to a club; Newsies is how they defined themselves at Yale. Today's student will write one or two articles a week, when he can, and he defines himself as a student. I've never heard the word Newsie except at the banquet.

If I have described the modern undergraduate primarily as a driven creature who is largely ignoring the blithe spirit inside who keeps trying to come out and play, it's because that's where the crunch is, not only at Yale but throughout American education. It's why I think we should all be worried about the values that are nurturing a generation so fearful of risk and so goal-obsessed at such an early age.

46

I tell students that there is no one "right" way to get ahead — that each of them is a different person, starting from a different point and bound for a different destination. I tell them that change is a tonic and that all the slots are not codified nor the frontiers closed. One of my ways of telling them is to invite men and women who have achieved success outside the academic world to come and talk informally with my students during the year. They are heads of companies or ad agencies, editors of magazines, politicians, public officials, television magnates, labor leaders, business executives, Broadway producers, artists, writers, economists, photographers, scientists, historians — a mixed bag of achievers.

47

I ask them to say a few words about how they got started. The students assume that they started in their present profession and knew all along that it was what they wanted to do. Luckily for me, most of them got into their field by a circuitous route, to their surprise, after many detours. The students are startled. They can hardly conceive of a career that was not preplanned. They can hardly imagine allowing the hand of God or chance to nudge them down some unforeseen trail.

48

• • •

Comprehension

1. What advice does Zinsser give students when they bring their problems to him?
2. What does Zinsser wish for his students? Why does he believe his wish is naive?
3. What four kinds of pressure does Zinsser identify?
4. Whom does Zinsser blame for the existence of these pressures? Explain.
5. How, according to Zinsser, is his evaluation of students different from their own and from their potential employers' assessments?
6. Why does Zinsser believe that women are probably under even more pressure than men? Do you think this is true today?
7. How does what Zinsser calls the "new pauperism" (38) affect professors?

8. Who, according to Zinsser, is ultimately responsible for eliminating college pressures? Explain.

9. In what sense are sports and other extracurricular activities another source of anxiety for students? How do students adapt to this pressure?

Purpose and Audience

1. In your own words, state Zinsser's thesis. Is his intent in this essay simply to expose a difficult situation or does he want to effect change? What makes you think so?

2. On what kind of audience do you think this essay would have the most significant impact: students, teachers, parents, potential employers, graduate school admissions committees, or college administrators? Why?

3. What do you think Zinsser hopes to accomplish in paragraphs 42–46? How would the essay be different without this section?

4. What assumptions does Zinsser make about his audience? Do you think these assumptions are valid? Explain.

Style and Structure

1. Evaluate the essay's introductory strategy. What impact do you think the notes to Carlos are likely to have on readers?

2. Identify the boundaries of Zinsser's actual classification. How does he introduce the first category? How does he indicate that his treatment of the final category is complete?

3. What function do paragraphs 22 and 31 serve in the essay?

4. Zinsser is careful to explain that when he refers to students as *he*, he includes female students as well. However, he also refers to professors as *he* (for example, in paragraphs 35–37). Assuming that not all professors at Yale are male, what other stylistic options does Zinsser have?

5. At various points in the essay, Zinsser quotes deans and students at Yale. What is the effect of these quotations?

6. Zinsser notes that his categories are "intertwined" (22, 31). In what ways do the categories overlap? Does this overlap weaken the essay? Explain.

7. What, if anything, seems to determine the order of Zinsser's categories? Is this order effective? Why, or why not?

Vocabulary Projects

1. Define each of the following words as it is used in this selection.

proverbial (5)	intangible (16)	blithe (46)
supplicants (9)	accrue (21)	tonic (47)
balm (9)	exhorted (21)	codified (47)
privy (11)	tenacity (23)	
venerated (14)	faculties (28)	

2. At times Zinsser uses religious language — *national god, sacred document* — to describe the students' quest for success. Identify other examples of such language, and explain why it is used.

Journal Entry

Which of the pressures Zinsser identifies has the strongest impact on you? Why? Do you have any other pressures Zinsser does not mention?

Writing Workshop

1. Zinsser describes problems students faced at an elite private college in the late 1970s. Are the pressures you experience as a college student similar to or different from the ones Zinsser identifies? Classify your own college pressures, and write an email to your academic advisor or dean. Include a thesis statement that takes a strong stand against the forces responsible for these pressures.

2. Write a classification essay supporting a thesis about college students' drive for success. Categorize students you know either by the degree of their need to succeed or by the different ways in which they wish to succeed. Include a reference to Zinsser's essay — or to Carolyn Foster Segal's essay on page 471 — to support your thesis. Be sure to include parenthetical documentation and a works-cited page. (See the Appendix for information on documentation formats.)

3. Zinsser takes a negative view of the college pressures he identifies. Using his four categories, write an essay arguing that, in the long run, these pressures are not only necessary but also valuable.

Combining the Patterns

Exemplification is an important secondary pattern in this classification-and-division essay. Identify as many passages of exemplification as you can. What do these examples add to Zinsser's essay? What other kinds of examples might be helpful to readers?

Thematic Connections

- "The 'Black Table' Is Still There" (page 345)
- "Suicide Note" (page 377)
- "I'm Your Teacher, Not Your Internet-Service Provider" (page 416)
- "The Dog Ate My Disk, and Other Tales of Woe" (page 471)

The Dog Ate My Disk, and Other Tales of Woe

Carolyn Foster Segal (b. 1950) teaches English at Cedar Crest College in Allentown, Pennsylvania. Segal has published poetry, fiction, and essays in a number of publications, including the *Chronicle of Higher Education,* where the following essay originally appeared. She sums up her ideas about writing as follows: "Writing — and it does not matter if it is writing about a feature of the landscape, an aspect of human nature, or a work of literature — begins with observation. The other parts are curiosity, imagination, and patience." She has received hundreds of responses from other instructors corroborating the experiences she describes here.

Background on academic integrity

While falsifying an excuse for being unprepared for class may seem like a minor infraction, it may still be considered a breach of academic integrity. At many colleges, honor codes attempt to define academic integrity and set penalties for those who violate its rules. The concept of college honor codes in the United States goes back to one developed by students at the University of Virginia in 1840, but reports of widespread cheating on college campuses in the early 1990s brought renewed interest in such codes. (Surveys show that more than three-quarters of college students have cheated at least once during their schooling, and an even greater number see cheating as the norm among successful students.) In 1992, the Center for Academic Integrity was established to help colleges and universities find ways to promote "honesty, trust, fairness, respect, and responsibility" among students and faculty members. Its original twenty-five-member group has grown to include more than two hundred institutions, and many other colleges have adopted its goals as well. The main focus of most honor codes revolves around discouraging plagiarism — copying the work of others and presenting the work of others as one's own — and various forms of cheating on tests. The Center for Academic Integrity sees promoting individual honesty as the fundamental issue underlying all of these concerns.

Taped to the door of my office is a cartoon that features a cat explaining to his feline teacher, "The dog ate my homework." It is intended as a gently humorous reminder to my students that I will not accept excuses for late work, and it, like the lengthy warning on my syllabus, has had absolutely no effect. With a show of energy and creativity that would be admirable if applied to the (missing) assignments in question, my students persist, week after week, semester after semester, year after year, in offering excuses about why their work is not ready. Those reasons fall into several 1 broad categories: the family, the best friend, the evils of dorm life, the evils of technology, and the totally bizarre.

The Family

The death of the grandfather/grandmother is, of course, the grand- 2
mother of all excuses. What heartless teacher would dare to question a student's grief or veracity? What heartless student would lie, wishing death on a revered family member, just to avoid a deadline? Creative students may win extra extensions (and days off) with a little careful planning and fuller plot development, as in the sequence of "My grandfather/grandmother is sick"; "Now my grandfather/grandmother is in the hospital"; and finally, "We could all see it coming — my grandfather/grandmother is dead."

Another favorite excuse is "the family emergency," which (always) goes 3
like this: "There was an emergency at home, and I had to help my family." It's a lovely sentiment, one that conjures up images of Louisa May Alcott's* little women rushing off with baskets of food and copies of *Pilgrim's Progress*,** but I do not understand why anyone would turn to my most irresponsible students in times of trouble.

The Best Friend

This heartwarming concern for others extends beyond the family to 4
friends, as in, "My best friend was up all night and I had to (a) stay up with her in the dorm, (b) drive her to the hospital, or (c) drive to her college because (1) her boyfriend broke up with her, (2) she was throwing up blood [no one catches a cold anymore; everyone throws up blood], or (3) her grandfather/grandmother died."

At one private university where I worked as an adjunct, I heard an inter- 5
esting spin that incorporated the motifs of both best friend and dead relative: "My best friend's mother killed herself." One has to admire the cleverness here: A mysterious woman in the prime of her life has allegedly committed suicide, and no professor can prove otherwise! And I admit I was moved, until finally I had to point out to my students that it was amazing how the simple act of my assigning a topic for a paper seemed to drive large numbers of otherwise happy and healthy middle-aged women to their deaths. I was careful to make that point during an off week, during which no deaths were reported.

The Evils of Dorm Life

These stories are usually fairly predictable; almost always feature the 6
evil roommate or hallmate, with my student in the role of the innocent

---

* EDS. NOTE — Nineteenth-century sentimental novelist, author of *Little Women*.
** EDS. NOTE — Eighteenth-century allegory by John Bunyan describing a Christian's journey from the City of Destruction to the Celestial City.

victim; and can be summed up as follows: My roommate, who is a horrible person, likes to party, and I, who am a good person, cannot concentrate on my work when he or she is partying. Variations include stories about the two people next door who were running around and crying loudly last night because (a) one of them had boyfriend/girlfriend problems; (b) one of them was throwing up blood; or (c) someone, somewhere, died. A friend of mine in graduate school had a student who claimed that his roommate attacked him with a hammer. That, in fact, was a true story; it came out in court when the bad roommate was tried for killing his grandfather.

The Evils of Technology

The computer age has revolutionized the student story, inspiring   7
almost as many new excuses as it has Internet businesses. Here are just a few electronically enhanced explanations:

- The computer wouldn't let me save my work.
- The printer wouldn't print.
- The printer wouldn't print this disk.
- The printer wouldn't give me time to proofread.
- The printer made a black line run through all my words, and I know you can't read this, but do you still want it, or wait, here, take my disk. File name? I don't know what you mean.
- I swear I attached it.
- It's my roommate's computer, and she usually helps me, but she had to go to the hospital because she was throwing up blood.
- I did write to the newsgroup, but all my messages came back to me.
- I just found out that all my other newsgroup messages came up under a diferent name. I just want you to know that its really me who wrote all those messages, you can tel which ones our mine because I didnt use the spelcheck! But it was yours truely :) Anyway, just in case you missed those messages or dont belief its my writting. I'll repeat what I sad: I thought the last movie we watched in clas was borring.

The Totally Bizarre

I call the first story "The Pennsylvania Chain Saw Episode." A com-   8
muter student called to explain why she had missed my morning class. She had gotten up early so that she would be wide awake for class. Having a bit of extra time, she walked outside to see her neighbor, who was cutting some wood. She called out to him, and he waved back to her with the saw. Wouldn't you know it, the safety catch wasn't on or was broken, and the blade flew right out of the saw and across his lawn and over her fence and across her yard and severed a tendon in her right hand. So she was calling

me from the hospital, where she was waiting for surgery. Luckily, she reassured me, she had remembered to bring her paper and a stamped envelope (in a plastic bag, to avoid bloodstains) along with her in the ambulance, and a nurse was mailing everything to me even as we spoke.

That wasn't her first absence. In fact, this student had missed most of the class meetings, and I had already recommended that she withdraw from the course. Now I suggested again that it might be best if she dropped the class. I didn't harp on the absences (what if even some of this story were true?). I did mention that she would need time to recuperate and that making up so much missed work might be difficult. "Oh, no," she said, "I can't drop this course. I had been planning to go on to medical school and become a surgeon, but since I won't be able to operate because of my accident, I'll have to major in English, and this course is more important than ever to me." She did come to the next class, wearing — as evidence of her recent trauma — a bedraggled Ace bandage on her left hand.

You may be thinking that nothing could top that excuse, but in fact I have one more story, provided by the same student, who sent me a letter to explain why her final assignment would be late. While recuperating from her surgery, she had begun corresponding on the Internet with a man who lived in Germany. After a one-week, whirlwind Web romance, they had agreed to meet in Rome, to rendezvous (her phrase) at the papal Easter Mass. Regrettably, the time of her flight made it impossible for her to attend class, but she trusted that I — just this once — would accept late work if the pope wrote a note.

· · ·

Comprehension

1. What is Segal's thesis? Does she state it in her essay? What exactly is she classifying here?

2. In paragraph 3, Segal says, "I do not understand why anyone would turn to my most irresponsible students in times of trouble." Do you see this comment as fair?

3. Which of the excuses Segal discusses do you see as valid? Which do you see as just excuses? Why?

4. Do you see Segal as rigid and unsympathetic, or do you think her frustration is justified? Do you think her students are irresponsible procrastinators or simply overworked?

5. What lessons do you think Segal would like her students to learn from her? Would reading this essay teach them what she wants them to learn?

Purpose and Audience

1. This essay was originally published in the *Chronicle of Higher Education,* a periodical for college teachers. How do you think these readers responded to the essay? How do you respond?

2. Do you see Segal's purpose here as to entertain, to let off steam, to warn, to criticize, or to change students' habits? Explain.

3. In paragraph 7, Segal lists some specific excuses in one category, paraphrasing students' remarks and even imitating their grammar and style. Why does she do this? Is it an effective strategy?

Style and Structure

1. In paragraph 1, Segal lists the five categories she plans to discuss. Is this list necessary?

2. Are Segal's categories mutually exclusive, or do they overlap? Could she combine any categories? Can you think of any categories she does not include?

3. What determines the order in which Segal introduces her categories? Is this order logical, or should she present her categories in a different order?

4. Does Segal discuss comparable points for each category? What points, if any, need to be added?

5. Segal frequently uses **sarcasm** in this essay. Give some examples. Given her original audience, do you think this tone is appropriate? How do you react to her sarcasm?

6. Throughout her essay, Segal returns again and again to two excuses: "my grandfather/grandmother died" and "throwing up blood." Locate different versions of these excuses in the essay. Why do you think she singles out these two excuses?

7. Although Segal deals with a serious academic problem, she includes many expressions — such as "Wouldn't you know it" (8) — that give her essay an informal tone. Identify some other examples. What is your reaction to the essay's casual, offhand tone?

8. Review the category Segal calls "The Evils of Technology." Can you add to her list? Can you create subcategories?

Vocabulary Projects

1. Define each of the following words as it is used in this selection.

feline (1)   adjunct (5)
veracity (2)   harp (9)
revered (2)   bedraggled (9)
conjures (3)   rendezvous (10)

2. Every profession has its own unique terms. What terms in this essay characterize the writer as a college professor?

Journal Entry

Do you think this essay is funny? Explain your reaction.

Writing Workshop

1. Write an email to Segal explaining why your English paper will be late, presenting several different kinds of excuses for your paper's lateness. Before you present your own superior excuses, be sure to acknowledge the inadequacies of the excuses Segal lists, quoting a few and including parenthetical documentation and a works-cited page. (See the Appendix for information on documentation formats.)

2. Write an essay identifying four or five categories of legitimate excuses for handing in work late. If you like, you can use narrative examples from your own life as a student to explain each category.

3. Using a light (or even sarcastic) tone, write an essay identifying several different categories of teachers in terms of their shortcomings — for instance, teachers who do not cover the assigned work or teachers who do not grade papers in a timely fashion. Be sure to give specific examples of teachers in each category.

Combining the Patterns

In paragraphs 8–10, Segal uses **narration** to tell two stories. What do these stories add to her essay? Do you think she should have added more stories like these to her essay? If so, where?

Thematic Connections

- "I'm Your Teacher, Not Your Internet-Service Provider" (page 416)
- "College Pressures" (page 462)
- "The Ways We Lie" (page 485)

Mother Tongue

Amy Tan was born in 1952 in Oakland, California, the daughter of recent Chinese immigrants. In 1984, when she began to write fiction, she started to explore the contradictions she faced as a Chinese American who was also the daughter of immigrant parents. Three years later, she published *The Joy Luck Club* (1987), a best-selling novel about four immigrant Chinese women and their American-born daughters. Later works include the novel *The Bonesetter's Daughter* (2001), two children's books, *The Opposite of Fate: A Book of Musings* (2003), and *Saving Fish from Drowning* (2005). In the following 1990 essay, Tan considers her mother's heavily Chinese-influenced English, as well as the different "Englishes" she herself uses, especially in communicating with her mother. She then discusses the potential limitations of growing up with immigrant parents who do not speak fluent English.

Background on Asian Americans and standardized tests

The children of Asian immigrants tend to be highly assimilated and are often outstanding students, in part because their parents expect them to work hard and do well. Most who were born in the United States speak and read English fluently. Yet on standardized tests, while they generally score much higher than average in math, their verbal scores are a bit lower than average. For example, average SAT scores for all student test-takers beginning college in 2004 were 528 on the verbal section and 531 on the math section; the average scores for Asian-American students were 507 on the verbal section and 577 on the math section. In some cases, this lower verbal score means that an Asian-American student's combined score may limit his or her college choices. Moreover, as Tan suggests, Asian-American students' performance on such standardized tests may lead teachers to discourage them from pursuing degrees in fields outside of math and science.

I am not a scholar of English or literature. I cannot give you much   1
more than personal opinions on the English language and its variations in
this country or others.

I am a writer. And by that definition, I am someone who has always   2
loved language. I am fascinated by language in daily life. I spend a great
deal of my time thinking about the power of language — the way it can
evoke an emotion, a visual image, a complex idea, or a simple truth. Language is the tool of my trade. And I use them all — all the Englishes I grew
up with.

Recently, I was made keenly aware of the different Englishes I do use. I   3
was giving a talk to a large group of people, the same talk I had already

given to half a dozen other groups. The nature of the talk was about my writing, my life, and my book, *The Joy Luck Club*. The talk was going along well enough, until I remembered one major difference that made the whole talk sound wrong. My mother was in the room. And it was perhaps the first time she had heard me give a lengthy speech, using the kind of English I have never used with her. I was saying things like, "The intersection of memory upon imagination" and "There is an aspect of my fiction that relates to thus-and-thus" — a speech filled with carefully wrought grammatical phrases, burdened, it suddenly seemed to me, with nominalized forms, past perfect tenses, conditional phrases, all the forms of standard English that I had learned in school and through books, the forms of English I did not use at home with my mother.

Just last week, I was walking down the street with my mother, and I again found myself conscious of the English I was using, and the English I do use with her. We were talking about the price of new and used furniture and I heard myself saying this: "Not waste money that way." My husband was with us as well, and he didn't notice any switch in my English. And then I realized why. It's because over the twenty years we've been together I've often used that same kind of English with him, and sometimes he even uses it with me. It has become our language of intimacy, a different sort of English that relates to family talk, the language I grew up with.   4

So you'll have some idea of what this family talk I heard sounds like,   5
I'll quote what my mother said during a recent conversation which I videotaped and then transcribed. During this conversation my mother was talking about a political gangster in Shanghai who had the same last name as her family's, Du, and how the gangster in his early years wanted to be adopted by her family, which was rich by comparison. Later, the gangster became more powerful, far richer than my mother's family, and one day showed up at my mother's wedding to pay his respects. Here's what she said in part:

"Du Yusong having business like fruit stand. Like off the street kind.   6
He is Du like Du Zong — but not Tsung-ming Island people. The local people call putong, the river east side, he belong to that side local people. The man want to ask Du Zong father take him in like become own family. Du Zong father wasn't looking down on him, but didn't take seriously, until that man big like become a mafia. Now important person very hard to inviting him. Chinese way, come only to show respect, don't stay for dinner. Respect for making big celebration, he shows up. Mean gives lots of respect. Chinese custom. Chinese social life that way. If too important won't have to stay too long. He come to my wedding. I didn't see. I heard it. I gone to boy's side, they have YMCA dinner. Chinese age I was nineteen."

You should know that my mother's expressive command of English   7
belies how much she actually understands. She reads the *Forbes* report, listens to *Wall Street Week*, converses daily with her stockbroker, reads all of Shirley MacLaine's books with ease — all kinds of things I can't begin to understand. Yet some of my friends tell me they understand 50 percent of

what my mother says. Some say they understand 80 to 90 percent. Some say they understand none of it, as if she were speaking pure Chinese. But to me, my mother's English is perfectly clear, perfectly natural. It's my mother's tongue. Her language, as I hear it, is vivid, direct, full of observation and imagery. This was the language that helped shape the way I saw things, expressed things, made sense of the world.

Lately, I've been giving more thought to the kind of English my mother speaks. Like others, I have described it to people as "broken" or "fractured" English. But I wince when I say that. It has always bothered me that I can think of no way to describe it other than "broken," as if it were damaged and needed to be fixed, as if it lacked a certain wholeness and soundness. I've heard other terms used, "limited English," for example. But they seem just as bad, as if everything is limited, including people's perceptions of the limited English speaker.

I know this for a fact, because when I was growing up, my mother's "limited" English limited *my* perception of her. I was ashamed of her English. I believed that her English reflected the quality of what she had to say. That is, because she expressed them imperfectly her thoughts were imperfect. And I had plenty of empirical evidence to support me: the fact that people in department stores, at banks, and at restaurants did not take her seriously, did not give her good service, pretended not to understand her, or even acted as if they did not hear her.

My mother has long realized the limitations of her English as well. When I was fifteen, she used to have me call people on the phone to pretend I was she. In this guise, I was forced to ask for information or even complain and yell at people who had been rude to her. One time it was a call to her stockbroker in New York. She had cashed out her small portfolio and it just so happened we were going to go to New York the next week, our very first trip outside California. I had to get on the phone and say in an adolescent voice that was not very convincing, "This is Mrs. Tan."

And my mother was standing in the back whispering loudly, "Why he don't send me check, already two weeks late. So mad he lie to me, losing me money."

And then I said in perfect English, "Yes, I'm getting rather concerned. You had agreed to send the check two weeks ago, but it hasn't arrived."

Then she began to talk more loudly. "What he want, I come to New York tell him front of his boss, you cheating me?" And I was trying to calm her down, make her be quiet, while telling the stockbroker, "I can't tolerate any more excuses. If I don't receive the check immediately I am going to have to speak to your manager when I'm in New York next week." And sure enough, the following week there we were in front of this astonished stockbroker, and I was sitting there red-faced and quiet, and my mother, the real Mrs. Tan, was shouting at his boss in her impeccable broken English.

We used a similar routine just five days ago, for a situation that was far less humorous. My mother had gone to the hospital for an appointment, to find out about a benign brain tumor a CAT scan had revealed a month ago. She said she had spoken very good English, her best English, no mistakes. Still, she said, the hospital did not apologize when they said they had lost the CAT scan and she had come for nothing. She said they did not seem to have any sympathy when she told them she was anxious to know the exact diagnosis, since her husband and son had both died of brain tumors. She said they would not give her any more information until the next time and she would have to make another appointment for that. So she said she would not leave until the doctor called her daughter. She wouldn't budge. And when the doctor finally called her daughter, me, who spoke in perfect English — lo and behold — we had assurances the CAT scan would be found, promises that a conference call on Monday would be held, and apologies for any suffering my mother had gone through for a most regrettable mistake.

I think my mother's English almost had an effect on limiting my pos- 15 sibilities in life as well. Sociologists and linguists probably will tell you that a person's developing language skills are more influenced by peers. But I do think that the language spoken in the family, especially in immigrant families which are more insular, plays a large role in shaping the language of the child. And I believe that it affected my results on achievement tests, IQ tests, and the SAT. While my English skills were never judged as poor, compared to math, English could not be considered my strong suit. In grade school I did moderately well, getting perhaps B's, sometimes B-pluses, in English and scoring perhaps in the sixtieth or seventieth percentile on achievement tests. But those scores were not good enough to override the opinion that my true abilities lay in math and science, because in those areas I achieved A's and scored in the ninetieth percentile or higher.

This was understandable. Math is precise; there is only one correct 16 answer. Whereas, for me at least, the answers on English tests were always a judgment call, a matter of opinion and personal experience. Those tests were constructed around items like fill-in-the-blank sentence completion, such as "Even though Tom was _____, Mary thought he was _____." And the correct answer always seemed to be the most bland combinations of thoughts, for example, "Even though Tom was shy, Mary thought he was charming," with the grammatical structure "even though" limiting the correct answer to some sort of semantic opposites, so you wouldn't get answers like, "Even though Tom was foolish, Mary thought he was ridiculous." Well, according to my mother, there were very few limitations as to what Tom could have been and what Mary might have thought of him. So I never did well on tests like that.

The same was true with word analogies, pairs of words in which you 17 were supposed to find some sort of logical, semantic relationship — for example, "*Sunset* is to *nightfall* as _____ is to _____." And here you would be presented with a list of four possible pairs, one of which showed the same kind of relationship: *red* is to *stoplight, bus* is to *arrival, chills* is to *fever, yawn* is to *boring*. Well, I could never think that way. I knew what the tests were asking, but I could not block out of my mind the images already created by the first pair, *"sunset* is to *nightfall"* — and I would see a burst of colors against a darkening sky, the moon rising, the lowering of a curtain of stars. And all the other pairs of words — red, bus, stoplight, boring — just threw up a mass of confusing images, making it impossible for me to sort out something as logical as saying: "A sunset precedes nightfall" is the same as "a chill precedes a fever." The only way I would have gotten that answer right would have been to imagine an associative situation, for example, my being disobedient and staying out past sunset, catching a chill at night, which turns into feverish pneumonia as punishment, which indeed did happen to me.

I have been thinking about all this lately, about my mother's English, about achievement tests. Because lately I've been asked, as a writer, why there are not more Asian Americans represented in American literature. Why are there few Asian Americans enrolled in creative writing programs? Why do so many Chinese students go into engineering? Well, these are broad sociological questions I can't begin to answer. But I have noticed in surveys — in fact, just last week — that Asian students, as a whole, always do significantly better on math achievement tests than in English. And this makes me think that there are other Asian-American students whose English spoken in the home might also be described as "broken" or "limited." And perhaps they also have teachers who are steering them away from writing and into math and science, which is what happened to me.   18

Fortunately, I happen to be rebellious in nature and enjoy the challenge of disproving assumptions made about me. I became an English major my first year in college, after being enrolled as pre-med. I started writing nonfiction as a freelancer the week after I was told by my former boss that writing was my worst skill and I should hone my talents toward account management.   19

But it wasn't until 1985 that I finally began to write fiction. And at first I wrote using what I thought to be wittily crafted sentences, sentences that would finally prove I had mastery over the English language. Here's an example from the first draft of a story that later made its way into *The Joy Luck Club,* but without this line: "That was my mental quandary in its nascent state." A terrible line, which I can barely pronounce.   20

Fortunately, for reasons I won't get into today, I later decided I should envision a reader for the stories I would write. And the reader I decided upon was my mother because these were stories about mothers. So with this reader in mind — and in fact she did read my early drafts — I began to write stories using all the Englishes I grew up with: the English I spoke to my mother, which for lack of a better term might be described as "simple"; the English she used with me, which for lack of a better term might be described as "broken"; my translation of her Chinese, which could certainly   21 be described as "watered down"; and what I imagined to be her translation of her Chinese if she could speak in perfect English, her internal language, and for that I sought to preserve the essence, but neither an English nor a Chinese structure. I wanted to capture what language ability tests can never reveal: her intent, her passion, her imagery, the rhythms of her speech and the nature of her thoughts.

Apart from what any critic had to say about my writing, I knew I had   22
succeeded where it counted when my mother finished reading my book and gave me her verdict: "So easy to read."

. . .

Comprehension

1. What is Tan classifying in this essay? What individual categories does she identify?

2. Where does Tan identify the different categories she discusses in "Mother Tongue"? Should she have identified these categories earlier? Explain your reasoning.

3. Does Tan illustrate each category she identifies? Does she treat all categories equally? If she does not, do you see this as a problem? Explain.

4. In what specific situations does Tan say her mother's "limited English" was a handicap? In what other situations might Mrs. Tan face difficulties?

5. What effects have her mother's English had on Tan's life?

6. How does Tan account for the difficulty she had in answering questions on achievement tests, particularly word analogies? Do you think her problems in this area can be explained by the level of her family's language skills, or might other factors also be to blame? Explain.

7. In paragraph 18, Tan considers the possible reasons for the absence of Asian Americans in the fields of language and literature. What explanations does she offer? What other explanations can you think of?

Purpose and Audience

1. Why do you suppose Tan opens her essay by explaining her qualifications? Why, for example, does she tell her readers she is "not a scholar of English or literature" (1) but a writer who is "fascinated by language in daily life" (2)?

2. Do you think Tan expects most of her readers to be Asian American? To be familiar with Asian-American languages and culture? How can you tell?

3. Is Tan's primary focus in this essay on language or on her mother? Explain your conclusion.

Style and Structure

1. This essay's style is relatively informal. For example, Tan uses *I* to refer to herself and addresses her readers as *you*. Identify other features that characterize her style as informal. Do you think a more formal style would strengthen her credibility? Explain your reasoning.

2. In paragraph 6, Tan quotes a passage of her mother's speech. What purpose does Tan say she wants this quotation to serve? What impression does it give of her mother? Do you think this effect is what Tan intended? Explain.

3. In paragraphs 10 through 13, Tan juxtaposes her mother's English with her own. What point do these quoted passages make?

4. The expression used in Tan's title, "Mother Tongue," is also used in paragraph 7. What does this expression generally mean? What does it seem to mean in this essay?

5. In paragraph 20, Tan quotes a "terrible line" from an early draft of part of her novel *The Joy Luck Club*. Why do you suppose she quotes this line? How is it different from the writing style she uses in "Mother Tongue"?

Vocabulary Projects

1. Define each of the following words as it is used in this selection.

nominalized (3)	guise (10)	semantic (16)
belies (7)	impeccable (13)	quandary (20)
empirical (9)	insular (15)	nascent (20)

2. In paragraph 8, Tan discusses the different words and phrases that might be used to describe her mother's spoken English. Which of these terms seems most accurate? Do you agree with Tan that these words are unsatisfactory? What other term for her mother's English would be both neutral and accurate?

Journal Entry

In paragraph 9, Tan says that when she was growing up she was sometimes ashamed of her mother because of her limited English proficiency. Have you ever felt ashamed of a parent (or a friend) because of his or her inability to "fit in" in some way? How do you feel now about your earlier reaction?

Writing Workshop

1. What different "Englishes" (or other languages) do you use in your day-to-day life as a student, employee, friend, and family member? Write a classification-and-division essay identifying, describing, and illustrating each kind of language and explaining the purpose it serves.

2. What kinds of problems does a person whose English is as limited as Mrs. Tan's face in the age of computers and instant communication? Write a classification-and-division essay that identifies and explains the kinds of problems you might encounter today if the level of your spoken English were comparable to Mrs. Tan's. Try to update some of the specific situations Tan describes, quoting Tan where necessary, and be sure to document any borrowed words or ideas and to include a works-cited page. (See the Appendix for information on documentation formats.)

3. Tan's essay focuses on spoken language, but people also use different kinds of *written* language in different situations. Write a classification-and-division essay that identifies and analyzes three different kinds of written English: one appropriate for your parents, one for a teacher or employer, and one for a friend. Illustrate each kind of language with a few sentences directed at each audience about your plans for your future. In your thesis statement, explain why all three kinds of language are necessary.

Combining the Patterns

Tan develops her essay with a series of anecdotes about her mother and about herself. How does this use of **narration** strengthen her essay? Could she have made her point about the use of different "Englishes" without these anecdotes? What other strategy could she have used?

Thematic Connections

- "Only Daughter" (page 97)
- "Sixty-Nine Cents" (page 102)
- "Words Left Unspoken" (page 172)
- "The Human Cost of an Illiterate Society" (page 248)

STEPHANIE ERICSSON

The Ways We Lie

Stephanie Ericsson (b. 1953) grew up in San Francisco and began writing as a teenager. She has been a screenwriter and an advertising copywriter and has published several books based on her own life. *Shamefaced: The Road to Recovery* and *Women of AA: Recovering Together* (both 1985) focus on her experiences with addiction; *Companion through the Darkness: Inner Dialogues on Grief* (1993) deals with the sudden death of her husband; and *Companion into the Dawn: Inner Dialogues on Loving* (1994) is a collection of essays.

Background on lies in politics and business
The following piece originally appeared as the cover article in the January 1993 issue of the *Utne Reader*, which was devoted to the theme of lies and lying. The subject had particular relevance after a year when the honesty of Bill Clinton — the newly elected U.S. president — had been questioned. (It also followed the furor surrounding the confirmation hearings of U.S. Supreme Court nominee Clarence Thomas, who denied allegations by attorney Anita Hill of workplace sexual harassment; here the question was who was telling the truth and who was not.) Six years later, President Clinton was accused of perjury and faced a Senate impeachment trial. More recently, lying was featured prominently in the news as executives at a number of major corporations were charged with falsifying records at the expense of employees and shareholders, and the Bush administration was accused of exaggerating the danger of weapons of mass destruction in Iraq to justify going to war.

The bank called today and I told them my deposit was in the mail, even though I hadn't written a check yet. It'd been a rough day. The baby I'm pregnant with decided to do aerobics on my lungs for two hours, our three-year-old daughter painted the living-room couch with lipstick, the IRS put me on hold for an hour, and I was late to a business meeting because I was tired. 1

I told my client the traffic had been bad. When my partner came home, his haggard face told me his day hadn't gone any better than mine, so when he asked, "How was your day?" I said, "Oh, fine," knowing that one more straw might break his back. A friend called and wanted to take me to lunch. I said I was busy. Four lies in the course of a day, none of which I felt the least bit guilty about. 2

We lie. We all do. We exaggerate, we minimize, we avoid confrontation, we spare people's feelings, we conveniently forget, we keep secrets, we justify lying to the big-guy institutions. Like most people, I indulge in small falsehoods and still think of myself as an honest person. Sure I lie, but it doesn't hurt anything. Or does it? 3

I once tried going a whole week without telling a lie, and it was paralyzing. I discovered that telling the truth all the time is nearly impossible. 4

It means living with some serious consequences: The bank charges me $60 in overdraft fees, my partner keels over when I tell him about my travails, my client fires me for telling her I didn't feel like being on time, and my friend takes it personally when I say I'm not hungry. There must be some merit to lying.

But if I justify lying, what makes me any different from slick politi-   5
cians or the corporate robbers who raided the S&L industry? Saying it's okay to lie one way and not another is hedging. I cannot seem to escape the voice deep inside me that tells me: When someone lies, someone loses.

What far-reaching consequences will I, or others, pay as a result of my   6
lie? Will someone's trust be destroyed? Will someone else pay *my* penance because I ducked out? We must consider the *meaning of our actions*. Deception, lies, capital crimes, and misdemeanors all carry meanings. *Webster's* definition of *lie* is specific:

> 1: a false statement or action especially made with the intent to deceive;
> 2: anything that gives or is meant to give a false impression.

A definition like this implies that there are many, many ways to tell a   7
lie. Here are just a few.

The White Lie

> A man who won't lie to a woman has very little consideration for
> her feelings.
> – BERGEN EVANS

The white lie assumes that the truth will cause more damage than a   8
simple, harmless untruth. Telling a friend he looks great when he looks like hell can be based on a decision that the friend needs a compliment more than a frank opinion. But, in effect, it is the liar deciding what is best for the lied to. Ultimately, it is a vote of no confidence. It is an act of subtle arrogance for anyone to decide what is best for someone else.

Yet not all circumstances are quite so cut-and-dried. Take, for instance,   9
the sergeant in Vietnam who knew one of his men was killed in action but listed him as missing so that the man's family would receive indefinite compensation instead of the lump-sum pittance the military gives widows and children. His intent was honorable. Yet for twenty years this family kept their hopes alive, unable to move on to a new life.

Facades

> Et tu, Brute?
> – CAESAR*

We all put up facades to one degree or another. When I put on a suit to   10
go to see a client, I feel as though I am putting on another face, obeying the

---

* EDS. NOTE — "And you, Brutus?" (Latin). In Shakespeare's play *Julius Caesar*, Caesar asks this question when he sees Brutus, whom he has believed to be his friend, among the conspirators who are stabbing him.

expectation that serious businesspeople wear suits rather than sweatpants. But I'm a writer. Normally, I get up, get the kid off to school, and sit at my computer in my pajamas until four in the afternoon. When I answer the phone, the caller thinks I'm wearing a suit (though the UPS man knows better).

But facades can be destructive because they are used to seduce others into an illusion. For instance, I recently realized that a former friend was a liar. He presented himself with all the right looks and the right words and offered lots of new consciousness theories, fabulous books to read, and fascinating insights. Then I did some business with him, and the time came for him to pay me. He turned out to be all talk and no walk. I heard a plethora of reasonable excuses, including in-depth descriptions of the big break around the corner. In six months of work, I saw less than a hundred bucks. When I confronted him, he raised both eyebrows and tried to convince me that I'd heard him wrong, that he'd made no commitment to me. A simple investigation into his past revealed a crowded graveyard of disenchanted former friends.

Ignoring the Plain Facts

> Well, you must understand that Father Porter is only human. . . .
> – A MASSACHUSETTS PRIEST

In the '60s, the Catholic Church in Massachusetts began hearing complaints that Father James Porter was sexually molesting children. Rather than relieving him of his duties, the ecclesiastical authorities simply moved him from one parish to another between 1960 and 1967, actually providing him with a fresh supply of unsuspecting families and innocent children to abuse. After treatment in 1967 for pedophilia, he went back to work, this time in Minnesota. The new diocese was aware of Father Porter's obsession with children, but they needed priests and recklessly believed treatment had cured him. More children were abused until he was relieved of his duties a year later. By his own admission, Porter may have abused as many as a hundred children.

Ignoring the facts may not in and of itself be a form of lying, but consider the context of this situation. If a lie is *a false action done with the intent to deceive,* then the Catholic Church's conscious covering for Porter created irreparable consequences. The church became a co-perpetrator with Porter.

Deflecting

> When you have no basis for an argument, abuse the plaintiff.
> – CICERO

I've discovered that I can keep anyone from seeing the true me by being selectively blatant. I set a precedent of being up-front about intimate issues, but I never bring up the things I truly want to hide; I just let people assume I'm revealing everything. It's an effective way of hiding.

Any good liar knows that the way to perpetuate an untruth is to deflect   15
attention from it. When Clarence Thomas exploded with accusations that
the Senate hearings were a "high-tech lynching," he simply switched the
focus from a highly charged subject to a radioactive subject. Rather than
defending himself, he took the offensive and accused the country of racism. It was a brilliant maneuver. Racism is now politically incorrect in official circles — unlike sexual harassment, which still rewards those who can
get away with it.

Some of the most skillful deflectors are passive-aggressive people who,   16
when accused of inappropriate behavior, refuse to respond to the accusations. This you-don't-exist stance infuriates the accuser, who, understandably, screams something obscene out of frustration. The trap is sprung
and the act of deflection successful, because now the passive-aggressive
person can indignantly say, "Who can talk to someone as unreasonable as
you?" The real issue is forgotten and the sins of the original victim become
the focus. Feeling guilty of name-calling, the victim is fully tamed and
crawls into a hole, ashamed. I have watched this fighting technique work
thousands of times in disputes between men and women, and what I've
learned is that the real culprit is not necessarily the one who swears the
loudest.

Omission

> The cruelest lies are often told in silence.
> – R. L. STEVENSON

Omission involves telling most of the truth minus one or two key facts   17
whose absence changes the story completely. You break a pair of glasses
that are guaranteed under normal use and get a new pair, without mentioning that the first pair broke during a rowdy game of basketball. Who
hasn't tried something like that? But what about omission of information
that could make a difference in how a person lives his or her life?

For instance, one day I found out that rabbinical legends tell of another   18
woman in the Garden of Eden before Eve. I was stunned. The omission of
the Sumerian goddess Lilith from Genesis — as well as her demonization
by ancient misogynists as an embodiment of female evil — felt like spiritual
robbery. I felt like I'd just found out my mother was really my stepmother.
To take seriously the tradition that Adam was created out of the same mud
as his equal counterpart, Lilith, redefines all of Judeo-Christian history.

Some renegade Catholic feminists introduced me to a view of Lilith   19
that had been suppressed during the many centuries when this strong goddess was seen only as a spirit of evil. Lilith was a proud goddess who defied
Adam's need to control her, attempted negotiations, and when this failed,
said adios and left the Garden of Eden.

This omission of Lilith from the Bible was a patriarchal strategy to   20
keep women weak. Omitting the strong-woman archetype of Lilith from
Western religions and starting the story with Eve the Rib has helped keep

Christian and Jewish women believing they were the lesser sex for thousands of years.

Stereotypes and Clichés

> Where opinion does not exist, the status quo becomes stereotyped
> and all originality is discouraged.
> — BERTRAND RUSSELL

21   Stereotype and cliché serve a purpose as a form of shorthand. Our need for vast amounts of information in nanoseconds has made the stereotype vital to modern communication. Unfortunately, it often shuts down original thinking, giving those hungry for the truth a candy bar of misinformation instead of a balanced meal. The stereotype explains a situation with just enough truth to seem unquestionable.

22   All the "isms" — racism, sexism, ageism, et al. — are founded on and fueled by the stereotype and the cliché, which are lies of exaggeration, omission, and ignorance. They are always dangerous. They take a single tree and make it a landscape. They destroy curiosity. They close minds and separate people. The single mother on welfare is assumed to be cheating. Any black male could tell you how much of his identity is obliterated daily by stereotypes. Fat people, ugly people, beautiful people, old people, large-breasted women, short men, the mentally ill, and the homeless all could tell you how much more they are like us than we want to think. I once admitted to a group of people that I had a mouth like a truck driver. Much to my surprise, a man stood up and said, "I'm a truck driver, and I never cuss." Needless to say, I was humbled.

Groupthink

> Who is more foolish, the child afraid of the dark, or the man afraid
> of the light?
> — MAURICE FREEHILL

23   Irving Janis, in *Victims of GroupThink,* defines this sort of lie as a psychological phenomenon within decision-making groups in which loyalty to the group has become more important than any other value, with the result that dissent and the appraisal of alternatives are suppressed. If you've ever worked on a committee or in a corporation, you've encountered groupthink. It requires a combination of other forms of lying — ignoring facts, selective memory, omission, and denial, to name a few.

24   The textbook example of groupthink came on December 7, 1941. From as early as the fall of 1941, the warnings came in, one after another, that Japan was preparing for a massive military operation. The Navy command in Hawaii assumed Pearl Harbor was invulnerable — the Japanese weren't stupid enough to attack the United States' most important base. On the other hand, racist stereotypes said the Japanese weren't smart enough to

invent a torpedo effective in less than 60 feet of water (the fleet was docked in 30 feet); after all, U.S. technology hadn't been able to do it.

On Friday, December 5, normal weekend leave was granted to all the   25
commanders at Pearl Harbor, even though the Japanese consulate in Hawaii was busy burning papers. Within the tight, good-ole-boy cohesiveness of the U.S. command in Hawaii, the myth of invulnerability stayed well entrenched. No one in the group considered the alternatives. The rest is history.

Out-and-Out Lies

The only form of lying that is beyond reproach is lying for its own sake.

– Oscar Wilde

Of all the ways to lie, I like this one the best, probably because I get   26
tired of trying to figure out the real meanings behind things. At least I can trust the bald-faced lie. I once asked my five-year-old nephew, "Who broke the fence?" (I had seen him do it.) He answered, "The murderers." Who could argue?

At least when this sort of lie is told it can be easily confronted. As the   27
person who is lied to, I know where I stand. The bald-faced lie doesn't toy with my perceptions — it argues with them. It doesn't try to refashion reality, it tries to refute it. *Read my lips.* . . . No sleight of hand. No guessing. If this were the only form of lying, there would be no such thing as floating anxiety or the adult-children of alcoholics movement.

Dismissal

Pay no attention to that man behind the curtain! I am the Great Oz!

– The Wizard of Oz

Dismissal is perhaps the slipperiest of all lies. Dismissing feelings, per-   28
ceptions, or even the raw facts of a situation ranks as a kind of lie that can do as much damage to a person as any other kind of lie.

The roots of many mental disorders can be traced back to the dismissal   29
of reality. Imagine that a person is told from the time she is a tot that her perceptions are inaccurate. *"Mommy, I'm scared."* "No, you're not, darling." *"I don't like that man next door, he makes me feel icky."* "Johnny, that's a terrible thing to say, of course you like him. You go over there right now and be nice to him."

I've often mused over the idea that madness is actually a sane reaction   30
to an insane world. Psychologist R. D. Laing supports this hypothesis in *Sanity, Madness & the Family,* an account of his investigations into families of schizophrenics. The common thread that ran through all of the families he studied was a deliberate, staunch dismissal of the patient's perceptions

from a very early age. Each of the patients started out with an accurate grasp of reality, which, through meticulous and methodical dismissal, was demolished until the only reality the patient could trust was catatonia.

Dismissal runs the gamut. Mild dismissal can be quite handy for for-   31
giving the foibles of others in our day-to-day lives. Toddlers who have just learned to manipulate their parents' attention sometimes are dismissed out of necessity. Absolute attention from the parents would require so much energy that no one would get to eat dinner. But we must be careful and attentive about how far we take our "necessary" dismissals. Dismissal is a dangerous tool, because it's nothing less than a lie.

Delusion

> We lie loudest when we lie to ourselves.
> – ERIC HOFFER

I could write the book on this one. Delusion, a cousin of dismissal, is   32
the tendency to see excuses as facts. It's a powerful lying tool because it fil-ters out information that contradicts what we want to believe. Alcoholics who believe that the problems in their lives are legitimate reasons for drink-ing rather than results of the drinking offer the classic example of deluded thinking. Delusion uses the mind's ability to see things in myriad ways to support what it wants to be the truth.

But delusion is also a survival mechanism we all use. If we were to fully   33
contemplate the consequences of our stockpiles of nuclear weapons or global warming, we could hardly function on a day-to-day level. We don't want to incorporate that much reality into our lives because to do so would be paralyzing.

Delusion acts as an adhesive to keep the status quo intact. It shame-   34
lessly employs dismissal, omission, and amnesia, among other sorts of lies. Its most cunning defense is that it cannot see itself.

> The liar's punishment . . . is that he cannot believe anyone else.
> – GEORGE BERNARD SHAW

These are only a few of the ways we lie. Or are lied to. As I said earlier,   35
it's not easy to entirely eliminate lies from our lives. No matter how pious we may try to be, we will still embellish, hedge, and omit to lubricate the daily machinery of living. But there is a world of difference between telling functional lies and living a lie. Martin Buber* once said, "The lie is the spirit committing treason against itself." Our acceptance of lies becomes a cultural cancer that eventually shrouds and reorders reality until moral garbage becomes as invisible to us as water is to a fish.

How much do we tolerate before we become sick and tired of being   36
sick and tired? When will we stand up and declare our *right* to trust? When

---

* EDS. NOTE — Austrian-born Judaic philosopher (1878–1965).

do we stop accepting that the real truth is in the fine print? Whose lips do we read this year when we vote for president? When will we stop being so reticent about making judgments? When do we stop turning over our personal power and responsibility to liars?

Maybe if I don't tell the bank the check's in the mail I'll be less tolerant   37
of the lies told me every day. A country song I once heard said it all for me: "You've got to stand for something or you'll fall for anything."

• • •

Comprehension

1. List and briefly define each of the ten kinds of lies Ericsson identifies.
2. Why, in Ericsson's view, is each kind of lie necessary?
3. According to Ericsson, what is the danger of each kind of lie?
4. Why does Ericsson like "out-and-out lies" (26–27) best?
5. Why is "dismissal" the "slipperiest of all lies" (28)?

Purpose and Audience

1. Is Ericsson's thesis simply that "there are many, many ways to tell a lie" (7)? Or is she defending — or attacking — the process of lying? Try to state her thesis in a single sentence.
2. Do you think Ericsson's choice of examples reveals a political bias? If so, do you think she expects her intended audience to share her views? Explain your conclusion.

Style and Structure

1. Despite the seriousness of her subject matter, Ericsson's essay is informal; her opening paragraphs are especially personal and breezy. Why do you think she uses this kind of opening? Do you think her decision makes sense?
2. Ericsson introduces each category of lie with a quotation. What function do these quotations serve? Do you think the essay would be more or less effective without them? Explain your conclusion.
3. In addition to a heading and a quotation, what other elements does Ericsson include in her treatment of each kind of lie? Are all the discussions parallel — that is, does each include *all* the standard elements and *only* those elements? If not, do you think this lack of balance is a problem? Explain.
4. What, if anything, determines the order in which Ericsson arranges her categories? Do you think any category should be relocated? If so, why?
5. Throughout her essay, Ericsson uses **rhetorical questions**. Why do you suppose she uses this stylistic device?

6. Ericsson occasionally cites the views of experts. Why does she do so? If she wished to cite additional experts, what professional backgrounds or fields of study do you think they should represent? Why?

7. In paragraph 29, Ericsson says, "Imagine that a person is told from the time she is a tot. . . ." Does she use *she* in similar contexts elsewhere in the essay? Do you find the feminine form of the personal pronoun appropriate or distracting? Explain.

8. Paragraphs 35–37 constitute Ericsson's conclusion. How does this conclusion parallel the essay's introduction in terms of style, structure, and content?

Vocabulary Projects

1. Define each of the following words as it is used in this selection.

travails (4)	deflectors (16)	staunch (30)
hedging (5)	passive-aggressive (16)	catatonia (30)
pittance (9)	misogynists (18)	gamut (31)
facades (10)	counterpart (18)	foibles (31)
plethora (11)	archetype (20)	reticent (36)
pedophilia (12)	nanoseconds (21)	
blatant (14)	obliterated (22)	

2. Ericsson uses many **colloquialisms** in this essay — for example, "I could write the book on this one" (32). Identify as many of these informed expressions as you can. Why do you think she uses colloquialisms instead of more formal expressions? Do they have a positive or negative effect on your reaction to her ideas? Explain.

Journal Entry

In paragraph 3, Ericsson says, "We lie. We all do." Later in the paragraph, she comments, "Sure I lie, but it doesn't hurt anything. Or does it?" Answer her question.

Writing Workshop

1. Choose three or four of Ericsson's categories, and write a classification-and-division essay called "The Ways I Lie." Base your essay on personal experience, and include an explicit thesis statement that defends these lies — or is sharply critical of their use. Be sure to document Ericsson's essay when you cite her categories, and to include a works-cited page. (See the Appendix for information on documentation formats.)

2. In paragraph 22, Ericsson condemns stereotypes. Write a classification-and-division essay with the following thesis statement: "Stereotypes are usually inaccurate, often negative, and always dangerous." In your essay, consider the stereotypes applied to three or four of the following groups:

people who are disabled, overweight, or elderly; teenagers; politicians; housewives; and immigrants.

3. Using the thesis provided in question 2, write a classification-and-division essay that considers the stereotypes applied to three or four of the following occupations: police officers, librarians, used-car dealers, flight attendants, lawyers, construction workers, rock musicians, accountants, and telemarketers.

Combining the Patterns

A dictionary **definition** is a familiar — even tired — strategy for an essay's introduction. Would you advise Ericsson to delete the definition in paragraph 6 for this reason, or do you believe it is necessary? Explain.

Thematic Connections

- " 'What's in a Name?' " (page 5)
- "Thirty-Eight Who Saw Murder Didn't Call the Police" (page 120)
- "The Hidden Life of Garbage" (page 177)
- "The Lottery" (page 311)
- "The Power of Words in Wartime" (page 363)

JONATHAN KOPPELL

On the Internet, There's No Place to Hide

An associate professor of politics and management at Yale University, Jonathan Koppell (b. 1971) studies the design and administration of complex organizations, such as government-created entities that operate in the marketplace to achieve public policy goals. He has published the book *The Politics of Quasi-Government* (2003), as well as numerous scholarly articles and essays for periodicals including the *New York Times*, the *Wall Street Journal*, and the *Atlantic Monthly*. The following essay was originally published in 2000 in *The Industry Standard*, a newsmagazine devoted to the Internet economy.

Background on "Big Brother" and government surveillance
In George Orwell's novel *Nineteen Eighty-Four* (1949), Big Brother is the dictatorial leader of the fictional Oceania, a totalitarian state whose citizens are under constant governmental surveillance and control. While there is some question in the novel as to whether Big Brother is an actual person or simply represents Oceania's power structure, his image is everywhere, accompanied by the constant exhortation "Big Brother is watching you." The name "Big Brother" has come to personify any powerful interests that attempt to exercise strict control through surveillance of citizens, employees, and the like. In the aftermath of the 9/11 attacks, the Bush administration and Congress significantly broadened the government's powers to secretly track U.S. citizens, leading critics to charge that the United States has become a Big Brother–style surveillance state.

In its early years, one of the most cherished characteristics the Internet 1 offered was anonymity. Online, no one knew your real name.

You were also anonymous in a deeper sense. In chat rooms or MUDs, 2 Net denizens could become anyone they wanted. A bored, thirtysomething middle manager could spend a few hours as a wealthy fashion model, big-game hunter, or eighteen-year-old college coed. Your imagination was the only constraint on your identity. In the words of the famous New Yorker cartoon, no one knew you were a dog.

Fifteen or so years later, the commercialization of the Internet is 3 assaulting both types of anonymity. Information about individuals is now a treasured commodity. A computer user could once hide his or her identity with ease. It can still be done, but it takes considerably more work.

The first type of anonymity — I'll call it "name anonymity" — has con- 4 sumed most of our attention. Privacy advocates have decried infringements on name anonymity by both government and business.

Big Brother certainly has the resources and, depending on whom you ask, the technology to track people as they move about the Web. This is genuinely disturbing. Suppose the friendly folks at the National Security Agency listen in on your Echelon transmissions and become interested in your frequent use of the word "revolution." They could follow your online activities, with staggering opportunities for invasion of privacy. They could punch up your eBay bids to search for suspicious items, see what seditious literature you were reviewing at Amazon.com, check out your dietary habits through your Webvan purchases. Before you know it, there's a knock on the door, and blammo! Janet Reno's* working your grandmother over with a garden hose. 5

Or maybe not. Call me naive but that possibility, in this country at least, still seems remote. For most people, the bigger threat is from profit-seeking data collectors, driven by an insatiable thirst among marketers for lists of promising customers. 6

Several companies are trying to efficiently amass data on individuals based on their online activities. So, for example, after you enter your name and address to win an online raffle, the data-gathering company will track your surfing habits to establish your likes and dislikes. In theory, this aggregated information can then be sold to companies that can send email and snail mail perfectly crafted to appeal to you. 7

So far, the promise of perfect information for Web-based marketers falls short of the reality. Even without action from Congress or the Federal Trade Commission, name anonymity seems relatively safe for the time being. 8

But don't get too comfortable. The second type of anonymity — the ability to hide and alter our defining characteristics — is very much under siege. I call this "profile anonymity." 9

It turns out that to marketers and advertisers, your name is not terribly important. Oh, they certainly would like to know your name, address, and so on. It makes direct mail that much more effective. But what matters most is your profile. They want to know what you are. 10

In what city do you live? How old are you? What is your race, religion, ethnicity? The answers to these questions define you as a consumer. With this kind of knowledge, advertisers can make refined pitches ostensibly crafted to persuade someone just like you, if not you. 11

Until the technology to accumulate large quantities of data linked to individuals is improved, the dominant techniques of building profiles are simple. For example, Internet users are being funneled through portals designed to attract consumers that fit a certain profile. There are portals for African Americans, women, gays, Latinos, and more. At many sites, people are induced by offers for goods and services to fill out questionnaires that help establish salient characteristics of interest to marketers. 12

---

* EDS. NOTE — Former United States attorney general.

This lets companies target types of people, even if they can't target   13
individuals. In this sense, your profile anonymity is eroded. Where once it
could be said that "no one knows you're a dog," that is no longer the case.
Indeed, a more contemporary caption to the New Yorker cartoon would
read, "On the Internet, everyone knows you're an aging, overweight,
malamute-retriever mix living in the Southwest, and with a preference for
rawhide."

So what? Is there any reason to care whether people are identified by   14
their Internet habits, especially if these cannot be linked to a name? After
all, if the worst thing that happens is that a fictitious FloraBonita.com targets left-handed gay and Latino gardeners for its Web ads, who cares?

I do. The commercial pressure to identify online individuals by their   15
demographic characteristics reinforces many of the schisms in society.
Instead of breaking down barriers by allowing people to escape predeter-
mined categories, the Internet now reinforces identities, swells their significance in a whole new context, and makes it more difficult to be seen as
an individual separate from racial, ethnic, or gender identifiers.

This means something in real terms. Consider services that attempt to   16
agglomerate computer users by customizing newspapers based on their
identifying traits. By limiting exposure to news that is not "relevant" to a
certain group, our biases and preconceptions may be hardened because
they will remain unquestioned.

There will always be discord in society, with or without the Internet.   17
Whether we are less likely to get together and sing "Kumbaya"* is of no
concern to me. But practically speaking, building consensus in a multiracial, multicultural world becomes increasingly difficult if society is fractured. While Web portals are not necessarily going to bring about social
disintegration tomorrow, they and similar devices of division encourage
some of our most antisocial tendencies.

Politicians are more likely to fuel this trend than combat it. Although   18
balkanization of the population inevitably makes policy-making more
contentious and challenging, splitting up the electorate has traditionally
served electoral purposes. The same logic that leads marketers to subdivide
audiences appeals to candidates seeking votes.

Candidate Web pages already solicit information from visitors and   19
direct them to particular areas within their sites. Thus the Jewish voter, the
soccer mom, or the blue-collar white male see different faces of the candidate. This makes possible a type of high-tech pandering. Without broadcasting potentially alienating views to all audiences, politicians can appeal
to the basest interests of supporters without broader accountability.

What made the Internet truly distinctive was its potential to corrode   20
superficial barriers, to let people escape the confines of identity. Currently, it is
relatively easy to avoid identification on the Web, but it has to be approached
consciously. Every time you check weather forecasts or movie times, for

---

* EDS. NOTE — Folk song popular in the American civil rights movement.

example, you disclose your location. Surfers have been single-minded in their concern for name anonymity, with little or no concern for profile anonymity. Privacy protection may keep our names and numbers from prying eyes, but we may never again be able to lose ourselves in cyberspace.

• • •

Comprehension

1. What two categories of anonymity does Koppell focus on in this essay?
2. Does Koppell define each type of anonymity? If so, where? If not, write a one-sentence definition for each.
3. What does Koppell see as the advantages of maintaining anonymity on the Internet?
4. What dangers does Koppell see in losing anonymity online?
5. Which of the two types of anonymity does Koppell think is more important? Why?
6. Do you think the scenario presented in paragraph 5 is a realistic one? Does Koppell?
7. In paragraph 10, Koppell says that marketers and advertisers "want to know what you are." What does he mean by "what you are"? *Why* do they want to know this?
8. In paragraphs 15–18 of this classification-and-division essay, Koppell expresses his concerns about the dangers of establishing categories of Internet users and classifying people on the basis of gender, race, income, and so on. What specific dangers does he envision?

Purpose and Audience

1. Is Koppell writing for a general audience or for an audience that is knowledgeable about computers? How can you tell?
2. What do you think Koppell hopes to accomplish by referring in paragraph 2 to the "famous *New Yorker* cartoon" (see page 499)? By bringing it up again in paragraph 13?
3. In your own words, state this essay's thesis.

Style and Structure

1. In paragraph 14, Koppell asks a series of questions, and he goes on to answer the last one in the following paragraph. Is his answer enough?
2. In paragraphs 15–18, when Koppell discusses his fears about dividing and classifying Internet users, he uses a number of words that suggest these related operations. For example, he uses the words *categories* (15), *division* (17), and *subdivide* (18). What other words suggest division and classification?
3. What does Koppell mean by "high-tech pandering" (19)? What connotations does the word *pandering* have?

4. Do you think Koppell's title suits his essay? Can you suggest a better title — for example, one that is more concise?

5. The *New Yorker* cartoon Koppell refers to is shown below. Do you think he should have included it in his essay? Why or why not?

"On the Internet, nobody knows you're a dog."

Vocabulary Projects

1. Define each of the following words as it is used in this selection.

denizens (2)	insatiable (6)	agglomerate (16)
decried (4)	salient (12)	balkanization (18)
infringements (4)	demographic (15)	pandering (19)
seditious (5)	schisms (15)	

2. List all the specialized computer terms Koppell uses in this essay. Which, if any, do you think need to be defined for a general audience?

Journal Entry

Reread paragraph 7. Do you think the scenario described here is alarming? Explain why (or why not).

Writing Workshop

1. Decide on a principle of classification for Internet users — for example, age or geographic location — and create three or four different categories. Name each category, and then write a classification-and-division essay in which you discuss what products or services online advertisers might like to sell to each group and how they might customize their approaches to reach them. In your thesis and in your conclusion, take a stand for or against this type of niche marketing, referring to paragraphs 15–18 of Koppell's essay. Be sure to document any of his words or ideas that you borrow and to include a works-cited page. (See the Appendix for information on documentation formats.)

2. Review some of your friends' Facebook or MySpace profiles. Then, write an essay in which you classify these profiles according to how "anonymous" (and how revealing) they are. In your thesis, express your opinion about what kind of profile you consider to be too revealing, and why.

3. Visit several Internet dating sites, such as Match.com or Eharmony.com. Consider what these sites say they do to protect subscribers' privacy — and what more you think they *should* do. Then, write a classification-and-division essay that considers the different kinds of problems that might be created by a loss of anonymity on a dating site. Give each category of problem a descriptive title.

Combining the Patterns

Although Koppell identifies two distinct categories of anonymity, he does not compare or contrast them. If he added a paragraph of **comparison and contrast** to his essay, what points of similarity or difference should it include? Where would the paragraph go? Do you think such a paragraph would be a good addition to the essay? Explain why or why not.

Thematic Connections

- "Thirty-Eight Who Saw Murder Didn't Call the Police" (page 120)
- "I'm Your Teacher, Not Your Internet-Service Provider" (page 416)
- "Friending, Ancient or Otherwise" (page 431)

Five Ways to Kill a Man (Poetry)

Edwin Brock (1927–1997) was born in London, England. As a young man, he served in the Royal Navy for two years, and he later worked as a police officer. His first poetry collection, *An Attempt at Exorcism,* was published in 1959. He went on to work as an advertising copywriter while publishing more than a dozen poetry collections. He is also the author of the novel *The Little White God* (1962) and the memoir *Here, Now, Always* (1977).

Background on the poem
In the following 1963 poem, the first stanza refers to the crucifixion of Jesus, as described in the New Testament. Nailing a victim to a pole or cross was a form of capital punishment practiced in ancient times, especially by the Romans. The second stanza refers to the battling of knights suited in armor during the European Middle Ages. The third stanza refers to the trench warfare and mustard-gas bombs used by German and British forces during World War I. These bombs caused severe blistering, blindness, and respiratory failure, resulting in many casualties. The fourth stanza refers to the aerial bombing conducted during World War II — the German attacks on London, the Japanese attack on Pearl Harbor, and the U.S. atomic bombs dropped on Hiroshima and Nagasaki in Japan.

There are many cumbersome ways to kill a man:
you can make him carry a plank of wood
to the top of a hill and nail him to it. To do this
properly you require a crowd of people
wearing sandals, a cock that crows, a cloak   5
to dissect, a sponge, some vinegar and one
man to hammer the nails home.

Or you can take a length of steel,
shaped and chased in a traditional way,
and attempt to pierce the metal cage he wears.   10
But for this you need white horses,
English trees, men with bows and arrows,
at least two flags, a prince and a
castle to hold your banquet in.

Dispensing with nobility, you may, if the wind   15
allows, blow gas at him. But then you need
a mile of mud sliced through with ditches,
not to mention black boots, bomb craters,
more mud, a plague of rats, a dozen songs
and some round hats made of steel.   20

In an age of aeroplanes, you may fly
miles above your victim and dispose of him by
pressing one small switch. All you then
require is an ocean to separate you, two
systems of government, a nation's scientists,   25
several factories, a psychopath and
land that no one needs for several years.

These are, as I began, cumbersome ways
to kill a man. Simpler, direct, and much more neat
is to see that he is living somewhere in the middle   30
of the twentieth century, and leave him there.

•   •   •

Reading Literature

1. What four ways to kill a man does the poem's speaker identify in stanzas 1–4? What method does he identify in the poem's final stanza?
2. What other examples can you give for each category?
3. When the speaker uses the word *you*, to whom is he referring?

Journal Entry

Why does the speaker see the first four methods of killing as "cumbersome" (1)? Why is the final method "Simpler, direct, and much more neat" (29)?

Thematic Connections

- "Ground Zero" (page 167)
- "Get It Right: Privatize Executions" (page 299)
- "The Lottery" (page 311)
- "Thanks to Modern Science" (page 573)
- "Torture's Terrible Toll" (page 696)

WRITING ASSIGNMENTS FOR CLASSIFICATION AND DIVISION

1. Choose a film you have seen recently, and list all the elements you consider significant — plot, direction, acting, special effects, and so on. Then, further subdivide each category (for instance, listing each of the special effects). Using this list as an outline, write a review of the film.

2. Write an essay classifying the teachers or bosses you have had into several distinct categories, and make a judgment about the relative effectiveness of the individuals in each group. Give each category a name, and be sure your essay has a thesis statement.

3. What fashion styles do you observe on your college campus? Establish four or five distinct categories, and write an essay classifying students on the basis of how they dress. Give each group of students a descriptive title.

4. Look through this book's thematic table of contents (page xxxi), and choose three essays on the same general subject. Then, write an essay discussing the different ways writers can explore the same theme. Be sure your topic sentences clearly define your three categories. Document all references to the essays you choose, and include a works-cited page. (See the Appendix for information on documentation formats.)

5. Many consider violence in sports a serious problem. Write an essay expressing your views on this problem. Using a classification-and-division structure, categorize information according to sources of violence (such as the players, the nature of the game, and the fans).

6. Classify television shows according to type (reality show, crime drama, and so forth), audience (preschoolers, school-age children, adults, and so on), or any other logical principle. Write an essay based on your system of classification, making sure to include a thesis statement. For instance, you might assert that the relative popularity of one kind of program over others reveals something about television watchers or that one kind of program shows signs of becoming obsolete.

7. Write a lighthearted essay discussing kinds of snack foods, cartoons, pets, status symbols, toys, shoppers, vacations, weight-loss diets, hairstyles, or drivers.

8. Write an essay assessing the relative merits of several different politicians, Web sites, news broadcasts, or academic majors.

9. What kinds of survival skills does a student need to get through college successfully? Write a classification-and-division essay identifying and discussing several kinds of skills and indicating why each category is important. If you like, you may write your essay in the form of an email to a beginning college student.

10. After attending a party or concert, write an essay dividing the people you observe there into categories according to some logical principle. Include a thesis statement that indicates how different the various groups are.

COLLABORATIVE ACTIVITY FOR CLASSIFICATION AND DIVISION

Working in a group of four students, devise a classification system encompassing all the different kinds of popular music the members of your group favor. You may begin with general categories, such as country, pop, and rhythm and blues, but you should also include more specific categories, such as rap and heavy metal, in your classification system. After you decide on categories and subcategories that represent the tastes of all group members, fill in examples for each category. Then, devise several different options for arranging your categories into an essay.

13
Definition

WHAT IS DEFINITION?

A **definition** tells what a term means and how it differs from other terms in its class. In the following paragraph from "Altruistic Behavior," anthropologist Desmond Morris defines *altruism,* the key term of his essay:

Topic sentence	Altruism is the performance of an unselfish act. As a pattern of behavior, this act must have two
Extended defini- **tion defines term** **by** *enumeration* **and** *negation*	properties: it must benefit someone else, and it must do so to the disadvantage of the benefactor. It is not merely a matter of being helpful; it is helpfulness at a cost to yourself.

Most people think of definition in terms of print or online dictionaries, which give brief, succinct explanations — called **formal definitions** — of what words mean. But definition also includes explaining what something, or even someone, *is* — that is, its essential nature. Sometimes a definition requires a paragraph, an essay, or even a whole book. These longer, more complex definitions are called **extended definitions**.

Understanding Formal Definitions

Look at any dictionary, and you will notice that all definitions have a standard three-part structure. First, they present the *term* to be defined, then the general *class* it is a part of, and finally the *qualities that differentiate it* from the other terms in the same class.

TERM	CLASS	DIFFERENTIATION
behaviorism	a theory	that regards the objective facts of a subject's actions as the only valid basis for psychological study

cell	a unit of protoplasm	with a nucleus, cytoplasm, and an enclosing membrane
naturalism	a literary movement	whose original adherents believed that writers should treat life with scientific objectivity
mitosis	a process	of nuclear division of cells, consisting of prophase, metaphase, anaphase, and telophase
authority	a power	to command and require obedience

Understanding Extended Definitions

Many extended-definition essays include short formal definitions like those in dictionaries. In such an essay, a brief formal definition can introduce readers to the extended definition, or it can help to support the essay's thesis. However, an extended definition does not follow a set **pattern of development**. Instead, it uses whatever strategies best suit the writer's purpose, the term being defined, and the writing situation. In fact, any one (or more than one) of the essay patterns illustrated in this book can be used to structure a definition essay.

USING DEFINITION

Providing a formal definition of each term you use is seldom necessary or desirable. Readers will either know what a word means or be able to look it up. Sometimes, however, defining your terms is essential. For example, when taking an exam, you are likely to encounter questions that require definitions. You might, for example, be asked to define *behaviorism*; tell what a *cell* is; explain the meaning of the literary term *naturalism*; include a comprehensive definition of *mitosis* in your answer; or define *authority*. Such exam questions cannot always be answered in a sentence or two. In fact, the definitions they call for often require a full paragraph — or even several paragraphs.

Extended definitions are useful in many academic assignments besides exams. For example, definitions can explain abstractions such as *freedom*, controversial terms such as *right to life*, or **slang** terms (informal expressions whose meanings may vary from locale to locale or change as time passes). In a particular writing situation, a definition may be essential because a term has more than one meaning, because you are using it in an unusual way, because you are fairly certain the term will be unfamiliar to your readers, or because it is central to your discussion.

PLANNING A DEFINITION ESSAY

Developing a Thesis Statement

The thesis of a definition essay should do more than simply identify the term to be defined — and more than just define it. The thesis statement needs to make clear to readers the larger purpose for which you are defining the term. For example, assume you set out to write an extended definition of *behaviorism*. If your goal is to show its usefulness for treating patients with certain psychological disorders, a statement like "This essay will define behaviorism" will not be very helpful. Even a formal definition — "Behaviorism is a theory that regards the objective facts of a subject's actions as the only valid basis for psychological study" — is not enough. Your thesis needs to suggest the *value* of this kind of therapy, not just tell what it is — for example, "Contrary to critics' objections, behaviorism is a valid approach for treating a wide variety of psychological dysfunctions."

Deciding on a Pattern of Development

You can organize a definition essay according to one or more of the patterns of development described in this book. As you plan your essay and jot down your ideas about the term or subject you will define, you will see which other patterns are most useful. For example, the formal definitions of the five terms discussed on pages 505–6 could be expanded with five different patterns of development:

- **Exemplification**   To explain *behaviorism*, you could give **examples**. Carefully chosen cases could show how this theory of psychology applies to different situations. These examples could help readers see exactly how behaviorism works and what it can and cannot account for. Often, examples are the clearest way to explain something. Defining dreams as "the symbolic representation of mental states" might convey little to readers who do not know much about psychology, but a few examples would help you make your meaning clear. Many students have dreams about taking exams — perhaps dreaming that they are late for the test, that they remember nothing about the course, or that they are writing their answers in disappearing ink. You might explain the nature of dreams by interpreting these particular dreams, which may reflect anxiety about a course or about school in general.

- **Description**   You can explain the nature of something by **describing** it. For example, the concept of a *cell* is difficult to grasp from just a formal definition, but your readers would understand the concept more clearly if you were to describe what a cell looks like, possibly with the aid of a diagram or two. Concentrating on the cell membrane, cytoplasm, and nucleus, you could detail each structure's appearance and function. These descriptions would enable readers to visualize the whole cell and understand its workings. Of course, description involves more than the visual: a definition of a tsunami might describe the sounds and the appearance of this enormous ocean wave, and a definition of Parkinson's disease might include a description of how its symptoms affect a patient.

• **Comparison and contrast**   An extended definition of *naturalism* could use a **comparison-and-contrast** structure. Naturalism is one of several major movements in American literature, so its literary aims could be contrasted with those of other literary movements, such as romanticism or realism. Or you might compare and contrast the plots and characters of several naturalistic works with those of romantic or realistic works. Anytime you need to define something unfamiliar, you can compare it to something familiar to your readers. For example, your readers may never have heard of the Chinese dish sweet-and-sour cabbage, but you can help them imagine it by saying it tastes something like cole slaw. You can also define a thing by contrasting it with something unlike it, especially if the two have some qualities in common. For instance, one way to explain the British sport of rugby is by contrasting it with American football, which is not as violent.

• **Process**   Because mitosis is a process, an extended definition of *mitosis* should be organized as a **process explanation**. By tracing the process from stage to stage, you would clearly define this type of cell division for your readers. Process is also a suitable pattern for objects that must be defined in terms of what they do. For example, because a computer carries out certain processes, an extended definition of a computer would probably include a process explanation.

• **Classification and division**   You could define *authority* by using **classification and division**. Basing your extended definition on the model developed by the German sociologist Max Weber, you could divide the class *authority* into the subclasses *traditional authority, charismatic authority,* and *legal-bureaucratic authority.* By explaining each type of authority, you could clarify this very broad term for your readers. In both extended and formal definitions, classification and division can be very useful. By identifying the class something belongs to, you are explaining what kind of thing it is. For instance, *monetarism* is an economic theory; *The Adventures of Huckleberry Finn* is a novel; and *emphysema* is a disease. Likewise, by dividing a class into subclasses, you are defining something more specifically. Emphysema, for instance, is a disease of the lungs and can therefore be classified with tuberculosis but not with appendicitis.

Phrasing Your Definition

Whatever form your definitions take, make certain that they clearly define your terms. Be sure to provide a true definition, not just a descriptive statement such as "Happiness is a four-day weekend." Also, remember that repetition is not definition, so don't include the term you are defining in your definition. For instance, the statement "abstract art is a school of artists whose works are abstract" clarifies nothing for your readers. Finally, define as precisely as possible. Name the class of the term you are defining — "mitosis is *a process* of cell division" — and define this class as narrowly and as accurately as you can, clearly differentiating your term from other members of its class. Careful attention to the language and structure of your definition will help readers understand your meaning.

STRUCTURING A DEFINITION ESSAY

Like other essays, a definition essay should have an introduction, a body, and a conclusion. Although a formal definition strives for objectivity, an extended definition usually does not. Instead, it is likely to define a term in a way that reflects your attitude toward the subject or your reason for defining it. For example, your extended-definition paper about literary *naturalism* might argue that the significance of this movement's major works has been underestimated by literary scholars. Similarly, your definition of *authority* might criticize its abuses. In such cases, the **thesis statement** provides a focus for your definition essay, telling readers *your* approach to the definition.

The **introduction** identifies the term to be defined, perhaps presents a brief formal definition, and goes on to state the essay's thesis. The body of the essay expands the definition, using any one (or several) of the patterns of development explained and illustrated in this text.

In addition to using various patterns of development, you can expand the **body** of your definition by using any of the following strategies:

- You can define a term by using **synonyms** (words with similar meanings).
- You can define a term by using **negation** (telling what it is *not*).
- You can define a term by using **enumeration** (listing its characteristics).
- You can define a term by using **analogies** (comparisons identifying similarities between the term and something dissimilar).
- You can define a term by discussing its **origin and development** (the -word's derivation, original meaning, and usages).

NOTE: If you are describing an object or situation that is unfamiliar to your readers, you can also include a **visual** — a drawing, painting, diagram, or photograph — to supplement your definition.

Your essay's **conclusion** reminds readers why you have chosen to define the term, perhaps restating your thesis.

Suppose your assignment is to write a short paper for your introductory psychology course. You decide to examine *behaviorism*. Of course, you can define the word in one sentence, or possibly two. But to explain the *concept* of behaviorism and its status in the field of psychology, you must go beyond the dictionary.

Now, you have to decide what kinds of explanations are most suitable for your topic and for your intended audience. If you are trying to define *behaviorism* for readers who know very little about psychology, you might use comparisons that relate behaviorism to your readers' experiences, such as how they were raised or how they train their pets. You might also use examples, but the examples would relate not to psychological experiments or clinical treatment but to experiences in everyday life. If, however, you are directing your paper to your psychology instructor, who obviously already knows what behaviorism is, your purpose is to show that you know, too. One way to do this is to compare behaviorism with other psychological theories; another way is to give examples of how behaviorism works in practice; still another is to briefly summarize the background and history of the theory. (In a long paper, you might use all of these strategies.)

After considering your paper's scope and audience, you might decide that because behaviorism is somewhat controversial, your best strategy is to supplement a formal definition with examples showing how behaviorist assumptions and methods are applied in specific situations. These examples, drawn from your class notes and textbook, would support your thesis that behaviorism is a valid approach for treating certain psychological dysfunctions. Together, your examples would define *behaviorism* as it is understood today.

An informal outline for your essay might look like this:

Introduction:	Thesis statement — Contrary to its critics' objections, behaviorism is a valid approach for treating a wide variety of psychological dysfunctions.
Background:	Definition of behaviorism, including its origins and evolution
First example:	The use of behaviorism to help psychotics function in an institutional setting
Second example:	The use of behaviorism to treat neurotic behavior, such as chronic anxiety, a phobia, or a pattern of destructive acts
Third example:	The use of behaviorism to treat normal but antisocial or undesirable behavior, such as heavy smoking or overeating
Conclusion:	Restatement of thesis or review of key points

Notice how the three examples in this paper define behaviorism with the kind of complexity, detail, and breadth that a formal definition could not duplicate. This definition is more like a textbook explanation — and, in fact, textbook explanations are often written as extended definitions.

REVISING A DEFINITION ESSAY

When you revise a definition essay, consider the items on the revision checklist on page 54. In addition, pay special attention to the items on the following checklist, which apply specifically to revising definition essays.

✓ **REVISION CHECKLIST: Definition**

- Does your assignment call for definition?
- Does your essay include a clearly stated thesis that identifies the term you will define and tells readers why you are defining it?
- Have you included a formal definition of your subject? Have you defined other key terms that may not be familiar to your readers?
- Have you used appropriate patterns of development to expand your definition?
- Do you need to use other strategies — such as synonyms, negation, enumeration, or analogies — to expand your definition?
- Do you need to discuss the origin and development of the term you are defining?
- Do you need to include a visual?

EDITING A DEFINITION ESSAY

When you edit your definition essay, follow the guidelines on the editing checklists on pages 71, 74, and 76. In addition, focus on the grammar, mechanics, and punctuation issues that are particularly relevant to definition essays. One of these issues — avoiding the phrases *is when* and *is where* in formal definitions — is discussed here.

GRAMMAR IN CONTEXT: Avoiding *is when* and *is where*

Many extended definitions include a one-sentence formal definition. As you have learned, such definitions must include the term you are defining, the class to which the term belongs, and the characteristics that distinguish the term from other terms in the same class.

Sometimes, however, when you are defining a term or concept, you may find yourself departing from this set structure and using the phrase *is when* or *is where*. If so, your definition is not complete because it omits the term's class. (In fact, the use of *is when* or *is where* indicates that you are actually presenting an example of the term and not a definition.)

(continued on next page)

(continued from previous page)

You can avoid this error by making certain that the form of the verb *be* in your definition is always followed by a noun.

INCORRECT: As described in the essay "The Untouchable," *prejudice* is when someone forms an irrational bias or negative opinion of a person or group (Mahtab 515).

CORRECT: As described in the essay "The Untouchable," *prejudice* is an irrational bias or negative opinion of a person or group (Mahtab 515).

INCORRECT: According to Meghan Daum, *celebrity* is where you don't buy your own groceries (532).

CORRECT: According to Meghan Daum, *celebrities* are "people who don't buy their own groceries" (532).

> For more practice in avoiding faulty constructions, visit Exercise Central at bedfordstmartins.com/patterns/faultyconstructions.

✓**EDITING CHECKLIST: Definition**

- Have you avoided using *is when* and *is where* in your formal definitions?
- Have you used the present tense for your formal definition — even if you have used the past tense elsewhere in your essay?
- In your formal definition, have you italicized the term you are defining (or underlined to indicate italics) and placed the definition itself in quotation marks?

A STUDENT WRITER: Definition

The following student essay, written by Ajoy Mahtab for a composition course, defines the untouchables, members of a caste that is shunned in India. In his essay, Ajoy, who grew up in Calcutta, presents a thesis that is sharply critical of the practice of ostracizing untouchables. Note that he includes a photograph to help readers understand the unfamiliar term he is defining.

The Untouchable

Introduction: background
A word that is extremely common in India yet uncommon to the point of incomprehension in the West is the word *untouchable*. It is a word that has had extremely

1

Fig. 1. Sean Sprague, "Untouchable woman sweeping in front of her house in a village in Tamil Nadu, India" (2003); *The Image Works* (web; 4 Nov. 2008).

sinister connotations throughout India's history. A rigorously worked-out caste system has traditionally existed in Indian society. At the top of the social ladder sat the Brahmins, the clan of the priesthood. These people had renounced the material world for a spiritual one. Below them came the Kshatriyas, or the warrior caste. This caste included the kings and all their nobles along with their armies. Third on the social ladder were the Vaishyas, who were the merchants of the land. Trade was their only form of livelihood. Last came the Shudras — the menials. Shudras were employed by the prosperous as sweepers and laborers. Originally a person's caste was determined only by his profession. Thus, if the son of a merchant joined the army, he automatically converted from a Vaishya to a Kshatriya. However, the system soon became hereditary and rigid. Whatever one's occupation, one's caste was determined from birth according to the caste of one's father.

Outside of this structure were a group of people, human beings treated worse than dogs and shunned far more than

2

lepers, people who were not considered even human, people who defiled with their very touch. These were the Achhoots: the untouchables, one of whom is shown in Fig. 1. The word *untouchable* is commonly defined as "that which cannot or should not be touched." In India, however, it was taken to a far greater extreme. The untouchables of a village lived in a separate community downwind of the borders of the village. They had a separate water supply, for they would make the village water impure if they were to drink from it. When they walked, they were made to bang two sticks together continuously so that passersby could hear them coming and thus avoid an untouchable's shadow. Tied to their waists, trailing behind them, was a broom that would clean the ground they had walked on. The penalty for not following these or any other rules was death for the untouchable and, in many instances, for the entire untouchable community.

Formal definition

Historical background

Present situation

One of the pioneers of the fight against untouchability was Mahatma Gandhi. Thanks to his efforts and those of many others, untouchability no longer presents anything like the horrific picture painted earlier. In India today, in fact, recognition of untouchability is punishable by law. Theoretically, there is no such thing as untouchability anymore. But old traditions linger on, and such a deep-rooted fear passed down from generation to generation cannot disappear overnight. Even today, caste is an important factor in most marriages. Most Indian surnames reveal a person's caste immediately, so it is a difficult thing to hide. The shunning of the untouchable is more prevalent in South India, where people are much more devout, than in the North. Some people would rather starve than share food and water with an untouchable. This concept is very difficult to accept in the West, but it is true all the same.

3

Example

I remember an incident from my childhood. I could not have been more than eight or nine at the time. I was on a holiday staying at my family's house on the river Ganges. A festival was going on, and, as is customary, we were giving the servants small presents. I was handing them out when an old lady, bent with age, slowly hobbled into the room. She stood in the far corner of the room all alone, and no one so much as looked at her. When the entire line ended, she stepped

4

hesitantly forward and stood in front of me, looking down at the ground. She then held a cloth stretched out in front of her. I was a little confused about how I was supposed to hand her her present, since both her hands were holding the cloth. Then, with the help of prompting from someone behind me, I learned that I was supposed to drop the gift into the cloth without touching the cloth itself. It was only later that I found out that she was an untouchable. This was the first time I had actually come face to face with such prejudice, and it felt like a slap in the face. That incident was burned into my memory, and I do not think I will ever forget it.

Conclusion begins   The word *untouchable* is not often used in the West, and   5
when it is, it is generally used as a complimentary term. For example, an avid fan might say of an athlete, "He was absolutely untouchable. Nobody could even begin to compare with him." It seems rather ironic that a word could be so favorable in one culture and so negative in another. Why does a word that gives happiness in one part of the world cause pain in another? Why does the same word have different meanings to different people around the globe? Why do certain words cause rifts and others forge bonds? I do not think anyone can tell me the answers to these questions.

Conclusion continues   No actual parallel can be found today that compares to   6
the horrors of untouchability. For an untouchable, life itself was a crime. The day was spent just trying to stay alive. From the
Thesis statement   misery of the untouchables, the world should learn a lesson: isolating and punishing any group of people is dehumanizing and immoral.

Points for Special Attention

Thesis Statement. Ajoy Mahtab's assignment was to write an extended definition of a term he assumed would be unfamiliar to his audience. Because he had definite ideas about the unjust treatment of the untouchables, Ajoy wanted his essay to have a strong thesis that communicated his disapproval. Still, because he knew his American classmates would need a good deal of background information before they would understand the context for such a thesis, he decided not to present it in his introduction. Instead, he decided to lead up to his thesis gradually and state it at the end of his essay. When other students in the class reviewed his draft, this subtlety was one of the points they reacted to most favorably.

Structure.   Ajoy's introduction establishes the direction of his essay by introducing the word he will define; he then places this word in context by explaining India's rigid caste system. In paragraph 2, he gives the formal definition of the word *untouchable* and goes on to sketch the term's historical background. Paragraph 3 explains the status of the untouchables in present-day India, and paragraph 4 gives a vivid example of Ajoy's first encounter with an untouchable. As he begins his conclusion in paragraph 5, Ajoy brings his readers back to the word his essay defines. Here he uses two strategies to add interest: he contrasts a contemporary American usage of *untouchable* with its pejorative meaning in India, and he asks a series of **rhetorical questions** (questions asked for effect and not meant to be answered). In paragraph 6, Ajoy presents a summary of his position to lead into his thesis statement.

Patterns of Development.   This essay uses a number of strategies commonly incorporated into extended definitions: it includes a formal definition, explains the term's origin, and explores some of the term's connotations. The essay also uses several familiar patterns of development. For instance, paragraph 1 uses classification and division to explain India's caste system; paragraphs 2 and 3 use brief examples to illustrate the plight of the untouchable; and paragraph 4 presents a narrative. Each of these patterns enriches the definition.

Visual.   Ajoy includes a **visual** — a photograph of an untouchable — to supplement his passages of description and to help readers understand this very unfamiliar concept. He places the photograph early in his essay, where it will be most helpful, and he refers to it with the phrase "one of whom is shown in Fig. 1." In addition, he includes a caption below the photo with full source information.

Focus on Revision

Because the term Ajoy defined was so unfamiliar to his classmates, many of the peer editing worksheets his classmates filled in asked for more information. One suggestion in particular — that he draw an **analogy** between the unfamiliar term *untouchable* and a more familiar concept — appealed to Ajoy as he planned his revision. Another student suggested that Ajoy could compare untouchables to other groups who are shunned — for example, people with AIDS. Although Ajoy states in his conclusion that no parallel exists, an attempt to find common ground between untouchables and other groups could make his essay more meaningful to his readers — and bring home to them a distinctly alien idea. Such a connection could also make his conclusion especially powerful.

📄   **PEER EDITING WORKSHEET: Definition**

1. What term is the writer defining? Does the essay include a formal definition? If so, where? If no formal definition is included, should one be added?

2. Why is the writer defining the term? Does the essay include a thesis statement that makes this purpose clear? If not, suggest revisions.

3. What patterns does the writer use to develop the definition? What other patterns could be used? Would a visual be helpful?

4. Does the essay define the term appropriately for its audience? Does the definition help you understand the meaning of the term?

5. Does the writer use **synonyms** to develop the definition? If so, where? If not, where could synonyms be used to help communicate the term's meaning?

6. Does the writer use **negation** to develop the definition? If so, where? If not, could the writer strengthen the definition by explaining what the term is not?

7. Does the writer use **enumeration** to develop the definition? If so, where? If not, where might the term's special characteristics be listed?

8. Does the writer use **analogies** to develop the definition? If so, where? Do you find these analogies helpful? What additional analogies might help readers understand the term more fully?

9. Does the writer explain the term's origin and development? If so, where? If not, do you believe this information should be added?

10. Reread the essay's introduction. If the writer uses a formal definition as an opening strategy, try to suggest an alternative opening.

The selections that follow use exemplification, description, narration, and other methods of developing extended definitions. The first selection, a visual text, is followed by questions designed to illustrate how definition can operate in visual form.

U.S. Census 2000 Form (Questionnaire)

→ **NOTE: Please answer BOTH Questions 7 and 8.**

7. Is Person 1 Spanish/Hispanic/Latino? *Mark* ☒ *the* ***"No"*** *box if* ***not*** *Spanish/Hispanic/Latino.*

☐ **No,** not Spanish/Hispanic/Latino   ☐ Yes, Puerto Rican

☐ Yes, Mexican, Mexican Am., Chicano   ☐ Yes, Cuban

☐ Yes, other Spanish/Hispanic/Latino — *Print group.* ↘

8. What is Person 1's race? *Mark* ☒ **one or more races** to *indicate what this person considers himself/herself to be.*

☐ White

☐ Black, African Am., or Negro

☐ American Indian or Alaska Native — *Print name of enrolled or principal tribe.* ↘

☐ Asian Indian   ☐ Japanese   ☐ Native Hawaiian

☐ Chinese   ☐ Korean   ☐ Guamanian or Chamorro

☐ Filipino   ☐ Vietnamese   ☐ Samoan

☐ Other Asian — *Print race.* ↘   ☐ Other Pacific Islander — *Print race.* ↘

☐ Some other race — *Print race.* ↘

• • •

Reading Images

1. In a single complete sentence, define yourself in terms of your race, religion, or ethnicity (whatever is most important to you).

2. Look at the U.S. Census questions above. Which boxes would you mark? Do you see this choice as an accurate expression of what you consider yourself to be? Explain.

3. Only recently has the Census Bureau permitted respondents to mark "one or more races" to indicate their ethnic identity. Do you think this option is a good idea?

Journal Entry

Why do you think the government needs to know "what [a] person considers himself/herself to be"? Do you think it is important for the government to know how people define themselves, or do you consider this information an unwarranted violation of a person's privacy? Explain.

Thematic Connections

- "Indian Education" (page 135)
- "Two Ways to Belong in America" (page 411)
- "Mother Tongue" (page 477)
- "Black *and* Latino" (page 537)
- "The Myth of the Latin Woman: I Just Met a Girl Named Maria" (page 730)

I Want a Wife

Judy Brady has published articles on many social issues. Diagnosed with breast cancer in 1980, she became active in the politics of cancer and has edited *Women and Cancer* (1990) and *One in Three: Women with Cancer Confront an Epidemic* (1991). She also helped found the Toxic Links Coalition, an organization devoted to lobbying for cancer and environmental issues.

Background on the status of women

Brady has been active in the women's movement since 1969, and "I Want a Wife" first appeared in the premiere issue of the feminist *Ms.* magazine in 1972. That year represented perhaps the height of the feminist movement in the United States. The National Organization for Women, established in 1966, had hundreds of chapters around the country. The Equal Rights Amendment, barring discrimination against women, passed in Congress (although it was ratified by only thirty-five of the necessary thirty-eight states), and Congress also passed Title IX of the Education Amendments Act, which required equal opportunity (in sports as well as academics) for all students in any school that receives federal funding. At that time, women accounted for just under 40 percent of the labor force (up from 23 percent in 1950), a number that has grown to almost 50 percent today. Of mothers with children under age eighteen, fewer than 40 percent were employed in 1970; today, three-quarters work, 38 percent of them full-time and year-round. As for stay-at-home fathers, their numbers have increased from virtually zero to more than three million.

I belong to that classification of people known as wives. I am A Wife. And, not altogether incidentally, I am a mother. 1

Not too long ago a male friend of mine appeared on the scene fresh from a recent divorce. He had one child, who is, of course, with his ex-wife. He is looking for another wife. As I thought about him while I was ironing one evening, it suddenly occurred to me that I, too, would like to have a wife. Why do I want a wife? 2

I would like to go back to school so that I can become economically independent, support myself, and, if need be, support those dependent upon me. I want a wife who will work and send me to school. And while I am going to school I want a wife to take care of my children. I want a wife to keep track of the children's doctor and dentist appointments. And to keep track of mine, too. I want a wife to make sure my children eat properly and are kept clean. I want a wife who will wash the children's clothes and keep them mended. I want a wife who is a good nurturant attendant to my children, who arranges for their schooling, makes sure that they have an adequate social life with their peers, takes them to the park, the zoo, etc. I 3 want a wife who takes care of the children when they are sick, a wife who arranges to be around when the children need special care, because, of course, I cannot miss classes at school. My wife must arrange to lose time at work and not lose the job. It may mean a small cut in my wife's income from time to time, but I guess I can tolerate that. Needless to say, my wife will arrange and pay for the care of the children while my wife is working.

I want a wife who will take care of *my* physical needs. I want a wife who will keep my house clean. A wife who will pick up after my children, a wife who will pick up after me. I want a wife who will keep my clothes clean, ironed, mended, replaced when need be, and who will see to it that my personal things are kept in their proper place so that I can find what I need the minute I need it. I want a wife who cooks the meals, a wife who is a *good* cook. I want a wife who will plan the menus, do the necessary grocery shopping, prepare the meals, serve them pleasantly, and then do the cleaning up while I do my studying. I want a wife who will care for me when I am sick and sympathize with my pain and loss of time from school. I want a wife to go along when our family takes a vacation so that someone can continue to care for me and my children when I need a rest and change of scene.

I want a wife who will not bother me with rambling complaints about a wife's duties. But I want a wife who will listen to me when I feel the need to explain a rather difficult point I have come across in my course of studies. And I want a wife who will type my papers for me when I have written them.

I want a wife who will take care of the details of my social life. When my wife and I are invited out by my friends, I want a wife who will take care of the babysitting arrangements. When I meet people at school that I like and want to entertain, I want a wife who will have the house clean, will prepare a special meal, serve it to me and my friends, and not interrupt when I talk about things that interest me and my friends. I want a wife who will have arranged that the children are fed and ready for bed before my guests arrive so that the children do not bother us. I want a wife who takes care of the needs of my guests so that they feel comfortable, who makes sure that they have an ashtray, that they are passed the hors d'oeuvres, that they are offered a second helping of the food, that their wine glasses are replenished when necessary, that their coffee is served to them as they like it. And I want a wife who knows that sometimes I need a night out by myself.

I want a wife who is sensitive to my sexual needs, a wife who makes love passionately and eagerly when I feel like it, a wife who makes sure that I am satisfied. And, of course, I want a wife who will not demand sexual attention when I am not in the mood for it. I want a wife who assumes the complete responsibility for birth control, because I do not want more children. I want a wife who will remain sexually faithful to me so that I do not have to clutter up my intellectual life with jealousies. And I want a wife who understands that *my* sexual needs may entail more than strict adherence to monogamy. I must, after all, be able to relate to people as fully as possible.

If, by chance, I find another person more suitable as a wife than the wife I already have, I want the liberty to replace my present wife with another one. Naturally, I will expect a fresh new life; my wife will take the children and be solely responsible for them so that I am left free.   8

When I am through with school and have a job, I want my wife to quit working and remain at home so that my wife can more fully and completely take care of a wife's duties.   9

My God, who *wouldn't* want a wife?   10

• • •

Comprehension

1. In one sentence, define what Brady means by *wife*. Does this ideal wife actually exist? Explain.

2. List some of the specific duties of the wife Brady describes. Into what five general categories does Brady arrange these duties?

3. What complaints does Brady apparently have about the life she actually leads? To what does she seem to attribute her problems?

4. Under what circumstances does Brady say she would consider leaving her wife? What would happen to the children if she left?

Purpose and Audience

1. This essay was first published in *Ms.* magazine. In what sense is it appropriate for the audience of this feminist publication? Where else can you imagine it appearing?

2. Does this essay have an explicitly stated thesis? If so, where is it? If the thesis is implied, paraphrase it.

3. Do you think Brady *really* wants the kind of wife she describes? Explain your response.

Style and Structure

1. Throughout the essay, Brady repeats the words "I want a wife." What is the effect of this repetition?

2. The first and last paragraphs of this essay are quite brief. Does this weaken the essay? Why, or why not?

3. In enumerating a wife's duties, Brady frequently uses the verb *arrange*. What other verbs does she use repeatedly? How do these verbs help her make her point?

4. Brady never uses the personal pronouns *he* or *she* to refer to the wife she defines. Why not?

5. Comment on Brady's use of phrases such as *of course* (2, 3, and 7), *needless to say* (3), *after all* (7), *by chance* (8), and *naturally* (8). What do these expressions contribute to the sentences where they appear? To the essay as a whole?

Vocabulary Projects

1. Define each of the following words as it is used in this selection.

   nurturant (3)   adherence (7)
   replenished (6)   monogamy (7)

2. Going beyond the dictionary definitions, decide what Brady means to suggest by each of the following words. Is she using any of these words sarcastically? Explain.

   proper (4)   necessary (6)   suitable (8)
   pleasantly (4)   demand (7)   free (8)
   bother (6)   clutter up (7)

Journal Entry

Is Brady's 1972 characterization of a wife still accurate today? Which of the characteristics she describes have remained the same? Which have changed? Why?

Writing Workshop

1. Write an essay defining your ideal boss, parent, teacher, or pet.
2. Write an essay titled "I Want a Husband." Taking an **ironic** stance, use society's notions of the ideal husband to help you shape your definition.
3. Write a definition essay called "The Ideal Couple," in which you try to divide household chores and other responsibilities equitably between the two partners. Your essay can be serious or humorous. Develop your definition with examples.

Combining the Patterns

Like most definition essays, "I Want a Wife" uses several patterns of development. Which ones does it use? Which of these do you consider most important for supporting Brady's thesis? Why?

Thematic Connections

- "My Mother Never Worked" (page 114)
- "Why Marriage Is Good for You" (page 227)
- "Sex, Lies, and Conversation" (page 436)
- Declaration of Sentiments and Resolutions (page 581)

JOSÉ ANTONIO BURCIAGA

Tortillas

José Antonio Burciaga (1940–1996) was the founder of *Diseños Literarios,* a publishing company in California, as well as the comedy troupe Culture Clash. He contributed fiction, poetry, and articles to many anthologies, as well as to journals and newspapers. He also published several books of poems, drawings, and essays, including the poetry collection *Undocumented Love* (1992) and the essay collection *Drink Cultura* (1993). "Tortillas," originally titled "I Remember Masa," was first published in *Weedee Peepo* (1988), a collection of essays in Spanish and English.

Background on tortillas

Tortillas have been a staple of Mexican cooking for thousands of years. These thin, round griddlecakes made of cornmeal *(masa)* are often eaten with every meal, and the art of making them is still passed from generation to generation (although they now are widely available commercially as well). The earliest Mexican immigrants introduced them to the United States, and in the past twenty-five years tortillas, along with many other popular items of Mexican cuisine, have entered the country's culinary landscape (as, over the decades, has a wide variety of other "ethnic" foods, such as pizza, egg rolls, bagels, sushi, and gyros). Still, tortillas have special meaning for Mexican Americans, and in this essay Burciaga discusses the role of the tortilla within his family's culture.

My earliest memory of *tortillas* is my *Mamá* telling me not to play with them. I had bitten eyeholes in one and was wearing it as a mask at the dinner table. 1

As a child, I also used *tortillas* as hand warmers on cold days, and my family claims that I owe my career as an artist to my early experiments with *tortillas.* According to them, my clowning around helped me develop a strong artistic foundation. I'm not so sure, though. Sometimes I wore a *tortilla* on my head, like a *yarmulke,* and yet I never had any great urge to convert from Catholicism to Judaism. But who knows? They may be right. 2

For Mexicans over the centuries, the *tortilla* has served as the spoon and the fork, the plate and the napkin. *Tortillas* originated before the Mayan civilizations, perhaps predating Europe's wheat bread. According to Mayan mythology, the great god Quetzalcoatl, realizing that the red ants knew the secret of using maize as food, transformed himself into a black ant, infiltrated the colony of red ants, and absconded with a grain of corn. (Is it any wonder that to this day, black ants and red ants do not get along?) Quetzalcoatl then put maize on the lips of the first man and woman, Oxomoco and Cipactonal, so that they would become strong. Maize festivals are still celebrated by many Indian cultures of the Americas. 3

When I was growing up in El Paso, *tortillas* were part of my daily life. I   4
used to visit a *tortilla* factory in an ancient adobe building near the open
mercado in Ciudad Juárez. As I approached, I could hear the rhythmic slap-
ping of the *masa* as the skilled vendors outside the factory formed it into
balls and patted them into perfectly round corn cakes between the palms
of their hands. The wonderful aroma and the speed with which the women
counted so many dozens of *tortillas* out of warm wicker baskets still linger
in my mind. Watching them at work convinced me that the most handsome and *deliciosas tortillas* are handmade. Although machines are faster,
they can never adequately replace generation-to-generation experience.
There's no place in the factory assembly line for the tender slaps that
give each *tortilla* character. The best thing that can be said about mass-
producing *tortillas* is that it makes it possible for many people to enjoy them.

In the *mercado* where my mother shopped, we frequently bought *taqui-*   5
tos de nopalitos, small tacos filled with diced cactus, onions, tomatoes, and
jalapeños. Our friend Don Toribio showed us how to make delicious,
crunchy *taquitos* with dried, salted pumpkin seeds. When you had no money
for the filling, a poor man's *taco* could be made by placing a warm *tortilla*
on the left palm, applying a sprinkle of salt, then rolling the *tortilla* up
quickly with the fingertips of the right hand. My own kids put peanut butter and jelly on *tortillas,* which I think is truly bicultural. And speaking of
fast foods for kids, nothing beats a *quesadilla,* a *tortilla* grilled-cheese sandwich.

Depending on what you intend to use them for, *tortillas* may be made   6
in various ways. Even a run-of-the-mill *tortilla* is more than a flat corn cake.
A skillfully cooked homemade *tortilla* has a bottom and a top; the top skin
forms a pocket in which you put the filling that folds your *tortilla* into a
taco. Paper-thin *tortillas* are used specifically for *flautas,* a type of taco that
is filled, rolled, and then fried until crisp. The name *flauta* means *flute,*
which probably refers to the Mayan bamboo flute; however, the only sound
that comes from an edible *flauta* is a delicious crunch that is music to the
palate. In México *flautas* are sometimes made as long as two feet and then
cut into manageable segments. The opposite of *flautas* is *gorditas,* meaning
little fat ones. These are very thick small *tortillas.*

The versatility of *tortillas* and corn does not end here. Besides being   7
tasty and nourishing, they have spiritual and artistic qualities as well. The
Tarahumara Indians of Chihuahua, for example, concocted a corn-based
beer called *tesgüino,* which their descendants still make today. And everyone
has read about the woman in New Mexico who was cooking her husband a
tortilla one morning when the image of Jesus Christ miraculously appeared
on it. Before they knew what was happening, the man's breakfast had
become a local shrine.

Then there is *tortilla* art. Various Chicano artists throughout the   8
Southwest have, when short of materials or just in a whimsical mood, used
a dry *tortilla* as a small, round canvas. And a few years back, at the height of
the Chicano movement, a priest in Arizona got into trouble with the

Church after he was discovered celebrating mass using a *tortilla* as the host. All of which only goes to show that while the *tortilla* may be a lowly corn cake, when the necessity arises, it can reach unexpected distinction.

· · ·

Comprehension

1. What exactly is a tortilla?
2. List the functions — both practical and whimsical — that tortillas serve.
3. In paragraph 7, Burciaga cites the "spiritual and artistic qualities" of tortillas. Do you think he is being serious? Explain your reasoning.

Purpose and Audience

1. Burciaga states his thesis explicitly in his essay's final sentence. Paraphrase this thesis. Why do you think he does not state it sooner?
2. Do you think Burciaga expects most of his readers to be of Hispanic descent? To be familiar with tortillas? How can you tell?
3. Why do you think Burciaga uses humor in this essay? Is it consistent with his essay's purpose? Could the humor have a negative effect on his audience? Explain.
4. Why are tortillas so important to Burciaga? Is it just their versatility he admires, or do they represent something more to him?

Style and Structure

1. Where does Burciaga provide a formal definition of *tortilla*? Why does he locate this formal definition at this point in his essay?
2. Burciaga uses many Spanish words, but he defines only some of them — for example, *taquitos de nopalitos* and *quesadilla* in paragraph 5 and *flautas* and *gorditas* in paragraph 6. Why do you think he defines some Spanish terms but not others? Should he have defined them all?
3. Does Burciaga use **synonyms** or **negation** to define *tortilla*? Does he discuss the word's **origin and development**? If so, where? If not, do you think any of these strategies would improve his essay? Explain.

Vocabulary Projects

1. Define each of the following words as it is used in this selection.

   yarmulke (2)   absconded (3)   concocted (7)
   maize (3)   adobe (4)

2. Look up each of the following words in a Spanish-English dictionary, or at Googles's Language Tools, and (if possible) supply its English equivalent.

   mercado (4)   deliciosas (4)
   masa (4)   jalapeños (5)

Journal Entry

Explore some additional uses — practical or frivolous — for tortillas that Burciaga does not discuss.

Writing Workshop

1. Write an essay defining a food that is important to your family, ethnic group, or circle of friends. Begin with your own "earliest memory" of the food, comparing it with Burciaga's, and use several patterns of development, as Burciaga does. Assume your audience is not familiar with the food you define. Your thesis should indicate why the food is so important to you. Be sure to document references to Burciaga's essay and to include a works-cited page. (See the Appendix for information on documentation formats.)

2. Relying primarily on description and exemplification, define a food that is sure to be familiar to all your readers. Do not name the food until your essay's last sentence.

3. Write an essay defining a food — but include a thesis statement that paints a very favorable portrait of a much-maligned food (for example, Spam or brussels sprouts) or a very negative picture of a popular food (for example, chocolate or ice cream).

Combining the Patterns

Burciaga uses several patterns of development in his extended definition. Where, for example, does he use **description**, **narration**, **process**, and **exemplification**? Does he use any other patterns?

Thematic Connections

- "Sixty-Nine Cents" (page 102)
- "Panacea" (page 162)
- "Once More to the Lake" (page 183)
- "The Park" (page 709)

GAYLE ROSENWALD SMITH

The Wife-Beater

Gayle Rosenwald Smith, an attorney, currently practices family law. She
has published articles in a variety of journals and periodicals and is coauthor of *What Every Woman Should Know about Divorce and Custody* (1998)
and *Divorce and Money: Everything You Need to Know* (2004). The following
essay appeared in the *Philadelphia Inquirer* in 2001.

Background on the "wife-beater" shirt

As Smith notes here, *wife-beater* is a slang term for a type of sleeveless
undershirt that has in recent years become fashionable. An Internet search
of the term found a number of businesses that actually market such shirts
as "wife-beaters." The corresponding shirts for women are often called
"boy-beaters." A Texas-based firm offers adult-sized shirts emblazoned
with the slogan, as well as "Lil' Wife Beater" shirts for babies. The firm's
Web site — accompanied by the beat of a rap recording about "smashing"
women — includes a background screen showing a woman being spanked
and provides a link to a "Wife Beater Hall of Fame." It also offers to send a
second shirt at half price to any customer convicted of domestic violence
(proof of conviction required, photos not acceptable). In another twist, a
feminist retail site has offered a "Wife Beater Beater" shirt with a cartoon
image of a woman kicking a man in the groin.

Everybody wears them. The Gap sells them. Fashion designers Dolce
and Gabbana have lavished them with jewels. Their previous greatest resurgence occurred in the 1950s, when Marlon Brando's Stanley Kowalski wore
one in Tennessee Williams' *A Streetcar Named Desire*. They are all the rage. [1]

What are they called? [2]

The name is the issue. For they are known as "wife-beaters." [3]

A Web search shows that kids nationwide are wearing the skinny-
ribbed white T-shirts that can be worn alone or under another shirt.
Women have adopted them with the same gusto as men. A search of bou-
tiques shows that these wearers include professionals who wear them,
adorned with designer accessories, under their pricey suits. They are available in all colors, sizes, and price ranges. [4]

Wearers under 25 do not seem to be disturbed by the name. But I
sure am. [5]

It's an odd name for an undershirt. And even though the ugly stereotypes behind the name are both obvious and toxic, it appears to be cool to
say the name without fear of (or without caring about) hurting anyone. [6]

That the name is fueled by stereotype is now an academically established fact, although various sources disagree on exactly when shirt and
name came together. The *Oxford Dictionary* defines the term *wife-beater* as: [7]

1. A man who physically abuses his wife and
2. Tank-style underwear shirts. Origin: based on the stereotype that physically abusive husbands wear that particular type of shirt.

The *World Book Dictionary* locates the origin of the term *wife-beater* in the 1970s, from the stereotype of the Midwestern male wearing an undershirt while beating his wife. The shirts are said to have been popular in the 1980s at all types of sporting events, especially ones at which one sits in the sun and develops "wife-beater marks." The undershirts also attained popularity at wet T-shirt contests, in which the wet, ribbed tees accentuated contestants' breasts. 8

In an article in the style section of the *New York Times,* Jesse Scheidlower, principal editor of the *Oxford English Dictionary*'s American office, says the association of the undershirt and the term *wife-beater* arose in 1997 from varied sources, including gay and gang subcultures and rap music. 9

In the article, some sources argued that the reference in the term was not to spousal abuse per se but to popular-culture figures such as Ralph Cramden and Tony Soprano. And what about Archie Bunker? 10

It's not just the name that worries me. Fashion headlines reveal that we want to overthrow '90s grunge and return to shoulder pads and hardware-studded suits. Am I reading too much into a fashion statement that the return is also to male dominance where physical abuse is acceptable as a means of control? 11

There has to be a better term. After all, it's a pretty rare piece of clothing that can make both men and women look sexier. You'd expect a term connoting flattery — not violence. 12

Wearers under 25 may not want to hear this, but here it is. More than 4 million women are victims of severe assaults by boyfriends and husbands each year. By conservative estimate, family violence occurs in 2 million families each year in the United States. Average age of the batterer: 31. 13

Possibly the last statistic is telling. Maybe youth today would rather ignore the overtones of the term *wife-beater.* It is also true, however, that the children of abusers often learn the behavior from their elders. 14

Therein lies perhaps the worst difficulty: that this name for this shirt teaches the wrong thing about men. Some articles quote women who felt the shirts looked great, especially on guys with great bodies. One woman stated that it even made guys look "manly." 15

So *manly* equals *violent*? Not by me, and I hope not by anyone on any side of age 25. 16

. . .

Comprehension

1. Why is Smith "disturbed" (5) by the name "wife-beater"? Do you think her concern is justified?

2. In paragraph 3, Smith says, "The name is the issue"; in paragraph 11, she says "It's not just the name that worries me." What does she mean by each statement? Does she contradict herself?

3. What relationship does Smith see between the name of a sleeveless undershirt and the prevalence of family violence? Does she believe a causal connection does — or could — exist? If so, which is the cause, and which is the effect?

4. In paragraph 12, Smith acknowledges that the shirt "can make both men and women look sexier." Does this remark in any way undercut her credibility? Explain.

5. How, according to Smith, does calling a shirt a wife-beater teach women "the wrong thing about men" (15)?

Purpose and Audience

1. How do you think Smith expects her audience to react to her opening statement ("Everybody wears them")?

2. Why do you think Smith wrote this essay? Is her purpose to change the name of the T-shirt, or does she seem to have a more ambitious purpose? Explain.

3. Twice in her essay, Smith mentions a group she calls "wearers under 25" (5, 13). Does she seem to direct her remarks at these young adults or at older readers? At wearers of the shirts or at a more general audience?

4. Restate Smith's thesis in your own words.

Style and Structure

1. Why do you think Smith begins her essay by explaining the popularity of sleeveless undershirts? Is this an effective opening strategy?

2. In paragraph 7, Smith reproduces a formal definition from the *Oxford Dictionary*. Why does she include this definition when she has already defined her term? What, if anything, does the formal definition add?

3. Where does Smith present information on the history of the wife-beater? Why does she include this kind of information?

4. Where does Smith quote statistics? Do you see this information as relevant or incidental to her argument?

Vocabulary Projects

1. Define each of the following words as it is used in this selection.

resurgence (1)	accentuated (8)
gusto (4)	per se (10)
toxic (6)	connoting (12)

2. In paragraph 12, Smith says, "There has to be a better term." Can you think of a "better term" — one that does not suggest violence — for the shirt Smith describes?

3. Visit several different Internet sites — for example, dictionary.com and Merriam-Webster Online at m-w.com — and compare their definitions of the term *wife beater*. How are these definitions alike? How are they different?

Journal Entry

Do you agree with Smith that the casual use of terms like *wife-beater* is dangerous, or do you think she is exaggerating the problem?

Writing Workshop

1. Relying primarily on description and exemplification, define an article of clothing that is essential to your wardrobe. Begin by checking Internet sites on fashion history, such as fashion-era.com, to learn the item's history and the origin of its name.

2. Using comparison and contrast to structure your essay, define what a particular item of clothing means to you — and what it means to one of your parents.

3. Do members of your religious or ethnic group wear an item of clothing that is not well known to others? Define the article of clothing, and explain its significance and its history in terms that outsiders can understand.

Combining the Patterns

Do you think Smith should have spent more time in this essay on developing the **cause-and-effect** relationship, if any, between the "wife-beater" shirt and family violence? What additional information would she have to provide?

Thematic Connections

Fame-iness

Essayist Megan Daum (b. 1970) has contributed pieces to the *New Yorker,* the *Village Voice,* the *New York Times Book Review,* *Vogue,* and *Harper's Bazaar,* among many other popular periodicals. Some of these articles were collected in her first book, *My Misspent Youth* (2001). She writes a regular column for the op-ed page of the *Los Angeles Times* and has appeared on public radio's *Morning Edition* and *This American Life.* Noted for her sharp wit and entertaining observations on American culture, Daum has also published a novel, *The Quality of Life Report* (2003), which was named a *New York Times* Notable Book.

Background on "fifteen minutes of fame"

In a 1968 catalog essay accompanying his first international retrospective exhibition, pop artist and cultural icon Andy Warhol predicted — somewhat tongue-in-cheek — that "in the future everyone will be world-famous for fifteen minutes." He was referring to the proliferation of mass media, particularly television, and the need to fill the airwaves with anything that would provide an audience for advertisers. (Warhol himself was obsessed with the concept of celebrity.) The slogan quickly became a catchphrase, with "fifteen minutes of fame" referring to any short-lived appearance in the limelight. Warhol couldn't have foreseen that, starting in the 1990s, reality television programs, the Internet, and a culture increasingly used to considering anyone a celebrity would bring his prediction even closer to reality.

Why is it that most celebrities in the culture today are people I've never heard of? I always thought fame had to do with being well known to the public, with being easily recognized on the street, with being, you know . . . *famous.* 1

If you asked me to name some famous people, I might offer up examples such as Bill Clinton, Meryl Streep, and Sting. If I spotted any one of them at the supermarket, it would probably warrant a call to my best friend to report what brand of peanut butter they were buying. 2

But these are also people who'd never go to the supermarket. The reason is that celebrities, at least according to my definition, don't buy their own groceries. They have their assistants do it, or they order special deliveries from organic farms or, more likely, they don't eat at all. 3

That's because they're not quite real people, which is exactly why we love them. Or at least we used to. These days it seems that only crotchety dinosaur types like me still harbor such provincial notions of what it means to be famous. 4

I know what you're thinking right about now: Here's another column   5
about the vulgarity of contemporary celebrity culture, with sentences that
start with phrases like "these days." Believe me, I feel your nausea.

But I've also been feeling something else lately that goes beyond my   6
cluelessness about who's on the cover of *In Touch Weekly*. Call it reverse
indifference. You know how you can walk into a room that smells like garbage, initially be bowled over with disgust but eventually grow immune to
the odor? That's the opposite of what's happened to my celebrity radar.
Whereas I used to merely ignore news about the faux famous and their
tabloid-targeted exploits, I now notice it and feel repulsed. And I'm pretty
sure that's the whole idea.

Obviously, celebrity repulsion has been in the air in recent weeks. I   7
don't need to name names, but suffice it to say that popular culture's
approval rating (and, in turn, that of the media that can't get enough of it)
is at an all-time low. Whether we're talking about a deceased gold-digger*
or an apparently deranged astronaut** (and, be honest, we're still talking
about both of them — all the time) it's pretty clear that it's never been a
worse time to be famous. For one thing, the competition is stiff. (The Dixie
Chicks, celebs with some old-school fame value, swept the Grammys, but
we're still more interested in paternity claims and NASA-issue diapers.) For
another thing, celebrity is just not as valuable as it used to be. By the look
of things, just about anyone can get it—or at least something closely
approximating it.

Not so long ago, you had to make a pretty strenuous effort to become well   8
enough known to register as famous. If you were an actor, you auditioned
your butt off. If you were a musician, you played in clubs for no money.
Part of the allure of fame was that access was limited. You pretty much had
to show up regularly on network television, in studio movies, or on top-40
radio. However, because that playing field was relatively small, once you
got there it wasn't too hard to become a household name—if only for the
allotted fifteen minutes.

Now I'm not sure there's such a thing as a household name anymore.   9
Instead of fifteen minutes of fame, we get personalities who are famous in
the eyes of maybe fifteen people. Fame is no longer about reaching the
masses but about finding a niche audience somewhere.

This can, of course, be a very good thing, since the masses have never   10
been known for their taste or intelligence. But there's a dangerous flip side
to the democratization of fame. The YouTube/*American Idol*/MySpace

---

* EDS. NOTE — Anna Nicole Smith, former model and *Playboy* playmate who married
an elderly billionaire and fought his children for his estate. After her death, several ex-
lovers claimed to be the father of her baby daughter.

** EDS. NOTE — Astronaut Lisa Marie Nowak, who faced kidnapping and attempted
murder charges in 2007 after she drove nine-hundred miles (reportedly wearing diapers
so she wouldn't have to stop along the way) to confront a romantic rival.

regime may be providing new opportunities for genuinely talented, less conventional people, but it's providing even more opportunities for untalented, often downright annoying people. "Celebrity" now connotes a mundanity that borders on tedium, not to mention that smelly territory of reverse indifference.

Merriam Webster's 2006 word of the year was Stephen Colbert's coinage of "truthiness," which describes our inclination to believe in ideas without regard to logic or evidence. Perhaps our definition of celebrity has taken a similar path. Now that the mystique of so many celebrities is rooted less in their accomplishments than in their ability to get our attention by provoking our disgust, perhaps it's not fame they're offering but "fame-iness."   11

Unlike actual fame, which involves some talent and hard work, "fame-iness" requires little more than a willingness to humiliate oneself. Instead of a reward for a job well done, it's more like a punishment for cutting corners. And guess what? The audience gets punished too.   12

Talk about dirty work—no wonder only the unskilled seem to be applying. Now if we could only stop reading their résumés.   13

• • •

Comprehension

1. According to Daum, what does it mean to be famous?
2. How does Daum define a celebrity?
3. What does Daum mean in paragraph 7 when she says, "it's pretty clear that it's never been a worse time to be famous"?
4. How does Daum see today's celebrities as different from those of years ago? Does she see this change as positive or negative?
5. What do you think Daum means in paragraph 6 by "tabloid-targeted exploits"? Can you give examples of such exploits?
6. In paragraph 9, Daum says, "Fame is no longer about reaching the masses but about finding a niche audience somewhere." Give some examples of what such a "niche audience" might be.
7. What does Daum see as the positive side of the "democratization of fame" (10)?
8. According to Daum, what is the difference between "actual fame" and "fame-iness"?

Purpose and Audience

1. This essay discusses fame and celebrities in general terms but gives very few examples. What examples does Daum provide? Why do you think she doesn't include more?
2. What is Daum's attitude toward her audience? How do you know? Does paragraph 5 offer any information that might help answer this question?

Style and Structure

1. Does Daum include a formal definition of *fame-iness* in her essay? If so, where? If not, supply one.
2. Where does Daum explain her term's origin?
3. Where does she define *fame-iness* by negation? By analogy?
4. What other terms are defined in this essay? Why?
5. What patterns of development does Daum use to develop her definition?
6. Evaluate Daum's opening and closing paragraphs. What strategies does she use? Should these paragraphs be developed further? If so, how?

Vocabulary Projects

1. Define each of the following words as it is used in this selection.

   warrant (2)   allotted (8)
   crotchety (4)   niche (9)
   provincial (4)   mundanity (10)
   suffice (7)

2. In addition to *fame-iness*, Daum coins several other terms in this essay, including "reverse indifference" (6), "faux famous" (6) and "celebrity repulsion" (7). In your own words, define these terms.

Journal Entry

Do you agree with Daum that today, "the mystique of so many celebrities is rooted less in their accomplishments than in their ability to get our attention by provoking our disgust" (11)? Explain your feelings on this issue.

Writing Workshop

1. Write your own extended definition of *fame-iness*. Begin by summarizing Daum's views on how fame has changed, and then provide a formal definition of *fame-iness*. Develop your definition with examples of present-day celebrities who help to define the term. Be sure to acknowledge, and document, Daum's words and ideas, and be sure to include a works-cited page. (See the Appendix for information on documentation formats.)
2. Write an extended definition of *fame*, using classification to develop your essay. Begin by establishing three or four categories of fame, based on how a person earned his or her celebrity — for example, through talent, heroism, or criminal activity. Then, give a series of examples for each category. In your thesis, communicate your opinion about which kind of fame is most deserved. Be sure to include a formal definition of *fame* early in your essay.

Combining the Patterns

Daum's essay includes very few **examples** of celebrities. In which specific sections of the essay would you add such examples? Which particular celebrities would best illustrate Daum's points?

Thematic Connections

- "Thirty-Eight Who Saw Murder Didn't Call the Police" (page 120)
- "Grant and Lee: A Study in Contrasts" (page 405)
- "Torture's Terrible Toll" (page 696)

ROBERTO SANTIAGO

Black *and* Latino

Born in New York's Spanish Harlem in 1964, Roberto Santiago was a member of the first class of New York University's prestigious Urban Journalism Workshop, a summer program designed to encourage minority high school students to consider a career in journalism. After graduating from Oberlin College, he established a distinguished career as a writer and editor with publications such as the *Cleveland Plain Dealer*, the *New York Daily News*, and, currently, the *Miami Herald*, where he is a senior staff writer and often focuses on issues of poverty and social justice. Santiago also edited *Boricuas: Influential Puerto Writings* (1995), a highly regarded anthology of prose, poetry, plays, and screenplays. The following essay originally appeared in *Essence* magazine, a popular African-American publication.

Background on racial definitions by the United States Census Bureau
As recently as 1950, the United States Census Bureau in surveying race relied on only three categories: white, Negro, and other. (Whites were asked to specify whether they were native- or foreign-born.) The 1960 census saw the addition of American Indian, Japanese, Chinese, and Filipino, and the 1970 form added Hawaiian and Korean. For the 1980 census, due largely to lobbying by New Mexico Senator Joseph Montoya, in addition to specifying race, the census form asked respondents to identify whether they were of Spanish or Hispanic origin. (In fact, the term *Hispanic* was coined largely for this purpose.) The next major change came with the 2000 census, which allowed respondents to check off more than one race from the list of White, Black/African-American, American Indian/Native Alaskan, Asian, and Native Hawaiian/Pacific Islander. (Some Other Race continued to be an option.)

"There is no way that you can be black and Puerto Rican at the same time." What? Despite the many times I've heard this over the years, that statement still perplexes me. I *am* both and always have been. My color is a blend of my mother's rich, dark skin tone and my father's white complexion. As they were both Puerto Rican, I spoke Spanish before English, but I am totally bilingual. My life has been shaped by my black and Latino heritages, and despite other people's confusion, I don't feel I have to choose one or the other. To do so would be to deny a part of myself.

There has not been a moment in my life when I did not know that I looked black — and I never thought that others did not see it, too. But growing up in East Harlem, I was also aware that I did not "act black," according to the African-American boys on the block.

My lighter-skinned Puerto Rican friends were less of a help in this department. "You're not black," they would whine, shaking their heads. "You're a *boriqua* [slang for Puerto Rican], you ain't no *moreno* [black]." If that was true, why did my mirror defy the rules of logic? And most of all, why did I feel that there was some serious unknown force trying to make me choose sides?

Acting black. Looking black. Being a real black. This debate among us is almost a parody. The fact is that I am black, so why do I need to prove it? 4

The island of Puerto Rico is only a stone's throw away from Haiti, and, no fooling, if you climb a palm tree, you can see Jamaica bobbing on the Atlantic. The slave trade ran through the Caribbean basin, and virtually all Puerto Rican citizens have some African blood in their veins. My grandparents on my mother's side were the classic *negro como carbón* (black as carbon) people, but despite the fact that they were as dark as can be, they are officially not considered black. 5

There is an explanation for this, but not one that makes much sense, or difference, to a working-class kid from Harlem. Puerto Ricans identify themselves as Hispanics — part of a worldwide race that originated from eons of white Spanish conquests — a mixture of white, African, and *Indio* blood, which, categorically, is apart from black. In other words, the culture is the predominant and determinant factor. But there are frustrations in being caught in a duo-culture, where your skin color does not necessarily dictate what you are. When I read Piri Thomas's searing autobiography, *Down These Mean Streets*, in my early teens, I saw that he couldn't figure out other people's attitudes toward his blackness, either. 6

My first encounter with this attitude about the race thing rode on horseback. I had just turned six years old and ran toward the bridle path in Central Park as I saw two horses about to trot past. "Yea! Horsie! Yea!" I yelled. Then I noticed one figure on horseback. She was white, and she shouted, "Shut up, you f — g nigger! Shut up!" She pulled back on the reins and twisted the horse in my direction. I can still feel the spray of gravel that the horse kicked at my chest. And suddenly she was gone. I looked back, and, in the distance, saw my parents playing Whiffle Ball with my sister. They seemed miles away. 7

They still don't know about this incident. But I told my Aunt Aurelia almost immediately. She explained what the words meant and why they were said. Ever since then I have been able to express my anger appropriately through words or action in similar situations. Self-preservation, ego, and pride forbid men from ever ignoring, much less forgetting, a slur. 8

Aunt Aurelia became, unintentionally, my source for answers I needed about color and race. I never sought her out. She just seemed to appear at my home during the points in my childhood when I most needed her for solace. "Puerto Ricans are different from American blacks," she told me once. "There is no racism between what you call white and black. Nobody even considers the marriages interracial." She then pointed out the difference in color between my father and mother. "You never noticed that," she said, "because you were not raised with that hang-up." 9

Aunt Aurelia passed away before I could follow up on her observation. But she had made an important point. It's why I never liked the attitude that says I should be exclusive to one race. 10

My behavior toward this race thing pegged me as an iconoclast of sorts.   11
Children from mixed marriages, from my experience, also share this attitude. If I have to beat the label of iconoclast because the world wants
people to be in set categories and I don't want to, then I will.

A month before Aunt Aurelia died, she saw I was a little down about   12
the whole race thing, and she said, "Roberto, don't worry. Even if — no
matter what you do — black people in this country don't, you can always
depend on white people to treat you like a black."

·   ·   ·

Comprehension

1. In Puerto Rico, according to Santiago, culture — not race — is central to a
   person's identity. Why, then, do you think it is so difficult for Santiago to
   consider his culture, rather than his race, the "predominant and determinant factor" (6) in defining his identity?

2. Why does Santiago include the information in paragraphs 4–5 in his
   essay? What does it contribute?

3. In paragraph 4, Santiago says, "This debate among us is almost a parody."
   What does he mean?

4. Find a plot summary of Piri Thomas's *Down These Mean Streets* (referred to
   in paragraph 6) at Amazon.com. How does this information help you to
   understand Santiago's dilemma?

5. In paragraph 8, Santiago says, "Self-preservation, ego, and pride forbid
   men from ever ignoring, much less forgetting, a slur." Instead, he
   believes, one should "express . . . anger appropriately through words or
   action. . . ." What might constitute an "appropriate" expression of anger
   in response to a slur that expresses racist, sexist, or homophobic attitudes?

6. What advantages might be associated with defining oneself as black
   rather than Latino? As Latino rather than black?

Purpose and Audience

1. Do you think Santiago is trying to inform, educate, or persuade his readers? Or do you think he is just trying to tell them how he feels? Explain
   your conclusion.

2. Do you think Santiago sees his audience as predominantly black, white,
   or Latino? How can you tell?

3. Santiago's essay has a clearly stated thesis. Where is it? Rephrase it in your
   own words.

Style and Structure

1. Santiago opens his essay with a quotation. Is this an effective strategy?
   Can you suggest a better one?

2. Why do you think Santiago italicizes the three phrases that open paragraph 4?

3. Why does Santiago include the expression "no fooling" in paragraph 5? Does it make you more or less likely to accept the information in this paragraph?

4. At several points in his essay, Santiago refers to "the race thing" (7, 11) or "the whole race thing" (12). What does he mean? Is this an effective term for the problem he describes? Can you think of a better one?

5. Do you think Aunt Aurelia meant her advice to Roberto (quoted in paragraph 12) to be **ironic**? Do you think he took it that way? What do you think her words mean?

Vocabulary Projects

1. Define each of the following words as it is used in this selection.

   parody (4)   solace (9)
   categorically (6) iconoclast (11)
   searing (6)

2. In paragraph 7, when Santiago quotes the racial slur hurled at him, he spells out the slur but abbreviates the profane modifier as "f___g." Do you think this makes sense, or do you think he should have abbreviated both words — or neither?

3. Go online to research the terms *Latino*, *Hispanic*, and *Chicano*, all of which are used by Americans of Spanish descent. Which groups in the United States tend to prefer which term? How do Puerto Ricans generally refer to themselves? What do you conclude about how Americans of Spanish origin define themselves?

Journal Entry

Do you believe that someone who has roots in more than one culture or ethnic group has to "choose one or the other"? Or, can a person really be, for example, both black and Latino?

Writing Workshop

1. Write an essay in which you define yourself in terms of your race or ethnicity. If you believe that two or more racial or ethnic groups compete for your loyalty, write about how you attempt to reconcile their demands as you define your cultural identity. Use a modified version of Santiago's thesis as your thesis statement, acknowledging and documenting his words and including a works-cited page. (See the Appendix for information on documentation formats.)

2. Write an essay in which you define yourself in terms of the community with which you identify — for example, your school, your neighborhood, or your city.

3. Write an essay in which you define yourself as a member of your family (either your nuclear family or your extended family). Begin by defining what it means to be (for example) a Santiago, and expand your definition with examples of qualities that different family members exemplify. (You may use some narrative examples as well.)

Combining the Patterns

What does the **narrative** in paragraph 7 add to this essay? Why is it important? What other kinds of narrative passages could be added to enrich this essay?

Thematic Connections

- "Just Walk On By" (page 236)
- "The 'Black Table' Is Still There" (page 345)
- U.S. Census Bureau (Questionnaire) (page 518)
- "American Dreams, Foreign Flags" (page 650)
- "The Myth of the Latin Woman: I Just Met a Girl Named Maria" (page 730)

What Work Is (Poetry)

Philip Levine (b. 1928) teaches at New York University. Levine published his first volume of poetry, *On the Edge,* in 1961 and is the author of some fifteen more, including *Not This Pig* (1968); *Ashes: Poems New and Old* (1979), which received the National Book Critics' Circle Award; *What Work Is* (1991), which won the National Book Award; *The Simple Truth* (1994), which won the Pulitzer Prize; and, most recently, *Breath* (2004). He has also published a collection of essays, *The Bread of Time: Toward an Autobiography* (1994). A manual laborer during most of his early life, Levine eventually drew on those experiences for his poetry: "It's ironic that while I was a worker in Detroit, which I left when I was twenty-six, my sense was that the thing that's going to stop me from being a poet is the fact that I'm doing this crummy work. . . . The irony is, going to work every day became the subject of probably my best poetry. But I couldn't see that at the time. And it took me another ten years to wake up to it. That I had a body of experience that nobody else had."

Background on the poem

As Levine relates in a commentary on the poem, "What Work Is" was inspired by an experience from his youth. In need of a job and responding to an employment ad that required applicants to be at the plant at eight A.M. on a Monday morning, he arrived to find that the employment office didn't open until ten A.M. He stood in the rain with some two hundred others until employment personnel showed up at about twenty of ten to unlock the doors. "Then they locked them in our faces," Levine observes. "I realized that they had done this on purpose. They required a test of our docility. If we hadn't waited for two hours, we weren't right for this [crummy] job. It angered me. I carried that anger with me for many, many years." When he finally got to the front of the line, a man behind a desk asked Levine what kind of work he wanted. Levine replied, "I'd like your job," meaning, he says, "I'd like to dump on people the way you do." Levine continues: "He said, 'Next,' and that was the end of that. So my big mouth again." (The brother he refers to in "What Work Is," and who turns up in many of Levine's poems, is his twin.)

We stand in the rain in a long line
waiting at Ford Highland Park. For work.
You know what work is — if you're
old enough to read this you know what
work is, although you may not do it.   5
Forget you. This is about waiting,
shifting from one foot to another.
Feeling the light rain falling like mist

into your hair, blurring your vision
until you think you see your own brother   10
ahead of you, maybe ten places.
You rub your glasses with your fingers,
and of course it's someone else's brother,
narrower across the shoulders than
yours but with the same sad slouch, the grin   15
that does not hide the stubbornness,
the sad refusal to give in to
rain, to the hours wasted waiting,
to the knowledge that somewhere ahead
a man is waiting who will say, "No,   20
we're not hiring today," for any
reason he wants. You love your brother,
now suddenly you can hardly stand
the love flooding you for your brother,
who's not beside you or behind or   25
ahead because he's home trying to
sleep off a miserable night shift
at Cadillac so he can get up
before noon to study his German.
Works eight hours a night so he can sing   30
Wagner,* the opera you hate most,
the worst music ever invented.
How long has it been since you told him
you loved him, held his wide shoulders,
opened your eyes wide and said those words,   35
and maybe kissed his cheek? You've never
done something so simple, so obvious,
not because you're too young or too dumb,
not because you're jealous or even mean
or incapable of crying in   40
the presence of another man, no,
just because you don't know what work is.

•   •   •

Reading Literature

1. How does this poem define *work*? Do you think it really explains "what
   work is"? Why, or why not?

2. Who is the poem's speaker? Where is he, and what is he doing? What do
   you think the speaker means when he says, "you think you see your own

---

* EDS. NOTE — Richard Wagner (1813–1883), groundbreaking German composer
whose works many singers still find difficult.

brother / ahead of you" (lines 10–11) but "of course it's someone else's brother" (line 13)?

3. How do you explain the poem's last few lines? How does the speaker's ignorance of what work is keep him from telling his brother he loves him? What is the connection?

Journal Entry

In lines 3–5, the speaker says, "You know what work is — if you're / old enough to read this you know what / work is, although you may not do it." Do you know "what work is"?

Thematic Connections

- "My Mother Never Worked" (page 114)
- "Midnight" (page 209)
- "The Peter Principle" (page 216)
- "Down and Out in Discount America" (page 638)

WRITING ASSIGNMENTS FOR DEFINITION

1. Choose a document or ritual that is a significant part of your religious or cultural heritage. Define it, using any pattern or combination of patterns you choose, but be sure to include a formal definition somewhere in your essay. Assume your readers are not familiar with the term you are defining.

2. Define an abstract term — for example, *stubbornness, security, courage,* or *fear* — by making it concrete. You can develop your definition with a series of brief examples or with an extended narrative that illustrates the characteristic you are defining.

3. The readings in this chapter define (among other things) a food, a family role, and an item of clothing. Write an essay using examples and description to define one of these topics — for instance, ramen noodles (food), a stepmother (family role), or a chador (item of clothing).

4. Do some research on webmd.com (for adult health issues) or kidshealth .org (for childen's health issues) to learn the meaning of one of these medical conditions: angina, migraine, Down syndrome, attention deficit disorder, schizophrenia, autism, or Alzheimer's disease. Then, write an extended definition essay explaining the condition to an audience of high school students. Be sure to quote (and document) any material you borrow from your source. (See the Appendix for information on documentation formats.)

5. Use a series of examples to support a thesis in an essay that defines *racism, sexism, ageism, homophobia,* or another type of bigoted behavior.

6. Choose a term that is central to one of your courses — for instance, *naturalism, behaviorism,* or *authority* — and write an essay defining the term. Assume your audience is made up of students who have not yet taken the course. You may begin with an overview of the term's origin if you believe this is appropriate. Then, develop your essay with examples and **analogies** that will facilitate your audience's understanding of the term. Your purpose is to convince readers that understanding the term you are defining is important.

7. Assume your audience is from a culture unfamiliar with modern American children's pastimes. Write a definition essay for this audience describing the form and function of a Frisbee, a Barbie doll, an action figure, a skateboard, or a video game.

8. Review any one of the following narrative essays from Chapter 6, and use it to help you develop an extended definition of one of the following terms.

   "Only Daughter" or "Finishing School" — prejudice

   "My Mother Never Worked" — work

   "Thirty-Eight Who Saw Murder Didn't Call the Police" — apathy

   "Shooting an Elephant" — power

9. What constitutes an education? Define the term *education* by identifying several different sources of knowledge, formal or informal, and explaining what each contributes. You might read — or reread — "Finishing

School" (page 107), "Indian Education" (page 135), "The Socks" (page 95), or "The Human Cost of an Illiterate Society" (page 248).

10. What qualifies someone as a hero? Developing your essay with a series of examples, define the word *hero*. Include a formal definition, and try to incorporate at least one paragraph defining the term by explaining and illustrating what a hero is *not*.

COLLABORATIVE ACTIVITY FOR DEFINITION

Working as a group, choose one of the following words to define: *pride, hope, sacrifice,* or *justice*. Then, define the term with a series of extended examples drawn from films your group members have seen, with each of you developing an illustrative paragraph based on a different film. (Before beginning, your group may decide to focus on one particular genre of film.) When everyone in the group has read each paragraph, work together to formulate a thesis that asserts the vital importance of the quality your examples have defined. Finally, write suitable opening and closing paragraphs for the essay, and arrange the body paragraphs in a logical order, adding transitions where necessary.

14
Argumentation

WHAT IS ARGUMENTATION?

Argumentation is a process of reasoning that asserts the soundness of a debatable position, belief, or conclusion. Argumentation takes a stand — supported by evidence — and urges people to share the writer's perspective and insights. In the following paragraph from his essay "Holding Cell," Jerome Groopman argues that with its decision to limit therapeutic cloning, the President's Council on Bioethics has prevented scientists from carrying out important medical research that could possibly save lives:

Issue identified

The President's Council on Bioethics, chaired by Dr. Leon R. Kass, presented its long-awaited report on human cloning to the White House. . . . The council unanimously advised against "cloning to produce children," commonly called "reproductive cloning." But on "cloning for biomedical research" — therapeutic cloning to produce stem cells to try to ameliorate disease — it split. Of the seventeen members, ten (including Kass) voted against it. They couched their rejection as a compromise since they called not for a permanent ban but for a four-year moratorium. This moratorium, according to the letter accompanying the report, would allow "a thorough federal review . . . to clarify the issues and foster a public consensus about how to proceed." It would also give researchers time to seek alternative ways to generate stem cells. But for scientists and, more importantly, for the millions of patients with incurable maladies, the compromise is a painful disappointment. It shackles potentially lifesaving research and provides no clear framework to advance the ethical debate.

Background presents both sides of issue

Topic sentence (takes a stand)

Argumentation can be used to convince other people to accept (or at least acknowledge the validity of) your position; to defend your position, even if you cannot convince others to agree; or to question or refute a position you believe to be misguided, untrue, dangerous, or evil (without necessarily offering an alternative).

UNDERSTANDING ARGUMENTATION AND PERSUASION

Although the terms *persuasion* and *argumentation* are frequently used interchangeably, they do not mean the same thing. **Persuasion** is a general term that refers to how a writer influences an audience to adopt a belief or follow a course of action. To persuade an audience, a writer relies on various kinds of appeals — appeals based on emotion (*pathos*), appeals based on logic (*logos*), and appeals based on the character reputation of the writer (*ethos*).

Argumentation is the appeal to reason. In an argument, a writer connects a series of statements so that they lead logically to a conclusion. Argumentation is different from persuasion in that it does not try to move an audience to action; its primary purpose is to demonstrate that certain ideas are valid and others are not. Moreover, unlike persuasion, argumentation has a formal structure: an argument makes points, supplies evidence, establishes a logical chain of reasoning, refutes opposing arguments, and accommodates the audience's views.

As the selections in this chapter demonstrate, however, most effective arguments combine two or more appeals: even though their primary appeal is to reason, they may also appeal to emotions. For example, you could use a combination of logical and emotional appeals to argue against lowering the drinking age in your state from twenty-one to eighteen. You could appeal to *reason* by constructing an argument leading to the conclusion that the state should not condone policies that have a high probability of injuring or killing citizens. You could support your conclusion by presenting statistics showing that alcohol-related traffic accidents kill more teenagers than disease does. You could also cite a study showing that when the drinking age was raised from eighteen to twenty-one, fatal accidents declined. In addition, you could include an appeal to the *emotions* by telling a particularly sad story about an eighteen-year-old alcoholic or by pointing out how an increased number of accidents involving drunk drivers would cost some innocent people their lives. These appeals to your audience's emotions could strengthen your argument by widening its appeal. Keep in mind, however, that in an effective argument emotion does not take the place of logic; it supports and reinforces it.

The appeals you choose and how you balance them depend in part on your purpose and your sense of your audience. As you consider what strategies to use, remember that some extremely effective appeals are unfair. Although most people would agree that lies, threats, misleading statements, and appeals to greed and prejudice are unacceptable ways of reaching an audience, such appeals are used in daily conversation, in political campaigns, and even in international diplomacy. Nevertheless, in your college writing you should use only those appeals that most people would consider fair. To do otherwise will undercut your audience's belief in your trustworthiness and weaken your argument.

PLANNING AN ARGUMENTATIVE ESSAY

Choosing a Topic

In an argumentative essay, as in all writing, choosing the right topic is important. Ideally, you should have an intellectual or emotional stake in your topic. Still, you should be open-minded and willing to consider all sides of a question. If the evidence goes against your position, you should be willing to change your thesis. You should also be able, from the outset, to consider your topic from other people's viewpoints; this will help you determine what their beliefs are and how they are likely to react. You can then use this knowledge to build your case and to refute opposing viewpoints. If you cannot be open-minded, you should choose another topic you can deal with more objectively.

Other factors should also influence your selection of a topic. First, you should be well informed about your topic. In addition, you should choose an issue narrow enough to be treated in the space available to you or be willing to confine your discussion to one aspect of a broad issue. It is also important to consider your **purpose** — what you expect your argument to accomplish and how you wish your audience to respond. If your topic is so far-reaching that you cannot identify what you want to convince readers to think, or if your purpose is so idealistic that your expectations of their response are impossible or unreasonable, your essay will suffer.

Developing a Thesis

After you have chosen your topic, you are ready to state the position you will argue in the form of a **thesis**. Keep in mind that in an argumentative essay, your thesis must take a stand — in other words, it must be **debatable**. A good argumentative thesis states a proposition that at least some people will object to. Arguing a statement of fact or an idea that most people accept as self-evident is pointless. Consider the following thesis statement:

> Education is the best way to address the problem of increased drug use among teenagers.

This thesis statement says that increased drug use is a problem among teenagers, that more than one possible solution to this problem exists, and that education is a better solution than any other. In your argument, you will have to support each of these three points logically and persuasively.

A good way to test the suitability of your thesis for an argumentative essay is to formulate an **antithesis**, a statement that asserts the opposite position. If you think that some people would support the antithesis, you can be certain your thesis is indeed debatable.

Thesis:	Education is the best way to address the problem of increased drug use among teenagers.
Antithesis:	Education is not the best way to address the problem of increased drug use among teenagers.
Thesis:	Because immigrants have contributed much to the development of the United States, immigration quotas should be relaxed.
Antithesis:	Even though immigrants have contributed much to the development of the United States, immigration quotas should not be relaxed.

Analyzing Your Audience

Before writing any essay, you should analyze the characteristics, values, and interests of your audience. In argumentation, it is especially important to consider what beliefs or opinions your readers are likely to have and whether your audience is likely to be friendly, neutral, or hostile to your thesis.

It is probably best to assume that some, if not most, of your readers are at least **skeptical** — that they are open to your ideas but need to be convinced. This assumption will keep you from making claims you cannot support. If your position is controversial, you should assume that an informed and determined opposition is looking for holes in your argument.

In an argumentative essay, you face a dual challenge. You must appeal to readers who are neutral or even hostile to your position, and you must influence those readers so that they are more receptive to your viewpoint. For example, it would be relatively easy to convince college students that tuition should be lowered or instructors that faculty salaries should be raised. You could be reasonably sure, in advance, that each group would agree with your position. But argument requires more than just telling people what they already believe. It would be much harder to convince college students that tuition should be raised to pay for an increase in instructors' salaries or to persuade instructors to forgo raises so that tuition can remain the same. Remember, your audience will not just take your word for the claims you make. You must provide evidence that will support your thesis and reasoning that will lead logically to your conclusion.

Gathering and Documenting Evidence

All the points you make in your paper must be supported. If they are not, your audience will dismiss them as unfounded, irrelevant, or unclear. Sometimes you can support a statement with appeals to emotion, but most of the time you support your argument's points by appealing to reason — by providing **evidence**: facts and opinions in support of your position.

As you gather evidence and assess its effectiveness, keep in mind that evidence in an argumentative essay never proves anything conclusively. If it did, there would be no debate — and hence no point in arguing. The best that evidence can do is convince your audience that an assertion is reasonable and worth considering.

Kinds of Evidence. Evidence can be *fact* or *opinion*. **Facts** are statements that most people agree are true and that can be verified independently. Facts — including statistics — are the most commonly used type of evidence. It is a fact, for example, that fewer people per year were killed in U.S. automobile accidents in 2008 than in 1975. Facts may be drawn from your own experience as well as from reading and observation. It may, for instance, be a fact you have had a serious automobile accident. Quite often, facts are more convincing when they are supplemented by **opinions**, or interpretations of facts. To connect your facts about automobile accidents to the assertion that the installation of side-impact airbags in all small trucks and SUVs, as well as in cars, could reduce deaths still further, you could cite the opinions of an expert — consumer advocate Ralph Nader, for example. His statements, along with the facts and statistics you have assembled and your own interpretations of those facts and statistics, could convince readers that your solution to the problem of highway deaths is reasonable.

Keep in mind that not all opinions are equally convincing. The opinions of experts are more convincing than are those of individuals who have limited knowledge of an issue. Your personal opinions can be excellent evidence (provided you are knowledgeable about your subject), but they are usually less convincing to your audience than an expert's opinion. In the final analysis, what is important is not just the quality of the evidence but also the credibility of the person offering it.

What kind of evidence might change readers' minds? That depends on the readers, the issue, and the facts at hand. Put yourself in the place of your readers, and ask what would make them receptive to your thesis. Why, for example, should a student agree to pay higher tuition? You might concede that tuition is high but point out that it has not been raised for three years while the college's costs have kept going up. The cost of heating and maintaining the buildings has increased, and professors' salaries have not, with the result that several excellent teachers have recently left the college for higher-paying jobs. Furthermore, cuts in federal and state funding have already caused a reduction in the number of courses offered. Similarly, how could you convince a professor to agree to accept no raise at all, especially in light of the fact that faculty salaries have not kept up with inflation? You could say that because cuts in government funding have already reduced course offerings and because the government has also reduced funds for student loans, any further rise in tuition to pay faculty salaries would cause some students to drop out — and that in turn would eventually cost some instructors their jobs. As you can see, the evidence you use in an argument depends to a great extent on whom you want to persuade and what you know about them.

Criteria for Evidence.   As you select and review material, choose your evidence with the following three criteria in mind:

1. Your evidence should be **relevant**. It should support your thesis and be pertinent to your argument. As you present evidence, be careful not to concentrate so much on a specific example that you lose sight of the point you are supporting. Such digressions may confuse your readers. For example, in arguing for mandatory HIV testing for all health-care workers, one student made the point that AIDS is at epidemic proportions. To illustrate this point, he offered a discussion of the bubonic plague in fourteenth-century Europe. Although interesting, this example was not relevant. To show its relevance, the student would have to link his discussion to his assertions about AIDS, possibly by comparing the spread of the bubonic plague in the fourteenth century to the spread of AIDS in Africa today.

2. Your evidence should be **representative**. It should represent the full range of opinions about your subject, not just one side. For example, in an essay arguing against the use of animals in medical experimentation, you would not just use information provided by animal rights activists. You would also use information supplied by medical researchers, pharmaceutical companies, and perhaps medical ethicists.

The examples and expert opinions you include should also be **typical**, not aberrant. Suppose you are writing an essay in support of building a trash-to-steam plant in your city. To support your thesis, you present the example of Baltimore, which has a successful trash-to-steam program. As you consider your evidence, ask yourself if Baltimore's experience with trash-to-steam is typical. Did other cities have less success? Take a close look at the opinions that disagree with the position you plan to take. If you understand your opposition, you can refute it effectively when you write your paper.

3. Your evidence should be **sufficient**. It should include enough facts, opinions, and examples to support your claims. The amount of evidence you need depends on the length of your paper, your audience, and your thesis. It stands to reason that you would use fewer examples in a two-page paper than in a ten-page research assignment. Similarly, an audience that is favorably disposed to your thesis might need only one or two examples to be convinced, whereas a skeptical audience would need many more. As you develop your thesis, think about the amount of support you will need to write your paper. You may decide that a narrower, more limited thesis will be easier to support than a more inclusive one.

Documentation of Evidence.   After you decide on a topic, you should begin to gather evidence. Sometimes you can use your own ideas and observations to support your claims. Most of the time, however, you will have to use the print and electronic resources of the library or search the Internet to locate the information you need.

Whenever you use such evidence in your paper, you have to **document** it by providing the source of the information. (When documenting sources, follow the documentation format recommended by the Modern Language Association, which is explained in the Appendix of this book.) If you don't document your sources, your readers are likely to dismiss your evidence, thinking that it may be inaccurate, unreliable, or simply false. **Documentation** gives readers the ability to evaluate the sources you cite and to consult them if they wish. When you document sources, you are telling your readers that you are honest and have nothing to hide.

Documentation also helps you avoid **plagiarism** — presenting the ideas or words of others as if they were your own. Certainly you don't have to document every idea you use in your paper. For example, **common knowledge** — information you could easily find in several reference sources — can be presented without documentation, and so can your own ideas. You must, however, document any use of a direct quotation and any ideas, statistics, charts, diagrams, or pictures that you obtain from your source. (See the Appendix for information on documentation formats.)

Dealing with the Opposition

When gathering evidence, keep in mind that you should not ignore arguments against your position. In fact, you should specifically address the most obvious — and sometimes the not-so-obvious — objections to your position. By directly addressing these objections in your essay, you will help convince readers that your arguments are sound. This part of an argument, called **refutation**, is essential to making the strongest case possible.

You can **refute** opposing arguments by showing that they are unsound, unfair, or weak. Frequently, you will present evidence to show the weakness of your opponent's points and to reinforce your own case. Careful use of definition and cause-and-effect analysis may also prove effective. In the following passage from the classic essay "Politics and the English Language," George Orwell refutes an opponent's argument:

> I said earlier that the decadence of our language is probably curable. Those who deny this would argue, if they produced an argument at all, that language merely reflects existing social conditions, and that we cannot influence its development by any direct tinkering with words and constructions. So far as the general tone or spirit of a language goes, this may be true, but it is not true in detail. Silly words and expressions have often disappeared, though not through any evolutionary process but owing to the conscious actions of a minority.

Orwell begins by stating the point he wants to make, goes on to define the argument against his position, and then identifies its weakness. Later in the essay, Orwell bolsters his argument by presenting examples that support his point.

When an opponent's argument is so compelling that it cannot be easily dismissed, you should **concede** its strength (admit that is is valid). By acknowledging that a point is well taken, you reinforce the impression that you are a fair-minded person. If possible, identify the shortcomings of the opposing position, and then move your argument to more solid ground. (Often an opponent's strong point addresses only *one* facet of a multifaceted problem.) Notice in the example on page 553 that Orwell concedes an opposing argument when he says, "So far as the general tone or spirit of a language goes, this may be true." Later in his discussion, he refutes this argument by pointing out its shortcomings.

When planning an argumentative essay, write down all the arguments against your thesis that you can think of. Then, as you gather your evidence, decide which points you will refute, keeping in mind that careful readers will expect you to refute the most compelling of your opponent's arguments. Be careful, however, not to distort an opponent's argument by making it seem weaker than it actually is. This technique, called creating a **straw man**, can backfire and actually turn fair-minded readers against you.

Understanding Rogerian Argument

Not all arguments are (or should be) confrontational. Psychologist Carl Rogers has written about how to argue without assuming an adversarial relationship. According to Rogers, traditional strategies of argument rely on confrontation — trying to prove that an opponent's position is wrong. With this method of arguing, one person is "wrong" and one is "right." By attacking an opponent and repeatedly hammering home the message that his or her arguments are incorrect or misguided, a writer forces the opponent into a defensive position. The result is conflict, disagreement, and frequently ill will and hostility.

Rogers recommends that you think of those who disagree with you as colleagues, not adversaries. With this approach, now known as **Rogerian argument**, you enter into a cooperative relationship with opponents. Instead of aggressively refuting opposing arguments, you emphasize points of agreement and try to find common ground. You thus collaborate to find mutually satisfying solutions. By adopting a conciliatory attitude, you demonstrate your respect for opposing viewpoints and your willingness to compromise and work toward a position that both you and those who disagree with you will find acceptable. To use a Rogerian strategy in your writing, follow the guidelines on page 555.

USING DEDUCTIVE AND INDUCTIVE ARGUMENTS

In an argument, you move from evidence to a conclusion in two ways. One method, called **deductive reasoning**, proceeds from a general premise or assumption to a specific conclusion. Deduction is what most people

> ✓ **CHECKLIST:** **Guidelines for Using Rogerian Argument**
>
> - Begin by summarizing opposing viewpoints.
> - Carefully consider the position of those who disagree with you. What are their legitimate concerns? If you were in their place, how would you react?
> - Present opposing viewpoints accurately and fairly. Demonstrate your respect for the ideas of those who disagree with you.
> - Concede the strength of a compelling opposing argument.
> - Acknowledge the concerns you and your opposition share.
> - Point out to readers how they will benefit from the position you are defining.
> - Present the evidence that supports your viewpoint.

mean when they speak of logic. Using strict logical form, deduction holds that if all the statements in the argument are true, the conclusion must also be true.

The other method of moving from evidence to conclusion is called **inductive reasoning**. Induction proceeds from individual observations to a more general conclusion and uses no strict form. It requires only that all the relevant evidence be stated and that the conclusion fit the evidence better than any other conclusion would. Most written arguments use a combination of deductive and inductive reasoning, but it is simpler to discuss and illustrate them separately.

Using Deductive Arguments

The basic form of a deductive argument is a **syllogism**. A syllogism consists of a **major premise**, which is a general statement; a **minor premise**, which is a related but more specific statement; and a **conclusion**, which is drawn from those premises. Consider the following example:

Major premise:	All Olympic runners are fast.
Minor premise:	Jesse Owens was an Olympic runner.
Conclusion:	Therefore, Jesse Owens was fast.

As you can see, if you grant both the major and minor premises, then you must also grant the conclusion. In fact, it is the only conclusion you can properly draw. You cannot reasonably conclude that Jesse Owens was slow because that conclusion contradicts the premises. Nor can you conclude (even if it is true) that Jesse Owens was tall because that conclusion goes beyond the premises.

Of course, this argument seems obvious, and it is much simpler than an argumentative essay would be. In fact, a deductive argument's premises can be fairly elaborate. The Declaration of Independence, which appears later in this chapter, has at its core a deductive argument that could be summarized in this way:

Major premise:	Tyrannical rulers deserve no loyalty.
Minor premise:	King George III is a tyrannical ruler.
Conclusion:	Therefore, King George III deserves no loyalty.

The major premise is a statement that the Declaration claims is **self-evident** — so obvious that it needs no proof. Much of the Declaration consists of evidence to support the minor premise that King George is a tyrannical ruler. The conclusion, because it is drawn from those premises, has the force of irrefutable logic: the king deserves no loyalty from his American subjects, who are therefore entitled to revolt against him.

When a conclusion follows logically from the major and minor premises, then the argument is said to be **valid**. But if the syllogism is not logical, the argument is not valid, and the conclusion is not sound. For example, the following syllogism is not logical:

Major premise:	All dogs are animals.
Minor premise:	All cats are animals.
Conclusion:	Therefore, all dogs are cats.

Of course, the conclusion is absurd. But how did we wind up with such a ridiculous conclusion when both premises are obviously true? The answer is that the syllogism actually contains two major premises. (Both the major and minor premises begin with *all*.) Therefore, the syllogism is defective, and the argument is invalid. Consider the following example of an invalid argument:

Major premise:	All dogs are animals.
Minor premise:	Ralph is an animal.
Conclusion:	Therefore, Ralph is a dog.

Here, an error in logic occurs because the minor premise refers to a term in the major premise that is **undistributed** — it covers only some of the items in the class it denotes. (To be valid, the minor premise must refer to the term in the major premise that is **distributed** — it covers *all* the items in the class it denotes.) In the major premise, *dogs* is the distributed term; it designates *all dogs*. The minor premise, however, refers to *animals,* which is undistributed because it refers only to animals that are dogs. As the minor premise establishes, Ralph is an animal, but it does not follow that he is a dog. He could be a cat, a horse, or even a human being.

Even if a syllogism is valid — that is, correct in its form — its conclusion will not necessarily be **true**. The following syllogism draws a false conclusion:

Major premise:	All dogs are brown.
Minor premise:	My poodle Toby is a dog.
Conclusion:	Therefore, Toby is brown.

As it happens, Toby is black. The conclusion is false because the major premise is false: many dogs are *not* brown. If Toby were actually brown, the conclusion would be correct, but only by chance, not by logic. To be **sound**, a syllogism must be both logical and true.

The advantage of a deductive argument is that if you convince your audience to accept your major and minor premises, the force of logic should bring them to accept your conclusion. Therefore, you should try to select premises that you know your audience accepts or that are self-evident — that is, premises that most people believe to be true. Do not assume, however, that "most people" refers only to your friends and acquaintances. Consider, too, those who may hold different views. If you think your premises are too controversial or difficult to establish firmly, you should use inductive reasoning.

Using Inductive Arguments

Inductive arguments move from specific examples or facts to a general conclusion. Unlike deduction, induction has no distinctive form, and its conclusions are less definitive than those of syllogisms. Still, much inductive thinking (and writing based on that thinking) tends to follow a particular process.

- First, you decide on a question to be answered — or, especially in the sciences, a tentative answer to such a question, called a **hypothesis**.
- Then, you gather the evidence that is relevant to the question and that may be important to finding the answer.
- Finally, you move from your evidence to your conclusion by making an **inference** — a statement about the unknown based on the known — that answers the question and takes the evidence into account.

Here is a very simple example of the inductive process:

Question:	How did that living-room window get broken?
Evidence:	There is a baseball on the living-room floor.
	The baseball was not there this morning.
	Some children were playing baseball this afternoon.
	They were playing in the vacant lot across from the window.
	They stopped playing a little while ago.
	They aren't in the vacant lot now.
Conclusion:	One of the children hit or threw the ball through the window; then, they all ran away.

The conclusion, because it takes all of the evidence into account, seems obvious. But if it turned out that the children had been playing volleyball, not baseball, that one additional piece of evidence would make the conclusion doubtful — and the true answer could not be inferred. Even if the conclusion is believable, you cannot necessarily assume it is true: after all, the window could have been broken in some other way. For example, perhaps a bird flew against it, and perhaps the baseball in the living room had gone unnoticed all day, making the second piece of "evidence" on the list not true.

Considering several possible conclusions is a good way to avoid reaching an unjustified or false conclusion. In the preceding example, a hypothesis like this one might follow the question:

Hypothesis: One of those children playing baseball broke the living-room window.

Many people stop reasoning at this point, without considering the evidence. But when the gap between your evidence and your conclusion is too great, you may reach a hasty conclusion or one that is not supported by the facts. This well-named error is called **jumping to a conclusion** because it amounts to a premature inductive leap. In induction, the hypothesis is merely the starting point. The rest of the inductive process continues as if the question were still to be answered — as in fact it is until all the evidence has been taken into account.

Because inductive arguments tend to be more complicated than the example on pages 557–58, it is not always easy to move from the evidence you have collected to a sound conclusion. Of course, the more information you gather, the smaller the gap between your evidence and your conclusion. Still, whether large or small, the crucial step from evidence to conclusion always involves what is called an **inductive leap**. For this reason, it is important to remember that inductive conclusions are not facts. **Facts** are verifiable statements, but inductive conclusions are inferences and opinions that, at best, are never certain, only highly probable.

Using Toulmin Logic

Another approach for structuring arguments has been advanced by philosopher Stephen Toulmin. Known as **Toulmin logic**, this method is an effort to describe how the argumentative strategies a writer uses lead readers to respond the way they do. Toulmin puts forth a model that divides arguments into three parts: the *claim*, the *grounds*, and the *warrant*.

- The **claim** is the main point of the essay. Usually the claim is stated directly as the thesis, but in some arguments it may be implied.
- The **grounds** — the material a writer uses to support the claim — can be evidence (facts or expert opinion) or appeals to the emotions or values of the audience.

- The **warrant** is the inference that connects the claim to the grounds. It can be a belief that is taken for granted or an assumption that underlies the argument.

In its simplest form, an argument following Toulmin logic would look like this:

Claim: Carol should be elected class president.

Grounds: Carol is an honor student.

Warrant: A person who is an honor student would make a good class president.

When you formulate an argument using Toulmin logic, you can still use inductive and deductive reasoning. You derive your claim inductively from facts and examples, and you connect the grounds and warrant to your claim deductively. For example, the deductive argument in the Declaration of Independence that was summarized on page 556 can be represented this way:

Claim: King George III deserves no loyalty.

Grounds: King George III is a tyrannical ruler.

Warrant: Tyrannical rulers deserve no loyalty.

As Toulmin points out, the clearer your warrant, the more likely readers will be to agree with it. Notice that in the two preceding examples, the warrants are very explicit.

Recognizing Fallacies

Fallacies are illogical statements that may sound reasonable or true but are actually deceptive and dishonest. When careful readers detect them, such statements can turn even a sympathetic audience against your position. Here are some of the more common fallacies that you should avoid.

Begging the Question.   Begging the question is a logical fallacy that assumes in the premise what the arguer should be trying to prove in the conclusion. This tactic asks readers to agree that certain points are self-evident when in fact they are not.

Unfair and shortsighted legislation that limits free trade is a threat to the American economy.

Restrictions against free trade may or may not be unfair and shortsighted, but emotionally loaded language does not constitute proof. The statement begs the question because it assumes what it should be proving — that legislation that limits free trade is unfair and shortsighted.

Argument from Analogy.   An **analogy** is a form of comparison that explains something unfamiliar by comparing it to something familiar. Although analogies can explain abstract or unclear ideas, they do not constitute proof. An argument based on an analogy frequently ignores important dissimilarities between the two things being compared. When this occurs, the argument is fallacious.

> The overcrowded conditions in some parts of our city have forced people together like rats in a cage. Like rats, they will eventually turn on one another, fighting and killing until a balance is restored. It is therefore necessary that we vote to appropriate funds to build low-cost housing.

No evidence is offered to establish that people behave like rats under these or any other conditions. Just because two things have some characteristics in common, you should not assume they are alike in other respects.

Personal Attack (Argument *Ad Hominem*). This fallacy tries to divert attention from the facts of an argument by attacking the motives or character of the person making the argument.

> The public should not take seriously Dr. Mason's plan for improving county health services. He is a former alcoholic whose wife recently divorced him.

This attack on Dr. Mason's character says nothing about the quality of his plan. Sometimes a connection exists between a person's private and public lives — for example, in a case of conflict of interest. However, no evidence of such a connection is presented here.

Hasty or Sweeping Generalization. Sometimes called *jumping to a conclusion,* this fallacy occurs when a conclusion is reached on the basis of too little evidence.

> Because our son benefited from home schooling, every child should be educated in this way.

Perhaps other children would benefit from home schooling, and perhaps not, but no conclusion about children in general can be reached on the basis of just one child's experience.

False Dilemma (Either/Or Fallacy). This fallacy occurs when a writer suggests that only two alternatives exist even though there may be others.

> We must choose between life and death, between intervention and genocide. No one can be neutral on this issue.

An argument like this oversimplifies an issue and forces people to choose between extremes instead of exploring more moderate positions.

Equivocation. This fallacy occurs when the meaning of a key term changes at some point in an argument. Equivocation makes it seem as if a conclusion follows from premises when it actually does not.

ARGUMENTATION **561**

As a human endeavor, computers are a praiseworthy and even remarkable accomplishment. But how human can we hope to be if we rely on computers to make our decisions?

The use of *human* in the first sentence refers to the entire human race. In the second sentence, *human* means "merciful" or "civilized." By subtly shifting this term to refer to qualities characteristic of people as opposed to machines, the writer makes the argument seem more sound than it is.

Red Herring. This fallacy occurs when the focus of an argument is shifted to divert the audience from the actual issue.

The mayor has proposed building a new sports stadium. How can he even consider allocating millions of dollars to this scheme when so many professional athletes are being paid such high salaries?

The focus of this argument should be the merits of the sports stadium. Instead, the writer shifts to the irrelevant issue of athletes' high salaries.

You Also (*Tu Quoque*). This fallacy asserts that an opponent's argument has no value because the opponent does not follow his or her own advice.

How can that judge favor stronger penalties for convicted drug dealers? During his confirmation hearings, he admitted smoking marijuana when he was a student.

Appeal to Doubtful Authority. Often people will attempt to strengthen an argument with references to experts or famous people. These appeals are valid when the person referred to is an expert in the area being discussed. They are not valid, however, when the individuals cited have no expertise on the issue.

According to Diane Sawyer, interest rates will remain low during the next fiscal year.

Although Diane Sawyer is a respected journalist, she is not an expert in business or finance. Therefore, her pronouncements about interest rates are no more than a personal opinion or, at best, an educated guess.

Misleading Statistics. Although statistics are a powerful form of factual evidence, they can be misrepresented or distorted in an attempt to influence an audience.

Women will never be competent firefighters; after all, 50 percent of the women in the city's training program failed the exam.

Here, the writer has neglected to mention that there were only two women in the program. Because this statistic is not based on a large enough sample, it cannot be used as evidence to support the argument.

Post Hoc, Ergo Propter Hoc (**After This, Therefore Because of This**). This fallacy, known as *post hoc* **reasoning**, assumes that because two events occur close together in time, the first must be the cause of the second.

> Every time a Republican is elected president, a recession follows. If we want to avoid another recession, we should elect a Democrat.

Even if it were true that recessions always occur during the tenure of Republican presidents, no causal connection has been established. (See pages 326–27.)

Non Sequitur (**It Does Not Follow**). This fallacy occurs when a statement does not logically follow from a previous statement.

> Disarmament weakened the United States after World War I. Disarmament also weakened the United States after the Vietnam War. For this reason, the city's efforts to limit gun sales will weaken the United States.

The historical effects of disarmament have nothing to do with current efforts to control the sale of guns. Therefore, the conclusion is a *non sequitur.*

Using Transitions

Transitional words and **phrases** are extremely important in argumentative essays. Without these words and phrases, readers will find it difficult to follow your logic and could easily lose track of your argument.

Argumentative essays use transitions to signal a shift in focus. For example, paragraphs that present the specific points in support of your argument can signal this purpose with transitions such as *first, second, third, in addition,* and *finally.* In the same way, paragraphs that refute opposing arguments can signal this purpose with transitions such as *still, nevertheless,*

USEFUL TRANSITIONS FOR ARGUMENTATION

all in all	in conclusion
as a result	in other words
finally	in short
first, second, third	in summary
for example	nevertheless
for instance	on the one hand . . . on the other hand
for these reasons	still
however	therefore
in addition	thus
in brief	yet

A more complete list of transitions appears on page 43.

however, and *yet.* Transitional words and phrases — such as *therefore* and *for these reasons* — are also useful when you are presenting your argument's conclusions.

STRUCTURING AN ARGUMENTATIVE ESSAY

An argumentative essay, like other kinds of essays, has an **introduction**, a **body**, and a **conclusion**. However, an argumentative essay has its own special structure, one that ensures that ideas are presented logically and convincingly. The Declaration of Independence follows the typical structure of many classic arguments:

Introduction: Introduces the issue
        States the thesis

Body: Induction — offers evidence to support the thesis
        Deduction — uses syllogisms to support the thesis
        States the arguments against the thesis and refutes
        them

Conclusion: Restates the thesis in different words
        Makes a forceful closing statement

Jefferson begins the Declaration by presenting the issue that the document addresses: the obligation of the people of the American colonies to tell the world why they must separate from Great Britain. Next, Jefferson states his thesis that because of the tyranny of the British king, the colonies must replace his rule with another form of government. In the body of the Declaration, he offers as evidence twenty-eight examples of injustice endured by the colonies. Following the evidence, Jefferson refutes counterarguments by explaining how again and again the colonists have appealed to the British for redress, but without result. In his concluding paragraph, he restates the thesis and reinforces it one final time. He ends with a flourish: speaking for the representatives of the United States, he explicitly dissolves all political connections between England and America.

Not all arguments, however, follow this pattern. Your material, your thesis, your purpose, your audience, the type of argument you are writing, and the limitations of your assignment all help you determine the strategies you use. If your thesis is especially novel or controversial, for example, the refutation of opposing arguments may come first. In this instance, opposing positions might even be mentioned in the introduction — provided they are discussed more fully later in the argument.

Suppose your journalism instructor gives you the following assignment:

Select a controversial topic that interests you, and write a brief editorial about it. Direct your editorial to readers who do not share your views, and try to convince them that your position is reasonable. Be sure to acknowledge the view your audience holds and to refute possible criticisms of your argument.

You are well informed about one local issue because you have just read a series of articles on it. A citizens' group is lobbying for a local ordinance that would authorize government funding for religious schools. Since you have also recently studied the constitutional doctrine of separation of church and state in your American government class, you know you could argue fairly and strongly against the position taken by this group.

An informal outline of your essay might look like this:

Issue introduced:	Should public tax revenues be spent on aid to religious schools?
Thesis statement:	Despite the pleas of citizen groups like Religious School Parents United, using tax dollars to support church-affiliated schools violates the U.S. Constitution.
Evidence (deduction):	Explain general principle of separation of church and state in the Constitution.
Evidence (induction):	Present recent examples of court cases interpreting and applying this principle.
Evidence (deduction):	Explain how the Constitution and the court cases apply to your community's situation.
Opposition refuted:	Identify and respond to arguments used by Religious School Parents United. Concede the point that religious schools educate many children who would otherwise have to be educated in public schools at taxpayers' expense.
Conclusion:	Restate the thesis; end with a strong closing statement.

REVISING AN ARGUMENTATIVE ESSAY

When you revise an argumentative essay, consider the items on the revision checklist on page 54. In addition, pay special attention to the items on the following checklist, which apply specifically to argumentative essays.

✓ **REVISION CHECKLIST: Argumentation**

- Does your assignment call for argumentation?
- Have you chosen a topic you can argue about effectively?
- Do you have a debatable thesis?
- Have you considered the beliefs and opinions of your audience?
- Is your evidence relevant, representative, and sufficient?
- Have you documented evidence you have gathered from sources? Have you included a works-cited page?
- Have you made an effort to address your audience's possible objections to your position?

- Have you refuted opposing arguments?
- Have you used inductive or deductive reasoning (or a combination of the two) to move from your evidence to your conclusion?
- Have you avoided logical fallacies?
- Have you used appropriate transitional words and phrases?

EDITING AN ARGUMENTATIVE ESSAY

When you edit your argumentative essay, follow the guidelines on the editing checklists on pages 71, 74, and 76. In addition, focus on the grammar, mechanics, and punctuation issues that are particularly relevant to argumentative essays. One of these issues — using coordinating and subordinating conjunctions to link ideas — is discussed in the pages that follow.

GRAMMAR IN CONTEXT: Using Coordinating and Subordinating Conjunctions

When you write an argumentative essay, you often have to use **conjunctions** — words that join other words or groups of words — to express the logical and sequential relationships between ideas in your sentences. Conjunctions are especially important because they help readers follow the logic of your argument. For this reason, you should be certain that the conjunctions you select clearly and accurately communicate the connections between the ideas you are discussing.

Using Coordinating Conjunctions A **compound sentence** is made up of two or more independent clauses (simple sentences) connected by a coordinating conjunction. **Coordinating conjunctions** join two independent clauses that express ideas of equal importance, and they also indicate how those ideas are related.

independent clause   *independent clause*
[People can disobey unjust laws], <u>or</u> [they can be oppressed by them].

COORDINATING CONJUNCTIONS

and (*indicates addition*)
but, yet (*indicate contrast or contradiction*)
or (*indicates alternatives*)
nor (*indicates an elimination of alternatives*)
so, for (*indicate a cause-and-effect connection*)

(continued on next page)

(continued from previous page)

According to Thomas Jefferson, the king has refused to let governors pass important laws, <u>and</u> he has imposed taxes without the consent of the people (576–77).

Elizabeth Cady Stanton says that women are equal to men, <u>but</u> men think that they are superior (584).

Martin Luther King Jr. does not believe that all laws are just, <u>nor</u> does he believe that it is wrong to protest unjust laws (592).

When you use a coordinating conjunction to join two independent clauses, always place a comma before the coordinating conjunction.

Using Subordinating Conjunctions A **complex sentence** is made up of one independent clause (simple sentence) and one or more dependent clauses. (A dependent clause cannot stand alone as a sentence.) Subordinating conjunctions link dependent and independent clauses that express ideas of unequal importance, and they also indicate how those ideas are related.

independent clause
[According to Liza Featherstone, Wal-Mart has to pay low wages]

dependent clause
[<u>so that</u> it can keep its prices down] (640).

SUBORDINATING CONJUNCTIONS

SUBORDINATING CONJUNCTION	RELATIONSHIP BETWEEN CLAUSES
after, before, since, until, when, whenever, while	Time
as, because, since, so that	Cause or effect
even if, if, unless	Condition
although, even though, though	Contrast

"All segregation statutes are unjust <u>because</u> segregation distorts the soul and damages the personality" (King 593).

"<u>If</u> this philosophy had not emerged, by now many streets of the South would, I am convinced, be flowing with blood" (King 596).

"<u>Before</u> the pen of Jefferson etched the majestic words of the Declaration of Independence across the pages of history, we were here" (King 599).

"Because Wal-Mart sells the things that people need at very low prices, they love to shop there" (De Coster and Edmonds 634).

When you use a subordinating conjunction to join two clauses, place a comma after the dependent clause when it comes *before* the independent clause. Do not use a comma when the dependent clause comes *after* the independent clause.

When they signed the Declaration of Independence, Thomas Jefferson and the others knew they were committing treason. (*comma*)

Thomas Jefferson and the others knew they were committing treason when they signed the Declaration of Independence. (*no comma*)

For more practice in using coordinating and subordinating conjunctions, visit Exercise Central at bedfordstmartins.com/patterns/conjunctions.

✓ **EDITING CHECKLIST: Argumentation**

- Have you used coordinating conjunctions correctly to connect two or more independent clauses?
- Do the coordinating conjunctions accurately express the relationship between the ideas in the independent clauses?
- Have you placed a comma before the coordinating conjunction?
- Have you used subordinating conjunctions correctly to connect an independent clause and one or more dependent clauses?
- Do the subordinating conjunctions accurately express the relationship between the ideas in the dependent and independent clauses?
- Have you placed a comma after the dependent clause when it comes before the independent clause?
- Have you remembered not to use a comma when the dependent clause comes after the independent clause?

A STUDENT WRITER: Argumentation

The following editorial, written by Matt Daniels for his college newspaper, illustrates the techniques discussed earlier in this chapter.

An Argument against the Anna Todd Jennings Scholarship

Introduction   Recently, a dispute has arisen over the "Caucasian-   1

Summary of controversy   restricted" Anna Todd Jennings scholarship.* Anna Jennings

---

* EDS. NOTE — This essay discusses an actual situation, but the name of the scholarship has been changed here.

died in 1955, and her will established a trust that granted a scholarship of up to $15,000 for a deserving student. Unfortunately, Jennings, who had certain racist views, limited her scholarship to "Caucasian students." After much debate with family and friends, I, a white, well-qualified, and definitely deserving student, have decided not to apply for the

Thesis statement scholarship. It is my view that despite arguments to the contrary, applying for the Anna Todd Jennings scholarship furthers the racist ideas held by its founder.

Argument (deductive) Most people would agree that racism in any form is an evil 2 that should be opposed. The Anna Todd Jennings scholarship is a subtle but nonetheless dangerous expression of racism. It explicitly discriminates against African Americans, Asians, Latinos, Native Americans, and others. By providing a scholarship for whites only, Anna Jennings frustrates the aspirations of groups who until recently had been virtually kept out of the educational mainstream. On this basis alone, students should refuse to apply and should actively work to encourage the school to challenge the racist provisions of Anna Todd Jennings's will. According to one expert, such challenges have been upheld by the courts: the striking down of a similar clause in the will of the eighteenth-century financier Stephen Girard, which limited admission to white male orphans, is just one example.

Argument (inductive) The school itself must share some blame in this case. 3 Students who applied for the Anna Todd Jennings scholarship

Evidence were unaware of its restrictions. The director of the financial aid office has acknowledged that he knew about the racial restrictions of the scholarship but thought that students should have the right to apply anyway. The materials distributed by the financial aid office also gave no indication that the award was limited to Caucasians. Students were required to fill out forms, submit financial statements, and forward transcripts. In addition to this material, all students were told to attach a recent photograph to their application. Little did the applicants know that the sole purpose of this innocuous little picture was to distinguish whites from nonwhites. By keeping secret the scholarship's restrictions, the school has put students in the position of unwittingly endorsing Anna Jennings's racism. Thus, both the school and the unsuspecting students have been in collusion with the administrators of the Anna Todd Jennings trust.

Refutation of opposing argument

The question students face is this: What is the best way to deal with the generosity of a racist? A recent edition of the school paper contained several letters saying that students should accept Anna Jennings's scholarship money. One student said, "If we do not take that money and use our education to topple the barriers of prejudice, we are giving the money to those who will use the money in the opposite fashion." This argument, although attractive, is flawed. If an individual accepts a scholarship with racial restrictions, then he or she is actually endorsing the principles behind it. If a student does not want to appear to endorse racism, then he or she should reject the scholarship, even if this action causes hardship or gives adversaries a momentary advantage. To do otherwise is to further the cause of the individual who set up the scholarship. The best way to register a protest is to work to change the requirement for the scholarship and to encourage others not to apply as long as the racial restrictions exist.

Refutation of opposing argument

Another letter to this newspaper made the point that a number of other restricted scholarships are available at the school and no one seems to question them. For example, one is for the children of veterans, another is for women, and yet another is earmarked for African Americans. Even though these scholarships have restrictions, to assume that all restrictions are the same is to make a hasty generalization. Women, African Americans, and the children of veterans are groups that many believe deserve special treatment. Both women and African Americans have been discriminated against for years, and, as a result, educational opportunities have been denied them. Earmarking scholarships for them is simply a means of restoring some measure of equality. The children of veterans have been singled out because their parents have performed an extraordinary service for their country. Whites, however, do not fall into either of these categories. Special treatment for them is based solely on race and has nothing to do with any objective standard of need or merit.

Conclusion

Restatement of thesis

I hope that by refusing to apply for the Anna Todd Jennings scholarship, I have encouraged other students to think about the issues involved in their own decisions. All of us have a responsibility to ourselves and to society. If we truly believe

4

5

6

Concluding statement   that racism in all its forms is evil, then we have to make a choice between sacrifice and hypocrisy. Faced with these options, our decision should be clear: accept the loss of funds as an opportunity to explore your values and fight for your principles; if you do, this opportunity is worth far more than any scholarship.

Points for Special Attention

Gathering Evidence. Because of his involvement with his subject, Matt Daniels could support his points with examples from his own experience. Still, Matt did have to review the requirements for the scholarship and decide on the arguments he would make. In addition, he reviewed an article that appeared in the school newspaper and the letters students wrote in response to the article. He then chose material that would add authority to his arguments.

Certainly, statistics, studies, and expert testimony, if they exist, would strengthen Matt's argument. But even without such evidence, an argument such as this one, based on solid reasoning, personal experience, and some research can be quite compelling.

Documentation. Matt used material from several outside sources in his editorial. For example, he used information from a government Web site when he discussed Stephen Girard's will. He also used information from an article in his school newspaper as well as from letters to the editor. Matt knew that newspaper editorials like his do not usually include documentation. As he wrote his editorial, however, he used phrases like "According to one expert" to make sure that readers would know when he used information from a source.

Before Matt submitted his editorial for his journalism class, where it would be part of his writing portfolio, he had added documentation. Here are two sentences from this version of the editorial, along with the proper documentation.

> According to one expert, such challenges have been upheld by the courts: the striking down of a similar case in the will of eighteenth-century financier Stephen Girard is just one example (St. John 12).

> One student said, "If we do not take that money and use our education to topple the barriers of prejudice, we are giving the money to those who will use the money in the opposite fashion" (Divakaan).

Refuting Opposing Arguments. Matt devotes two paragraphs to summarizing and refuting arguments made by those who believe qualified students should apply for the scholarship despite its racial restrictions. He begins this section by asking a **rhetorical question** — a question asked not to elicit an answer but to further the argument. He goes on to refute what he considers the two best arguments against his thesis — that students should take the money and work to fight racism and that other scholarships at the school have restrictions. Matt counters these arguments by identifying a flaw in the logic of the first argument and by pointing to a fallacy, a hasty generalization, in the second.

Audience. Because he wrote his essay as an editorial for his college newspaper, Matt assumed his audience would be familiar with the issue he was discussing. Letters to the editor of the paper convinced him that his position was controversial, so he decided that his readers, mostly students and instructors, would have to be persuaded that his points were valid. To achieve this purpose, he carefully presents himself as a reasonable person, explains issues he believes are central to his case, and avoids *ad hominem* attacks. In addition, he avoids sweeping generalizations and name-calling and includes many details to support his assertions and convince readers that his points are worth considering.

Organization. Matt uses several strategies discussed earlier in this chapter. He begins his essay by introducing the issue he is going to discuss and then states his thesis: "Applying for the Anna Todd Jennings scholarship furthers the racist ideas held by its founder."

Because Matt had given a good deal of thought to his subject, he was able to construct two fairly strong arguments to support his position. His first argument is deductive. He begins by stating a premise he believes is self-evident — racism should be opposed. The rest of this argument follows a straightforward deductive pattern:

Major premise:	Racism should be opposed.
Minor premise:	The Anna Todd Jennings scholarship is racist.
Conclusion:	Therefore, the Anna Todd Jennings scholarship should be opposed.

Matt ends his first argument with factual evidence that reinforces his conclusion: the successful challenge to the will of financier Stephen Girard, which limited admittance to Girard College in Philadelphia to white male orphans.

Matt's second argument is inductive, asserting that the school has put students in the position of unknowingly supporting racism. The argument begins with Matt's hypothesis and presents the fact that even though the school is aware of the racist restrictions of the scholarship, it has not made students aware of them. According to Matt, the school's knowledge (and tacit approval) of the situation leads to the conclusion that the school is in collusion with those who manage the scholarship.

In his fourth and fifth paragraphs, Matt refutes two opposing arguments. Although his conclusion is rather brief, it does effectively reinforce and support his main idea. Matt ends his essay by recommending a course of action to his fellow students.

Focus on Revision

Matt constructed a solid argument that addressed his central issue very effectively. However, some students on the newspaper's editorial board thought he should add a section giving more information about Anna Todd Jennings and her bequest. These students believed that such information would help them better understand the implications of accepting her money. As it now stands, the essay dismisses Anna Todd Jennings as a racist, but biographical material and excerpts from her will — both of which appeared in the school paper — would enable readers to grasp the extent of her prejudice. Matt decided to follow up on this advice and to strengthen his conclusion as well. He thought that including the exact words of Anna Todd Jennings would help him to reinforce his points forcefully and memorably.

📄 **PEER EDITING WORKSHEET: Argumentation**

1. Does the essay take a stand on an issue? What is it? At what point does the writer state his or her thesis? Is the thesis debatable?
2. What evidence does the writer include to support his or her position? What additional evidence could the writer supply?
3. Has the writer used information from outside sources? If so, is parenthetical documentation included? Identify any information that the writer should have documented but did not.
4. Does the essay summarize and refute the opposing arguments? List these arguments.
5. How effective are the writer's refutations? Should the writer address any other arguments?
6. Does the essay use inductive reasoning? Deductive reasoning? Both? Provide an example of each type of reasoning used in the essay.
7. Does the essay include any logical fallacies? How would you correct these fallacies?
8. Do coordinating and subordinating conjunctions convey the logical and sequential connections between ideas?
9. How could the introduction be improved?
10. How could the conclusion be improved?

The essays that follow represent a wide variety of topics, and the purpose of each essay is to support a controversial thesis. Each of the three debates pairs two essays that take opposing stands on the same issue. In the two casebooks, four essays on a single topic offer a greater variety of viewpoints. The first selection, a visual text, is followed by questions designed to illustrate how argumentation can operate in visual form.

Thanks to Modern Science . . . (Ad)

• • •

Reading Images

1. What points does the ad's headline make? Does the rest of the ad support these points?
2. How would you describe the picture that accompanies the text? How does the picture reinforce the message of the text?
3. Does this ad appeal primarily to logic, to emotions, or to both? Explain.
4. List the specific points the ad makes. Which points are supported by evidence? Which points should be supported by evidence but are not? How does this lack of support affect your response to the ad?

Journal Entry

Overall, do you find this ad convincing? Write an email to the ACLU presenting your position. Be sure to refer to specific parts of the ad to support your argument.

Thematic Connections

- "Thirty-Eight Who Saw Murder Didn't Call the Police" (page 120)
- "Get It Right: Privatize Executions" (page 299)
- "Guns and Grief" (page 350)
- "Five Ways to Kill a Man" (page 501)

THOMAS JEFFERSON

The Declaration of Independence

Thomas Jefferson was born in 1743 in what is now Albemarle County, Virginia. A lawyer, he was elected to Virginia's colonial legislature in 1769 and began a distinguished political career that strongly influenced the early development of the United States. In addition to his participation in the Second Continental Congress of 1775–1776, which ratified the Declaration of Independence, he served as governor of Virginia; as minister to France; as secretary of state under President George Washington; as vice president under John Adams; and, finally, as president from 1801 to 1809. After his retirement, he founded the University of Virginia. He died on July 4, 1826.

Background on the struggle for American independence

By the early 1770s, many residents of the original thirteen American colonies were convinced that King George III and his ministers, both in England and in the New World, wielded too much power over the colonists. In particular, they objected to a series of taxes imposed on them by the British Parliament, and, being without political representation, they asserted that "taxation without representation" amounted to tyranny. In response to a series of laws Parliament passed in 1774 to limit the political and geographic freedom of the colonists, representatives of each colony met at the Continental Congress of 1774 to draft a plan of reconciliation, but it was rejected.

As cries for independence increased, British soldiers and state militias began to engage in armed conflict, which by 1776 had become a full-fledged civil war. On June 11, 1776, the Second Continental Congress chose Jefferson, Benjamin Franklin, and several other delegates to draft a declaration of independence. The draft was written by Jefferson, with suggestions and revisions contributed by other commission members. Jefferson's Declaration of Independence challenges a basic assumption of its time — that the royal monarch ruled by divine right — and, in so doing, became one of the most important political documents in world history.

As you read, keep in mind that to the British, the Declaration of Independence was a call for open rebellion. For this reason, the Declaration's final sentence, in which the signatories pledge their lives, fortunes, and honor, is no mere rhetorical flourish. Had England defeated the colonists, everyone who signed the Declaration of Independence would have been arrested, charged with treason or sedition, stripped of his property, and probably hanged.

When in the course of human events, it becomes necessary for one people to dissolve the political bonds which have connected them with another, and to assume among the powers of the earth, the separate and equal station to which the Laws of Nature and of Nature's God entitle them, a decent respect to the opinions of mankind requires that they should declare the causes which impel them to the separation.

We hold these truths to be self-evident, that all men are created equal, that they are endowed by their Creator with certain unalienable rights, that among these are life, liberty, and the pursuit of happiness. That to secure these rights, governments are instituted among men, deriving their just powers from the consent of the governed. That whenever any form of government becomes destructive to these ends, it is the right of the people to alter or to abolish it, and to institute new government, laying its foundation on such principles and organizing its powers in such form, as to them shall seem most likely to effect their safety and happiness. Prudence, indeed, will dictate that governments long established should not be changed for light and transient causes; and accordingly all experience hath shown, that mankind are more disposed to suffer, while evils are sufferable, than to right themselves by abolishing the forms to which they are accustomed. But when a long train of abuses and usurpations, pursuing invariably the same object, evinces a design to reduce them under absolute despotism, it is their right, it is their duty, to throw off such government, and to provide new guards for their future security. Such has been the patient sufferance of these Colonies; and such is now the necessity which constrains them to alter their former systems of government. The history of the present king of Great Britain is a history of repeated injuries and usurpations, all having in direct object the establishment of an absolute tyranny over these States. To prove this, let facts be submitted to a candid world.   2

He has refused his assent to laws, the most wholesome and necessary for the public good.   3

He has forbidden his Governors to pass laws of immediate and pressing importance, unless suspended in their operation till his assent should be obtained; and when so suspended, he has utterly neglected to attend to them.   4

He has refused to pass other laws for the accommodation of large districts of people, unless those people would relinquish the right of representation in the legislature, a right inestimable to them and formidable to tyrants only.   5

He has called together legislative bodies at places unusual, uncomfortable, and distant from the depository of their public records, for the sole purpose of fatiguing them into compliance with his measure.   6

He has dissolved representative houses repeatedly, for opposing with manly firmness his invasions on the rights of people.   7

He has refused for a long time, after such dissolutions, to cause others to be elected; whereby the legislative powers, incapable of annihilation, have returned to the people at large for their exercise; the State remaining in the meantime exposed to all the dangers of invasion from without, and convulsions within.   8

He has endeavoured to prevent the population of these states; for that   9
purpose obstructing the laws for naturalization of foreigners; refusing to
pass others to encourage their migration hither, and raising the conditions
of new appropriations of lands.

He has obstructed the administration of justice, by refusing his assent   10
to laws for establishing judiciary powers.

He has made judges dependent on his will alone, for the tenure of their   11
offices, and the amount and payment of their salaries.

He has erected a multitude of new offices, and sent hither swarms of   12
officers to harass our people, and eat out their substance.

He has kept among us, in times of peace, standing armies without the   13
consent of our legislatures.

He has affected to render the military independent of and superior to   14
the civil power.

He has combined with others to subject us to a jurisdiction foreign to   15
our constitution, and unacknowledged by our laws; giving his assent to
their acts of pretended legislation:

For quartering large bodies of troops among us: 16

For protecting them, by a mock trial, from punishment for any mur-   17
ders which they should commit on the inhabitants of these States:

For cutting off our trade with all parts of the world: 18

For imposing taxes on us without our consent: 19

For depriving us in many cases, of the benefits of trial by jury: 20

For transporting us beyond seas to be tried for pretended offences: 21

For abolishing the free system of English laws in a neighbouring   22
Province, establishing therein an arbitrary government, and enlarging its
boundaries so as to render it at once an example and fit instrument for
introducing the same absolute rule into these Colonies:

For taking away our Charters, abolishing our most valuable laws, and   23
altering fundamentally the forms of our governments:

For suspending our own legislatures, and declaring themselves invested   24
with power to legislate for us in all cases whatsoever.

He has abdicated government here, by declaring us out of his protec-   25
tion and waging war against us.

He has plundered our seas, ravaged our coasts, burnt our towns, and   26
destroyed the lives of our people.

He is at this time transporting large armies of foreign mercenaries to   27
complete the works of death, desolation and tyranny, already begun with
circumstances of cruelty and perfidy scarcely paralleled in the most barbarous ages, and totally unworthy the head of a civilized nation.

He has constrained our fellow citizens taken captive on the high seas   28
to bear arms against their country, to become the executioners of their
friends and brethren, or to fall themselves by their hands.

He has excited domestic insurrections amongst us, and has endeav-   29
oured to bring on the inhabitants of our frontiers, the merciless Indian

savages, whose known rule of warfare, is an undistinguished destruction of all ages, sexes, and conditions.

In every stage of these oppressions we have petitioned for redress in the most humble terms: our repeated petitions have been answered only by repeated injury. A prince whose character is thus marked by every act which may define a tyrant, is unfit to be the ruler of a free people. 30

Nor have we been wanting in attentions to our British brethren. We have warned them from time to time of attempts by their legislature to extend an unwarrantable jurisdiction over us. We have reminded them of the circumstances of our emigration and settlement here. We have appealed to their native justice and magnanimity, and we have conjured them by the ties of our common kindred to disavow these usurpations, which, would inevitably interrupt our connections and correspondence. They too have been deaf to the voice of justice and of consanguinity. We must, therefore, acquiesce in the necessity, which denounces our separation, and hold them, as we hold the rest of mankind, enemies in war, in peace friends. 31

We, therefore, the Representatives of the United States of America, in General Congress, assembled, appealing to the Supreme Judge of the world for the rectitude of our intentions, do, in the name, and by authority of the good people of these Colonies, solemnly publish and declare, That these United Colonies are, and of right ought to be Free and Independent States; that they are absolved from all allegiance to the British Crown, and that all political connection between them and the state of Great Britain, is and ought to be totally dissolved; and that as Free and Independent States, they have full power to levy war, conclude peace, contract alliances, establish commerce, and to do all other acts and things which Independent States may of right do. And for the support of this declaration, with a firm reliance on the protection of divine Providence, we mutually pledge to each other our lives, our fortunes, and our sacred honor. 32

•   •   •

Comprehension

1. What "truths" does Jefferson say are "self-evident"?
2. What does Jefferson say is the source from which governments derive their powers?
3. What reasons does Jefferson give to support his premise that the United States should break away from Great Britain?
4. What conclusions about British rule does Jefferson draw from the evidence he presents?

Purpose and Audience

1. What is the major premise of Jefferson's argument? Should Jefferson have done more to establish the truth of this premise?

2. The Declaration of Independence was written during a period now referred to as the Age of Reason. In what ways has Jefferson tried to make his document appear reasonable?

3. For what audience (or audiences) was the document intended? Which groups of readers would have been most likely to accept it? Explain.

4. How effectively does Jefferson anticipate and refute the opposition?

5. In paragraph 31, following the list of grievances, why does Jefferson address his "British brethren"?

6. At what point does Jefferson state his thesis? Why does he state it where he does?

Style and Structure

1. Does the Declaration of Independence rely primarily on inductive or deductive reasoning? Identify examples of each.

2. What techniques does Jefferson use to create smooth and logical transitions from one paragraph to another?

3. Why does Jefferson list all of his twenty-eight grievances? Why doesn't he just summarize them or mention a few representative grievances?

4. Jefferson begins the last paragraph of the Declaration of Independence with "We, therefore." How effective is this conclusion? Explain.

Vocabulary Projects

1. Define each of the following words as it is used in this selection.

station (1)	evinces (2)	tenure (11)
impel (1)	despotism (2)	jurisdiction (15)
self-evident (2)	sufferance (2)	arbitrary (22)
endowed (2)	candid (2)	insurrections (29)
deriving (2)	depository (6)	disavow (31)
prudence (2)	dissolutions (8)	consanguinity (31)
transient (2)	annihilation (8)	rectitude (32)
usurpations (2)	appropriations (9)	levy (32)

2. Underline ten words that have negative connotations. How does Jefferson use these words to help him make his point? Do you think words with more neutral connotations would strengthen or weaken his case? Why?

3. What words does Jefferson use that are rarely used today? Would the Declaration of Independence be more meaningful to today's readers if it were updated, with more familiar words substituted? To help you formulate your response, try rewriting a paragraph or two, and assess your updated version. Look up any unfamiliar words in an online dictionary such as dictionary.com.

Journal Entry

Do you think Jefferson is being fair to the king? Do you think he should be?

Writing Workshop

1. Following Jefferson's example, write a declaration of independence from your school, job, family, or any other institution with which you are associated.

2. Go to the Web site ushistory.org/declaration/document/congress.htm and look at the revisions that Congress made to Jefferson's original draft of the Declaration of Independence. Decide which version you think is better. Then, write an essay in which you present your case. Make sure you document all words and ideas that you borrow from both versions of the Delcaration. In addition, include a works-cited page. (See the Appendix for information on documentation formats.)

3. In an argumentative essay written from the viewpoint of King George III, answer Jefferson. Try to convince the colonists that they should not break away from Great Britain. If you can, refute some of the points Jefferson makes. Make sure that you document all words and ideas that you borrow from the Declaration and that you include a works-cited page. (See the Appendix for information on documentation formats.)

Combining the Patterns

The middle section of the Declaration of Independence is developed by means of **exemplification**: it presents a series of examples to support Jefferson's assertion that the colonists have experienced "repeated injuries and usurpations" (2). Are these examples relevant? Representative? Sufficient? What other pattern of development could Jefferson have used to support his assertion?

Thematic Connections

- "The 'Black Table' Is Still There" (page 345)
- "The Power of Words in Wartime" (page 363)
- "Grant and Lee: A Study in Contrasts" (page 405)
- "Letter from Birmingham Jail" (page 588)

Declaration of Sentiments and Resolutions, Seneca Falls Convention, 1848

Elizabeth Cady was born in Johnstown, New York, in 1815 and attended the Troy Female Seminary. At the age of twenty-five, she married the writer and abolitionist Henry Brewster Stanton, joining him in the struggle to end slavery. She also became active in the woman suffrage movement, lobbying for the right of women to vote. This movement had its beginnings in the United States at the first Woman's Rights Convention, which was organized by Stanton and other early petitioners for women's rights and held in Seneca Falls, New York, in July 1848. There, the following declaration was first presented, amended, and then unanimously adopted by the three hundred delegates. (All the resolutions were passed unanimously except for the one calling for women's right to vote, which was thought by some to be extreme enough to discredit the larger feminist movement.) Stanton went on to lead the National Woman Suffrage Movement from 1869 to 1890 and to coedit *Revolution,* a feminist periodical. A popular lecturer and skilled writer, she continued to work toward the goal of equality for women until her death in 1902.

Background on the women's suffrage movement

In 1848, women were considered inferior to men in terms of intelligence and rationality, so the Founding Fathers' "all men are created equal" did not seem to apply to them. In fact, the idea for the Seneca Falls Convention was spurred by Stanton's experiences at the 1840 World Anti-Slavery Convention in London, which she attended with her husband and which refused to admit women delegates to the floor. When made public, the Declaration of Sentiments was universally derided by the press and by contemporary religious leaders — even Henry Stanton thought his wife had gone too far. The Civil War interrupted the budding women's rights movement, but at its close, when emancipated African-American men were granted the right to vote, the movement picked up steam again. Its leaders lobbied for an amendment to the U.S. Constitution allowing women to vote and pressed state legislatures for voting rights as well. It was a long road, however. By 1913, only twelve states had extended voting rights to women, and not until the Nineteenth Amendment to the Constitution was ratified in 1920 did all American women gain this right.

Declaration of Sentiments

When, in the course of human events, it becomes necessary for one portion of the family of man to assume among the people of the earth a position different from that which they have hitherto occupied, but one to

1

which the laws of nature and of nature's God entitle them, a decent respect to the opinions of mankind requires that they should declare the causes that impel them to such a course.

We hold these truths to be self-evident: that all men and women are created equal; that they are endowed by their Creator with certain inalienable rights; that among these are life, liberty, and the pursuit of happiness; that to secure these rights governments are instituted, deriving their just powers from the consent of the governed. Whenever any form of government becomes destructive of these ends, it is the right of those who suffer from it to refuse allegiance to it, and to insist upon the institution of a new government, laying its foundation on such principles, and organizing its powers in such form, as to them shall seem most likely to effect their safety and happiness. Prudence, indeed, will dictate that governments long established should not be changed for light and transient causes; and accordingly all experience hath shown that mankind are more disposed to suffer, while evils are sufferable, than to right themselves by abolishing the forms to which they were accustomed. But when a long train of abuses and usurpations, pursuing invariably the same object, evinces a design to reduce them under absolute despotism, it is their duty to throw off such government, and to provide new guards for their future security. Such has been the patient sufferance of the women under this government, and such is now the necessity which constrains them to demand the equal station to which they are entitled.

2

The history of mankind is a history of repeated injuries and usurpations on the part of man toward woman, having in direct object the establishment of an absolute tyranny over her. To prove this, let facts be submitted to a candid world.

3

He has never permitted her to exercise her inalienable right to the elective franchise.

4

He has compelled her to submit to laws, in the formation of which she had no voice.

5

He has withheld from her rights which are given to the most ignorant and degraded men — both natives and foreigners.

6

Having deprived her of this first right of a citizen, the elective franchise, thereby leaving her without representation in the halls of legislation, he has oppressed her on all sides.

7

He has made her, if married, in the eye of the law, civilly dead.

8

He has taken from her all right in property, even to the wages she earns.

9

He has made her, morally, an irresponsible being, as she can commit many crimes with impunity, provided they be done in the presence of her husband. In the covenant of marriage, she is compelled to promise obedience to her husband, he becoming, to all intents and purposes, her master — the law giving him power to deprive her of her liberty, and to administer chastisement.

10

He has so framed the laws of divorce, as to what shall be the proper causes, and in case of separation, to whom the guardianship of the children shall be given, as to be wholly regardless of the happiness of

11

women — the law, in all cases, going upon the false supposition of the supremacy of man, and giving all power into his hands.

After depriving her of all rights as a married woman, if single, and the owner of property, he has taxed her to support a government which recognizes her only when her property can be made profitable to it. 12

He has monopolized nearly all the profitable employments, and from those she is permitted to follow, she receives but a scanty remuneration. He closes against her all the avenues to wealth and distinction which he considers most honorable to himself. As a teacher of theology, medicine, or law, she is not known. 13

He has denied her the facilities for obtaining a thorough education, all colleges being closed against her. 14

He allows her in Church, as well as State, but a subordinate position, claiming Apostolic authority for her exclusion from the ministry, and, with some exceptions, from any public participation in the affairs of the Church. 15

He has created a false public sentiment by giving to the world a different code of morals for men and women, by which moral delinquencies which exclude women from society, are not only tolerated, but deemed of little account in man. 16

He has usurped the prerogative of Jehovah himself, claiming it as his right to assign for her a sphere of action, when that belongs to her conscience and to her God. 17

He has endeavored, in every way that he could, to destroy her confidence in her own powers, to lessen her self-respect, and to make her willing to lead a dependent and abject life. 18

Now, in view of this entire disenfranchisement of one-half the people of this country, their social and religious degradation — in view of the unjust laws above mentioned, and because women do feel themselves aggrieved, oppressed, and fraudulently deprived of their most sacred rights, we insist that they have immediate admission to all the rights and privileges which belong to them as citizens of the United States. 19

In entering upon the great work before us, we anticipate no small amount of misconception, misrepresentation, and ridicule; but we shall use every instrumentality within our power to effect our object. We shall employ agents, circulate tracts, petition the State and National legislatures, and endeavor to enlist the pulpit and the press in our behalf. We hope this Convention will be followed by a series of Conventions embracing every part of the country. 20

Resolutions

Whereas, The great precept of nature is conceded to be, that "man shall pursue his own true and substantial happiness." Blackstone* in his 21

---

* EDS. NOTE — Sir William Blackstone (1723–80), English jurist. Many regard his *Commentaries* (1765–69) as the most thorough treatment of English law ever produced.

Commentaries remarks, that this law of Nature being coeval with mankind, and dictated by God himself, is of course superior in obligation to any other. It is binding over all the globe, in all countries and at all times; no human laws are of any validity if contrary to this, and such of them as are valid, derive all their force, and all their validity, and all their authority, mediately and immediately, from this original; therefore,

 Resolved, That such laws as conflict, in any way, with the true and sub-   22
stantial happiness of woman, are contrary to the great precept of nature and of no validity, for this is "superior in obligation to any other."

 Resolved, That all laws which prevent woman from occupying such a   23
station in society as her conscience shall dictate, or which place her in a position inferior to that of man, are contrary to the great precept of nature, and therefore of no force or authority.

 Resolved, That woman is man's equal — was intended to be so by the   24
Creator, and the highest good of the race demands that she should be recognized as such.

 Resolved, That the women of this country ought to be enlightened in   25
regard to the laws under which they live, that they may no longer publish their degradation by declaring themselves satisfied with their present position, nor their ignorance, by asserting that they have all the rights they want.

 Resolved, That inasmuch as man, while claiming for himself intellec-   26
tual superiority, does accord to woman moral superiority, it is preeminently his duty to encourage her to speak and teach, as she has an opportunity, in all religious assemblies.

 Resolved, That the same amount of virtue, delicacy, and refinement of   27
behavior that is required of woman in the social state, should also be required of man, and the same transgressions should be visited with equal severity on both man and woman.

 Resolved, That the objection of indelicacy and impropriety, which is so   28
often brought against woman when she addresses a public audience, comes with a very ill-grace from those who encourage, by their attendance, her appearance on the stage, in the concert, or in feats of the circus.

 Resolved, That woman has too long rested satisfied in the circumscribed   29
limits which corrupt customs and a perverted application of the Scriptures have marked out for her, and that it is time she should move in the enlarged sphere which her great Creator has assigned her.

 Resolved, That it is the duty of the women of this country to secure to   30
themselves their sacred right to the elective franchise.

 Resolved, That the equality of human rights results necessarily from the   31
fact of the identity of the race in capabilities and responsibilities.

 Resolved, therefore, That, being invested by the Creator with the same   32
capabilities, and the same consciousness of responsibility for their exercise, it is demonstrably the right and duty of woman, equally with man, to promote every righteous cause by every righteous means; and especially in regard to the great subjects of morals and religion, it is self-evidently her right to participate with her brother in teaching them, both in private and

in public, by writing and by speaking, by any instrumentalities proper to be used, and in any assemblies proper to be held; and this being a self-evident truth growing out of the divinely implanted principles of human nature, any custom or authority adverse to it, whether modern or wearing the hoary sanction of antiquity, is to be regarded as a self-evident falsehood, and at war with mankind.

Resolved, That the speedy success of our cause depends upon the zeal- 33
ous and untiring efforts of both men and women, for the overthrow of the monopoly of the pulpit, and for the securing to woman an equal participation with men in the various trades, professions, and commerce.*

• • •

Comprehension

1. According to Stanton, why is it necessary for women to declare their sentiments?
2. What truths does Stanton say are "self-evident" (2)?
3. What injuries does Stanton list? Which injuries seem most important?
4. What type of reception does Stanton expect the Declaration of Sentiments and Resolutions to receive? What does she propose to do about this reception?
5. What conclusion does Stanton draw? According to her, what self-evident right do women have? What does she believe should be regarded as "a self-evident falsehood" (32)?

Purpose and Audience

1. Is Stanton addressing men, women, or both? How can you tell? Does she consider one segment of her audience more receptive to her ideas than another? Explain.
2. What strategies does Stanton use to present herself as a reasonable person? Do you think she is successful? Explain.
3. What is Stanton's thesis? At what point does she state it? Why do you think she states it when she does?
4. What is Stanton's purpose? Do you think she actually expects to change people's ideas and behavior, or does she have some other purpose in mind?

Style and Structure

1. Does Stanton present her argument inductively or deductively? Why do you think she chose this arrangement?

---

* EDS. NOTE — This last resolution was given by Lucretia Mott at the actual convention. All the previous resolutions were drafted earlier by Elizabeth Cady Stanton.

2. The Declaration of Sentiments and Resolutions imitates the tone, style, and, in some places, even the wording of the Declaration of Independence. What are the advantages of this strategy? What are the disadvantages?

3. In paragraphs 2 and 32, Stanton mentions "self-evident" truths. Are these truths really self-evident? Should she have done more to establish the validity of these statements?

4. What are the major and minor premises of Stanton's argument? Do these premises lead logically to her conclusion?

5. How do transitional words and phrases help Stanton move readers from one section of her argument to another? Are the transitions effective?

6. Should Stanton have specifically refuted arguments against her position? Could she be accused of ignoring her opposition?

Vocabulary Projects

1. Define each of the following words as it is used in this selection.

hitherto (1)	station (2)	validity (21)
impel (1)	franchise (4)	transgressions (27)
inalienable (2)	degraded (6)	indelicacy (28)
allegiance (2)	impunity (10)	impropriety (28)
dictate (2)	chastisement (10)	circumscribed (29)
sufferable (2)	subordinate (15)	sphere (29)
invariably (2)	delinquencies (16)	antiquity (32)
sufferance (2)	abject (18)	zealous (33)
constrains (2)	disenfranchisement (19)	

2. Today, many people would consider the style of some of the passages in the Declaration of Sentiments and Resolutions stiff and overly formal. Find a paragraph that fits this description, and rewrite it using less formal diction. What is lost in your revision, and what is gained?

Journal Entry

Review Stanton's list of injuries to women. How many of these wrongs have been corrected? How many have yet to be addressed?

Writing Workshop

1. Choose an issue you care about, and write your own Declaration of Sentiments and Resolutions. Like Stanton, echo the phrasing of the Declaration of Independence in your essay.

2. Reread your journal entry, and select one of the injuries to women that has not yet been corrected. Write an email to the editor of your school newspaper arguing that this issue needs to be resolved. In your email, refer specifically to the Declaration of Sentiments and Resolutions.

3. When the Declaration of Sentiments and Resolutions was voted on at the Seneca Falls Convention in 1848, the only resolution not passed unanimously was the one that called for women to win the right to vote (30). Write a letter to the convention calling on the delegates to vote for this resolution. Make sure you refute the main argument against this resolution — that it would alienate so many people that it would discredit the entire feminist movement.

4. Go to the Web site ushistory.org/declaration/document/congress.htm and look at the revisions that Congress made to Jefferson's original draft of the Declaration of Independence. Decide which version you think is better. Then, write an essay in which you present your case. Make sure you document all words and ideas that you borrow from both versions of the Declaration. In addition, include a works-cited page. (See the Appendix for information on documentation formats.)

Combining the Patterns

Like the Declaration of Independence, the Declaration of Sentiments and Resolutions is partly developed by **exemplification**. A series of examples supports Stanton's assertion that women now "demand the equal station to which they are entitled" (2). How effective are these examples? Are they relevant? Representative? Sufficient?

Thematic Connections

- "My Mother Never Worked" (page 114)
- "A Peaceful Woman Explains Why She Carries a Gun" (page 357)
- "I Want a Wife" (page 520)
- The Declaration of Independence (page 575)

Letter from Birmingham Jail

Martin Luther King Jr. was born in Atlanta, Georgia, in 1929. After receiving his doctorate in theology from Boston University in 1955, he became pastor of the Dexter Avenue Baptist Church in Montgomery, Alabama. There, he organized a 382-day bus boycott that led to the 1956 Supreme Court decision outlawing segregation on Alabama's buses. As leader of the Southern Christian Leadership Conference, he was instrumental in securing the civil rights of black Americans, using methods based on a philosophy of nonviolent protest. His books include *Stride towards Freedom* (1958) and *Why We Can't Wait* (1964). In 1964, he was awarded the Nobel Peace Prize. He was assassinated in 1968 in Memphis, Tennessee.

Background on racial segregation

In 1896, the Supreme Court ruled in *Plessy v. Ferguson* that "separate but equal" accommodations on railroad cars gave African Americans the equal protection guaranteed by the Fourteenth Amendment of the Constitution. This decision was used to justify separate public facilities — including schools — for blacks and whites well into the twentieth century.

In the mid-1950s, state support for segregation and discrimination against blacks had begun to be challenged. Supreme Court decisions in 1954 and 1955 declared segregation in public schools and other publicly financed venues unconstitutional, while blacks and whites alike were calling for an end to discrimination. Their actions took the form of marches, boycotts, and sit-ins (organized protests whose participants refuse to move from a public area). Many whites, however, particularly in the South, vehemently resisted any change in race relations.

By 1963, when Martin Luther King Jr. organized a campaign against segregation in Birmingham, Alabama, tensions ran deep. He and his followers met fierce opposition from the police, as well as from white moderates, who considered him an "outside agitator." During the demonstrations, King was arrested and jailed for eight days. While imprisoned, he wrote his "Letter from Birmingham Jail" to white clergymen to explain his actions and answer those who urged him to call off the demonstrations.

April 16, 1963

My Dear Fellow Clergymen:

While confined here in the Birmingham city jail, I came across your recent statement calling my present activities "unwise and untimely." Seldom do I pause to answer criticism of my work and ideas. If I sought to answer all the criticisms that cross my desk, my secretaries would have little time for anything other than such correspondence in the course of the day, and I would have no time for constructive work. But since I feel that you

1

are men of genuine good will and that your criticisms are sincerely set forth, I want to try to answer your statement in what I hope will be patient and reasonable terms.

I think I should indicate why I am here in Birmingham, since you have been influenced by the view which argues against "outsiders coming in." I have the honor of serving as president of the Southern Christian Leadership Conference, an organization operating in every southern state, with headquarters in Atlanta, Georgia. We have some eighty-five affiliated organizations across the South, and one of them is the Alabama Christian Movement for Human Rights. Frequently we share staff, educational, and financial resources with our affiliates. Several months ago the affiliate here in Birmingham asked us to be on call to engage in a nonviolent direct-action program if such were deemed necessary. We readily consented, and when the hour came we lived up to our promise. So I, along with several members of my staff, am here because I was invited here. I am here because I have organizational ties here.

But more basically, I am in Birmingham because injustice is here. Just as the prophets of the eighth century B.C. left their villages and carried their "thus saith the Lord" far beyond the boundaries of their home towns, and just as the Apostle Paul left his village of Tarsus and carried the gospel of Jesus Christ to the far corners of the Greco-Roman world, so am I compelled to carry the gospel of freedom beyond my own home town. Like Paul, I must constantly respond to the Macedonian call for aid.

Moreover, I am cognizant of the interrelatedness of all communities and states. I cannot sit idly by in Atlanta and not be concerned about what happens in Birmingham. Injustice anywhere is a threat to justice everywhere. We are caught in an inescapable network of mutuality, tied in a single garment of destiny. Whatever affects one directly, affects all indirectly. Never again can we afford to live with the narrow, provincial, "outside agitator" idea. Anyone who lives inside the United States can never be considered an outsider anywhere within its bounds.

You deplore the demonstrations taking place in Birmingham. But your statement, I am sorry to say, fails to express a similar concern for the conditions that brought about the demonstrations. I am sure that none of you would want to rest content with the superficial kind of social analysis that deals merely with effects and does not grapple with underlying causes. It is unfortunate that demonstrations are taking place in Birmingham, but it is even more unfortunate that the city's white power structure left the Negro community with no alternative.

In any nonviolent campaign there are four basic steps: collection of the facts to determine whether injustices exist; negotiation; self-purification; and direct action. We have gone through all these steps in Birmingham. There can be no gainsaying the fact that racial injustice engulfs this community. Birmingham is probably the most thoroughly segregated city in the United States. Its ugly record of brutality is widely known. Negroes have experienced grossly unjust treatment in courts. There have been more unsolved bombings of Negro homes and churches in Birmingham than in any other city in the nation. These are the hard, brutal facts of the case. On the basis of these conditions, Negro leaders sought to negotiate with the city fathers. But the latter consistently refused to engage in good-faith negotiation.

Then, last September, came the opportunity to talk with leaders of Birmingham's economic community. In the course of the negotiations, certain promises were made by the merchants — for example, to remove the stores' humiliating racial signs. On the basis of these promises, the Reverend Fred Shuttlesworth and the leaders of the Alabama Christian Movement for Human Rights agreed to a moratorium on all demonstrations. As the weeks and months went by, we realized that we were the victims of a broken promise. A few signs, briefly removed, returned; the others remained. 7

As in so many past experiences, our hopes had been blasted, and the shadow of deep disappointment settled upon us. We had no alternative except to prepare for direct action, whereby we would present our very bodies as means of laying our case before the conscience of the local and the national community. Mindful of the difficulties involved, we decided to undertake a process of self-purification. We began a series of workshops on nonviolence, and we repeatedly asked ourselves: "Are you able to accept blows without retaliating?" "Are you able to endure the ordeal of jail?" We decided to schedule our direct-action program for the Easter season, realizing that except for Christmas, this is the main shopping period of the year. Knowing that a strong economic-withdrawal program would be the by-product of direct action, we felt that this would be the best time to bring pressure to bear on the merchants for the needed change. 8

Then it occurred to us that Birmingham's mayoral election was coming up in March, and we speedily decided to postpone action until after election day. When we discovered that the Commissioner of Public Safety, Eugene "Bull" Connor, had piled up enough votes to be in the run-off, we decided again to postpone action until the day after the run-off so that the demonstrations could not be used to cloud the issues. Like many others, we waited to see Mr. Connor defeated, and to this end we endured postponement after postponement. Having aided in this community need, we felt that our direct-action program could be delayed no longer. 9

You may well ask, "Why direct action? Why sit-ins, marches, and so forth? Isn't negotiation a better path?" You are quite right in calling for negotiation. Indeed, this is the very purpose of direct action. Nonviolent direct action seeks to create such a crisis and foster such a tension that a community which has constantly refused to negotiate is forced to confront the issue. It seeks so to dramatize the issue that it can no longer be ignored. My citing the creation of tension as part of the work of the nonviolent-resistor may sound rather shocking. But I must confess that I am not afraid of the word "tension." I have earnestly opposed violent tension, but there is a type of constructive, nonviolent tension which is necessary for growth. 10

Just as Socrates felt that it was necessary to create a tension in the mind so that individuals could rise from the bondage of myths and half-truths to the unfettered realm of creative analysis and objective appraisal, so must we see the need for nonviolent gadflies to create the kind of tension in society that will help men rise from the dark depths of prejudice and racism to the majestic heights of understanding and brotherhood.

The purpose of our direct-action program is to create a situation so 11 crisis-packed that it will inevitably open the door to negotiation. I therefore concur with you in your call for negotiation. Too long has our beloved Southland been bogged down in a tragic effort to live in monologue rather than dialogue.

One of the basic points in your statement is that the action that I and 12 my associates have taken in Birmingham is untimely. Some have asked: "Why didn't you give the new city administration time to act?" The only answer that I can give to this query is that the new Birmingham administration must be prodded about as much as the outgoing one, before it will act. We are sadly mistaken if we feel that the election of Albert Boutwell as mayor will bring the millennium to Birmingham. While Mr. Boutwell is a much more gentle person than Mr. Connor, they are both segregationists, dedicated to maintenance of the status quo. I have hoped that Mr. Boutwell will be reasonable enough to see the futility of massive resistance to desegregation. But he will not see this without pressure from devotees of civil rights. My friends, I must say to you that we have not made a single gain in civil rights without determined legal and nonviolent pressure. Lamentably, it is an historical fact that privileged groups seldom give up their privileges voluntarily. Individuals may see the moral light and voluntarily give up their unjust posture; but, as Reinhold Niebuhr* has reminded us, groups tend to be more immoral than individuals.

We know through painful experience that freedom is never voluntarily 13 given by the oppressor; it must be demanded by the oppressed. Frankly, I have yet to engage in a direct-action campaign that was "well timed" in the view of those who have not suffered unduly from the disease of segregation. For years now I have heard the word "Wait!" It rings in the ear of every Negro with piercing familiarity. This "Wait" has almost always meant "Never." We must come to see, with one of our distinguished jurists, that "justice too long delayed is justice denied."

We have waited for more than 340 years for our constitutional and 14 God-given rights. The nations of Asia and Africa are moving with jetlike speed toward gaining political independence, but we still creep at horse-and-buggy pace toward gaining a cup of coffee at a lunch counter. Perhaps it is easy for those who have never felt the stinging darts of segregation to say, "Wait." But when you have seen vicious mobs lynch your mothers and fathers at will and drown your sisters and brothers at whim; when you have seen hate-filled policemen curse, kick, and even kill your black brothers

---

* EDS. NOTE — American religious and social thinker (1892–1971).

and sisters; when you see the vast majority of your twenty million Negro brothers smothering in an airtight cage of poverty in the midst of an affluent society; when you suddenly find your tongue twisted and your speech stammering as you seek to explain to your six-year-old daughter why she can't go to the public amusement park that has just been advertised on television, and see tears welling up in her eyes when she is told that Funtown is closed to colored children, and see ominous clouds of inferiority beginning to form in her little mental sky, and see her beginning to distort her personality by developing an unconscious bitterness toward white people; when you have to concoct an answer for a five-year-old son who is asking, "Daddy, why do white people treat colored people so mean?"; when you take a cross-country drive and find it necessary to sleep night after night in the uncomfortable corners of your automobile because no motel will accept you; when you are humiliated day in and day out by nagging signs reading "white" and "colored"; when your first name becomes "nigger," your middle name becomes "boy" (however old you are), and your last name becomes "John," and your wife and mother are never given the respected title "Mrs."; when you are harried by day and haunted at night by the fact that you are a Negro, living constantly at tiptoe stance, never quite knowing what to expect next, and are plagued with inner fears and outer resentments; when you are forever fighting a degenerating sense of "nobodiness" — then you will understand why we find it difficult to wait. There comes a time when the cup of endurance runs over, and men are no longer willing to be plunged into the abyss of despair. I hope, sirs, you can understand our legitimate and unavoidable impatience.

You express a great deal of anxiety over our willingness to break laws.   15
This is certainly a legitimate concern. Since we so diligently urge people to obey the Supreme Court's decision of 1954 outlawing segregation in the public schools, at first glance it may seem rather paradoxical for us consciously to break laws. One may well ask: "How can you advocate breaking some laws and obeying others?" The answer lies in the fact that there are two types of laws: just and unjust. I would be the first to advocate obeying just laws. One has not only a legal but a moral responsibility to obey just laws. Conversely, one has a moral responsibility to disobey unjust laws. I would agree with St. Augustine* that "an unjust law is no law at all."

Now, what is the difference between the two? How does one determine   16
whether a law is just or unjust? A just law is a man-made code that squares with the moral law or the law of God. An unjust law is a code that is out of harmony with the moral law. To put it in the terms of St. Thomas Aquinas:** An unjust law is a human law that is not rooted in eternal law and natural law. Any law that uplifts human personality is just. Any law

---

* EDS. NOTE — Early church father and philosopher (354–430).
** EDS. NOTE — Italian philosopher and theologian (1225–1274).

that degrades human personality is unjust. All segregation statutes are unjust because segregation distorts the soul and damages the personality. It gives the segregator a false sense of superiority and the segregated a false sense of inferiority. Segregation, to use the terminology of the Jewish philosopher Martin Buber, substitutes an "I-it" relationship for an "I-thou" relationship and ends up relegating persons to the status of things. Hence segregation is not only politically, economically, and sociologically unsound, it is morally wrong and sinful. Paul Tillich* has said that sin is separation. Is not segregation an existential expression of man's tragic separation, his awful estrangement, his terrible sinfulness? Thus it is that I can urge men to obey the 1954 decision of the Supreme Court, for it is morally right; and I can urge them to disobey segregation ordinances, for they are morally wrong.

Let us consider a more concrete example of just and unjust laws. An   17
unjust law is a code that a numerical or power majority group compels a minority group to obey but does not make binding on itself. This is *difference* made legal. By the same token, a just law is a code that a majority compels a minority to follow and that it is willing to follow itself. This is *sameness* made legal.

Let me give another explanation. A law is unjust if it is inflicted on a   18
minority that, as a result of being denied the right to vote, had no part in enacting or devising the law. Who can say that the legislature of Alabama which set up that state's segregation laws was democratically elected? Throughout Alabama all sorts of devious methods are used to prevent Negroes from becoming registered voters, and there are some counties in which, even though Negroes constitute a majority of the population, not a single Negro is registered. Can any law enacted under such circumstances be considered democratically structured?

Sometimes a law is just on its face and unjust in its application. For   19
instance, I have been arrested on a charge of parading without a permit. Now, there is nothing wrong in having an ordinance which requires a permit for a parade. But such an ordinance becomes unjust when it is used to maintain segregation and to deny citizens the First-Amendment privilege of peaceful assembly and protest.

I hope you are able to see the distinction I am trying to point out. In no   20
sense do I advocate evading or defying the law, as would the rabid segregationist. That would lead to anarchy. One who breaks an unjust law must do so openly, lovingly, and with a willingness to accept the penalty. I submit that an individual who breaks a law that conscience tells him is unjust, and who willingly accepts the penalty of imprisonment in order to arouse the conscience of the community over its injustice, is in reality expressing the highest respect for law.

---

* EDS. NOTE — American philosopher and theologian (1886–1965).

Of course, there is nothing new about this kind of civil disobedience. 21
It was evidenced sublimely in the refusal of Shadrach, Meshach, and
Abednego* to obey the laws of Nebuchadnezzar, on the ground that a
higher moral law was at stake. It was practiced superbly by the early Christians, who were willing to face hungry lions and the excruciating pain of
chopping blocks rather than submit to certain unjust laws of the Roman
Empire. To a degree, academic freedom is a reality today because Socrates
practiced civil disobedience. In our own nation, the Boston Tea Party represented a massive act of civil disobedience.

We should never forget that everything Adolph Hitler did in Germany 22
was "legal" and everything the Hungarian freedom fighters did in Hun-
gary was "illegal." It was "illegal" to aid and comfort a Jew in Hitler's Germany. Even so, I am sure that, had I lived in Germany at the time, I would
have aided and comforted my Jewish brothers. If today I lived in a Communist country where certain principles dear to the Christian faith are suppressed, I would openly advocate disobeying that country's antireligious
laws.

I must make two honest confessions to you, my Christian and Jewish 23
brothers. First, I must confess that over the past few years I have been
gravely disappointed with the white moderate. I have almost reached the
regrettable conclusion that the Negro's great stumbling block in his stride
toward freedom is not the White Citizens Counciler or the Ku Klux Klan-
ner, but the white moderate, who is more devoted to "order" than to justice; who prefers a negative peace which is the absence of tension to a
positive peace which is the presence of justice; who constantly says, "I agree
with you in the goal you seek, but I cannot agree with your methods of
direct action"; who paternalistically believes he can set the timetable for
another man's freedom; who lives by a mythical concept of time and who
constantly advises the Negro to wait for a "more convenient season." Shal-
low understanding from people of good will is more frustrating than absolute misunderstanding from people of ill will. Lukewarm acceptance is
much more bewildering than outright rejection.

I had hoped that the white moderate would understand that law and 24
order exist for the purpose of establishing justice and that when they fail in
this purpose they become the dangerously structured dams that block the
flow of social progress. I had hoped that the white moderate would understand that the present tension in the South is a necessary phase of the
transition from an obnoxious negative peace, in which the Negro passively
accepted his unjust plight, to a substantive and positive peace, in which all
men will respect the dignity and worth of human personality. Actually, we
who engage in nonviolent direct action are not the creators of tension.
We merely bring to the surface the hidden tension that is already alive. We
bring it out in the open, where it can be seen and dealt with. Like a boil

---

* EDS. NOTE — In the Book of Daniel, three men who were thrown into a blazing fire
for refusing to worship a golden statue.

that can never be cured so long as it is covered up but must be opened with all its ugliness to the natural medicines of air and light, injustice must be exposed, with all the tension its exposure creates, to the light of human conscience and the air of national opinion, before it can be cured.

In your statement you assert that our actions, even though peaceful, must be condemned because they precipitate violence. But is this a logical assertion? Isn't this like condemning a robbed man because his possession of money precipitated the evil act of robbery? Isn't this like condemning Socrates because his unswerving commitment to truth and his philosophical inquiries precipitated the act by the misguided populace in which they made him drink hemlock? Isn't this like condemning Jesus because his unique God-consciousness and never-ceasing devotion to God's will precipitated the evil act of crucifixion? We must come to see that, as the federal courts have consistently affirmed, it is wrong to urge an individual to cease his efforts to gain his basic constitutional rights because the quest may precipitate violence. Society must protect the robbed and punish the robber.

I had also hoped that the white moderate would reject the myth concerning time in relation to the struggle for freedom. I have just received a letter from a white brother in Texas. He writes: "All Christians know that the colored people will receive equal rights eventually, but it is possible that you are in too great a religious hurry. It has taken Christianity almost two thousand years to accomplish what it has. The teachings of Christ take time to come to earth." Such an attitude stems from a tragic misconception of time, from the strangely irrational notion that there is something in the very flow of time that will inevitably cure all ills. Actually, time itself is neutral; it can be used either destructively or constructively. More and more I feel that the people of ill will have used time much more effectively than have the people of good will. We will have to repent in this generation not merely for the hateful words and actions of the bad people, but for the appalling silence of the good people. Human progress never rolls in on wheels of inevitability; it comes through the tireless efforts of men willing to be coworkers with God, and without this hard work, time itself becomes an ally of the forces of social stagnation. We must use time creatively, in the knowledge that the time is always ripe to do right. Now is the time to make real the promise of democracy and transform our pending national elegy into a creative psalm of brotherhood. Now is the time to lift our national policy from the quicksand of racial injustice to the solid rock of human dignity.

You speak of our activity in Birmingham as extreme. At first I was rather disappointed that fellow clergymen would see my nonviolent efforts as those of an extremist. I began thinking about the fact that I stand in the middle of two opposing forces in the Negro community. One is a force of complacency, made up in part of Negroes who, as a result of long years of oppression, are so drained of self-respect and a sense of "somebodiness" that they have adjusted to segregation; and in part of a few middle-class

Negroes who, because of a degree of academic and economic security and because in some ways they profit by segregation, have become insensitive to the problems of the masses. The other force is one of bitterness and hatred, and it comes perilously close to advocating violence. It is expressed in the various black nationalist groups that are springing up across the nation, the largest and best-known being Elijah Muhammad's Muslim movement. Nourished by the Negro's frustration over the continued existence of racial discrimination, this movement is made up of people who have lost faith in America, who have absolutely repudiated Christianity, and who have concluded that the white man is an incorrigible "devil."

I have tried to stand between these two forces, saying that we need   28
emulate neither the "do-nothingism" of the complacent nor the hatred and despair of the black nationalist. For there is the more excellent way of love and nonviolent protest. I am grateful to God that, through the influence of the Negro church, the way of nonviolence became an integral part of our struggle.

If this philosophy had not emerged, by now many streets of the South   29
would, I am convinced, be flowing with blood. And I am further convinced that if our white brothers dismiss as "rabble-rousers" and "outside agitators" those of us who employ nonviolent direct action, and if they refuse to support our nonviolent efforts, millions of Negroes will, out of frustration and despair, seek solace and security in black-nationalist ideologies — a development that would inevitably lead to a frightening racial nightmare.

Oppressed people cannot remain oppressed forever. The yearning for   30
freedom eventually manifests itself, and that is what has happened to the American Negro. Something within has reminded him of his birthright of freedom, and something without has reminded him that it can be gained. Consciously or unconsciously, he has been caught up by the *Zeitgeist*, and with his black brothers of Africa and his brown and yellow brothers of Asia, South America, and the Caribbean, the United States Negro is moving with a sense of great urgency toward the promised land of racial justice. If one recognizes this vital urge that has engulfed the Negro community, one should readily understand why public demonstrations are taking place. The Negro has many pent-up resentments and latent frustrations, and he must release them. So let him march; let him make prayer pilgrimages to the city hall; let him go on freedom rides — and try to understand why he must do so. If his repressed emotions are not released in nonviolent ways, they will seek expression through violence; this is not a threat but a fact of history. So I have not said to my people, "Get rid of your discontent." Rather, I have tried to say that this normal and healthy discontent can be channeled into the creative outlet of nonviolent direct action. And now this approach is being termed extremist.

But though I was initially disappointed at being categorized as an   31
extremist, as I continued to think about the matter I gradually gained a measure of satisfaction from the label. Was not Jesus an extremist for love: "Love your enemies, bless them that curse you, do good to them that hate

you, and pray for them which despitefully use you, and persecute you." Was not Amos an extremist for justice: "let justice roll down like waters and righteousness like an everflowing stream." Was not Paul an extremist for the Christian gospel: "I bear in my body the marks of the Lord Jesus." Was not Martin Luther an extremist: "Here I stand; I cannot do otherwise, so help me God." And John Bunyan: "I will stay in jail to the end of my days before I make a butchery of my conscience." And Abraham Lincoln: "This nation cannot survive half slave and half free." And Thomas Jefferson: "We hold these truths to be self-evident, that all men are created equal. . . ." So the question is not whether we will be extremists, but what kind of extremists we will be. Will we be extremists for hate or for love? Will we be extremists for the preservation of injustice or for the extension of justice? In that dramatic scene of Calvary's hill three men were crucified. We must never forget that all three were crucified for the same crime — the crime of extremism. Two were extremists for immorality, and thus fell below their environment. The other, Jesus Christ, was an extremist for love, truth, and goodness, and thereby rose above his environment. Perhaps the South, the nation, and the world are in dire need of creative extremists.

I hoped that the white moderate would see this need. Perhaps I was too   32
optimistic; perhaps I expected too much. I suppose I should have realized that few members of the oppressor race can understand the deep groans and passionate yearnings of the oppressed race, and still fewer have the vision to see that injustice must be rooted out by strong, persistent, and determined action. I am thankful, however, that some of our white brothers in the South have grasped the meaning of this social revolution and committed themselves to it. They are still all too few in quantity, but they are big in quality. Some — such as Ralph McGill, Lillian Smith, Harry Golden, James McBride Dabbs, Ann Braden, and Sarah Patton Boyle — have written about our struggle in eloquent and prophetic terms. Others have marched with us down nameless streets of the South. They have languished in filthy, roach-infested jails, suffering the abuse and brutality of policemen who view them as "dirty nigger-lovers." Unlike so many of their moderate brothers and sisters, they have recognized the urgency of the movement and sensed the need for powerful "action" antidotes to combat the disease of segregation.

Let me take note of my other major disappointment. I have been so   33
greatly disappointed with the white church and its leadership. Of course, there are some notable exceptions. I am not unmindful of the fact that each of you has taken some significant stands on this issue. I commend you, Reverend Stallings, for your Christian stand on this past Sunday, in welcoming Negroes to your worship service on a nonsegregated basis. I commend the Catholic leaders of this state for integrating Spring Hill College several years ago.

But despite these notable exceptions, I must honestly reiterate that I   34
have been disappointed with the church. I do not say this as one of those negative critics who can always find something wrong with the church. I

say this as a minister of the gospel, who loves the church; who was nurtured in its bosom; who has been sustained by its spiritual blessings and who will remain true to it as long as the cord of life shall lengthen.

When I was suddenly catapulted into the leadership of the bus protest   35
in Montgomery, Alabama, a few years ago, I felt we would be supported by the white church. I felt that the white ministers, priests, and rabbis of the South would be among our strongest allies. Instead, some have been outright opponents, refusing to understand the freedom movement and misrepresenting its leaders; all too many others have been more cautious than courageous and have remained silent behind the anesthetizing security of stained-glass windows.

In spite of my shattered dreams, I came to Birmingham with the hope   36
that the white religious leadership of this community would see the justice of our cause and, with deep moral concern, would serve as the channel through which our just grievances could reach the power structure. I had hoped that each of you would understand. But again I have been disappointed.

There was a time when the church was very powerful — in the time   37
when the early Christians rejoiced at being deemed worthy to suffer for what they believed. In those days the church was not merely a thermometer that recorded the ideas and principles of popular opinion; it was a thermostat that transformed the mores of society. Whenever the early Christians entered a town, the people in power became disturbed and immediately sought to convict the Christians for being "disturbers of the peace" and "outside agitators." But the Christians pressed on, in the conviction that they were "a colony of heaven," called to obey God rather than man. Small in number, they were big in commitment. They were too God-intoxicated to be "astronomically intimidated." By their effort and example they brought an end to such ancient evils as infanticide and gladiatorial contests.

Things are different now. So often the contemporary church is a weak,   38
ineffectual voice with an uncertain sound. So often it is an archdefender of the status quo. Far from being disturbed by the presence of the church, the power structure of the average community is consoled by the church's silent — and often even vocal — sanction of things as they are.

But the judgment of God is upon the church as never before. If today's   39
church does not recapture the sacrificial spirit of the early church, it will lose its authenticity, forfeit the loyalty of millions, and be dismissed as an irrelevant social club with no meaning for the twentieth century. Every day I meet young people whose disappointment with the church has turned into outright disgust.

Perhaps I have once again been too optimistic. Is organized religion   40
too inextricably bound to the status quo to save our nation and the world? Perhaps I must turn my faith to the inner spiritual church, the church

within the church, as the true *ekklesia** and the hope of the world. But again I am thankful to God that some noble souls from the ranks of organized religion have broken loose from the paralyzing chains of conformity and joined us as active partners in the struggle for freedom. They have left their secure congregations and walked the streets of Albany, Georgia, with us. They have gone down the highways of the South on tortuous rides for freedom. Yes, they have gone to jail with us. Some have been dismissed from their churches, have lost the support of their bishops and fellow ministers. But they have acted in the faith that right defeated is stronger than evil triumphant. Their witness has been the spiritual salt that has preserved the true meaning of the gospel in these troubled times. They have carved a tunnel of hope through the dark mountain of disappointment.

I hope the church as a whole will meet the challenge of this decisive hour. But even if the church does not come to the aid of justice, I have no despair about the future. I have no fear about the outcome of our struggle in Birmingham, even if our motives are at present misunderstood. We will reach the goal of freedom in Birmingham and all over the nation, because the goal of America is freedom. Abused and scorned though we may be, our destiny is tied up with America's destiny. Before the pilgrims landed at Plymouth, we were here. Before the pen of Jefferson etched the majestic words of the Declaration of Independence across the pages of history, we were here. For more than two centuries our forebears labored in this country without wages; they made cotton king; they built the homes of their masters while suffering gross injustice and shameful humiliation — and yet out of a bottomless vitality they continued to thrive and develop. If the inexpressible cruelties of slavery could not stop us, the opposition we now face will surely fail. We will win our freedom because the sacred heritage of our nation and the eternal will of God are embodied in our echoing demands.   41

Before closing I feel impelled to mention one other point in your statement that has troubled me profoundly. You warmly commended the Birmingham police for keeping "order" and "preventing violence." I doubt that you would have so warmly commended the police force if you had seen its dogs sinking their teeth into unarmed, nonviolent Negroes. I doubt that you would so quickly commend the policemen if you were to observe their ugly and inhumane treatment of Negroes here in the city jail; if you were to watch them push and curse old Negro women and young Negro girls; if you were to see them slap and kick old Negro men and young boys; if you were to observe them, as they did on two occasions, refuse to give us food because we wanted to sing our grace together. I cannot join you in your praise of the Birmingham police department.   42

It is true that the police have exercised a degree of discipline in handling the demonstrators. In this sense they have conducted themselves   43

* EDS. NOTE — Greek word for the early Christian church.

rather "nonviolently" in public. But for what purpose? To preserve the vile system of segregation. Over the past few years I have consistently preached that nonviolence demands that the means we use must be as pure as the ends we seek. I have tried to make clear that it is wrong to use immoral means to attain moral ends. But now I must affirm that it is just as wrong, or perhaps even more so, to use moral means to preserve immoral ends. Perhaps Mr. Connor and his policemen have been rather nonviolent in public, as was Chief Pritchett in Albany, Georgia, but they have used the moral means of nonviolence to maintain the immoral end of racial injustice. As T. S. Eliot has said, "The last temptation is the greatest treason: To do the right deed for the wrong reason."

I wish you had commended the Negro sit-inners and demonstrators of 44 Birmingham for their sublime courage, their willingness to suffer, and their amazing discipline in the midst of great provocation. One day the South will recognize its real heroes. They will be the James Merediths,* with the noble sense of purpose that enables them to face jeering and hostile mobs, and with the agonizing loneliness that characterizes the life of the pioneer. They will be old, oppressed, battered Negro women, symbolized in a seventy-two-year-old woman in Montgomery, Alabama, who rose up with a sense of dignity and with her people decided not to ride segregated buses, and who responded with ungrammatical profundity to one who inquired about her weariness: "My feets is tired, but my soul is at rest." They will be the young high school and college students, the young ministers of the gospel and a host of their elders, courageously and nonviolently sitting in at lunch counters and willingly going to jail for conscience's sake. One day the South will know that when these disinherited children of God sat down at lunch counters, they were in reality standing up for what is best in the American dream and for the most sacred values in our Judaeo-Christian heritage, thereby bringing our nation back to those great wells of democracy which were dug deeply by the founding fathers in their formulation of the Constitution and the Declaration of Independence.

Never before have I written so long a letter. I'm afraid it is much too 45 long to take your precious time. I can assure that it would have been much shorter if I had been writing from a comfortable desk, but what else can one do when he is alone in a narrow jail cell, other than write long letters, think long thoughts, and pray long prayers?

If I have said anything in this letter that overstates the truth and indi- 46 cates an unreasonable impatience, I beg you to forgive me. If I have said anything that understates the truth and indicates my having a patience that allows me to settle for anything less than brotherhood, I beg God to forgive me.

I hope this letter finds you strong in the faith. I also hope that circum- 47 stances will soon make it possible for me to meet each of you, not as an

---

* EDS. NOTE — James Meredith was the first African American to enroll at the University of Mississippi.

integrationist or a civil-rights leader but as a fellow clergyman and a Christian brother. Let us all hope that the dark clouds of racial prejudice will soon pass away and the deep fog of misunderstanding will be lifted from our fear-drenched communities, and in some not too distant tomorrow the radiant stars of love and brotherhood will shine over our great nation with all their scintillating beauty.

> Yours for the cause of Peace and Brotherhood,
> Martin Luther King Jr.

• • •

Comprehension

1. King says he seldom answers criticism. Why not? Why, then, does he decide to do so in this instance?
2. Why do the other clergymen consider King's activities to be "'unwise and untimely'" (1)?
3. What reasons does King give for the demonstrations? Why does he think it is too late for negotiations?
4. What does King say *wait* means to black people?
5. What are the two types of laws King defines? What is the difference between the two?
6. What does King find illogical about the claim that the actions of his followers precipitate violence?
7. Why is King disappointed in the white church?

Purpose and Audience

1. Why, in the first paragraph, does King establish his setting (the Birmingham city jail) and define his intended audience?
2. Why does King begin his letter with a reference to his audience as "men of genuine good will" (1)? Is this phrase **ironic** in light of his later criticism of them? Explain.
3. What indicates that King is writing his letter to an audience other than his fellow clergymen?
4. What is the thesis of this letter? Is it stated or implied?

Style and Structure

1. Where does King seek to establish that he is a reasonable person?
2. Where does King address the objections of his audience?
3. As in the Declaration of Independence, transitions are important in King's letter. Identify the transitional words and phrases that connect the different parts of his argument.

4. Why does King cite Jewish, Catholic, and Protestant philosophers to support his position?

5. King relies heavily on appeals to authority (Augustine, Aquinas, Buber, Tillich, and so forth). Why do you think he uses this strategy?

6. King uses both induction and deduction in his letter. Find an example of each, and explain how they function in his argument.

7. Throughout the body of his letter, King criticizes his audience of white moderates. In his conclusion, however, he seeks to reestablish a harmonious relationship with them. How does he do this? Is he successful?

Vocabulary Projects

1. Define each of the following words as it is used in this selection.

affiliate (2)	devotees (12)	reiterate (34)
cognizant (4)	estrangement (16)	intimidated (37)
mutuality (4)	ordinances (16)	infanticide (37)
provincial (4)	anarchy (20)	inextricably (40)
gainsaying (6)	elegy (26)	scintillating (47)
unfettered (10)	incorrigible (27)	
millennium (12)	emulate (28)	

2. Locate five **allusions** to the Bible in this essay. Look up these allusions in an online Bible dictionary such as http://eastonsbibledictionary.com. Then, determine how these allusions help King express his ideas.

3. In paragraph 14, King refers to his "cup of endurance." What is this a reference to? How is the original phrase worded?

Journal Entry

Do you believe King's remarks go too far? Do you believe they do not go far enough? Explain.

Writing Workshop

1. Write an argumentative essay supporting a deeply held belief of your own. Assume that your audience, like King's, is not openly hostile to your position.

2. **Synthesis** Assume you are a militant political leader responding to Martin Luther King Jr. Argue that King's methods do not go far enough. Be sure to address potential objections to your position. You might want to consult a Web site such as standford.edu/group/King/about_king/encyclopedia/x_malcolm.htm or read some newspapers and magazines from the 1960s to help you prepare your argument. (Be sure to document all material you borrow from your sources, and include a works-cited page. (See the Appendix for information on documentation formats.)

3. **Synthesis** Read your local newspaper for several days, collecting articles about a controversial subject that interests you. Using information from

the articles, take a position on the issue, and write an essay supporting it. (Be sure to document all material you borrow from your sources. See the Appendix for information on documentation formats.)

Combining the Patterns

In "Letter from Birmingham Jail," King includes several passages of **narration**. Find two of these passages, and discuss what use King makes of narration. Why do you think narration plays such an important part in King's argument?

Thematic Connections

- "Finishing School" (page 107)
- "The 'Black Table' Is Still There" (page 345)
- "Two Ways to Belong in America" (page 411)

DEBATE

What Is a Hate Crime?

A hate crime, also called a bias-related crime, is a crime committed against an individual or group of individuals that is motivated by bias regarding race, color, religion, or ethnic/national origin (some hate-crimes statutes also include gender, disability, and sexual orientation). The first state statute against hate crimes, the Massachusetts Civil Rights Act, was passed in 1979 in the wake of violent attempts on the part of white parents in Boston to prevent black students from being bused to their neighborhood schools. Three years later, in 1981, the Anti-Defamation League (ADL) drafted model legislation designed to increase penalties for vandalism of churches and crimes against individuals or groups based on bigotry.

The issue of hate crimes came to wide public attention in 1982 when a Chinese-American man in Michigan was beaten to death with a baseball bat by a laid-off white auto worker and his uncle because they thought he was Japanese. (At the time, Japanese auto companies were starting to take business away from American companies.) Three years later, the United States Congress began hearings on the subject of hate crimes, and in 1990 legislation was enacted requiring the collection of statistics on such crimes. In 1993, the United States Supreme Court upheld a Wisconsin statute based on the ADL model, and today all but three states have some sort of hate crimes legislation on the books.

In addition, Congress has passed the Hate Crimes Sentencing Enhancement Act, which increases penalties for some federal crimes when they are motivated by bias. Attempts to add sexual orientation to the federal statute began shortly after the brutal murder of young Matthew Sheppard in Wyoming, apparently because of his homosexuality. The murder sparked national outrage, but the proposed changes to the statute have so far failed. The Local Law Enforcement Enhancement Act, which would strengthen the ability of federal, state, and local governments to investigate and prosecute hate crimes, has also failed to pass.

Supporters of hate-crime legislation charge that the federal government has done little to stem hate crimes — in fact, the yearly number of hate-crimes charges brought by the Justice Department dropped from seventy-six in 1996 to twenty-two ten years later. On the other hand, critics of hate-crime legislation claim that such laws single out some groups for "special-victim" status, violating the equal protection language of the Fourteenth Amendment to the Constitution, and that they punish offenders for their beliefs, a violation of freedom of expression. It is likely that hate-crimes legislation will continue to evolve as these competing viewpoints redefine the terms of the debate.

As the following debate suggests, major questions arise over whether to define particular actions as hate crimes. The writers (who are both African American) agree about the need for hate-crime laws, but they disagree about whether these laws should be applied to the widespread appearance of nooses across the United States in the latter part of 2007. Alarmed by what he sees as a "symbol of domestic terrorism," columnist George Curry argues that these actions should be seen as more than simply pranks. Ellis Cose, however, argues that nooses pose no real threat and that to get upset about them is to "grant them an importance that they do not deserve."

GEORGE CURRY

Calling Nooses What
They Are — Terrorism

George Curry is editor-in-chief of the National Newspaper Publishers
Association news service and BlackPressUSA.com. A one-time *Sports Illustrated* writer, Curry is the author of *Jake Gaither: America's Most Famous Black
Coach* (1977). He has also edited several anthologies. A past president of
the American Society of Magazine Editors, Curry was the first African
American to hold that position. He appears frequently as a commentator
on national news programs and also writes a weekly opinion column syndicated in more than two hundred newspapers nationwide.

Background on lynching and nooses

As early as 1845, *Webster's Dictionary* defined *lynching* as "the practice of
punishing men for crimes by private unauthorized persons, without a
legal trial . . . to inflict punishment without forms of law, as by a mob."
Many communities during the late nineteenth and early twentieth centuries condoned lynching, particularly in the South, where the greatest number took place. Historically, both whites and blacks were victims of
lynching, but according to statistics compiled by the NAACP in 1921, of
the 3,224 recorded lynchings in the United States between 1889 and 1918,
2,522 were of black people, predominantly black men; other sources bear
out this disparity. Lynchings took a number of violent forms: victims
could be tied up and lashed with whips until senseless, shot repeatedly
with firearms, mutilated or castrated, dragged behind autos, and even
burned alive. But public hangings were most common; thus, the noose
became a potent symbol of this barbarous act. As actual lynchings began
to disappear, the appearance of a noose came to serve as a threat, particularly during the Civil Rights era, when African Americans were beginning
to claim their equal place in society. Long associated with white suprema-
cist groups such as the Ku Klux Klan, symbolic nooses are a powerful
reminder of the racism that pervaded — and may still pervade — some
parts of the United States.

Hardly a week passes without reports of some incident involving a   1
noose: On a doorknob of an African American professor at Columbia University; inside a black Coast Guard cadet's bag; in a Home Depot store
under construction in Elgin, Illinois; in a Long Island, New York, police
locker room; and in a tree outside a cultural center at the University of
Maryland. On October 1, a white construction worker shook a noose at a
black worker on the Comcast Tower construction site in Center City.

The very symbol of domestic terrorism was even found outside a post   2
office near Ground Zero in Manhattan.

It is difficult to grasp the severity of these post–Jena 6 outbreaks without recognizing what the noose symbolizes. In early American history, most lynching victims were white. But that changed as of 1886, when there were seventy-four recorded lynchings of blacks and sixty-four of whites. In every year since the end of the Civil War, the number of blacks lynched has easily exceeded whites put to death outside of the law.   3

Statistics compiled by Tuskegee Institute (now Tuskegee University) in Alabama show that from 1882 through 1944, when lynchings first began to drop significantly, there were 3,417 reported lynchings of blacks and 1,291 of whites.   4

As Philip Dray notes in his excellent book, *At the Hands of Persons Unknown: The Lynching of Black America*, lynching became "a systematized reign of terror that was used to maintain the power whites had over blacks, a way to keep blacks fearful and to forestall black progress and miscegenation."   5

It should come as no surprise that lynching became largely a southern phenomenon. In Gunnar Myrdal's 1944 landmark study *An American Dilemma: The Negro Problem and Modern Democracy*, he observed the South's "fixation on the purity of white womanhood." He noted, "The South has an obsession with sex which helps make this region quite irrational in dealing with Negroes generally."   6

At any crossing of the color line, real or perceived, white mobs assumed the role of judge, jury, and executioner.   7

Ralph Ginzburg's book *100 Years of Lynchings*, first published in 1962 and reissued by Black Classic Press in Baltimore, provides a compilation of newspaper stories about lynchings. Among them: 8

HARTWELL, Georgia, Jan. 2 — Two negroes were lynched and a negro woman was badly beaten as the result of a remark to a white girl in Anderson County, South Carolina, according to reports received here tonight.   9

The three negroes were riding in a buggy when they passed the girl. One of the men made a remark to the white girl, at which she took offense. She reported the encounter to a group of white men who quickly caught up with the blacks, lynched the men, beat the woman, and ordered her out of the state.   10

Reports concerning the nature of the alleged insulting remarks are conflicting. Officials of Georgia county say that one of the negro men yelled out, "Hello, Sweetheart." The negro woman asserts that all they said was "Hello."   — *Philadelphia Inquirer*, January 3, 1916   11

MUSKOGEE, Oklahoma, March 31 — Marie Scott, a negro woman, was taken from the Wagoner County jail early today and hanged from a telephone pole. A mob of at least a dozen armed men overpowered the jailer, a one-armed man, threw a rope over the screaming woman's head, dragged her out of her cell, and strung her up from the jail.   12

Marie Scott was charged with driving a knife into the heart of Lemuel Peace, a youthful white man who, in the company with other young white men, had gone to the negro quarter of Wagoner last Saturday night.   13
    — *Seattle Times*, March 31, 1914

CEDAR BLUFF, Mississippi, March 31 — Jeff Brown was lynched by a mob   14
here late Saturday afternoon. Brown was walking down the street near the
car tracks and saw a moving freight train going in the direction in which
he wanted to go. He started to run to board the moving train. On the sidewalk was the daughter of a white farmer. Brown accidently brushed against
her and she screamed. A gang quickly formed and ran after him, jerking
him off the moving train. He was beaten into insensibility and then hung
to a tree. The sheriff has made no attempt to find out who the members of
the mob were. Picture cards of the body are being sold on the streets at five
cents apiece.   —*Birmingham Voice of the People*, April 1, 1916

Far from being merely a prank, the hanging of nooses harks back to a   15
shameful period in American history. It was not until 1952 that the United
States went a whole year without a single lynching. If we're ever going to
bridge the racial divide, we must acknowledge that for more than a century, if an African American was thought to have violated a social code, he
or she could be killed for it. That's not a laughing matter.

•   •   •

Comprehension

1. In paragraph 3, Curry says, "It is difficult to grasp the severity of those
   post–Jena 6 outbreaks without recognizing what the noose symbolizes."
   What does he mean? Do you think he is correct?

2. In paragraph 5, Curry cites a source who refers to lynching as "a systematized reign of terror." According to this source, what was the purpose of
   this "reign of terror," and how did it manifest itself?

3. Curry quotes a 1944 source that refers to the South as "quite irrational in
   dealing with Negroes generally" (6). What point is Curry making here and
   in the paragraph that follows?

4. What does Curry call for in his closing paragraph?

Purpose and Audience

1. Why does Curry open his essay as he does? What does this opening suggest about his intended audience?

2. Based on paragraph 3, how would you summarize Curry's purpose? Do
   you think the essay succeeds in achieving this purpose?

3. How effective is Curry's title? Can you suggest an alternative title?

Style and Structure

1. What is the effect of paragraph 2, a single-sentence paragraph following a
   much longer opening paragraph?

2. Curry presents statistics on lynchings in paragraphs 3 and 4. Do these
   statistics effectively make the case he wants to make? If so, why? If not,
   why not?

3. Much of Curry's essay consists of quotations from outside sources. Why do you suppose he decided to rely so heavily on such sources as evidence to support his position? Should he have included other kinds of evidence?

4. Why do you think Curry arranges the three newspaper accounts of lynchings in the order he does?

5. Where in the essay does Curry acknowledge those who disagree with him? Do you think he successfully refutes this position?

6. What is the effect of Curry's brief final sentence?

Vocabulary Projects

1. Define each of the following words as it is used in this selection.

severity (3) executioner (7)
miscegenation (5) insensibility (14)
irrational (6) violated (15)

2. Curry refers to the display of nooses as "domestic terrorism" (2). Does this seem to be an accurate characterization, or do you think he is exaggerating?

3. What does the phrase "any crossing of the color line, real or perceived" (7) suggest about race relations in the late nineteenth and early twentieth centuries?

Journal Entry

What do you think motivates people to display nooses? What should be done to those who do this? What might be the best way to discourage (or end) this practice?

Writing Workshop

1. **Synthesizing Sources** Write an essay in which you respond to the display of nooses as a threat. For example, do you agree with Curry that they are an act of "terrorism"? Do you believe such displays should be considered hate crimes (and therefore illegal), or do you see them as a protected form of free speech? You might want to look at cnn.com/2007/US/11/01/nooses/index.html to get some additional information about nooses and hate crimes. Be sure to document all words and ideas that you borrow from your sources and to include a works-cited page. (See the Appendix for information on documentation formats.)

2. Do you agree with Curry that there is a "racial divide" (15) in the United States? If so, how do you think it might best be bridged? If not, how would you convince Curry and those who agree with him that their views are inaccurate? Write an email to Curry in which you present your case.

3. Curry writes about African Americans in the past being killed for violating "a social code" (15). Give some examples of today's social codes, and explain what happens when people violate them.

Combining the Patterns

Note the places in his essay where Curry includes paragraphs of **exemplification**. How well do these examples help him make his point? Does he include enough examples? Too many examples?

Thematic Connections

- "Finishing School" (page 107)
- "Just Walk On By" (page 236)
- "The 'Black Table' Is Still There" (page 345)

ELLIS COSE

Ignore the Noose Makers

Ellis Cose (b. 1951) has been a contributing editor at *Newsweek* since 1993 and was formerly chair of the editorial board and op-ed page editor at the *Daily News* in New York City. President of the Institute for Journalism Education, Cose in 2002 received the New York Association of Black Journalists' lifetime achievement award. He is also the author of more than ten books, including his best-selling *The Rage of a Privileged Class: Why Are Middle-Class Blacks Angry? Why Should America Care?* (1994) and, most recently, *Bone to Pick: On Forgiveness, Reconciliation, Reparations, and Revenge* (2004). A frequent guest on television news shows, Cose produces the syndicated radio program *Against the Odds*, which focuses on individuals who have triumphed over extreme adversity.

Background on the "Jena 6"

In late August of 2006, on the campus of Jena High School in the small town of Jena, Louisiana, nooses appeared hanging from a tree a day after a group of black students chose to sit under the tree, a spot generally claimed by white students. The principal recommended expulsion for those white students found responsible but was overruled by the predominantly white school board. Racial tensions escalated over the next several months, and in late November a black student was attacked off-campus by white students; one of the attackers was later charged with simple battery and released on probation. Four days after the attack, a white student taunted the black victim of the attack and then was himself attacked by a group of black students. The white student lost consciousness, but he was able to attend a school event that evening. The black students were subsequently charged with attempted second-degree murder. Over the next seven months, the story spread through email and Internet postings, but not until late summer of 2007 did it receive nationwide press coverage. A protest drew thousands to Jena in late September. The charges against the six black students had by this point been reduced, but the severity of the original charges (as compared to the minor charges brought against the white students) continues to spark controversy.

In an age when lynching is no longer accepted, what is the meaning of a noose? When a twisted rope, evocative of such a hideous history, hangs so far away from the horrors that defined it, is it still worth getting worked up about? Or when nooses appear on trees, on doors and in well-traveled public places, should we dismiss them as tasteless diversions? Cries for attention from sick, benighted souls? If only the questions were purely hypothetical. In the past few weeks, nooses have appeared in numerous

1

places, spawning an orgy of coverage along with questions about their significance and potential harm.

The catalyst seems to be the brouhaha in Jena, Louisiana. Last year six black students there were accused of beating up a white student after three nooses were found hanging from a tree outside a school. The blacks were charged with attempted murder. Though the charges were subsequently reduced, outrage over the students' being charged with such a serious crime culminated in a demonstration last month that drew an estimated 10,000 protesters to the tiny town of 3,000.

Now, it appears, nooses have become the totem of choice for some troubled people. Earlier this month a black professor at Columbia University's Teachers College found a noose hanging from her office door. *USA Today* recently cataloged an array of such incidents: nooses at the University of Maryland, in a Long Island, New York, police locker room and in a bus-maintenance garage in Pittsburgh, to name a few. RACIAL CRISIS? OR JUST ROPE IN THE HANDS OF FOOLS? asked the headline atop a *New York Times* column.

I'd lay odds on the latter. This is an outbreak of copycat idiocy perpetrated by mean-spirited people who get a thrill out of seeing others riled up. And a lot of people have taken the bait. At Columbia, the noose spawned a rally in support of the targeted professor. In her State of the College address, president Susan H. Fuhrman said the perpetrator had "targeted all of us who believe in diversity."

It's unclear exactly what effect the noose was supposed to have. But it *is* clear that it stirred emotions out of proportion to its threat. The reason, of course, has to do with the history of the noose — or, to be more precise, the legacy of lynching.

Between 1882 and 1951, more than 5,000 people were lynched in the United States, according to statistics kept by the Tuskegee Institute. Not all were black. Roughly a fourth were white, Mexican, or Asian. But lynchings of blacks were different from lynchings of whites. Many were "spectacle" lynchings, public rituals designed to make the point that "black bodies still belonged to white people," writes Cynthia Carr in "Our Town," which explores a 1930 lynching in Marion, Indiana. Newspapers and public officials frequently egged on the lynch mobs, plying them with lurid (and often false) details. "Stories of sexual assault, insatiable black rapists, tender white virgins . . . were the bodice rippers of their day. . . . The cumulative impression was of a world made precarious by Negroes," reports historian Philip Dray in *At the Hands of Persons Unknown.*

Because of lynching's violent, racist, and sexually charged history, the mere invocation of it can make people insanely angry — or, as Clarence Thomas demonstrated during his Senate confirmation hearings (when he referred to his treatment as a "high-tech lynching"), silence a roomful of normally loquacious politicians. Still, 2007 is different from 1907.

Hate crimes didn't even have a name then. It was reasonable to believe, especially in the South, that "uppity," or even just random blacks, could be lynched with impunity. In 1990, Congress mandated the attorney general to collect data on hate crimes, and the FBI pledged to work with local officials to prosecute such transgressions. More important, lynchings and other hate crimes — be they anti-Semitic, anti-gay, or anti-black — no longer have broad public support.

People still engage in hateful behavior: the FBI recorded 7,163 bias incidents in 2005, the last year for which statistics are available, down slightly from the 7,947 recorded a decade earlier. The majority were racial incidents, mostly against blacks. Still, no one really believes a Columbia professor is about to be lynched.   9

A position paper by the American Psychological Association concluded that most hate crimes were the work of "otherwise law-abiding young people." Their actions were sometimes fueled by alcohol or drugs, "but the main determinant appears to be personal prejudice," which blinds aggressors "to the immorality of what they are doing." Extreme crimes "tend to be committed by people with a history of antisocial behavior."   10

Maybe it's time to stop getting so upset about these stupid gestures. Use them as occasions to educate — to revisit and extract lessons from history. And in cases where prosecutable crimes are committed, make the fools feel the full impact of the law. But to treat their acts as a serious expression of anything other than cruelty is to grant them an importance that they do not deserve.   11

•   •   •

Comprehension

1. According to Cose, what motivated the "copycat" behavior (4) of those who displayed nooses in the weeks before his essay was written?
2. How does Cose describe the response to the rash of noose displays he writes about? How does he explain this response?
3. In what ways does Cose say the situation today is different from the situation a century ago in terms of what the display of a noose suggests? Do you agree?
4. According to Cose, what is the appropriate response to displays of nooses? Why?

Purpose and Audience

1. How does Cose think his readers have responded to the stories of noose displays that have appeared in the media? How can you tell?
2. What is the purpose of the essay's second and third paragraphs? Why are they located where they are?
3. Why does Cose quote from a paper issued by the American Psychological Association regarding hate crimes (10)? What effect does he hope the quotation will have?

Style and Structure

1. Where in the essay does Cose first suggest his thesis? How does this state-ment relate to the series of questions he poses in his opening paragraph? How does it relate to the questions he quotes in paragraph 3 from a head-line in the *New York Times*?
2. Where does Cose actually state his thesis? Why do you suppose he chooses this point in the essay to do so?
3. The middle of Cose's argument focuses on the subject of lynching (6–7). In what sense does this section act as a transition from the first part of his essay to the conclusion?
4. Why do you think Cose does not address opposing arguments in any detail? Do you think his failure to do so weakens his essay?

Vocabulary Projects

1. Define each of the following words as it is used in this selection.

evocative (1)	brouhaha (2)	precarious (6)
diversions (1)	culminated (2)	invocation (7)
benighted (1)	perpetrator (4)	loquacious (7)
spawning (1)	insatiable (6)	impunity (8)
catalyst (2)	cumulative (6)	anti-Semitic (8)

2. In paragraph 7, Cose writes that any reminder of lynching "can make people insanely angry." What do you think Cose is trying to accomplish by using this language? Do you find the language too strong, or does it seem appropriate to you?

Journal Entry

In his final paragraph, Cose refers to displays of nooses as "stupid gestures." What is your response to this characterization? What do you think is the best way to respond to this kind of act?

Writing Workshop

1. **Synthesizing Sources** Who do you think makes a better argument, Curry or Cose? Write an essay briefly summarizing the positions of the two writers and then taking a stand in support of one or the other. Include your reasons for supporting one over the other, and use material from both essays to support your thesis. Be sure to document your sources and to include a works-cited page. (See the Appendix for informa-tion on documentation formats.)
2. Do you think it might be possible for Curry and Cose to reach some sort of agreement on how to respond to displays of nooses and what they sym-bolize? Write an essay in which you argue that "terrorism" is too strong a term for such displays but that to call them simply "stupid gestures" is to

treat them too lightly. In your view, what motivates such displays, and what are the most effective ways of responding to them?

3. According to the quotation Cose cites from the American Psychological Association, most bias-related crimes are perpetrated by "otherwise law-abiding young people." Develop an educational program to be implemented in schools to help stem the number of hate crimes committed by young people. Then, write an essay in which you explain your program and argue for its implementation in your local school system. You might want to look at cnn.com/2007/US/11/01/nooses/index.html to get some additional information about nooses and hate crimes. Be sure to document all words and ideas that you borrow from your sources and to include a works-cited page. (See the Appendix for information on documentation formats.)

Combining the Patterns

Where in his essay does Cose rely on **cause and effect**? On **comparison and contrast**? How does each of these strategies help him develop his argument?

Thematic Connections

- "Fatwa City" (page 242)
- "The Power of Words in Wartime" (page 363)
- "Letter from Birmingham Jail" (page 588)

DEBATE

How Big a Threat Is Global Warming?

Faced with evidence that the earth had in the past undergone periods of extremely cold weather, the so-called Ice Ages, nineteenth-century scientists sought to understand the causes of these climate changes. It was suggested as early as 1859 that changes in the concentration of gases in the earth's atmosphere could bring about climate change, and in 1896 the Swedish scientist Svante Arrhenius suggested a direct link between atmospheric carbon dioxide levels and temperatures at the earth's surface (later called the "greenhouse effect"). Arrhenius even went so far as to claim that increases in atmospheric carbon dioxide concentrations, brought about by the burning of coal and other fossil fuels, would in the future noticeably increase the earth's average temperature. His findings raised little concern at the time because he expected, based on the emissions levels of his day, that even a doubling of carbon dioxide levels would take three thousand years or more.

Throughout the twentieth century, scientists continued to speculate about the causes of climate change, and various models were developed showing both a cooling trend and a warming trend occurring. It was not until the late 1970s that a scientific consensus began to develop around the idea that increased levels of chlorofluorocarbons (CFCs) and certain gases produced in the industrialized world were contributing to global warming. By 1981, the warmest year on record to that point, a clear warming trend seemed to be occurring (though not all experts agreed that it was the result of carbon dioxide emissions or that it was a matter of any real concern). This trend has continued, with eleven of the world's warmest years occurring in the thirteen years prior to 2008.

While skeptics remain — including those who insist that evidence of warming over the last few decades is not proof of warming on a larger scale and those who hold that global warming is a naturally occurring trend — the majority of experts accept human-induced global warming as a reality. At the same time, the extent of the threat of global warming and the kinds of policies that should be enacted to deal with it remain a subject of serious debate, as the following two readings suggest. In "The Time to Act Is Now," former vice president Al Gore argues that "we face a deepening global crisis that requires us to act boldly, quickly, and wisely." In "Global Warming Delusions," environmental scientist Daniel Botkin claims that if we panic over global warming as a crisis, "we are going to spend our money unwisely, we will take actions that are counterproductive, and we will fail to do many of the things that will benefit the environment and ourselves."

AL GORE

The Time to Act Is Now

Vice president for two terms under Bill Clinton, Al Gore (b. 1948) served as an army military journalist in Vietnam, after which he took a job as a reporter for Nashville's *The Tennessean*. He was elected to the U.S. House of Representatives in 1976 and to the Senate in 1984. Following his terms as vice president, he ran for president in 2000, winning the popular vote but losing very narrowly to George Bush in a disputed election. Having been an advocate in the fight against global warming since the 1970s and author of one of the first books to lay out the issue for a popular audience (*Earth in the Balance*, 1992), Gore now turned his attention to the cause full-time, forming a company to encourage environmentally responsible corporate investment and lecturing on the subject worldwide. A documentary based on his live presentation, *An Inconvenient Truth*, won an Academy Award in 2007, and that same year Gore shared the Nobel Peace Prize for his "efforts to build up and disseminate greater knowledge about man-made climate change, and to lay the foundations for the measures that are needed to counteract such change."

Background on the politics of global warming

The 1992 United Nations Conference on Environment and Development (popularly known as the Earth Summit) produced, among other agreements, an international treaty aimed at reducing carbon dioxide and other greenhouse gases as a means of reducing global warming. It set no specific limits or timetable but laid the groundwork for a 1997 summit, known as the Kyoto Protocol, which produced a treaty requiring developed nations to cut greenhouse gas emissions by 5.2 percent of 1990 levels by 2012 (although the actual percentages varied by nation). President Clinton signed the agreement but did not submit it to Congress for ratification, and President Bush entered office strongly opposed to the pact on the grounds that mandatory limits could be economically harmful and that developing countries (in particular, China and India, whose greenhouse gas production is growing rapidly) are exempted. The treaty has now been ratified by 165 nations, including every "developed nation" except for the United States.

It is now clear that we face a deepening global climate crisis that 1 requires us to act boldly, quickly and wisely. "Global warming" is the name it was given a long time ago. But it should be understood for what it is: a planetary emergency that now threatens human civilization on multiple fronts. Stronger hurricanes and typhoons represent only one of many new dangers as we begin what someone has called "a nature hike through the Book of Revelation."

As I write, my heart is heavy due to the suffering the people of the Gulf 2 Coast have endured. In Florida, Alabama, Mississippi, Louisiana, and

Texas, and particularly in New Orleans, thousands have experienced losses beyond measure as our nation and the world witnessed scenes many of us thought we would never see in this great country. But unless we act quickly, this suffering will be but a beginning.

The science is extremely clear: global warming may not affect the frequency of hurricanes, but it makes the average hurricane stronger, magnifying its destructive power. In the years ahead, there will be more storms like Katrina, unless we change course. Indeed, we have had two more Category 5 storms since Katrina — including Wilma, which before landfall was the strongest hurricane ever measured in the Atlantic. 3

We know that hurricanes are heat engines that thrive on warm water. We know that heat-trapping gases from our industrial society are warming the oceans. We know that, in the past thirty years, the number of Category 4 and 5 hurricanes globally has almost doubled. It's time to connect the dots: 4

- Last year, the science textbooks had to be rewritten. They used to say, "It's impossible to have a hurricane in the South Atlantic." We had the first one last year, in Brazil. Japan also set an all-time record for typhoons last year: ten. The previous record was seven.

- This summer, more than two hundred cities in the United States broke all-time heat records. Reno, Nevada, set a new record with ten consecutive days above one hundred degrees. Tucson, Arizona, tied its all-time record of thirty-nine consecutive days above one hundred degrees. New Orleans — and the surrounding waters of the Gulf — also hit an all-time high.

- This summer, parts of India received record rainfall — thirty-seven inches fell in Mumbai in twenty-four hours, killing more than one thousand people.

- The new extremes of wind and rain are part of a larger pattern that also includes rapidly melting glaciers worldwide, increasing desertification, a global extinction crisis, the ravaging of ocean fisheries, and a growing range for disease "vectors" like mosquitoes, ticks, and many other carriers of viruses and bacteria harmful to people.

All of these are symptoms of a deeper crisis: the "Category 5" collision between our civilization — as we currently pursue it — and the earth's environment. 5

Sixty years ago, Winston Churchill wrote about another kind of gathering storm. When Neville Chamberlain tried to wish that threat away with appeasement, Churchill said, "This is only the beginning of the reckoning. This is only the first sip, the first foretaste, of a bitter cup which will be proffered to us year by year — unless by a supreme recovery of moral health and martial vigor, we rise again and take our stand for freedom." 6

For more than fifteen years, the international community has conducted a massive program to assemble the most accurate scientific assess- 7 ment on global warming. Two thousand scientists, in a hundred countries, have produced the most elaborate, well-organized scientific collaboration in the history of humankind and have reached a consensus as strong as it ever gets in science. As Bill McKibben points out, there is no longer any credible basis to doubt that the earth's atmosphere is warming because of human activities. There is no longer any credible basis to doubt that we face a string of terrible catastrophes unless we prepare ourselves and deal with the underlying causes of global warming.

Scientists around the world are sounding a clear and urgent warning. Global warming is real, it is already under way, and the consequences are totally unacceptable.   8

Why is this happening? Because the relationship between humankind and the earth has been utterly transformed. To begin with, we have quadrupled the population of our planet in the past hundred years. And secondly, the power of the technologies now at our disposal vastly magnifies the impact each individual can have on the natural world. Multiply that by six and a half billion people, and then stir into that toxic mixture a mind-set and an attitude that say it's OK to ignore scientific evidence — that we don't have to take responsibility for the future consequences of present actions — and you get this violent and destructive collision between our civilization and the earth.   9

There are those who say that we can't solve this problem — that it's too big or too complicated or beyond the capacity of political systems to grasp.   10

To those who say this problem is too difficult, I say that we have accepted and met such challenges in the past. We declared our liberty, and then won it. We designed a country that respected and safeguarded the freedom of individuals. We abolished slavery. We gave women the right to vote. We took on Jim Crow and segregation. We cured fearsome diseases, landed on the moon, won two wars simultaneously — in the Pacific and in Europe. We brought down communism, we defeated apartheid. We have even solved a global environmental crisis before: the hole in the stratospheric ozone layer.   11

So there should be no doubt that we can solve this crisis too. We must seize the opportunities presented by renewable energy, by conservation and efficiency, by some of the harder but exceedingly important challenges such as carbon capture and sequestration. The technologies to solve the global-warming problem exist, if we have the determination and wisdom to use them.   12

But there is no time to wait. In the 1930s, Winston Churchill also wrote of those leaders who refused to acknowledge the clear and present danger: "They go on in strange paradox, decided only to be undecided, resolved to be irresolute, adamant for drift, solid for fluidity, all powerful to be impotent. The era of procrastination, of half-measures, of soothing and baffling expedients, of delays, is coming to a close. In its place, we are entering a period of consequences."   13

With Hurricane Katrina, the melting of the Arctic ice cap and careless 14
ecological mayhem, we, too, are entering a period of consequences. This is
a moral moment. This is not ultimately about any scientific debate or
political dialogue. Ultimately it is about who we are as human beings. It is
about our capacity to transcend our own limitations.

The men and women honored as warriors and heroes have risen to this 15
new occasion. On the surface, they share little in common: scientists, ministers, students, politicians, activists, lawyers, celebrities, inventors, world
leaders. But each of them recognized the threat that climate change poses
to the planet — and responded by taking immediate action to stop it. Their
stories should inspire and encourage us to see with our hearts, as well as
our heads, the unprecedented response that is now called for.

As these heroes demonstrate, we have everything we need to face this 16
urgent challenge. All it takes is political will. And in our democracy, political will is a renewable resource.

• • •

Comprehension

1. Why do you suppose Gore says that global warming should be seen as a
   "planetary emergency" (1)?
2. According to Gore, what is the effect of global warming on hurricanes?
   What explains this effect?
3. What other effects of global warming does Gore enumerate?
4. What point is Gore making in paragraph 6, and what role does this point
   play in his argument?
5. What, according to Gore, are the causes of global warming? What solutions does he suggest are possible?
6. What does Gore mean when he writes, "This is a moral moment" (14)?

Purpose and Audience

1. What seems to be Gore's purpose in this essay? Is he writing to change
   people's minds, to alter their behavior, or for some other purpose? What
   makes you think so?
2. Where does Gore acknowledge opposition to his position? How does he
   deal with this opposition?
3. What does paragraph 11 suggest to you about Gore's intended audience?
4. How does Gore reach out to readers in his final two paragraphs?

Style and Structure

1. How do you respond to the language of Gore's opening paragraph? Why
   do you think he might have chosen such a strongly worded opening?

2. What impression of himself does Gore attempt to create in paragraph 2? Do you think he succeeds?

3. What repeated sentence structure does Gore use in paragraph 4? What is the effect of this repetition?

4. Why do you think Gore decided to use a bulleted list following paragraph 4? How would your reading of the list be different if the points were not bulleted?

5. Gore brackets paragraphs 6–13 with two quotations by British statesman Winston Churchill, writing in the 1930s about the impending threat of Nazi Germany. How do paragraphs 6–13 relate to these quotations? Why do you think Gore includes the quotations? Do you think their use of quotations is justified?

Vocabulary Projects

1. Define each of the following words as it is used in this selection.

desertification (4)	catastrophe (7)	adamant (13)
vectors (4)	quadrupled (9)	procrastination (13)
appeasement (6)	stratospheric (11)	expedients (13)
proffered (6)	sequestration (12)	mayhem (14)
martial (6)	paradox (13)	unprecedented (15)

2. What **allusion** is Gore making in paragraph 5 when he refers to a "'Category Five' collision between our civilization . . . and the Earth's environment"?

3. In his final paragraph, why is Gore's use of the phrase "a renewable resource" to describe the political will of a democracy particularly apt?

Journal Entry

What did you know about global warming before reading this essay? Has reading the essay changed your views on the subject in any way? If so, how? If not, why not?

Writing Workshop

1. **Synthesizing Sources**   Write an essay in which you present your own views about the threat of global warming. You may draw on information presented in Gore's essay as well as in the opposing argument by Daniel Botkin on page 623, but be sure to state a clear argumentative thesis and to present your supporting evidence in your own words. Include appropriate documentation and a works-cited page. (See the Appendix for information on documentation formats.)

2. How do you think individuals might go about making a contribution to reductions in greenhouse gases? Outline a possible course of action, and try to convince your readers to take the steps that you recommend. Before writing your essay, look at the Environmental Protection Agency's Web

site at epa.gov/climatechange/wycd/index.html, which deals with this issue. Make sure you document all words and ideas that you borrow from this source. In addition, include a works-cited page. (See the Appendix for information on documentation formats.)

3. Write an essay focusing on another environmental issue: air or water pollution, hazardous waste disposal, human encroachment on natural habitats, sustainable land use, ecotourism, water conservation, wetlands preservation, or another topic that interests you. In your essay, take a strong stand on the issue you select. Refer to Gore's essay, making sure to include documentation and a works-cited page. (See the Appendix for information on documentation formats.)

Combining the Patterns

The list following paragraph 4 is developed primarily through **exemplification**. Do you think Gore uses enough examples? What purpose do these examples serve?

Thematic Connections

- "The Hidden Life of Garbage" (page 177)
- "Once More to the Lake" (page 183)
- "Swollen Expectations" (page 422)

DANIEL B. BOTKIN

Global Warming Delusions

Daniel Botkin calls himself "a scientist who studies life from a planetary perspective." With degrees in physics, biology, and literature, he is professor emeritus in the Department of Ecology, Evolution, and Marine Biology at the University of California, Santa Barbara. He is also president and founder of the Center for the Study of the Environment, a non-profit research and education organization, and serves on the board of the Environmental Literacy Council. Botkin has advised the World Bank about tropical forests, biological diversity, and sustainability and advised the Rockefeller Foundation about global environmental issues. A pioneer in the study of ecosystems and wilderness, Botkin developed the first successful computer simulation in ecology, a highly influential computer model of forest growth. His first important book was *Discordant Harmonies: A New Ecology for the 21st Century*, written in 1990, and since then he has published nine more, including, with E. A. Keller, the popular introductory college textbook *Environmental Sciences: The Earth as a Living Planet* (2007, 6th edition). The following essay was first published in the week following the announcement that Al Gore and the Intergovernmental Panel on Climate Change had been awarded the 2007 Nobel Peace Prize.

Background on the predicted effects of global warming

Those concerned about global warming claim that it will have a variety of negative, even disastrous, effects on life on earth. The United Nations Intergovernmental Panel on Climate Change, for example, claims that as many as 30 percent of species will be at increasing risk of extinction. Extended summer heat spells will increase the risk of heat stroke, especially among the elderly, the chronically ill, and young children. Drought and inland flooding may become more severe. In addition, rising sea levels will result in severe coastal flooding affecting millions more people each year, and up to 30 percent of coastal wetlands could be lost. Others concerned about the threat of global warming suggest that because of warming summers, insect infestations will destroy plant life, and diseases carried by mosquitoes will spread. Hurricanes and other storms that form over water are likely to be stronger because of higher ocean temperatures. The melting of freshwater ice caps will likely affect sea life negatively, and habitat changes will force many species into cooler regions where adaptation may be difficult. In the following essay, Botkin questions the validity of such claims, which he thinks are at best exaggerated and at worst alarmist.

Global warming doesn't matter except to the extent that it will affect life — ours and that of all living things on Earth. And contrary to the latest news, the evidence that global warming will have serious effects on life is thin. Most evidence suggests the contrary.

1

Case in point: this year's United Nations report on climate change and other documents say that 20 percent to 30 percent of plant and animal species will be threatened with extinction in this century due to global warming — a truly terrifying thought. Yet, during the past 2.5 million years, a period that scientists now know experienced climatic changes as rapid and as warm as modern climatological models suggest will happen to us, almost none of the millions of species on Earth went extinct. The exceptions were about twenty species of large mammals (the famous mega-fauna of the last ice age — saber-tooth tigers, hairy mammoths, and the like), which went extinct about 10,000 to 5,000 years ago at the end of the last ice age, and many dominant trees and shrubs of northwestern Europe. But elsewhere, including North America, few plant species went extinct, and few mammals.

We're also warned that tropical diseases are going to spread, and that we can expect malaria and encephalitis epidemics. But scientific papers by Prof. Sarah Randolph of Oxford University show that temperature changes do not correlate well with changes in the distribution or frequency of these diseases; warming has not broadened their distribution and is highly unlikely to do so in the future, global warming or not.

The key point here is that living things respond to many factors in addition to temperature and rainfall. In most cases, however, climate-modeling-based forecasts look primarily at temperature alone, or temperature and precipitation only. You might ask, "Isn't this enough to forecast changes in the distribution of species?" Ask a mockingbird. *The New York Times* recently published an answer to a query about why mockingbirds were becoming common in Manhattan. The expert answer was: food — an exotic plant species that mockingbirds like to eat had spread to New York City. It was this, not temperature or rainfall, the expert said, that caused the change in mockingbird geography.

You might think I must be one of those know-nothing naysayers who believes global warming is a liberal plot. On the contrary, I am a biologist and ecologist who has worked on global warming, and been concerned about its effects, since 1968. I've developed the computer model of forest growth that has been used widely to forecast possible effects of global warming on life — I've used the model for that purpose myself, and to forecast likely effects on specific endangered species.

I'm not a naysayer. I'm a scientist who believes in the scientific method and in what facts tell us. I have worked for forty years to try to improve our environment and improve human life as well. I believe we can do this only from a basis in reality, and that is not what I see happening now. Instead, like fashions that took hold in the past and are eloquently analyzed in the classic nineteenth-century book *Extraordinary Popular Delusions and the Madness of Crowds*, the popular imagination today appears to have been captured by beliefs that have little scientific basis.

Some colleagues who share some of my doubts argue that the only way to get our society to change is to frighten people with the possibility of a catastrophe, and that therefore it is all right and even necessary for scientists to exaggerate. They tell me that my belief in open and honest assessment is naïve. "Wolves deceive their prey, don't they?" one said to me recently. Therefore, biologically, he said, we are justified in exaggerating to get society to change.

The climate modelers who developed the computer programs that are being used to forecast climate change used to readily admit that the models were crude and not very realistic, but were the best that could be done with available computers and programming methods. They said our options were to either believe those crude models or believe the opinions of experienced, data-focused scientists. Having done a great deal of computer modeling myself, I appreciated their acknowledgment of the limits of their methods. But I hear no such statements today. Oddly, the forecasts of computer models have become our new reality, while facts such as the few extinctions of the past 2.5 million years are pushed aside, as if they were not our reality.

A recent article in the well-respected journal *American Scientist* explained why the glacier on Mt. Kilimanjaro could not be melting from global warming. Simply from an intellectual point of view it was fascinating — especially the author's Sherlock Holmes approach to figuring out what was causing the glacier to melt. That it couldn't be global warming directly (i.e., the result of air around the glacier warming) was made clear by the fact that the air temperature at the altitude of the glacier is below freezing. This means that only direct radiant heat from sunlight could be warming and melting the glacier. The author also studied the shape of the glacier and deduced that its melting pattern was consistent with radiant heat but not air temperature. Although acknowledged by many scientists, the paper is scorned by the true believers in global warming.

We are told that the melting of the arctic ice will be a disaster. But during the famous medieval warming period — A.D. 750 to 1230 or so — the Vikings found the warmer northern climate to their advantage. Emmanuel Le Roy Ladurie addressed this in his book *Times of Feast, Times of Famine: A History of Climate Since the Year 1000*, perhaps the greatest book about climate change before the onset of modern concerns with global warming. He wrote that Erik the Red "took advantage of a sea relatively free of ice to sail due west from Iceland to reach Greenland. . . . Two and a half centuries later, at the height of the climatic and demographic fortunes of the northern settlers, a bishopric of Greenland was founded at Gardar in 1126."

Ladurie pointed out that "it is reasonable to think of the Vikings as unconsciously taking advantage of this [referring to the warming of the Middle Ages] to colonize the most northern and inclement of their conquests, Iceland and Greenland." Good thing that Erik the Red didn't have Al Gore or his climatologists as his advisers.

Should we therefore dismiss global warming? Of course not. But we should make a realistic assessment, as rationally as possible, about its cultural, economic, and environmental effects. As Erik the Red might have told you, not everything due to a climatic warming is bad, nor is everything that is bad due to a climatic warming.

We should approach the problem the way we decide whether to buy insurance and take precautions against other catastrophes — wildfires, hurricanes, earthquakes. And as I have written elsewhere, many of the actions we would take to reduce greenhouse-gas production and mitigate global-warming effects are beneficial anyway, most particularly a movement away from fossil fuels to alternative solar and wind energy. 13

My concern is that we may be moving away from an irrational lack of concern about climate change to an equally irrational panic about it. 14

Many of my colleagues ask, "What's the problem? Hasn't it been a good thing to raise public concern?" The problem is that in this panic we are going to spend our money unwisely, we will take actions that are counterproductive, and we will fail to do many of those things that will benefit the environment and ourselves. 15

For example, right now the clearest threat to many species is habitat destruction. Take the orangutans, for instance, one of those charismatic species that people are often fascinated by and concerned about. They are endangered because of deforestation. In our fear of global warming, it would be sad if we fail to find funds to purchase those forests before they are destroyed, and thus let this species go extinct. 16

At the heart of the matter is how much faith we decide to put in science — even how much faith scientists put in science. Our times have benefited from clear-thinking, science-based rationality. I hope this prevails as we try to deal with our changing climate. 17

• • •

Comprehension

1. How does Botkin dispute claims that global warming will lead to the threat of plant and animal extinction and the spread of tropical diseases?

2. What does Botkin say most climate-modeling–based forecasts focus on? What does he see as the limitations of this focus?

3. According to Botkin, how were the computer programs used in climate modeling and prediction regarded by those who used them in the past? How has that changed?

4. What is the point of Botkin's references in paragraphs 10–11 to Viking travels during the "famous medieval warming period"?

5. Why does Botkin think that overstated concerns about global warming are a problem? What specific example does he offer to explain his point?

Purpose and Audience

1. What does Botkin seem to think his readers believe about global warming?

2. What is Botkin's purpose in paragraph 5? What effect do you suppose he hopes this paragraph will have on readers?

3. This essay originally appeared on the op-ed page of the *Wall Street Journal*, a newspaper whose editorial policy tends to favor corporate interests. Does this knowledge affect your response to Botkin's argument in any way?

Style and Structure

1. Why do you suppose Botkin opens his essay as he does, moving directly into his argument without providing background information? Do you find this opening effective, or do you think he should have provided more background?

2. Where does Botkin present the opposing argument that exaggerating the threat of global warming is a good thing? Why do you think he might have chosen to present it where he does?

3. What kinds of evidence does Botkin present in this essay? How convincing do you find this evidence? What other kinds of evidence could he have presented?

4. Botkin opens paragraph 12 with a question, which he quickly answers. What is the effect of this question/answer structure?

5. Paragraph 14 is only one sentence long. Why do you suppose Botkin chose to isolate this sentence?

Vocabulary Projects

1. Define each of the following words as it is used in this selection.

megafauna (2)	demographic (10)	mitigate (13)
correlate (3)	bishopric (10)	irrational (14)
eloquently (6)	inclement (11)	deforestation (16)

2. In paragraph 5, Botkin argues that he is not one of the "know-nothing naysayers who [believe] global warming is a liberal plot." What is his purpose in using such language?

3. In his final paragraph, Botkin writes about dealing with "our changing climate" rather than using the term "global warming." How do the **connotations** of these two phrases differ?

Journal Entry

Botkin suggests in paragraphs 11–12 that global warming may well have beneficial aspects. According to Botkin, what might some of these benefits be?

Writing Workshop

1. **Synthesizing Sources**   Write an essay in which you briefly summarize the arguments made by Gore and Botkin and then go on to explain which writer you find more convincing. Include a strong argumentative thesis and provide specific evidence from each essay to support your position. Be sure to document your sources and to include a works-cited page. (See the Appendix for information on documentation formats.)

2. Botkin writes that "the popular imagination today appears to have been captured by beliefs that have little scientific basis" (6), a statement that could apply to other topics besides global warming. Discuss a few of these topics in an argumentative essay. Why do you think contemporary popular culture might tend to avoid "clear-thinking, science-based rationality" in favor of beliefs that scientists say are not supported by hard evidence? How might this viewpoint be changed?

3. **Synthesizing Sources**   What do you think of the argument that "the only way to get our society to change is to frighten people with the possibility of a catastrophe" (7)? How can people best be persuaded to act in terms of the long-term interests of the earth instead of in terms of their own self-interest? Write an opinion piece for your local newspaper in which you present your case. Before you begin, review the essays in this debate as well as the Environmental Protection Agency's Web site's pages that deal with climate change (epa.gov/climatechange/index.html). Be sure to document all words and ideas that you borrow from your sources and to include a works-cited page. (See the Appendix for information on documentation formats.)

Combining the Patterns

Where in the essay does Botkin rely on **cause and effect**? Why is this pattern particularly appropriate for his argument?

Thematic Connections

- "The Storm" (page 190)
- "Earth without People" (page 368)
- "The Ways We Lie" (page 485)

DEBATE

Is Wal-Mart Good for America?

Not only is Wal-Mart the largest retailer in the United States, but it is also the largest retailer in the world, with stores in Canada, Mexico, South and Central America, Europe, the United Kingdom, China, and Korea. In the United States, more than 100 million people shop at Wal-Mart every week. In 2000, Wal-Mart opened a new store almost every two days, and in 2004, it began opening a new store almost every day. (This does not include Wal-Mart discount stores and SAM'S Clubs.) Most Wal-Mart stores are "megastores," measuring more than 200,000 square feet, and include groceries, pharmacies, and hardware and garden supply areas. With over 1.2 million employees and more than 3,600 stores, Wal-Mart is the largest employer in the United States after the federal government. Given the size and scope of Wal-Mart, the humble beginnings of Sam Walton, the founder of the Wal-Mart empire, come as something of a surprise.

Sam Walton began his career in 1940 at J. C. Penney as a management trainee at a salary of seventy-five dollars a month. After serving in the military during World War II, Walton borrowed twenty thousand dollars from his father-in-law and opened a variety store. The store was a success, largely because Walton stocked his shelves with low-priced merchandise and experimented with buying directly from wholesalers and passing the savings on to his customers. After selling the variety store, Walton bought a 5 & 10 cent store. By 1962, he, his father-in-law, and his brother had opened sixteen other stores, including several larger stores called Walton's Family Centers. In these stores, Walton instituted a number of innovations, such as special promotions, profit sharing for employees, and limited partnerships for managers.

In 1962, Walton and his brother opened the first Wal-Mart — a discount store that sold name brands at low prices. Soon, Wal-Marts had sprung up all across rural America. Walton believed that the reason for Wal-Mart's success was its hometown identity. He also believed that each store should reflect the values both of its customers and of the community it served. Walton actively managed his company, overseeing its expansion, until his death in 1992.

Because of its size and its dominance of the discount market, it is not surprising that Wal-Mart has attracted its share of controversy. Critics point out, for example, that given its large sales volume, Wal-Mart does not contribute enough to charity. (Recently, Wal-Mart has taken steps to counter this charge. For example, in 2006, it launched a national partnership with America's Second Harvest, a leading anti-hunger group.) Another criticism is that despite a "Made in the USA" advertising campaign, the majority of products Wal-Mart sells are made overseas, often in sweatshops in developing nations. In addition, critics assert that Wal-Mart keeps its prices down and its profits up by paying low wages and by not providing health care for many of its workers. (Wal-Mart says that 90 percent of its employees are insured either through the company's policies or elsewhere. Critics, however, challenge this claim.) They point to the fact that even though Wal-Mart's starting salary is similar to that of other discount retailers, salaries are significantly lower than its competitors' at the end of an employee's second year. Critics also condemn many of Wal-Mart's other employment practices. At this point, Wal-Mart has lost a class-action sex-discrimination lawsuit and has also been fined by the government for employing undocumented workers and for not allowing some workers to take mandated meal breaks. Finally, it has doggedly opposed unions whenever they have attempted to organize workers.

The writers in this debate hold very different opinions about Wal-Mart. In "The Case for Wal-Mart," Karen De Coster and Brad Edmonds attempt to refute many of the criticisms leveled at Wal-Mart. According to them, by enabling low-income people to buy a host of products at very low prices, Wal-Mart performs a service to the low-wage communities it serves. In "Down and Out in Discount America," Liza Featherstone disagrees with this assessment, pointing out that Sam Walton's business model requires a large number of low-wage customers. For this reason, says Featherstone, it is in Wal-Mart's best interest to keep the wages of its employees low so that they, too, will have to shop at Wal-Mart and will further increase its customer base.

KAREN DE COSTER AND BRAD EDMONDS

The Case for Wal-Mart

Karen De Coster is a Michigan-based certified public accountant and a member of the Mackinac Center for Public Policy Board of Scholars. As a freelance writer, she has contributed articles and essays to the libertarian Web sites LewRockwell.com and Mises.org as well as to publications such as *The Free Market, Liberty,* the *Washington Times,* and a number of Michigan newspapers. Brad Edmonds, an Alabama-based banker, holds a master's degree in industrial psychology and a doctorate in musical arts.

Background on big-box retailing

Large discount department stores as we know them today had their beginnings in the five-and-dime variety-store chains popular in small-town America beginning in the early part of the twentieth century. The first discount department stores can be traced to 1962, when the F. W. Woolworth corporation opened its first Woolco (now defunct), the S. S. Kresge corporation opened its first Kmart, the Dayton Hudson corporation opened its first Target, and Sam Walton opened the first Wal-Mart. Kmart grew most rapidly, opening 250 locations by 1967; Wal-Mart, by contrast, had only eighteen locations by that year. By the early 1970s, Kmart had become a major competitor of mainstream department stores such as Sears.

The 1980s saw the introduction nationwide of specialty "big-box" retailers: Lowe's hardware supplies, which had begun as a chain of regular-sized hardware stores in the 1950s, began to expand its retail space in new locations to as much as 160,000 square feet; Home Depot, a new venture in 1979, similarly opened huge hardware and building supply showrooms; Barnes and Noble, a New York book-selling institution since the 1800s, began expanding its market with the opening of mega-bookstores in free-standing malls; and Toys "Я" Us started its chain of "full-scale toy-store extravaganzas" (in the words of its Web site). Many others followed. By the late 1990s, Wal-Mart had eclipsed them all, becoming the country's largest retailer — due, in part, to the introduction of the massive SAM'S Clubs, originally geared toward small businesses, and Wal-Mart Super Centers, combinaion department and grocery stores that are almost twice as large as traditional Wal-Marts. While some communities have fought the development of such big-box chains, in much of the United States they have become a familiar part of the landscape.

The accusations against Wal-Mart are numerous, and they include: 1 paying overseas workers too little; not paying benefits to part-time workers; refusing to sell items that don't fall within its criteria for being "family-oriented"; not giving enough back to the community; and discriminating against women.

All the accusations leveled against Wal-Mart can be applied to just   2
about any large corporation in America, as frequently is the case. For
example, Kathie Lee Gifford was almost run out of the country for indirectly giving jobs to otherwise unemployable, Third World workers.

In addition, most retail and service sector employees still do not get   3
paid full job benefits, so what makes Wal-Mart so distinctive in that case?
What's more, Wal-Mart management has indeed made decisions to refrain
from selling certain items that did not live up to its moral standards — including certain music CDs and a brand of barbecue sauce sold
by a man who promoted his Confederate heritage — but what's wrong with
a private company exercising its own moral discretion according to its
stated values? Accordingly, the marvelous ways of the free market allow us
to move on elsewhere for our purchases when we are dissatisfied with what
we perceive as corporate nonsense.

Wal-Mart is an employer that pays relatively low wages compared to   4
most jobs or careers, and that engenders a sense of loathing from people
getting paid those wages. But Wal-Mart is not unlike any other retailer in
the respect that it, for the most part, provides jobs and not careers. Other
gigantic corporations such as General Electric or General Motors, on the
other hand, employ executives, college graduates, and skilled laborers, so
they avoid much of the wage-related scrutiny given to retail employers. Add
to that the labor union organizers' inability to unionize Wal-Mart and you
have the perfect recipe for resentment and scorn.

The overriding charges one comes across amid the many Wal-Mart   5
rants are "too large" and "too powerful." Thus it's just more anti-industry,
anti-free market claptrap. Along with that are the hoots and hollers about
this great chain "destroying small towns" by way of buying property in rural
areas and opening its doors to townsfolk so they have access to convenient,
one-stop shopping, an ample supply of products, and unbeatable prices.

However, there is one prevailing phenomenon that makes Wal-Mart a   6
unique target for contempt and that is its "bigness." Americans, generally
speaking, like to attack bigness. There are things associated with bigness
that Americans aren't keen on, like clout and domination.

In fact, the favorite indictment of Wal-Mart is that they dominate the   7
market wherever they go and sell goods at prices that are too low (gasp!).
This in turn — say the naysayers — drives small, local competitors out of
business because they can't compete with Wal-Mart's pricing or product
selection.

Suppose it's true that Wal-Mart went around opening giant stores in   8
small towns, pricing goods below their own cost long enough to drive local
stores out of business. Even if this were correct, Wal-Mart would only be
selling its own property. Suppose you want to sell a house you inherited,
and quickly. Should you not be allowed to set the price as low as you want?

The theory goes that Wal-Mart could then set prices high, and make   9
monopoly profits. How plausible is this, really? First, Wal-Mart executives
would have to be able to see the future — they'd have to know about how

long it would take to drive everyone out of business in advance, and know whether they could afford to price goods below cost for long enough to corner the market. Then, through trial and error, they'd have to find the point at which they could set prices low enough to keep customers from driving to another town, but high enough to recoup the losses from the earlier below-cost pricing.

It gets less plausible the more you think about it: The smaller the town, 10 the easier it would be to drive competitors out of business. Then again, a town small enough for this would be small enough to have bitter memories of the pricing strategy and small enough to boycott Wal-Mart before the strategy succeeded. And a very small town would not support a giant Wal-Mart anyway. The larger the town, the less feasible it would be to drive others out of business in that town — Wal-Mart would have to drive their prices far below those of large grocery and department stores, which would be much more difficult.

Further, where is there evidence of Wal-Mart ever driving up prices 11 after becoming established in a market? Wal-Mart has indeed set prices low enough to drive mom and pop stores out of business all over the country and kept the prices that low forever. Yet a journalist for the *Cleveland Scene* said about Wal-Mart's pricing policy: "That's 100 million shoppers a week lured by 'Always Low Prices.'" Lured — as if consumers really don't want low prices; they are just tricked into thinking they do!

In a free market, large suppliers of nearly everything will drive most 12 small suppliers out of business. The only people who can afford to do business on a small scale are people at the top of their fields or in a niche: McDonald's has to keep prices low, and economies of scale do this, while Brennan's restaurant in New Orleans can keep prices high. People who produce house paint and wallpaper must compete on price with other suppliers, while famous artists can keep their prices high. General Motors must keep prices low, while Rolls-Royce doesn't have to.

Nobody complains that there aren't family auto manufacturers, but 13 the powerful farmers' political lobby makes sure we pay inflated prices to keep inefficient farmers in business. Of course, giant agribusinesses don't complain that their weaker competition is kept in the market, because the giant agribusinesses enjoy the inflated prices just as do the family farmers, some of whom are paid to leave their fields fallow.

Nobody complains that there aren't family pharmaceutical manu- 14 facturers, but people complain when Wal-Mart drives a corner drug store out of business. Yet if the corner drug store owners had the same political lobbying power farmers have, you can bet we'd be paying $20 for Q-tips.

If the truth be told, Wal-Mart improves the lives of people in rural 15 areas because it gives them access to a lifestyle that they otherwise would not have — a gigantic store showcasing the world's greatest choice of products from groceries to music to automotive products. When it comes to prices and service, try finding 70 percent off clearances at your local mom-and-pop store or try going to that same store and returning shoes you've worn for three months for a full-price refund with no questions asked.

On the whole, if one doesn't like Wal-Mart and finds it to be of greater utility to support their local mom-and-pop stores for an assortment of cultural and non-economic reasons, then they may do so. If consumers wish to obstruct the development of a Wal-Mart store in their small town, they have scores of non-bullying options to pick from in order to try and persuade their fellow townsfolk that a new Wal-Mart is not the best option. 16

Still, it is not always easy to convince folks to eschew ultra-convenience for the sake of undefined, moral purposes. Consumers most often shop with their wallet, not with political precepts. For that reason, the anti–Wal-Mart crowd uses political coercion and an assortment of anti-private property decrees — such as zoning manipulation — in order to stave off the construction of a new Wal-Mart store in their town. 17

Hating Wal-Mart is the equivalent of hating Bill Gates.* Sam Walton had a grandiose vision for himself, and sought to realize that vision by providing something people want — low prices. He has done every bit as much for your lifestyle as Bill Gates. 18

Families who shop carefully at Wal-Mart can actually budget more for investing, children's college funds, or entertainment. And unlike other giant corporations, Wal-Mart stores around the country make an attempt to provide a friendly atmosphere by spending money to hire greeters, who are often people who would have difficulty finding any other job. This is a friendly, partial solution to shoplifting problems; the solution K-mart applied ("Hey, what's in that bag?") didn't work as well. 19

It's interesting to observe that the consumers who denounce Wal-Mart are often the same folks who take great joy in reaping the rewards of corporate bigness, such as saving money with sales, clearances, and coupons, being able to engage in comparative shopping, and taking advantage of generous return policies. 20

When all's said and done, Wal-Mart employs lots of people; provides heaps of things you need in one place at the lowest prices you'll find; and gives millions to charities every year. Add up the charitable giving of all the mom and pop stores in the country and it probably won't equal that of one giant corporation. 21

To be sure, if Americans didn't love Wal-Mart so much it wouldn't be sitting at the top of the 2002 Fortune 500** with $219 billion in revenues. And we do love Wal-Mart. We love it because it gives us variety and abundance. We love it because it saves us time and wrangling. And we love it because no matter where we are, it's always there when we need it. 22

•   •   •

---

* EDS. NOTE — Multibillionaire chairman and chief software architect of Microsoft Corporation.

** EDS. NOTE — *Fortune* magazine's yearly list of the country's five hundred most profitable companies.

Comprehension

1. What are critics' major accusations against Wal-Mart? According to De Coster and Edmonds, how does Wal-Mart compare to other large American corporations?

2. What is the difference between a corporation that provides a job and one that provides a career? Which type of corporation is Wal-Mart? How does this fact explain the relatively low wages Wal-Mart pays to its workers?

3. According to Wal-Mart's critics, what problems does Wal-Mart create by being "'too large' and 'too powerful'" (5)? How do De Coster and Edmonds respond to this charge?

4. How, according to De Coster and Edmonds, does Wal-Mart improve the lives of people in rural areas? How does Wal-Mart help families save money?

5. What do De Coster and Edmonds mean when they say, "Hating Wal-Mart is the equivalent of hating Bill Gates" (18)?

Purpose and Audience

1. Do De Coster and Edmonds expect readers to be familiar with Wal-Mart? How can you tell?

2. What was the writers' purpose in writing this essay?

3. The title of this essay leaves no doubt about the writers' position. Was this choice a good idea? Should they have used a title that was not so explicit? Explain.

4. What is the writers' attitude toward Wal-Mart's critics? What words and phrases convey their attitude?

Style and Structure

1. De Coster and Edmonds introduce their essay by listing the accusations against Wal-Mart. Why do they begin this way? Is this a good strategy?

2. In paragraph 2, De Coster and Edmonds say, "All the accusations leveled against Wal-Mart can be applied to just about any large corporation in America." Does this response adequately deal with the issue? Does it constitute a **logical fallacy**? Explain.

3. What arguments against Wal-Mart do De Coster and Edmonds address? How convincingly do they refute them?

4. In paragraph 20, De Coster and Edmonds say, "It's interesting to observe that the consumers who denounce Wal-Mart are often the same folks who take great joy in reaping the rewards of corporate bigness." Is this statement a **logical fallacy**? Explain.

5. Are there any places where you think De Coster and Edmonds overstate their case? If so, how do you react to these overstatements?

6. De Coster and Edmonds end their essay by saying, "if Americans didn't love Wal-Mart so much it wouldn't be sitting at the top of the 2002

Fortune 500 with $219 billion in revenues." Is this a logical conclusion? Can Wal-Mart's financial success be explained in any other way?

Vocabulary Projects

1. Define each of these words as it is used in this selection.

   accusations (1)   agribusinesses (13)
   distinctive (3)   utility (16)
   scrutiny (4)   eschew (17)
   claptrap (5)   precepts (17)
   indictment (7)   grandiose (18)
   feasible (10)

2. In paragraph 22, De Coster and Edmonds repeat the word *love* five times. What is the meaning of this word as it is used here? What is the point of this repetition?

Journal Entry

What do you think of Wal-Mart? Do you love it, as De Coster and Edmonds say Americans do, or do you have another opinion of it?

Writing Workshop

1. Write an essay agreeing or disagreeing with the statement, "If the truth be told, Wal-Mart improves the lives of people in rural areas because it gives them access to a lifestyle that they otherwise would not have" (15). Be sure to document all material that you borrow from your sources and to include a works-cited page. (See the Appendix for information on documentation formats.)

2. Assume you are the regional manager of a Wal-Mart attempting to open a store in a small town. To do so, you must get approval from the local zoning board. Write an email to the zoning board discussing the benefits the store would bring to the community. In your discussion, acknowledge some of the problems that might result, but make sure you make your case that, on the whole, Wal-Mart would be good for the local economy. Use material from "The Case for Wal-Mart" to support your points.

3. **Synthesizing Sources**   In her essay "Down and Out in Discount America" (page 638), Liza Featherstone says that organized labor should oppose Wal-Mart "not just because Wal-Mart is a grave threat to unionized workers' jobs (which it is) but because it threatens all American ideals that are at odds with profit — ideals such as justice, equality, and fairness" (28). Write a response from De Coster and Edmonds to Featherstone's statement, using material from both essays to support your points. Be sure to document all material that you borrow from your sources and to include a works-cited page. (See the Appendix for information on documentation formats.)

Combining the Patterns

Paragraphs 9 through 11 are developed by means of **cause and effect**. How does this strategy help De Coster and Edmonds support their argument?

Thematic Connections

- "My Mother Never Worked" (page 114)
- "The Peter Principle" (page 216)
- "Swollen Expectations" (page 422)

LIZA FEATHERSTONE

Down and Out in Discount America

Journalist Liza Featherstone has written frequently about student and youth activism for progressive periodicals such as the *Nation, Lingua Franca,* San Francisco's *Bay Guardian, Left Business Observer, Dissent,* and the *Columbia Journalism Review.* Featherstone has also published articles in *Ms., Salon, Nerve, US,* and *Rolling Stone,* among others, and is the coauthor of *Students against Sweatshops: The Making of a Movement* (2002) and author of *Selling Women Short: The Landmark Battle for Workers' Rights at Wal-Mart* (2004). The following essay appeared in the *Nation.*

Background on efforts to unionize Wal-Mart

Labor unions have a long history in the United States. These official organizations of workers within an industry grant their elected officials the power to negotiate salaries, benefits, and working conditions with employers. They are largely responsible for the significant improvement in working conditions for union members for the first half of the twentieth century. Critics argue, however, that by driving up salaries and the cost of medical benefits, unions place companies at a disadvantage, discourage employment nationally, and contribute to the cost of goods for consumers.

  In response to the decline in union membership (from close to half the workforce in the 1940s to less than 12 percent in 2006), efforts at unionizing have been stepped up in recent years. As the largest private employer in the United States, Wal-Mart has been a prime target of these efforts — and Wal-Mart has fought back vigorously. Handbooks for managers are full of antiunion advice, and potential employees are screened to exclude those who have been members of unions or whose personality type suggests they might be open to union membership. While Wal-Mart officials deny the charges, critics claim that the corporation has illegally barred efforts by employees to promote a union in stores, forced employees to sign forms pledging not to support union efforts, and fired employees sympathetic to unions. (Such actions violate federal law, which permits workers to lobby other workers in their workplace to form a labor union.) When meat cutters in a Texas Wal-Mart Supercenter voted to form a union in their department, the company eliminated their jobs by switching to selling precut and packaged meat. And, when a Canadian Wal-Mart store voted to unionize, the company promptly closed the store.

On the day after Thanksgiving, the biggest shopping day of the year, Wal-Mart's many progressive critics — not to mention its business competitors — finally enjoyed a bit of schadenfreude* when the retailer had to

1

* Eds. note — Taking pleasure in the misfortune of others.

admit to "disappointing" sales. The problem was quickly revealed: Wal-Mart hadn't been discounting aggressively enough. Without low prices, Wal-Mart just isn't Wal-Mart.

That's not a mistake the big-box behemoth is likely to make again. Wal-Mart knows its customers, and it knows how badly they need the discounts. Like Wal-Mart's workers, its customers are overwhelmingly female, and struggling to make ends meet. Betty Dukes, the lead plaintiff in Dukes v. Wal-Mart,* the landmark sex-discrimination case against the company, points out that Wal-Mart takes out ads in her local paper the same day the community's poorest citizens collect their welfare checks. "They are promoting themselves to low-income people," she says. "That's who they lure. They don't lure the rich. . . . They understand the economy of America. They know the haves and have-nots. They don't put Wal-Mart in Piedmonts.** They don't put Wal-Mart in those high-end parts of the community. They plant themselves right in the middle of Poorville."

Betty Dukes is right. A 2000 study by Andrew Franklin, then an economist at the University of Connecticut, showed that Wal-Mart operated primarily in poor and working-class communities, finding, in the bone-dry language of his discipline, "a significant negative relationship between median household income and Wal-Mart's presence in the market." Although fancy retailers noted with chagrin during the 2001 recession that absolutely everybody shops at Wal-Mart — "Even people with $100,000 incomes now shop at Wal-Mart," a PR flack for one upscale mall fumed — the Bloomingdale's set is not the discounter's primary market, and probably never will be. Only 6 percent of Wal-Mart shoppers have annual family incomes of more than $100,000. A 2003 study found that 23 percent of Wal-Mart Supercenter customers live on incomes of less than $25,000 a year. More than 20 percent of Wal-Mart shoppers have no bank account, long considered a sign of dire poverty. And while almost half of Wal-Mart Supercenter customers are blue-collar workers and their families, 20 percent are unemployed or elderly.

Al Zack, who until his retirement in 2004 was the United Food and Commercial Workers' vice president for strategic programs, observes that appealing to the poor was "Sam Walton's real genius. He figured out how to make money off of poverty. He located his first stores in poor rural areas and discovered a real market. The only problem with the business model is that it really needs to create more poverty to grow." That problem is cleverly solved by creating more bad jobs worldwide. In a chilling reversal of Henry Ford's strategy, which was to pay his workers amply so they could buy Ford cars, Wal-Mart's stingy compensation policies — workers make, on average, just over $8 an hour, and if they want health insurance, they

---

* EDS. NOTE — Case of seven California women — current and former Wal-Mart employees — charging the company with systematic sex discrimination in promotions, assignments, training, and pay.

** EDS. NOTE — Fertile agricultural regions.

must pay more than a third of the premium — contribute to an economy in which, increasingly, workers can only afford to shop at Wal-Mart.

To make this model work, Wal-Mart must keep labor costs down. It does this by making corporate crime an integral part of its business strategy. Wal-Mart routinely violates laws protecting workers' organizing rights (workers have even been fired for union activity). It is a repeat offender on overtime laws; in more than thirty states, workers have brought wage-and-hour class-action suits against the retailer. In some cases, workers say, managers encouraged them to clock out and keep working; in others, managers locked the doors and would not let employees go home at the end of their shifts. And it's often women who suffer most from Wal-Mart's labor practices. Dukes v. Wal-Mart, which is the largest civil rights class-action suit in history, charges the company with systematically discriminating against women in pay and promotions.

Solidarity across the Checkout Counter

Given the poverty they have in common, it makes sense that Wal-Mart's workers often express a strong feeling of solidarity with the shoppers. Wal-Mart workers tend to be aware that the customers' circumstances are similar to their own, and to identify with them. Some complain about rude customers, but most seem to genuinely enjoy the shoppers.

One longtime department manager in Ohio cheerfully recalls her successful job interview at Wal-Mart. Because of her weight, she told her interviewers, she'd be better able to help the customer. "I told them I wanted to work in the ladies department because I'm a heavy girl." She understands the frustrations of the large shopper, she told them: "'You know, you go into Lane Bryant and some skinny girl is trying to sell you clothes.' They laughed at that and said, 'You get a second interview!'"

One plaintiff in the Dukes lawsuit, Cleo Page, who no longer works at Wal-Mart, says she was a great customer service manager because "I knew how people feel when they shop, so I was really empathetic."

Many Wal-Mart workers say they began working at their local Wal-Mart because they shopped there. "I was practically born in Wal-Mart," says Alyssa Warrick, a former employee now attending Truman State University in Missouri. "My mom is obsessed with shopping. . . . I thought it would be pretty easy since I knew where most of the stuff was." Most assumed they would love working at Wal-Mart. "I always loved shopping there," enthuses Dukes plaintiff Dee Gunter. "That's why I wanted to work for 'em."

Shopping is traditionally a world of intense female communication and bonding, and women have long excelled in retail sales in part because of the identification between clerk and shopper. Page, who still shops at Wal-Mart, is now a lingerie saleswoman at Mervyn's (owned by Target). "I do enjoy retail," she says. "I like feeling needed and I like helping people, especially women."

Betty Dukes says, "I strive to give Wal-Mart customers one hundred   11
percent of my abilities." This sentiment was repeated by numerous other
Wal-Mart workers, always with heartfelt sincerity. Betty Hamilton, a
61-year-old clerk in a Las Vegas Sam's Club, won her store's customer service award last year. She is very knowledgeable about jewelry, her favorite
department, and proud of it. Hamilton resents her employer — she complains about sexual harassment and discrimination, and feels she has been
penalized on the job for her union sympathies — but remains deeply
devoted to her customers. She enjoys imparting her knowledge to shoppers
so "they can walk out of there and feel like they know something." Like
Page, Hamilton feels she is helping people. "It makes me so happy when I
sell something that I know is an extraordinarily good buy," she says. "I feel
like I've done somebody a really good favor."

The enthusiasm of these women for their jobs, despite the workplace   12
indignities many of them have faced, should not assure anybody that the
company's abuses don't matter. In fact, it should underscore the tremendous debt Wal-Mart owes women: This company has built its vast profits
not only on women's drudgery but also on their joy, creativity, and genuine
care for the customer.

Why Boycotts Don't Always Work

Will consumers return that solidarity and punish Wal-Mart for dis-   13
criminating against women? Do customers care about workers as much as
workers care about them? Some women's groups, like the National Organization for Women and Code Pink, have been hoping that they do, and
have encouraged the public not to shop at Wal-Mart. While this tactic
could be fruitful in some community battles, it's unlikely to catch on
nationwide. A customer saves 20–25 percent by buying groceries at Wal-
Mart rather than from a competitor, according to retail analysts, and poor
women need those savings more than anyone.

That's why many women welcome the new Wal-Marts in their commu-   14
nities. The *Winona* (Minnesota) *Post* extensively covered a controversy over
whether to allow a Wal-Mart Supercenter into the small town; the letters to
the editor in response offer a window into the female customer's loyalty to
Wal-Mart. Though the paper devoted substantial space to the sex discrimination case, the readers who most vehemently defended the retailer were
female. From the nearby town of Rollingstone, Cindy Kay wrote that she
needed the new Wal-Mart because the local stores didn't carry large-enough
sizes. She denounced the local anti-Wal-Mart campaign as a plot by rich
and thin elites: "I'm glad those people can fit into and afford such clothes.
I can barely afford Shopko and Target!"

A week later, Carolyn Goree, a preschool teacher also hoping for a Win-   15
ona Wal-Mart, wrote in a letter to the *Post* editor that when she shops at
most stores, $200 fills only a bag or two, but at Wal-Mart, "I come out with
a cart full top and bottom. How great that feels." Lacking a local Wal-Mart,

Goree drives over the Wisconsin border to get her fix. She was incensed by an earlier article's lament that some workers make only $15,000 yearly. "Come on!" Goree objected. "Is $15,000 really that bad of a yearly income? I'm a single mom and when working out of my home, I made $12,000 tops and that was with child support. I too work, pay for a mortgage, lights, food, everything to live. Everything in life is a choice. . . . I am for the little man/woman — I'm one of them. So I say stand up and get a Wal-Mart."

Sara Jennings, a disabled Winona reader living on a total of $8,000, heartily concurred. After paying her rent, phone, electric and cable bills, Jennings can barely afford to treat herself to McDonald's. Of a recent trip to the LaCrosse, Wisconsin, Wal-Mart, she raved, "Oh boy, what a great treat. Lower prices and a good quality of clothes to choose from. It was like heaven for me." She, too, strongly defended the workers' $15,000 yearly income: "Boy, now that is a lot of money. I could live with that." She closed with a plea to the readers: "I'm sure you all make a lot more than I. And I'm sure I speak for a lot of seniors and very-low-income people. We need this Wal-Mart. There's nothing downtown." 16

From Consumers to Workers and Citizens

It is crucial that Wal-Mart's liberal and progressive critics make use of the growing public indignation at the company over sex discrimination, low pay and other workers' rights issues, but it is equally crucial to do this in ways that remind people that their power does not stop at their shopping dollars. It's admirable to drive across town and pay more for toilet paper to avoid shopping at Wal-Mart, but such a gesture is, unfortunately, not enough. As long as people identify themselves as consumers and nothing more, Wal-Mart wins. 17

The invention of the "consumer" identity has been an important part of a long process of eroding workers' power, and it's one reason working people now have so little power against business. According to the social historian Stuart Ewen, in the early years of mass production, the late nineteenth and early twentieth centuries, modernizing capitalism sought to turn people who thought of themselves primarily as "workers" into "consumers." Business elites wanted people to dream not of satisfying work and egalitarian societies — as many did at that time — but of the beautiful things they could buy with their paychecks. 18

Business was quite successful in this project, which influenced much early advertising and continued throughout the twentieth century. In addition to replacing the "worker," the "consumer" has also effectively displaced the citizen. That's why, when most Americans hear about the Wal-Mart's worker-rights abuses, their first reaction is to feel guilty about shopping at the store. A tiny minority will respond by shopping elsewhere — and only a handful will take any further action. A worker might call her union and organize a picket. A citizen might write to her congressman or local news- 19 paper, or galvanize her church and knitting circle to visit local management. A consumer makes an isolated, politically slight decision: to shop or not to shop. Most of the time, Wal-Mart has her exactly where it wants her, because the intelligent choice for anyone thinking as a consumer is not to make a political statement but to seek the best bargain and the greatest convenience.

To effectively battle corporate criminals like Wal-Mart, the public must   20
be engaged as citizens, not merely as shoppers. What kind of politics could encourage that? It's not clear that our present political parties are up to the job. Unlike so many horrible things, Wal-Mart cannot be blamed on George W. Bush. The Arkansas-based company prospered under the state's native son Bill Clinton when he was governor and President. Sam Walton and his wife, Helen, were close to the Clintons, and for several years Hillary Clinton, whose law firm represented Wal-Mart, served on the company's board of directors. Bill Clinton's "welfare reform" has provided Wal-Mart with a ready workforce of women who have no choice but to accept its poverty wages and discriminatory policies.

Still, a handful of Democratic politicians stood up to the retailer. Cali-   21
fornia Assemblywoman Sally Lieber, who represents the 22nd Assembly District and is a former mayor of Mountain View, was outraged when she learned about the sex discrimination charges in Dukes v. Wal-Mart, and she smelled blood when, tipped off by dissatisfied workers, her office discovered that Wal-Mart was encouraging its workers to apply for public assistance, "in the middle of the worst state budget crisis in history!" California had a $38 billion deficit at the time, and Lieber was enraged that taxpayers would be subsidizing Wal-Mart's low wages, bringing new meaning to the term "corporate welfare."

Lieber was angry, too, that Wal-Mart's welfare dependence made it   22
nearly impossible for responsible employers to compete with the retail giant. It was as if taxpayers were unknowingly funding a massive plunge to the bottom in wages and benefits — quite possibly their own. She held a press conference in July 2003, to expose Wal-Mart's welfare scam. The Wal-Mart documents — instructions explaining how to apply for food stamps, Medi-Cal (the state's healthcare assistance program), and other forms of welfare — were blown up on posterboard and displayed. The morning of the press conference, a Wal-Mart worker who wouldn't give her name for fear of being fired snuck into Lieber's office. "I just wanted to say, right on!" she told the assemblywoman.

Wal-Mart spokespeople have denied that the company encourages   23
employees to collect public assistance, but the documents speak for themselves. They bear the Wal-Mart logo, and one is labeled "Wal-Mart: Instructions for Associates." Both documents instruct employees in procedures for applying to "Social Service Agencies." Most Wal-Mart workers I've interviewed had co-workers who worked full time for the company and received public assistance, and some had been in that situation themselves. Public

assistance is very clearly part of the retailer's cost-cutting strategy. (It's ironic that a company so dependent on the public dole supports so many right-wing politicians who'd like to dismantle the welfare state.)

Lieber, a strong supporter of the social safety net who is now assistant speaker pro tempore of the California Assembly, last year passed a bill that would require large and mid-sized corporations that fail to provide decent, affordable health insurance to reimburse local governments for the cost of providing public assistance for those workers. When the bill passed, its opponents decided to kill it by bringing it to a statewide referendum. Wal-Mart, which just began opening Supercenters in California this year, mobilized its resources to revoke the law on election day this November, even while executives denied that any of their employees depended on public assistance. 24

Citizens should pressure other politicians to speak out against Wal-Mart's abuses and craft policy solutions. But the complicity of both parties in Wal-Mart's power over workers points to the need for a politics that squarely challenges corporate greed and takes the side of ordinary people. That kind of politics seems, at present, strongest at the local level. 25

Earlier this year, labor and community groups in Chicago prevented Wal-Mart from opening a store on the city's South Side, in part by pushing through an ordinance that would have forced the retailer to pay Chicago workers a living wage. In Hartford, Connecticut, labor and community advocates just won passage of an ordinance protecting their free speech rights on the grounds of the new Wal-Mart Supercenter, which is being built on city property. Similar battles are raging nationwide, but Wal-Mart's opponents don't usually act with as much coordination as Wal-Mart does, and they lack the retail behemoth's deep pockets. 26

With this in mind, SEIU* president Andy Stern has recently been calling attention to the need for better coordination — and funding — of labor and community anti-Wal-Mart efforts. Stern has proposed that the AFL-CIO allocate $25 million of its royalties from purchases on its Union Plus credit card toward fighting Wal-Mart and the "Wal-Martization" of American jobs. 27

Such efforts are essential not just because Wal-Mart is a grave threat to unionized workers' jobs (which it is) but because it threatens all American ideals that are at odds with profit — ideals such as justice, equality, and fairness. Wal-Mart would not have so much power if we had stronger labor laws, and if we required employers to pay a living wage. The company knows that, and it hires lobbyists in Washington to vigorously fight any effort at such reforms — indeed, Wal-Mart has recently beefed up this political infrastructure substantially, and it's likely that its presence in Washington will only grow more conspicuous. 28

The situation won't change until a movement comes together and builds the kind of social and political power for workers and citizens that 29

* EDS. NOTE — Service Employees International Union.

can balance that of Wal-Mart. This is not impossible: In Germany, unions are powerful enough to force Wal-Mart to play by their rules. American citizens will have to ask themselves what kind of world they want to live in. That's what prompted Gretchen Adams, a former Wal-Mart manager, to join the effort to unionize Wal-Mart. She's deeply troubled by the company's effect on the economy as a whole and the example it sets for other employers. "What about our working-class people?" she asks. "I don't want to live in a Third World country." Working people, she says, should be able to afford "a new car, a house. You shouldn't have to leave the car on the lawn because you can't afford that $45 part."

•　•　•

Comprehension

1. What are Featherstone's major complaints against Wal-Mart? How does Betty Dukes epitomize Wal-Mart's abuses?

2. What does Al Zack mean when he says that Sam Walton's genius was to discover "how to make money off of poverty" (4). How is Walton's strategy different from that of Henry Ford?

3. What do Wal-Mart shoppers and employees have in common? What, according to Featherstone, is the "tremendous debt Wal-Mart owes women" (12)?

4. Why does Featherstone think boycotting Wal-Mart will not work? What strategy does she think people should use to punish Wal-Mart?

5. Why does Featherstone single out Assemblywoman Sally Lieber for praise?

6. According to Featherstone, how is Wal-Mart a threat to American ideals? What does she think should be done to change the situation? How is Germany a model for action against Wal-Mart?

Purpose and Audience

1. What is Featherstone's purpose in writing this essay? To change readers' ideas? To move people to action? Something else? Explain.

2. Does Featherstone consider her readers friendly, hostile, or neutral? What political leanings does she expect her readers to have? How can you tell?

3. Where does Featherstone state her thesis? Should she have used a more explicit thesis statement?

4. In paragraph 20, Featherstone calls Wal-Mart a corporate criminal. Do you think this strategy helps her case, hurts it, or has no effect at all?

Style and Structure

1. Featherstone introduces her essay by describing a sex-discrimination lawsuit brought by an employee. Why does she begin this way? Is this a successful opening strategy?

2. Featherstone supports her points with a number of quotations from women who work or shop at Wal-Mart. How effective are these quotations as support? Should she have used a greater variety of evidence — such as additional statistics like those she introduces in paragraph 3 — to support her points? If so, what evidence should she have used?

3. In paragraph 4, Featherstone uses deductive reasoning to reach the conclusion that "Wal-Mart's stingy compensation policies . . . contribute to an economy in which, increasingly, workers can only afford to shop at Wal-Mart." Examine the logic of this paragraph — perhaps creating a **syllogism** — and determine whether or not Featherstone's conclusion is logical.

4. How clearly does Featherstone lay out the case against Wal-Mart? What points, if any, need further explanation or illustration?

5. In paragraph 28, Featherstone says that Wal-Mart "threatens all American ideals that are at odds with profit — ideals such as justice, equality, and fairness." How is profit at odds with "justice, equality, and fairness"? Does Featherstone need to present evidence to support this statement, or is it self-evident?

6. While acknowledging Wal-Mart's low prices, Featherstone does not concede any other points in opposition to her position. Should she have? What other concessions would have strengthened her argument?

Vocabulary Projects

1. Define each of these words as it is used in this selection.

behemoth (2)	bonding (10)	deficit (21)
median (3)	indignities (12)	subsidizing (21)
chagrin (3)	drudgery (12)	dismantle (23)
recession (3)	fruitful (13)	referendum (24)
dire (3)	indignation (17)	revoke (24)
stingy (4)	elites (18)	infrastructure (28)
integral (5)	displaced (19)	

2. In paragraph 2 of her essay, Featherstone quotes Betty Dukes, plaintiff in a sexual-discrimination lawsuit against Wal-Mart: "'They are promoting themselves to low-income people,' she says. 'That's who they lure. They don't lure the rich.'" What is the **denotation** of *lure*? What are its **connotations**? In what sense could Wal-Mart be said to "lure" people? Do you think the use of the word *lure* here is accurate? (You might want to consult a Web site such as dictionary.com to help you answer this question.)

Journal Entry

Do you think Featherstone makes a strong case against Wal-Mart?

Writing Workshop

1. Do you, like Featherstone, believe that Wal-Mart does a great deal of damage to low-income people? Or, do you believe that the inexpensive goods and services Wal-Mart provides outweigh any problems the company might create? Write a short essay presenting your position.

2. **Synthesizing Sources**   Assume you own a small business in a town where Wal-Mart is trying to open. Before they can open, however, they have to get approval from the local zoning board. Write an email to the zoning board explaining why Wal-Mart should not be allowed to come to your town. In your essay, concede some of the benefits Wal-Mart would bring, but make the point that, on the whole, the store would do more harm than good. Be specific, and talk about the effect Wal-Mart would have on local business. Use material from "Down and Out in Discount America" to support your points. Before you begin your essay, you might also want to read an article on the PBS Web site pbs.org/wgbh/pages/frontline/shows/walmart/transform/protest.html that examines the effect of Wal-Mart on small communities.

3. **Synthesizing Sources**   In "The Case for Wal-Mart" (page 631), De Coster and Edmonds say, "If the truth be told, Wal-Mart improves the lives of people in rural areas because it gives them access to a lifestyle that they otherwise would not have" (15). Write an essay considering how Featherstone would respond to this statement. Use ideas from both essays to support your points. Be sure to document all material that you borrow from your sources and to include a works-cited page. (See the Appendix for information on documentation formats.)

Combining the Patterns

Paragraphs 18 and 19 are developed by **definition**. What words is Featherstone defining? How do these definitions help her further her argument?

Thematic Connections

- "My Mother Never Worked" (page 114)
- "The Peter Principle" (page 216)
- "What Work Is" (page 542)

CASEBOOK

How Open Should Our Borders Be?

It is often said that the United States is a nation of immigrants. In ways both large and small, immigrants from around the world have contributed to the fabric of American culture, its economic and physical growth, its political power, and its reputation as a beacon to the world.

Until the turn of the twentieth century, immigrant numbers averaged four to five hundred thousand yearly, first primarily from northern Europe and later from southern and eastern Europe. The California Gold Rush brought an influx of Chinese immigrants beginning in the middle of the nineteenth century, sparking the first law restricting immigration, California's so-called Coolie Labor Law; legislation twenty years later further restricted Chinese immigration. Otherwise, immigration was largely unregulated until 1891, when the federal government assumed responsibility for processing those seeking to enter the United States, rejecting those seen as unfit. The first processing center opened on Ellis Island in New York in 1892. Still, the years between 1901 and 1914 saw a doubling of yearly immigration rates spurred by America's general prosperity in relation to much of the rest of the world. Following a downturn during World War I, a series of regulatory laws was enacted between 1917 and 1924, including those establishing caps on immigrants by country. As a result, immigrant numbers fell to pre-1900 levels, and they sank even lower in the years before and after World War II.

New legislation in 1965 retained caps by country (though redistributing the numbers so they no longer favored northern and western Europe) but gave preference to relatives of U.S. citizens and of legal permanent residents, with unlimited numbers allowed for spouses and children of citizens and, in more limited numbers, for extended family members. Since then, the face of the United States has changed dramatically. Not only has immigration returned to levels not seen since the first decade of the twentieth century (about a million people a year since the 1980s), but first- and second-generation Americans today are much more likely to come from Central and South America and Asia than from Europe. While this greater diversity is celebrated by some, others charge that this new wave of immigrants does not always share the core cultural values of traditional European immigrants — in particular, the goals of assimilation and learning English — and that, in some cases, their lower educational achievement is detrimental to American society.

The years since 1965 have also seen a rise in illegal immigration. By 1980, it was estimated that some 3 million people were in the country illegally. The number grew to 5 million by 1987, when legislation aimed at curtailing illegal immigration granted amnesty to some 3 million illegals, allowing them to remain in the country legally while at the same time making it more difficult for employers to hire undocumented workers. As critics have pointed out, the measure was a complete failure, and today there are an estimated 11.6 million illegal immigrants in the country, up from 8.5 million as recently as 2000.

The four essays in this casebook consider a number of issues in the immigration debate. In "American Dreams, Foreign Flags," Linda Chavez argues that Latinos can most effectively lobby for immigration reform not by presenting themselves as "an aggrieved foreign presence," but by showing other Americans that they share common values and aspirations. In her 2006 congressional "Statement of Support for Comprehensive Immigration Reform," Senator Dianne Feinstein presents her case for an immigration reform bill that includes funding for tighter border patrols and, more controversially, a mechanism whereby people already in the country illegally may receive permission to remain here legally and work toward full citizenship. Herbert Meyer's "Why Americans Hate This 'Immigration' Debate" argues that too many current immigrants are not immigrants in the traditional sense at all — that is, people here to assimilate and "put the old country behind them" — but are here "solely for jobs" and so don't play by the same rules others play by. Finally, in "To Reunite a Nation," Pat Buchanan, as a 2000 presidential candidate, proposes an immigration reform policy that would significantly reduce the number of entry visas granted each year and would allocate visas based on a point system that includes education and job skills, not just the fact that an applicant has relatives in the United States.

LINDA CHAVEZ

American Dreams, Foreign Flags

Linda Chavez is chairman of the Center for Equal Opportunity, a Virginia-based public policy research organization. In 1983, President Ronald Reagan named her staff director of the U.S. Commission on Civil Rights. She subsequently held a number of government posts, including chair of the National Commission on Migrant Education. Chavez is the author of three books: *Out of the Barrio: Toward a New Politics of Hispanic Assimilation* (1991), *An Unlikely Conservative: The Transformation of an Ex-Liberal, or How I Became the Most Hated Hispanic in America* (2002), and *Betrayal: How Union Bosses Shake Down Their Members and Corrupt American Politics* (2004). In 2000, Chavez was named a Library of Congress "Living Legend" for her contributions to America's cultural and social heritage.

Background on the presence of Hispanics in the United States
Settlements of Spanish-speaking people in what is now the United States predate the earliest English-speaking settlement by five hundred years, and much of the Southwest remained under Spanish or Mexican control — and thus populated primarily by Spanish speakers — until the middle of the nineteenth century. When the United States acquired this territory in 1848 at the end of the Mexican-American War, most of the existing Hispanic population chose to remain and become U.S. citizens. Despite the terms of the treaty ending the war, which guaranteed the property rights of the former Mexican citizens, many landowners lost title to their land as a result of lawsuits and subsequently passed legislation. In addition, Hispanics in the Southwest suffered considerable discrimination at the hands of the new settlers from the East and remained a largely marginal population, mostly isolated from the economic mainstream. The first real influx of Mexican nationals into the United States did not occur until the mid-twentieth century, when World War II created a need for unskilled labor. Many of these so-called *braceros*, officially "guest workers," eventually sought citizenship, but caps by country on the number of immigrants allowed into the United States kept Hispanic immigration (unlike migration from Puerto Rico, a U.S. commonwealth) relatively low. Federal immigration reform in 1965 that provided opportunities for family members of citizens and resident aliens to apply to immigrate led to a boom in immigration from Latin America, particularly Mexico. As a result, Hispanics have made up the largest group of immigrants to the United States since the 1970s. According to 2005 statistics, more than 40 million Americans, almost 17 million of these foreign-born, identify themselves as Hispanic (up 20 percent from five years earlier).

Hundreds of thousands of flag-waving demonstrators took to the streets in Denver, Los Angeles, Phoenix, and dozens of other cities in the last week to protest harsh legislation passed by the House that would make

1

felons of the 12 million illegal aliens living in the United States — along with anyone who provides them with shelter, food, or other services. It didn't take long for a bipartisan majority on the Senate Judiciary Committee to get the message and take a softer tack.

On Monday, four Republicans joined all eight committee Democrats to vote down the controversial penalties. Their proposal also calls for admitting more legal immigrants and temporary workers, allowing illegal aliens already in the country to remain here and earn citizenship if they pay a fine, learn English, and study American civics.

The Senate bill has a long way to go before becoming law, however. Despite their victory in this round, supporters of comprehensive immigration reform must be careful in their tactics, including what symbols they embrace. Although American flags were widely visible among the crowd of a half-million in downtown Los Angeles (organizers had asked marchers to bring them), reports indicated that they were outnumbered by those of Mexico, Guatemala, El Salvador, and other countries. And if history is any guide, those foreign banners could spur an anti-immigrant reaction.

That's what happened in 1994, when 70,000 people marched in Los Angeles, many waving Mexican flags, to show their distaste for Proposition 187, a California ballot initiative that denied social services to illegal aliens and their children. Initially favored by more than 70 percent of voters, the measure was losing steam as the election approached, with a poll a week before the election showing it ahead by only one point. But that sea of green, white, and red Mexican flags flooding the streets just before the election signaled to many Californians that those demanding equal treatment were more attached to their native country than to the United States. The proposition scored a surprisingly strong 59 percent of the vote, although the courts eventually declared it unconstitutional.

Similar dynamics are playing out today. For all the talk of national security and the economic costs of immigration, the underlying issue driving the current anti-immigrant frenzy is a deep suspicion that this latest group of newcomers won't do what others before them did: learn English and embrace American identity.

Unfortunately, many Latino leaders play right into the hands of those who claim they are different from the Germans, Italians, Poles, Jews, Irish, and others who came here in another era. With shouts of "Sí, se puede!" (Yes, we can!) — an old United Farm Workers rallying cry — and signs announcing "We didn't cross the border, the border crossed us," the demonstrators are likely to turn off more Americans than they win over. And the sight of thousands of angry Hispanic students from California to Virginia pouring out of schools to join protest marches will only reinforce stereotypes that Latinos care little about education.

Instead of presenting themselves as an aggrieved, foreign presence, immigration advocates ought to be explaining how similar Latinos are to other Americans in their values, aspirations, and achievements. It's an easy case to make.

Mexican-born men, for example, are more likely to be in the labor force   8
than any other racial or ethnic group, according to the Census Bureau.
Nearly half of Latino immigrants own their own homes. While most immigrants from Latin America, especially Mexico and Central America, lag in
educational attainment, their children are far more likely to stay in school:
according to research by the Pew Hispanic Center, 80 percent of second-
generation Latinos graduate from high school. Almost half of second-
generation Latinos ages 25 to 44 have attended college, and those who
graduate earn more on average than non-Hispanic white workers.

Latino immigrants are also starting their own businesses at a rapid   9
pace. The Census Bureau reported that entrepreneurship among Latinos is
increasing at a rate three times faster than that of other Americans. Americans of Hispanic descent now own 1.6 million businesses generating $222
billion annually; and while Census data didn't distinguish between immigrants and American-born Hispanics, it suggested that much of this
growth occurred in heavily immigrant communities.

Like every generation of immigrants before them, Latinos start out on   10
the bottom rungs of the economic ladder, but they don't stay there. They
are learning English as quickly as their predecessors, perhaps more quickly
thanks to television (a majority of third-generation Latinos speak only
English). They are intermarrying at faster rates than earlier ethnic groups,
too, with about one-third of married American-born Latinos having a non-
Hispanic spouse.

These facts, if they were more widely known, would go a long way to   11
calming fears about Latino immigration. If Latino advocates hope to influence the outcome of the Senate debate on immigration over the next two
weeks, they would do well to spread the word — and trade their ancestral
flags for the Stars and Stripes.

•   •   •

Comprehension

1. What inspired the demonstrations Chavez refers to in her opening paragraph, and what was the apparent result of those demonstrations?
2. Why is Chavez concerned about the appearance of flags from Central
   American countries in the demonstrations she writes about?
3. What suggestions does Chavez have for Latino immigration advocates?
4. What does Chavez say happens to Latino immigrants over time?

Purpose and Audience

1. It is likely that Chavez has both a dual purpose and a dual audience in
   mind for this essay. What are these purposes and audiences?
2. Where does Chavez state her thesis? Why do you think she chose to state
   it there? Is this the most effective location?

3. Chavez does not specifically address any opposing arguments. Do you think this omission weakens her argument?

Style and Structure

1. Throughout the essay, Chavez mentions the waving of flags. Identify such references, and explain how they support her argument.
2. Why do you suppose Chavez focuses on statistics in paragraphs 8–10? What do these statistics contribute to her argument?
3. Evaluate Chavez's final paragraph. Does it seem to be a fitting conclusion to her argument?

Vocabulary Projects

1. Define each of the following words as it is used in this selection.

   bipartisan (1)   entrepreneurship (9)
   frenzy (5)   ancestral (11)
   aggrieved (7)

2. In paragraph 4, Chavez refers to "a sea of green, white, and red Mexican flags flooding the streets" of Los Angeles. What is the effect of this **metaphor**?

Journal Entry

Chavez writes about legislation that would create criminal penalties for "anyone who provides [illegal immigrants] with shelter, food, or other services" (1). How do you respond to the idea of such legislation?

Writing Workshop

1. What advice would you offer to immigrants and their leaders who wish to sway public opinion in favor of making immigration easier and providing more opportunities for immigrants? Write an essay in which you address public concerns about immigrants and reassure those who feel threatened by immigration.
2. People of Irish descent celebrate St. Patrick's Day with displays of Irish flags and other symbols that suggest their devotion to their native country, and Italian-Americans display Italian flags on Columbus Day. Are these displays different from displays of Mexican and other Central American flags in pro-immigration demonstrations? Why are the former not seen as offensive while the latter, according to Chavez, are, at least by some? Write an email to Chavez in which you present your opinion.
3. Chavez makes the claim in paragraph 10 that Latinos "are learning English as quickly as their predecessors." Considerable controversy surrounds immigrants' use of English, including issues such as offering

bilingual education, providing public information in languages other than English, and requiring workers to use English in the workplace. Write an essay in which you present your views on how to accommodate those whose first language is not English.

Combining the Patterns

Where in the essay does Chavez use **narration** and **description**? What do these passages contribute to the essay?

Thematic Connections

- "Only Daughter" (page 97)
- "Black *and* Latino" (page 537)
- "The Myth of the Latin Woman: I Just Met a Girl Named Maria" (page 730)

Statement in Support of Comprehensive Immigration Reform

San Francisco native Dianne Feinstein has been a U.S. senator from California since 1992. In 1969, she was elected to the San Francisco Board of Supervisors and became the first woman in history to serve as its president. She assumed the position of mayor of San Francisco in 1978 (again, a first for a woman) after the sitting mayor was assassinated, and she went on to be elected to the post for two terms. Her accomplishments as a senator include successfully lobbying for legislation prohibiting the manufacture and sale of nineteen types of military-style assault weapons, working to significantly increase funding for breast cancer research, and introducing the California Desert Protection Act, the largest designation of protected land in the country's history. As a member of the Senate Judiciary Committee, Feinstein chairs the Terrorism, Technology, and Homeland Security Subcommittee and sits on the subcommittee for Immigration, Border Control, and Citizenship.

Background on United States citizenship and legal residency

A person is automatically a citizen of the United States if he or she is born in the United States (an 1898 Supreme Court ruling stipulated that this is the case even if someone's parents are not citizens, and this ruling has been construed as applying even if the parents are in the country illegally) or born outside of the United States to parents who are citizens. (Foreign-born children adopted by U.S. citizens also become citizens automatically.) The path to citizenship for those who are not citizens by birth begins with applying for status as a permanent legal resident ("green card" holder). Foreign-born spouses, minor children, and parents of U.S. citizens are automatically eligible, and there is no limit as to how many can apply. Other family members of citizens — such as adult children and brothers and sisters — as well as spouses and children of those who are already permanent legal residents are also eligible although only a limited number are allowed to apply yearly. Workers in certain categories (generally those who are highly skilled) may also apply, again with yearly limits in each category. A person can also apply through a lottery system that confers green cards on 55,000 randomly selected people a year from countries with low rates of immigration to the United States. In addition, people admitted to the country as refugees or granted political asylum are eligible for citizenship. An applicant for citizenship must have a valid green card and have lived in the United States for at least five years (three years if married to a citizen or serving in the armed forces); prove literacy in English; pass a test on U.S. history and government; display "good moral character"; and swear an oath of allegiance to the United States.

Mr. President, shortly the Senate is going to be confronted with a vote on two bills, one of them being the leader's bill which deals with enforcement on the border, and the other the Judiciary Committee bill which essentially incorporates provisions of the McCain-Kennedy bill into a broad and comprehensive bill which will, I believe, be before the Senate for discussion and amendment. 1

The bill approved by the Judiciary Committee is a bipartisan bill. . . . It is the first step forward in a very difficult and consequential process to address what has become one of the most contentious issues in American life. . . . 2

Any legislation approved by Congress, I think, has to take into consideration the reality of today's immigration world in America. It is very different from the 1990s, it is very different from the 1980s, and it is very different from the 1970s. There are very strongly held views on both sides. Most, though, of what is attempted by Federal agencies responsible for the administration of immigration services today and responsible for the protection of our borders has more often than not failed, and we have to deal with that failure. 3

Employer sanctions, which are the seed of current immigration laws, have failed. Border control is spotty at best. Naturalization takes years. Detention facilities are inadequate. And despite our attempts to gain operational control of our border and to secure the interior of the United States so that everyone plays by the rules, the government has essentially failed. 4

We now have 10 million to 12 million undocumented people living in the United States. They have come here illegally. They live furtively. Many of them have been here for twenty to thirty years. I know many. They own their homes. They pay taxes. Their children were born in this country and educated in this country. This is the only home they know. They want to live by the law, but they have no way currently to live by the law. 5

Employer sanctions, I mentioned, do not and, I believe, in our global economy, will not work. That is evidenced by the fact that in 2004, only forty-six employers in the United States were criminally convicted for employer sanctions out of 3,258 cases initiated. 6

I have watched in California. On the few occasions where immigration officials have gone to agricultural worksites and arrested employers, the public reaction has been entirely negative. 7

Both you and I know, Mr. President, that a law is only as good as the ability to enforce it. There is virtually today no ability to enforce employer sanctions in the United States of America. Therefore, a more punitive immigration philosophy that is based and dependent upon employer sanctions as working doesn't work and clearly creates a situation whereby there is disorganized chaos in the immigration world. 8

Another reason for this is our borders are a sieve, porous through and through. The Senator from Arizona correctly mentioned there are fourteen miles on the California border with Mexico where there is a two-layer fence. It is an immigration border control process known as Operation 9

Gatekeeper. It was very controversial when put into play, but it works. And he is correct, immigrants coming in illegally in that corridor have been deterred.

But what has happened is, it has simply pushed them east into unfenced portions of the border, and those portions of the border where the desert and the heat wreak considerable destruction upon anybody crossing.

A concern with porous borders has also brought attention to a classification of aliens known as "other than Mexicans." In 2005, Border Patrol agents apprehended 165,175 "other than Mexicans" at the border, 155,000 of them on the southern border.

The concern here is that many of these people are increasingly from terrorist-supporting countries, and that presents a real potential national security threat to our country.

We continue to have a catch-and-release policy with respect to this limited category of people, but we don't have sufficient detention facilities. Consequently, they are released on their own recognizance pending a hearing. They are expected to show up at the hearing. More often than not, they do not show up. They simply disappear into the fabric of America, gone for all time.

I can go on and on, but I think this gives an accurate view of what has become an extraordinarily dysfunctional immigration system, and it has also made me realize that while we need strong border enforcement, it alone is not the only solution to the problem of illegal immigration.

The House bill, which focuses only on enforcement and criminalization of undocumented aliens, isn't the solution. We need to be much more realistic and comprehensive.

Mr. President, the Senate Judiciary Committee passed a bill, and I must tell you, I regret the way it was done. It was a kind of forced march, hour after hour of amendments on a bill that is very complicated, that I believe has actually come to the floor somewhat prematurely. I don't believe there is yet a consensus in this body, and I hope the debate that takes place can be a respectful debate so members will feel free to open their minds and then to change them if the facts warrant that.

But this bill is a beginning. It seeks to address the overall problem in a much more comprehensive and practical way.

First with regard to border enforcement. The bill doubles the number of Border Patrol agents. It adds 12,000 over five years. Senator Kyl and I had testimony in the Terrorism and Technology Subcommittee from the head of Border Patrol that today there are 11,300 Border Patrol agents. This more than doubles that number over the next five years.

It also would add an additional 2,500 new ports of entry inspectors in this same period so that the ports of entry are strengthened and legal immigration is able to be handled in a more prompt manner.

It criminalizes the act of constructing or financing a tunnel or subterranean passage across an international border into the United States. Most people don't know this, but this has become a real problem. There are forty such tunnels that have been built since 9/11, and the great bulk of them are on the southern border. Large-scale smuggling of drugs, weapons, and immigrants takes place today through these tunnels.   .

I recently visited a tunnel running from San Diego to Tijuana, and I was struck by the inordinate sophistication of the tunnel. It was a half mile long. It went sixty to eighty feet deep, eight feet tall. It had a concrete floor. It was wired for electricity. It had drainage. At one end, three hundred pounds of marijuana were found, and at the other end, three hundred pounds of marijuana.   21

What was interesting is that the California entry into the tunnel was a very modern warehouse, a huge warehouse compartmented but empty and kept empty for a year. You went into one office, and there was a hatch in the floor. It looked much like the hatch which Saddam had secreted himself in. But when you lifted that hatch and you looked underground, you saw a very sophisticated tunnel. It went under other buildings all the way across the double fence into Mexico and up in Mexico in a building as well.   22

Today, interestingly enough, at this time, there is no law that makes building or financing such a tunnel a crime. A provision in this bill includes language from the Feinstein-Kyl Border Tunnel Prevention Act which would make the building or financing of a cross-border tunnel a crime punishable by up to twenty years.   23

This bill also authorizes additional unmanned aerial vehicles, modern cameras, sensors, and other new technologies to allow the Department of Homeland Security to work with the Department of Defense so the latter can carry out surveillance activities at the border to prevent illegal immigration.   24

So this bill is very strong on border enforcement. But it doesn't just leave it there, as the majority leader's bill does. It says, that is only half the problem; you have to deal with the other half of the problem, and there is the rub. That is the difficult part, and that is the controversial part as well.   25

The bill we have from the Judiciary Committee seeks to remedy the very real needs of our economy which, as much as we might want to, cannot be ignored. Our global economy has changed the face of the American workforce. I am not going to comment on whether this is good or bad. In some cases, it is one or the other. In some cases, it is mixed. But the fact of the matter is the needs are different and the workforce is somewhat different.   26

Let me give you a large industry: agriculture. There are about 1,600,000 workers in this country who work in agriculture. In my state, there are 566,000. I would hazard an informed guess that half of the 566,000 are here in undocumented status. I have had farmer after farmer, grower after grower tell me they cannot farm, they cannot grow without this workforce. I didn't believe it, so I got in touch with fifty-eight—we have fifty-eight counties—fifty-eight welfare departments and asked them to post notices   27 saying: Please, there are jobs in agriculture. Here is where to come. Here is what to expect. Guess what. Not a single person responded anywhere in the fifty-eight counties of California.

That was pretty convincing evidence to me that Americans don't 28 choose to do this work. It is the undocumented workforce who has been the mainstay of American agriculture, whether through the H-2A program coming cyclically or whether it is through a large contingent of undocumented workers who remain in this country year after year and do this work.

Under this program . . . an undocumented worker could apply for a 29 blue card if that worker could demonstrate that he or she has worked in American agriculture for at least 150 workdays within the previous two years before December 31, 2005. After receiving blue cards, individuals who have then worked an additional period in American agriculture for three years, 150 workdays per year, or 100 workdays per year for five years, would be eligible for a green card. Their spouses could work, and their children could remain in the country with them.

What would be the result of this? The result is that American agricul- 30 ture would have a stable base of employment which is legal, which has the opportunity to bring people out of the shadows into the bright light of day, assume additional responsibilities, grow in the process, and raise their families. I think that is healthy for America, not unhealthy.

Also, we reform the current H-2A program, which is the agricultural 31 guest worker program, which employs, I would say around thirty thousand people and is used largely in the tobacco-producing States. The way this is reformed is it makes it easier for an employer to apply for workers through an attestation system, the paperwork is simpler, the housing requirements are changed to make it easier. In general, the bill updates the H-2A agricultural program.

Returning to the larger bill, I suppose the most contentious part is 32 what should happen to the 12 million people who are living here in the shadows, undocumented. Many would say they are here illegally; they ought to go back. Well, they are not going to go back. They are going to remain living furtively, and they are going to remain in the shadows. And most of them work.

The question before this body is: does that make sound public policy 33 sense over a substantial period of time? These immigrants live furtively. They are subject to work abuse, exploitation, threats, and blackmail. This bill would provide them with an opportunity to come into the light of day. But it wouldn't be easy for them. It is not an amnesty. An amnesty is instant forgiveness with no conditions. There are conditions on this. They must pay a fine of $2,000, they must learn English, they must have paid all back taxes, and they must be evaluated as neither a criminal or a national security threat to this nation.

Also, they would not go in front of anybody in the line. There are pres- 34 ently 3.3 million people waiting in other countries legally for green cards, and those people should and will be processed first. It is estimated it will take, believe it or not, up to six years to process 3.3 million. These workers, these undocumented 12 million would go at the end of that line, and then one by one, they would come through that line. If they have worked steadily for the six-year period, if they can show they have paid all back taxes, if they have avoided any criminal convictions, if they have learned English in that time, they would be granted a green card. Therefore, they come out of a furtive lifestyle, hidden and in secret, living in fear that tomorrow they could or might be deported.

Over the years in the Senate, one of the things that we can do is put forward a private bill. If we see a family or an individual who we believe is an exceptional circumstance, we can try and get a private bill passed for them, and when we introduce the bill, their deportation is stayed. It is very hard to get a private bill through. Many Members don't do private bills. I met some of the families. I want to give you three cases that I think are eloquent testimony to what is happening amongst the 12 million.   35

Let me share with you a family. Their last name is Arreola. They live in Porterville, California. I have filed a private immigration relief bill for them over two sessions. I didn't get the bill passed, but their deportation has been stayed. Mr. and Mrs. Arreola came to the United States from Mexico illegally in the 1980s to work in agriculture. They have five children, two brought to the United States as toddlers, and three born in the United States. They range from eight years old today to nineteen, and they know no other home but this country.   36

Their eldest daughter, Nayely, is a bright, engaging student. I have met her and talked with her. She is the embodiment of the American dream and what can happen when we give children a chance to excel in a loving, nurturing environment. She was the first in her family to graduate from high school and the first to go to college. And on a full scholarship. She goes to Fresno Pacific University. Mrs. Arreola works as a produce packer and Mr. Arreola now has an appliance repair business. They have no criminal background. They own their home. They pay their taxes. For Nayely, this bill offers a glimmer of hope that her family, once and for all, can come out of the shadows. They don't have to have that daily fear of deportation. They have been here for twenty years. They are and will be legal, productive citizens.   37

One other example. Shigeru Yamada is a twenty-one-year-old Japanese national living in Chula Vista, California. He is facing removal from this country due to a tragic circumstance relating to the death of his mother. He entered the United States with his mother and two sisters in 1992 at the age of ten. He fled from an alcoholic father who had been physically abusive to his mother, the children, and even his own parents.   38

Tragically, Shigeru's mother was killed in a car crash in 1995, and he was orphaned at the age of thirteen. The death of his mother also served to impede the process for him to legalize his status. He could not legalize his status. At the time of her death, his family was living legally in the United   39

States. His mother had acquired a student visa for herself and her children. Her death revoked his legal status in the United States.

In addition, his mother was also engaged to an American citizen at the time of her death. Had she survived, her son would have become an American citizen through this marriage. Instead, today, he is an illegal immigrant leading a model American life. He graduated with honors from Eastlake High School in 2000. He has earned a number of awards, including being named an "Outstanding English Student" his freshman year. He is an All-American Scholar, and he is earning the United States National Minority Leadership Award. He was vice president of the associated student body his senior year of high school. He is popular and he is trustworthy. He is an athlete. He was named the "Most Inspirational Player of the Year" in junior varsity baseball and football as well as varsity football. After graduating, he volunteered for four years to help coach the school's girl's softball team. 40

Sending him back to Japan today would be an enormous hardship. He doesn't speak the language. He is unaware of the nation's cultural trends. He is American, raised here, educated here. He is one who is deserving, who would be helped by this legislation. . . . 41

Let me give a third example of the type and character of individuals that this bill would legalize. The Plascencias are Mexican nationals living in San Bruno, California. They are undocumented. They face removal from the country due to the fact that they have received ineffective assistance of counsel. They have four children, all born in this country. The mother and father are subject to deportation; the children are not. They arrived in this country in 1988, and they have worked hard. Mrs. Plascencia studied English. She is now taking nursing classes at the College of San Mateo. She worked for four years in the oncology department of Kaiser Permanente Hospital, where she was a medical assistant. 42

Mr. Plascencia works at Vince's Shellfish Market. During the last thirteen years he has worked his way up from part-time employee to his current supervisory position. He is now the foreman in charge of the packing department. 43

The Plascencia family has struggled to become legal residents for many years. Based on the advice of counsel, whom they were later forced to fire for gross incompetence, they applied for asylum. The application was denied, and they were placed in removal proceedings. 44

Their children—Christina, thirteen; Erika, nine; Alfredo, seven; and Daisy, two—are entitled to remain. Their eldest daughter, Christina, is enrolled in Parkside Intermediate School in San Bruno, where she is an honor student. Erika and Alfredo are enrolled in Belle Air Elementary School. They are doing well. They have received praise from their teachers. 45

This family has worked hard to achieve the financial security their children now enjoy. This includes a home they purchased three years ago in San Bruno, California. They own their car. They have medical insurance. And they have paid their taxes. 46

It is very clear to me and I think to a majority of Americans that this 47
family has embraced the American dream and their continued presence in
our country would do much to enhance the values we hold dear. So I believe
that by presenting a pathway for the 12 million to become legal, this bill
offers the only realistic option. Think about it. How do you find 12 million
people, and what do you do when you find them, if you do? If brought
across the border, they return the next day. This is their home. This is their
work. There are no adequate facilities to detain them. And most, today,
have become a vital and necessary part of the American workforce—in agriculture, in restaurants, in hotels, in landscaping, and throughout our
economy.

We need to build a border infrastructure that is modern and effective. 48
We can do that. Operation Gatekeeper has shown irrefutably we can, in
fact, enforce our borders if we have the will to do so and we are willing to
spend the money to do so. But we also need to find an orderly way to allow
those people who are already here, who are embedded in our communities
and in our workforce, to be able to continue to remain. This bill does that.

I know this is tough for everybody because I know emotions run high 49
and it is really hard to change your mind on this subject because there are
so many conflicting pressures. But we have an opportunity to chart a new
destiny for a lot of people. We have an opportunity to do something which
has a chance to work, which is real, which meets the needs of real people
out there, and which can stop the illegal infusion through our borders in
the future if we act wisely, well, and effectively.

•   •   •

Comprehension

1. What argument does Feinstein make about current immigration legislation and border enforcement? Why is this point important to her larger
   argument?
2. What issues does the first part of the bill passed by the Senate Judiciary
   Committee address? How does Feinstein say this bill will make a difference?
3. What point is Feinstein making in paragraphs 26–28?
4. What issues does the second part of the bill passed by the Senate Judiciary Committee address? Why does she think the measures in the bill are
   necessary?
5. Is Feinstein optimistic or pessimistic about the Senate's ability to address
   the problems of illegal immigration? Explain.

Purpose and Audience

1. Feinstein spends considerably more time dealing with the aspects of the
   bill that concern immigration reform than with those that concern border enforcement. Why do you think this might be the case?

2. What does Feinstein concede in paragraph 16? What is her purpose here?

3. In paragraphs 1, 9, and 18 Feinstein refers to other members of the Senate. Why do you think she does so?

4. Why does Feinstein conclude her essay the way she does? Would another closing strategy be more effective?

Style and Structure

1. What stylistic characteristics suggest that Feinstein's statement is an oral rather than a written presentation?

2. Feinstein's statement can be divided into six sections: paragraphs 1–2, 3–14, 15–17, 18–28, 29–47, and 48–49. What is the central function of each section? Can you identify subsections within any of these sections?

3. Feinstein acknowledges opposing arguments in paragraphs 15, 27, and 32–34. How does she do so? Does she refute these arguments effectively?

4. A significant part of Feinstein's speech is devoted to describing three situations involving illegal aliens in her home state (35–46). Why do you think this section comes at the end of Feinstein's argument rather than earlier in her speech? *Should* it have come earlier?

5. What is the function of paragraph 47?

Vocabulary Projects

1. Define each of the following words as it is used in this selection.

bipartisan (2)	dysfunctional (14)	exploitation (33)
sanctions (4)	amendments (16)	deportation (35)
furtively (5)	consensus (16)	asylum (44)
chaos (8)	inordinate (21)	irrefutably (48)
porous (9)	attestation (31)	embedded (48)

2. In paragraphs 32 and 33, Feinstein refers to "people who are living here in the shadows" being given "an opportunity to come into the light of day." What effect does she hope this **metaphor** will have on her audience?

3. In the first two sentences of the final paragraph of her statement, Feinstein uses informal language such as "tough," "really hard," and "a lot." Is this language appropriate for her audience and purpose?

Journal Entry

How do you respond to the examples Feinstein presents in paragraphs 36–46? Do you think these are typical examples? What do they contribute to your evaluation of her argument?

Writing Workshop

1. What is your response to the proposal Feinstein presents here regarding a pathway to citizenship for workers who are in the country illegally? Write

an email to Feinstein in which you take a stand on this legislation. Be sure to summarize and refute opposing arguments.

2. **Synthesizing Sources** In paragraph 27, Feinstein makes the point that most illegal workers in the country are working in jobs that employers cannot find Americans to fill. Write an essay in which you agree or disagree with Feinstein's assessment. Before you write your essay, read the summary of a Pew Hispanic Center Report at pewhispanic.org/newsroom/releases/release.php?ReleaseID=33 that examines the condition of illegal undocumented Hispanic immigrants in the United States. Be sure to document all words and ideas that you borrow from your sources and to include a works-cited page. (See the Appendix for information on documentation formats.)

3. In paragraph 26, Feinstein makes the point that the "global economy has changed the face of the American workforce" both for the better and for the worse. How has the global economy affected you, your family members, and people you know? Has it been mostly for the better or mostly for the worse? Write an opinion piece for your local newspaper in which you support your position on this issue.

Combining the Patterns

In paragraphs 29–30, Feinstein uses **cause and effect** to make her case. Summarize this cause-and-effect argument.

Thematic Connections

- "My Mother Never Worked" (page 114)
- "Two Ways to Belong in America" (page 411)

HERBERT MEYER

Why Americans Hate
This "Immigration" Debate

During the Reagan administration, Herbert Meyer served as special assistant to the director of Central Intelligence and vice chairman of the CIA's National Intelligence Council. A former editor at *Fortune* magazine and a frequent contributor to the *Wall Street Journal, National Review,* and other periodicals, Meyer is the author of several books, including *Real-World Intelligence* (1991) and *Hard Thinking: The Fusion of Politics and Science* (1993).

Background on undocumented workers

The American farm industry has depended on Mexican labor since World War II, when the United States worked out an agreement with Mexico to allow Mexican nationals into the country as temporary workers called *braceros.* Once the program ended in 1964, some workers were able to gain legal permanent residency status, but many of those who did not remained in the United States and continued to be employed illegally. Critics of U.S. immigration policy believe that unless the government can somehow prevent U.S. businesses from employing undocumented workers, or unless Mexico and other countries somehow improve their economies for their poorest people, no amount of border policing — whether in the form of more border agents and checkpoints, more high-tech surveillance equipment, or even a 2,000-mile-long fence or wall — will deter workers from seeking illegal entry into the country. Recognizing this problem and tacitly admitting that American business relies on foreign labor, former President Bush in 2004 proposed a "guest worker" program that would allow undocumented immigrants currently living in the United States to apply for a work permit for up to three years if they can prove that their employer could not find a U.S. citizen willing to take the job. Criticized both by those who prefer deportation and those who support a path to permanent citizenship, the proposal had little support and eventually died.

One of the most striking features of the immigration debate now raging in Washington is that none of the Democratic or Republican proposals seem to hold any appeal for ordinary Americans — which is why this debate is generating so much frustration among voters that no matter which proposal Congress adopts, the issue itself threatens to shatter both parties' bases and dominate the November elections.   1

Simply put, the debate in Washington isn't about "immigration" at   2
all — and that's the problem.

To ordinary Americans, the definition of "immigration" is very spe- 3
cific: you come here with absolutely nothing except a burning desire to be
an American. You start off at some miserable, low-paying job that at least
puts a roof over your family's head and food on the table. You put your
kids in school, tell them how lucky they are to be here — and make darn
sure they do well even if that means hiring a tutor and taking a second, or
third, job to pay for it. You learn English, even if you've got to take classes
at night when you're dead tired. You play by the rules — which means you
pay your taxes, get a driver's license, and insure your car so that if yours
hits mine, I can recover the cost of the damages. And you file for citizenship the first day you're eligible.

Do all this and you become an American like all the rest of us. Your 4
kids will lose their accents, move into the mainstream, and retain little of
their heritage except a few words of your language and — if you're
lucky — an irresistible urge to visit you now and then for some of mom's
old-country cooking.

This is how the Italians made it, the Germans made it, the Dutch made 5
it, the Poles made it, the Jews made it, and more recently how the Cubans
and the Vietnamese made it. The process isn't easy — but it works and
that's the way ordinary Americans want to keep it.

The Two Hispanic Groups

But the millions of Hispanics who have come to our country in the last 6
several decades—and it's the Hispanics we're talking about in this debate,
not those from other cultures — are, in fact, two distinct groups. The first
group is comprised of "immigrants" just like all the others, who have put
the old country behind them and want only to be Americans. They aren't
the problem. Indeed, most Americans welcome them among us, as we have
welcomed so many other cultures.

The problem is the second group of Hispanics. *They aren't immi-* 7
grants — which is what neither the Democratic or Republican leadership
seems to understand, or wants to acknowledge. They have come here solely
for jobs, which isn't the same thing at all. (And many of them have come
here illegally.) Whether they remain in the U.S. for one year, or ten
years — or for the rest of their lives — they don't conduct themselves like
immigrants. Yes, they work hard to put roofs above their heads and food
on their tables — and for this we respect them. But they have little interest
in learning English themselves, and instead demand that we make it possible for them to function here in Spanish. They put their children in our
schools, but don't always demand as much from them as previous groups
demanded of their kids. They don't always pay their taxes — or insure their
cars.

In short, they aren't playing by the rules that our families played by 8
when they immigrated to this country. And to ordinary Americans this
behavior is deeply — very deeply — offensive. We see it unfolding every day

in our communities, and we don't like it. This is what none of our politicians either understands, or dares to say aloud. Instead, they blather on — and on — about "amnesty" and "border security" without ever coming to grips with what is so visible, and so offensive, to so many of us — namely, all these foreigners among us who aren't behaving like immigrants.

The phrase we use to describe foreigners who come here not as "immigrants" but merely for jobs is "guest workers." And we are told — incessantly — that we need these "guest workers" because they take jobs that Americans don't want and won't take themselves. This is true, but it's also disingenuous. Throughout our country's history, immigrants have always taken jobs that Americans don't want and won't take themselves. For crying out loud, no foreigner has ever come to our country out of a blazing ambition to dig ditches, mow lawns, bag groceries, sew clothing, or clean other people's houses. If we hadn't always had a huge number of these miserable jobs available that none of "us" would do — there wouldn't have been a way for immigrants throughout the nineteenth and twentieth centuries to step off the boat and find work.

A willingness by "immigrants" to start at the bottom — so they can move up the economic ladder or at least give their kids a shot at the higher rungs — is precisely how the system is supposed to work. And it always has. (My own family is one of the tens of millions that did precisely this. My grandfather came from Poland and found work as a pocket-maker in New York's garment district. The pay was low, the hours were long, and when the old man finally retired he could hardly move his fingers or see without thick glasses. Yet one of his sons, my uncle, became a lawyer with a fancy practice on Manhattan's Upper East Side. His kids did even better; his son wound up chairman of Stanford University's history department, and his daughter became a famous art critic, moved to London, and married an Englishman who became a member of the House of Lords. What is astonishing about this story is that — it isn't astonishing. It's the sort of thing that happens all the time, and it's why ordinary Americans don't want to change the system that made it possible.)

Blame the Birth Rate

One fact that hasn't been part of the immigration debate is this: during the past two decades our national birth rate has dropped to just below the 2.1 births-per-woman replacement rate. So we really do need to "import" people because — to put it bluntly — we haven't bred enough of them ourselves to do all the work that needs to be done in an affluent, ageing society like ours. But then, we've always needed "more" people to do the work we want done. And we've always brought them in from elsewhere—as immigrants.

Yet today we have millions of foreigners among us who have come here to work, but not to immigrate. Our politicians tell us that we must accept this because — for the first time in our history — we've reached that point when we need "guest workers" who aren't immigrants to keep our economy growing. If this is true — and isn't it odd that no one has troubled to explain why it's true — then we must find some way to distinguish between "immigrants" and "guest workers" so that they aren't treated the same just because they both are here. And if it isn't true that our continued economic growth requires "guest workers" who aren't immigrants — then the entire concept of "guest workers" that lies at the core of virtually every proposal now before Congress, including amnesty for those who are here illegally, must be abandoned in favor of something that makes sense.

Until our elected officials come to grips with the real issue that's troubling ordinary Americans — not a growing population of foreigners among us, but rather a growing population of foreigners among us who aren't behaving like immigrants — public frustration will grow no matter what bill Congress passes in the coming weeks. It could lead to the kind of political explosion that none of us really wants.   13

•   •   •

Comprehension

1. How does Meyer define *immigration*? What does he say is the end result of the process?
2. What does Meyer see as the two different groups of Hispanics now in the United States? Why does he think the behavior of the second group he describes is so "offensive" (8)?
3. What is Meyer's point in paragraph 10?
4. What problem does Meyer identify in this essay? What does he believe should be done to remedy this problem? What does he say might be the result of not facing the problem?

Purpose and Audience

1. How would you define Meyer's intended audience? Does he seem to assume that this audience generally agrees with him or disagrees with him? What makes you think so?
2. What effect do you think Meyer hopes his argument will have on "the immigration debate now raging in Washington" (1)?
3. To whom does Meyer seem to be appealing in paragraph 3? What purpose does this paragraph serve in his larger argument?

Style and Structure

1. Meyer's second paragraph consists of just one sentence. Why might he have chosen not to conclude the preceding paragraph or open the following paragraph with this sentence?

2. In paragraphs 2, 3, 6, 8, 9, 10, 11, and 12, Meyer places specific words and phrases in quotation marks, particularly "immigrants" and "guest workers." Why does he do so? What is his intended effect?

3. Meyer waits until his final paragraph to state his thesis. What reason might he have for doing so? Do you think this was a wise decision?

4. Meyer does not acknowledge any potential objections to his argument. Why might he not have felt the need to do so? Do you think his argument would be strengthened if he had?

5. Meyer mixes relatively formal language with informal phrases such as "make darn sure they do" (3), "dead tired" (3), "kids" (4, 10), "blather on" (8), and "for crying out loud" (9). What is the effect of his inclusion of such informal language?

Vocabulary Projects

1. Define each of the following words as it is used in this selection.

   irresistible (4)   incessantly (9)
   comprised (6)   disingenuous (9)
   amnesty (8)

2. In his opening and in his conclusion, Meyer uses very strong language to describe the potential outcome of the immigration issue he is writing about ("shatter both parties' bases," "the kind of political explosion none of us really wants"). Do you think the argument he presents justifies such strong language? Why, or why not?

Journal Entry

In paragraph 3, Meyer summarizes how "ordinary Americans" define *immigration*. Do you think this definition is accurate, or do you think it stereotypes immigrants?

Writing Workshop

1. **Synthesizing Sources**   Meyer's essay was written partly in response to the proposed legislation summarized in Dianne Feinstein's statement before the Senate. How might Feinstein respond to Meyer? Write a brief essay in which you use Feinstein's stance on this issue and the evidence she presents to critique Meyer's position. Include parenthetical documentation and a works-cited page. (See the Appendix for information on documentation formats.)

2. Do you agree with Meyer's statement that the children of immigrants will ultimately "lose their accents, move into the mainstream, and retain little of their heritage except a few words of [their parents'] language" (4)? Should becoming an American mean losing any but the most distant connection with one's heritage? Write an essay in which you take a

position on this issue. Before you write your essay, you might want to look at wikihow.com/Lose-Your-Accent, a Web site that gives immigrants tips on how to lose their accents.

3. Write an email to your congressional representative in which you offer your views on the concept of guest workers. Do you feel that the U.S. economy needs such workers? What benefits should be available to them? What should be expected of them?

Combining the Patterns

The heart of Meyer's argument is developed as a **comparison and contrast**. How does he go about developing this comparison? Why is it essential to the presentation of his case?

Thematic Connections

- "Indian Education" (page 135)
- "Suicide Note" (page 377)
- "Tortillas" (page 524)

To Reunite a Nation

Outspoken conservative columnist and commentator Patrick Buchanan began his career in 1961 as a reporter with the *St. Louis Globe-Democrat*. Following Nixon's election to the presidency in 1968, Buchanan joined the new administration as a special assistant and speechwriter. When Nixon resigned in 1974, Buchanan briefly advised President Gerald Ford before leaving the White House to return to his role as a newspaper, radio, and television commentator. After a brief stint as director of communications for Ronald Reagan, Buchanan, again a popular columnist, ran unsuccessfully for the Republican presidential nomination in 1992. Then, in 2000, he ran for president on the Reform Party ticket, ultimately receiving less than 1 percent of the vote. Buchanan is now a political commentator for MSNBC and a regular on PBS's *The McLaughlin Group*. He also contributes to a variety of conservative publications and has published nine books, most recently *Day of Reckoning: How Hubris, Ideology, and Greed Are Tearing America Apart* (2007). In the following speech, delivered in 2000 during his presidential campaign, Buchanan proposes a plan for immigration reform.

Background on race and ethnicity in the United States
The most recent figures from the U.S. Census Bureau show that 73.9 percent of Americans identify themselves as white, 12.4 percent as black or African American, 4.4 percent as Asian, 0.8 percent as American Indian or Alaskan native, 0.1 percent as Native Hawaiian or other Pacific Islander, 6.3 percent as some other race, and 2 percent as two or more races. In addition, some 15 percent of respondents identify as Hispanic or Latino, regardless of race, with more than half of these claiming Mexican heritage. So, clearly, the United States remains by a large majority a predominantly white, non-Hispanic nation. Why, then, is there a perception among some that the population of Hispanic immigrants and their children and grandchildren is so high? One reason is that there are more Hispanics than ever before, so they are more visible. Another reason is that Hispanics are concentrated in certain parts of the country, giving the impression that they are more numerous than they acutally are. For example, almost 35 percent of Californians identify as Hispanic. Compare those numbers with Pennsylvania, another populous state, where fewer than 5 percent identify as Hispanic. In fact, in only eight states do Hispanics constitute 15 percent or more of the population. Everywhere else, their percentages are lower than average, with the population of twenty-four states being under 5 percent Hispanic.

Let me begin with a story: in 1979, Deng Xiaoping arrived here on an official visit. China was emerging from the Cultural Revolution, and poised to embark on the capitalist road. When President Carter sat down with Mr. Deng, he told him he was concerned over the right of the Chinese people to emigrate. The Jackson-Vanik amendment, Mr. Carter said, prohibited granting most favored nation trade status to regimes that did not allow their people to emigrate.

"Well, Mr. President," Deng cheerfully replied, "just how many Chinese do you want? Ten million? Twenty million? Thirty million?" Deng's answer stopped Carter cold. In a few words, the Chinese leader had driven home a point Mr. Carter seemed not to have grasped: hundreds of millions of people would emigrate to America in an eyelash, far more than we could take in, far more than our existing population of 270 million, if we threw open our borders. And though the United States takes in more people than any other nation, it still restricts immigration to about one million a year, with three or four hundred thousand managing to enter every year illegally.

There is more to be gleaned from this encounter. Mr. Carter's response was a patriotic, or, if you will, a nationalistic response. Many might even label it xenophobic. The president did not ask whether bringing in 10 million Chinese would be good for them. He had suddenly grasped that the real issue was how many would be good for America? Mr. Carter could have asked another question: Which Chinese immigrants would be best for America? It would make a world of difference whether China sent over 10 million college graduates or 10 million illiterate peasants, would it not?

Since the Carter-Deng meeting, America has taken in 20 million immigrants, many from China and Asia, many more from Mexico, Central America, and the Caribbean, and a few from Europe. Social scientists now know a great deal about the impact of this immigration.

Like all of you, I am awed by the achievements of many recent immigrants. Their contributions to Silicon Valley are extraordinary. The overrepresentation of Asian-born kids in advanced high school math and science classes is awesome, and, to the extent that it is achieved by a superior work ethic, these kids are setting an example for all of us. The contributions that immigrants make in small businesses and hard work in tough jobs that don't pay well merits our admiration and deepest respect. And, many new immigrants show a visible love of this country and an appreciation of freedom that makes you proud to be an American.

Northern Virginia, where I live, has experienced a huge and sudden surge in immigration. It has become a better place, in some ways, but nearly unrecognizable in others, and no doubt worse in some realms, a complicated picture over all. But it is clear to anyone living in a state like California or Virginia that the great immigration wave, set in motion by the Immigration Act of 1965, has put an indelible mark upon America.

We are no longer a biracial society; we are now a multiracial society. We no longer struggle simply to end the divisions and close the gaps between black and white Americans; we now grapple, often awkwardly, with an unprecedented ethnic diversity. We also see the troubling signs of a national turning away from the idea that we are one people, and the emergence of a radically different idea, that we are separate ethnic nations within a nation.

Al Gore caught the change in a revealing malapropism. Mr. Gore trans- 8
lated the national slogan, "E Pluribus Unum," which means "Out of many, one," into "Out of one, many." Behind it, an inadvertent truth: America is Balkanizing as never before.

Five years ago, a bipartisan presidential commission, chaired by 9
Barbara Jordan, presented its plans for immigration reform. The commission called for tighter border controls, tougher penalties on businesses that hire illegal aliens, a new system for selecting legal immigrants, and a lowering of the annual number to half a million. President Clinton endorsed the recommendations. But after ethnic groups and corporate lobbies for foreign labor turned up the heat, he backed away.

The data that support the Jordan recommendations are more refined 10
today. We have a National Academy of Sciences report on the economic consequences of immigration, a Rand study, and work by Harvard's George Borjas and other scholars. All agree that new immigration to the United States is heavily skewed to admitting the less skilled. Unlike other industrialized democracies, the United States allots the vast majority of its visas on the basis of whether new immigrants are related to recent immigrants, rather than whether they have the skills or education America needs. This is why it is so difficult for Western and Eastern Europeans to come here, while almost entire villages from El Salvador have come in.

Major consequences flow from having an immigration stream that 11
ignores education or skills. Immigrants are now more likely than native-born Americans to lack a high school education. More than a quarter of our immigrant population receives some kind of welfare, compared to 15 percent of native-born. Before the 1965 bill, immigrants were less likely to receive welfare. In states with many immigrants, the fiscal impact is dramatic. The National Academy of Sciences contends that immigration has raised the annual taxes of each native household in California by $1,200 a year. But the real burden is felt by native-born workers, for whom mass immigration means stagnant or falling wages, especially for America's least skilled.

There are countervailing advantages. Businesses can hire new immi- 12
grants at lower pay; and consumers gain because reduced labor costs produce cheaper goods and services. But, generally speaking, the gains from high immigration go to those who use the services provided by new immigrants.

If you are likely to employ a gardener or housekeeper, you may be 13
financially better off. If you work as a gardener or housekeeper, or at a factory job in which unskilled immigrants are rapidly joining the labor force, you lose. The last twenty years of immigration have thus brought about a redistribution of wealth in America, from less-skilled workers and toward employers. Mr. Borjas estimates that one half of the relative fall in the

wages of high school graduates since the 1980s can be traced directly to mass immigration.

At some point, this kind of wealth redistribution, from the less well off   14
to the affluent, becomes malignant. In the 1950s and '60s, Americans with low reading and math scores could aspire to and achieve the American Dream of a middle class lifestyle. That is less realistic today. Americans today who do poorly in high school are increasingly condemned to a low-wage existence; and mass immigration is a major reason why.

There is another drawback to mass immigration: a delay in the assimi-   15
lation of immigrants that can deepen our racial and ethnic divisions. As in Al Gore's "Out of One, Many."

Concerns of this sort are even older than the Republic itself. In 1751,   16
Ben Franklin asked: "Why should Pennsylvania, founded by the English, become a Colony of Aliens, who will shortly be so numerous as to German-ize us instead of our Anglifying them?" Franklin would never find out if his fears were justified. German immigration was halted by the Seven Years War; then slowed by the Great Lull in immigration that followed the Amer-ican Revolution. A century and half later, during what is called the Great Wave, the same worries were in the air.

In 1915 Theodore Roosevelt told the Knights of Columbus: "There is   17
no room in this country for hyphenated Americanism. . . . The one abso-lutely certain way of bringing this nation to ruin, of preventing all possibil-ity of its continuing to be a nation at all, would be to permit it to become a tangle of squabbling nationalities." Congress soon responded by enacting an immigration law that brought about a virtual forty-year pause to digest, assimilate, and Americanize the diverse immigrant wave that had rolled in between 1890 and 1920.

Today, once again, it is impossible not to notice the conflicts generated   18
by a new "hyphenated Americanism." In Los Angeles, two years ago, there was an anguishing afternoon in the Coliseum where the U.S. soccer team was playing Mexico. The Mexican-American crowd showered the U.S. team with water bombs, beer bottles, and trash. The Star Spangled Banner was hooted and jeered. A small contingent of fans of the American team had garbage hurled at them. The American players later said that they were bet-ter received in Mexico City than in their own country.

Last summer, El Cenizo, a small town in south Texas, adopted Spanish   19
as its official language. All town documents are now to be written, and all town business conducted, in Spanish. Any official who cooperates with U.S. immigration authorities was warned he or she would be fired. To this day, Governor Bush is reluctant to speak out on this de facto secession of a tiny Texas town to Mexico.

Voting in referendums that play a growing part in the politics of Cali-   20
fornia is now breaking down sharply on ethnic lines. Hispanic voters opposed Proposition 187 to cut off welfare to illegal aliens, and they rallied against it under Mexican flags. They voted heavily in favor of quotas and ethnic preferences in the 1996 California Civil Rights Initiative, and, again,

to keep bilingual education in 1998. These votes suggest that in the California of the future, when Mexican-American voting power catches up with Mexican-American population, any bid to end racial quotas by referendum will fail. A majority of the state's most populous immigrant group now appears to favor set-asides and separate language programs, rather than to be assimilated into the American mainstream.

The list of troubling signs can be extended. One may see them in   21
the Wen Ho Lee nuclear secrets case, as many Chinese-Americans immediately concluded the United States was prosecuting Mr. Lee for racist reasons.

Regrettably, a cultural Marxism called political correctness is taking   22
root that makes it impossible to discuss immigration in any but the most glowing terms. In New York City billboards that made the simple point that immigration increases crowding and that polls show most Americans want immigration rates reduced were forced down under circumstances that came very close to government-sponsored censorship. The land of the free is becoming intolerant of some kinds of political dissent.

Sociologist William Frey has documented an out-migration of black   23
and white Americans from California, some of them seeking better labor market conditions, others in search of a society like the one they grew up in. In California and other high immigration states, one also sees the rise of gated communities where the rich close themselves off from the society their own policies produce.

I don't want to overstate the negatives. But in too many cases the   24
American Melting Pot has been reduced to a simmer. At present rates, mass immigration reinforces ethnic subcultures, reduces the incentives of newcomers to learn English, and extends the life of linguistic ghettos that might otherwise be melded into the great American mainstream. If we want to assimilate new immigrants — and we have no choice if we are to remain one nation — we must slow down the pace of immigration.

Whatever its shortcomings, the United States has done far better at   25
alleviating poverty than most countries. But an America that begins to think of itself as made up of disparate peoples will find social progress far more difficult. It is far easier to look the other way when the person who needs help does not speak the same language, or share a common culture or common history.

Americans who feel it natural and right that their taxes support the   26
generation that fought World War II — will they feel the same way about those from Fukien Province or Zanzibar? If America continues on its present course, it could rapidly become a country with no common language, no common culture, no common memory, and no common identity. And that country will find itself very short of the social cohesion that makes compassion possible.

None of us are true universalists: we feel responsibility for others   27
because we share with them common bonds — common history and a common fate. When these are gone, this country will be a far harsher place.

That is why I am proposing immigration reform to make it possible to fully assimilate the 30 million immigrants who have arrived in the last thirty years. As President, I will ask Congress to reduce new entry visas to 300,000 a year, which is enough to admit immediate family members of new citizens, with plenty of room for many thousands with the special talents or skills our society needs. If after several years, it becomes plain that the United States needs more immigrants because of labor shortages, it should implement a point system similar to that of Canada and Australia, and allocate visas on a scale which takes into account education, knowledge of English, job skills, age, and relatives in the United States. 28

I will also make the control of illegal immigration a national priority. Recent reports of thousands of illegals streaming across the border into Arizona, and the sinister and cruel methods used to smuggle people by ship into the United States, demand that we regain control of our borders. For a country that cannot control its borders isn't fully sovereign; indeed, it is not even a country anymore. 29

Without these reforms, America will begin a rapid drift into uncharted waters. We shall become a country with a dying culture and deepening divisions along the lines of race, class, income, and language. We shall lose for our children and for the children of the 30 million who have come here since 1970 the last best hope of earth. We will betray them all — by denying them the great and good country we were privileged to grow in. We just can't do that. 30

With immigration at the reduced rate I recommend, America will still be a nation of immigrants. We will still have the benefit of a large, steady stream of people from all over the world whose life dream is to be like us — Americans. But, with this reform, America will become again a country engaged in the mighty work of assimilation, of shaping new Americans, a proud land where newcomers give up their hyphens, the great American melting pot does its work again, and scores of thousands of immigrant families annually ascend from poverty into the bosom of Middle America to live the American dream. 31

• • •

Comprehension

1. What is the point of the story about Jimmy Carter and Deng Xiaoping with which Buchanan opens his essay?
2. How, according to Buchanan, has the United States changed since "the great immigration wave, set in motion by the Immigration Act of 1965" (6)?
3. What does Buchanan see as the disadvantages and advantages of current immigration policy? Does he think one outweighs the other?
4. What is Buchanan's point in paragraphs 18–21?
5. What concerns does Buchanan raise in paragraphs 24–27?

6. Summarize what Buchanan proposes to do as president to reform immigration policies.

Purpose and Audience

1. Knowing that this selection was written during Buchanan's bid for the presidency in 2000, what do you think its purpose was?
2. Does Buchanan think his audience's views on current U.S. immigration policy are neutral, positive, or negative? What makes you think so?
3. To whom is Buchanan appealing in paragraphs 13–14? Does this group seem like a natural political constituency for him? Explain.
4. In paragraph 27, Buchanan writes, "None of us are true universalists." What does he mean?

Style and Structure

1. One could say that Buchanan's thesis is, "The United States should enact comprehensive immigration reform." Where in his argument does he come closest to stating this thesis?
2. Buchanan organizes his argument into seven sections: paragraphs 1–3, 4–8, 9–15, 16–17, 18–23, 24–27, and 28–31. What is the focus of each section, and why are they presented in the order in which they are?
3. How would you describe Buchanan's writing style? Consider the level of formality of his language, his sentence and paragraph length, and the image he presents of himself.
4. Buchanan acknowledges in paragraph 5 what he admires about "the achievements of many recent immigrants." Why does he do this early in the essay rather than later? Do you see this as the most effecive strategy?
5. Evaluate Buchanan's last paragraph. How does his language change here, and why do you suppose it does?

Vocabulary Projects

1. Define each of the following words as it is used in this selection.

xenophobic (3)	stagnant (11)	referendums (20)
unprecedented (7)	countervailing (12)	linguistic (24)
malapropism (8)	redistribution (13)	alleviating (25)
inadvertent (8)	malignant (14)	cohesion (26)
Balkanizing (8)	assimilation (15)	sovereign (29)
skewed (10)		

2. In paragraph 22, Buchanan refers to "political correctness." Go to the Web site reference.com and determine what this phrase means and how it is generally used. What role does the phrase play in Buchanan's overall argument?

Journal Entry

What is your view of the American Melting Pot that Buchanan writes about in paragraph 24? How would you define this concept? Do you agree with Buchanan that the Melting Pot is something Americans should try to achieve but are failing to do so? Or do you take a different position?

Writing Workshop

1. **Synthesizing Sources** Based on the essays in this casebook as well as your own observations and experiences, write an essay in which you present your proposal for immigration reform. Do you think immigration levels should be reduced, be expanded, or remain the same? Would you change the way applicants for green cards are determined? How would you propose dealing with illegal immigrants currently living in the United States? What is your view of guest worker policy? Consider any of these topics, as well as others that strike you as important. Be sure to include parenthetical documentation for the essays you cite and to include a works-cited page. (See the Appendix for information on documentation formats.)

2. **Synthesizing Sources** How might Buchanan respond to Dianne Feinstein's Senate statement regarding immigration reform? Write an essay based on Buchanan's stance here that critiques the proposals Feinstein articulates. Be sure to document your references to Feinstein and Buchanan and to include a works-cited page. (See the Appendix for information on documentation formats.)

3. Buchanan criticizes the current state of "hyphenated Americanism" (18). What does he mean by this phrase? (You might want to go to the Web site urbandictionary.com to get a full definition of *hyphenated Americans*.) What are your views on the many groups within the greater U.S. community that define themselves as hyphenated Americans? Write an essay in which you describe the results of "hyphenated Americanism" as positive, negative, or both.

Combining the Patterns

What patterns does Buchanan use to develop the topic sentence that begins paragraph 18?

Thematic Connections

- "Sixty-Nine Cents" (page 102)
- "Mother Tongue" (page 477)
- "Tortillas" (page 524)

CASEBOOK

Is There a Case for Torture?

Torture, from the Latin for "to twist," has a long history in the West. In ancient Greece, slaves could be tortured to elicit evidence at trial, and Roman law allowed torture to obtain evidence of treason or crimes against the state. In the Middle Ages, a form of torture known as the ordeal was sometimes used to determine an accused person's innocence or guilt; in the case of ordeal by fire, for example, those accused were required to walk barefoot across hot coals and would be judged innocent if they escaped unhurt, guilty if they did not. In 1252, the Roman Catholic Church, influenced by Roman law regarding treason, sanctioned the use of torture to elicit confessions from accused heretics, as well as to force them to accuse others. With the church as their model, civil tribunals across Europe adopted torture as a means of coercing confessions for certain crimes although the practice had died out by 1800.

In the twentieth century, the Nazis' Gestapo developed what were called "sharpened interrogation" techniques to be used on prisoners who were deemed sources of information regarding hostilities toward the state; these initially included "deprivation of sleep, exhaustion exercises, but also the resort to blows with a stick (in case of more than twenty blows a doctor must be present)." Testimony following World War II detailed the Gestapo's use of various torture implements, beatings, and ice-cold baths to elicit information. Nazi atrocities led to the adoption of the United Nations Universal Declaration of Human Rights in 1948. Article 5 of that document reads: "No one shall be subjected to torture or to cruel, inhuman, or degrading treatment or punishment." The 1949 Geneva Convention pact on the treatment of prisoners of war also includes specific protections against torture: "Prisoners of war must at all times be humanely treated. . . . Likewise, prisoners of war must at all times be protected, particularly against acts of violence or intimidation and against insults and public curiosity" (Article 13). "No physical or mental torture, nor any other form of coercion, may be inflicted on prisoners of war to secure from them information of any kind whatever. Prisoners of war who refuse to answer may not be threatened, insulted, or exposed to any unpleasant or disadvantageous treatment of any kind" (Article 17).

Still, in the intervening years, repressive regimes — from Stalinist Russia to current-day Zimbabwe — have resorted to torture to intimidate dissidents and subversives, to punish those seen as disloyal, and to maintain power. Some historians go so far as to suggest that the years since the turn of the twentieth century have seen more widespread instances of torture than in any other era.

The issue has hit home especially hard in the United States in the aftermath of the terrorist bombings of September 11, 2001. In waging its worldwide war on terror, the Bush administration came under heavy fire for setting aside long-standing policies against torture. Shocking videos of abuse by U.S. military personnel in the Iraqi prison camp at Abu Ghraib, the alleged mistreatment of suspected terrorists being held indefinitely at Guantanamo, and the administration's admission of sanctioning a torture technique known as waterboarding to elicit confessions from Al-Qaeda members have all led to a fierce debate about the morality and even the effectiveness of torture as a defensive tool.

That debate is reflected in the readings in this casebook. "The Case for Torture," written by philosophy professor Michael Levin in 1982 and therefore not prompted by the events since 9/11, argues that "there are situations in which torture is not merely permissible but morally manda-tory," as when authorities capture a terrorist who has hidden an atomic bomb in a major metropolitan area. In "The Case for Torture Warrants," attorney Alan Dershowitz a argues for granting law enforcement person-nel warrants in advance giving them the authority to use torture to elicit information from particular suspects. In "How Much Torture Is OK?," columnist Cathy Young urges that the United States maintain a "'no tor-ture' stance . . . with tacit acknowledgement that, under narrow and extreme circumstances, the rules may be bent." Finally, Senator John McCain, who experienced torture as a prisoner of war in Vietnam, argues that, Levin's position notwithstanding, no "scenario requires us to write into law an exception to our treaty and moral obligations that would per-mit cruel, inhumane, and degrading treatment."

MICHAEL LEVIN

The Case for Torture

Michael Levin (b. 1944) is a professor of philosophy at the City College of New York. His academic focus is on theories of knowledge, but he has sparked considerable controversy because of his negative stances regarding feminism and homosexuality and his belief that genetic differences are responsible for IQ disparities between the races. The author of articles in a variety of academic journals, he has also contributed to conservative periodicals aimed at a popular audience, such as *Commentary* and the *National Review*, and has published several books, including *Feminism and Freedom* (1987), *Why Race Matters* (1997), and, with Laurence Thomas, *Sexual Orientation and Human Rights* (1999). The following essay originally appeared in *Newsweek* in 1982, long before the terrorist acts of 2001 brought the question of torture to wide public attention.

Background on torture purposes and techniques

Broadly speaking, governments and governmental authorities have used torture for four purposes: to obtain a confession; to elicit information about other criminalized activities and accomplices or to lead authorities to where something has been hidden; to inflict punishment; and to intimidate the prisoner or others into certain actions or behaviors. In places where there is little respect for human rights, the infliction of physical pain through violence is a common practice, whether through beating and kicking, burning, mutilation, or worse. In instances where evidence of the torture would create trouble for authorities, pain may be inflicted through electroshock instruments or by trussing the prisoner up in a grossly unnatural position, then tightening the bonds to make the position increasingly painful. Prisoners may also be forced to stand or to hold an uncomfortable position for many hours. Psychological torture includes sleep deprivation, depriving prisoners of oxygen by submerging them underwater or covering their heads with a tight-fitting bag, staged executions, making the prisoner listen to the screams of family members or other detainees in another room, and sexual humiliation.

It is generally assumed that torture is impermissible, a throwback to a more brutal age. Enlightened societies reject it outright, and regimes suspected of using it risk the wrath of the United States. 1

I believe this attitude is unwise. There are situations in which torture is not merely permissible but morally mandatory. Moreover, these situations are moving from the realm of imagination to fact. 2

Suppose a terrorist has hidden an atomic bomb on Manhattan Island which will detonate at noon on July 4 unless . . . (here follow the usual demands for money and release of his friends from jail). Suppose, further, that he is caught at 10 A.M. of the fateful day, but — preferring death to 3 failure — won't disclose where the bomb is. What do we do? If we follow due process — wait for his lawyer, arraign him — millions of people will die. If the only way to save those lives is to subject the terrorist to the most excruciating possible pain, what grounds can there be for not doing so? I suggest there are none. In any case, I ask you to face the question with an open mind.

Torturing the terrorist is unconstitutional? Probably. But millions of 4 lives surely outweigh constitutionality. Torture is barbaric? Mass murder is far more barbaric. Indeed, letting millions of innocents die in deference to one who flaunts his guilt is moral cowardice, an unwillingness to dirty one's hands. If you caught the terrorist, could you sleep nights knowing that millions died because you couldn't bring yourself to apply the electrodes?

Once you concede that torture is justified in extreme cases, you have 5 admitted that the decision to use torture is a matter of balancing innocent lives against the means needed to save them. You must now face more realistic cases involving more modest numbers. Someone plants a bomb on a jumbo jet. He alone can disarm it, and his demands cannot be met (or if they can, we refuse to set a precedent by yielding to his threats). Surely we can, we must, do anything to the extortionist to save the passengers. How can we tell three hundred, or one hundred, or ten people who never asked to be put in danger, "I'm sorry, you'll have to die in agony, we just couldn't bring ourselves to . . ."

Here are the results of an informal poll about a third, hypothetical, 6 case. Suppose a terrorist group kidnapped a newborn baby from a hospital. I asked four mothers if they would approve of torturing kidnappers if that were necessary to get their own newborns back. All said yes, the most "liberal" adding that she would like to administer it herself.

I am not advocating torture as punishment. Punishment is addressed 7 to deeds irrevocably past. Rather, I am advocating torture as an acceptable measure for preventing future evils. So understood, it is far less objectionable than many extant punishments. Opponents of the death penalty, for example, are forever insisting that executing a murderer will not bring back his victim (as if the purpose of capital punishment were supposed to be resurrection, not deterrence or retribution). But torture, in the cases described, is intended not to bring anyone back but to keep innocents from being dispatched. The most powerful argument against using torture as a punishment or to secure confessions is that such practices disregard the rights of the individual. Well, if the individual is all that important — and he is — it is correspondingly important to protect the rights of individuals threatened by terrorists. If life is so valuable that it must never be taken, the lives of the innocents must be saved even at the price of hurting the one who endangers them.

Better precedents for torture are assassination and preemptive attack. 8 No Allied leader would have flinched at assassinating Hitler, had that been possible. (The Allies did assassinate Heydrich.) Americans would be angered to learn that Roosevelt could have had Hitler killed in 1943 —

thereby shortening the war and saving millions of lives — but refused on moral grounds. Similarly, if nation A learns that nation B is about to launch an unprovoked attack, A has a right to save itself by destroying B's military capability first. In the same way, if the police can by torture save those who would otherwise die at the hands of kidnappers or terrorists, they must.

There is an important difference between terrorists and their victims   9
that should mute talk of the terrorists' "rights." The terrorist's victims are at risk unintentionally, not having asked to be endangered. But the terrorist knowingly initiated his actions. Unlike his victims, he volunteered for the risks of his deed. By threatening to kill for profit or idealism, he renounces civilized standards, and he can have no complaint if civilization tries to thwart him by whatever means necessary.

Just as torture is justified only to save lives (not extort confessions or   10
recantations), it is justifiably administered only to those known to hold innocent lives in their hands. Ah, but how can the authorities ever be sure they have the right malefactor? Isn't there a danger of error and abuse? Won't We turn into Them?

Questions like these are disingenuous in a world in which terrorists   11
proclaim themselves and perform for television. The name of their game is public recognition. After all, you can't very well intimidate a government into releasing your freedom fighters unless you announce that it is your group that has seized its embassy. "Clear guilt" is difficult to define, but when 40 million people see a group of masked gunmen seize an airplane on the evening news, there is not much question about who the perpetrators are. There will be hard cases where the situation is murkier. Nonetheless, a line demarcating the legitimate use of torture can be drawn. Torture only the obviously guilty, and only for the sake of saving innocents, and the line between Us and Them will remain clear.

There is little danger that the Western democracies will lose their way   12
if they choose to inflict pain as one way of preserving order. Paralysis in the face of evil is the greater danger. Someday soon a terrorist will threaten tens of thousands of lives, and torture will be the only way to save them. We had better start thinking about this.

· · ·

Comprehension

1. What point does Levin concede in paragraph 1? Why do you think he does this?

2. Under what specific circumstances does Levin call for torture?

3. How realistic are the situations Levin presents? Does the low probability of their happening diminish his case for the use of torture?

4. How does Levin address the possibility that the wrong people might be tortured?

Purpose and Audience

1. What is Levin's purpose in writing this essay? Do you think he has achieved his purpose? Are you convinced by his argument?
2. Who is Levin's intended audience? How can you tell?
3. What is Levin's thesis? Where does he state it? Why do you think he states it at that point?
4. Characterize the tone of the essay. Is it reasonable? Does the essay's tone help Levin to make his point?

Style and Structure

1. Explain Levin's use of the "ticking time bomb" scenario in paragraph 3. Is this a convincing example? Why, or why not?
2. In paragraph 4, Levin asks three questions and answers the first two but not the third. What is the effect of this strategy? Do you see any problems in his using such a strategy?
3. In paragraph 5, Levin writes, "Once you concede that torture is justified in extreme cases, you have admitted . . ." Is this a fair statement, or is Levin **begging the question**?
4. Levin provides three scenarios where he thinks torture might be appropriate: the atomic bomb in paragraph 3, the bomb on the jet in paragraph 5, and the kidnapped baby in paragraph 6. What is Levin's purpose in presenting these scenarios in this order?

Vocabulary Projects

1. Define each of the following words as it is used in this selection.

impermissible (1)	concede (5)	idealism (9)
fateful (3)	hypothetical (6)	recantations (10)
deference (4)	advocating (7)	murkier (11)

2. In paragraph 4, Levin says, "letting millions of innocents die in deference to one who flaunts his guilt is moral cowardice." Go to the Web site dictionary.com, and look up *flaunts*. How is the meaning of *flaunt* different from the meaning of *flout*, a word with which it is frequently confused?

Journal Entry

Consider the ways popular culture has influenced how we think about torture. You might consider television shows that include scenes of torture, such as *Lost, The Sopranos,* and *24*. Are such portrayals realistic? Why or why not?

Writing Workshop

1. Levin claims that the situations that call for torture are "moving from the realm of imagination to fact" (2). Is he correct? Write an essay in which you cite some examples to support your position.

2. In paragraph 11, Levin proposes the following: "Torture only the obviously guilty, and only for the sake of saving innocents, and the line between Us and Them will remain clear" (11). Is Levin guilty of **begging the question**? Is the situation really as simple as he says it is? Explain your reasoning in an argumentative essay.

3. Levin writes, "I am not advocating torture as punishment. Punishment is addressed to deeds irrevocably past" (7). Do you agree with the distinction that Levin makes between punishment and torture? Do you think there is ever a case where torture is an appropriate punishment for a crime? Explain your answer.

Combining the Patterns

In paragraphs 3, 5, and 6, Levin uses **examples** of cases where he feels that torture would be appropriate. What is the purpose of these examples? Would his argument succeed without them? Would it even be possible without them? Why or why not?

Thematic Connections

- "The Power of Words in Wartime" (page 363)
- "The Ways We Lie" (page 485)

ALAN M. DERSHOWITZ

The Case for Torture Warrants

Alan Dershowitz (b. 1938) is the Felix Frankfurter Professor of Law at Harvard Law School. Long a proponent of civil liberties, he has taken on many controversial cases, often involving celebrities such as junk bond king Michael Milken, televangelist Jim Bakker, and heavyweight boxing champion Mike Tyson. Dershowitz also advised the team that secured O.J. Simpson's acquittal in his wife's murder trial. Since 1982, Dershowitz has published more than twenty books, including *Reasonable Doubts: The Criminal Justice System and the O. J. Simpson Case* (1996), *Why Terrorism Works: Understanding the Threat, Responding to the Challenge* (2002), *Shouting Fire: Civil Liberties in a Turbulent Age* (2002), *The Case for Israel* (2003), and *Blasphemy: How the Religious Right Is Hijacking the Declaration of Independence* (2007). He has also written more than three hundred op-ed columns, contributed to a variety of newsmagazines, and appeared as a commentator on numerous television news programs. The following essay was published some six months after the terrorist attacks of 2001.

Background on the effectiveness of torture in eliciting information
In the absence of any recent significant scientific research (due partly to the fact that, given the nature of the subject, hard unbiased information is difficult to come by), experts differ as to the effectiveness of torture as a means of eliciting information from prisoners. On the one hand are those like retired army Colonel Jack Jacobs, now an analyst for MSNBC, who says, "You need to be aggressive to get the information you want, but if you treat people inhumanely, they're just going to tell you what they think you want to hear. They'll do anything just to get the mistreatment to stop, so you get nothing from mistreatment." Jacobs goes on to say that while working as an intelligence officer in Vietnam he got the most useful information by giving detainees "cigarettes, medical care, food, and water. Almost always, you get the best success from treating people properly." On the other hand is the position articulated by Robert Kaplan, writing in a review of the 2004 book *The Interrogators: Inside the Secret War against Al Qaeda* authored pseudonymously by an Army interrogator: "Sadly, it is no use saying torture never works, because as the French authorities learned in Algeria, as the Filipinos learned with their own Muslim insurgents, and as the Dubai authorities learned with a Qaeda terrorist, it periodically does work, and in some instances can possibly avert a major attack. While it is true that the threat of torture . . . induces more anxiety among detainees than torture itself, that threat over time will carry little weight if it becomes widely known that the jailers have no record of following through."

Now that it has been disclosed that our government had information of "undetermined reliability," from an agent whose code name is Dragon- 1 fire, that New York City may have been targeted for a ten-kiloton nuclear weapon, the arguments for empowering law enforcement officials to do everything necessary to prevent a catastrophic terrorist attack are becoming more compelling. In the immediate aftermath of the September 11th attacks, FBI officials leaked a story about their inability to obtain information from suspected terrorists by conventional means, such as buying the information by offers of cash or leniency, or compelling the information by grants of immunity and threats of imprisonment for contempt of court. Those who leaked the story suggested that there may come a time when law enforcement officials might have to resort to unconventional means, including nonlethal torture. Thus began one of the most unusual debates in American legal and political history: should law enforcement be authorized to torture suspects who are thought to have information about a ticking bomb?

This ticking bomb scenario had long been a staple of legal and political philosophers who love to debate hypothetical cases that test the limit of absolute principles, such as the universal prohibition against the use of torture which has long been codified by international treaties. The ticking bomb case has also been debated, though not as a hypothetical case, in Israel, whose security services long claimed the authority to employ "moderate physical pressure" in order to secure real time intelligence from captured terrorists believed to know about impending terrorist acts. The moderate physical pressure employed by Israel was tougher than it sounds, but not nearly as tough as the brutal methods used by the French in interrogating suspected terrorists during the Algerian uprisings. The Israeli security service would take a suspected terrorist, tie him to a chair in an uncomfortable position for long periods of time with loud music blaring in the background, and then place a smelly sack over his head and shake him violently. Many tongues were loosened by this process and several terrorist acts prevented, without any suspects being seriously injured.

Torture, it turns out, can sometimes produce truthful information. The Israeli experience suggested that information obtained as a result of torture should never be believed, unless it can be independently confirmed, but such information can sometimes be self-proving, as when the subject leads law enforcement to the actual location of the bomb.

Nonetheless, the Israeli Supreme Court outlawed all use of even moderate, nonlethal physical pressure. It responded to the ticking bomb scenario by saying that if a security agent thought it was necessary to use physical pressure in order to prevent many deaths, he could take his chances, be prosecuted, and try to raise a defense of "necessity." In my book *Shouting Fire*, I wrote critically of this decision on the ground that it places security officials in an impossible dilemma. It would be better if any such official could seek an *advanced* ruling from a judge, as to whether physical pressure is warranted under the specific circumstances, in order to avoid being subject to an after the fact risk of imprisonment. Thus was born the proposal for a torture warrant.

Actually it was a rebirth, because half a millennium ago torture warrants were part of the law of Great Britain. They could be sought only in cases involving grave threats to the Crown or the Empire and were granted in about one case a year. Judges, even in those times, were extremely reluctant to authorize the thumb screw. 5

Why then should we even think about returning to an old practice that was abolished in England many years ago? The reason is because if we ever did have a ticking bomb case — especially a ticking nuclear bomb case — law enforcement officials would in fact resort to physical force, even torture, as a last resort. In speaking to numerous audiences since September 11th — audiences reflecting the entire breadth of the political and ideological spectrum — I have asked for a show of hands as to how many would favor the use of nonlethal torture in an actual ticking bomb case. The vast majority of audience members responded in the affirmative. So have law enforcement officials to whom I have spoken. If it is true that torture would in fact be used in such a case, then the important question becomes: is it better to have such torture done under the table, off the books, and below the radar screen — or in full view, with accountability and as part of our legal system? This is a very difficult question with powerful arguments on both sides. On the one hand, we have had experience with off the book policies such as President Nixon's "plumbers" and Oliver North's "foreign policy initiatives." In a democracy, accountability and visibility must be given high priorities. On the other hand, to legitimate torture and make it part of our legal system, even in extreme cases, risks reversion to a bad old time when torture was routine. 6

One key question is whether the availability of a torture warrant would, in fact, increase or decrease the actual amount of torture employed by law enforcement officials. I believe, though I cannot prove, that a formal requirement of a judicial warrant as a prerequisite to nonlethal torture would decrease the amount of physical violence directed against suspects. Judges would require compelling evidence before they would authorize so extraordinary a departure from our constitutional norms, and law enforcement officials would be reluctant to seek a warrant unless they had compelling evidence that the suspect had information needed to prevent an imminent terrorist attack. Moreover the rights of the suspect would be better protected with a warrant requirement. He would be granted immunity, told that he was now compelled to testify, threatened with imprisonment if he refuses to do so, and given the option of providing the requested information. Only if he refused to do what he was legally compelled to do — provide necessary information which could not incriminate him because of the immunity — would he be threatened with torture. Knowing that such a threat was authorized by the law, he might well provide the information. If he still refused to, he would be subjected to judicially monitored physical measures designed to cause excruciating pain without leaving any lasting damage. A sterilized needle underneath the nail might be 7 one such approved method. This may sound brutal, but it does not compare in brutality with the prospect of thousands of preventable deaths at the hands of fellow terrorists.

Let me cite two examples to demonstrate why I think there would be 8 less torture with a warrant requirement than without one. Recall the case of the alleged national security wiretap being placed on the phones of Martin Luther King by the Kennedy administration in the early 1960s. This was in the days when the attorney general could authorize a national security wiretap without a warrant. Today no judge would issue a warrant in a case as flimsy as that one. When Zaccarias Moussaui was detained after trying to learn how to fly an airplane, without wanting to know much about landing it, the government did not even seek a national security wiretap because its lawyers believed that a judge would not have granted one. If Moussaui's computer could have been searched without a warrant, it almost certainly would have been.

It is a great tragedy that we have to be discussing the horrors of tor- 9 ture. Some even believe that any discussion of this issue is beyond the pale of acceptable discourse in twenty-first-century America. But it is far better to discuss in advance the kinds of tragic choices we may encounter if we ever confront an actual ticking bomb terrorist case, than to wait until the case arises and let somebody make the decision in the heat of the moment.

An analogy to the shooting down of a passenger-filled hijacked airliner 10 heading toward a crowded office building will be instructive. Prior to September 11th it might have been a debatable issue whether the plane should be shot down. Today that is no longer debatable. But would anyone suggest that the decision should be made by a low ranking police officer? Of course not. We all agree that this should be a decision made at the highest level possible — by the President or the Secretary of Defense, if there is time to have such a dreadful decision made by accountable public figures. The use of torture in the ticking bomb case, like the shooting down of the hijacked airplane, involves a horrible choice of evils. In my view this choice should be made with visibility and accountability, either by a judicial officer or by the President of the United States. It should not be made by nameless and unaccountable law enforcement officials, risking imprisonment if they guess wrong.

• • •

Comprehension

1. What is the "ticking bomb scenario" (2)?
2. What is a torture warrant? According to Dershowitz, is a torture warrant a new idea?
3. According to Dershowitz, what is the purpose of a torture warrant, and who should be authorized to order one?

4. In paragraph 2, Dershowitz refers to "moderate physical pressure." How is that different from torture? When does it become torture? Where do you draw the line?

5. Why does Dershowitz think it is better to discuss torture now rather than to wait until we "confront an actual ticking bomb terrorist case" (9)?

Purpose and Audience

1. Why do you think Dershowitz wrote this essay? Is it successful as an argument? Why, or why not?

2. Identify Dershowitz's thesis. Where does it appear in the essay? If you had written this essay, would you have placed it there? Explain.

3. "Torture," Dershowitz writes in paragraph 3, "can sometimes produce truthful information." Does the use of the word *sometimes* help or harm his statement?

Style and Structure

1. Dershowitz begins by suggesting that "New York City may have been targeted for a ten-kiloton nuclear weapon . . ." Is this an effective opening? Why or why not? What does it accomplish?

2. At the end of paragraph 1, Dershowitz states the main question of his essay: "Should law enforcement be authorized to torture suspects who are thought to have information about a ticking bomb?" What is the purpose of including this question early in his essay? Do you think this is a good strategy?

3. In paragraph 5, Dershowitz looks back to the law of Great Britain five hundred years ago. How does this help his argument? Why do you suppose he didn't start with this information?

4. In paragraph 9, Dershowitz writes, "It is a great tragedy that we have to be discussing the horrors of torture." What is the effect of this statement? In your view, is it true?

Vocabulary Projects

1. Define each of the following words as it is used in this selection.

kiloton (1)	affirmative (6)
empowering (1)	requirement (7)
staple (2)	judicially (7)
warranted (4)	cite (8)
millennium (5)	discourse (9)
abolished (6)	accountable (10)

2. In his final paragraph, Dershowitz writes that using torture in the ticking bomb case "involves a horrible choice of evils." What is the effect of his using such strong language?

Journal Entry

In paragraph 2, Dershowitz refers to Israel's use of "moderate physical pressure" as support for his argument that the United States should in some cases authorize the use of torture. Do you think the actions of other countries are relevant to whether the United States should use torture? Explain your response.

Writing Workshop

1. **Synthesizing Sources**   Dershowitz is writing his essay after having read Michael Levin's "The Case for Torture." How can you tell? Point out places where you believe Dershowitz shows the influence of Levin's thinking. Be sure to document your references to Dershowitz and Levin and to include a works-cited page. (See the Appendix for information on documentation formats.)

2. Interview a veteran, and get his or her perspective on torture. Investigate the ways your subject's experiences with the military affect his or her position. Does your subject agree with the distinction that Levin makes between punishment and torture? Do you?

3. Reread the "Recognizing Fallacies" section of this chapter (page 559), and consider whether Dershowitz's essay contains any logical fallacies. For example, does Dershowitz make a **hasty generalization** when he justifies the use of torture in the United States by citing the actions of Israel and the French? Does he commit the **either/or fallacy** when he discusses the "ticking bomb" dilemma? Write an argumentative essay in which you present your findings.

Combining the Patterns

In paragraph 8, Dershowitz provides two **examples**. How do these examples contribute to his argument?

Thematic Connections

- "Thirty-Eight Who Saw Murder Didn't Call the Police" (page 120)
- "Get It Right: Privatize Executions" (page 299)
- "Five Ways to Kill a Man" (page 501)

CATHY YOUNG

How Much Torture Is OK?

Journalist Cathy Young was born in Russia in 1963 and immigrated to the United States in 1980. Author of articles and reviews for the *Washington Post*, the *New York Times*, *Newsday*, and the *New Republic*, among other periodicals, Young has also appeared as a commentator on NPR's *Talk of the Nation*, *CNN & Company*, and the *Today* show. In addition, Young has published two books, *Growing Up in Moscow: Memories of a Soviet Girlhood* (1989) and *Ceasefire!: Why Women and Men Must Join Forces to Achieve True Equality* (1999). The following essay appeared in the *Boston Globe* in late 2005.

Background on U.S.-sanctioned methods of torture

According to Darius Rejali, a professor of political science at Reed College, the three methods of torture apparently approved by the Bush administration for suspected terrorists and Iraqi insurgents have been used in various places throughout the twentieth century ("a tradition that includes colonial imperialists, Stalin's secret police, and the Gestapo"). The first involves choking a prisoner with water. This can be done either by forcing water down a prisoner's throat, thereby stretching the internal organs until he experiences extreme pain, or by holding a prisoner under water almost to the point of drowning (in one CIA technique, called waterboarding, prisoners are strapped to boards before having water poured over their faces). In the second, a prisoner is forced to stand for long periods, causing the ankles to swell and blisters to form, making any movement painful. The third method is sleep deprivation, which also may involve exposing the prisoner to extremes of heat or cold and which causes disorientation, hallucinations, and paranoia. What the three methods have in common is that they leave no marks. The army's latest field manual on intelligence now bans these practices.

It is a shocking sign of the times that we are having a debate about the appropriateness of torture. Some would say that it's a sign of our democracy's moral decline; others, of the desperate times that have driven us to desperate measures. Either way, those of us who do not want the free world to lose its soul to terrorism must stand up and be counted. 1

Credible reports that detainees in Afghanistan and Iraq have been abused in U.S. custody have generated widespread outrage, as have revelations that the White House and the Justice Department had authorized "coercive interrogation" techniques — some of which are widely regarded as forms of torture — for some prisoners held by the CIA. Senator John McCain has spearheaded an amendment to the annual defense appropriations bill banning "cruel, inhuman, and degrading treatment" of prisoners by any U.S. personnel. In October, the Republican-controlled Senate passed this amendment by a vote of 90–9. The Bush administration, meanwhile, 2 insists that it does not authorize torture — even as it seeks to block the McCain legislation. The issue has bitterly divided conservatives.

It is said, rightly, that torture degrades both its victims and its perpe- 3 trators. The debate has also degraded the moral caliber of discourse among supporters of the war on terror. Outrageously, the editorial page of the *Wall Street Journal* has argued that such techniques as exposure to extreme heat or cold, or "waterboarding" (which induces a drowning sensation), are not torture but merely "psychological techniques."

A much more thoughtful "antiantitorture" argument is made by 4 Charles Krauthammer in the *Weekly Standard*. Krauthammer agrees that torture is "terrible and monstrous," and he does not deny that such practices as "waterboarding" are torture. But he also asserts that some forms of this monstrous thing must remain permissible in extreme cases: the "ticking time bomb" scenario, in which a captured terrorist knows the location of a bomb that could kill thousands; and the high-level terrorist who possesses a treasure trove of information about the terror network and its plots.

Yet the "ticking time bomb" scenario is not only extremely improbable, 5 it's also one in which torture is most likely to be useless. If the terrorist knows the bomb will go off in two hours, all he has to do is stall by giving false information until it does go off. And with high-level terrorists, psychological manipulation may prove much more effective in extracting *accurate* information than physical suffering.

McCain has cited Israel as a model of fighting terror without resorting 6 to torture: physical coercion in interrogations was banned by the Israeli Supreme Court in 1999. Krauthammer disagrees, pointing out that since the start of the second Palestinian uprising, coercive tactics toward detainees in Israel have been commonly used under the radar, with widespread acceptance from the public.

But the 2004 *Washington Post* article Krauthammer cites actually dem- 7 onstrates two things. First, while interrogations in Israel were toughened, there has been no return to pre-1999 techniques that included physical brutality; today, Israeli interrogators rely mainly on psychological pressure (including sleep deprivation). Second, the allegations of physical abuse in the story involve maltreatment of detainees by soldiers, not interrogators. The allegations, if true, are troubling and suggest that acceptance of abuse "for a good cause" may foster a climate of abuse with no information-extracting purposes.

Krauthammer also notes that McCain's opposition is not as absolutist 8 as he makes it out to be. The senator has said that in a "ticking time bomb" emergency, the president may be able to authorize the use of illegal techniques. Legal experts also believe the ban on "cruel, inhuman, or degrading" treatment may allow the harshness of interrogation methods to be calibrated to the urgency of the situation. Krauthammer concludes that McCain's uncompromising stance is partly for show. He urges us to abandon "moral preening" and honestly admit that sometimes, "we must all be prepared to torture."

Yet what good will such honesty accomplish? Yes, a "no torture" stance 9
is likely to be qualified with tacit acknowledgment that, under narrow and
extreme circumstances, the rules may be bent. That seems vastly preferable
to open endorsement of torture. If we start with a "thou shalt not torture"
absolute, we are likely to be vigilant about lapses from this commandment,
limiting them only to absolute necessity. If we start with the premise that
torture is sometimes acceptable, there's no telling how low we're going to
go on that slippery slope.

* * *

Comprehension

1. Briefly summarize Young's position on torture. Is she totally in favor of
   it, in favor of it under certain circumstances, or totally opposed to it?
2. Explain why Young feels the way she does about torture.
3. What does Young think about the "ticking time bomb" scenario (4)?

Purpose and Audience

1. Young's essay appeared originally in the online version of the *Boston Globe*.
   What characteristics identify it as a newspaper opinion piece?
2. How would you characterize the tone of this essay? How does her tone
   help Young to make her point?
3. What is Young's thesis? Restate this thesis in your own words.
4. What is Young's purpose in writing this essay? Do you think she achieves
   her purpose? Are you convinced by her argument?

Style and Structure

1. Young begins by claiming that debating the use of torture is "shocking."
   How does this set the tone for her piece? Is it an effective start?
2. Young writes that there are "those of us who do not want the free world
   to lose its soul to terrorism" (1). What does Young mean by the phrase
   "lose its soul"?
3. Young cites John McCain in paragraphs 2, 6, and 8 and Charles
   Krauthammer in paragraphs 4, 6, 7, and 8. What is the purpose of mentioning McCain and Krauthammer and their views? Is Young's discussion
   of them effective? How does it help her argument?
4. Reread Young's concluding paragraph. How does it sum up and extend
   her position?

Vocabulary Projects

1. Define each of the following words as it is used in this selection.

   detainees (2)   spearheaded (2)
   coercive (2)   degrades (3)

waterboarding (4)   ban (8)
manipulation (5)   tacit (9)
cites (7)

2. In paragraph 4, Young uses the term "ticking time bomb," which is also used in other essays in this casebook. What does this term mean? What does it suggest?

Journal Entry

Consider possible ways, other than torture, to get information from an enemy in a time of war. What are the benefits and drawbacks of each method?

Writing Workshop

1. Young lists a number of interrogation methods in her essay, including the following:

   • abuse
   • psychological pressure
   • exposure to extreme heat or cold
   • coercive tactics
   • physical brutality
   • maltreatment
   • cruel, inhuman, and degrading treatment

   Provide examples of each of these interrogation methods. Which do you see as torture, and which do you think are not?

2. **Synthesizing Sources**   In her last paragraph, Young warns that the use of torture puts us on a "slippery slope." Consulting an online dictionary such as dictionary.com, define *slippery slope*, and explain how it fits into Young's argument. Do you agree with Young that allowing torture in some instances puts us on a "slippery slope"? If so, where does it lead? Compare her view with that of Alan Dershowitz. Does he think the use of torture puts us on a "slippery slope"? Be sure to include parenthetical documentation and a works-cited page. (See the Appendix for information on documentation formats.)

Combining the Patterns

Young cites two **examples** in paragraph 4. What are they? How essential are they to her argument?

Thematic Connections

• "Fatwa City" (page 242)
• "Calling Nooses What They Are — Terrorism" (page 606)

JOHN McCAIN

Torture's Terrible Toll

Born into a distinguished naval family (his father and grandfather were admirals), John McCain (b. 1936) graduated from the U.S. Naval Academy at Annapolis and trained as a navy pilot. In the mid-1960s, he volunteered for combat duty in Vietnam, flying low-altitude attack missions, and was shot down in 1967 over the North Vietnamese capital of Hanoi. Offered early release because of his status as the son of a high-ranking American officer, McCain refused and spent five and a half years in a series of prison camps, where he was beaten and tortured. On his release at the end of the war, he tried to return to flying duty, but the physical impairments resulting from his years in prison effectively ended his combat career. In 1982, he was elected to the U.S. House of Representatives. Four years later he was elected to fill the seat of retiring Barry Goldwater in the Senate. A conservative willing to challenge his fellow Republicans when his beliefs differed from the party line, McCain has earned a reputation as a political maverick. Popular with the public and the press, he made a strong showing in the 2000 Republican presidential primary, eventually losing to George W. Bush, and in 2008 he became his party's candidate for president.

Background on the Geneva Conventions

The Geneva Conventions are four international treaties, signed by the United States, that focus on the humane treatment of civilians and certain combatants during times of war and political conflict. The first was ratified in 1864 in conjunction with the establishment of the International Red Cross. It protects humanitarian workers and establishes protocols for the treatment of casualties of war. The second was a 1949 treaty extending the terms of the first. That year also saw the ratification of the third Convention, dealing with prisoners of war, and the fourth, dealing with "civilian persons." According to the third Convention, "Prisoners of war must . . . be humanely treated. Any unlawful act or omission by the Detaining Power causing death or seriously endangering the health of a prisoner of war . . . is prohibited. . . . Likewise, prisoners of war must at all times be protected, particularly against acts of violence or intimidation and against insults and public curiosity. . . . Every prisoner of war, when questioned on the subject, is bound to give only his surname, first names and rank, date of birth, and army, regimental, personal or serial number, or failing this, equivalent information. . . . No physical or mental torture, nor any other form of coercion, may be inflicted on prisoners of war to secure from them information of any kind whatever. Prisoners of war who refuse to answer may not be threatened, insulted, or exposed to unpleasant or disadvantageous treatment of any kind." The fourth Convention prohibits "violence to life and person, in particular murder of all kinds, mutilation, cruel treatment, and torture," and "outrages upon personal dignity, in particular humiliating and degrading treatment."

The debate over the treatment of enemy prisoners, like so much of the increasingly overcharged partisan debate over the war in Iraq and the global war against terrorists, has occasioned many unserious and unfair charges about the administration's intentions and motives. With all the many competing demands for their attention, President Bush and Vice President Cheney have remained admirably tenacious in their determination to prevent terrorists from inflicting another atrocity on the American people, whom they are sworn to protect. It is certainly fair to credit their administration's vigilance as a substantial part of the reason that we have not experienced another terrorist attack on American soil since September 11, 2001.

It is also quite fair to attribute the administration's position — that U.S. interrogators be allowed latitude in their treatment of enemy prisoners that might offend American values — to the president's and vice president's appropriate concern for acquiring actionable intelligence that could prevent attacks on our soldiers or our allies or on the American people. And it is quite unfair to assume some nefarious purpose informs their intentions. They bear the greatest responsibility for the security of American lives and interests. I understand and respect their motives just as I admire the seriousness and patriotism of their resolve. But I do, respectfully, take issue with the position that the demands of this war require us to accord a lower station to the moral imperatives that should govern our conduct in war and peace when they come in conflict with the unyielding inhumanity of our vicious enemy.

Obviously, to defeat our enemies we need intelligence, but intelligence that is reliable. We should not torture or treat inhumanely terrorists we have captured. The abuse of prisoners harms, not helps, our war effort. In my experience, abuse of prisoners often produces bad intelligence because under torture a person will say anything he thinks his captors want to hear — whether it is true or false — if he believes it will relieve his suffering. I was once physically coerced to provide my enemies with the names of the members of my flight squadron, information that had little if any value to my enemies as actionable intelligence. But I did not refuse, or repeat my insistence that I was required under the Geneva Conventions to provide my captors only with my name, rank, and serial number. Instead, I gave them the names of the Green Bay Packers' offensive line, knowing that providing them false information was sufficient to suspend the abuse. It seems probable to me that the terrorists we interrogate under less than humane standards of treatment are also likely to resort to deceptive answers that are perhaps less provably false than that which I once offered.

Our commitment to basic humanitarian values affects — in part — the willingness of other nations to do the same. Mistreatment of enemy prisoners endangers our own troops who might someday be held captive. While some enemies, and Al Qaeda surely, will never be bound by the principle of reciprocity, we should have concern for those Americans captured by more traditional enemies, if not in this war then in the next. Until about 1970, North Vietnam ignored its obligations not to mistreat the Americans they held prisoner, claiming that we were engaged in an unlawful war against them and thus not entitled to the protections of the Geneva Conventions. But when their abuses became widely known and incited unfavorable international attention, they substantially decreased their mistreatment of us. Again, Al Qaeda will never be influenced by international sensibilities or open to moral suasion. If ever the term "sociopath" applied to anyone, it applies to them. But I doubt they will be the last enemy America will fight, and we should not undermine today our defense of international prohibitions against torture and inhumane treatment of prisoners of war that we will need to rely on in the future.

To prevail in this war we need more than victories on the battlefield.   5 This is a war of ideas, a struggle to advance freedom in the face of terror in places where oppressive rule has bred the malevolence that creates terrorists. Prisoner abuses exact a terrible toll on us in this war of ideas. They inevitably become public, and when they do they threaten our moral standing, and expose us to false but widely disseminated charges that democracies are no more inherently idealistic and moral than other regimes. This is an existential fight, to be sure. If they could, Islamic extremists who resort to terror would destroy us utterly. But to defeat them we must prevail in our defense of American political values as well. The mistreatment of prisoners greatly injures that effort.

The mistreatment of prisoners harms us more than our enemies. I   6 don't think I'm naive about how terrible are the wages of war, and how terrible are the things that must be done to wage it successfully. It is an awful business, and no matter how noble the cause for which it is fought, no matter how valiant their service, many veterans spend much of their subsequent lives trying to forget not only what was done to them, but some of what had to be done by them to prevail.

I don't mourn the loss of any terrorist's life. Nor do I care if in the   7 course of serving their ignoble cause they suffer great harm. They have pledged their lives to the intentional destruction of innocent lives, and they have earned their terrible punishment in this life and the next. What I do mourn is what we lose when by official policy or official neglect we allow, confuse, or encourage our soldiers to forget that best sense of ourselves, that which is our greatest strength — that we are different and better than our enemies, that we fight for an idea, not a tribe, not a land, not a king, not a twisted interpretation of an ancient religion, but for an idea that all men are created equal and endowed by their Creator with inalienable rights.

Now, in this war, our liberal notions are put to the test. Americans of   8 good will, all patriots, argue about what is appropriate and necessary to combat this unconventional enemy. Those of us who feel that in this war, as in past wars, Americans should not compromise our values must answer those Americans who believe that a less rigorous application of those values is regrettably necessary to prevail over a uniquely abhorrent and dangerous enemy. Part of our disagreement is definitional. Some view more coercive interrogation tactics as something short of torture but worry that they might be subject to challenge under the "no cruel, inhumane, or degrading" standard. Others, including me, believe that both the prohibition on torture and the cruel, inhumane, and degrading standard must remain intact. When we relax that standard, it is nearly unavoidable that some objectionable practices will be allowed as something less than torture because they do not risk life and limb or do not cause very serious physical pain.

For instance, there has been considerable press attention to a tactic   9
called "waterboarding," where a prisoner is restrained and blindfolded while an interrogator pours water on his face and into his mouth — causing the prisoner to believe he is being drowned. He isn't, of course; there is no intention to injure him physically. But if you gave people who have suffered abuse as prisoners a choice between a beating and a mock execution, many, including me, would choose a beating. The effects of most beatings heal. The memory of an execution will haunt someone for a very long time and damage his or her psyche in ways that may never heal. In my view, to make someone believe that you are killing him by drowning is no different than holding a pistol to his head and firing a blank. I believe that it is torture, very exquisite torture.

Those who argue the necessity of some abuses raise an important   10
dilemma as their most compelling rationale: the ticking-time-bomb scenario. What do we do if we capture a terrorist who we have sound reasons to believe possesses specific knowledge of an imminent terrorist attack?

In such an urgent and rare instance, an interrogator might well try   11
extreme measures to extract information that could save lives. Should he do so, and thereby save an American city or prevent another 9/11, authorities and the public would surely take this into account when judging his actions and recognize the extremely dire situation which he confronted. But I don't believe this scenario requires us to write into law an exception to our treaty and moral obligations that would permit cruel, inhumane, and degrading treatment. To carve out legal exemptions to this basic principle of human rights risks opening the door to abuse as a matter of course, rather than a standard violated truly in extremis. It is far better to embrace a standard that might be violated in extraordinary circumstances than to lower our standards to accommodate a remote contingency, confusing personnel in the field and sending precisely the wrong message abroad about America's purposes and practices.

The state of Israel, no stranger to terrorist attacks, has faced this   12
dilemma, and in 1999 the Israeli Supreme Court declared cruel, inhumane, and degrading treatment illegal. "A democratic, freedom-loving society," the court wrote, "does not accept that investigators use any means for the purpose of uncovering truth. The rules pertaining to investigators are important to a democratic state. They reflect its character."

I've been asked often where did the brave men I was privileged to serve   13
with in North Vietnam draw the strength to resist to the best of their abilities the cruelties inflicted on them by our enemies. They drew strength
from their faith in each other, from their faith in God, and from their faith
in our country. Our enemies didn't adhere to the Geneva Conventions.
Many of my comrades were subjected to very cruel, very inhumane, and
degrading treatment, a few of them unto death. But every one of us — every
single one of us — knew and took great strength from the belief that we
were different from our enemies, that we were better than them, that we, if
the roles were reversed, would not disgrace ourselves by committing or
approving such mistreatment of them. That faith was indispensable not
only to our survival, but to our attempts to return home with honor. For
without our honor, our homecoming would have had little value to us.

The enemies we fight today hold our liberal values in contempt, as they   14
hold in contempt the international conventions that enshrine them. I
know that. But we are better than them, and we are stronger for our faith.
And we will prevail. It is indispensable to our success in this war that those
we ask to fight it know that in the discharge of their dangerous responsibilities to their country they are never expected to forget that they are
Americans, and the valiant defenders of a sacred idea of how nations
should govern their own affairs and their relations with others — even our
enemies.

Those who return to us and those who give their lives for us are entitled   15
to that honor. And those of us who have given them this onerous duty are
obliged by our history, and the many terrible sacrifices that have been
made in our defense, to make clear to them that they need not risk their or
their country's honor to prevail; that they are always — through the violence, chaos, and heartache of war, through deprivation and cruelty and
loss — they are always, always, Americans, and different, better, and stronger than those who would destroy us.

• • •

Comprehension

1. What is McCain's position on torture?
2. What reasons does McCain give for his stand on the use of torture in
   interrogations?
3. What examples does McCain provide of nonphysical abuse that he nevertheless feels is torture?

Purpose and Audience

1. What is McCain's purpose in writing this essay? Do you think he achieves
   his purpose? Why or why not?

2. McCain's essay appeared in *Newsweek*, a magazine for a general audience. How do the essay's style and tone indicate that it is aimed at a general audience rather than an audience of politicians or military officers?

3. Paraphrase McCain's thesis.

Style and Structure

1. In the first two paragraphs of his essay, McCain sets the stage for what follows. What does he do in those first two paragraphs, and what do they accomplish?

2. McCain says that he and other American prisoners during the Vietnam War believed that they "were different from [their] enemies, that [they] were better than them" (13); he believes, in regard to "the enemies we fight today," that "we are better than them" (14); and that Americans are "different, better, and stronger than those who would destroy us" (15). What is the purpose of these claims? Why does he repeat them?

Vocabulary Projects

1. Define each of the following words as it is used in this selection.

overcharged (1)	undermine (4)	dilemma (10)
partisan (1)	prevail (5)	urgent (11)
attribute (2)	naïve (6)	pertaining (12)
nefarious (2)	ignoble (7)	comrades (13)
coerced (3)	notions (8)	valiant (14)
humanitarian (4)	interrogator (9)	deprivation (15)

2. In paragraph 9, McCain calls waterboarding "very exquisite torture." Look up the word *exquisite* in an online dictionary. Which of the meanings listed there do you think McCain had in mind? Why?

Journal Entry

John McCain was himself tortured as a prisoner during the Vietnam War. What does that experience allow him to add to his argument? Does knowing that he was tortured affect your reaction to his essay?

Writing Workshop

1. **Synthesizing Sources**   Rank the four writers in this casebook in order from those who feel most strongly against torture to those who feel most strongly that it should be allowed. Briefly summarize each position. Then, explain whose position you support, and why. Be sure to include parenthetical documentation and a works-cited page. (See the Appendix for information on documentation formats.)

2. McCain cites several reasons why torture does not work. He says it "harms . . . our war effort" (3), "endangers our own troops" (4), and

threatens our "moral standing" (5). Which of these reasons do you find most persuasive and why?

3. **Synthesizing Sources**   Identify McCain's position on torture warrants as he explains it in paragraph 11, and compare it to the position held by Alan Dershowitz. How do McCain's and Dershowitz's views relate to those of Cathy Young? Whose arguments on authorizing torture do you find most convincing? Why? Be sure to document references to Dershowitz, McCain, and Young and to include a works-cited page. (See the Appendix for information on documentation formats.)

Combining the Patterns

In paragraph 3, McCain provides an **example** of his response to his own torture as a prisoner of war. Rather than identifying the members of his flight squadron, he gave the names of players on a professional football team. What purpose does this example serve? Is it effective?

Thematic Connections

- "Get It Right: Privatize Executions" (page 299)
- "Five Ways to Kill a Man" (page 501)
- "Calling Nooses What They Are — Terrorism" (page 606)

WRITING ASSIGNMENTS FOR ARGUMENTATION

1. Write an essay discussing whether parents have a right to spank their children. If your position is that they do, under what circumstances? What limitations should exist? If your position is that they do not, how should parents discipline children? How should they deal with inappropriate behavior?

2. Go to the American Library Association's Web site at ala.org/ala/pio/ piopresskits/bbbwpresskit/bannedchallenged.htm, and look at the list of the most frequently banned books of the twentieth century. After reviewing the list, choose a book that you have read. Assume that a library in your town has decided that the book you have chosen was objectionable and has removed it from the shelves. Write an email to your local newspaper arguing for or against the library's actions. Make a list of the major arguments that might be advanced against your position, and try to refute some of them in your email.

3. In Great Britain, cities began installing video surveillance systems in public areas in the 1970s. Police departments claim that these cameras help them do their jobs more efficiently. For example, such cameras enabled police to identify and capture terrorists who bombed the London subway in 2005. Opponents of the cameras say that the police are creating a society that severely compromises the right of personal privacy. How do you feel about this issue? Assume that the police department in your city is proposing to install cameras in the downtown and other pedestrian areas. Write an editorial for your local paper presenting your views on the topic.

4. Write an essay discussing under what circumstances, if any, animals should be used for scientific experimentation.

5. During his campaign for president, candidate Bill Clinton promised to allow all people, regardless of sexual orientation, to serve in the United States military. This measure went against the previous policy that banned openly gay individuals from serving. In 1993, then-President Clinton accepted a compromise measure, which came to be called "don't ask, don't tell." In essence, this policy said that as long as lesbians and gay men kept their sexual orientations secret, they could remain in the military. Write an essay in which you argue for or against the continuation of this policy. Should "don't ask, don't tell" be continued, or is it, as many of its detractors claim, unrealistic, unworkable, and ultimately discriminatory? Before you write your essay, go to the Internet to find out more about this policy as well as about gay men and lesbians in the military.

6. Go to deathpenalty.org, and research some criminal cases that resulted in the death penalty. Write an essay using these accounts to support your arguments either for or against the death penalty. Be sure to document your sources and to include a works-cited page. (See the Appendix for information about documentation.)

7. Write an argumentative essay discussing under what circumstances a nation has an obligation to go (or not to go) to war.

8. Since the events of September 11, 2001, the idea of arming pilots of commercial passenger planes has been debated. Those opposed to arming pilots claim that the risks — that a gun will fall into the hands of

hijackers or that a passenger will be accidentally shot — outweigh any benefits. Those who support the idea say that the pilot is the last line of defense and must be able to defend the cockpit from terrorists. Due to public pressure in favor of arming pilots, a small trial program has been instituted. Do you think all pilots of commercial airplanes should be armed? Write an essay presenting your views on this subject.

9. In the Declaration of Independence, Jefferson says that all individuals are entitled to "life, liberty and the pursuit of happiness." Write an essay arguing that these rights are not absolute.

10. Write an argumentative essay on one of these topics:

   - Should high school students be required to recite the Pledge of Allegiance at the start of each school day?
   - Should college students be required to do community service?
   - Should public school teachers be required to pass periodic competency tests?
   - Should the legal drinking age be raised (or lowered)?
   - Should states be required to educate the children of illegal immigrants?

COLLABORATIVE ACTIVITY FOR ARGUMENTATION

Working with three other students, select a controversial topic — one not covered in any of the debates in this chapter — that interests all of you. (You can review the previous Writing Assignments for Argumentation to get ideas.) State your topic the way a topic is stated in a formal debate:

Resolved: The United States should censor Internet content.

Then, divide into two two-member teams, and decide which team will take the pro position and which will take the con. Each team should list the arguments on its side of the issue and then write two or three paragraphs summarizing its position. Finally, each team should stage a ten-minute debate — five minutes for each side — in front of the class. (The pro side presents its argument first.) At the end of each debate, the class should discuss which team has presented the stronger arguments.

15

Combining the Patterns

Many paragraphs combine several patterns of development. In the following paragraph, for example, Paul Hoffman uses narration, exemplification, and cause and effect to explain why we tend to see numbers as more than "instruments of enumeration":

Topic sentence

Narration

Exemplification

Cause and effect

The idea that numbers are not mere instruments of enumeration but are sacred, perfect, friendly, lucky, or evil goes back to antiquity. In the sixth century B.C. Pythagoras, whom schoolchildren associate with the famous theorem that in a right triangle the square of the hypotenuse always equals the sum of the squares of its sides, not only performed brilliant mathematics but made a religion out of numbers. In numerology, the number 12 has always represented completeness, as in the 12 months of the year, the 12 signs of the zodiac, the 12 hours of the day, the 12 gods of Olympus, the 12 labors of Hercules, the 12 tribes of Israel, the 12 apostles of Jesus, the 12 days of Christmas, and, more recently perhaps, the 12 eggs in an egg carton. Since 13 exceeds 12 by only one, the number lies just beyond completeness and, hence, is restless to the point of being evil.

Like paragraphs, essays do not usually follow a single pattern of development; in fact, nearly every essay, including those in this text, combines a variety of patterns. Even though an essay may be organized according to one dominant pattern, it is still likely to include paragraphs, and even groups of paragraphs, shaped by other patterns of development. For example, a process essay can use **cause and effect** to show the results of the process, and a cause-and-effect essay can use **exemplification** (to illustrate possible effects) or **comparison and contrast** of two events (to assess possible causes). In many cases, a dominant pattern is supported by other patterns; in fact, combining various patterns in a single essay gives writers the flexibility to express their ideas most effectively. For this reason, each essay in Chapters 6 through 14 of this text is followed by Combining the Patterns questions that focus on how the essay uses (or might use) other patterns of development along with its dominant pattern.

STRUCTURING AN ESSAY BY COMBINING THE PATTERNS

Essays that combine various patterns of development, like essays structured primarily by a single pattern, include an **introduction**, several **body paragraphs**, and a **conclusion**. The introduction typically ends with the thesis statement that gives the essay its focus, and the conclusion often restates that thesis or summarizes the essay's main points. Each body paragraph (or group of paragraphs) is structured according to the pattern of development that best suits the material it develops.

Suppose you are planning your answer to the following question on a take-home essay exam for a sociology of religion course:

> What factors attract people to cults? Why do they join? Support your answer with specific examples that illustrate how cults recruit and retain members.

The wording of this exam question ("for what reasons") suggests that the essay's dominant pattern of development will be **cause and effect**; the wording also suggests that this cause-and-effect structure will include **exemplification**. In addition, you may decide to develop your essay with **definition** and **process**.

An informal outline for your essay might look like this:

Introduction:	Definition of *cult* (defined by negation — telling what it is *not* — and by comparison and contrast with *religion*). Thesis statement (suggests cause and effect): Using aggressive recruitment tactics and isolating potential members from their families and past lives, cults appeal to new recruits by offering them a highly structured environment.
Cause and effect:	Why people join cults
Process:	How cults recruit new members
Exemplification:	Tactics various cults use to retain members (series of brief examples)
Conclusion:	Restatement of thesis or review of key points.

COMBINING THE PATTERNS: REVISING AND EDITING

When you revise an essay that combines several patterns of development, consider the items on the revision checklist on page 54, as well as any of the more specific revision checklists in Chapters 6 through 14 that apply to the patterns in your essay. As you edit your essay, refer to the editing checklists on pages 71, 74, and 76, and to the individual editing checklists in Chapters 6 through 14. You may also wish to consult the Grammar in Context sections that appear throughout the book, as well as the one that follows.

GRAMMAR IN CONTEXT: Agreement with Indefinite Pronouns

A **pronoun** is a word that takes the place of a noun or another pronoun in a sentence. Unlike most pronouns, an **indefinite pronoun** (*anyone, either, each,* and so on) does not refer to a specific person or thing.

Subject-Verb Agreement.   Pronoun subjects must agree in number with their verbs: singular pronouns (*I, he, she, it,* and so on) take singular verbs, and plural pronouns (*we, they,* and so on) take plural verbs.

"I have learned much as a scavenger" (Eighner 715).

"We were free like comets in the heavens" (Truong 710).

Indefinite pronoun subjects also must agree in number with their verbs: singular indefinite pronouns take singular verbs, and plural indefinite pronouns take plural verbs. Most indefinite pronouns are singular, but some are plural.

SUBJECT–VERB AGREEMENT WITH INDEFINITE PRONOUN SUBJECTS

SINGULAR INDEFINITE PRONOUNS

another	anyone	everyone	one	each
either	neither	anything	everything	

"Everyone was darker or lighter than we were" (Truong 711).

"Everything seems to stink" (Eighner 720).

PLURAL INDEFINITE PRONOUNS

both	many	few	several	others

"Many are discarded for minor imperfections that can be pared away" (Eighner 717).

NOTE: A few indefinite pronouns — *some, all, any, more, most,* and *none* — may be either singular or plural, depending on their meaning in the sentence.

SINGULAR: According to David Kirby, some of the history of tattoos is surprising. (*Some* refers to *history,* so the verb is singular.)

(continued on next page)

(continued from previous page)

PLURAL: <u>Some</u> of the tattoos David Kirby discusses <u>serve</u> as a kind of "record book," while others create a "canvas" (741). (*Some* refers to *tattoos*, so the verb is plural.)

Pronoun-Antecedent Agreement.   An **antecedent** is the noun or pronoun a pronoun refers to in a sentence. Pronouns must agree in number with their antecedents.

Use a singular pronoun to refer to a singular indefinite pronoun antecedent.

<u>Each</u> day has <u>its</u> surprises for Lars Eighner and his dog Lizbeth.

Use a plural pronoun to refer to a plural indefinite pronoun antecedent.

<u>Many</u> of the people who pass Eighner and Lizbeth avert <u>their</u> eyes.

NOTE: Although the indefinite pronoun *everyone* is singular, it is often used with a plural pronoun in everyday speech and informal writing.

INFORMAL: <u>Everyone</u> turns <u>their</u> heads when Eighner and Lizbeth walk by.

This usage is generally acceptable in informal situations, but college writing requires correct pronoun-antecedent agreement.

CORRECT: <u>People</u> turn <u>their</u> heads when Eighner and Lizbeth walk by.

> For more practice in avoiding agreement problems with indefinite pronouns, visit Exercise Central at **bedfordstmartins.com/patterns/indefinitepronouns.**

The essays in this chapter illustrate how different patterns of development work together in a single piece of writing. The first two essays — "The Park" by Michael Huu Truong, a student, and "On Dumpster Diving" by Lars Eighner — include annotations that identify the various patterns these writers use. Truong's essay relies primarily on narration, but he also uses description and exemplification to convey his memories of childhood. Eighner's combines sections of definition, exemplification, classification and division, cause and effect, comparison and contrast, and process; at the same time, he tells the story (narration) and provides vivid details (description) of his life as a homeless person.

Following these annotated essays are three additional selections that combine patterns: Judith Ortiz Cofer's "The Myth of the Latin Woman: I

Just Met a Girl Named Maria," David Kirby's "Inked Well," and Jonathan Swift's classic satire "A Modest Proposal." Each of the essays in this chapter is followed by the same types of questions that accompany the reading selections that appear elsewhere in the text.

A STUDENT WRITER: Combining the Patterns

This essay was written by Michael Huu Truong for a first-year composition course in response to the assignment "Write an essay about the person and/or place that defined your childhood."

The Park

Background

My childhood did not really begin until I came to this country from the jungle of Vietnam. I can't really remember much from this period, and the things I do remember are vague images that I have no desire or intention to discuss. However, my childhood in the States was a lot different, especially after I met my friend James. While it lasted, it was paradise.   1

Thesis statement

Narrative begins

Description: effects of cold

It was a cold wintry day in February after a big snowstorm — the first I'd ever seen. My lips were chapped, my hands were frozen stiff, and my cheeks were burning from the biting wind, and yet I loved it. I especially loved the snow. I had come from a country where the closest things to snow were white paint and cotton balls. But now I was in America. On that frosty afternoon, I was determined to build a snowman. I had seen them in books, and I had heard they could talk. I knew they could come alive, and I couldn't wait.   2

Comparison and contrast: U.S. vs. Vietnam

Description: James

"Eyryui roeow ierog," said a voice that came out of nowhere. I turned around, and right in my face was a short, red-faced (probably from the cold wind) Korean kid with a dirty, runny nose. I responded, "Wtefkjkr ruyjft gsdfr" in my own tongue. We understood each other perfectly, and we expressed our understanding with a smile. Together, we built our first snowman. We were disappointed that evening when the snowman just stood there; however, I was happy because I had made my first friend.   3

Narration: the first day

Analogies

Ever since then we've been a team like Abbott and Costello (or, when my cousin joined us, The Three Stooges). The two of us were inseparable. We could've made the greatest Krazy Glue commercial ever.   4

Narration: what they did that summer

The summer that followed the big snowstorm, from what   5
I can recall, was awesome. We were free like comets in the
heavens, and we did whatever our hearts wanted. For the most
part, our desires were fulfilled in a little park across the street.
This park was ours; it was like our own planet guarded by our
own robot army (disguised as trees). Together we fought against
the bigger people who always tried to invade and take over our
world. The enemy could never conquer our fortress because they
would have to destroy our robots, penetrate our force field, and
then defeat us; this last feat would be impossible.

Narrative continues

Examples: what they banished

This park was our fantasy land where everything we   6
wished for came true and everything we hated was banished
forever. We banished vegetables, cheese, bigger people,
and — of course — girls. The land was enchanted, and we could
be whatever we felt like. We were super ninjas one day and
millionaires the next; we became the heroes we idolized and

Examples: superhero fantasies

lived the lives we dreamed about. I had the strength of Bruce
Lee and Superman; James possessed the power of Clint
Eastwood and the Bionic Man. My weapons were the skills of
Bruce and a cape. James, however, needed a real weapon for
Clint, and the weapon he made was awesome. The Death Ray
could destroy a building with one blast, and it even had a shield
so that James was always protected. Even with all his mighty
weapons and gadgets, though, he was still no match for
Superman and Bruce Lee. Every day, we fought until death (or
until our parents called us for dinner).

Narrative continues

When we became bored with our super powers, the park   7
became a giant spaceship. We traveled all over the Universe,
conquering and exploring strange new worlds and mysterious
planets. Our ship was a top-secret indestructible space warship

Examples: new worlds and planets

called the X–007. We went to Mars, Venus, Pluto, and other
alien planets, destroying all the monsters we could find. When
necessary, our spacecraft was transformed into a submarine for
deep-sea adventures. We found lost cities, unearthed treasures,
and saved Earth by destroying all the sea monsters that were
plotting against us. We became heroes — just like Superman,
Bruce Lee, the Bionic Man, and Clint Eastwood.

Cause and effect: prospect of school leads to problems

James and I had the time of our lives in the park that   8
summer. It was great — until we heard about the horror of
starting school. Shocked and terrified, we ran to our fortress to

escape. For some reason, though, our magic kingdom had lost its powers. We fought hard that evening, trying to keep the bigger people out of our planet, but the battle was soon lost. Bruce Lee, Superman, the Bionic Man, and Clint Eastwood had all lost their special powers.

Narrative continues

9 School wasn't as bad as we'd thought it would be. The first day, James and I sat there with our hands folded. We didn't talk or move, and we didn't dare look at each other (we would've cracked up because we always made these goofy faces). Even though we had pens that could be transformed into weapons, we were still scared.

Description: school

10 Everyone was darker or lighter than we were, and the teacher was speaking a strange language (English). James and I giggled as she talked. We giggled softly when everyone else talked, and they laughed out loud when it was our turn to speak.

Narrative continues

11 The day dragged on, and all we wanted to do was go home and rebuild our fortress. Finally, after an eternity, it was almost three o'clock. James and I sat at the edge of our seats as we counted under our breath: "10, 9, 8, 7, 6, 5, 4, 3, 2, 1." At last, the bell sounded. We dashed for the door and raced home and across the street — and then we stopped. We stood still in the middle of the street with our hearts pounding like the beats of a drum. The cool September wind began to pick up, and everything became silent. We stood there and watched the metal of the fence reflect the beautiful colors of the sun. It was beautiful, and yet we hated everything about it. The new metal fence separated us from our fortress, our planet, our spaceship, our submarine — and, most important of all, from our heroes and our dreams.

Description: the fence

12 We stood there for a long time. As the sun slowly turned red and sank beneath the ground, so did our dreams, heroes, and hearts. Darkness soon devoured the park, and after a while we walked home with only the memories of the summer that came after the big snowstorm.

Points for Special Attention

Writing a Personal Experience Essay. Michael's instructor specified that he was to write an essay about a person or place to help his readers — other students — understand what his childhood was like.

Because it was a personal experience essay, Michael was free to use the first-person pronouns *I* and *we,* as well as contractions, although neither would be acceptable in a more formal essay.

Thesis Statement.   Because Michael's primary purpose in this essay was to communicate personal feelings and impressions, an argumentative thesis statement (such as "If every television in the United States disappeared, more people would have childhoods like mine") would have been inappropriate. Still, Michael states his thesis explicitly in order to unify his essay around the dominant impression he wants to convey: "While it lasted, it was paradise."

Combining the Patterns.   Michael also had more specific purposes, and these determined the patterns that shape his essay. His essay's dominant pattern is *narration,* but to help students visualize the person (James) and the place (the park) he discusses, he includes sections that *describe* and give concrete, specific *examples* as well as summarize his daily routine. These patterns work together to create an essay that conveys the nature of his childhood to readers.

Transitions.   The transitions between the individual sentences and paragraphs of Michael's essay — "now," "Ever since," "The summer that followed the big snowstorm" — serve primarily to move readers through time. This is appropriate because narration is the dominant pattern that determines his essay's overall structure.

Detail.   Michael's essay is full of specific detail — for example, quoted bits of dialogue in paragraph 3 and names of his heroes and of particular games (and related equipment and weapons) elsewhere. The descriptive details that re-create the physical scenes — in particular, the snow, cold, frost, and wind of winter and the sun reflected in the fence — are vivid enough to help readers visualize the places Michael writes about.

Figures of Speech.   Michael's essay describes a time when his imagination wandered without the restraints of adulthood. Appropriately, he uses **simile**, **metaphor**, and **personification** — "We were free like comets in the heavens"; "The park became a giant spaceship"; "We found lost cities, unearthed treasures, and saved Earth"; "Darkness soon devoured the park" — to evoke the time and place he describes.

Focus on Revision

Michael's assignment asked him to write about his childhood, and he chose to focus on his early years in the United States. When his peer editing group discussed his essay, however, a number of students were curious about his life in Vietnam. Some of them thought he should add a paragraph summarizing the "vague images" he remembered of his earlier childhood, perhaps contrasting it with his life in the United States, as he does in passing in paragraph 2. An alternate suggestion, made by one classmate, was that Michael consider deleting the sentence in paragraph 1 that states he has "no desire or intention to discuss" this part of his life, since it raises issues his essay does not address. After thinking about these ideas, Michael decided to delete this sentence in his next draft and to add a brief paragraph about his life in Vietnam, contrasting the park and his friendship with James with some of his earlier, less idyllic memories.

📄 **PEER EDITING WORKSHEET: Combining the Patterns**

1. Using the annotations for "The Park" (page 709) or "On Dumpster Diving" (page 714) as a guide, annotate the essay to identify the patterns of development it uses.
2. What is the essay's thesis? If it is not explicitly stated, state it in your own words. What pattern or patterns of development are suggested by the wording of the thesis statement?
3. What dominant pattern of development determines the essay's overall structure?
4. What patterns does the writer use to develop the body paragraphs of the essay? Explain why each pattern is used in a particular paragraph or group of paragraphs.
5. What patterns are not used? Where, if anywhere, might one of these patterns serve the writer's purpose?
6. Review the essay's topic sentences. Is the wording of each topic sentence consistent with the particular pattern that structures the paragraph? If not, suggest possible ways some of the topic sentences might be reworded.

Each of the following essays combines several patterns, blending strategies to achieve the writer's purpose.

On Dumpster Diving

Lars Eighner (b. 1948) dropped out of the University of Texas at Austin after his third year and took a job at a state mental hospital. After leaving his job over a policy dispute in 1988 and falling behind in his rent payments, Eighner became homeless. For three years, he traveled between Austin and Los Angeles with his dog, Lizbeth, earning what money he could from writing stories for magazines. Eighner's memories of his experiences living on the street, *Travels with Lizbeth* (1993), was written on a computer he found in a Dumpster. The following chapter from that book details the practical dangers as well as the many possibilities he discovered in his "Dumpster diving." Eighner now lives in Austin and works as a freelance writer and writing coach.

Background on the homeless

Although the number of homeless people is difficult to measure accurately, homelessness has become a highly visible issue in the past two decades. It is estimated, for example, that as many as ten million people experienced homelessness in this country in the late 1980s alone. This surge in homelessness has a number of causes. Perhaps most important, a booming real estate market led to a significant drop in affordable housing in many areas of the country. In several cities, single-room-occupancy hotels, which had long provided cheap lodging, were demolished or converted into luxury apartments. At the same time, new technologies left many unskilled workers jobless. Government policies against detaining the nondangerous mentally ill against their will also played a significant role. (About a quarter of all homeless people are thought to be mentally ill.) Currently, the U.S. Department of Health and Human Services estimates that homelessness affects two to three million Americans each year.

This chapter was composed while the author was homeless. The present tense has been preserved.

Definition: Dumpster

Long before I began Dumpster diving I was impressed with Dumpsters, enough so that I wrote the Merriam-Webster research service to discover what I could about the word *Dumpster*. I learned from them that it is a proprietary word belonging to the Dempsey Dumpster company. Since then I have dutifully capitalized the word, although it was lowercased in almost all the citations Merriam-Webster photocopied for me. Dempsey's word is too apt. I have never heard these things called anything but Dumpsters. I do not know anyone who knows the generic name for these

1

objects. From time to time I have heard a wino or hobo give some corrupted credit to the original and call them Dipsy Dumpsters.

Narration: Eighner's story begins

I began Dumpster diving about a year before I became homeless. 2

Definition: Dumpster diving

I prefer the word *scavenging* and use the word *scrounging* when I mean to be obscure. I have heard people, evidently meaning to be polite, use the word *foraging*, but I prefer to reserve that word for gathering nuts and berries and such, which I do also according to the season and the opportunity. *Dumpster diving* seems to me to be a little too cute and, in my case, inaccurate because I lack the athletic ability to lower myself into the Dumpsters as the true divers do, much to their increased profit. 3

I like the frankness of the word *scavenging*, which I can hardly think of without picturing a big black snail on an aquarium wall. I live from the refuse of others. I am a scavenger. I think it a sound and honorable niche, although if I could I would naturally prefer to live the comfortable consumer life, perhaps — and only perhaps — as a slightly less wasteful consumer, owing to what I have learned as a scavenger. 4

Narration: story continues

While Lizbeth and I were still living in the shack on Avenue B as my savings ran out, I put almost all my sporadic income into rent. The necessities of daily life I began to extract from Dumpsters. Yes, we ate from them. Except for jeans, all my clothes came from Dumpsters. Boom boxes, candles, bedding, toilet paper, a virgin male love doll, medicine, books, a typewriter, dishes, furnishings, and change, sometimes amounting to many dollars — I acquired many things from Dumpsters. 5

Exemplification: things found in Dumpsters

Thesis statement

I have learned much as a scavenger. I mean to put some of what I have learned down here, beginning with the practical art of Dumpster diving and proceeding to the abstract. 6

What is safe to eat? 7

After all, the finding of objects is becoming something of an urban art. Even respectable employed people will sometimes find something tempting sticking out of a Dumpster or standing beside one. Quite a number of people, not all of them of the bohemian type, are willing to brag that they found this or that piece of trash. But eating from Dumpsters is 8 what separates the dilettanti from the professionals. Eating safely from the Dumpsters involves three principles: using the senses and common sense to evaluate the condition of the found materials, knowing the Dumpsters of a given area and checking them regularly, and seeking always to answer the question "Why was this discarded?"

Comparison and contrast: Dumpster divers vs. others

Perhaps everyone who has a kitchen and a regular supply of groceries has, at one time or another, made a sandwich and eaten half of it before discovering mold on the bread or got a mouthful of milk before realizing the milk had turned. Nothing of the sort is likely to happen to a Dumpster diver because he is constantly reminded that most food is discarded for a reason. Yet a lot of perfectly good food can be found in Dumpsters. 9

Classification and division: different kinds of food found in Dumpsters and their relative safety

Canned goods, for example, turn up fairly often in the Dumpsters I frequent. All except the most phobic people will be willing to eat from a can, even if it came from a Dumpster. Canned goods are among the safest foods to be found in Dumpsters but are not utterly foolproof. 10

Although very rare with modern canning methods, botulism is a possibility. Most other forms of food poisoning seldom do lasting harm to a healthy person, but botulism is almost certainly fatal and often the first symptom is death. Except for carbonated beverages, all canned goods should contain a slight vacuum and suck air when first punctured. Bulging, rusty, and dented cans and cans that spew when punctured should be avoided, especially when the contents are not very acidic or syrupy. 11

Heat can break down the botulin, but this requires much more cooking than most people do to canned goods. To the extent that botulism occurs at all, of course, it can occur in cans on pantry shelves as well as in cans from Dumpsters. Need I say that home-canned goods are simply too risky to be recommended. 12

From time to time one of my companions, aware of the source of my provisions, will ask, "Do you think these crackers are really safe to eat?" For some reason it is most often the crackers they ask about. 13

This question has always made me angry. Of course I would not offer my companion anything I had doubts about. But more than that, I wonder why he cannot evaluate the condition of the crackers for himself. I have no special knowledge and I have been wrong 14 before. Since he knows where the food comes from, it seems to me he ought to assume some of the responsibility for deciding what he will put in his mouth. For myself I have few qualms about dry foods such as crackers, cookies, cereal, chips, and pasta if they are free of visible contaminates and still dry and crisp. Most often such things are found in the original packaging, which is not so much a positive sign as it is the absence of a negative one.

Raw fruits and vegetables with intact skins seem   15
perfectly safe to me, excluding of course the obviously rotten. Many are discarded for minor imperfections that can be pared away. Leafy vegetables, grapes, cauliflower, broccoli, and similar things may be contaminated by liquids and may be impractical to wash.

Candy, especially hard candy, is usually safe if it has   16
not drawn ants. Chocolate is often discarded only because it has become discolored as the cocoa butter de-emulsified. Candying, after all, is one method of food preservation because pathogens do not like very sugary substances.

All of these foods might be found in any Dumpster   17
and can be evaluated with some confidence largely on the basis of appearance. Beyond these are foods that cannot be correctly evaluated without additional information.

I began scavenging by pulling pizzas out of the   18
Dumpster behind a pizza delivery shop. In general, prepared food requires caution, but in this case I knew when the shop closed and went to the Dumpster as soon as the last of the help left.

Such shops often get prank orders; both the orders   19
and the products made to fill them are called *bogus*. Because help seldom stays long at these places, pizzas are often made with the wrong topping, refused on delivery for being cold, or baked incorrectly. The products to be discarded are boxed up because inventory is kept by counting boxes: A boxed pizza can be written off; an unboxed pizza does not exist.

I never placed a bogus order to increase the supply   20
of pizzas and I believe no one else was scavenging in this Dumpster. But the people in the shop became suspicious and began to retain their garbage in the shop overnight. While it lasted I had a steady supply of fresh, sometimes warm pizza. Because I knew the Dumpster I knew the source of the pizza, and because I

visited the Dumpster regularly I knew what was fresh and what was yesterday's.

The area I frequent is inhabited by many affluent   21
college students. I am not here by chance; the Dumpsters in this area are very rich. Students throw out many good things, including food. In particular they tend to throw everything out when they move at the end of a semester, before and after breaks, and around midterm, when many of them despair of college. So I find it advantageous to keep an eye on the academic calendar.

Cause and effect: why Eighner visits certain Dumpsters; why students throw out food

Students throw food away around breaks because   22
they do not know whether it has spoiled or will spoil before they return. A typical discard is a half jar of peanut butter. In fact, nonorganic peanut butter does not require refrigeration and is unlikely to spoil in any reasonable time. The student does not know that, and since it is Daddy's money, the student decides not to take a chance. Opened containers require caution and some attention to the question "Why was this discarded?" But in the case of discards from student apartments, the answer may be that the item was thrown out through carelessness, ignorance, or wastefulness. This can sometimes be deduced when the item is found with many others, including some that are obviously perfectly good.

Some students, and others, approach defrosting a   23
freezer by chucking out the whole lot. Not only do the circumstances of such a find tell the story, but also the mass of frozen goods stays cold for a long time and items may be found still frozen or freshly thawed.

Yogurt, cheese, and sour cream are items that are   24
often thrown out while they are still good. Occasionally I find cheese with a spot of mold, which of course I just pare off, and because it is obvious why such a cheese was discarded, I treat it with less suspicion than an apparently perfect cheese found in similar circumstances. Yogurt is often discarded, still sealed, only because the expiration date on the carton had passed. This is one of my favorite finds because yogurt will keep for several days, even in warm weather.

Students throw out canned goods and staples at   25
the end of semesters and when they give up college at midterm. Drugs, pornography, spirits, and the like are often discarded when parents are expected — Dad's Day, for example. And spirits also turn up after big

party weekends, presumably discarded by the newly reformed. Wine and spirits, of course, keep perfectly well even once opened, but the same cannot be said of beer.

My test for carbonated soft drinks is whether they 26 still fizz vigorously. Many juices or other beverages are too acidic or too syrupy to cause much concern, provided they are not visibly contaminated. I have discovered nasty molds in the vegetable juices, even when the product was found under its original seal; I recommend that such products be decanted slowly into a clear glass. Liquids always require some care. One hot day I found a large jug of Pat O'Brien's Hurricane mix. The jug had been opened but was still ice cold. I drank three large glasses before it became apparent to me that someone had added rum to the mix, and not a little rum. I never tasted the rum, and by the time I began to feel the effects I had already ingested a very large quantity of the beverage. Some divers would have considered this a boon, but being suddenly intoxicated in a public place in the early afternoon is not my idea of a good time.

Examples: liquids that require care

I have heard of people maliciously contaminating 27 discarded food and even handouts, but mostly I have heard of this from people with vivid imaginations who have had no experience with Dumpsters themselves. Just before the pizza shop stopped discarding its garbage at night, jalapeños began showing up on most of the thrown-out pizzas. If indeed this was meant to discourage me, it was a wasted effort because I am a native Texan.

For myself, I avoid game, poultry, pork, and egg- 28 based foods, whether I find them raw or cooked. I seldom have the means to cook what I find, but when I do I avail myself of plentiful supplies of beef, which is often in very good condition. I suppose fish becomes disagreeable before it becomes dangerous. Lizbeth is happy to have any such thing that is past its prime and, in fact, does not recognize fish as food until it is quite strong.

Home leftovers, as opposed to surpluses from 29 restaurants, are very often bad. Evidently, especially among students, there is a common type of personality that carefully wraps up even the smallest leftover and shoves it into the back of the refrigerator for six months or so before discarding it. Characteristic of this type are the reused jars and margarine tubs to which the remains are committed. I avoid ethnic foods I am unfamiliar with. If I do not know what it is supposed to look like when it is good, I cannot be certain I will be able to tell if it is bad.

No matter how careful I am I still get dysentery at least once a month, oftener in warmer weather. I do not want to paint too romantic a picture. Dumpster diving has serious drawbacks as a way of life. 30

Process: how to scavenge

I learned to scavenge gradually, on my own. Since then I have initiated several companions into the trade. I have learned that there is a predictable series of stages a person goes through in learning to scavenge. 31

At first the new scavenger is filled with disgust and self-loathing. He is ashamed of being seen and may lurk around, trying to duck behind things, or he may try to dive at night. (In fact, most people instinctively look away from a scavenger. By skulking around, the novice calls attention to himself and arouses suspicion. Diving at night is ineffective and needlessly messy.) 32

Every grain of rice seems to be a maggot. Everything seems to stink. He can wipe the egg yolk off the found can, but he cannot erase from his mind the stigma of eating garbage. 33

That stage passes with experience. The scavenger finds a pair of running shoes that fit and look and smell brand-new. He finds a pocket calculator in perfect working order. He finds pristine ice cream, still frozen, more than he can eat or keep. He begins to understand: People throw away perfectly good stuff, a lot of perfectly good stuff. 34

At this stage, Dumpster shyness begins to dissipate. The diver, after all, has the last laugh. He is finding all manner of good things that are his for the taking. Those who disparage his profession are the fools, not he. 35

He may begin to hang on to some perfectly good things for which he has neither a use nor a market. Then he begins to take note of the things that are not perfectly good but are nearly so. He mates a Walkman with broken earphones and one that is missing a battery cover. He picks up things that he can repair. 36

At this stage he may become lost and never recover. Dumpsters are full of things of some potential value to someone and also of things that never have much 37 intrinsic value but are interesting. All the Dumpster divers I have known come to the point of trying to acquire everything they touch. Why not take it, they reason, since it is all free? This is, of course, hopeless. Most divers come to realize that they must restrict themselves to items of relatively immediate utility. But in some cases the diver simply cannot control himself. I have met several of these pack-rat types. Their ideas of the values of various pieces of junk verge on the psychotic. Every bit of glass may be a diamond, they think, and all that glisters,* gold.

Cause and effect: why Eighner gains weight when he scavenges

I tend to gain weight when I am scavenging. Partly   38
this is because I always find far more pizza and doughnuts than water-packed tuna, nonfat yogurt, and fresh vegetables. Also I have not developed much faith in the reliability of Dumpsters as a food source, although it has been proven to me many times. I tend to eat as if I have no idea where my next meal is coming from. But mostly I just hate to see food go to waste and so I eat much more than I should. Something like this drives the obsession to collect junk.

As for collecting objects, I usually restrict myself to   39
collecting one kind of small object at a time, such as pocket calculators, sunglasses, or campaign buttons.

Cause and effect: why Eighner saves items

To live on the street I must anticipate my needs to a certain extent: I must pick up and save warm bedding I find in August because it will not be found in Dumpsters in November. As I have no access to health care, I often hoard essential drugs, such as antibiotics and antihistamines. (This course can be recommended only to those with some grounding in pharmacology. Antibiotics, for example, even when indicated are worse than useless if taken in insufficient amounts.) But even if I had a home with extensive storage space, I could not save everything that might be valuable in some contingency.

I have proprietary feelings about my Dumpsters. As   40
I have mentioned, it is no accident that I scavenge from ones where good finds are common. But my limited

Comparison and contrast: Dumpsters in rich and poorer areas

experience with Dumpsters in other areas suggests to me that even in poorer areas, Dumpsters, if attended with sufficient diligence, can be made to yield a livelihood. The rich students discard perfectly good kiwi fruit; poorer people discard perfectly good apples.

* Eds. note — Glitters.

Slacks and Polo shirts are found in one place; jeans and T-shirts in the other. The population of competitors rather than the affluence of the dumpers most affects the feasibility of survival by scavenging. The large number of competitors is what puts me off the idea of trying to scavenge in places like Los Angeles.

Curiously, I do not mind my direct competition, 41 other scavengers, so much as I hate the can scroungers.

Cause and effect: why people scrounge cans

People scrounge cans because they have to have a 42 little cash. I have tried scrounging cans with an able-bodied companion. Afoot a can scrounger simply cannot make more than a few dollars in a day. One can extract the necessities of life from the Dumpsters directly with far less effort than would be required to accumulate the equivalent value in cans. (These observations may not hold in places with container redemption laws.)

Can scroungers, then, are people who must have 43 small amounts of cash. These are drug addicts and winos, mostly the latter because the amounts of cash are so small. Spirits and drugs do, like all other commodities, turn up in Dumpsters and the scavenger will from time to time have a half bottle of a rather good wine with his dinner. But the wino cannot survive on these occasional finds; he must have his daily dose to stave off the DTs. All the cans he can carry will buy about three bottles of Wild Irish Rose.

Comparison and contrast: can scroungers vs. true scavengers

I do not begrudge them the cans, but can scroungers 44 tend to tear up the Dumpsters, mixing the contents and littering the area. They become so specialized that they can see only cans. They earn my contempt by passing up change, canned goods, and readily hockable items.

There are precious few courtesies among scavengers. 45 But it is common practice to set aside surplus items: pairs of shoes, clothing, canned goods, and such. A true scavenger hates to see good stuff go to waste, and what he cannot use he leaves in good condition in plain sight.

Can scroungers lay waste to everything in their 46 path and will stir one of a pair of good shoes to the bottom of a Dumpster, to be lost or ruined in the muck. Can scroungers will even go through individual garbage cans, something I have never seen a scavenger do.

Individual garbage cans are set out on the public 47 easement only on garbage days. On the other days going through them requires trespassing close to a dwelling. Going through individual garbage cans without scattering litter is almost impossible. Litter is likely to reduce the public's tolerance of scavenging. Individual cans are simply not as productive as Dumpsters; people in houses and duplexes do not move so often and for some reason do not tend to discard as much useful material. Moreover, the time required to go through one garbage can that serves one household is not much less than the time required to go through a Dumpster that contains the refuse of twenty apartments.

Cause and effect: why scavengers do not go through individual garbage cans

But my strongest reservation about going through individual garbage cans is that this seems to me a very personal kind of invasion to which I would object if I were a householder. Although many things in Dumpsters are obviously meant never to come to light, a Dumpster is somehow less personal. 48

I avoid trying to draw conclusions about the people who dump in the Dumpsters I frequent. I think it would be unethical to do so, although I know many people will find the idea of scavenger ethics too funny for words. 49

Examples: things found in Dumpsters

Dumpsters contain bank statements, correspondence, and other documents, just as anyone might expect. But there are also less obvious sources of information. Pill bottles, for example. The labels bear the name of the patient, the name of the doctor, and the name of the drug. AIDS drugs and antipsychotic medicines, to name but two groups, are specific and are seldom prescribed for any other disorders. The plastic compacts for birth-control pills usually have complete label information. 50

Despite all of this sensitive information, I have had only one apartment resident object to my going through the Dumpster. In that case it turned out the resident was a university athlete who was taking bets and who was afraid I would turn up his wager slips. 51

Occasionally a find tells a story. I once found a small paper bag containing some unused condoms, several partial tubes of flavored sexual lubricants, a partially used compact of birth-control pills, and the torn pieces of a picture of a young man. Clearly she was through with him and planning to give up sex altogether. 52

Dumpster things are often sad — abandoned teddy bears, shredded wedding books, despaired-of sales kits. 53

I find many pets lying in state in Dumpsters. Although I hope to get off the streets so that Lizbeth can have a long and comfortable old age, I know this hope is not very realistic. So I suppose when her time comes she too will go into a Dumpster. I will have no better place for her. And after all, it is fitting, since for most of her life her livelihood has come from the Dumpster. When she finds something I think is safe that has been spilled from a Dumpster, I let her have it. She already knows the route around the best ones. I like to think that if she survives me she will have a chance of evading the dog catcher and of finding her sustenance on the route.

Silly vanities also come to rest in the Dumpsters. I am a rather accomplished needleworker. I get a lot of material from the Dumpsters. Evidently sorority girls, hoping to impress someone, perhaps themselves, with their mastery of a womanly art, buy a lot of embroider-by-number kits, work a few stitches horribly, and eventually discard the whole mess. I pull out their stitches, turn the canvas over, and work an original design. Do not think I refrain from chuckling as I make gifts from these kits. 54

I find diaries and journals. I have often thought of compiling a book of literary found objects. And perhaps I will one day. But what I find is hopelessly commonplace and bad without being, even unconsciously, camp. College students also discard their papers. I am horrified to discover the kind of paper that now merits an A in an undergraduate course. I am grateful, however, for the number of good books and magazines the students throw out. 55

In the area I know best I have never discovered vermin in the Dumpster, but there are two kinds of kitty surprise. One is alley cats whom I meet as they leap, claws first, out of Dumpsters. This is especially thrilling when I have Lizbeth in tow. The other kind of kitty surprise is a plastic garbage bag filled with some ponderous, amorphous mass. This always proves to be used cat litter. 56

City bees harvest doughnut glaze and this makes the Dumpster at the doughnut shop more interesting. My faith in the instinctive wisdom of animals is always shaken whenever I see Lizbeth attempt to catch a bee in her mouth, which she does whenever bees are present. Evidently some birds find Dumpsters profitable, for 57 birdie surprise is almost as common as kitty surprise of the first kind. In hunting season all kinds of small game turn up in Dumpsters, some of it, sadly, not entirely dead. Curiously, summer and winter, maggots are uncommon.

The worst of the living and near-living hazards of the Dumpsters are the fire ants. The food they claim is not much of a loss, but they are vicious and aggressive. It is very easy to brush against some surface of the Dumpster and pick up half a dozen or more fire ants, usually in some sensitive area such as the underarm. One advantage of bringing Lizbeth along as I make Dumpster rounds is that, for obvious reasons, she is very alert to ground-based fire ants. When Lizbeth recognizes a fire-ant infestation around our feet, she does the Dance of the Zillion Fire Ants. I have learned not to ignore this warning from Lizbeth, whether I perceive the tiny ants or not, but to remove ourselves at Lizbeth's first *pas de bourée.** All the more so because the ants are the worst in the summer months when I wear flip-flops if I have them. (Perhaps someone will misunderstand this. Lizbeth does the Dance of the Zillion Fire Ants when she recognizes more fire ants than she cares to eat, not when she is being bitten. Since I have learned to react promptly, she does not get bitten at all. It is the isolated patrol of fire ants that falls in Lizbeth's range that deserves pity. She finds them quite tasty.) 58

Process: how to go through a Dumpster

By far the best way to go through a Dumpster is to lower yourself into it. Most of the good stuff tends to settle at the bottom because it is usually weightier than the rubbish. My more athletic companions have often demonstrated to me that they can extract much good material from a Dumpster I have already been over. 59

To those psychologically or physically unprepared to enter a Dumpster, I recommend a stout stick, preferably with some barb or hook at one end. The hook can be used to grab plastic garbage bags. When I find canned goods or other objects loose at the bottom of a Dumpster, I lower a bag into it, roll the desired object into the bag, and then hoist the bag out — a procedure more easily described than executed. Much Dumpster diving is a matter of experience for which nothing will do except practice. 60

---

* Eds. note — A ballet step.

Dumpster diving is outdoor work, often surprisingly pleasant. It is not entirely predictable; things of interest turn up every day and some days there are finds of great value. I am always very pleased when I can turn up exactly the thing I most wanted to find. Yet in spite of the element of chance, scavenging more than most other pursuits tends to yield returns in some proportion to the effort and intelligence brought to bear. It is very sweet to turn up a few dollars in change from a Dumpster that has just been gone over by a wino.

61

The land is now covered with cities. The cities are full of Dumpsters. If a member of the canine race is ever able to know what it is doing, then Lizbeth knows that when we go around to the Dumpsters, we are hunting. I think of scavenging as a modern form of self-reliance. In any event, after having survived nearly ten years of government service, where everything is geared to the lowest common denominator, I find it refreshing to have work that rewards initiative and effort. Certainly I would be happy to have a sinecure again, but I am no longer heartbroken that I left one.

62

Cause and effect: results of Eighner's experiences as a scavenger

I find from the experience of scavenging two rather deep lessons. The first is to take what you can use and let the rest go by. I have come to think that there is no value in the abstract. A thing I cannot use or make useful, perhaps by trading, has no value however rare or fine it may be. I mean useful in some broad sense — some art I would find useful and some otherwise.

63

I was shocked to realize that some things are not worth acquiring, but now I think it is so. Some material things are white elephants that eat up the possessor's substance. The second lesson is the transience of material being. This has not quite converted me to a dualist,* but it has made some headway in that direction. I do not suppose that ideas are immortal, but certainly mental things are longer lived than other material things.

64

Once I was the sort of person who invests objects with sentimental value. Now I no longer have those objects, but I have the sentiments yet.

65

Many times in our travels I have lost everything but the clothes I was wearing and Lizbeth. The things I find in Dumpsters, the love letters and rag dolls of so many

66

---

* EDS. NOTE — Someone who believes that the world consists of two opposing forces, such as mind and matter.

lives, remind me of this lesson. Now I hardly pick up a thing without envisioning the time I will cast it aside. This I think is a healthy state of mind. Almost everything I have now has already been cast out at least once, proving that what I own is valueless to someone.

Anyway, I find my desire to grab for the gaudy bauble has been largely sated. I think this is an attitude I share with the very wealthy — we both know there is plenty more where what we have came from. Between us are the rat-race millions who nightly scavenge the cable channels looking for they know not what.   67

I am sorry for them.   68

•   •   •

Comprehension

1. In your own words, give a one-sentence definition of *Dumpster diving.*
2. List some of Eighner's answers to the question, "Why was this discarded?" (8). What additional reasons can you think of?
3. What foods does Eighner take particular care to avoid? Why?
4. In paragraph 30, Eighner comments, "Dumpster diving has serious drawbacks as a way of life." What drawbacks does he cite in his essay? What additional drawbacks are implied? Can you think of others?
5. Summarize the stages in the process of learning to scavenge.
6. In addition to food, what else does Eighner scavenge for? Into what general categories do these items fall?
7. Why does Eighner hate can scroungers?
8. What lessons has Eighner learned as a Dumpster diver?

Purpose and Audience

1. In paragraph 6, Eighner states his purpose: to record what he has learned as a Dumpster diver. What additional purposes do you think he had in setting his ideas down on paper?
2. Do you think most readers are apt to respond to Eighner's essay with sympathy? Pity? Impatience? Contempt? Disgust? How do you react? Why?
3. Why do you think Eighner chose not to provide much background about his life — his upbringing, education, or work history — before he became homeless? Do you think this decision was a wise one? How might such information (for example, any of the details in the headnote that precedes the essay) have changed readers' reactions to his discussion?
4. In paragraph 8, Eighner presents three principles one must follow to eat safely from a Dumpster; in paragraphs 59–60 he explains how to go through a Dumpster; and throughout the essay he includes many

cautions and warnings. Clearly, he does not expect his audience to take up Dumpster diving. What, then, is his purpose in including such detailed explanations?

5. When Eighner begins paragraph 9 with "Perhaps everyone who has a kitchen," he encourages readers to identify with him. Where else does he make efforts to help readers imagine themselves in his place? Are these efforts successful? Explain your response.

6. What effect do you think the essay's last sentence is calculated to have on readers? What effect does it have on you?

Style and Structure

1. Eighner opens his essay with a fairly conventional strategy: extended definitions of *Dumpster* and *Dumpster diving*. What techniques does he use in paragraphs 1 through 3 to develop these definitions? Is beginning with definitions the best strategy for this essay? Explain your answer.

2. This long essay contains three one-sentence paragraphs. Why do you think Eighner isolates these sentences? Do you think any of them should be combined with an adjacent paragraph? Explain your reasoning.

3. As the introductory note explains, Eighner chose to retain the present tense even though he was no longer homeless when the essay was published. Why do you think he decided to preserve the present tense?

4. Eighner's essay includes a number of lists that catalog items he came across (for example, in paragraphs 5 and 50). Identify as many of these lists as you can. Why do you think Eighner includes such extensive lists?

Vocabulary Projects

1. Define each of the following words as it is used in this selection.

proprietary (1)	decanted (26)	feasibility (40)
niche (4)	ingested (26)	stave (43)
sporadic (5)	avail (28)	commonplace (55)
bohemian (8)	skulking (32)	vermin (56)
dilettanti (8)	stigma (33)	sinecure (62)
phobic (10)	pristine (34)	transience (64)
pared (15)	dissipate (35)	gaudy (67)
pathogens (16)	intrinsic (37)	bauble (67)
staples (25)	contingency (39)	

2. In paragraph 3, Eighner suggests several alternative words for *diving* as he uses it in his essay. Consult an unabridged dictionary to determine the connotations of each of his alternatives. What are the pros and cons of substituting one of these words for *diving* in Eighner's title and throughout the essay?

Journal Entry

In paragraphs 21–25, Eighner discusses the discarding of food by college students. Does your own experience support his observations? Do you think he is being too hard on students, or does his characterization seem accurate?

Writing Workshop

1. Write an essay about a homeless person you have seen in your community. Use any patterns you like to structure your paper. When you have finished, annotate your essay to identify the patterns you have used.
2. Write an email to your school's dean of students recommending steps that can be taken on your campus to redirect discarded (but edible) food to the homeless. Use process and exemplification to structure your message, and use information from Eighner's essay to support your points. (Be sure to acknowledge your source.)
3. Taking Eighner's point of view and using information from his essay, write an argumentative essay with a thesis statement that takes a strong stand against homelessness and recommends government or private measures to end it. If you like, you may write your essay in the form of a statement by Eighner to a congressional committee. Document any words or ideas you borrow from Eighner, and include a works-cited page. (See the Appendix for information on documentation formats.)

Combining the Patterns

Review the annotations that identify each pattern of development used in this essay. Which patterns seem to be most effective in helping you understand and empathize with the life of a homeless person? Why?

Thematic Connections

- "The Human Cost of an Illiterate Society" (page 248)
- "The Power of Words in Wartime" (page 363)
- "The Untouchable" (page 512)
- The Declaration of Independence (page 575)

JUDITH ORTIZ COFER

The Myth of the Latin Woman: I Just Met a Girl Named Maria

Born in Puerto Rico in 1952, Judith Ortiz Cofer moved to New Jersey with her family when she was four. She is now Regents' and Franklin Professor of English and Creative Writing at the University of Georgia. Widely anthologized, Ortiz Cofer has published three collections of poetry, including *A Love Story Beginning in Spanish* (2005); three essay collections, including *Silent Dancing* (1990) and *The Latin Deli* (1993); three novels, including the young adult novel *Call Me Maria* (2006); and the short story collection *An Island Like You: Stories of the Barrio* (1995). In a recent interview, she commented on her early writing: "Poetry allowed me to become intimate with English. And it allowed me to master the one skill that I try to teach my students — and if that's the only thing I accomplish, I consider it a success — and that is succinctness: economy and concentration of language. Why use fifteen words when one clear, elegant sentence will do it?"

Background on images of Hispanic women in film

During the era of silent film, Hispanic performers found a particular niche with the popularity of the stereotypical "Latin lover." Although Hispanic actors enjoyed much greater success, a handful of Hispanic actresses, such as Myrtle Gonzalez and Beatriz Michelina, played in leading roles that did not always cast them as Latina. For example, Mexican-born Dolores del Rio, the only Hispanic actress to achieve international stardom during the period, played characters named Evelyn Iffield and Jeanne Lamont as well as Carlotta de Silva and Carmelita de Granados. However, in the late 1920s, the advent of sound brought many fewer movie roles for Hispanic actresses. Some who found success during the thirties and forties conformed to broad stereotypes — for example "Mexican Spitfire" Lupe Velez, Carmen "the Lady in the Tutti-Frutti Hat" Miranda, and Maria Montez's hot-blooded seductresses. Others gave up any sense of themselves as Hispanic on screen (as was the case for Margarita Carmen Cansino, whose hair was dyed, eyebrows heavily plucked, and skin lightened to make her into the movie star Rita Hayworth). In the fifties and sixties, actresses with star quality such as Katy Jurado and Rita Moreno (who won a supporting actress Academy Award for her fiery Anita in *West Side Story*) were generally relegated to "exotic" or comic roles and rarely played leads. The sixties saw the stardom of bombshell Raquel Welch (born Jo Raquel Tejada), who, like Hayworth, played down her Hispanic roots; but it was not really until the nineties that young performers such as Jessica Alba, Jennifer Lopez, Penelope Cruz, and Salma Hayek could come into their own, playing Hispanics who are more than one-dimensional stereotypes or characters whose ethnicity is not important.

On a bus trip to London from Oxford University where I was earning   1
some graduate credits one summer, a young man, obviously fresh from a
pub, spotted me and as if struck by inspiration went down on his knees in
the aisle. With both hands over his heart he broke into an Irish tenor's ren-
dition of "Maria" from *West Side Story*.* My politely amused fellow passengers gave his lovely voice the round of gentle applause it deserved. Though
I was not quite as amused, I managed my version of an English smile: no
show of teeth, no extreme contortions of the facial muscles — I was at this
time of my life practicing reserve and cool. Oh, that British control, how I
coveted it. But "Maria" had followed me to London, reminding me of a
prime fact of my life: you can leave the island, master the English language,
and travel as far as you can, but if you are a Latina, especially one like me
who so obviously belongs to Rita Moreno's** gene pool, the island travels
with you.

This is sometimes a very good thing — it may win you that extra min-   2
ute of someone's attention. But with some people, the same things can
make *you* an island — not a tropical paradise but an Alcatraz, a place
nobody wants to visit. As a Puerto Rican girl living in the United States†
and wanting like most children to "belong," I resented the stereotype that
my Hispanic appearance called forth from many people I met.

Growing up in a large urban center in New Jersey during the 1960s, I   3
suffered from what I think of as "cultural schizophrenia." Our life was
designed by my parents as a microcosm of their *casas*‡ on the island. We
spoke in Spanish, ate Puerto Rican food bought at the *bodega*,§ and practiced strict Catholicism at a church that allotted us a one-hour slot each
week for mass, performed in Spanish by a Chinese priest trained as a missionary for Latin America.

As a girl I was kept under strict surveillance by my parents, since my   4
virtue and modesty were, by their cultural equation, the same as their
honor. As a teenager I was lectured constantly on how to behave as a proper
senorita. But it was a conflicting message I received, since the Puerto Rican
mothers also encouraged their daughters to look and act like women and
to dress in clothes our Anglo friends and their mothers found too "mature"
and flashy. The difference was, and is, cultural; yet I often felt humiliated
when I appeared at an American friend's party wearing a dress more suitable to a semi-formal than to a playroom birthday celebration. At Puerto
Rican festivities, neither the music nor the colors we wore could be too
loud.

---

* EDS. NOTE — A Broadway musical, based on *Romeo and Juliet*, about two rival New
York street gangs, one Anglo and one Puerto Rican.

** EDS. NOTE — Puerto Rico–born actress who won an Oscar for her role in the 1960
movie version of *West Side Story*.

† EDS. NOTE — Although it is an island, Puerto Rico is part of the United States.

‡ EDS. NOTE — Homes.

§ EDS. NOTE — Small grocery store.

I remember Career Day in our high school, when teachers told us to come dressed as if for a job interview. It quickly became obvious that to the Puerto Rican girls "dressing up" meant wearing their mother's ornate jewelry and clothing, more appropriate (by mainstream standards) for the company Christmas party than as daily office attire. That morning I had agonized in front of my closet, trying to figure out what a "career girl" would wear. I knew how to dress for school (at the Catholic school I attended, we all wore uniforms), I knew how to dress for Sunday mass, and I knew what dresses to wear for parties at my relatives' homes. Though I do not recall the precise details of my Career Day outfit, it must have been a composite of these choices. But I remember a comment my friend (an Italian American) made in later years that coalesced my impressions of that day. She said that at the business school she was attending, the Puerto Rican girls always stood out for wearing "everything at once." She meant, of course, too much jewelry, too many accessories. On that day at school we were simply made the negative models by the nuns, who were themselves not credible fashion experts to any of us. But it was painfully obvious to me that to the others, in their tailored skirts and silk blouses, we must have seemed "hopeless" and "vulgar." Though I now know that most adolescents feel out of step much of the time, I also know that for the Puerto Rican girls of my generation that sense was intensified. The way our teachers and classmates looked at us that day in school was just a taste of the cultural clash that awaited us in the real world, where prospective employers and men on the street would often misinterpret our tight skirts and jingling bracelets as a "come-on."

Mixed cultural signals have perpetuated certain stereotypes — for example, that of the Hispanic woman as the "hot tamale" or sexual firebrand. It is a one-dimensional view that the media have found easy to promote. In their special vocabulary, advertisers have designated "sizzling" and "smoldering" as the adjectives of choice for describing not only the foods but also the women of Latin America. From conversations in my house I recall hearing about the harassment that Puerto Rican women endured in factories where the "boss-men" talked to them as if sexual innuendo was all they understood, and worse, often gave them the choice of submitting to their advances or being fired.

It is custom, however, not chromosomes, that leads us to choose scarlet over pale pink. As young girls, it was our mothers who influenced our decisions about clothes and colors — mothers who had grown up on a tropical island where the natural environment was a riot of primary colors, where showing your skin was one way to keep cool as well as to look sexy. Most important of all, on the island, women perhaps felt freer to dress and move more provocatively since, in most cases, they were protected by the traditions, mores, and laws of a Spanish/Catholic system of morality and machismo whose main rule was: *You may look at my sister, but if you touch her I will kill you.* The extended family and church structure could provide a young woman with a circle of safety in her small pueblo on the island; if a man "wronged" a girl, everyone would close in to save her family honor.

My mother has told me about dressing in her best party clothes on Saturday nights and going to the town's plaza to promenade with her girlfriends in front of the boys they liked. The males were thus given an opportunity to admire the women and to express their admiration in the form of *piropos*: erotically charged street poems they composed on the spot. (I have myself been subjected to a few *piropos* while visiting the island, and they can be outrageous, although custom dictates that they must never cross into obscenity.) This ritual, as I understand it, also entails a show of studied indifference on the woman's part; if she is "decent," she must not acknowledge the man's impassioned words. So I do understand how things can be lost in translation. When a Puerto Rican girl dressed in her idea of what is attractive meets a man from the mainstream culture who has been trained to react to certain types of clothing as a sexual signal, a clash is likely to take place. I remember the boy who took me to my first formal dance leaning over to plant a sloppy, over-eager kiss painfully on my mouth; when I didn't respond with sufficient passion, he remarked resentfully: "I thought you Latin girls were supposed to mature early," as if I were expected to *ripen* like a fruit or vegetable, not just grow into womanhood like other girls.

It is surprising to my professional friends that even today some people, including those who should know better, still put others "in their place." It happened to me most recently during a stay at a classy metropolitan hotel favored by young professional couples for weddings. Late one evening after the theater, as I walked toward my room with a colleague (a woman with whom I was coordinating an arts program), a middle-aged man in a tuxedo, with a young girl in satin and lace on his arm, stepped directly into our path. With his champagne glass extended toward me, he exclaimed "Evita!"*

Our way blocked, my companion and I listened as the man half-recited, half-bellowed "Don't Cry for Me, Argentina." When he finished, the young girl said: "How about a round of applause for my daddy?" We complied, hoping this would bring the silly spectacle to a close. I was becoming aware that our little group was attracting the attention of the other guests. "Daddy" must have perceived this too, and he once more barred the way as we tried to walk past him. He began to shout-sing a ditty to the tune of "La Bamba" — except the lyrics were about a girl named Maria whose exploits rhymed with her name and gonorrhea. The girl kept saying "Oh, Daddy" and looking at me with pleading eyes. She wanted me to laugh along with the others. My companion and I stood silently waiting for the man to end his offensive song. When he finished, I looked not at him but at his daughter. I advised her calmly never to ask her father what he had done in the

8

9

10

---

* EDS. NOTE — A Broadway musical about Eva Duarte de Perón, the former first lady of Argentina.

army. Then I walked between them and to my room. My friend complimented me on my cool handling of the situation, but I confessed that I had really wanted to push the jerk into the swimming pool. This same man — probably a corporate executive, well-educated, even worldly by most standards — would not have been likely to regale an Anglo woman with a dirty song in public. He might have checked his impulse by assuming that she could be somebody's wife or mother, or at least *somebody* who might take offense. But, to him, I was just an Evita or a Maria: merely a character in his cartoon-populated universe.

Another facet of the myth of the Latin woman in the United States is   11
the menial, the domestic — Maria the housemaid or countergirl. It's true that work as domestics, as waitresses, and in factories is all that's available to women with little English and few skills. But the myth of the Hispanic menial — the funny maid, mispronouncing words and cooking up a spicy storm in a shiny California kitchen — has been perpetuated by the media in the same way that "Mammy" from *Gone with the Wind* became America's idea of the black woman for generations. Since I do not wear my diplomas around my neck for all to see, I have on occasion been sent to that "kitchen" where some think I obviously belong.

One incident has stayed with me, though I recognize it as a minor   12
offense. My first public poetry reading took place in Miami, at a restaurant where a luncheon was being held before the event. I was nervous and excited as I walked in with notebook in hand. An older woman motioned me to her table, and thinking (foolish me) that she wanted me to autograph a copy of my newly published slender volume of verse, I went over. She ordered a cup of coffee from me, assuming that I was the waitress. (Easy enough to mistake my poems for menus, I suppose.) I know it wasn't an intentional act of cruelty. Yet of all the good things that happened later, I remember that scene most clearly, because it reminded me of what I had to overcome before anyone would take me seriously. In retrospect I understand that my anger gave my reading fire. In fact, I have almost always taken any doubt in my abilities as a challenge, the result most often being the satisfaction of winning a convert, of seeing the cold, appraising eyes warm to my words, the body language change, the smile that indicates I have opened some avenue for communication. So that day as I read, I looked directly at that woman. Her lowered eyes told me she was embarrassed at her faux pas, and when I willed her to look up at me, she graciously allowed me to punish her with my full attention. We shook hands at the end of the reading and I never saw her again. She has probably forgotten the entire incident, but maybe not.

Yet I am one of the lucky ones. There are thousands of Latinas without   13
the privilege of an education or the entrees into society that I have. For them life is a constant struggle against the misconceptions perpetuated by the myth of the Latina. My goal is to try to replace the old stereotypes with a much more interesting set of realities. Every time I give a reading, I hope the stories I tell, the dreams and fears I examine in my work, can

achieve some universal truth that will get my audience past the particulars of my skin color, my accent, or my clothes.

I once wrote a poem in which I called all Latinas "God's brown daugh- 14 ters." This poem is really a prayer of sorts, offered upward, but also, through the human-to-human channel of art, outward. It is a prayer for communication and for respect. In it, Latin women pray "in Spanish to an Anglo God/with a Jewish heritage," and they are "fervently hoping/that if not omnipotent,/at least He be bilingual."

• • •

Comprehension

1. What does Cofer mean by "cultural schizophrenia" (3)?
2. What "conflicting message" (4) did Cofer receive from her family?
3. What points does Cofer make by including each of the following in her essay?
   - The story about the young man in Oxford (1)
   - The story about Career Day (5)
   - The story about the poetry reading (12)
4. According to Cofer, what stereotypes are commonly applied to Latinas?
5. How does Cofer explain why she and other Puerto Rican women like to dress as they do? Why do outsiders think they dress this way?
6. What exactly is "the myth of the Latin woman" (11)?
7. How does Cofer hope to help people see beyond the stereotypes she describes? Is she successful?

Purpose and Audience

1. Which of the following do you think is Cofer's thesis? Why?
   - "[I]f you are a Latina, especially one like me who so obviously belongs to Rita Moreno's gene pool, the island travels with you" (1).
   - "As a Puerto Rican girl living in the United States. . . . I resented the stereotype that my Hispanic appearance called forth from many people I met" (2).
   - "My goal is to try to replace the old stereotypes with a much more interesting set of realities" (13).
2. Why does Cofer begin paragraph 13 with, "Yet I am one of the lucky ones"? How do you think she expects her audience to react to this statement?
3. Despite its use of Spanish words, this essay is directed at an Anglo audience. How can you tell?
4. How might you expect non-Latinas — or men — to respond to this essay?

Style and Structure

1. Cofer opens her essay with a story about an incident in her life. Considering her subject matter and her audience, is this an effective opening strategy? Why, or why not?

2. In paragraphs 1–2, Cofer uses the word *island* to suggest several different things. What positive connotations — and what negative ones — does this word have for her?

3. What do you think Cofer means to suggest with these expressions in paragraph 8?
   - "erotically charged"
   - "studied indifference"
   - "lost in translation"
   - "mainstream culture"

4. Cofer does not introduce the stereotype of the Latina as "the menial, the domestic" until paragraph 11, when she devotes two paragraphs to this part of the stereotype. Why does she wait so long? Should this discussion have appeared earlier? Should it have been deleted altogether? Explain your reasoning.

5. Several of Cofer's paragraphs — for example, paragraphs 5, 8, 10, and 12 — are quite long. Do you think any of these paragraphs should be divided into two separate paragraphs? If so, where would you divide each paragraph, and why?

6. How do you interpret the lines of poetry that Cofer quotes in her conclusion? Is this an effective concluding strategy? Why or why not?

Vocabulary Projects

1. Define each of the following words as it is used in this selection.

coveted (1)	innuendo (6)	complied (10)
microcosm (3)	machismo (7)	regale (10)
coalesced (5)	pueblo (7)	faux pas (12)
firebrand (6)	promenade (8)	

2. Cofer uses Spanish words throughout this essay, and she does not define them. Find definitions of these words in a Spanish/English dictionary, such as SpanishDict.com, or at Google Language Tools. Would the English equivalents be just as effective as — or even more effective than — the Spanish words?

Journal Entry

On the basis of what she writes here, it seems as if Cofer does not confront the people who stereotype her and does not show anger, even in the incident described in paragraphs 9–10. Do you think she should have acted differently, or do you admire her restraint?

Writing Workshop

1. What stereotypes are applied by outsiders to your racial or ethnic group (or to people of your gender, intended profession, or geographic region)? Write an exemplification essay in which you argue that these stereotypes are untrue and potentially harmful. Support your thesis with passages of narration, comparison and contrast, and cause and effect.

2. Think of some books, films, advertisements, or TV shows that feature characters of your own racial or ethnic group. Write a classification essay in which you discuss the different ways in which these characters are portrayed. Use exemplification and description to explain your categories. In your thesis, evaluate the accuracy of these characterizations.

3. In paragraph 1 of her essay, Cofer says, "you can leave the island, master the English language, and travel as far as you can, but if you are a Latina, especially one like me who so obviously belongs to Rita Moreno's gene pool, the island travels with you." Editing this statement to suit your own "gene pool," use it as the thesis of an essay about the problems you have fitting in to some larger segment of society. Be sure to acknowledge Cofer as your source and to document your version of her statement as well as any words you quote.

Combining the Patterns

What patterns of development does Cofer use? Annotate the essay to identify each pattern. Use the annotations accompanying "On Dumpster Diving" (page 714) as a guide.

Thematic Connections

- "Only Daughter" (page 97)
- "Sixty-Nine Cents" (page 102)
- "Just Walk On By" (page 236)
- "The Power of Words in Wartime" (page 363)

Inked Well

Poet David Kirby is a long time professor of English at Florida State University, where he teaches nineteenth-century American literature and creative writing. He has authored or coauthored twenty-nine books, including the poetry collections *The House on Boulevard Street* (2007) and *The Ha-Ha* (2003), literary studies such as *Mark Strand and the Poet's Place in Contemporary Culture* (1990) and *Herman Melville* (1993), and the essay collection *Ultra-Talk: Johnny Cash, the Mafia, Shakespeare, Drum Music, St. Teresa of Avila, and 17 Other Colossal Topics of Conversation* (2007).

Background on tattoos

People have sported tattoos for more than five thousnd years. In some cultures, tattoos have marked a rite of passage into adulthood. They have also symbolized spiritual protection, status within a clan, fertility, and social ostracism, among other things. (Interestingly, the teachings of both Judaism and Islam specifically prohibit tattooing.) In modern Western culture, tattoos primarily serve as body adornment, although there are exceptions — for example, the Nazis forcibly tattooed identifying numbers on many Jews, and members of some street gangs wear tattoos that signify membership. In the United States today, the most popular tattoos are abstract tribal designs based on motifs that originated among Polynesian Islanders (historically, some of the most heavily tattooed people in the world), as well as Celtic designs, flowers and butterflies, angels, stars, dragons, Chinese characters, and swallows and anchors, once staples among sailors and now making a comeback. Increasingly, tattoo artists are being taken seriously, and an original design may be worth thousands of dollars, or even more. Today conventions of tattoo enthusiasts, such as the traveling Bodyart Expo, draw millions of participants each year. The cost of getting a tattoo can be as much as a hundred dollars an hour. (Getting *rid* of a tattoo can cost considerably more.)

Some tattooed people are easier to read than others. 1

When Richard Costello tried to sell stolen motorcycle parts on eBay 2 earlier this year, he put the items on the floor and photographed them, though the photos also included his bare feet, with the word *White* tattooed on one and *Trash* on the other. The bike's lawful owner did a Web search, found what appeared to be the stolen parts, and notified the Clearwater, Florida, police department. Since jail records typically include identifying marks, it didn't take long for local detectives to identify Mr. Costello and set up a sting. He was arrested after showing up with a van full of stolen parts and is now facing trial. According to Sgt. Greg Stewart, Mr. Costello "just tiptoed his way back to jail."

L'Affaire White Trash confirmed just about everything that I thought about tattoos until recently; namely, that in addition to being nasty and unsanitary, tattoos only grace the skins of either bottom feeders or those who want to pretend they are. Richard Costello's phenomenal act of self-betrayal wouldn't have been a surprise at all to modernist architect Adolph Loos, whose influential 1908 essay "Ornament and Crime" is still cited today as a potent argument against frills and fancy stuff. Mr. Loos wrote in effect a manifesto opposing decoration, which he saw as a mark of primitive cultures, and in favor of simplicity, which is a sign of, well, modernism. Thus, Mr. Loos reasoned, it's OK for a Pacific Islander to cover himself and all his possessions with ink and carvings, whereas "a modern person [i.e., a European] who tattoos himself is either a criminal or a degenerate. . . . People with tattoos not in prison are either latent criminals or degenerate aristocrats."

So, presuming the kid with a Tweety Bird tattoo on his forearm who delivered your pizza last night isn't a down-on-his-luck baronet who's trying to earn enough money to return to his ancestral estate in Northumberland and claim his seat on the Queen's Privy Council, does the fact that he's slinging pies mean that he simply hasn't lived long enough to commit his first murder? Not necessarily: tattoos have a richer social history than one might think.

Tattoos were brought to Europe from Polynesia by eighteenth-century British explorers, as Margo DeMello writes in *Bodies of Inscription: A Cultural History of the Modern Tattoo Community* (2000). Europeans who had tattoos in those days were not social bottom dwellers. And as Charles C. Mann points out in *1491* (2005), Americans first saw tattoos in the New World on their conflicted Indian hosts as early as 1580. To Protestants of ascetic temperaments, these exotic displays were of a piece with the colonists' propensity to see Indians as primeval savages.

Perhaps predictably, however, tattoos came ultimately to signify patriotism rather than exoticism in the United States. The first known professional tattoo artist in the United States was one Martin Hildebrandt, who set up shop in New York City in 1846. Mr. Hildebrandt became instrumental in establishing the tradition of the tattooed serviceman by practicing his craft on soldiers and sailors on both sides in the Civil War as he migrated from one camp to another.

And then occurred one of those curious little shifts that make history so delicious. Tattoos became fashionable among members of the European aristocracy, who encountered the practice during nineteenth-century trips to the Far East.

By the beginning of World War I, though, the lords and ladies had all but abandoned bodily decoration. Why? Because by then, anybody could get a tattoo. The laborious process involving hand-tapping ink into the skin with a single needle was made obsolete with the invention of the electric tattoo machine in 1891. Tattooing suddenly became easier, less painful, and, mainly, cheaper. This led to the speedy spread of the practice throughout the working class and its abandonment by the rich.

By the middle of the twentieth century, tattooing seemed largely the province of bikers, convicts, and other groups on the margins of society, much as Mr. Loos had predicted. Except for all those patriotic servicemen, a century ago tattoos were the tribal marks that you paid somebody to cut into your skin so that everyone would know you belonged to a world populated by crooks and creeps, along with a few bored aristocrats who would probably have been attracted to living a life of crime had their trust funds not rendered it redundant. And if things had stayed that way, I wouldn't be writing this essay: tattoos would be simply one more way of differentiating "Them" from "Us."

9

But "We" are the ones who are tattooed now: in the late twentieth century, the middle class began showing up in droves at tattoo parlors. A study in the June 2006 issue of the *Journal of the American Academy of Dermatology* reveals that as many as 24 percent of men and women between the ages of eighteen and fifty have one or more tattoos — up from just 15 to 16 percent in 2003. Men and women are equally likely to be tattooed, though the women surveyed are more likely to have body piercings, as well.

10

How did this change come to pass? Those of us who are certain we'll never get a tattoo will always shudder with joy when we read about knuckleheads like Richard Costello. But more and more people who wouldn't have dreamed of being tattooed a few years back are paying good money to have sketches of boom boxes, court jesters, and spider webs incised into their hides. Why, and what does it say about the world we live in?

11

To answer these questions, I walked the streets of Tallahassee, Florida, accosting total and sometimes menacing-looking strangers with the intent of asking them questions about the most intimate parts of their bodies. Any stereotypes of tattooed "victims" I had fell by the wayside rather quickly.

12

One of my first lessons was that people can get the biggest, most colorful tattoos either for exceedingly complex reasons or none at all. Jen (I'll use first names only), a pretty, slender brunette in her late twenties, said getting a tattoo was simply on a list of things she wanted to do. Melissa, a grad student in modern languages whom I spied in a bookstore wearing a pair of low-slung jeans, got a black and blue love knot high on one hip because she and her friend wanted identical tattoos, "even though she's not my friend anymore." Becky wanted a tattoo that would be a means of "making a promise to myself that I would become the person I wanted to be, that I would improve my life through hard work."

13

Of the dozen or so subjects I interviewed, Jodie was the sweetest, the most articulate, and the most heavily inked — her arms were fully sleeved in tattoos, and she was making plans to get started on her hands and neck. Jodie explained that she had been a "cutter" who "was having a lot of trouble with hurting myself physically for various reasons, so I began to get tattooed. It didn't take me long to realize that getting tattooed was quite comparable to cutting myself; it was a way for me to 'bleed out' the emotional pains which I was unable to deal with otherwise."

14

Jodie is smart as well as troubled. She knew she was hurting herself and would continue to do so, so she sublimated her self-destruction and made art of it, as surely as, say, poet Sylvia Plath* did — temporarily, anyway.   15

It seems that more and more people from every walk of life in these United States are getting tattooed. These pioneers are "deterritorializing" tattoos, in Ms. DeMello's words, liberating them from patriotic sailors and dim-bulb motorcycle thieves and making them available to soccer moms and dads.   16

Tattoos have always been a means of identifying oneself, notes Ms. DeMello, and are always meant to be read — even a tattoo that's hidden becomes a secret book of sorts. When you get a tattoo, you write yourself, in a manner of speaking, and make it possible for others to read you, which means that every tattoo has a story.   17

There are primarily two types of tattoo narratives, the Record Book and the Canvas. Melissa, the young woman who got her tattoo to signify bonding with a friend, was capturing a relationship as one might with a photograph. In the pop music world, rap artists and other musicians sometimes get tattoos of friends or relatives who have died violently or merely passed away. The Dixie Chicks agreed to get a little chick footprint on the insteps of their feet for every No. 1 album they had.   18

If your body is a Record Book, then you and everyone who sees you is looking back at the events depicted there. But if you see your body as a Canvas, then the story you tell is, at least in its conception and execution, as inner-driven as any by Faulkner or Hemingway. Jodie, for example, is going over every inch of her body, using it as a way to tell herself a story she's beginning to understand only gradually. The more she understands, the more she "revises," just as any other artist might: her first tattoo was "a horrible butterfly thing," she told me, "which has since been covered up with a lovely raven."   19

Every person with a tattoo is a link in a chain of body modification that goes back to the dawn of human history. Researchers have found sharpened pieces of manganese dioxide — black crayons, really — that Neanderthals may have used to color animal skins as well as their own. The ancient Egyptians practiced simple tattooing. Today, radically different cultures share an obsession with body remodeling that goes far beyond mere tattooing. African tribes pierce and scar the body routinely; weightlifters pump their pecs until they bulge like grapefruit; women pay for cosmetic breast enlargement or reduction. And if that's not enough evidence that body modification is endemic, I have one word for you: *Botox.*   20

The point of all this is self-expression — and we seem to be living in a time where that's what nearly everybody (word carefully chosen) wants to do, in one way or another. As with all lifestyle changes, the tricky part is knowing when to stop.   21

---

* EDS. NOTE — American confessional poet who committed suicide in 1963 at the age of thirty-one.

As I said, I used to think tattoos were for either lowlifes or those who   22
wanted to pretend they were, but my mind now stands changed by the
thoughtful, articulate people I talked to and the spectacular designs that
had been inked into their bodies. In a word, tattoos are now officially OK
by me.

Does that mean I'd get one? Not on your life.   23

• • •

Comprehension

1. Kirby opens his essay with a narrative that recounts "L'Affaire White Trash" (3). Why does he begin with this narrative? What does it illustrate about tattoos?

2. Where does Kirby present information on the history of tattoos? Why does he include this background? Is it necessary? Why does he return to this historical background in paragraph 20?

3. According to Kirby, how has the tattooed population changed over the years? What factors explain these changes?

4. What does Kirby mean when he says that "'We' are the ones who are tattooed now" (10)?

5. What two kinds of "tattoo narratives" does Kirby identify? How are they different?

6. According to Kirby, for what reasons do people get tattoos? Can you think of additional reasons?

7. How have Kirby's ideas about tattoos changed over the years? *Why* have they changed?

Purpose and Audience

1. Is Kirby's primary purpose to provide information about tattoos, to entertain readers, to explore his own feelings about tattoos, or to persuade readers to consider getting tattoos? Explain.

2. In paragraph 4, Kirby says, "Tattoos have a richer social history than one might think." Is this his essay's thesis? If not, what is the thesis of "Inked Well"?

3. Why do you think Kirby mentions the universal "obsession with body remodeling" in paragraph 20? How do you think he expects this reference to affect his audience's reactions to his thesis? How do you react?

Style and Structure

1. What do you see as this essay's dominant pattern of development? Why?

2. Kirby's first and last paragraphs are each just one sentence long. Are the short introduction and conclusion effective? If you were to expand them, what would you add? Why?

3. Where does Kirby cite experts? Where does he include statistics? What do these kinds of information add to his essay?

Vocabulary Projects

1. Define each of the following words as it is used in this selection.

sting (2)   droves (10)
ascetic (5)   incised (11)
propensity (5)   endemic (20)
primeval (5)

2. Explain the possible meanings of "Inked Well," the essay's title.

3. Go to a professional tattoo Web site such as tattoos.com, and list some words and phrases that are part of the vocabulary of the tattoo industry. Define several of these words and expressions in layperson's terms. Does Kirby use any of these terms? If not, why not?

4. What is the origin of the word *tattoo*? Check an online dictionary to find out.

Journal Entry

Do you see tattoos as art or as a kind of defacement or self-mutilation? Explain your feelings.

Writing Workshop

1. Find pictures of tattoos on Google Image. Then, write a classification-and-division essay that discusses the kinds of tattoos you find there. (You might want to begin by looking at "Four Tattoos," page 214). Be sure your essay has a thesis statement that makes a point about tattoos, and use exemplification, description, and comparison and contrast to support your thesis. If you like, you may illustrate your essay with photos or drawings you find on the Web, but if you do, remember to document your source.

2. In paragraph 11, Kirby asks what the prevalence of tattoos says about the world we live in. Using cause and effect as your dominant pattern of development, write an essay that tries to explain what accounts for this phenomenon. Use description and exemplification to support your points.

3. In paragraph 17, Kirby says, "When you get a tattoo, you write yourself, in a manner of speaking, and make it possible for others to read you, which means that every tattoo has a story." What story would you like your own tattoo (or tattoos) to tell?

Combining the Patterns

What patterns of development does Kirby use? Annotate the essay to identify each pattern. Use the annotations accompanying "On Dumpster Diving" (page 714) as a guide.

Thematic Connections

JONATHAN SWIFT

A Modest Proposal

Jonathan Swift (1667–1745) was born in Dublin, Ireland, and spent much of his life journeying between his homeland, where he had a modest income as an Anglican priest, and England, where he wished to be part of the literary establishment. The author of many satires and political pamphlets, he is best known today for *Gulliver's Travels* (1726), a sharp satire that, except among academics, is now read primarily as a fantasy for children.

Background on the English-Irish conflict

At the time Swift wrote "A Modest Proposal," Ireland had been essentially under British rule since 1171, with the British often brutally suppressing rebellions by the Irish people. When Henry VIII of England declared a Protestant Church of Ireland, many of the Irish remained fiercely Roman Catholic, and this led to even greater contention. By the early 1700s, the English-controlled Irish Parliament had passed laws that severely limited the rights of Irish Catholics, and British trade policies had begun to seriously depress the Irish economy. A fierce advocate for the Irish people in their struggle under British rule, Swift published several works supporting the Irish cause. The following sharply ironic essay was written during the height of a terrible famine in Ireland, when the British were proposing a devastating tax on the impoverished Irish citizenry. Note that Swift does not write in his own voice here but adopts the persona of one who does not recognize the barbarity of his "solution."

It is a melancholy object to those who walk through this great town* or travel in the country, when they see the streets, the roads, and cabin doors, crowded with beggars of the female sex, followed by three, four, or six children, all in rags and importuning every passenger for an alms. These mothers, instead of being able to work for their honest livelihood, are forced to employ all their time in strolling to beg sustenance for their helpless infants, who, as they grow up, either turn thieves for want of work, or leave their dear native country to fight for the Pretender in Spain, or sell themselves to the Barbadoes.**

I think it is agreed by all parties that this prodigious number of children in the arms, or on the backs, or at the heels of their mothers, and frequently of their fathers, is in the present deplorable state of the kingdom a very great additional grievance; and therefore whoever could find out a fair, cheap, and easy method of making these children sound, useful

---

* EDS. NOTE — Dublin.

** EDS. NOTE — Many young Irishmen left their country to fight as mercenaries in Spain's civil war or to work as indentured servants in the West Indies.

members of the commonwealth would deserve so well of the public as to have his statue set up for a preserver of the nation.

But my intention is very far from being confined to provide only for the children of professed beggars; it is of a much greater extent, and shall take in the whole number of infants at a certain age who are born of parents in effect as little able to support them as those who demand our charity in the streets.

As to my own part, having turned my thoughts for many years upon this important subject, and maturely weighed the several schemes of the other projectors, I have always found them grossly mistaken in their computation. It is true, a child just dropped from its dam may be supported by her milk for a solar year, with little other nourishment; at most not above the value of two shillings, which the mother may certainly get, or the value in scraps, by her lawful occupation of begging; and it is exactly at one year old that I propose to provide for them in such a manner as instead of being a charge upon their parents or the parish, or wanting food and raiment for the rest of their lives, they shall on the contrary contribute to the feeding, and partly to the clothing, of many thousands.

There is likewise another great advantage in my scheme, that it will prevent those involuntary abortions, and that horrid practice of women murdering their bastard children, alas, too frequent among us, sacrificing the poor innocent babies, I doubt, more to avoid the expense than the shame, which would move tears and pity in the most savage and inhuman breast.

The number of souls in this kingdom being usually reckoned one million and a half, of these I calculate there may be about two hundred thousand couples whose wives are breeders, from which number I subtract thirty thousand couples who are able to maintain their own children, although I apprehend there cannot be so many under the present distress of the kingdom; but this being granted, there will remain an hundred and seventy thousand breeders. I again subtract fifty thousand for those women who miscarry, or whose children die by accident or disease within the year. There only remain an hundred and twenty thousand children of poor parents annually born. The question therefore is, how this number shall be reared and provided for, which, as I have already said, under the present situation of affairs, is utterly impossible by all the methods hitherto proposed. For we can neither employ them in handicraft nor agriculture; we neither build houses (I mean in the country) nor cultivate land. They can very seldom pick up livelihood by stealing till they arrive at six years old, except where they are of towardly parts,* although I confess they learn the rudiments much earlier, during which time they can however be looked upon only as probationers, as I have been informed by a principal gentleman in the country of Cavan, who protested to me that he never knew

3

4

5

6

---

* EDS. NOTE — Precocious.

above one or two instances under the age of six, even in a part of the kingdom so renowned for the quickest proficiency in that art.

I am assured by our merchants that a boy or a girl before twelve years old is no salable commodity; and even when they come to this age, they will not yield above three pounds, or three pounds and half a crown at most on the Exchange; which cannot turn to account either to the parents or the kingdom, the charge of nutriment and rags having been at least four times that value. 7

I shall now therefore humbly propose my own thoughts, which I hope will not be liable to the least objection. 8

I have been assured by a very knowing American of my acquaintance in London, that a young healthy child well nursed is at a year old a most delicious, nourishing, and wholesome food, whether stewed, roasted, baked, or boiled; and I make no doubt that it will equally serve in fricasee or a ragout. 9

I do therefore humbly offer it to public consideration that of the hundred and twenty thousand children, already computed, twenty thousand may be reserved for breed, whereof only one fourth part to be males, which is more than we allow to sheep, black cattle, or swine; and my reason is that these children are seldom the fruits of marriage, a circumstance not much regarded by our savages, therefore one male will be sufficient to serve four females. That the remaining hundred thousand may at a year old be offered in sale to the persons of quality and fortune through the kingdom, always advising the mother to let them suck plentifully in the last month, so as to render them plump and fat for a good table. A child will make two dishes at an entertainment for friends; and when the family dines alone, the fore or hind quarter will make a reasonable dish, and seasoned with a little pepper or salt, will be very good boiled on the fourth day, especially in winter. 10

I have reckoned upon a medium that a child just born will weigh twelve pounds, and in a solar year if tolerably nursed increaseth to twenty-eight pounds. 11

I grant this food will be somewhat dear, and therefore very proper for landlords, who, as they have already devoured most of the parents, seem to have the best title to the children. 12

Infant's flesh will be in season throughout the year, but more plentiful in March, and a little before and after. For we are told by a grave author, an eminent French physician,* that fish being a prolific diet, there are more children born in Roman Catholic countries about nine months after Lent, than at any other season; therefore, reckoning a year after Lent, the markets will be more glutted than usual, because the number of popish infants is at least three to one in this kingdom; and therefore it will have one other collateral advantage, by lessening the number of Papists** among us. 13

---

* EDS. NOTE — François Rabelais, a sixteenth-century satirical writer.
** EDS. NOTE — Roman Catholics.

I have already computed the charge of nursing a beggar's child (in 14 which list I reckon all cottagers, laborers, and four fifths of the farmers) to be about two shillings per annum, rags included; and I believe no gentleman would repine to give ten shillings for the carcass of a good fat child, which, as I have said, will make four dishes of excellent nutritive meat, when he hath only some particular friend or his own family to dine with him. Thus the squire will learn to be a good landlord, and grow popular among the tenants; the mother will have eight shillings net profit, and be fit for work till she produces another child.

Those who are more thrifty (as I must confess the times require) may 15 flay the carcass; the skin of which artificially* dressed will make admirable gloves for ladies, and summer boots for fine gentlemen.

As to our city of Dublin, shambles** may be appointed for this purpose in the most convenient parts of it, and butchers we may be assured 16 will not be wanting; although I rather recommend buying the children alive, and dressing them hot from the knife as we do roasting pigs.

A very worthy person, a true lover of his country, and whose virtues I 17 highly esteem, was lately pleased in discoursing on this matter to offer a refinement upon my scheme. He said that many gentlemen of his kingdom, having of late destroyed their deer, he conceived that the want of venison might be well supplied by the bodies of young lads and maidens, not exceeding fourteen years of age nor under twelve, so great a number of both sexes in every county being now ready to starve for want of work and service; and these to be disposed of by their parents, if alive, or otherwise by their nearest relations. But with due deference to so excellent a friend and so deserving a patriot I cannot be altogether in his sentiments; for as to the males, my American acquaintance assured me from frequent experience that their flesh was generally tough and lean, like that of our schoolboys, by continual exercise, and their taste disagreeable; and to fatten them would not answer the charge. Then as to the females, it would, I think with humble submission, be a loss to the public, because they soon would become breeders themselves; and besides, it is not improbable that some scrupulous people might be apt to censure such a practice (although indeed very unjustly) as a little bordering upon cruelty; which, I confess, hath always been with me the strongest objection against any project, how well soever intended.

But in order to justify my friend, he confessed that this expedient was 18 put into his head by the famous Psalmanazar,† a native of the island Formosa, who came from thence to London above twenty years ago, and in conversation told my friend that in his country when any young person happened to be put to death, the executioner sold the carcass to the persons

---

* EDS. NOTE — Skillfully.
** EDS. NOTE — A slaughterhouse or meat market.
† EDS. NOTE — Frenchman who passed himself off as a native of Formosa (present-day Taiwan).

of quality as a prime dainty; and that in his time the body of a plump girl of fifteen, who was crucified for an attempt to poison the emperor, was sold to the Imperial Majesty's prime minister of state, and other great mandarins of the court, in joints from the gibbet, at four hundred crowns. Neither indeed can I deny that if the same use were made of several plump young girls in this town, who without one single groat to their fortunes cannot stir abroad without a chair,* and appear at the playhouse and assemblies in foreign fineries which they never will pay for, the kingdom would not be the worse.

Some persons of a desponding spirit are in great concern about the vast number of poor people who are aged, diseased, or maimed, and I have been desired to employ my thoughts what course may be taken to ease the nation of so grievous an encumbrance. But I am not in the least pain upon that matter, because it is very well known that they are every day dying and rotting by cold and famine, and filth and vermin, as fast as can be reasonably expected. And as to the younger laborers, they are now in almost as hopeful a condition. They cannot get work, and consequently pine away for want of nourishment to a degree that if any time they are accidentally hired to common labor, they have not strength to perform it; and thus the country and themselves are happily delivered from the evils to come. 19

I have too long digressed, and therefore shall return to my subject. I think the advantages by the proposal which I have made are obvious and many, as well as of the highest importance. 20

For first, as I have already observed, it would greatly lessen the number of Papists, with whom we are yearly overrun, being the principal breeders of the nation as well as our most dangerous enemies; and who stay at home on purpose to deliver the kingdom to the Pretender, hoping to take their advantage by the absence of so many good Protestants, who have chosen rather to leave their country than to stay at home and pay tithes against their conscience to an Episcopal curate. 21

Secondly, the poorer tenants will have something valuable of their own, which by law may be made liable to distress,** and help to pay their landlord's rent, their corn and cattle being already seized and money a thing unknown. 22

Thirdly, whereas the maintenance of an hundred thousand children, from two years old and upwards, cannot be computed at less than ten shillings a piece per annum, the nation's stock will be thereby increased fifty thousand pounds per annum, besides the profit of a new dish introduced to the tables of all gentlemen of fortune in the kingdom who have any refinement in taste. And the money will circulate among ourselves, the goods being entirely of our own growth and manufacture. 23

---

* EDS. NOTE — A sedan chair; that is, a portable covered chair designed to seat one person and then to be carried by two men.

** EDS. NOTE — Property could be seized by creditors.

Fourthly, the constant breeders, besides the gain of eight shillings sterling per annum by the sale of their children, will be rid of the charge for maintaining them after the first year. 24

Fifthly, this food would likewise bring great custom to taverns, where the vintners will certainly be so prudent as to procure the best receipts* for dressing it to perfection, and consequently have their houses frequented by all the fine gentlemen, who justly value themselves upon their knowledge in good eating; and a skillful cook, who understands how to oblige his guests, will contrive to make it as expensive as they please. 25

Sixthly, this would be a great inducement to marriage, after which all wise nations have either encouraged by rewards or enforced by laws and penalties. It would increase the care and tenderness of mothers toward their children, when they were sure of a settlement for life to the poor babes, provided in some sort by the public, to their annual profit instead of expense. We should see an honest emulation among the married women, which of them could bring the fattest child to the market. Men would become as fond of their wives during the time of pregnancy as they are now of their mares in foal, their cows in calf, or sows when they are ready to farrow; nor offer to beat or kick them (as is too frequent a practice) for fear of miscarriage. 26

Many other advantages might be enumerated. For instance, the addition of some thousand carcasses in our exportation of barreled beef, the propagation of swine's flesh, and improvements in the art of making good bacon, so much wanted among us by the great destruction of pigs, too frequent at our tables, which are no way comparable in taste or magnificence to a well-grown, fat, yearling child, which roasted whole will make a considerable figure at a lord mayor's feast or other public entertainment. But this and many others I omit, being studious of brevity. 27

Supposing that one thousand families in this city would be constant customers for infants' flesh, besides others who might have it at merry meetings, particularly weddings and christenings, I compute that Dublin would take off annually about twenty thousand carcasses, and the rest of the kingdom (where probably they will be sold somewhat cheaper) the remaining eighty thousand. 28

I can think of no one objection that will possibly be raised against this proposal, unless it should be urged that the number of people will be thereby much lessened in the kingdom. This I freely own, and it was indeed one principal design in offering it to the world. I desire the reader will observe; that I calculate my remedy for this one individual kingdom of Ireland and for no other that ever was, is, or I think ever can be upon earth. Therefore, let no man talk to me of other expedients: of taxing our absentees at five shillings a pound: of using neither clothes nor household furniture except what is of our own growth and manufacture: of utterly rejecting the materials and instruments that promote foreign luxury: of 29

---

* EDS. NOTE — Recipes.

curing the expensiveness of pride, vanity, idleness, and gaming in our women: of introducing a vein of parsimony, prudence, and temperance: of learning to love our country, in the want of which we differ even from Low-landers and the inhabitants of Topinamboo:* of quitting our animosities and factions, nor acting any longer like the Jews,** who were murdering one another at the very moment their city was taken: of being a little cau-tious not to sell our country and conscience for nothing: of teaching land-lords to have at least one degree of mercy toward their tenants: lastly, of putting a spirit of honesty, industry, and skill into our shopkeepers; who, if a resolution could now be taken to buy only our native goods, would imme-diately unite to cheat and exact upon us in the price, the measure, and the goodness, nor could ever yet be brought to make one fair proposal of just dealing, though often and earnestly invited to it.

Therefore, I repeat, let no man talk to me of these and the like expedi-ents, till he hath at least some glimpse of hope that there will ever be some hearty and sincere attempt to put them in practice.† 30

But as to myself, having been wearied out for many years with offering vain, idle, visionary thoughts, and at length utterly despairing of success, I fortunately fell upon this proposal, which, as it is wholly new, so it hath something solid and real, of no expense and little trouble, full in our own power, and whereby we can incur no danger in disobliging England. For this kind of commodity will not bear exploration, the flesh being of too tender a consistence to admit a long continuance in salt, although perhaps I could name a country which would be glad to eat up our whole nation without it. 31

After all, I am not so violently bent upon my own opinion as to reject any offer proposed by wise men, which shall be found equally innocent, cheap, easy, and effectual. But before something of that kind shall be advanced in contradiction to my scheme, and offering a better, I desire the author or authors will be pleased maturely to consider two points. First, as things now stand, how they will be able to find food and raiment for an hundred thousand useless mouths and backs. And secondly, there being a round million of creatures in human figure throughout this kingdom, whose sole subsistence put into a common stock would leave them in debt two million of pounds sterling, adding those who are beggars by profes-sion to the bulk of farmers, cottagers, and laborers, with their wives and children who are beggars in effect; I desire those politicians who dislike my overture, and may perhaps be so bold to attempt an answer, that they will first ask the parents of these mortals whether they would not at this day think it a great happiness to have been sold for food at a year old in this manner I prescribe, and thereby have avoided such a perpetual scene of 32

---

* EDS. NOTE — A place in the Brazilian jungle.
** EDS. NOTE — In the first century B.C., the Roman general Pompey could conquer Jerusalem in part because the citizenry was divided among rival factions.
† EDS. NOTE — Note that these measures represent Swift's true proposal.

misfortunes as they have since gone through by the oppression of landlords, the impossibility of paying rent without money or trade, the want of
common sustenance, with neither house nor clothes to cover them from
the inclemencies of the weather, and the most inevitable prospect of entail-
ing the like or greater miseries upon their breed forever.

    I profess, in the sincerity of my heart, that I have not the least personal   33
interest in endeavoring to promote this necessary work, having no other
motive than the public good of my country, by advancing our trade, providing for infants, relieving the poor, and giving some pleasure to the rich.
I have no children by which I can propose to get a single penny; the young-
est being nine years old, and my wife past childbearing.

• • •

Comprehension

1. What problem does Swift identify? What general solution does he recommend?
2. What advantages does Swift see in his plan?
3. What does he see as the alternative to his plan?
4. What clues indicate that Swift is not serious about his proposal?
5. In paragraph 29, Swift lists and rejects a number of "other expedients."
   What are they? Why do you think he presents and rejects these ideas?

Purpose and Audience

1. Swift's target here is the British government, in particular its poor treatment of the Irish. How would you expect British government officials to
   respond to his proposal? How would you expect Irish readers to react?
2. What do you think Swift hoped to accomplish in this essay? Do you
   think his purpose was simply to amuse and shock, or do you think he
   wanted to change people's minds — or even inspire them to take some
   kind of action? Explain.
3. In paragraphs 6, 14, 23, and elsewhere, Swift presents a series of mathe-
   matical calculations. What effect do you think he expected these compu-
   tations to have on his readers?
4. Explain why each of the following groups might have been offended by
   this essay: women, Catholics, butchers, and the poor.
5. How do you think Swift expected the appeal in his conclusion to affect
   his audience?

Style and Structure

1. In paragraph 6, Swift uses the word *breeders* to refer to fertile women.
   What connotations does this word have? Why does he use this word
   rather than a more neutral alternative?

2. What purpose does paragraph 8 serve in the essay? Do the other short paragraphs have the same function? Explain.

3. Swift's remarks are presented as an argument. Where, if anywhere, does he anticipate and refute his readers' objections?

4. Swift applies to infants many words usually applied to animals who are slaughtered to be eaten — for example, *fore or hind quarter* (10) and *carcass* (15). Identify as many examples of this kind of usage as you can. Why do you think Swift uses such words?

5. Throughout his essay, Swift cites the comments of others — "our merchants" (7), "a very knowing American of my acquaintance" (9), and "an eminent French physician" (13), for example. Find some additional examples. What, if anything, does he accomplish by referring to these people?

6. A **satire** is a piece of writing that uses wit, **irony**, and ridicule to attack foolishness, incompetence, or evil. How does "A Modest Proposal" fit this definition of satire?

7. Evaluate the strategy Swift uses to introduce each advantage he cites in paragraphs 21 through 26.

8. Swift uses a number of parenthetical comments in his essay — for example, in paragraphs 14, 17, and 26. Identify as many of these parenthetical comments as you can, and consider what they contribute to the essay.

9. Swift begins paragraph 20 with the words, "I have too long digressed, and therefore shall return to my subject." Has he in fact been digressing? Explain.

Vocabulary Projects

1. Define each of the following words as it is used in this selection.

importuning (1)	rudiments (6)	encumbrance (19)
alms (1)	nutriment (7)	tithes (21)
prodigious (2)	repine (14)	vintners (25)
professed (3)	flay (15)	expedients (29)
dam (4)	scrupulous (17)	parsimony (29)
reckoned (6)	censure (17)	temperance (29)
apprehend (6)	desponding (19)	raiment (32)

2. The title states that Swift's proposal is a "modest" one; elsewhere he says he proposes his ideas "humbly" (8). Why do you think he chooses these words? Does he really mean to present himself as modest and humble?

Journal Entry

What is your emotional reaction to this essay? Do you find it amusing or offensive? Why?

Writing Workshop

1. Write a "modest proposal," either straightforward or satirical, for solving a problem in your school or community.
2. Write a "modest proposal" for achieving one of these national goals:
   - Providing universal health care
   - Banning assault weapons
   - Eliminating binge drinking on college campuses
   - Eliminating childhood obesity
   - Promoting sexual abstinence among teenagers
   - Banning SUVs
3. Write a letter to an executive of the tobacco industry, a television network, or an industry that threatens the environment. In your letter, set forth a "modest proposal" for making the industry more responsible.

Combining the Patterns

What patterns of development does Swift use in his argument? Annotate the essay to identify each pattern. Use the annotations accompanying "On Dumpster Diving" (page 714) as a guide.

Thematic Connections

- "The Embalming of Mr. Jones" (page 304)
- "The Irish Famine, 1845–1849" (page 333)
- "Earth without People" (page 368)
- "I Want a Wife" (page 520)

WRITING ASSIGNMENTS FOR COMBINING THE PATTERNS

1. Reread Michael Huu Truong's essay at the beginning of this chapter. Responding to the same assignment he was given ("Write an essay about the person and/or place that defined your childhood"), use several different patterns to communicate to readers what your own childhood was like.

2. Write an essay about the political, social, or economic events that you believe have dominated and defined your life (or a stage of your life). Use cause and effect and any other patterns you think are appropriate to explain and illustrate why these events were important to you and how they affected you.

3. Develop a thesis statement that draws a general conclusion about the nature, quality, or effectiveness of advertising in print media (in news-papers or magazines or on billboards). Write an essay that supports this thesis statement with a series of very specific paragraphs. Use the patterns of development that best help you to characterize particular advertisements.

4. Exactly what do you think it means to be an American? Write a definition essay that answers this question, developing your definition with what-ever patterns best serve your purpose.

5. Many of the essays in this text recount the writers' personal experiences. Identify one essay that describes experiences that are either similar to your own or in sharp contrast to your own. Then, write a comparison-and-contrast essay *either* comparing *or* contrasting your experiences with those of the writer. Use several different patterns to develop your essay.

COLLABORATIVE ACTIVITY FOR COMBINING THE PATTERNS

Working in pairs, choose an essay from Chapters 6 through 14 of this text. Then, working individually, identify the various patterns of development used in the essay. When you have finished, compare notes with your classmate. Have both of you identified the same patterns in the essay? If not, try to reach a consensus. Working together, write a paragraph summarizing why each pattern is used and explaining how the various patterns combine to support the essay's thesis.

Using Research in Your Writing

In some essays — such as narrative and descriptive essays — you can use your own ideas to support your points. In other essays — such as argumentative essays — you may have to supplement your own ideas with **research**: material from books, articles, television programs, the Internet, and your library's electronic databases. As you research and write, remember what you have learned about the writing process, and keep in mind that your main task is to present ideas clearly and convincingly. You will have an easier time writing a research paper if you follow an orderly process:

1. Choose a topic.
2. Test your topic.
3. Do research.
4. Evaluate sources.
5. Take notes.
6. Watch out for plagiarism.
7. Draft a thesis statement.
8. Make an outline.
9. Write your essay.
10. Document your sources.

STEP 1: CHOOSING A TOPIC

The first step in writing an essay that calls for research is finding a topic to write about. Before you decide on a topic, ask yourself the following questions:

- What is my page limit?
- When is my paper due?
- How many sources am I expected to use?

The answers to these questions can help you make sure your topic is neither too broad nor too narrow.

Philip Lau, a student in a college composition course, was asked to write a paper of about 1,500 words that would be due in five weeks and would require some research. The assignment further specified that the paper focus on a topic related to the Internet.

Philip decided right away that he wanted to write about Wikipedia. This general subject interested him because while he had always found Wikipedia to be a very useful site, his teachers had warned students that it was not trustworthy; in fact, some teachers had even banned its use as a research source.

Philip realized at once that "Wikipedia" would be too broad a topic and "my teachers' view of Wikipedia" would be too narrow. However, he thought that "The drawbacks of open-source Internet sites like Wikipedia" might work well. Not only did the topic interest him, but he felt he would be able to discuss it in the required number of words and complete his paper within the time limit.

STEP 2: TESTING YOUR TOPIC

Before you choose a topic, you should test it to see if it will work — in other words, if you can find enough to write about. Begin by going to the Internet and doing a keyword search. You should also survey the resources of your library. (You might find it helpful to meet with a college librarian, who can answer questions and point you toward useful resources.)

In the library, begin by looking at the online central information system to see what books and articles about your topic are listed there. (Frequently, the online central information system contains the library's catalog as well as a number of databases you can search.) For example, under the general topic "Wikipedia and reliability," Philip discovered a number of books and articles that focused on this topic. Many of these articles included serious criticisms of Wikipedia, including attacks on its policy of using anonymous writers and editors.

STEP 3: DOING RESEARCH

Finding Information in the Library

The best place to start your research is in your college library. It contains print and electronic resources you cannot find anywhere else — including on the free Internet. For the best results, you should do your library research systematically: begin by looking at reference works; then, search the library's catalog and periodical indexes; and, finally, look for any additional facts or statistics you need to support your ideas.

GUIDELINES FOR USING LIBRARY RESOURCES

Reference Works   Begin your research by consulting works that will give you an overview of your topic as well as key facts, dates, and names to use in your paper. **General encyclopedias** — like the *New Encyclopaedia Britannica* — contain articles on a wide variety of topics. **Specialized encyclopedias** contain articles that give you detailed information about a specific field — psychology or sociology, for example. Other reference works — such as *Who's Who in America* — provide information about people's lives. (Many of these reference works are available in both print and electronic form.)

The Library's Catalog   Once you get a general sense of your topic, you can consult the library's catalog. Most libraries have replaced print catalogs with **online catalogs** that enable you to search all the resources held by the library. By typing in words or phrases related to your topic on computer terminals located around the library, you can find books, periodicals and other materials to use in your paper. If you know exactly what you are looking for, you can find it by typing in the title of a book or the name of its author.

Periodical Indexes   After consulting the online catalog, you may want to look at the periodical indexes your library subscribes to. **Periodical indexes** are databases that access information from newspapers, magazines, and journals. Some indexes list just citations, while others provide the full text of articles. You can usually search the periodical indexes on the same computer terminals you use to search the library's online catalog. Many college libraries have classes that teach you how to access articles in periodical indexes.

Sources for Facts and Statistics   As you write your paper, you may find that you need certain facts or statistics to support particular points. Reference works such as *Facts on File*, the *Information Please Almanac*, and the *Statistical Abstract of the United States* can help you get such information. These resources are available in the reference section of your college library, where a librarian can help you find sources of factual and statistical information specific to your topic. (They are also available online.)

Finding Information on the Internet

The Internet can give you access to a great deal of information that you can use to help you support the points you make. To search the Internet, you need a **search engine**, a program that enables you to sort through the millions of documents available on the Internet. The most popular search engines are Google and Yahoo.

There are three ways to use a search engine to find information.

1. *You can enter a Web site's URL.* All search engines have a box in which you can enter a Web site's electronic address, or **URL** (uniform resource

locator). When you click on the URL — or hit your computer's Enter or Return key — the search engine connects you to the Web site. For example, to find information about family members who entered the United States through Ellis Island, you would type in the URL ellisislandrecords.com.

2. *You can do a keyword search.* All search engines enable you to do a **keyword search**. You type a term into a box, and then the search engine looks for documents that contain the term. If you type a broad term like *civil war,* you might get millions of hits — far too many to consider. If this occurs, narrow your search by using a more specific term — *Battle of Gettysburg,* for example. You can focus your term even further by putting quotation marks around the term ("*Battle of Gettysburg*"). When you do this, the search engine will search only for documents that contain this specific phrase.

3. *You can do a subject search.* Many search engines, such as Yahoo, let you do a subject search. First, you click on a broad subject from a list of subjects: *The Humanities, The Arts, Entertainment, Business,* and so on. Each of these general subjects leads you to a list of more specific subjects, until, eventually, you get to the subtopic you want. For example, you could start your search by clicking on the general topic *Entertainment.* Clicking on this would lead you to *Movies* and then to *Movie Reviews.* Finally, you would get to a list of movie reviews that might link to the specific movie you were interested in.

When Philip searched the periodical index in his college library for the term "Wikipedia's reliability," he found an article in *Reason* magazine that discussed this question. His instructor told him that *Reason* was well respected and usually reliable, so he could assume the writer was someone who knew a lot about her subject.

STEP 4: EVALUATING SOURCES

Once you find information, you still have to **evaluate** it — that is, determine its usefulness. To evaluate a source, ask the following questions:

- *Is the source **respected**?* For example, an article in a national newspaper such as the *New York Times* or the *Wall Street Journal* is usually much more trustworthy than one from a tabloid such as the *National Enquirer.* In the same way, a scholarly publication is generally more respected than a source aimed at general readers.

- *Is the source **reliable**?* Is the information in your source factual, or does it consist mostly of opinions? Has the author documented information so that you can check it, or are facts and conclusions mostly presented without documentation?

- *Is the source **current**?* For example, a book or article on stem-cell research that is ten years old may contain information that is outdated and possibly incorrect.

- *Is the author of the source **credible**?* Often, a quick Google search can tell you a lot about an author's credibility. For example, does the author's background suggest a particular bias? Is the author an expert or simply a reporter? What other articles and books has the author written? What do they tell you about his or her credibility?

Because anyone can put information on the Internet, you need to be especially careful when you use information from Internet sites. Just as you would with any source, you have to make certain that Internet sources are reliable and that they contain information that is both accurate and verifiable.

LIBRARY DATABASES

In most cases, the information you get from your library's electronic databases is more reliable than information you download from the free Internet. Because your librarian has researched the reliability of the databases to which the library subscribes, you can be certain that they contain information that you can trust. For this reason, a trip to the library — in person or online — is usually the best way to start your research project.

STEP 5: TAKING NOTES

Once you have gathered and evaluated the material you will need, read it carefully, writing down any information you think you can use in your essay. As you take notes, record relevant information in a computer file you set up for your paper.

When you use information from a source in your paper, you do not always *quote* the exact words of your source. In fact, most often you *paraphrase* or *summarize* a source, putting its ideas into your own words. For this reason, most of your notes should be in the form of paraphrase or summary.

Paraphrasing

When you **paraphrase**, you present the main ideas of a source in your own words, but you keep the order and emphasis of the original. You paraphrase when you want to present a slightly condensed version of the source but not the author's exact words. Paraphrasing is useful when you want to make a difficult discussion easier to understand while still conveying an accurate sense of the original.

Begin by reading the source until you are sure you understand it. As you write, go through the source sentence by sentence, writing down ideas in the order in which they occur. Include only the author's ideas; keep your own opinions to yourself. As you write, follow your source closely. Be sure to present only the passage's main idea and key supporting points, eliminating examples and asides that are not essential to meaning. Remember, *because a paraphrase expresses the original ideas of the source's author, it must be documented.*

GUIDELINES FOR WRITING A PARAPHRASE

1. Read the passage you intend to paraphrase until you understand it.
2. Jot down the main idea of the passage, and list all supporting points.
3. As you write, follow the order and emphasis of the original.
4. When you revise, make sure you have used your own words and phrases, not the words or sentence structure of the original.
5. Document your source.

Here is a passage from page 22 of "Wikipedia and Beyond: Jimmy Wales's Sprawling Vision" by Katherine Mangu-Ward, an article Philip uses in his paper, followed by his paraphrase:

Original

An obvious question troubled, and continues to trouble many people: how could an "encyclopedia that anyone can edit" possibly be reliable? Can truth be reached by a consensus of amateurs? Can a community of volunteers aggregate and assimilate knowledge . . .?

Paraphrase

According to Katherine Mangu-Ward, there are serious questions about the reliability of Wikipedia's articles because any user can add, change, or delete information. There is some doubt about whether Wikipedia's unpaid and nonprofessional writers and editors can work together to create an accurate encyclopedia (22).

Summarizing

Unlike a paraphrase, which restates the ideas of a source in detail, a **summary** is a restatement, in your own words, of a passage's main idea. Because it is so general, a summary is always much shorter than the original. Unlike a paraphrase, a summary does not follow the order or emphasis of the original.

Before you begin to write, make sure you understand the passage you want to summarize. Read it several times, identifying the writer's main idea. As you write, use your own words, not those of your source. Keep in mind that a summary can be one sentence or several sentences in length, depending on the ideas in the original passage. As you revise, make sure your summary expresses just the main idea of your source, not your own opinions or conclusions. Remember, *because a summary expresses the original ideas of the source's author, it must be documented.*

GUIDELINES FOR WRITING A SUMMARY

1. Read the passage you intend to summarize until you understand it.

2. Jot down the main idea of the passage.

3. As you write, make sure you use your own words, not those of your source.

4. When you revise, make sure your summary contains only the ideas of the source.

5. Document your source.

Here is Philip's summary of the passage from the Mangu-Ward article reproduced on the previous page:

Summary

According to Katherine Mangu-Ward, Wikipedia's reliability is open to question because anyone can write or edit its articles (22).

Quoting

When you **quote**, you use the author's exact words as they appear in the source, including all punctuation, capitalization, and spelling. Enclose all words from your source in quotation marks — *followed by appropriate documentation.* Because quotations distract readers, use them only when you think the author's exact words will add something to your discussion. As a rule, unless you have a definite reason to quote a source, you should paraphrase or summarize it.

GUIDELINES FOR QUOTING SOURCES

1. Quote when the original language is so memorable that paraphrasing would lessen the impact of the writer's ideas.

2. Quote when a paraphrase or summary would change the meaning of the original.

3. Quote when the original language adds authority to your discussion. The exact words of an expert on your topic can help you make your point convincingly.

Introduce paraphrases, summaries, and quotations with a phrase that identifies the source or its author. You can place this **identifying phrase** at various points in a sentence. Instead of always using the same words to introduce source material — *says* or *states*, for example — try using different words and phrases — *points out*, *observes*, *comments*, *notes*, *remarks*, or *concludes*.

Identifying Phrase at the Beginning

According to Jonathan Dee, Wikipedia is "either one of the noblest experiments of the Internet age or a nightmare embodiment of relativism and the withering of intellectual standards" (36).

Identifying Phrase at the End

Wikipedia is "either one of the noblest experiments of the Internet age or a nightmare embodiment of relativism and the withering of intellectual standards," Jonathan Dee observes (36).

Identifying Phrase in the Middle

Wikipedia is "either one of the noblest experiments of the Internet age," Jonathan Dee comments, "or a nightmare embodiment of relativism and the withering of intellectual standards" (36).

Synthesizing Sources

When you write a **synthesis**, you combine material from two or more sources with your own ideas to convey an original viewpoint. In this sense, your research paper is actually a long synthesis in which you show your readers how the views of your sources are alike and different and how they support or do not support your ideas. For this reason, when you write a synthesis, it is important that you differentiate your ideas from those of your sources and that you clearly show what information comes from which source.

Paragraph 6 of Philip Lau's research paper, reproduced on page 765, is a good example of a synthesis. This paragraph discusses a common problem with wikis: the potential for harm when false information is inserted into articles. The paragraph begins with the student writer's own ideas, and the rest of the paragraph contains information from research sources that supports these ideas. (The examples that mention George W. Bush, George Soros, L. Ron Hubbard, abortion, and the Holocaust are not documented because they are **facts** — in other words, they can be found in several sources.) The main example in the paragraph has to do with the case of John Seigenthaler Sr., who was lied about in a Wikipedia article. The paragraph ends with a long quotation from Jane Kirtley that conveys the idea that because Wikipedia's writers are anonymous, they do not take responsibility for what they produce. This paragraph synthesizes several sources as it discusses a single problem of Wikipedia and other open-source Web sites.

Another problem with Wikipedia is the ease with which entries can be edited. Because the content of wikis can be altered by anyone, individuals can easily vandalize content by inserting incorrect information, obscene language, or even nonsense into articles. Writers who are more interested in presenting their personal opinions than presenting reliable information frequently target certain entries. For example, entries for controversial people, such as President George W. Bush, financier George Soros, or Scientology founder L. Ron Hubbard, or for controversial subjects, such as abortion and the Holocaust, are routinely vandalized. Sometimes this vandalism can be extremely harmful. One notorious case of vandalism involved John Seigenthaler Sr., a journalist who was falsely accused in a Wikipedia entry of being involved in the assassinations of John Kennedy and Robert Kennedy. As Seigenthaler's son has reported, the false information stayed on the site for more than four months and also appeared on at least two other sites that had used Wikipedia as their source (Seigenthaler). This incident as well as many others has caused people to question the reliability of Wikipedia. According to Jane Kirtley, the issue of reliability poses a real problem for the users of Wikipedia:

> It's hard to defend an anonymous poster who uploads a damaging falsehood about someone on a Web site that purports to provide facts from a "neutral point of view. . . ." Either accuracy matters, or it doesn't. If the denizens of cyberspace want to be taken seriously, they might want to be responsible for what they produce. (66)

GUIDELINES FOR WRITING A SYNTHESIS

1. Identify the main issues.
2. Identify the evidence that your sources have used to support their views on these issues.
3. Group the sources that deal with each issue.
4. Decide whether the sources agree or disagree on the issue.
5. Clearly report what each source says, using summaries, paraphrases, and quotations. (Be sure to document your sources.)
6. Show how the sources are related to one another. For instance, do they agree on everything? Do they show directly opposite views, or do they agree on some points and disagree on others? Do they overlap in any way?
7. Decide on your own viewpoint on the issue, and show how the sources are related to your viewpoint.

STEP 6: WATCHING OUT FOR PLAGIARISM

As a rule, **document** (provide source information for) all words, ideas, pictures, or statistics from an outside source. (It is not necessary, however, to document **common knowledge** — information most readers will probably know or factual information widely available in reference works.) When you present information from another source as if it were your own (whether intentionally or unintentionally), you are committing **plagiarism** — and plagiarism is theft. You can avoid plagiarism by understanding what you must document and what you do not have to document.

GUIDELINES FOR AVOIDING PLAGIARISM

YOU MUST DOCUMENT

- All word-for-word quotations from a source
- All summaries and paraphrases of material from a source
- All ideas — opinions, judgments, and insights — that are not your own
- All tables, graphs, charts, and statistics you get from a source

YOU DO NOT NEED TO DOCUMENT

- Your own ideas
- Common knowledge
- Familiar quotations

Avoiding Common Errors That Lead to Plagiarism

The following paragraph is from *The Cult of the Amateur: How Today's Internet Is Killing Our Culture* by Andrew Keen, a source that Philip found during his research. This paragraph, and the four rules listed after it, will help you understand and avoid the most common causes of plagiarism.

Original

The simple ownership of a computer and an Internet connection doesn't transform one into a serious journalist any more than having access to a kitchen makes one into a serious cook. But millions of amateur journalists think that it does. According to a June 2006 study by the Pew Internet and American Life Project, 34 percent of the 12 million bloggers in America consider their online "work" to be a form of journalism. That adds up to millions of unskilled, untrained, unpaid, unknown "journalists" — a thousandfold growth between 1996 and 2006 — spewing their (mis)information out in the cyberworld. (Andrew Keen. *The Cult of the Amateur: How Today's Internet Is Killing Our Culture*. New York: Doubleday, 2007. 47. Print.)

1. Identify Your Source

Plagiarism

One-third of the people who post material on Internet blogs think of themselves as serious journalists.

he writer does not quote Keen directly, but he still must identify Keen as the source of his paraphrased material. He can do this by adding an identifying phrase and parenthetical documentation.

Correct

According to Andrew Keen, one-third of the people who post material on Internet blogs think of themselves as serious journalists (47).

2. Place Borrowed Words in Quotation Marks

Plagiarism

According to Andrew Keen, the simple ownership of a computer and an Internet connection doesn't transform one into a serious journalist any more than having access to a kitchen makes one into a serious cook (47).

Although the writer cites Keen as his source, the passage incorrectly uses Keen's exact words without putting them in quotation marks. The writer must either place the borrowed words in quotation marks or paraphrase them.

Correct (Borrowed Words in Quotation Marks)

According to Andrew Keen, "the simple ownership of a computer and an Internet connection doesn't transform one into a serious journalist any more than having access to a kitchen makes one into a serious cook" (47).

3. Use Your Own Wording

Plagiarism

According to Andrew Keen, having a computer that can connect to the Internet does not make someone a real reporter, just as having a kitchen does not make someone a real cook. However, millions of these people think that they are real journalists. A Pew Internet and American Life study in June 2006 showed that about 4 million bloggers think they are journalists when they write on their blogs. Thus, millions of people who have no training may be putting erroneous information on the Internet (47).

Even though the writer acknowledges Keen as his source and provides parenthetical documentation, and even though he does not use Keen's exact words, his passage closely follows the order, emphasis, syntax, and phrasing of the original. In the following passage, the writer uses his own wording, quoting one distinctive phrase from his source.

Correct

According to Andrew Keen, although millions of American bloggers think of themselves as journalists, they are wrong. As Keen notes, "simple ownership of a computer and an Internet connection doesn't transform one into a serious journalist any more than having access to a kitchen makes one into a serious cook" (47).

4. Distinguish Your Own Ideas from Your Source's Ideas

Plagiarism

The anonymous writers of Wikipedia articles are, in some ways, similar to those who put material on personal blogs. Although millions of American bloggers think of themselves as journalists, they are wrong. "The simple ownership of a computer and an Internet connection doesn't transform one into a serious journalist any more than having access to a kitchen makes one into a serious cook" (Keen 47).

In the preceding passage, it appears that only the quotation in the last sentence is borrowed from Keen's book. In fact, however, the ideas in the second sentence are also Keen's. The writer should use an identifying phrase (such as "According to Keen") to acknowledge the borrowed material in this sentence and to indicate where it begins.

Correct

The anonymous writers of Wikipedia articles are, in some ways, similar to those who put material on personal blogs. According to Andrew Keen, although millions of American bloggers think of themselves as journalists, they are wrong. As Keen notes, the "simple ownership of a computer and an Internet connection doesn't transform one into a serious journalist any more than having access to a kitchen makes one into a serious cook" (47).

Avoiding Plagiarism with Online Sources

Most students know that using long passages (or entire articles) from a print source without documenting the source is plagiarism. Unfortunately, many students assume that borrowing material found on a Web site or elsewhere online without documentation is acceptable. However, such borrowing is also plagiarism.

Perhaps students feel differently about online borrowing because it is so easy to cut and paste from an online source into a text document. They may also see copying online material as acceptable because — with authors often unidentified online — no one appears to take credit for the source. No matter what the explanation is for this casual treatment of online sources, instructors consider the use of undocumented words or ideas from online sources to be plagiarism. Therefore, just as you do for print sources, you must document words or ideas you get from online sources.

NOTE: It goes without saying that downloading entire papers from Web sites and turning them in as your own work is plagiarism. Such conduct is unfair to you, your instructor, and your fellow students, and it undercuts the learning process.

STEP 7: DRAFTING A THESIS STATEMENT

After you have taken notes, review the information you have gathered, and draft a **thesis statement** — a single sentence that states the main idea of your paper and tells readers what to expect.

After completing his research, Philip Lau came up with the following thesis statement for his paper on Wikipedia.

> Although Wikipedia may be a good starting point for general information on a topic, college-level research papers should rely on more authoritative sources.

STEP 8: MAKING AN OUTLINE

Once you have drafted a thesis statement, you are ready to make an outline from your notes. Your outline, which covers just the body paragraphs of your paper, can be either a *topic outline* (each idea is expressed in a word or short phrase) or a *sentence* outline (each idea is expressed in a complete sentence). When it is finished, your outline will be your guide as you write your paper.

After reviewing his notes, Philip Lau constructed the following sentence outline for his paper. Notice that he uses roman numerals for first-level headings, capital letters for second-level headings, and arabic numerals for third-level headings.

> Although Wikipedia may be a good starting point for general information on a topic, college-level research papers should rely on more authoritative sources.

> I. Wikis are easy to access and easy to use.
>   A. Anyone can write and edit wikis quickly.
>   B. Wikipedia is free to its users.
>   C. All revisions are visible.
> II. Wikipedia publishes both facts and opinions.
>   A. Wikipedia values accuracy.
>   1. Wikipedia wants information to come from standard sources whose reliability is widely accepted.

   2. At Wikipedia no one person is responsible for fact checking.
   B. Wikipedia values objectivity.
      1. With controversial subjects, the various sides should be shown.
      2. Wikipedia warns readers against uncritically accepting what they read on a Web site.

III. Wikipedia is open to certain kinds of errors.
   A. It favors the community of knowledge over the views of individual experts.
      1. Wikipedia writers and editors may be "anti-elitist" and not respect expertise.
      2. Misinformation can be perpetuated.
   B. Because articles can be easily edited, vandalism may occur.
      1. Controversial people and subjects are often the targets of vandals.
      2. Vandalism can damage peoples' reputations.
   C. Wikipedia's articles may include bias.

IV. Wikipedia has tried to deal with its problems.
   A. Writers and editors now have to provide their user names to the site.
   B. Blocks can prevent changes to certain sites.

V. Wikipedia has been compared to its competitor, the traditional encyclopedia.
   A. Both reference sources have errors.
   B. Wikipedia's articles suffer from the lack of an editor.
      1. Editors have skills and experience.
      2. Editors assure the reader that articles are written clearly and logically.

VI. Peer-reviewed journals also have faults.
   A. Editors and reviewers may have conflicts of interest.
   B. The slow peer-review process means journals may not be up-to-date.

VII. Only the most reliable sources should be used for college research papers.
   A. At times, Wikipedia may be useful.
      1. Content may introduce readers to a variety of topics.
      2. Very current subjects may be covered only in Wikipedia.
      3. Wikipedia's reference lists may direct students to additional sources.
   B. In most cases, however, Wikipedia is not a reliable source for serious research.

STEP 9: WRITING YOUR ESSAY

Once you have decided on a thesis and written an outline, you are ready to write a draft of your essay. Start by arranging your notes in the order in which you will use them. Follow your outline as you write, but don't be afraid to depart from it if new ideas occur to you.

Begin your essay with an **introduction** that includes your **thesis statement**. Usually your introduction will be a single paragraph, but sometimes it will be longer.

In the **body** of your essay, you support your thesis statement, with each body paragraph developing a single idea. Support your points with summaries, paraphrases, and quotations from your sources as well as with your own ideas and opinions. Your body paragraphs should have clear **topic sentences** so that your readers will know exactly what points you are making, and you should use transitional words and phrases to help readers follow the progression of your ideas.

Finally, your **conclusion** should give readers a sense of completion. Like your introduction, your conclusion is usually a single paragraph, but it can be longer. It should reinforce your thesis statement and your paper's main ideas and should end with a sentence that will stay with readers.

Once you have drafted your essay, you should consider adding **visuals** — photographs, charts, graphs, and so on. Because they have such an immediate impact on readers, visuals can make your essay more memorable and more persuasive. But to be effective, they must clearly relate to the points you are making. Used effectively, visuals are another type of evidence that can support your thesis statement; used ineffectively, however, visuals will distract readers.

You can get visuals online, from print documents that you can scan, from digital cameras, and from commercially available software packages. Remember, however, that not all visuals will be suitable for (or effective in) your essay. You must evaluate the appropriateness of the visuals you intend to use, just as you would with a print source. And, of course, you must include full documentation for any visual you use.

Once you select a visual, you have to decide how to use it in your essay. The following guidelines should make this task easier for you.

GUIDELINES FOR USING VISUALS

- *Use a sentence to introduce the visual.* Visuals should never be carelessly dropped into your paper. Make sure that the relationship between the visual and the discussion is clear.

- *When you introduce the visual, refer to it parenthetically in the text.* Example: "This collaboration enables Wikipedia to publish a wide variety of entries on unusual, specialized topics (see fig. 1)."

- *Place the visual as close as possible to the relevant portion of the discussion.* Ideally, you want to insert the visual at the point where you discuss it. If that is not possible (because, for example, the visual is too large to fit on the page), put it at the top of the following page.

- *Document the visual.* Remember, you must give source information for all visual material that you get from a source.

Keep in mind that you will probably write several drafts of your essay before you submit it. You can use the revision checklist on page 54 to help you revise and edit your paper.

Philip Lau's completed essay on Wikipedia appears on page 782.

STEP 10: DOCUMENTING YOUR SOURCES

When you **document** a source, you tell readers where you have found the information you have used in your essay. The Modern Language Association (MLA) recommends the following documentation style for essays that use research.* This format consists of *parenthetical references* in the body of the paper that refer to a *works-cited* list at the end of the paper.

Parenthetical References in the Text

A parenthetical reference should include enough information to guide readers to a specific entry in your works-cited list. A typical parenthetical reference consists of the author's last name and the page number: (Mangu-Ward 21). If you use more than one work by the same author, include a shortened form of the title in the parenthetical reference: (Mangu-Ward, "Wikipedia & Beyond" 25). Notice that the parenthetical references do not include a comma after the title or "p." before the page number.

Whenever possible, introduce information with a phrase that includes the author's name. (If you do this, include only the page number in parentheses.)

> According to Andrew Keen, the absence of professional reporters and editors leads to erroneous information on Wikipedia (4).

Place documentation so that it does not interrupt the flow of your ideas, preferably at the end of a sentence.

The format for parenthetical references departs from these guidelines in the following special situations:

1. When you are citing a work by two authors

> It is impossible to access all Web sites by means of a single search engine (Sherman and Price 53).

2. When you are citing a work without a listed author

> The technology of wikis is important, but many users are not aware of it ("7 Things").

3. When you are citing an indirect source

If you use a statement by one author that is quoted in the work of another author, indicate this by including the abbreviation qtd. in ("quoted in").

> Marshall Poe notes that information on Wikipedia is "not exactly expert knowledge; it's common knowledge" (qtd. in Keen 39).

---

* For further information, see the seventh edition of the *MLA Handbook for Writers of Research Papers* (New York: Mod. Lang. Assn., 2009) or the MLA Web site at mla.org.

4. When you are citing an electronic source

Sources from the Internet or from library databases frequently do not contain page numbers. If the electronic source uses paragraph, section, or screen numbers, use the abbreviation par. or sec., or the full word screen, followed by the corresponding number, in your documentation. (If the citation includes an author's name, place a comma after the name.)

> On its Web site, Wikipedia warns its writers and editors to inspect sources carefully when they make assertions that are not generally held in academic circles ("Verifiability," sec. 3).

If the electronic source has no page numbers or markers of any kind, include just the name(s) of the author(s). Readers can tell that the citation refers to an electronic source when they consult the works-cited list.

> A Wikipedia entry can be very deceptive, but some users may not realize that its information may not be reliable (McHenry).

GUIDELINES FOR FORMATTING QUOTATIONS

SHORT QUOTATIONS   Quotations of no more than four typed lines are run in with the text of your paper. End punctuation comes after the parenthetical reference (which follows the quotation marks).

> According to Andrew Keen, on Wikipedia, "the voice of a high school kid has equal value to that of an Ivy League scholar of a trained profession" (42).

LONG QUOTATIONS   Quotations of more than four lines are set off from the text of your paper. Indent a long quotation one inch from the left-hand margin, and do not enclose the passage in quotation marks. The first line of a long quotation is not indented even if it is the beginning of a paragraph. If a quoted passage has more than one paragraph, indent the first line of each paragraph after the first one one-quarter inch. Introduce a long quotation with a colon, and place the parenthetical reference one space *after* the end punctuation.

> According to Katherine Mangu-Ward, Wikipedia has changed the world:
>> Wikipedia was born as an experiment in aggregating information. But the reason it works isn't that the world was clamoring for a new kind of encyclopedia. It took off because of the robust, self-policing community it created. . . . Despite its critics, it is transforming our everyday lives; as with Amazon, Google, and eBay, it is almost impossible to remember how much more circumscribed our world was before it existed. (21)

NOTE: Ellipsis points indicate that the student has deleted words from the quotation.

The Works-Cited List

The works-cited list includes all the works you **cite** (refer to) in your paper. Use the following guidelines to help you prepare your list.

> **GUIDELINES FOR PREPARING THE WORKS-CITED LIST**
>
> - Begin the works-cited list on a new page after the last page of your paper.
> - Number the works-cited page as the next page of the paper.
> - Center the heading Works Cited one inch from the top of the page; do not underline the heading or put it in quotation marks.
> - Double-space the list.
> - List entries alphabetically according to the author's last name.
> - Alphabetize unsigned articles according to the first major word of the title.
> - Begin each entry flush with the left-hand margin.
> - Indent second and subsequent lines one-half inch (or five spaces).
> - Separate each division of the entry — author, title, and publication information — by a period and one space.

The following sample works-cited entries cover the situations you will encounter most often. Follow the formats exactly as they appear here.

Books

BOOKS BY ONE AUTHOR

List the author with last name first. Italicize the title. Include the city of publication and a shortened form of the publisher's name — for example, *Bedford* for *Bedford/St. Martin's*. Use the abbreviation *UP* for *University Press*, as in *Princeton UP* and *U of Chicago P*. List the date of publication followed by a period, and then list the medium of publication (*Print*).

Goldsmith, Martin. *The Beatles Come to America*. Hoboken: Wiley, 2004. Print.

BOOKS BY TWO OR THREE AUTHORS

List authors in the order in which they are listed on the book's title page. List second and subsequent authors with first names first.

Bigelow, Fran, and Helene Siegel. *Pure Chocolate*. New York: Broadway, 2004. Print.

BOOK BY MORE THAN THREE AUTHORS

List only the first author, followed by the abbreviation *et al.* ("and others").

Ordeman, John T., et al. *Artists of the North American Wilderness: George and Belmore Browne*. New York: Warwick, 2004. Print.

TWO OR MORE BOOKS BY THE SAME AUTHOR

List two or more books by the same author in alphabetical order according to title. In each entry after the first, use three unspaced hyphens (followed by a period) instead of the author's name.

Angelou, Maya. *Hallelujah! The Welcome Table: A Lifetime of Memories with Recipes*. New York: Random, 2004. Print.

---. *I Know Why the Caged Bird Sings*. New York: Bantam, 1985. Print.

EDITED BOOK

Whitman, Walt. *The Portable Walt Whitman*. Ed. Michael Warner. New York: Penguin, 2004. Print.

TRANSLATION

García Márquez, Gabriel. *Living to Tell the Tale*. Trans. Edith Grossman. New York: Knopf, 2004. Print.

REVISED EDITION

Bjelajac, David. *American Art: A Cultural History*. 2nd ed. New York: Prentice, 2004. Print.

ANTHOLOGY

Kirszner, Laurie G., and Stephen R. Mandell, eds. *Patterns for College Writing: A Rhetorical Reader and Guide*. 11th ed. New York: Bedford, 2010. Print.

ESSAY IN AN ANTHOLOGY

Meyer, Herbert. "Why Americans Hate This 'Immigration' Debate." *Patterns for College Writing: A Rhetorical Reader and Guide*. 11th ed. Ed. Laurie G. Kirszner and Stephen R. Mandell. New York: Bedford, 2010. 665-68. Print.

MORE THAN ONE ESSAY IN THE SAME ANTHOLOGY

List each essay separately with a cross-reference to the entire anthology.

Feinstein, Dianne. "Statement in Support of Comprehensive Immigration Reform." Kirszner and Mandell 655-62.

Kirszner, Laurie G., and Stephen R. Mandell, eds. *Patterns for College Writing: A Rhetorical Reader and Guide*. 11th ed. New York: Bedford, 2010. Print.

Meyer, Herbert. "Why Americans Hate This 'Immigration' Debate." Kirszner and Mandell 665-68.

SECTION OR CHAPTER OF A BOOK

Gordimer, Nadine. "Loot." *"Loot" and Other Stories*. New York: Farrar, 2004. 1-6. Print.

INTRODUCTION, PREFACE, FOREWORD, OR AFTERWORD

Ingham, Patricia. Introduction. *Martin Chuzzlewit*. By Charles Dickens. London: Penguin, 1999. x-xxxii. Print.

MULTIVOLUME WORK

Malory, Thomas. *Le Morte D'Arthur*. Ed. Janet Cowen. 2 vols. London: Penguin, 1986. Print.

ARTICLE IN A REFERENCE WORK

For familiar reference works that publish new editions regularly, include only the edition (if given) and the year of publication.

"Civil Rights." *The World Book Encyclopedia*. 2006 ed. Print.

For less familiar reference works, provide a full citation.

Wagle, Greta. "Geisel, Theodor [Seuss]." *The Encyclopedia of American Literature*. Ed. Steven R. Serafin. New York: Continuum, 1999. Print.

Periodicals

Journals.   A **journal** is a publication aimed at readers who know a lot about a particular subject — English or history, for example.

ARTICLE IN A JOURNAL WITH CONTINUOUS PAGINATION THROUGHOUT AN ANNUAL VOLUME

Some scholarly journals have continuous pagination; that is, one issue might end on page 234, and the next would then begin with page 235. In this case, provide the volume number followed by a period and the issue number. Leave no space after the period between the volume and issue numbers. List the date of publication (in parentheses), the pages of the article, and the medium of publication.

Markley, Robert. "Gulliver and the Japanese: The Limits of the Postcolonial Past." *Modern Language Quarterly* 65.3 (2004): 457-80. Print.

ARTICLE IN A JOURNAL WITH SEPARATE PAGINATION IN EACH ISSUE

For a journal with each issue beginning on page 1, also include the volume and issue number, publication date, page numbers, and medium.

> Rushdie, Salman. "The Ministry of False Alarms." *Virginia Quarterly Review* 80.4 (2004): 7-23. Print.

Magazines.   A **magazine** is a publication aimed at general readers. For this reason, it contains articles that are easier to understand than those in journals.

ARTICLE IN A MONTHLY OR BIMONTHLY MAGAZINE

Frequently, an article in a magazine does not appear on consecutive pages — for example, it might begin on page 43, skip to page 47, and continue on page 49. If this is the case, include only the first page, followed by a plus sign.

> Edwards, Owen. "Kilroy Was Here." *Smithsonian* Oct. 2004: 40+. Print.

ARTICLE IN A WEEKLY OR BIWEEKLY MAGAZINE (SIGNED OR UNSIGNED)

> Schley, Jim. "Laid Off, and Working Harder than Ever." *Newsweek* 20 Sept. 2004: 16. Print.

> "Real Reform Post-Enron." *Nation* 4 Mar. 2002: 3. Print.

ARTICLE IN A NEWSPAPER

> Bykowicz, Julie. "Man Faces Identity Theft Counts; College Worker Accused of Taking Students' Data." *Sun* [Baltimore] 18 Sept. 2004: 2B. Print.

EDITORIAL OR LETTER TO THE EDITOR

> "An Un-American Way to Campaign." Editorial. *New York Times* 25 Sept. 2004, late ed.: A14. Print.

REVIEW IN A NEWSPAPER

> Scott, A. O. "Forever Obsessing about Obsession." Rev. of *Adaptation*, dir. Spike Jonze. *New York Times* 6 Dec. 2002: F1+. Print.

REVIEW IN A WEEKLY OR BIWEEKLY MAGAZINE

> Urquhart, Brian. "The Prospect of War." Rev. of *The Threatening Storm: The Case for Invading Iraq*, by Kenneth M. Pollack. *New York Review of Books* 19 Dec. 2002: 16-22. Print.

REVIEW IN A MONTHLY MAGAZINE

Jones, Kent. "The Lay of the Land." Rev. of *Sunshine State*, dir. John
    Sayles. *Film Commentary* May/June 2002: 22-24. Print.

Internet Sources

When citing Internet sources appearing on the World Wide Web,
include the following: the name of the author or editor of the Internet site;
the title of the site (italicized); the site's sponsor or publisher (if no sponsor or publisher is identified write *N.p.*); the date of electronic publication
(if no publication date is available, write *n.d.*); and the date you accessed
the source. Include the medium of publication, *Web*, between the update
date and the date of access.

ENTIRE INTERNET SITE (SCHOLARLY PROJECT, INFORMATION DATABASE, JOURNAL, OR PROFESSIONAL WEB SITE)

International Dialects of English Archive. Dept. of Theatre and Film, U of
    Kansas, 2004. Web. 4 Dec. 2008.

The Dickens Project. Ed. Jon Michael Varese. U of California, Santa Cruz,
    2004. Web. 2 Dec. 2008.

Words of the Year. Amer. Dialect Soc., 2008. Web. 18 Feb. 2008.

DOCUMENT WITHIN A WEB SITE

"Child and Adolescent Violence Research at the NIMH." *National Institute
    of Mental Health*, NIMH, 2005. Web. 2 Apr. 2008.

PERSONAL WEB SITE

Lynch, Jack. Home page. Jack Lynch, n.d. Web. 2 Jan. 2005.

ENTIRE ONLINE BOOK

Fielding, Henry. *The History of Tom Jones, a Foundling*. Ed. William Allan
    Nielson. New York: Collier, 1917. *Bartleby.com: Great Books Online*.
    Web. 29 Nov. 2008.

Austen, Jane. *Pride and Prejudice*. 1813. *The Literature Network*. Web. 30
    Nov. 2008.

PART OF AN ONLINE BOOK

Radford, Dollie. "At Night." *Poems*. London, 1910. *Victorian Women Writers
    Project*. Web. 17 Mar. 2008.

ARTICLE IN AN ONLINE SCHOLARLY JOURNAL

Condie, Kent C., and Jane Silverstone. "The Crust of the Colorado Plateau:
New Views of an Old Arc." *Journal of Geology* 107.4 (1999): 387-397.
Web. 9 Aug. 2008.

ARTICLE IN AN ONLINE REFERENCE BOOK OR ENCYCLOPEDIA

"Croatia." *The World Factbook 2004*. CIA, 30 Mar. 2004. Web. 30 Dec. 2007.

ARTICLE IN AN ONLINE NEWSPAPER

Krim, Jonathan. "FCC Preparing to Overhaul Telecom, Media Rules."
Washingtonpost.com. Washington Post, 3 Jan. 2003. Web. 6 Jan.
2007.

ONLINE EDITORIAL

"Ersatz Eve." Editorial. *New York Times on the Web*. New York Times, 28 Dec.
2002. Web. 5 Jan. 2006.

ARTICLE IN AN ONLINE MAGAZINE

Press, Eyal, and Jennifer Washburn. "The At-Risk-Youth Industry." *Atlantic
Online*. Atlantic Monthly Group, Dec. 2002. Web. 3 Jan. 2008.

REVIEW IN AN ONLINE PERIODICAL

Chocano, Carina. "Sympathy for the Misanthrope." Rev. of *Curb Your
Enthusiasm*, dir. Robert Weide, prod. Larry David. *Salon*. Salon Media
Group, 4 Dec. 2002. Web. 17 Sept. 2005.

POSTING TO A DISCUSSION LIST

Thune, W. Scott. "Emotion and Rationality in Argument." *CCCC/97 Online*.
N.p., 23 Mar. 1997. Web. 11 Nov. 2000.

Other Internet Sources

A PAINTING ON THE INTERNET

O'Keeffe, Georgia. *Evening Star, III*. 1917. Museum of Mod. Art, New York.
MoMA: The Museum of Modern Art. Web. 9 Nov. 2007.

A PHOTOGRAPH ON THE INTERNET

Cartier-Bresson, Henri. *William Faulkner, 1947*. *Tête à tête: Portraits by
Henri Cartier-Bresson*. Nat. Portrait Gallery, n.d. Web. 8 Oct. 2008.

A CARTOON ON THE INTERNET

Trudeau, Garry. "Doonesbury." Comic strip. *Washingtonpost.com.*
Washington Post, 7 Apr. 2005. Web. 5 May 2008.

A MAP OR CHART ON THE INTERNET

"Fort Worth, Texas." Map. *US Gazetteer.* US Census Bureau, n.d. Web. 26
Oct. 2008.

MATERIAL ACCESSED ON A CD-ROM, DISKETTE, OR MAGNETIC TAPE

In addition to the publication information, include the medium (CD-
ROM, for example) and the distribution vendor, if relevant (UMI-Proquest,
for example).

Aristotle. "Poetics." *The Complete Works of Aristotle.* Ed. Jonathan Barnes.
2 vols. Princeton: Princeton UP, 1984. CD-ROM. Clayton: InteLex,
1994.

"Feminism." *The Oxford English Dictionary.* 2nd ed. New York: Oxford UP,
1992. CD-ROM. Vers. 3.1. 2004.

EMAIL

Sullivan, John. "Re: Headnotes." Message to Laurie G. Kirszner. 13 Dec.
2008. E-mail.

COMPUTER SOFTWARE OR VIDEO GAME

Provide the name of the author or developer of the software, if available; the title of the software, italicized; the publisher or distributor and
publication date; and the software platform (for example, Xbox 360 or
PlayStation 3).

Sid Meier's Civilization IV: Colonization. Take 2 Interactive, 2008. Windows.

MATERIAL FROM A DATABASE SERVICE

For material retrieved from a database service such as *InfoTrac, Lexis-
Nexis, ProQuest,* or *EBSCOhost,* list the publication information for the
source and provide the name of the database (such as *LexisNexis Academic*),
italicized; the publication medium; and the date you accessed the source.

Benjamin, Roy. "The Stone of Stumbling in Finnegans Wake." *Journal of
Modern Literature* 31.2 (2008): 66-78. *Academic OneFile.* Web. 7 Apr.
2009.

Carter, Jeff. "The Missing Piece of Education Reform." *Washington Post* 18 May 2008, regional ed.: B8. *LexisNexis Academic*. Web. 31 March 2009.

Prince, Stephen. "Why Do Film Scholars Ignore Media Violence?" *Chronicle of Higher Education* 10 Aug. 2001: B18. *Academic Research Premier*. Web. 14 Feb. 2007.

Other Nonprint Sources

TELEVISION OR RADIO PROGRAM

"Prime Suspect 3." Writ. Lynda La Plante. *Mystery!* PBS. WNET, New York, 28 Apr. 1994. Television.

FILM, DVD, OR CD

Doubt. Dir. John Patrick Shanley. Perf. Meryl Streep, Philip Seymour Hoffman, Amy Adams, and Viola Davis. Miramax, 2008. DVD.

Man on Wire. Dir. James Marsh. Perf. Philippe Petit. Discovery Films, 2008. Film.

PERSONAL INTERVIEW

Garcetti, Gilbert. Personal interview. 7 May 2000.

SAMPLE STUDENT RESEARCH ESSAY IN MLA STYLE

Philip Lau's essay on Wikipedia begins on page 782.

Lau 1

Philip Lau
Professor Carroll
ENG 101
23 Nov. 2008

The Limitations of Wikipedia

Introduction

When they get a research assignment, many students immediately go to the Internet to find sources. Searching the Web, they may discover a useful Wikipedia article on their topic. But is Wikipedia a reliable reference source for a research paper? There is quite a controversy over the use of Wikipedia as a source, but the answer seems to be no. Although Wikipedia may be a good starting point for general information about a topic, college-level research papers should rely on more authoritative sources.

Thesis statement

A wiki is software that allows people to collaborate in forming the content of a Web site. With a wiki, anyone with a browser can edit, modify, rearrange, or delete the site content. It is not necessary to know HTML (hypertext mark-up language) or to work in HTML code. The word *wiki* comes from the word *wikiwiki*, which means "quick" or "fast" in Hawaiian. The most popular wiki is Wikipedia, a free, Internet-based encyclopedia that relies on the collaboration, consensus, openness, and trust of those who post and edit entries. Anyone can write a Wikipedia article by clicking on "How to write an article" or edit an entry by clicking on "Edit this entry." All the revisions are visible to everyone who clicks on "history" ("Verifiability"). According to Katherine Mangu-Ward, the success of Wikipedia "springs largely from [its founder's] willingness to trust large aggregations of human beings to produce good outcomes . . ." (26). This collaboration enables Wikipedia to publish a wide variety of entries on unusual, specialized topics (see Fig. 1). So far, there are over four million Wikipedia articles (Rothenberg).

Paragraph combines factual information, found in more than one source, with quotations from "Verifiability" and Mangu-Ward, and a statistic from Rothenberg

Wikipedia includes two kinds of content. The first kind of content is factual — that is, information that can be verified or

Lau 2

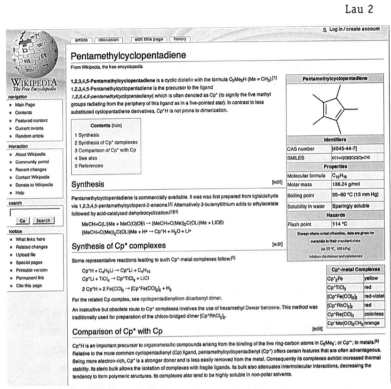

Fig. 1. Wikipedia entry for a chemical compound. Reproduced under the terms of the GNU Free Document License.

Paragraph combines Philip's own ideas with quotations and paraphrases from "Verifiability"

proved true. Factual material from reliable sources is more trustworthy than material from other sources. In fact, Wikipedia's own site states, "In general, the most reliable sources are peer-reviewed journals and books published in university presses; university-level textbooks; magazines, journals, and books published by respected publishing houses; and mainstream newspapers" ("Verifiability"). Most reliable publications have someone whose job it is to check facts. However, because Wikipedia relies on a community of people to write articles, no single person or group of people is responsible for checking facts. The theory is that after enough people have worked on an article, any errors in fact will have been found and corrected. However, this assumption is not necessarily true.

Lau 3

The second kind of content consists of opinions. Because an opinion is a belief or judgment, opinions, by definition, tend to be one-sided. So, since Wikipedia entries are supposed to be objective, Wikipedia's policy statement says that entries for controversial topics should include opinions that reflect the various sides of the issue ("Verifiability"). In addition, Wikipedia warns users against believing everything they read, even what they read on its own site: "Anyone can create a website or pay to have a book published, then claim to be an expert . . ." ("Verifiability"). It also advises readers to examine sources carefully, especially when they present controversial opinions or make claims that contradict established academic views ("Verifiability"). However, it is all up to the users; no one checks to make sure that these guidelines are followed.

Paragraph combines quotation and paraphrases from "Verifiability" with Philip's own ideas

In spite of its stated policies, then, Wikipedia is open to certain kinds of errors. One of Wikipedia's problems comes from its assumption that the knowledge of the community is more valuable than the knowledge of acknowledged experts in a field. Larry Sanger, one of the founders of Wikipedia, who has since left the project, concedes that Wikipedia has a problem with "anti-elitism, or lack of respect for expertise"; in fact, he refers to its "horror of the traditional deference to experience," which he claims explains why acknowledged experts avoid writing or editing articles in Wikipedia. Those who criticize Wikipedia often point to its irrational trust in the knowledge of the community. According to Andrew Keen, Wikipedia is virtually "the blind leading the blind — infinite monkeys providing infinite information for infinite readers, perpetuating the cycle of misinformation and ignorance" (4). On Wikipedia, Keen complains, "the voice of a high school kid has equal value to that of an Ivy League scholar . . ." (42).

Paragraph combines quotation and paraphrase from Sanger with a quotation from Keen

Another problem with Wikipedia is the ease with which entries can be edited. Because the content of wikis can be altered by anyone, individuals can easily vandalize content by inserting incorrect information, obscene language, or even

Lau 4

nonsense into articles. Writers who are more interested in presenting their personal opinions than presenting reliable information frequently target certain entries. For example, entries for controversial people, such as President George W. Bush, financier George Soros, or Scientology founder L. Ron Hubbard, or for controversial subjects, such as abortion and the Holocaust, are routinely vandalized. Sometimes this vandalism can be extremely harmful. One notorious case of vandalism involved John Seigenthaler Sr., a journalist who was falsely accused in a Wikipedia entry of being involved in the assassinations of John Kennedy and Robert Kennedy. As Seigenthaler's son has reported, the false information stayed on the site for more than four months and also appeared on at least two other sites that had used Wikipedia as their source (Seigenthaler). This incident, as well as many others, has caused people to question the reliability of Wikipedia. According to Jane Kirtley, the issue of reliability poses a real problem for the users of Wikipedia:

> It's hard to defend an anonymous poster who uploads a damaging falsehood about someone on a Web site that purports to provide facts from a "neutral point of view. . . ." Either accuracy matters, or it doesn't. If the denizens of cyberspace want to be taken seriously, they might want to be responsible for what they produce. (66)

Bias is another problem for Wikipedia. Some critics have accused Wikipedia of having a liberal bias; in fact, a competitor, Conservapedia, lists many examples of liberal bias in Wikipedia entries. Accusing Wikipedia of being anti-American and anti-Christian ("Examples"), Conservapedia questions the true agenda of the Wikipedia community. In a *Time* article, Jimmy Wales, founder of Wikipedia, denies this liberal bias and accuses Conservapedia of having a conservative bias (6). Still, such accusations raise questions about the credibility of Wikipedia.

Paragraph contains a long quotation from Kirtley, Philip's summary of the Seigenthaler article, and facts that were found in several sources

Paragraph contains paraphrases from "Examples" and Wales as well as Philip's own conclusions

Lau 5

Wikipedia has tried to correct some of the problems that its critics have pointed out. In response to criticism of its policy of allowing writers and editors to remain anonymous, Jimmy Wales changed Wikipedia's policy. Now, writers and editors have to provide their user names and thus take responsibility for the content they contribute. In addition, Wikipedia has made it possible for administrators to block certain sites from those wishing to edit them and to prevent certain writers and editors from posting or changing information. In addition, users must now be registered with Wikipedia for four days before they can change certain controversial entries (Hafner). However, authorship is still a problem. Most readers have no idea who has written an article that they are reading or whether or not that person can be trusted. Given Wikipedia's basic philosophy, there is no way to solve this problem.

Paragraph combines ideas found in several sources, a paraphrase from Hafner, and Philip's own ideas

Of course, even traditional encyclopedias have shortcomings. For example, a study by the journal *Nature* found that although Wikipedia included errors, the *Encyclopedia Britannica* also did. Nevertheless, Robert McHenry, a former editor of *Britannica*, points out that Wikipedia articles often do not get better through editing; instead, they frequently get worse. He goes on to say that Wikipedia suffers because it lacks the oversight that only a good editor can provide: "skills, knowledge, experience, and maybe a touch of talent." McHenry observes that out of concern for *Britannica*'s reputation, at least four people check every article for accuracy. He points out that professional editors do more than just check spelling and grammar; they also stand in "for the eventual reader in order to assure that what was written was clear, logical, and to the point." Since Wikipedia has no professional editors, its writing may be ungrammatical, stylistically awkward, or unclear.

Paragraph combines ideas found in several sources with paraphrases and quotations from McHenry

Supporters of Wikipedia defend the site against those charges, noting that more traditional sources, such as respected peer-reviewed journals, also have their problems. For example,

Lau 6

Paragraph contains ideas found in several sources and Philip's own conclusions

very new material is likely to be underrepresented or even omitted by a traditional print encyclopedia, which is published only every few years. In addition, some reviewers of articles that appear in peer-reviewed journals may have conflicts of interest. For example, a reviewer might reject an article that challenges his or her own work, or editors may favor certain authors over others. Also, it may be possible for reviewers to identify the work of a competitor, especially if the number of people working in a field is relatively small, and therefore let bias influence their evaluation of an article. Another problem is that it takes a long time for articles in peer-reviewed journals to get into print. Critics point out that by the time an article in a peer-reviewed journal gets into print, it may be outdated. As a result, peer-reviewed journals may not be as objective or as up-to-date as readers think they are.

Conclusion

Wikipedia is easy to access and easy to use. It includes information on just about any topic a researcher might want to explore. Still, it is not a reliable source for serious research. For one thing, many questions have been raised about the reliability of its articles. Also, librarians have complained that the continual editing of Wikipedia articles makes it impossible to document them correctly. As a result of these and other problems, many high schools and colleges do not allow students to cite Wikipedia as a source. Granted, there are times when Wikipedia can be useful. For example, visitors to the site can skim articles on a variety of topics, and this preliminary reading can help them find or narrow a research topic. In addition, students can often find general information on Wikipedia about very current topics that may not be treated anywhere else. Finally, the computer links that appear at the end of most Wikipedia articles can be a good starting point for research. In general, however, because of the questionable authorship of its entries and the lack of expertise and objectivity of some (if not many) of its contributors, Wikipedia is not a reliable source.

Lau 7

Works Cited

"Examples of Bias in Wikipedia." *Conservapedia*. Conservapedia, 27 Dec. 2007. Web. 28 Dec. 2007.

Hafner, Katie. "Growing Wikipedia Refines Its 'Anyone Can Edit' Policy." *New York Times*. New York Times, 17 June 2006. Web. 23 Dec. 2007.

Keen, Andrew. *The Cult of the Amateur: How Today's Internet Is Killing Our Culture*. New York: Doubleday, 2007. Print.

Kirtley, Jane. "Web of Lies: A Vicious Wikipedia Entry Underscores the Difficulty of Holding Anyone Responsible for Misinformation on the Internet." *American Journalism Review* 28.1 (2006): 66. Print.

Mangu-Ward, Katherine. "Wikipedia and Beyond: Jimmy Wales's Sprawling Vision." *Reason* June 2007: 20-29. Print.

McHenry, Robert. "The Faith-Based Encyclopedia Blinks." *TCS Daily*. TCS Daily, 14 Dec. 2005. Web. 21 Dec. 2007.

Rothenberg, Jennie. "Common Knowledge." *Atlantic.com*. Atlantic Monthly Group, 1 Aug. 2006. Web. 22 Dec. 2007.

Sanger, Larry. "Why Wikipedia Must Jettison Its Anti-Elitism." *Kuro5hin.org*. Kuro5hin, 31 Dec. 2004. Web. 21 Dec. 2007.

Seigenthaler, John. "A False Wikipedia 'Biography.'" *USAToday*. USA Today, 29 Nov. 2005. Web. 21 Dec. 2007.

"Verifiability." *Wikipedia*. Wikimedia Foundation, 22 Dec. 2007. Web. 24 Dec. 2007.

Wales, Jimmy. "10 Questions." *Time* 2 April 2007: 6. Print.

Glossary

Abstract/Concrete language   Abstract language names concepts or qualities that cannot be directly seen or touched: *love, emotion, evil, anguish*. Concrete language denotes objects or qualities that the senses can perceive: *fountain pen, leaky, shouting, rancid*. Abstract words are sometimes needed to express ideas, but they are very vague unless used with concrete supporting detail. The abstract phrase "The speaker was overcome with emotion" could mean almost anything, but the addition of concrete language clarifies the meaning: "He clenched his fist and shook it at the crowd" (anger).

Allusion   A brief reference to literature, history, the Bible, mythology, popular culture, and so on that readers are expected to recognize. An allusion evokes a vivid impression in very few words. "The gardener opened the gate, and suddenly we found ourselves in Eden" suggests in one word (*Eden*) the stunning beauty of the garden.

Analogy   A form of comparison that explains an unfamiliar element by comparing it to another that is more familiar. Analogies also enable writers to put abstract or technical information in simpler, more concrete terms: "The effect of pollution on the environment is like that of cancer on the body."

Annotating   The technique of recording one's responses to a reading selection by writing notes in the margins of the text. Annotating a text might involve asking questions, suggesting possible parallels with other selections or with the reader's own experience, arguing with the writer's points, commenting on the writer's style, or defining unfamiliar terms or concepts.

Antithesis   A viewpoint opposite to one expressed in a *thesis*. In an argumentative essay, the thesis must be debatable. If no antithesis exists, the writer's thesis is not debatable. (See also **Thesis**.)

Antonym   A word opposite in meaning to another word. *Beautiful* is the antonym of *ugly*. *Synonym* is the antonym of *antonym*.

Argumentation   The form of writing that takes a stand on an issue and attempts to convince readers by presenting a logical sequence of points supported by evidence. Unlike *persuasion*, which uses a number of different appeals, argumentation is primarily an appeal to reason. (See Chapter 14.)

Audience   The people "listening" to a writer's words. Writers who are sensitive to their audience will carefully choose a tone, examples, and allusions that their readers will understand and respond to. For instance, an effective article attempting to persuade high school students not to drink alcohol would use examples and allusions pertinent to a teenager's life. Different examples would be chosen if the writer were addressing middle-aged members of Alcoholics Anonymous.

Basis for comparison   A fundamental similarity between two or more things that enables a writer to compare them. In a comparison of how two towns react to immigrants, the basis of comparison might be that both towns have a rapidly expanding immigrant population. (If one of the towns did not have any immigrants, this comparison would be illogical.)

Body paragraphs   The paragraphs that develop and support an essay's thesis.

Brainstorming   An invention technique that can be done individually or in a group. When writers brainstorm on their own, they jot down every fact or idea that relates to a particular topic. When they brainstorm in a group, they discuss a topic with others and write down the useful ideas that come up.

Causal chain   A sequence of events when one event causes another event, which in turn causes yet another event.

Cause and effect   The pattern of development that discusses either the reasons for an occurrence or the observed or predicted consequence of an occurrence. Often both causes and effects are discussed in the same essay. (See Chapter 10.)

Causes   The reasons for an event, situation, or phenomenon. An *immediate cause* is an obvious one; a *remote cause* is less easily perceived. The *main cause* is the most important cause, whether it is immediate or remote. Other, less important causes that nevertheless encourage the effect in some way (for instance, by speeding it up or providing favorable circumstances for it) are called *contributory causes.*

Chronological order   The time sequence of events. Chronological order is often used to organize a narrative; it is also used to structure a process essay.

Claim   In Toulmin logic, the thesis or main point of an essay. Usually the claim is stated directly, but sometimes it is implied. (See also **Toulmin logic**.)

Classification and division   The pattern of development that uses these two related methods of organizing information. *Classification* involves searching for common characteristics among various items and grouping them accordingly, thereby imposing order on randomly organized information. *Division* breaks up an entity into smaller groups or elements. Classification generalizes; division specifies. (See Chapter 12.)

Cliché   An overused expression, such as *beauty is in the eye of the beholder, the good die young,* or *a picture is worth a thousand words.*

Clustering   A method of invention whereby a writer groups ideas visually by listing the main topic in the center of a page, circling it, and surrounding it with words or phrases that identify the major points to be addressed. The writer then circles these words or phrases, creating new clusters or ideas for each of them.

Coherence   The tight relationship between all the parts of an effective piece of writing. Such a relationship ensures that the writing will make sense to readers. For a piece of writing to be coherent, it must be logical and orderly, with effective *transitions* making the movement between sentences and paragraphs clear. Within and between paragraphs, coherence may also be enhanced by the repetition of key words and ideas, by the use of pronouns to refer to nouns mentioned previously, and by the use of parallel sentence structure.

Colloquialisms   Expressions that are generally appropriate for conversation and informal writing but not usually acceptable for the writing you do in college, business, or professional settings. Examples of colloquial language include contractions; clipped forms (*fridge* for *refrigerator*); vague expressions such as *kind of* and *sort of;* conversation fillers such as *you know;* and other informal words and expressions, such as *get across* for *communicate* and *kids* for *children.*

Common knowledge   Factual information that is widely available in reference sources, such as the dates of important historical events. Writers do not need to document common knowledge.

Comparison and contrast   The pattern of development that focuses on similarities and differences between two or more subjects. In a general sense, *comparison* shows how two or more subjects are alike; *contrast* shows how they are different. (See Chapter 11.) (See also **Point-by-point comparison**; **Subject-by-subject comparison**.)

Conclusion   The group of sentences or paragraphs that brings an essay to a close. To *conclude* means not only "to end" but also "to resolve." Although a conclusion does not review all the issues discussed in an essay, the conclusion is the place to show that those issues have been resolved. An effective conclusion indicates that the writer is committed to what has been expressed, and it is the writer's last chance to leave an impression or idea with readers.

Concrete language   See **Abstract/Concrete language**.

Connotation   The associations, meanings, or feelings a word suggests beyond its literal meaning. Literally, the word *home* means one's place of residence, but *home* also connotes warmth and a sense of belonging. (See also **Denotation**.)

Contributory cause   See **Causes**.

Deductive reasoning   The method of reasoning that moves from a general premise to a specific conclusion. Deductive reasoning is the opposite of *inductive reasoning.* (See also **Syllogism**.)

Definition   An explanation of a word's meaning; the pattern of development in which a writer explains what something or someone is. (See Chapter 13.) (See also **Extended definition; Formal definition**.)

Denotation   The literal meaning of a word. The denotation of *home* is "one's place of residence." (See also **Connotation**.)

Description   The pattern of development that presents a word picture of a thing, a person, a situation, or a series of events. (See Chapter 7; see also **Objective description; Subjective description**.)

Digression   A remark or series of remarks that wanders from the main point of a discussion. In a personal narrative, a digression may be entertaining because of its irrelevance, but in other kinds of writing it is likely to distract and confuse readers.

Division See **Classification and division**.

Documentation The formal way of giving credit to the sources a writer borrows words or ideas from. Documentation allows readers to evaluate a writer's sources and to consult them if they wish. Papers written for literature and writing classes use the documentation style recommended by the Modern Language Association (MLA). (See Appendix.)

Dominant impression The mood or quality that is central to a piece of writing.

Essay A short work of nonfiction writing on a single topic that usually expresses the author's impressions or opinions. An essay may be organized around one of the patterns of development presented in Chapters 6 through 14 of this book, or it may combine several of these patterns.

Euphemism A polite term for an unpleasant concept. (*Passed on* is a euphemism for *died.*)

Evidence Facts and opinions used to support a statement, position, or idea. *Facts,* which may include statistics, may be drawn from research or personal experience; *opinions* may represent the conclusions of experts or the writer's own ideas.

Example A concrete illustration of a general point.

Exemplification The pattern of development that uses a single extended *example* or a series of shorter examples to support a thesis. (See Chapter 8.)

Extended definition A paragraph-, essay-, or book-length definition developed by means of one or more of the rhetorical strategies discussed in this book.

Fallacy A statement that resembles a logical argument but is actually flawed. Logical fallacies are often persuasive, but they unfairly manipulate readers to win agreement. Fallacies include begging the question; argument from analogy; personal (*ad hominem*) attacks; hasty or sweeping generalizations; false dilemmas (the either/or fallacy); equivocation; red herrings; you also (*tu quoque*); appeals to doubtful authority; distorting statistics; *post hoc* reasoning; and *non sequiturs*. See the section on "Recognizing Fallacies" (page 559) for explanations and examples.

Figures of speech (also known as *figurative language*) Imaginative language used to suggest a special meaning or create a special effect. Three of the most common figures of speech are *similes, metaphors,* and *personification.*

Formal definition A brief explanation of a word's meaning as it appears in the dictionary.

Freewriting A method of invention that involves writing without stopping for a fixed period — perhaps five or ten minutes — without paying attention to spelling, grammar, or punctuation. The goal of freewriting is to let ideas flow and get them down on paper.

Grounds In Toulmin logic, the material that a writer uses to support a claim. Grounds may be evidence (facts or expert opinions) or appeals to the emotions or values of an audience. (See also **Toulmin logic**.)

Highlighting   A technique used by a reader to record responses to a reading selection by marking the text with symbols. Highlighting a text might involve underlining important ideas, boxing key terms, numbering a series of related points, circling unfamiliar words (or placing question marks next to them), drawing vertical lines next to an interesting or important passage, drawing arrows to connect related points, or placing asterisks next to discussions of the selection's central issues or themes.

Hyperbole   Deliberate exaggeration for emphasis or humorous effect: "I froze to death out in the storm"; "She has hundreds of boyfriends"; "Senior year passed by in a second." The opposite of hyperbole is *understatement.*

Imagery   A set of verbal pictures of sensory experiences. These pictures, conveyed through concrete details, make a description vivid and immediate to the reader. Some images are literal ("The cows were so white they almost glowed in the dark"); others are more figurative ("The black and white cows looked like maps, with the continents in black and the seas in white"). A pattern of imagery (repeated images of, for example, shadows, forests, or fire) may run through a piece of writing.

Immediate cause   See **Causes**.

Inductive reasoning   The method of reasoning that moves from specific evidence to a general conclusion based on this evidence. Inductive reasoning is the opposite of *deductive reasoning.*

Instructions   A kind of process essay whose purpose is to enable readers to *perform* a process. Instructions use the present tense and speak directly to readers: "Walk at a moderate pace for twenty minutes."

Introduction   An essay's opening. Depending on the length of an essay, the introduction may be one paragraph or several paragraphs. In an introduction, a writer tries to encourage the audience to read the essay that follows. Therefore, the writer must choose tone and diction carefully, indicate what the paper is about, and suggest to readers what direction it will take.

Invention (also known as *prewriting*)   The stage of writing when a writer explores the writing assignment, focuses ideas, and ultimately decides on a thesis for an essay. A writer might begin by thinking through the requirements of the assignment — the essay's purpose, length, and audience. Then, using one or more methods of invention — such as *freewriting, questions for probing, brainstorming, clustering,* and *journal writing* — the writer can formulate a tentative thesis and begin to write the essay.

Irony   Language that points to a discrepancy between two different levels of meaning. *Verbal irony* is characterized by a gap between what is stated and what is really meant, which often has the opposite meaning — for instance, "his humble abode" (referring to a millionaire's estate). *Situational irony* points to a discrepancy between what actually happens and what readers expect will happen. This kind of irony is present, for instance, when a character, trying to frighten a rival, ends up frightening himself. *Dramatic irony* occurs when the reader understands more about what is happening in a story than the character who is telling the story does. For example, a narrator might tell an anecdote that he intends to illustrate how clever he is, while it is obvious to the reader from the story's events that the narrator has made a fool of himself because of his gullibility. (See also **Sarcasm**.)

Jargon The specialized vocabulary of a profession or academic field. Although the jargon of a particular profession is an efficient means of communication within that field, it may not be clear or meaningful to readers outside that profession.

Journal writing A method of invention that involves recording ideas that emerge from reading or other experiences and then exploring them in writing.

Looping A method of invention that involves isolating one idea from a piece of freewriting and using this idea as a focus for a new piece of freewriting.

Main cause See **Causes**.

Metaphor A comparison of two dissimilar things that does not use the words *like* or *as* ("The small waves were the same, chucking the rowboat under the chin . . ." — E. B. White).

Narration The pattern of development that tells a story. (See Chapter 6.)

Objective description A detached, factual picture presented in plain and direct manner. Although pure objectivity is impossible to achieve, writers of science papers, technical reports, and news articles, among others, strive for precise language that is free of value judgments.

Paradox A statement that seems self-contradictory or absurd but is nonetheless true.

Paragraph The basic unit of an essay. A paragraph is composed of related sentences that together express a single idea. This main idea is often stated in a single *topic sentence*. Paragraphs are also graphic symbols on the page, mapping the progress of the ideas in the essay and providing visual breaks for readers.

Parallelism The use of similar grammatical elements within a sentence or sentences. "I like hiking, skiing, and to cook" is not parallel because *hiking* and *skiing* are gerund forms (*-ing*) while *to cook* is an infinitive form. Revised for parallelism, the sentence could read either "I like hiking, skiing, and cooking" or "I like to hike, to ski, and to cook." As a stylistic technique, parallelism can provide emphasis through repetition — for example, "Walk groundly, talk profoundly, drink roundly, sleep soundly" (William Hazlitt). Parallelism is also a powerful oratorical technique: "Until justice is blind to color, until education is unaware of race, until opportunity is unconcerned with the color of men's skins, emancipation will be a proclamation but not a fact" (Lyndon B. Johnson). Finally, parallelism can increase *coherence* within a paragraph or an essay.

Paraphrase The restatement of another person's words in one's own words, following the order and emphasis of the original. Paraphrase is frequently used in source-based papers, where the purpose is to use information gathered during research to support the ideas in the paper. For example, Jonathan Kozol's "Illiterates cannot travel freely. When they attempt to do so, they encounter risks that few of us can dream of" (page 252) might be paraphrased like this: "According to Jonathan Kozol, people who cannot read find travel extremely dangerous."

Personification   Describing concepts or objects as if they were human ("the chair slouched"; "the wind sighed outside the window").

Persuasion   The method a writer uses to move an audience to adopt a belief or follow a course of action. To persuade an audience, a writer relies on the various appeals — to the emotions, to reason, or to ethics. Persuasion is different from *argumentation,* which appeals primarily to reason.

Plagiarism   Presenting the words or ideas of someone else as if they were one's own (whether intentionally or unintentionally). Plagiarism should always be avoided.

Point-by-point comparison   A comparison in which the writer first makes a point about one subject and then follows it with a comparable point about the other subject. (See also **Subject-by-subject comparison**.)

Post hoc **reasoning**   A logical fallacy that involves looking back at two events that occurred in chronological sequence and wrongly assuming that the first event caused the second. For example, just because a car will not start after a thunderstorm, one cannot automatically assume that the storm caused the problem.

Prewriting   See **Invention**.

Principle of classification   In a classification-and-division essay, the quality the items have in common. For example, if a writer were classifying automobiles, one principle of classification might be "repair records."

Process   The pattern of development that presents a series of steps in a procedure in chronological order and shows how this sequence of steps leads to a particular result. (See Chapter 9.)

Process explanation   A kind of process essay whose purpose is to enable readers to understand a process rather than perform it.

Purpose   A writer's reason for writing. A writer's purpose may, for example, be to entertain readers with an amusing story, to inform them about a dangerous disease, to move them to action by enraging them with an example of injustice, or to change their perspective by revealing a hidden dimension of a person or situation.

Quotation   The exact words of a source, enclosed in quotation marks. A quotation should be used only to present a particularly memorable statement or to avoid a paraphrase that would change the meaning of the original.

Refutation   The attempt to counter an opposing argument by revealing its weaknesses. Three of the most common weaknesses are logical flaws in the argument, inadequate evidence, and irrelevance. Refutation greatly strengthens an argument by showing that the writer is aware of the complexity of the issue and has considered opposing viewpoints.

Remote cause   See **Causes**.

Rhetorical question   A question asked for effect and not meant to be answered.

Rogerian argument   A strategy put forth by psychologist Carl Rogers that rejects the adversarial approach that characterizes many arguments. Rather than attacking the opposition, Rogers suggests acknowledging the validity of opposing positions. By finding areas of agreement, a Rogerian argument reduces conflict and increases the chance that the final position will satisfy all parties.

Sarcasm   Deliberately insincere and biting irony — for example, "That's okay — I love it when you borrow things and don't return them."

Satire   Writing that uses wit, irony, and ridicule to attack foolishness, incompetence, or evil in a person or idea. Satire has a different purpose from comedy, which usually intends simply to entertain. For a classic example of satire, see Jonathan Swift's "A Modest Proposal," page 745.

Sexist language   Language that stereotypes people according to gender. Writers often use plural constructions to avoid sexist language. For example, *the doctors . . . they* can be used instead of *the doctor . . . he*. Words such as *police officer* and *firefighter* can be used instead of *policeman* and *fireman*.

Simile   A comparison of two dissimilar things using the words *like* or *as* ("Hills Like White Elephants" — Ernest Hemingway).

Slang   Informal words whose meanings vary from locale to locale or change as time passes. Slang is frequently associated with a particular group of people — for example, bikers, musicians, or urban youth. Slang is inappropriate in college writing.

Subject-by-subject comparison   A comparison that discusses one subject in full and then goes on to discuss the next subject. (See also **Point-by-point comparison**.)

Subjective description   A description that contains value judgments (*a saintly person*, for example). Whereas objective language is distanced from an event or object, *subjective language* is involved. A subjective description focuses on the author's reaction to the event, conveying not just a factual record of details but also their significance. Subjective language may include poetic or colorful words that impart a judgment or an emotional response (*stride, limp, meander, hobble, stroll, plod*, or *shuffle* instead of *walk*). Subjective descriptions often include *figures of speech*.

Summary   The ideas of a source as presented in one's own words. Unlike a paraphrase, a summary conveys only a general sense of a passage, without following the order and emphasis of the original.

Syllogism   A basic form of deductive reasoning. Every syllogism includes three parts: a major premise that makes a general statement ("Confinement is physically and psychologically damaging"); a minor premise that makes a related but more specific statement ("Zoos confine animals"); and a conclusion drawn from these two premises ("Therefore, zoos are physically and psychologically damaging to animals").

Symbol   A person, event, or object that stands for something more than its literal meaning.

Synonym   A word with the same basic meaning as another word. A synonym for *loud* is *noisy*. Most words in the English language have several synonyms, but each word has unique nuances or *connotations*.

Thesis   An essay's main idea; the idea that all the points in the body of the essay support. A thesis may be implied, but it is usually stated explicitly in the form of a *thesis statement*. In addition to conveying the essay's main idea, the thesis statement may indicate the writer's approach to the subject and the writer's purpose. It may also indicate the pattern of development that will structure the essay.

Topic sentence   A sentence stating the main idea of a paragraph. Often, but not always, the topic sentence opens the paragraph.

Toulmin logic   A method of structuring an argument according to the way arguments occur in everyday life. Developed by philosopher Stephen Toulmin, Toulmin logic divides an argument into three parts: the *claim*, the *grounds*, and the *warrant*.

Transitions   Words or expressions that link ideas in a piece of writing. Long essays frequently contain *transitional paragraphs* that connect one part of the essay to another. Writers use a variety of transitional expressions, such as *afterward, because, consequently, for instance, furthermore, however,* and *likewise*. See the list of transitions on page 43.

Understatement   Deliberate deemphasis for effect: "The people who live near the Mississippi River are not exactly looking forward to more flooding"; "Emily was a little upset about failing math." The opposite of understatement is *hyperbole*.

Unity   The desirable attribute of a paragraph in which every sentence relates directly to the paragraph's main idea. This main idea is often stated in a *topic sentence*.

Warrant   In Toulmin logic, the inference that connects the claim to the grounds. The warrant can be a belief that is taken for granted or an assumption that underlies the argument. (See also **Toulmin logic**.)

Writing process   The sequence of tasks a writer undertakes when writing an essay. During *invention*, or *prewriting*, the writer gathers information and ideas and develops a thesis. During the *arrangement* stage, the writer organizes material into a logical sequence. During *drafting and revision*, the essay is actually written and then rewritten. Finally, during *editing*, the writer puts the finishing touches on the essay by correcting misspellings, checking punctuation, searching for grammatical inaccuracies, and so on. These stages occur in no fixed order; many effective writers move back and forth among them. (See Chapters 2–5.)

Philip Levine. "What Work Is." From *What Work Is: Poems*. Copyright © 1992 by Philip Levine. Used by permission of Alfred A. Knopf, a division of Random House, Inc.

Herbert Meyer. "Why Americans Hate This 'Immigration' Debate." From www.AmericanThinker .com, April 3, 2006. Reprinted with the permission of the author.

Arthur Miller. "Get It Right: Privatize Executions." First published in the *New York Times* (May 8, 1992). Copyright © 1992 by Arthur Miller. Reprinted with the permission of The Wylie Agency, Inc.

Janice Mirikitani. "Suicide Note." From *Shredding Silence*. Copyright © 1987 by Janice Mirikitani. Reprinted by permission of Celestial Arts, an imprint of Ten Speed Press, Berkeley, CA, www .tenspeed.com.

Jessica Mitford. "The Embalming of Mr. Jones." From *The American Way of Death*. Copyright © 1963, 1978 by Jessica Mitford. Reprinted by permission of The Estate of Jessica Mitford.

Bharati Mukherjee. "Two Ways to Belong in America." From the *New York Times,* September 22, 1996. Copyright © 1996 by The New York Times Company. Reprinted with permission.

Cullen Murphy. "Fatwa City." From the *Atlantic,* November 2005. Copyright © 2005. Reprinted with permission of the publisher.

George Orwell. "Shooting an Elephant." From *Shooting an Elephant and Other Essays*. Copyright 1950 by Harcourt, Inc. and renewed © 1978 by Sonia Brownell Orwell. Reprinted with the permission of Harcourt, Inc. Copyright © George Orwell 1936 by permission of Bill Hamilton as the Literary Executor of the Estate of the Late Sonia Brownell Orwell and Seeker & Warburg Ltd.

Grace Paley. "Samuel." From *Enormous Changes at the Last Minute*. Copyright © 1971, 1974 by Grace Paley. Reprinted with the permission of Farrar, Straus & Giroux, LLC.

Laurence J. Peter and Raymond Hull. "The Peter Principle." Excerpt from *The Peter Principle*. Copyright © 1969 by William Morrow & Company, Inc. Reprinted with the permission of HarperCollins Publishers.

Joshua Piven, David Borgenicht, and Jennifer Worick. "How to Escape from a Bad Date." From *The Worst-Case Scenario Survival Handbook: Dating and Sex*. Copyright © 2001 by Joshua Piven, David Borgenicht, and Jennifer Worick. Used with permission of Chronicle Books LLC, San Francisco. Visit www.chroniclebooks.com.

Heather Rogers. "The Hidden Life of Garbage." Excerpt from *Gone Tomorrow: The Hidden Life of Garbage*. Copyright © 2005 by Heather Rogers. Reprinted with the permission of The New Press.

Lillian B. Rubin. "Guns and Grief." From *Dissent* (Summer 2007). Copyright © 2007 by the Foundation for the Study of Independent Social Ideas. Reprinted with permission.

Roberto Santiago. "Black *and* Latino." From *Essence* (November 1989). Reprinted with the permission of the author.

Carolyn Foster Segal. "The Dog Ate My Disk, and Other Tales of Woe." From the *Chronicle of Higher Education* (August 11, 2000). Reprinted with the permission of Carolyn Foster Segal.

Gary Shteyngart. "Sixty-Nine Cents." Copyright © 2007. First appeared in the *New Yorker*, September 3, 2007. Reprinted with permission of the Denise Shannon Literary Agency, Inc. All rights reserved.

Bonnie Smith-Yackel. "My Mother Never Worked." Reprinted with the permission of the author.

Gayle Rosenwald Smith. "The Wife-Beater." From the *Philadelphia Inquirer*, July 2, 2001. Copyright © 2001. Reprinted with the permission of the author.

Brent Staples. "Just Walk On By: A Black Man Ponders His Power to Alter Public Space." From *Harper's Magazine* (December 1986). Copyright © 1986. Reprinted with the permission of the author.

Amy Tan. "Mother Tongue." Originally published in the *Threepenny Review*. Copyright © 1990 by Amy Tan. Reprinted with the permission of the Sandra Dijkstra Literary Agency.

Deborah Tannen. "Sex, Lies, and Conversation." From *You Just Don't Understand*. Copyright © 1990 by Deborah Tannen. The adaptation appeared in the *Washington Post*, June 24, 1990. Reprinted by permission of HarperCollins Publishers and International Creative Management, Inc.

Alan Weisman. "Earth without People." From *Discover* (February 2005). Copyright © 2005 by Alan Weisman. Reprinted with the permission of the author.

Photo Credits

Index

subject-by-subject comparison, 387–88, 391–97
  defined, 387, 796
subjective description, 146–48
  defined, 146, 796
  subjective language, 147–48, 158
subject of writing
  general, 22
  See also topic selection
subject/verb agreement, 67–68, 707–8
subordinating conjunctions, functions of, 89, 566–67
"Suicide Note" (Mirikitani), 377–79
summary
  defined, 796
  transitional words/phrases for, 43
  writing guidelines, 762–63
support
  defined, 44
  documenting, 45
  effective, requirements of, 44–45
  techniques for, 44–45
surprising statement, in introduction, 40
Swift, Jonathan ("A Modest Proposal"), 745–52
"Swollen Expectations" (de Graff, Wann, and Naylor), 422–28
syllogism, 555–57
  and distributed versus undistributed terms, 556
  elements of, 555–56, 796
  false conclusions, 556–57
symbol, defined, 796
synonyms
  defined, 796
  defining terms with, 157, 509
synthesis, 764–65
  writing guidelines, 765

Tan, Amy ("Mother Tongue"), 477–82
Tannen ("Sex, Lies, and Conversation"), 436–40
television programs, MLA Works-Cited list, 781
tense of verbs. *See* verb tense
tentative thesis, 33
than/as, 391

"Thanks to Modern Science . . ." (American Civil Liberties Union), 573–74
thesis, 31–35
  and body paragraphs, 45–46
  and conclusion, 47
  defined, 31, 797
  explicitly stated thesis, 149
  expressive, 34
  formulating, 33
  implied thesis, 35, 149
  informative, 34
  and introduction, 31–32, 39–40
  persuasive, 34
  revising, 54
  stating in essay, 33–35
  and structure of essay, 31–32
  tentative thesis, 33
  wording of, 34–35
thesis statement
  argumentation, 549–50
  cause-and-effect essay, 328–31
  classification and division, 450, 457–58
  combining patterns, 712
  comparison and contrast, 386–88
  definition, 507, 509–10, 515
  description, 149
  development of, 32–33
  in exemplification, 201–2
  narrative, 84, 86–87, 91–92
  process essay, 265–66
  research paper, 769
third person, 264, 268
"Thirty-Eight Who Saw Murder Didn't Call the Police" (Gansberg), 120–23
time, transitional words for, 43, 86, 92
"Time to Act is Now, The" (Gore), 617–20
title of works, italics for, 77
titles of essays
  choosing, 62
  quotation marks for, 73
tone, of introduction, 40
topic outline, 49–50
topic selection, 22–29
  brainstorming, 26–28
  freewriting, 25–26
  journal writing, 27, 29